The National Underwriter Company

Homeowners Coverage Guide, 4th Edition
By Diane W. Richardson, CPCU

Highlights of the 4th Edition

This edition of the *Homeowners Coverage Guide* covers the most important aspects, and provides analysis, of the Insurance Services Office Homeowners form. It focuses on the 2011 ISO homeowners coverage form (effective in May 2011) and the 2008 AAIS homeowners forms.

The book expands the ever-popular "Coverage Scenarios," which provide real life as well as technical information on some of the most problematic of homeowners insurance issues. The Agents' Miscellany is updated to provide the agent with checklists and pertinent information needed to tailor a homeowners policy to a particular client's or prospect's needs. These checklists serve a dual purpose in helping to satisfy client needs while protecting agents against possible E&O exposure.

The newest release of this industry standard delivers significant information, including these key topics:

- Comparison between ISO's 2000 and 2011 homeowners forms
- Comparison between ISO's 2011 and AAIS 2008 homeowners forms
- New coverage scenarios
- Discussion of new case law (and its implications).
- Enhancements to the Agent's Miscellany
- Analysis of three new "Hot Topics," which contain references to various court rulings discussing:
  1. the policy term "where you reside"
  2. alcohol, drugs, and the homeowners exclusion
  3. malicious prosecution

For customer service questions or to place additional orders, please call 1-800-543-0874.

4th Edition

Homeowners Coverage Guide

Personal Lines Series

Diane W. Richardson, CPCU

The National Underwriter Company

This publication is designed to provide accurate and authoritative information in regard to the subject matter covered. It is sold with the understanding that the publisher is not engaged in rendering legal, accounting, or other professional service. If legal advice or other expert assistance is required, the services of a competent professional person should be sought.—from a Declaration of Principles jointly adopted by a Committee of the American Bar Association and a Committee of Publishers and Associations.

THE NATIONAL UNDERWRITER COMPANY
P.O. Box 14367
Cincinnati, Ohio 45250-0367

Fourth Edition, June 2011

International Standard Book Number: 978-936362-44-8
Library of Congress Control Number: 2011929709

Printed in the United States of America

About Summit Business Media

Summit Business Media (SBM) is the leading B2B media and information company serving the insurance, investment advisory, professional services, and mining investment markets through a variety of channels, including print, online, and live events. Through its Media and Reference Divisions, the company publishes 18 magazines and 150 reference titles. The Event Division hosts a dozen conferences in support of Summit's magazine brands. SBM's Data Division, comprised of Highline Data, Judy Diamond Associates, Agent Media, and Kirschner's, is the leading data provider of financial and marketing information on insurance companies, life and property-casualty agents, and investment advisors.

Summit employs nearly 400 employees in a dozen offices across the United States. For more information, please visit summitbusinessmedia.com.

About The National Underwriter Company

For over 110 years, The National Underwriter Company has been the first in line with the targeted tax, insurance, and financial planning information you need to make critical business decisions. Boasting nearly a century of expert experience, our reputable Editors are dedicated to putting accurate and relevant information right at your fingertips. With Tax Facts, Tools & Techniques, Advanced Markets AdvisorFX, Field Guide, FC&S®, and other resources available in print, on CD, and online, you can be assured that as the industry evolves National Underwriter will be at the forefront with the thorough and easy-to-use resources you rely on for success.

The National Underwriter Company
Update Service Notification

This National Underwriter Company publication is regularly updated to include coverage of developments and changes that affect the content. If you did not purchase this publication directly from The National Underwriter Company and you want to receive these important updates sent on a 30-day review basis and billed separately, please contact us at (800) 543-0874. Or you can mail your request with your name, company, address, and the title of the book to:

The National Underwriter Company
5081 Olympic Boulevard
Erlanger, KY 41018

If you purchased this publication from The National Underwriter Company directly, you have already been registered for the update service.

National Underwriter Company Contact Information

To order any National Underwriter Company title, please

- call 1-800-543-0874, 8-6 ET Monday – Thursday and 8 to 5 ET Friday
- online bookstore at www.nationalunderwriter.com, or
- mail to The National Underwriter Company, Orders Department, 5081 Olympic Blvd, Erlanger, KY 41018

Preface

About three years ago, when writing the preface to the Third Edition, it seemed as if home sales were steady. Now, however, sales of new homes have flattened, while sales of existing homes, after remaining stagnant for months, increased slightly. Mortgage rates are at an all time low, but many homeowners have found that they are "underwater" since their home's value is now less than the mortgage. Certainly this is a gloomy picture. Prior to the recent home foreclosure implosion, there were more new homes to insure. Builders could hardly keep pace with demand. That was the good news. The bad news is that now, many of those new homes are empty since their in-debt owners have been forced out. The good news is that those with good credit can find homes to purchase.

For the insurance professional, the market remains fairly constant with opportunities for sales. But with so much information (and points of purchase) available on the Internet, the insurance industry can no longer be complacent. Insurers—underwriters and claims adjusters—must be more aware than ever of problem areas; agents must make themselves ever more knowledgeable to better serve clients. This Coverage Guide, therefore, is written to help those in the industry have a better understanding of the homeowners policies.

The current Insurance Services Office (ISO) HO 00 03 and the American Association of Insurance Services (AAIS) HO 0003 are the basis for much of the following discussion, since these are the most commonly used homeowners forms. ISO has filed a revision the forms and endorsements to be effective May, 2011. However, not all jurisdictions might have adopted the revisions as of this book's publication, so be sure to check the applicable form prior to making any coverage determinations. Hawaii, North Carolina, Virginia, and Washington forms are promulgated by the various states' bureaus, although the forms incorporate much ISO material.

In discussing the forms, therefore, we will be comparing the ISO 2000 forms with the 2011 forms, as well as with the AAIS form. We will primarily be looking at the 2006 AAIS forms, except when we discuss the exclusion for water damage. Here, we will add the AAIS 2008 form to the mix, since AAIS has extensively revised the water damage exclusion—no doubt taking some of Katrina's lessons to heart.

Some housekeeping details. First, for the sake of convenience we will follow this naming: ISO forms will be designated HO 00 03 (for example) while the equivalent AAIS form will be designated as HO 0003. Second, the legal cases used in this book are for example. Interpretation varies, so if alluding to any of the court cases please make sure that they are valid in your jurisdiction. See, for example, the New Jersey's rejoinder to a Florida court's ruling on a waterbed, discussed in Chapter 5. Third, the icon (agents tip)(PC style) denotes a tip specifically directed to agents.

Finally, a *caveat*. The discussion is limited to the standard forms exclusive of the various states' amendatory provisions. For example, Nevada special provisions (HO 01 27) contains a sublimit of $10,000 for statutorily imposed vicarious parental liability not otherwise excluded. Kentucky special provisions (HO 01 16) amends the intentional loss exclusion so that it will not serve to deny payment to an innocent coinsured under certain circumstances. Please, therefore, consult the provisions for the state before determining coverage.

About the Author

Diane Richardson, CPCU, began her insurance career as a personal lines underwriter. She also worked as a state filings supervisor and as an agent. Diane retired from The National Underwriter Company, where she was an Associate Editor of *FC&S* Bulletins. She continues to consult for *FC&S*.

Her publications include *Insuring to Value* (co-authored with Marshall-Swift/Boeck), *The Homeowners Coverage Guide* (First through Fourth Editions), *The Personal Umbrella Coverage Guide*, and *The Home-Based Business Coverage Guide*.

She earned a BA from the University of Vermont and an EdM from Harvard.

Acknowledgement

I would like to thank **Christine Barlow, CPCU, Associate Editor, *FC&S Bulletins***, for her editing skills, patience, knowledge, and, above all, her sense of humor. Without her there would be no Fourth Edition.

About the Editors

Editors

Christine G. Barlow, CPCU, is an associate editor of *FC&S®*, the premiere coverage interpretative service in the country. She also wrote *Personal Lines Unlocked: The Key to Personal Lines Underwriting,* published by The National Underwriter Company, and has edited a number of the company's Reference Division publications.

Ms. Barlow has fifteen years experience in the insurance industry, beginning as a claims adjuster and then working as an underwriter and underwriting supervisor for personal lines. Before joining *FC&S*, Christine worked as an Underwriting Supervisor for Maryland Auto Insurance Fund, and as Senior Underwriter/Underwriter for companies Montgomery Mutual, Old American, Charter Group, and Nationwide.

She contributes to a number of other publications, including *Claims* magazine and ProducersWEB, and speaks at professional insurance seminars and workshops. Ms. Barlow graduated Cum Laude from Towson University.

Editorial Director

Diana B. Reitz, **CPCU, AAI**, is the editorial director of the Reference Division of The National Underwriter Company. As such she is responsible for the overall integrity of all division publications. She previously was the Director of the Property & Casualty Publishing Department of the Reference Division.

Ms. Reitz has been with The National Underwriter Company since 1998, when she was named editor of the Risk Financing and Self-Insurance manuals and associate editor of the *FC&S Bulletins*®. She also is co-author of the National Underwriter publication, *Workers Compensation Coverage Guide,* and has edited and contributed to numerous other books and publications, including *The Tools & Techniques of Risk Management and Insurance, Claims* magazine, ProducersWEB, and *National Underwriter Property & Casualty* newsweekly.

Prior to joining The National Underwriter she was with a regional insurance broker, concentrating on commercial insurance. She is a graduate of the University of Maryland and St. Francis College.

The Homeowners Coverage Guide: Interpretation and Analysis

Table of Contents

Chapter 1

An Overview

Introduction

The modern homeowners policies are package policies in that they cover dwelling, contents, personal liability, and medical payments exposures. Previously, coverage for these exposures had to be provided through separate contracts, notably fire and comprehensive personal liability policies. The dwelling fire and comprehensive personal liability coverages were combined in the first homeowners policies in the 1950s. Simplified language policies, in much the same format that is in use today, were introduced by the Insurance Services Office (ISO) in the Homeowners '76 program late in 1975.

The numbering system of the ISO homeowners forms was revised with the 2000 edition. Forms were numbered HO 00 03 10 00, for example, and this numbering system continues into the 2011 edition. The current AAIS homeowners forms were revised in the 2006 edition; forms are numbered HO 0003 09 08. To avoid confusion, we will refer to the forms as either the ISO HO 00 03, or the AAIS HO 0003. We will not include references in this book to either ISO or AAIS prior forms, such as the 1991 ISO HO 00 03 or the AAIS Form 3, edition 2. One further note: AAIS forms previously could be used to insure mobile homes and the homeowners forms included references to mobile homes. This is no longer the case; an endorsement to use with the forms will be introduced.

Forms Overview

The ISO homeowners program consists of six forms, each designed to meet a different need. There are progressively broader levels of coverage with respect to the perils insured against. The perils common to all forms are: fire or lightning, windstorm or hail, explosion, riot or civil commotion, aircraft, vehicles, smoke, vandalism or malicious mischief, theft, and volcanic eruption. Form HO 00 08 includes these named perils, although coverage for smoke and theft is restricted, as we will see in Chapter 12. Basic homeowners form HO 00 01, which also contained coverage for these perils, has been withdrawn and is no longer supported in the ISO program. AAIS form HO 0008 is extremely limited as to use, and so many of the endorsements previously offered will no longer be available. However, AAIS continues to offer form HO 0001.

The AAIS standard homeowners program includes seven forms, as opposed to ISO's six. AAIS HO 0008 includes the named perils of fire or lightning, windstorm or hail, explosion, riot or civil commotion, aircraft, vehicles, smoke, sinkhole collapse (a peril not included in the ISO forms except by endorsement or where mandated by law, as in Florida), vandalism, theft, and volcanic eruption. As in the ISO form, coverage for theft and smoke is restricted. Form HO 0001 includes these same named perils.

The second level of coverage is provided in ISO forms HO 00 02, HO 00 04, HO 00 06, and the personal property coverage of special form HO 00 03. The equivalent AAIS forms are HO 0002, HO 0004, HO 0006, and HO 0003. This level of coverage incorporates the *broad form* perils listed previously plus both *additional perils* not covered in the basic forms and *expanded definitions* of some of the basic perils. The added perils are falling objects; weight of ice, snow, or sleet; plumbing discharge; rupture of steam or hot water heating systems, air conditioning systems, or water heaters; freezing of plumbing or similar devices; and damage from artificially generated electricity. There is *broader* coverage than is provided in the basic forms under the perils of vehicles and, in ISO HO 00 08 and AAIS HO 0001 and HO 0008, for smoke.

The third level of coverage is *open perils* coverage for dwelling and other structures in special forms ISO HO 00 03 and AAIS HO 0003. Open perils coverage for dwelling, other structures, and personal property is provided by ISO HO 00 05 and AAIS HO 0005. *Open perils* coverage is also available for unit owners coverage A, which in a condominium includes such items of real property as alterations, appliances, fixtures and the like, and for personal property when ISO endorsements HO 17 32 and HO 17 31 are attached, respectively. This same level of coverage is available in the AAIS program through endorsements HO 7032 and HO 7029. Under the ISO homeowners 2000 program, *open perils* coverage for personal property became available to a tenant homeowner when endorsement HO 05 24 was added to an HO 00 04; under the AAIS program, HO 2730 is added to an HO 0004. AAIS has also introduced an endorsement, HO 4941, that can be attached to an HO 0003 to provide open perils coverage for personal property. Coverage is broader, however, under the HO 0005.

Perils at this level of coverage are not named, but restrictions on coverage are specified through exclusions, limitations, and exceptions applying to certain causes of loss and categories of property. Loss to insured property not reached by one of these restrictions is covered. This level of coverage, whether homeowners or other property insurance, was traditionally referred to as *all risks* because the coverage agreements formerly insured against all risks of physical loss (other than those subject to an exclusion). Current editions of homeowners forms delete the word *all* from this coverage agreement to avoid the implication that coverage is more sweeping than the policy as a whole actually provides.

Eligibility: Homeowners Forms

Policies that include coverage on the dwelling structure itself–ISO forms or AAIS forms–may be issued to the following:

1) For ISO, owner-occupants of one- to four-family dwellings used primarily for residential purposes. Some incidental occupancies are permitted as well as certain home-based businesses. For example, an insurance agent may maintain an in-home office although the agency itself is actually located elsewhere. In addition, a one-family dwelling may not be occupied by more than one additional family or two roomers or boarders. In a two-, three- or four-family dwelling, each individual unit may not be occupied by more than two families or one family with two roomers or boarders.

   In the AAIS program, owner-occupants of one- to four-family dwellings used principally for private residential purposes, are eligible. Each family unit may be occupied by no more than one family with no more than two boarders or roomers, or two families with no boarders or roomers.

   Some home-based businesses are permissible at the residence premises, as well as incidental occupancies. For more information on both the AAIS and ISO home-based business coverages, see *The Home-Based Business Coverage Guide* (The National Underwriter Company, 2002, FC&S Online).

2) In each program, resident co-owners of a two-, three-, or four-family dwelling may be written provided each occupies distinct living quarters with separate entrances. In that instance one owner is written on a homeowners policy; the other on tenant homeowners or contents policies. Their interest in the structure is then protected by means of an additional insured endorsement.

3) For both programs, occupants who are purchasing the dwelling on a long-term installment basis, such as under a land contract, may be written. Under this arrangement, the seller maintains title to the property until the terms of the contract are completed but does not function as a mortgagee. The seller's interest is covered through an additional insured endorsement. AAIS rules state that policy issuance is at the option of the company.

4) For both programs, intended owner-occupants of dwellings that are under construction and intended for private residential use.

5) For both programs, occupants of a dwelling under a life estate arrangement. ISO includes that the amount of building coverage must be at least 80 percent of the dwelling's replacement cost. A life estate arrangement is one in which an individual's interest in a piece of property is limited to the individual's life. For example, an insured may leave a residence to an elderly relative with the provision that, at the relative's death, the property reverts to the insured's children. AAIS rules state that policy issuance is at the option of the company.

6) For both programs, properties held in trust may be insured. Heretofore, the method of insuring such property was somewhat haphazard and depended upon the insurer's willingness to write property titled in the name of a trustee, which might well be a banking establishment. Both AAIS and ISO now offer means to insure this property on the standard homeowners forms by attaching endorsements. For more information, see Chapter 13.

Eligibility: Tenant Homeowners

In both the ISO and AAIS programs, the eligibility requirements for ISO HO 00 04 and AAIS HO 0004 contain the same stipulations as to residential use of the premises and incidental occupancies or a home-based business. Up to one additional family or two boarders or roomers are allowed.

Tenants of apartments, single family dwellings, or mobile homes are most commonly insured by form 4, but owner-occupants of structures that are ineligible for the other homeowners policies can make use of this form. As noted above, a tenant homeowners form may be used to insure the co-owner of a two-or-more family dwelling when each owner occupies distinct living quarters.

Residences held in trust may not be insured on a tenant homeowners form since real property, not personal property, is often the subject of these arrangements.

Eligibility: Unit Owners

In both AAIS and ISO programs, an owner of a condominium or cooperative unit is eligible to purchase an AAIS form HO 0006 or ISO HO 00 06 provided that the unit is primarily used for a residence and does not house more than one additional family or two boarders or roomers. Incidental occupancies and home-based businesses are permitted here as with the other homeowners forms. Unit owners forms are discussed in more detail in Chapter 12.

A condominium unit, since it is real property, may be held in trust. When this is the case, the unit owners form may be endorsed to cover the arrangement.

Eligibility: Seasonal Property

In the ISO program, an insured with a seasonal or second residence–whether in or out of state–must insure it separately. As an exception to the requirement that homeowners policies must be issued with all the available section I property and section II liability coverages, it is acceptable to write a policy for a second residence containing only section I coverage if the same insurer provides coverage on both the primary and secondary residences. Liability coverage for a secondary residence can be supplied by making a charge under section II of the homeowners policy covering the primary dwelling.

Seasonal or second residences may be insured using the usual homeowners forms. The dwellings must meet eligibility requirements as set forth by individual insurers. When both the primary and secondary or seasonal residences are in the same state, the AAIS rules allow the secondary location to be added by endorsement. Otherwise, a separate policy must be issued. In both programs, final acceptance of a seasonal or secondary residence is determined by the insurer.

Eligibility: Farm Property

Neither homeowners program is designed to be used when more than incidental farming takes place on the residence premises. The ISO program offers optional section II liability coverages for use only when the insured has a farm away from the residence premises and farming is not the insured's primary occupation, or if the farming conducted on the premises is incidental to the use of the premises as a residence. Under the AAIS program, farming may take place on the residence premises, but farming cannot be the business of the insured. The AAIS program offers a broader spectrum of endorsements than ISO for various aspects of incidental farming activities.

Eligibility: Mobile Homes

In the ISO program, mobile homes may be written by attaching endorsements to the homeowners forms. In the AAIS program, the previous edition's forms must be used for those wishing to insure mobile homes. Unlike the ISO forms, these forms include references to mobile homes so that they do not need to be specifically endorsed. For example, in Form 2 edition 2.0, the definition of "residence" is "a one- to four-family house, a townhouse, a row house, or a one- or two-family mobile home used mainly for family residential purposes."

Many insurers do not wish to insure mobile homes. As stated, both ISO and AAIS forms allow for coverage to be written; however, eligibility requirements should be reviewed before proceeding. For more information, see Chapter 12.

Eligibility: Incidental Occupancy

Dwellings with incidental business occupancy are eligible for homeowners coverage in both programs. However, the premises must be occupied principally as a dwelling (reiterating a primary requirement for homeowners eligibility). Permitted incidental occupancies include, but are not limited to, business or professional offices and private schools or studios that provide instruction in music, dance, or photography. It is possible for one residence premises to have both a permitted incidental occupancy *and* a home-based business, but it would be advisable to obtain an insurer's input on this. However, under no circumstances are these endorsements to be used to insure a home day care operation.

Unless the policy is endorsed, an incidental business occupancy limits property coverage and eliminates premises liability coverage for losses arising out of or connected to the business. Furthermore, coverage B (other structures) does not apply to other structures in which a business is conducted unless coverage is added back by endorsement. One of two endorsements may be added: ISO endorsement HO 04 42, permitted incidental occupancies (residence premises), which is also used if the business is conducted in another structure on the premises; or HO 24 43, permitted incidental occupancies (other residence). AAIS uses endorsement HO 3542 for incidental business on the insured premises, and endorsement HO 6243 for incidental business at another location. As discussed in Chapter 13, these endorsements remove the $2,500 limit that applies to business property on the residence premises and allow the full coverage C personal property limit to apply.

There are no specific requirements in the homeowners rules about increasing the personal property limit when an incidental occupancy exists, but agents and their clients are well advised to examine the coverage C amount closely to be sure it is sufficient to absorb the additional values of the business furnishings and equipment.

Eligibility: Home-Based Business

It is increasingly common for persons to start businesses in their homes. In these instances, the homeowners actually own the business and are not telecommuting. Both ISO and AAIS have developed programs to insure various types of businesses. Among the eligible businesses are office services, crafts, and, under the AAIS program, bed-and-breakfast operations. As noted above, the rules allow both a permitted incidental occupancy and a home-based business exposure to coexist; however, this is subject to insurer underwriting guidelines.

The home-based business endorsements will be discussed briefly in Chapter 13. For more information, see *The Home-Based Business Coverage Guide* (The National Underwriter Company, 2002, FC&S Online).

Limits of Liability

Insurers differ in their underwriting requirements for the minimum amount of coverage they will accept on a dwelling. One way of encouraging business in an insurer's target market is through rates. For example, the best rates of a given insurer might be for dwellings with replacement values of from $150,000 to $350,000. Dwellings with replacement values below or above those amounts will be charged proportionately more for coverage. Another insurer may specialize in dwellings with much higher values; another, much lower. The same is often true for tenant homeowners or for unit owners.

Although the limit for coverage A, dwelling, varies, the percentages for coverages B, C, and D remain constant unless changed by endorsement or, as is sometimes the case, by the insurer as part of its homeowners program. For ISO, these are:

Coverage B–Other Structures
HO 00 02, HO 00 03, HO 00 05, HO 00 08
10% of A, one- and two-family dwelling
5% of A, three- and four-family dwelling

Coverage C–Personal Property
HO 00 02, HO 00 03, HO 00 05, HO 00 08

50% of A, one- and two-family dwelling
30% of A, three-family dwelling
25% of A, four-family dwelling

Coverage D–Loss of Use
HO 00 02, HO 00 03, HO 00 05
30% of A
HO 00 04
30% of C
HO 00 06
50% of C
HO 00 08
10% of A

In the AAIS program, the limits are as follows:

Coverage B–Other Structures
HO 0001, HO 0002, HO 0003
10% of A
HO 0008, refer to company

Coverage C–Personal Property
HO 0001, HO 0002, HO 0003, HO 0008
50% of A, one- and two-family dwelling
30% of A, three- or four-family dwelling
HO 0005
70% of A, one- and two-family dwelling
50% of A, three- and four-family dwelling

Coverage D–Additional Living Costs
HO 0001, HO 0002, HO 0003
30% of A, one or two family dwelling
20% of A, three or four family dwelling
HO 0004
40% of C
HO 0005
30% of A, one or two family dwelling
20% of A, three or four family dwelling
HO 0008
20% of A, one- and two-family dwelling
10% of A, three- and four-family dwelling
HO 0006
40% of C

The rules governing ISO form HO 00 06 and AAIS form HO 0006 are slightly different in that coverage A is generally less than coverage C. Remember that, in condominium ownership, the unit owner generally has purchased airspace, with an interest in areas owned in common with other unit owners. For this reason, coverage A usually will apply to items such as wall-to-wall carpeting, wallpaper, lighting fixtures, or built-ins. In the AAIS program there is a limit of 10 percent of the coverage C amount applying to coverage A. In the ISO program, $5,000 is automatically provided in the coverage form. Both programs allow this amount to be increased.

Both programs allow additional insurance to be written on specified structures under coverage B. Coverage C may be increased or, in some cases, reduced to no less than 40 percent of coverage A. The prudent agent will use this option carefully, however. Insureds often accumulate many more possessions then they realize–that is, until a loss. Additional amounts of coverage D also may be written.

Rating Information

The AAIS manual contains program information, submission and rating instructions, loss costs, and explanations of available coverage options. Generally, the rating approach is similar to ISO homeowners rating. There are some differences to note, however. The ISO manual may be used countrywide, with state exception pages included for a particular state. AAIS provides a separate manual for each state.

The AAIS program uses a simplified fire protection classification. Instead of the usual ten classes as in the ISO program, AAIS uses three: protected, partially protected, and unprotected. Protected buildings are those located within five miles of a responding fire department and within 1,000 feet of a fire hydrant. Alternatively, the building may be within 1,000 feet of a year-round water source of at least 3,500 gallons and the responding fire department must have pumper truck capabilities; or the responding fire department must have a pumper/tanker truck capable of carrying at least 3,500 gallons. Partially protected buildings are those located within five road miles of a responding fire department, but the protected class water source requirements are not met. Unprotected buildings are those not meeting any of the above requirements (similar to class 10 in the usual classification system). Of course, this classification system does not mean that dwellings located in any class are automatically eligible for coverage; the underwriting guidelines of each company should be consulted.

ISO includes as part of the rating procedure a building code effectiveness grading. Grades of from one to ten are assigned based on adequacy of the community building code and the effectiveness of the community's enforcement of that code. Policies that cover windstorm, hail, or earthquake exposures in these communities may receive a credit. Complete information is available in the ISO countrywide manual and state exception pages.

The rating procedures differ between ISO and AAIS. (Note, however, that neither program furnishes rates. Both programs include loss costs, which then must be multiplied by the individual company's multiplier to obtain a final rate.) The ISO rating procedure consists of finding a key premium based on territory; multiplying this by a form factor; multiplying the result by the protection-construction factor; and, finally, multiplying the result by the key factor. The company multiplier is then applied. In the AAIS procedure, the precalculated loss cost, which reflects the territory, form, construction, and fire protection class, is multiplied by the amount of insurance. In both rating procedures any additional premium for optional coverages must be added separately.

Chapter 2

What's Covered

Introduction

Throughout the following discussion we will be referring to the 2008 AAIS homeowners and the 2011 ISO homeowners forms. As noted in the previous chapter, when referring to the specific forms we will always use "AAIS HO 0003" and for the ISO forms we will use ISO HO 00 03. We will compare and contrast the forms in each program as we discuss the coverages and exclusions. Since many words and terms that are defined in the forms are necessary for complete understanding of the insurance contract, we will begin each chapter with relevant definitions. The ISO and AAIS forms are reproduced in Appendix B (ISO 2011 HO 00 03; ISO 2011 HO 00 02 and HO 00 05, property coverages only; and AAIS 2008 HO 0003 and HO 0005, property coverages only) for ready reference to coverages, exclusions, and provisions.

As noted in the preface, the discussion refers to the homeowners forms exclusive of state mandatory and amendatory provisions. Therefore, if uncertain whether a particular provision applies, check the applicable amendatory provisions.

Definitions

The AAIS form covers a residence on the described location:

> "Described location" means the one- to four-family house, the townhouse, or the row house where "you" reside and which is shown on the "declarations" as the "described location". It includes related private structures and grounds at that location.

> However, if the "described location" is a townhouse or a row house, it includes only related private structures and grounds at that location that are used or occupied solely by "your" household for residential purposes.

The ISO form defines residence premises as:

> a. The one-family dwelling where you reside;
>
> b. The two-, three- or four-family dwelling where you reside in at least one of the family units; or
>
> c. That part of any other building where you reside;
>
> and which is shown as the "residence premises" in the Declarations.
>
> "Residence premises" also includes other structures and grounds at that location.

An interesting difference between the AAIS and ISO definitions is that the AAIS form refers to "related private structures." Thus, any structures on the described location should have some relationship to the residence itself—whether a garage, a gazebo, or a garden gate. The ISO form simply states that other structures and grounds at the residence premises location are included within the definition. But because restrictions apply to other structures, such as for business use, there does not appear to be a need to reinforce that the other structures must have some connection to the residence.

Sometimes what the geographic area of a residence premises actually encompasses is open to question. For example, is it a typical quarter acre lot? What about ten or twenty acres of woodland, with a cleared area for the dwelling? Is the residence premises then just the cleared area? The forms do not address this. Therefore, the residence premises may be any size. It is left to the individual insurer, if it so chooses, to make an underwriting determination as to what size premises it wishes to insure. The problem with a large premises is usually not one of property coverage, but a liability issue.

Coverage A, Dwelling

In the ISO forms, coverage A applies to the dwelling, which may be a one- to four-family building. Structures attached to the dwelling fall under the coverage A limit. For example, an attached garage or a deck firmly secured to the dwelling is considered part of the dwelling for coverage A purposes. Coverage A also applies to materials and supplies located either on or next to the residence premises and intended for use in construction, alteration, or repair of the dwelling or other structure. In the AAIS form, coverage A applies to the residence–including attached additions and built-in components and fixtures–as well as building materials and supplies located on or adjacent to the described location for use in construction, alteration, or repair of the residence or related private structures. By including within the coverage grant for the dwelling *built-in components and fixtures*, the AAIS form clarifies that items such as built-in dishwashers and microwaves, or sinks and toilets, are part of the dwelling for coverage purposes. (Loss settlement for appliances, however, is not the same as for the dwelling.) The ISO form does not state this, but custom dictates the same interpretation. Items that are built in or otherwise affixed to the building, such as a furnace or wall-to-wall carpet, are considered part of the dwelling.

There is a difference here between the two programs in the coverage grant. The ISO forms refer to *structures attached to the dwelling*, while the AAIS form refers to *additions*. In theory these are identical, since *Webster's Collegiate Dictionary* defines *addition* as "a part added (as to a building or residential section)." Therefore, the addition could be a deck, balcony, solarium, or carport. Both forms cover materials and supplies *on or next to* the residence premises.

The question sometimes arises as to whether a structure attached to another structure which is in turn attached to the dwelling also falls under coverage A. The policy language for both forms indicates that this is not the case. The ISO form for coverage A states that the insurer covers the "dwelling… including structures attached to the dwelling." For AAIS, coverage A states that it "includes additions attached to the residence…" The intent is thus that structures which might be attached to structures attached to the dwelling should be covered under coverage B.

Land, including land upon which the dwelling is situated, is not covered except, as we shall see, in the AAIS form. The AAIS form adds that underground water and surface water are not covered property; the ISO form includes *water or steam* in the list of property not covered.

Some independently filed homeowners forms do, in fact, provide limited coverage for land. Often the land restoration must be necessitated by a covered loss to the dwelling itself, and the cost is usually included within the dwelling limit of liability. For example, if the force of water from fire hoses caused land to wash away from a landscaped berm, these independent forms would respond.

Coverage for Land

An insured was raking pine needles in the front yard of his newly purchased home. There seemed to be quite a lot of broken glass among the needles, but he did not give it much thought. Shortly thereafter, he began to dig out land in the back to install a fish pond and realized that there was broken glass to a depth of thirteen feet.

The prior owner had worked for a waste management company and used waste glass to level his land. He dumped the glass and then put a thin layer of soil and sod over it.

Although the presence of the glass presents a danger to the inhabitants, the glass has not damaged covered property. Since the AAIS and ISO forms do not provide coverage for land, removal of the glass is not covered.

Coverage B, Other Structures

ISO coverage B insures other structures on the residence premises set aside from the dwelling by clear space. This includes structures connected to the dwelling by only a fence, utility line, or similar connection. Materials and supplies used to construct, alter, or repair the other structures are also covered if they are located on or next to the residence premises. Land, including land upon which the structure is located, is not covered.

Coverage B in earlier editions insured appurtenant structures, a term more specific–and therefore somewhat more restrictive–than other structures. Appurtenant structures are generally understood to be permanently affixed to the land and therefore a part of the realty, title to which passes with the title to the land itself. By this definition, an in-ground swimming pool, for example, is an appurtenant structure, but an above-ground pool is not. Simplified language homeowners coverage B applies to *any* unexcluded structure, a term that refers (according to standard dictionary definitions) to the very broad category of *something constructed.* By this definition, an other structure can include a storage shed or an ornamental rock garden.

AAIS coverage B is similar to that of ISO in that related private structures on the described location are covered. As with the ISO form, structures connected to the residence by only a fence, a utility line, or similar connection are not considered *attached.* The coverage also specifically applies to fences, driveways, sidewalks, and other permanently installed outdoor fixtures–a brick barbecue pit, for example. Having driveways and sidewalks specifically listed as coverage B answers the question as to where a damaged driveway, say, should be covered.

Both forms cover materials or supplies intended for use in construction, repair, or alteration of a related private structure. Both forms, however, provide coverage under coverage A, not under coverage B. There is no coverage for land, including the land on which the structure is situated (except, as we shall discuss, in the AAIS form), or for underground or surface water.

The standard limit of liability applying to other structures is 10 percent of the limit of liability applying to coverage A in both programs. This amount can be increased.

What is Included Under Coverage A

In the southern states, notably Florida, it is common to have a swimming pool with concrete leading from the dwelling to the pool and a screen enclosure over the pool. Does this make the patio/walkway and the enclosure part of the dwelling? The patio/walkway would not be attached to the dwelling, even though it would abut it. Arguing that it would be part of the dwelling would thus lead to the conclusion that the pool should be part of the dwelling and thus insured under coverage A—a conclusion that would hardly be supported by common definitions of *dwelling* and *pool.* Often, though, the enclosure itself is firmly attached to the dwelling. A case could then be made for coverage for the enclosure under A.

In the AAIS form, the use of "driveways and sidewalks" would make the insured reasonably conclude that a concrete patio would be a similar item and thus insured under coverage B. But with regard to the enclosure, coverage would be under A if the structure is attached to the dwelling. If the structure is not attached to the dwelling, but affixed to the patio, then it would be a permanently installed outdoor fixture, and covered under B.

It is important for insureds, as well as agents, to realize that substantial alterations or additions can affect insurance-to-value. For example, endorsements that offer an increase in coverage A should a loss exceed the policy limit frequently require notification to the insurer when additions or alterations are greater than 5 percent of the coverage A limit of liability.

Coverage B Limitations

The coverage for other structures has certain limitations, although each program treats other structures somewhat differently. Both programs limit coverage for business activities associated with the other structure. The AAIS program considers that a structure rented to a tenant of the insured residence that is not used for business, or a structure used solely as a private garage, are exceptions; therefore coverage applies. The ISO program states only that the other structure may be rented to a nontenant of the premises if used solely as a private garage. Both the AAIS and ISO forms preclude coverage for other structures "used, in whole or in part, for the direction or operation of a 'business'" (AAIS) or "other structures from which any 'business' is conducted" (ISO). Both ISO and AAIS now define a "business" as not including any activity generating no more than $2,500 (AAIS) or $2,000 (ISO) in any 12 month period, for any one insured, prior to the policy term. For example, an insured might have a woodworking hobby and sell some furniture. So long as the amount he or she earns is less than the amount indicated in the policy, the activity will not be considered a "business." We will discuss this in more detail in Chapter 4.

Both forms cover other structures used to store business property. (However, as we will discuss in Chapter 4, a special limit applies to property primarily used in business that is on the residence premises.) The business property may be owned either by an insured or a tenant of the dwelling, but the property cannot consist of or contain gaseous or liquid fuel, other than fuel in a permanently installed fuel tank on a vehicle or watercraft parked or stored in the structure. The AAIS form goes on to state that fuel in a portable container designed to hold fuel and no more than 5 U.S. gallons is acceptable. The AAIS form also states that "business" property that consists of a private passenger auto, a pickup, a van, or a motorized vehicle designed for grounds maintenance such as lawn mowing or snow plowing may be stored in the other structure with no denial of coverage. Under the earlier forms, it would have been possible (though not necessarily prudent) for an insurer to deny coverage if the insured kept an auto used in business in his or her detached garage.

As noted, both the ISO and the AAIS programs preclude coverage for an other structure when a business is conducted from it. If the business is a permitted incidental occupancy, such as an office or studio, then insurance on the other structure must be specified and an additional charge made. (See Chapter 13.) If the business is a home day care center, then specific insurance must also be arranged. See, as well, *The Home-Based Business Coverage Guide* (The National Underwriter Company, 2002, FC&S Online) if the business entails more than an incidental occupancy.

The exclusion of coverage for an other structure used in business has been analyzed by many courts, with no clear-cut conclusions. As of this writing, there have been no cases focusing on the current ISO or AAIS language which does not consider an amount earned under $2,000 or $2,500 a business. One case, however, would have led to the same outcome even with the new language, since the insured earned approximately $4,000 in each of three consecutive winters. The insured rented her barn to a marina for winter boat storage and it burned. The insured argued that her conduct had not led to the barn's destruction, but the court said the exclusion held regardless of whether her conduct created an unacceptable risk. The case is *Smith v. State Farm Fire and Casualty Company*, 656 N.W.2d 432 (Minn. App. 2003).

In *Byers v. Motorists Insurance Companies,* 863 N.E.2d 196 (Oh. App. 3d, 2006), the court found the exclusion for a structure used in whole or in part for business to be vague and thus construed against the insurer. The insured and her fiancé occasionally used her garage to assemble and store parts for satellite dishes. The garage burned and the insurer denied coverage. However, the court said this usage was so minimal as to not invoke the exclusion. The court said the policy did not distinguish active, ongoing business pursuits and passive activities that were remotely related to employment. Further, the court said, in opposition to *Smith*, above, the occasional use was so minimal as to not increase the risk to the garage and did not cause the loss or damage. Therefore, there was coverage for the loss.

Coverage B Limit of Liability

Coverage B applies to any number of other structures situated on the residence premises. The amount specified in the declarations (normally 10 percent of coverage A) as the limit of liability for this coverage is a blanket amount that may be applied to one or several structures as the nature of the loss dictates. The amount of insurance does not apply separately to each separate structure; it applies as a single amount over all. It is important to understand this. In event of a covered loss, the most that will be paid is 10 percent of the coverage A amount unless additional insurance has been arranged. For example, if the coverage A amount is $100,000, then $10,000 applies to coverage B. But if an insured has an in-ground pool, a three-car detached garage, and a brick wall with an ornate gate for a total value of $45,000, the most that will be paid is still $10,000. When the insurable value of all other structures on the premises exceeds the limit of insurance for coverage B, specific *additional* amounts of coverage may be scheduled by endorsement.

Sometimes an insured owns other structures that are not located on the residence premises. So long as they are used in connection with the residence premises and not used for residential purposes, coverage may be purchased. For example, an insured may own a garden plot elsewhere with a small storage shed. In the ISO program, either of two endorsements–one extending the blanket coverage already in place, and one for additional amounts of insurance–would provide necessary protection. These are the HO 04 91 and HO 04 92 respectively. In the AAIS program, the comparable endorsements are the HO 6217 and HO 6218. For more information see Chapter 13.

Coverage C, Personal Property

Personal Property Owned or Used by an Insured

Generally, coverage C applies worldwide to personal property owned or *used by* an insured. Each program has an exception to this. AAIS form HO 0008 covers personal property away from the described location, but limits coverage to 10 percent of the coverage C limit or $1,000, whichever is greater (there are two exceptions: removal of property while the residence is undergoing repairs, or removal to a newly acquired principal residence). ISO form HO 00 08 only covers personal property while it is on the residence premises. We will look at these and other differences in Chapter 12, but now will discuss the more common homeowners forms.

Two kinds of personal property, therefore, are covered. The first, of course, is the personal property owned by the insured. Although it is common to think of personal property covered by a homeowners policy as *contents* such as clothing or furniture, remember that personal property encompasses many other items–for example, a private passenger auto, a jet ski, or even a Cessna aircraft might be personal property. Therefore, the homeowners forms include limited coverage for some items and do not cover others at all. We will discuss this in Chapter 4.

The second type of covered personal property is that used by an insured. So, for example, if an insured borrows a riding lawnmower and while it is in his garage it catches fire and burns, the loss is covered under coverage C of the borrower's homeowners policy. In fact, as will be discussed in Chapter 9, the coverage for damage to property of others in the ISO form states that the insurer will not pay for "property damage" to the extent of any amount recoverable under Section I.

In the lawnmower scenario, of course, the deductible applies. The *other insurance* provision would also affect settlement in that if the one lending the mower has insurance covering it, then the two insurers would settle the loss on a *pro rata* basis. Take another example. A kind neighbor loans her new boat, a Chris Craft Crowne sport cruiser ($43,000) to a friend. The friend, who carries homeowners insurance, moors the boat under a cliff face, and a large boulder (which becomes a falling object and therefore a coverage C named peril) rolls down the cliff and demolishes the boat. The boat is personal property of another in the care of the insured, so there is coverage under the friend's homeowners policy. But in this case, the limitation for watercraft applies, which limits coverage to $1,500 (or $2,500 in the AAIS HO 0005).

Personal Property of Others

Coverage C also applies, at the named insured's request, to personal property of others while it is on the part of the residence premises occupied by an insured. (If the insured is a tenant, this coverage applies only to property in the insured's part of the dwelling or the insured's own apartment, not to portions of the building not occupied by the insured.) Also covered, if the insured wishes, is property owned by guests and residence employees while the property is in any residence occupied by any insured, although the AAIS HO 0008 and the ISO HO 00 08 do not provide this coverage. Because some homeowners forms state that coverage applies at the insured's request, some insurers have taken the position that the insured had to notify the insurer prior to a loss that others' or guests' property was to be covered–a somewhat difficult proposition. The ISO 2011 forms clarify the matter by declaring that coverage is provided for others' or guests' property "after a loss and at your request, we will cover property owned by others… or a guest…" Note that a guest's or residence employee's property need not be at the insured residence premises; it could be at the insured's mother's lakeside cottage, just so long as the insured is occupying that residence.

As we will see in Chapters 4 and 5, there are some limitations of coverage that apply to an insured's personal property while an insured premises is rented to others. Methods for insuring this property will be discussed in later chapters.

Property at Other Locations

In the 2011 edition, ISO has changed the limitations for property located away from the residence premises. For property usually situated at a residence of the insured, *other than* the residence premises, coverage is limited to the greater of 10 percent of the full coverage C limit or $1,000. (This limitation has not changed.) The limit applies to property at another *residence*, not at another location. (That is not the case with the ISO HO 00 08 or the AAIS HO 0008. These forms limit coverage for property that is away from the insured premises at *any other* location to the greater of 10 percent of coverage C or $1,000. The limitation does not apply, however, when property is moved because the insured residence is undergoing reconstruction or repair and is not fit to live in or store property in, or when property is moved to a newly acquired principal residence.) This limitation affects the amount of coverage available, for example, for the furniture at the insured's vacation cottage. However, other property, such as clothing that the insured takes along to the cottage even for an extended vacation, is not limited so long as the clothing is usually located at the residence premises. The limitation also applies to a student's property away at school except for items that normally accompany the student while away from the premises; e.g., a purse, a wallet, or clothing.

Note also that the limitation applies to the property wherever it is located at the time of loss as long as it is property that is *usually* situated at the other residence. Suppose an insured is moving from one secondary residence to another. Neither place is the insured residence premises, so the insured has only 10 percent (or $1,000) coverage on the property wherever it is actually located, including while in transit.

The 2011 ISO homeowners now includes a 10 percent, or $1,000 (whichever is greater) limitation on property located in a self-storage facility. This limit is separate from the 10 percent or $1,000 limit imposed on property at an insured's other residence. An insured could therefore have property in both a seasonal residence and a self-storage unit; should a loss occur in both places, 10 percent (or $1,000) of the coverage C amount would be available in each location. As with property in an insured's other residence, the limit does not apply if the property is in the self-storage unit because the residence premises is being repaired, renovated, or rebuilt, and not fit to live in or store property in. This amount may be increased by attaching endorsement HO 06 14 (increased amount of insurance for personal property located in a self-storage facility).

In both the AAIS and ISO programs, the limitation does not apply to personal property in a newly acquired principal residence for thirty days during the course of the move. The coverage C limit applies in full to this personal property during the thirty-day period. This provision gives the insured a chance to arrange for proper coverage.

Both programs also acknowledge that personal property must often be moved out of a dwelling if the dwelling is undergoing alteration, reconstruction, or repair, and is unfit either for use as a residence or as a place to store property. For example, an insured could sustain a house fire, necessitating a move into an apartment for three months while the insured residence is being repaired. The insured now has the full amount of coverage C available to cover personal property located in the apartment; the limitations for property usually located in a residence other than the residence premises or thirty days for property in a newly acquired principal residence do not apply under this circumstance. There is no requirement that the dwelling, however, has to have sustained a covered loss for this provision to apply. The ISO form refers to "renovation" and the AAIS form refers to "alteration." Neither of these terms would be used if, say, the dwelling had to be repaired or reconstructed following a loss; thus, if the insureds moved to an apartment while a new kitchen, deck, and family room was being added to the insured dwelling, there would be coverage.

Coverage for Personal Property

The following situation has arisen several times. Say a family insured on an HO 00 03 moves to a different city and the new residence is not ready when they arrive. What usually happens is that the family moves into an apartment and puts the bulk of their personal belongings into a self-storage facility. The policy on their former home is not cancelled. We know that they have the full coverage C limit for belongings in the apartment for thirty days from the time they start the move (after which the limit is reduced to 10 percent of the coverage C limit). Assuming that they have not closed on the new home nor even bought a new home when they arrive, is their property in storage protected until they move to the new permanent residence?

The answer depends on which edition of the HO 00 03 is in force. If the form is the ISO HO 00 03 05 11 edition, then coverage is limited to 10 percent of the limit of the coverage C limit of liability. In that event, endorsement HO 06 14 should be attached to the policy to provide additional coverage for the stored personal property.

If the form is the HO 00 03 10 00, then the insureds' personal belongings in self-storage are covered under the full coverage C limit until they can move into their new home. Personal property is insured *anywhere in the world.* Full coverage for personal property in a newly acquired principal residence lasts for thirty days from the time they begin to move the property there. The storage facility is not a newly acquired principal residence, nor is it an uninsured secondary residence, where the 10 percent limitation applies. However, if the stay in the apartment shows signs of continuing, the personal property becomes *usually* located at the apartment, and an insurer would have a strong case for denying coverage on that property should a loss occur. A safer course of action would be to arrange for coverage rather than rely on the not-yet-cancelled homeowners policy on the previous home.

The answer is the same if the insureds cancel the policy on the original home so long as they purchase insurance on the new home or as tenants under form HO 00 04.

Coverage D, Loss of Use

Additional Living Expense

Both the ISO and AAIS forms contain three related coverages grouped under the title "Loss of Use," or, in the AAIS forms, "Additional Living Costs and Loss of Rent" as homeowners coverage D. The first of these is coverage for additional living expense or costs. The period for which additional living expense will be paid is limited to the shortest time required to repair or replace the premises or, if the household moves to a new permanent residence, the shortest time required for the relocation to be completed. These coverage periods apply even if the policy expires in the meantime.

It is important to remember that the coverage is for any *increase* in living expenses and not to reimburse ordinary pre-loss expenses. For example, a covered fire damages an insured's home so the family must reside in a motel and eat meals at restaurants. Continuing monthly mortgage payments are $950 and the average monthly food bill is $825; so ordinary living expense is $1,775. Residing in a motel (with a negotiated rate) costs $1,400 per month and meals at a restaurant are $1,750 per month, which totals $3,150. The insured is entitled to the sum of $1,400 for the accommodation and $925 for the meals, or $2325.

Loss of Rents

The second of the loss of use coverages is fair rental value. This coverage will pay the lost rental value if a part of the residence premises is rented or held for rental to others and a covered section I loss makes that part of the premises not fit to live in. To be deducted from the amount paid is any expense that does not continue during the time the rented premises is unfit to be occupied (the cost of disconnected utilities, for example). Loss or expense due to cancellation of a lease or agreement is not covered. Like additional living expense, this coverage provides payment only for the shortest period required to repair or replace the affected premises and is not terminated by expiration of the policy.

Earlier homeowners forms allowed the named insured to choose either additional living expense or fair rental value in the event a covered loss made the residence premises uninhabitable; some forms have retained this option. But in the current ISO and AAIS forms, fair rental value is available only if the insured premises is rented or held for rental. That is, the property must either be actively rented or it must be available to be rented by a willing tenant. The reason for this change is that rental values of nondamaged homes doubled, and even tripled, in some disaster areas, such as happened in the Northridge area following the earthquake of January 17, 1994. Accordingly, the increased loss payments under fair rental value exceeded, in many instances, the actual additional living expenses of insureds. Since the opportunity for a windfall profit was never the intent, this option was deleted.

Boarding a Pet–Additional Living Expense

HO 00 03 insureds recently suffered a substantial fire loss to their home, which required them to find other living quarters during restoration.

The insureds have owned a dog for some time. The dog is an outside dog, but the question arises as to the cost of caring for the pet during the restoration period.

The additional living expense clause covers any necessary increase in living expenses incurred by you so that your household can maintain its normal standard of living. Keeping a pet is a part of this household's normal standard of living, and the cost of maintaining the pet when the residence cannot be occupied is a legitimate additional living expense. Therefore, it would appear that the additional costs related to caring for the dog, including boarding costs, would be compensable.

The fact that the dog is an outside dog rather than a house pet does not seem to alter the situation. With no one able to occupy the house, the animal could not be cared for if left at home. Finding an outdoor alternative less expensive than a kennel–leaving the dog with a friend for a modest fee, for example–would seem inappropriate because the animal might very well attempt to go back home, with harmful consequences.

Prohibited Use Coverage

The third of the loss of use coverages is often called "prohibited use" coverage. Additional living expense and fair rental value coverages are normally triggered by a covered section I loss to the residence premises that make it unfit to occupy. But there are circumstances in which insureds might be barred from access to their own residences as a result of damage to neighboring premises (as in the case of major fires or windstorms) that leaves their own homes with little or no damage and fit for occupancy. Prohibited use coverage pays additional living expense or fair rental value when an insured is prohibited from the use of the residence premises by a civil authority as a result of damage from an insured peril to neighboring premises. The maximum period during which this coverage applies is two weeks. Like the other loss of use coverages, prohibited use coverage may continue beyond the expiration date of the policy.

Webster's Collegiate Dictionary defines neighboring as "adjoining immediately or lying relatively near to," which appears to make the coverage available in circumstances where the premises immediately next door to an insured premises is not damaged, but the peril encroaches on the community. An example of this is the summer of 2007 wildfires in Utah, which came dangerously close to some communities, forcing evacuation.

There have been several cases construing the meaning of "neighborhood," usually within a planning or zoning context. One such is *Clayman v. Prince George's County*, 292 A.2d 689 (Ct. App. Md., 1972). Here, applicants requested rezoning from rural to commercial use to develop a shopping center. Those opposed argued that property values would decline and the enjoyment of their respective properties would be impaired. An argument in favor of the rezoning was that the nature of the "neighborhood" had changed. In finding for the appellants that the neighborhood had not changed, the court said "the neighborhood in any area must be an area which reasonably constitutes the immediate environs of the subject property and not some area miles away."

The court in *Maurer v. Austin Square, Inc.*, 215 N.E.2d 724 (Ct. App. Oh., 1966) turned to *Webster's New International Dictionary, Third Edition* (1964) for assistance in determining what a neighborhood was. This case also involved a dispute over zoning. The court agreed with Webster: "a.: a number of people forming a loosely cohesive community within a larger unit (as a city, town) and living close or fairly close together in more or less familiar association with each other within a relatively small section or district of usually somewhat indefinite boundaries and usually having some common or fairly common identifying feature (as approximate equality or economic condition, similar social status, similar interests) and usually some degree of self-sufficiency as a group (as through local schools, churches, libraries, business establishments, cultural and recreational facilities); b.: the particular section or district that is lived in by these people and that is marked by individual features (as type of homes and public establishments) that together establish a distinctive appearance and atmosphere; c.: an area or region of usually vague limits that is usually marked by some fairly distinctive feature of the inhabitants or terrain."

The court in *McDonald v. City of Concord*, 655 S.E.2d 455 (N.C. App, 2008) also turned to *Webster's New International Dictionary* (unabridged, 1993) and noted that there are "several definitions given for the term… Specifically, a neighborhood is 'a number of people forming a loosely cohesive community within a larger unit (as a city, town).'" The court went on to agree with the definition as given in *Maurer*, above, in making its determination.

But however "neighboring" is defined, it is important to note the damage that triggers coverage must be caused by an insured peril. For example, if rising flood waters prevent access to the residence premises, there will be no coverage since flood is not a peril covered by the homeowners forms. Further, the threat of damage alone is not a trigger. Damage must actually occur.

For a detailed discussion of prohibited use, see the article in *FC&S* "By Order of Civil Authority."

Receipts for Additional Living Expense

The insureds had an extensive fire loss, and were unable to live in their house. For a time they resided in a motel; they had to rent two rooms because their daughter was also living with them. They ate meals in a restaurant. Friends, who had a large house, invited the family to stay with them until they could find decent accommodation. The friends even provided meals. The insureds stayed with their friends several days, and paid the friends from their own finances. But when they submitted this bill to the insurer, the insurer refused to pay, stating that the friends' house was not a legitimate motel or hotel, and even implied that the insureds and the friends must have colluded together to defraud the insurer. Surely, even if the friends were kind enough to put the insureds up for such a long period of time without payment, they should be entitled to something for the extra expense they incurred.

There is certainly nothing in the policy that states insureds must reside in a hotel, motel, or rented house while their damaged premises is being restored, rebuilt, or replaced. And, unless the insurer has definite proof of collusion (and therefore fraud) it is extremely unwise to open a potential bad faith suit. A recent (unpublished) court case, *Grossman v. Homesite Insurance Company*, 2010 WL 1233907 (Conn. Super. 2010) addressed this issue. Here, the insureds stayed with friends, and turned in a receipt marked [name withheld] Bed and Breakfast. The insurer objected, stating that the claim had to be inflated, and that the friends did not operate a licensed bed and breakfast. The court pointed out that Connecticut state law did not require licensing for these operations; further, the claim was much less than one submitted when the insureds had to reside in a hotel. There had been no attempt to defraud, and the legitimate claim should be paid.

Coverage D Limit of Liability

The limit of liability specified for coverage D in the policy declarations constitutes an aggregate limit for the three loss of use coverages. The policy deductible is applied to coverage D losses. Since an additional living expense or fair rental value claim can arise only in connection with an insured property loss substantial enough to make the premises uninhabitable, the standard policy deductible of $500 will, in virtually all cases, be used up by the direct loss itself. The deductible will be a factor, for the most part, only in the event of a prohibited use claim, which may occur without any other section I loss.

Loss Not Covered

Finally, neither the AAIS nor the ISO homeowners will respond to loss or expense resulting from cancellation of a lease or agreement. This provision makes it clear that only a covered peril or action of civil authority resulting from a covered peril will trigger this coverage.

Chapter 3

The Additional Coverages

Introduction

Homeowners forms contain coverage enhancements termed *additional coverages* in the ISO forms and *incidental coverages* in the AAIS forms. Insurers originally added these coverages to the basic fire and extended coverages as inducements to consumers. Now it is hard to imagine a homeowners form without them, although there is a premium cost. And, since insurance contracts are contracts of adhesion, an insured cannot elect to forego the coverages he determines are unnecessary.

The number and kind of additional coverages vary by type of form–dwelling or tenant–and by scope of form–open perils or limited named perils. In ISO forms HO 00 02, HO 00 03, and HO 00 05 (comprehensive form), twelve additional coverages round out the section I coverage agreements of the homeowners policy. ISO form HO 00 04 contains twelve; HO 00 06 contains eleven; and ISO form HO 00 08 contains eight.

AAIS forms HO 0002, HO 0003, and HO 0004 contain fifteen coverages; form HO 0005 (special building and contents form) contains sixteen. Form HO 0006 contains thirteen, as does form HO 0001. Form HO 0008 contains ten.

As we shall see, there are some differences between the AAIS and ISO programs. AAIS added three new coverages in the 2006 edition, and continues these coverages into the current 2008 edition. Although many of the coverages are the same, AAIS offers coverage for refrigerated property that is available on the ISO forms only by endorsement. Introductory language to the coverages in the AAIS forms states that all of the incidental coverages are additional amounts of insurance unless specified. In the ISO forms, whether or not the amount provided is additional insurance is stated within the coverage grant itself.

We will discuss all additional or incidental coverages offered in the AAIS and ISO forms, noting the forms in which they appear. We will discuss the coverages of both the ISO and AAIS forms in the order in which they appear in ISO form HO 00 03, and include the number of the coverage in the AAIS form HO 0003. In the AAIS forms, coverages are listed in alphabetical order, so, for example, while debris removal is number 4. in form HO 0003, it is number 3. in form HO 0001 (HO 0001 does not contain collapse coverage). Therefore, if reviewing a form other than AAIS HO 0003, remember that the number might not be the same. We will conclude this chapter with the coverages in the AAIS forms that are not included in the ISO forms.

Debris Removal

Debris Removal of Covered Property

The ISO first additional coverage, contained in all the homeowners forms, is for debris removal. Debris removal is incidental property coverage 4. of the AAIS form HO 0003. If a covered loss leaves debris of covered property that must be removed, this coverage pays for the reasonable cost of that removal. So, for example, if a flood damages the insured's residence so that debris of the home must be removed, there is no coverage since flood is an excluded peril.

The cost of debris removal is included in the limit of liability applicable to the covered property, except when payment of the covered loss exhausts the applicable coverage limit. In that case, ISO and AAIS debris removal coverage will pay up to an additional 5 percent of the exhausted limit. For example, if a pole barn valued at $40,000 burns, the entire amount applies to both the barn and the cost to remove its debris. If it costs the entire $40,000 to rebuild the pole barn, then $2,000 (5 percent of $40,000) is available for debris removal. Also included within this coverage is the cost of removing volcanic ash and dust that causes direct damage to a building or property within a building.

The AAIS form adds that the coverage does not include any expenses to test for, monitor, clean up, remove, or in any way respond to or assess the effects of "pollutants". (The subject of pollutants, and the definition, are discussed in Chapter 6.)

Debris Removal of Fallen Trees

There is coverage in both the AAIS and ISO forms for removal from the residence premises (ISO) or the described location (AAIS) of the insured's trees felled by windstorm or hail, or weight of ice, snow or sleet, or a neighbor's trees felled by any of the coverage C named perils. This is additional insurance in both forms.

The ISO forms provide $1,000 with a $500 per tree limit. Coverage triggers may be: 1) damage to a covered structure; 2) blockage of a driveway allowing motor vehicles registered for use on public roads to access the premises; or 3) blockage of a ramp or other fixture designed to assist a handicapped person to enter or leave the dwelling. As noted above, the trees must be felled by windstorm, hail, weight of ice, snow or sleet, or, in the case of a neighbor's trees, a coverage C named peril.

The AAIS forms' incidental coverage for tree debris removal is also $1,000 with a $500 per tree limit. It responds to fallen trees that damage a covered structure, obstruct a ramp or other fixture designed to assist the handicapped to access the described location, or that obstruct a driveway on the described location. Here, the language differs from ISO in that the trees must prevent a motorized vehicle registered for use on public roads *or property* from accessing the insured premises. So, because in many states snowmobiles must be registered for use on public lands, presumably a drive blocked so an insured could not get his or her snowmobile off or onto the described location would qualify. The peril felling the trees must be windstorm or hail, or weight of ice, snow, or sleet; in the case of a neighbor's trees falling on the insured's property the falling must be caused by one of the coverage C perils.

Two questions are often raised with regard to the additional coverage for removal of trees. First, does the limit apply to the cost of removing the part of the tree that rests on the damaged structure, or is that cost considered to be part of the cost of repairing the structure? For example, if a tree is uprooted by windstorm and falls onto the dwelling, causing extensive damage, no repairs can begin until the parts of the tree resting on the building are cut away. It would, therefore, seem logical to categorize such costs as repair costs. The policy language, if strictly interpreted, would appear to include those costs within the $1,000 (or $500) limit. Remember, though, that this is an *additional coverage*. If the insurance coverage for repairs is insufficient, this additional coverage (coverage *in addition* to that otherwise provided for in the policy) may be called on.

Second, can the limit be used to remove the tree from the grounds, or does the limit apply only to removing it from covered property? The ISO policy provides that the insurer will also pay the reasonable expense, up to $1,000, for the removal from the residence premises of trees felled by the described perils. "Residence premises" is defined in the policy as the one- to four-family dwelling, other structures, and grounds where the insured resides. Thus, the $1,000 limit appears to apply to the removal from the dwelling and other structures as well as to removal from the grounds. Similarly, the AAIS form refers to the cost to remove the tree(s) from the "described location," which means the one- to four-family house, related private structures and grounds at that location where the named insured resides.

Storm Damage and Debris Removal

Recently an unexpected powerful storm dumped some six inches of rain in our area, causing supposedly dry creek beds to overflow into basements. In some instances, the force of the water caused foundation walls to buckle and collapse, allowing even more water to enter. Some houses will have to be rebuilt. What coverage is available to these homeowners? If they don't have flood insurance, is there at least coverage for removing destroyed contents from basements? What about removing trees that have fallen because of the water? What about water that backed up into basements because the storm drains couldn't handle the runoff?

Let's consider these situations one at a time. Although each is attributable to a single cause–the storm–only some of the resulting damage is covered. First, even though creek beds may normally be dry, when they *do* fill with water the result is a flood. *Webster's Collegiate Dictionary* defines flood as "a rising and overflowing of a body of water esp. onto normally dry land; also: a condition of overflowing." Flood is an excluded cause of loss under homeowners forms. Second, homeowners forms also exclude water damage resulting from surface water, which is commonly held to be the runoff of rain or melting snow. Damage resulting from these forms of water is not covered, so it follows that the cost to remove debris from the water, such as contents in a flooded basement, is not covered.

Trees falling because the ground becomes saturated and the roots tear out of the ground might be a different story. If a tree falls against a dwelling because of this, there is coverage under coverage A to remove the tree and repair any damage. The additional coverage for removal of trees will also apply if the storm included heavy wind (as well as the rain). Note, the tree

(scenario continues next page)

must fall against a dwelling or covered structure or block a drive or ramp designed to assist a handicapped person. (See the previous discussion.)

As far as damage from water backing up into basements, coverage hinges on whether or not the insured has coverage for water backup and sump overflow, such as that provided by ISO endorsement HO 04 95 or AAIS endorsement HO 2708. If that is the case, there might be coverage. However, the current endorsements allows coverage only if the water backup is not the result of flood. For example, if the water backup results strictly from storm drains' inability to handle the runoff of the rain, there is coverage. But if a stream overflows into a storm drain and causes it to back up, there would be no coverage. Since it might be hard to distinguish which type of water backed up in some instances, the insured should at the very least receive some consideration of his or her claim.

If the water backup or sump overflow endorsement responds to a loss, then there will also be coverage for debris removal.

Reasonable Repairs

The second of the ISO additional coverages is for reasonable repairs taken, in event of a covered loss, to protect covered property from further damage. In the AAIS form it is number 13. When insured property has been damaged by a covered peril, this additional coverage pays the reasonable cost for necessary *measures* taken solely to protect covered property from further damage. Note that *measures* need not necessarily mean *repairs.* So, for example, the cost for tarps to temporarily cover the hole where a roof was blown away is covered. Payments under the additional coverage are part of the limit of liability applicable to the property being repaired. Further, the reasonable repairs coverage does not relieve the insured of duties as prescribed under later conditions; that is, at the time of a loss, to protect the property from further damage even if that involves making necessary repairs to protect the property. Therefore, the insured is obligated to make repairs to protect covered property but might not be able to recover all the money spent.

The difficulty with the policy language is that it would appear to force the insured to make a determination at the time of the loss as to whether or not the loss is covered. Both ISO and AAIS refer to damage from a "Peril Insured Against," but in an *open perils* form, exactly what is that? Since losses are not always clear-cut, this could present a problem when the insured expects to collect for the cost of repairs if a loss turns out not to be covered. Conversely, if an insured thinks a loss is not covered and fails to make emergency repairs, could the claim be denied because of failure to fulfill the conditions?

Reasonable repairs coverage is designed principally to address loss situations in which quick action must be taken to minimize the extent of a loss. An insured with a broken picture window or smashed door cannot wait to file a claim before getting the damage repaired since this damage exposes the interior of the building and its contents to additional loss. When such a loss results from a covered peril, the measures taken to protect any covered property from further damage that are made to insured property will be reimbursed. For example, an insured might purchase plywood to board up a broken picture window because the glazier cannot immediately repair the damage. The cost of the plywood will be reimbursed.

We should note that in the earlier ISO forms, the provision supported coverage for claims in some areas where coverage would not otherwise be clear cut. For example, coverage for the cost of digging down to a broken underground water line on the insured's property to repair a leak was not specifically addressed in homeowners forms, although the cost of tearing out part of a building when the leak was *indoors* was included in open perils coverage on the dwelling. The cost of getting at broken pipes in either case, however, constituted part of the cost of repairs to prevent further damage–the leakage of water owned by the insured–and thus was a subject of reasonable repairs coverage if coverage was not otherwise spelled out.

But the ISO 2000 edition virtually eliminated coverage for digging down to get to a leaking pipe, unless the water damaged a covered structure. Further, water is no longer covered property. (See Chapter 4.) Therefore, it cannot be argued that the insured is losing covered property through accidental discharge of a plumbing system. Also, there is coverage for tear-out of a building or other structure, but, in the case of an other structure, only when the water causes actual damage to a building. See Chapter 6 for more information.

Trees, Plants, Shrubs, and Lawns

ISO additional coverage 3. and AAIS incidental property coverage 15. are for trees, plants, shrubs, and lawns. All of the property forms contain a variation of this coverage. Property in this category, ineligible for either coverage A, as part of the dwelling, or coverage C (property affixed to the realty becomes part of the realty), is insured on a limited basis by this additional coverage. Trees, shrubs, plants, and lawns on the residence premises are covered only against the perils of fire, lightning, explosion, riot, civil commotion, aircraft, vehicles (if not owned or operated by a resident of the insured premises, or, in the AAIS form, an occupant of the described location—see below), vandalism, malicious mischief, and theft, but not for damage by wind, hail, weight of ice or snow, or any unnamed peril that would be covered under open perils coverage. The ISO forms provide 5 percent of the coverage A limit of liability but no more than $500 for any one tree, plant, or shrub. The exceptions are forms HO 00 04 and HO 00 06, which allow 10 percent of the coverage C limit of liability, and form HO 00 08, which allows 5 percent but no more than $250 for any one tree, plant, or shrub. The ISO forms do not include the cost to remove the debris of any tree, shrub, or plant within the coverage, unlike the AAIS forms. There is another difference between the forms, and that is that the AAIS forms state that the insurer will pay for "direct physical loss." The ISO forms, on the other hand, state that the insurer will pay for "loss." There is a possibility of a denial of coverage, then, under the AAIS form where there should be none under the ISO. For example, suppose in quenching a house fire the water washes away several shrubs, or the firefighters trample the shrubs underfoot. Fire is the efficient cause of loss; however, under the AAIS form the fire has not "directly" caused the damage.

The AAIS forms differ slightly in that the vehicle causing damage cannot be owned or operated by an occupant—a broader term than resident—of the insured premises. Under this form, therefore, damage caused by someone temporarily staying, but not residing, at the insured premises would not be covered. The AAIS forms provide 5 percent of the coverage A limit of liability, with no more than $500 for each tree, plant, or shrub, and include within this amount the cost to remove any debris of the covered item. Unlike ISO, AAIS does not restrict the amount per tree, shrub, or bush in HO 0001 or HO 0008, but provides $500.

In both homeowners programs, the coverage for trees, plants, and shrubs is an additional amount of insurance. Both programs preclude coverage for any of this property if grown for business purposes.

Coverage for Loss to Medical Marijuana?

An insured, who has a license for medical marijuana, has lost all her plants and medication in a house fire. The insurer has requested a copy of the license to grow, as well as the receipts she used to purchase her medication. Despite having these forms, the insurer has denied coverage under coverage C for the plants and medication, and for the additional cost to purchase new plants under ALE. If other prescription drugs in the medicine cabinet, prescribed by the same doctor, are covered, why not the medical marijuana?

The prescription drugs and the cannabis should be covered as personal property. They're legally prescribed by a physician, and are necessary for the insured's health. She probably has a state-issued ID card (only New

(scenario continues next page)

Mexico requires a license to grow medical marijuana). Under state law in your insured's state, she is allowed to have twelve plants and 2 and a half ounces of harvested drug. Since a covered peril (fire) caused the loss, and no exclusion applies, the dried drug is covered as personal property.

The plants themselves are a different story. They fall under the category for trees, shrubs, plants and lawns, since there is no exception for houseplants. The per-plant limit applies. It is possible that a court would determine that the plants are not affected by the per-plant limit, since the wording "trees, shrubs, plants or lawns" would seem to indicate only those items grown in the land. In that case, the plants would be covered as personal property. However, until such time as a court makes a definitive ruling, the per-plant limit (and cause of loss) applies.

Fire Department Service Charge

If the named insured is liable under a contract or other agreement for fire department charges when firefighters are called to protect covered property from an insured peril, ISO additional coverage 4. (AAIS coverage 6.) will pay up to $500 (free of deductible) for such charges. The ISO form contains the provision that coverage does not apply if the property is located within the governmental unit or protection district providing the fire protection, as does the AAIS form.

All of the homeowners forms contain this additional coverage.

Property Removed

ISO additional coverage 5. and AAIS coverage 5., emergency removal, apply to instances in which it becomes necessary to protect covered property from a covered peril by moving it to another location. This coverage is an important aspect of preventing greater loss, and it is in all the homeowners forms. This coverage applies anywhere, against loss from *any cause,* for up to thirty days while the property is removed. The coverage does not increase the limit of liability on the removed property. The property being removed must be covered, but there is no stipulation that it must be removed from a *covered premises*. Also, the peril insured against need only be *endangering* the premises on which the covered property is located. For example, an insured could have personal property stored in a lock-up storage facility. He learns a fire is spreading toward the facility, so he moves the property to another location, where ten days later it is damaged by a flood. The coverage C limit of liability applies to this loss. (Under the current ISO form, we assume that the value of the stored property is no greater than 10 percent of coverage C, or $1,000, whichever is greater.)

It is important to recognize that, once the thirty days has elapsed, coverage for personal property reverts to the coverage C named perils. The thirty days limitation is only for the open perils coverage–true open perils with no exclusions–for the contents that have been removed to protect them.

The AAIS forms, unlike the ISO forms, add the provision that the coverage does not extend past the expiration date of the policy. Also, although the ISO forms state that the coverage insures against damage from any cause, the AAIS form adds that *any cause* does not include loss resulting from any act committed by or at the direction of an insured with the intention of causing a loss. (The ISO forms include similar language within the section I exclusions, which would therefore apply to the additional coverages.)

Unauthorized Use of Credit Cards

Additional coverage 6. of the ISO forms and incidental property coverage 3. of the AAIS forms provide coverage for losses resulting from theft or unauthorized use of credit or fund transfer cards or access devices, forgery, and counterfeit money. All homeowners forms in the two programs contain this coverage, but the two coverages are not identical in their scope.

In the ISO forms, $500 of coverage is provided for four categories of loss: 1) the legal obligation of an insured to pay for unauthorized use of credit cards issued to an insured or registered in an insured's name; 2) loss resulting from theft or unauthorized use of an insured's fund transfer card (often referred to as an ATM card) or access device used for deposit, withdrawal, or transfer of funds; 3) loss caused by forgery or alteration of a check or negotiable instrument; and 4) loss caused by the good-faith acceptance of counterfeit United States or Canadian paper money. This is additional coverage; no deductible applies.

Losses involving use of a card by a member of the named insured's household or anyone who has been entrusted with the card are not covered. Losses arising out of business use or the dishonesty of an insured are also excluded. For losses involving credit cards, the insured must have complied with the terms and conditions under which the credit card is issued. The $500 limit, which may be increased, functions as an aggregate with respect to a series of acts committed by one person.

The AAIS forms provide $1,500 ($5,000 in form HO 0005) of coverage, which may be increased, for the same categories of loss. Excluded are losses in which an insured has not complied with the rules under which the card was issued; in which the loss results from an insured's dishonesty or from an insured's business; in which a resident of the named insured's household has used the card or device; or in which an insured consents to another's (a noninsured) use of the card or device.

Since this coverage has as its subject certain legal liabilities of the insured (to pay for purchases illicitly made by others through use of a stolen credit card, for instance, or to meet the obligations imposed by the amount of a forged or altered check), it also includes an element of defense coverage similar to that associated with liability insurance. The earlier AAIS forms did not contain provisions for defense under this coverage, but the current forms state that the insurer has the option to defend an insured or the insured's bank when checks, drafts, or negotiable instruments are forged or altered.

A common Internet scam is to target an unwary seller. The seller (usually a U.S. citizen) offers something for sale; a "buyer" (usually *not* a U.S. citizen) offers to pay more than the item is worth. The "seller" offers to send a cashier's or certified check. The seller receives the check, deposits it, and sends the merchandise. By the time the buyer's bank notifies the seller the check has been a forgery, in some cases the unwary seller is already "on the hook" for any overdraft charges due to thinking the check was real. This coverage could help defray such expenses.

Both forms state that all loss resulting from a series of acts committed by any one person is considered to be one loss.

Loss Assessment

Additional coverage 7. of ISO form HO 00 03 (incidental property coverage 11. of AAIS HO 0003) is for loss assessed against the named insured arising from direct physical loss to property owned in common by all members of a property owners association. Loss assessments charged against the insured as owner or tenant of the residence premises are covered for up to $1,000 (the AAIS forms provide $1,500). The assessment must be made by a corporation or association of property owners and result from direct loss to property owned by all members collectively. The limit is the maximum amount available for all assessments arising from any one loss.

Loss must be caused by a something that would be covered if the property sustaining the loss were owned by the named insured, other than earthquake or land shock waves or tremors before, during, or after volcanic eruption. (Coverage for loss assessment for earthquake is available by endorsement.) The *assessments* must occur during the policy period, but the event(s) causing the assessments may occur before the policy takes effect. Any loss assessment charged against the insured or the property owners association by any government body is excluded. For example, if a condominium building fails a building inspection after being rebuilt following a covered fire, and the property owners association is fined for each day the building fails to pass, any assessment resulting from the fire is covered but the assessment resulting from the government-imposed fine is not.

The ISO form states that the most the insurer will pay is $1,000 "with respect to any one loss, regardless of the number of assessments. We will only apply one deductible, per unit, to the total amount of any one loss to the property described above [that is, owned by all members of the association], regardless of the number of assessments." Thus, if the named insured is assessed twice for one loss, perhaps $500 and $500, only one deductible will applied, not two. Or, if the named insured was assessed once, and then rented his or her unit and the new tenant was assessed again for the same loss, only one deductible would be applied.

The ISO form does not state that the $1,000 cannot be applied for an assessment to cover an association's deductible. On the other hand, the AAIS form precludes payment for a deductible; however, AAIS has an incidental coverage for association deductible, thus freeing this entire amount to apply to loss assessment exclusive of an association's deductible. We will discuss this at the end of this chapter.

Collapse

Additional coverage 8. in ISO form HO 00 03 and coverage 2. in AAIS HO 0003 provide coverage for collapse. This coverage is not contained in ISO HO 00 08 or AAIS forms HO 0001 or HO 0008. Both forms define *collapse* as an abrupt falling down, caving in (AAIS includes "or giving way") of a building or any part of a building. This must prevent the building or part of a building from being occupied for its intended purpose. Previously, many jurisdictions held that collapse could entail structural impairment, such as when a floor sags but has not collapsed or as when, say, a room addition separates from the main dwelling. The current definition, however, clearly intends that a building or part of a building be reduced to a heap of rubble, or, at the very least, so damaged that it cannot be occupied.

Both AAIS and ISO state that collapse is covered only if caused by a coverage C named peril, hidden decay, unless the presence of the decay was known to an insured (or, in the AAIS form, decay that no insured could reasonably have suspected); hidden insect or vermin damage (AAIS adds rodent damage and defines "vermin," which ISO does not) weight of animals, equipment, people, or personal property; weight of rain on a roof; or use of defective materials or methods in construction or repair if the collapse occurs during the course of the construction or repair.

The AAIS forms add clarifications not found in the ISO form. The terms of the collapse coverage provision do not limit coverage for direct loss caused by a peril insured against under coverage C. For example, if a loss is caused by the weight of ice, sleet, or snow, or by fire, and the dwelling becomes structurally impaired, the collapse provision would not preclude coverage since those perils have precedence over the coverage for collapse. Additionally, the forms state that with respect to the collapse coverage, the coverage C named peril of "weight of ice, snow or sleet means the weight of ice, snow, or sleet that causes damage to a building." This is important since the coverage C peril refers to the weight as causing damage to property within a building. The bacteria, fungi, and wet or dry rot exclusion does not apply to the coverage, nor does the exclusion for errors and omissions and defects. This clarifies that the use of defective materials or methods of construction, if they result in collapse during construction or repair, will not preclude coverage. This exclusion will be discussed in Chapter 6.

Loss to certain items is not covered, unless the cause of loss is the collapse of a building or any part of a building. Among these are awnings, fences, swimming pools, underground pipes, and retaining walls. The AAIS form clarifies that underground pipes, awnings, decks, etc., are not considered to be buildings or parts of buildings even if the items are attached to or connected to one or more buildings. Thus, an insured cannot argue that a drain line has collapsed and the cost to repair it should be covered.

Although the provision states that the coverage trigger must be collapse of a building, it does not stipulate collapse of a *covered* building. Say, for example, the wall of a neighbor's townhouse collapses and damages an insured's deck. A part of a building has collapsed, and that is sufficient for coverage. But if an insured's deck collapsed from the weight of people upon it there would be no coverage.

Forms HO 00 05 and HO 0005 provide coverage for personal property on an *open perils* basis, so there are no exclusions or limitations for personal property that is the subject of collapse.

Collapse Coverage

The insured has an HO 00 03. He has wet rot damage caused by water seeping under the shingles that has led to a sagging roof. The support beams have sustained water damage over a period of time, which has in turn resulted in the sagging roof. Does the insurer owe for both the roof and the support beams?

(scenario continues next page)

For collapse to be covered on an HO 00 03, the cause of the collapse must be one of those named under additional coverage 8. collapse. One of the causes is "hidden decay," which is the wet rot. Now, "wet rot" damage is itself excluded, but an ensuing loss to covered property described in coverages A and B not excepted or excluded is covered. The roof, though, is sagging. It has not collapsed into a heap of rubble, nor is the insured unable to occupy the building for its intended purpose, although, of course, that might change if the underlying roof beams are not repaired.

Under earlier ISO and AAIS forms, the insured might have made a case for coverage, depending upon the jurisdiction, since some courts had held that structural impairment was enough to trigger coverage. But as it stands, the language is quite clear and the damage is not covered.

Glass or Glazing Material

ISO additional coverage 9., glass or safety glazing material, is incidental property coverage 7. in the AAIS form. This coverage is contained in all the homeowners forms; however, it is limited in ISO form HO 00 08 and AAIS forms HO 0001 and HO 0008 to $100 per occurrence. Both forms promise to pay for breakage of glass or safety glazing material that is part of a covered building, storm door, or window. Where required by law, glass will be replaced with safety glazing materials. Direct physical loss to covered property damaged by the glass breakage is also covered, as when the shards from a shattered picture window rip a nearby armchair. However, if because glass is broken rain enters and soaks the chair, there is no coverage for the damaged chair. Loss caused by earth movement to glass that is part of a building, storm door, or storm window is also covered. There is no coverage for loss if the dwelling or residence has been vacant for more than sixty days preceding the loss.

To be covered under ISO form HO 00 04, the glass must be that which would be covered under the additional coverage for building additions and alterations; to be covered under AAIS form HO 0004, the glass must be that which would be covered under tenant's improvements. To be covered under the condominium forms, the glass would have to be covered under coverage A. Although both forms exclude coverage for glass breakage if the dwelling has been vacant for sixty days preceding the loss, this exclusion does not apply if the breakage is caused by earth movement. (In the condominium forms, the entire building containing the covered units must be vacant.) The forms clarify that dwellings under construction are not to be considered vacant.

In neither the AAIS nor the ISO forms does the coverage increase the limit that applies to the damaged property. In other words, should a dwelling burn the insured cannot claim an additional amount for the destroyed windows.

Landlord's Furnishings

Additional coverage 10. in the ISO HO 00 03 is for landlord's furnishings. The AAIS form incidental coverage 12. is property in rental units. ISO forms HO 00 04, HO 00 06, and HO 00 08, and AAIS forms HO 0004, HO 0006, and HO 0008 do not contain this coverage. In both programs, up to $2,500 per apartment is provided for appliances, carpeting, and other household furnishings contained in an apartment on the residence premises that is regularly rented or held for rental to others. Coverage is provided on a named peril basis–the coverage C perils–with the exception of theft, which is not covered. Any deductible applies on a per-loss basis.

Additions and Alterations

Rather than coverage for landlord's furnishings, the ISO HO 00 04 provides an additional amount of insurance–10 percent of the coverage C limit of liability–for improvements, alterations, or installations made to the building at the tenant homeowner's expense. In AAIS form HO 0004, incidental property coverage 9. is called tenant's improvements, and allows 10 percent of the coverage C limit for tenant's improvements. The coverage C named perils apply.

Ordinance or Law

ISO HO 00 03 additional coverage 11. applies to increased costs incurred because of enforcement of ordinance or law. This is incidental coverage 9. in the AAIS form. Not all of the homeowners forms contain this coverage. It is not in ISO form HO 00 08 or in AAIS form HO 0008.

This coverage responds if a covered loss results in covered property–a covered building or other structure–having to be rebuilt, repaired, or demolished in accordance with the enforcement of any building code, law, or ordinance governing the rebuilding, repair, or demolishing. In the ISO forms, coverage is limited to 10 percent of the coverage A amount (10 percent of the building alterations amount in ISO form HO 00 04 and 10 percent of the tenant's improvements amount in AAIS HO 0004) and is an additional amount of insurance. Similarly in the AAIS HO 0003, 10 percent of the coverage A limit is available. The AAIS forms do not specifically state the insurer will cover the cost to demolish and reconstruct the undamaged part of a covered building if it must be demolished because of damage to another part of the covered building, nor, on the other hand, do they exclude this cost. This cost may be considered part of the increased cost resulting from enforcement of ordinance or law and, therefore, covered.

Both forms state that the coverage may also be used for increased costs to remove debris. This provision is set out in a separate provision from the provision regarding regulation of construction, repair, replacement, or demolition. Thus, the coverage for debris removal can be used even if no ordinance or law regulates the debris removal itself; the trigger is that the ordinance or law must regulate construction, demolition, remodeling, renovation, repair, or replacement. Note that this provision for debris removal is different from the additional coverage for debris removal. Under ordinance or law coverage, the cost for the debris removal must be directly related to the ordinance or law enforcement—or, as the AAIS forms state, the coverage responds to cover the increased cost of debris removal when the loss to an insured residence or structure is caused by a peril insured against, and a code, ordinance or law regulates the construction, repair, replacement, or demolition of the residence or structure.

Both forms exclude costs or expense resulting from any law or ordinance that requires testing for, monitoring for, or cleanup of any pollutants. So, for example, if a covered fire destroys an older home with asbestos-wrapped furnace pipes, the coverage will not respond to cleanup of the asbestos. Also, any loss in value resulting from the enforcement of any code, law, or ordinance is excluded. For example, if a building code states that those charming wooden shakes on a roof must be replaced with fiberglass shingles because of fire regulations, with the result that the scenic log house loses $5,000 in value, the coverage will not respond.

Both forms state that the insurer pays for the increased costs "you incur." The question thus arises as to whether an insured can claim this additional amount to apply, say, to a replacement residence if he or she decides just to walk away from an insured destroyed dwelling. *Webster's Collegiate Dictionary* defines "incur" as "to come into or acquire (something undesirable) /to *incur* a debt." Thus, if no rebuilding or repair takes place, no debt, as to a contractor, has been incurred. But if local ordinance requires the insured to remove the debris from the destroyed dwelling, the coverage can be called upon for the expense.

Are Association Bylaws Ordinance or Law?

Suppose an insured resides in an area governed by a homeowners association. The association has drawn up bylaws regulating such things as color of front doors, flagpoles, etc. The insured dwelling burns, and the bylaws state that he must replace his (grandfathered) siding with cedar shakes.

Will ordinance or law coverage pay for this increased cost?

The answer is no. Bylaws, according to *Webster's New World College Dictionary,* are "any of a set of rules adopted by an organization or assembly for governing its own meetings or affairs." This is in contrast with *law,* which is "all the rules of conduct established and enforced by the authority, legislation, or custom of a given community, state, or other group."

Agent Tip

Particularly in regards to older homes, the standard amount of ordinance or law coverage may be insufficient. For example, a home built in 1920, with a replacement cost of $100,000, partially burns. The systems were last updated in 1970. Now, however, the aluminum wiring must be replaced with Romex, and all remaining lead pipes with PVC, at a cost of $12,000. Or, perhaps the house is over 50 percent damaged and must be demolished at a cost of $22,000. The 10 percent allotted by the policy is now used up. While a careful review of local building codes often is not feasible, the safest practice is to increase the coverage if there is any doubt.

The Oakland Hills fire of October 1991 proved a harsh lesson as to the value of this coverage. Some insureds, believing that they had full replacement cost policies, found to their horror they were as much as 83% *underinsured* because of the changes in the building codes.

Grave Markers

Coverage for grave markers is now explicitly included in the homeowners forms. Although individual or family cemetery plots or burial vaults of an insured have always been considered insured locations for liability purposes, coverage for the vaults, markers, or monuments themselves has been the subject of confusion. Are they other structures? If so, must separate coverage be arranged unless they are on the insured premises? If the insured does not own the land upon which they stand, this approach does not seem logical. Or are they personal property? In that case, the full amount of coverage C was available in the earlier forms. Many, including the editors of *FC&S Bulletins* (The National Underwriter Company, Cincinnati, Ohio) are of this opinion.

But now, grave markers have additional coverage status, and therefore, may be perceived by some as having less coverage. The amount available is $5,000 for grave markers, including mausoleums, on or away from the residence premises. The coverage C named perils apply.

In the AAIS form, this is incidental coverage 8. Coverage is up to $2,500 ($5,000 in the HO 0005). The coverage C named perils apply.

Association Deductible

As noted in the beginning of this chapter, the AAIS forms offer coverages not included in the ISO forms. The first of these is called *association deductible*, and it is incidental coverage 1. It is a new coverage in the 2006 edition. The coverage, $1,500 per occurrence (which may be increased) responds to an association deductible charged against the named insured as owner or tenant of the described location. The incidental coverage for loss assessment no longer will reimburse an assessment for an association insurance deductible. The association deductible coverage applies when an association deductible is charged against the named insured as owner or tenant of the described location. The deductible must have resulted from direct loss to property that: would have been eligible for coverage if owned by the named insured. It must be covered by the association insurance, and caused by a peril insured against under coverage A in the named insured's policy, except for earthquake or land shock waves associated with volcanic eruption.

Liquid Fuel Remediation

The current AAIS forms HO 0002, HO 0003, HO 0004, HO 0005, and HO 0006 contain incidental coverage 10. liquid fuel remediation. The coverage, $10,000 (which may be increased), responds to loss to property covered under coverages A, B, or C; land; or property covered under the incidental coverage for trees, plants, shrubs, or lawns. The land must be within the described location, other than farmland, and the site of a residence insured under coverage A or a related private structure insured under coverage B. The loss must be caused directly or indirectly by discharge, dispersal, emission, escape, leaching, leakage, migration, release, seepage, or spillage of liquid fuel from the fuel system of a heating or air conditioning system, a water heater, or domestic appliance on the described location. Included as well are costs for temporary measures to stop the fuel escape, costs to prevent the spread of the fuel, debris removal costs, and costs to clean up fuel from property covered under coverages A, B, or C, land, or trees, plants, shrubs, or lawns. However, if the discharge, dispersal, etc., is caused by a coverage C named peril, terms a. through g. of the liquid fuel remediation additional coverage—notably the $10,000 limit—do not apply.

The total amount of coverage applies to all discharges, leakages, etc., that an insured first discovers or is made aware of during the policy period.

Coverage D, additional living expense, does not apply to a loss caused by liquid fuel escape. Rather, additional living expense coverage is included within the $10,000 amount. And, although the incidental coverage for trees, shrubs, plants and lawns is 5 percent of the coverage A limit, that amount as well is included within the liquid fuel remediation coverage. No more than $500 for any tree, shrub, plant, or lawn will be paid.

The coverage does not cover damages resulting in loss of value of property or land, loss of market value, or loss because of cancellation of a lease.

Refrigerated Food Spoilage

An AAIS incidental property coverage not found in the ISO forms is $500 for refrigerated food spoilage, number 14. The food must be in a refrigerator or freezer on the insured premises, and the spoilage must be caused by interruption of electrical service caused by damage to the generating or transmission equipment or by mechanical or electrical breakdown of the refrigeration equipment. Coverage is on a per occurrence basis. So, for example, if lightning strikes transmission wires leading to the insured premises and causes a power outage, spoilage of refrigerated food is covered for $500.

Many insureds do not understand that food spoilage is not direct physical damage from a covered peril; rather, it is a consequential loss. Therefore, this coverage is valuable. Of course, it can be added to ISO homeowners by attaching endorsement HO 04 98, refrigerated property coverage.

Lock and Garage Door Transmitter Coverages

AAIS form HO 0005, special building and contents form, contains lock and garage door transmitter replacement coverage, incidental coverage 11. The amount of $500 is available to replace locks on exterior doors or the portable transmitter to the insured's automatic garage door, if the keys or transmitter are lost or stolen. The insured must notify the insurer within seventy-two hours of discovering the loss.

Having this coverage means the following will not apply: 1) the pair and set clause, in which the insurer pays the difference in actual cash value of the pair or set before the loss and the actual cash value just after the loss; or 2) the loss to parts clause, wherein the insurer pays only for the value of the lost or damaged part or the cost to repair or replace it. We will discuss these in Chapter 7.

Chapter 4

Limitations; Property Not Covered

Introduction

Certain categories of personal property, although covered by standard homeowners insurance, are subject to special limits of liability that are much lower than the overall coverage C limit. Property items included in these categories, for the most part, are of potentially high value, compact and readily portable, and thus attractive to thieves. The average homeowner usually does not own property in excess of the values provided, and it is the "average" homeowner for whom the pricing structure is designed.

For insureds with values in excess of any of these limits, increased limits or separate inland marine coverage can be arranged at additional premium. See, in particular, Chapter 13 for a discussion of scheduling personal property. If the ISO insured has not purchased *open perils* coverage on personal property, coverage C special limits may be increased by adding endorsement HO 04 65. If the insured has open perils coverage on personal property–through the HO 00 05 comprehensive form, the HO 00 06 endorsed by HO 17 31, or HO 00 04 endorsed by HO 05 24—the special limits may be increased by adding HO 04 66. In the AAIS program, the HO 0005 provides *open perils* coverage for personal property. The HO 0006 can be endorsed with HO 7029 and the HO 0004 with HO 2730 to provide open perils coverage. The special limits may be increased by attaching endorsement HO 2565. These endorsements are described in Chapter 13.

The property subject to these internal limits in the policy and the restricted amounts of coverage provided are outlined below. It should be noted that the limit specified for each category is the total amount recoverable for one loss involving any or *all* of the kinds of property included in the category. Also, the special limits are not additional amounts of insurance. Rather, they are included in the total coverage C limit.

Since there are limitations on property used in business, we begin with the definitions of "business." (Obviously the definitions will be important with regard to liability coverage, but here our focus is on property.)

Definition of *Business*

Both ISO and AAIS have changed the definition of *business*. Earlier editions of the forms stated either that: "Business includes trade, profession or occupation" (ISO) or "Business means a trade, a profession, or an occupation including farming, all whether full or part time. This includes the rental of property to others. It does not include the occasional rental for residential purposes of the part of the 'insured premises' normally occupied solely by 'your' household" (AAIS). These definitions impacted, as we will see, the limitation for property used in business as well as liability coverage. But in the current programs, the definitions have been revised so that many activities an insured might engage in to earn a little extra money are exempt. The ISO definition reads:

> "Business" means:
>
> a. A trade, profession or occupation engaged in on a full-time, part-time or occasional basis; or
>
> b. Any other activity engaged in for money or other compensation, except the following:
>
> (1) One or more activities, not described in (2) through (4) below, for which no "insured" receives more than $2,000 in total compensation for the 12 months before the beginning of the policy period;
>
> (2) Volunteer activities for which no money is received other than payment for expenses incurred to perform the activity;
>
> (3) Providing home day care services for which no compensation is received, other than the mutual exchange of such services; or
>
> (4) The rendering of home day care services to a relative of an "insured".

> The AAIS definition of a business is:
>
> a. a trade, a profession, or an occupation, including farming, all whether full time, part time, or occasional. This includes the rental of property to others, but does not include:

1) the occasional rental for residential purposes of that part of the "described location" normally occupied solely by "your" household; or

2) the rental or holding for rental of a portion of that part of the "described location" normally occupied by "your" household to no more than two roomers or boarders for use as a residence; or

b. any other activity undertaken for money or other compensation, but this does not include:

1) providing care services to a relative of an "insured";

2) providing services for the care of persons who are not relatives of an "insured" and for which the only compensation is the mutual exchange of like services;

3) a volunteer activity for which:

a) an "insured" receives no compensation; or

b) an "insured's" only compensation is the reimbursement of expenses incurred to carry out the activity; or

4) an activity not described in 1) through 3) above for which no "insured's" total compensation for the 12 month period just before the first day of this policy period was more than $2,500.

A note of caution–coverage for home day care activities may still be excluded by an endorsement that many insurers attach as a matter of course to policies. So, despite the forms defining a business as not including an activity generating a certain amount of income, it is wise to check before assuming paid home day care will be a covered activity.

Limitations

Money

The first special limit in the ISO form is $200 applying to money, bank notes, bullion, gold and silver other than goldware or silverware, platinum other than platinumware, coins, and medals. The AAIS forms limit coverage to $250. Both programs add scrip, stored value cards, and smart cards to this category of property. These are items that can act as money; in other words, they serve as a medium of exchange. Scrip is often used by charitable organizations or schools to raise money. The purchaser pays a fraction of the redeemable value and the difference is donated by the retailer to the organization. Examples of stored value cards are gift certificates and phone cards. Smart cards are similar to credit or debit cards, but they also store information on the cardholder. The AAIS form clarifies the intent by adding "other devices on which a cash value is stored electronically."

Including these items within the category answers the question as to what the insurer will pay in event of a covered loss. For example, if an insured has received a $500 stored value card for a birthday present, the amount recoverable is $200, not $500.

The limit for gold and silver can be troublesome. Remember that this limit applies to loss resulting from any of the coverage C perils, such as fire. It appears that the limit is intended to apply to silver and gold as commodities; however, silver and gold can also apply to articles made of silver or gold, such as silver candelabra or figurines.

Agent Tip

There is another limit for theft of silverware, discussed subsequently. If any doubt whatsoever exists, the prudent agent will arrange for proper coverage.

Securities

The ISO form provides $1,500 for securities, accounts, deeds, evidences of debt, letters of credit (a letter from a bank asking that the holder of the letter be allowed to draw upon the account of the writer of the letter), notes other than bank notes, manuscripts, personal records, passports, tickets and stamps. The AAIS program also limits coverage to $1,500, except for form HO 0005, in which the limit is $2,500. This dollar limit applies to these categories regardless of the medium (such as paper or computer software) on which the material exists. The limit includes the cost to research, replace, or restore the information from the lost or damaged material.

Before the current AAIS and ISO editions, it was possible to argue that scrip or stored value cards were evidences of debt, and so the limit for this category of property could apply if an insured sustained a loss of both money and a stored value card. That argument can no longer be made since the limit for money specifically includes these items.

Watercraft

AAIS special limit c.5) provides $1,500 ($2,500 in form HO 0005) for watercraft, including their trailers, semitrailers, furnishings, equipment and outboard engines or motors. The limit applies in the aggregate. ISO's special limit 3.c. is also $1,500. This low limit, together with the exclusions for wind or hail loss to this property (unless in a fully enclosed building) or theft away from the premises, makes it generally better to provide separate coverage for watercraft and their accessories, either by a watercraft endorsement to the homeowners or by a separate policy. The AAIS form used to contain an exception for canoes and rowboats, providing coverage for loss resulting from windstorm or hail for such watercraft so long as they were on the insured premises, but that exception has been removed from the "windstorm or hail" peril. Neither AAIS nor ISO cover theft of watercraft away from the insured premises.

The AAIS forms add that this limit does not apply to model watercraft not designed or used to carry people or cargo, or to hovercraft. Hovercraft, as will be seen, are not covered at all.

Coverage for Fishing Equipment

The insured likes to go fly fishing, and has amassed a good collection of flies, rods and reels, as well as waterproof waders, tackle boxes, etc. Sometimes, though, he takes a rowboat out into the lake at his cabin with all his fishing gear. Because he has a considerable amount of money tied up in the fishing equipment, if the gear were to be lost in a fire would the limit apply?

The phrasing of the limitation on watercraft refers to "their equipment." The fishing gear does not equip the watercraft in the way, say, that oars or floating seat cushions do. The limitation should apply to items used specifically to equip the watercraft for its function as a watercraft. The fishing gear does not do this and is exempt from the limitation.

Trailers

ISO special limit 3.d. limits coverage on trailers not used with watercraft to $1,500, as does the AAIS special limit c.6). (The AAIS limit for this property in form HO 0005 is $2,500.) AAIS adds that this category includes semitrailers, but not trailers or semitrailers designed for or used with watercraft. There is no restriction as to type of trailer, so a horse trailer or pull-behind camper has coverage. However, there is no coverage under either program for *theft* occurring away from the insured premises. Trailers of greater value than that provided for in the homeowners forms–or when coverage for theft is desired–may be covered separately under the auto policy, depending upon underwriting criteria.

Jewelry, Watches, and Furs

The next three special limits apply to loss by *theft* only, except where noted. The first of these, ISO special limit 3.e., is $1,500 for loss by theft of jewelry, watches, furs, and precious and semi-precious stones. The larger AAIS limit c.7) of $2,500 adds gems to this list. Neither ISO form

HO 00 08 nor AAIS form HO 0008 contain limits on theft of jewelry, watches, furs, guns, or silver-, gold-, pewter-, or platinumware because the overall theft limit for all personal property in the forms themselves is $1,000. Although ISO HO 00 05 limits coverage to $1,500, loss by *misplacing* or *losing* is also covered. Misplacing or losing is also covered when HO 17 31 is attached to the HO 00 06 or the H0 05 24 is attached to the HO 00 04. AAIS form HO 0005 also includes loss by misplacing or losing; the limit is $2,500. In the AAIS program, adding HO 2730 to an HO 0004 achieves the same effect, as does adding HO 7029 to an HO 0006.

Remember, the limits for theft of jewelry, watches, furs, silver, and guns can be increased. ISO endorsement HO 04 65 or AAIS endorsement HO 2565 should be attached to the policy.

The stated limit applies to each theft of property in any or all of the named categories, so that if one theft results in loss of a $500 watch, a $1,000 necklace, and a $1200 mink, the ISO HO 00 03 insured's limit is still $1,500. Note the limit applies only to loss by theft (or misplacing or losing where added by endorsement). If the jewelry is damaged by fire, the full coverage C amount is available.

Disagreement sometimes arises as to the meaning of the term *jewelry*. The word is not defined in the policy, so a standard desktop dictionary provides guidance. Some dictionary definitions of *jewelry* make it applicable to costume jewelry as well as to items containing genuine stones or precious metals; for example, according to the *Random House Dictionary*: "any ornament for personal adornment…including those of base metals, glass, plastic and the like." *Webster's Collegiate Dictionary,* however, defines *jewelry* as "objects of precious metal often set with gems and worn for personal adornment." Costume jewelry would thus appear exempt from the limitation under this definition, but many jewelry items can be made with materials other than precious metals and be quite expensive. Think, for example, of an ivory bracelet. Some jewelry designers work in stainless steel but still charge high prices for their work. If there is any doubt, the safest approach is to schedule the items.

In the case of *Standard Fire Insurance Company v. Griggs*, 567 S.W.2d 60 (Tex. App. 1978), the court held that the trial court had erred when it determined that various items of value were not jewelry. The insured's home was burglarized, and among the items stolen were seven Indian concha belts (belts of leather with silver and turquoise mountings) and bolo ties decorated with silver and inlay work. One expert testified that the items were articles of clothing, while another considered them "objects of adornment" or jewelry.

With respect to the meaning of furs, courts have most often adopted an interpretation advantageous to the insured. In *Starry v. Horace Mann Insurance Co.*, 649 P.2d 937 (Alaska 1982), the court ruled that a bear hide wall mount worth $5,000 was not subject to the fur limitation since, in the court's opinion, the language of the limitation made it applicable only to "common, everyday effects in the nature of jewelry and fur-bearing garments."

On the other hand, an Indiana court in the case of *Asbury v. Indiana Union Mutual Insurance Co.*, 441 N.E.2d 232 (Ind. Ct. App. 1982) held that animal pelts acquired through the insured's hunting hobby had the status of furs within the scope of the limit. The insurer denied any coverage at all on the pelts, contending that they were excluded as business property held for sale. The insured did customarily sell the animal skins from his hunting trips. But the court found an ambiguity between the exclusion of furs when offered for sale as part of a business and the fur limitation which, it said, could be understood as a specific provision of coverage on furs of any kind in the limited amount. In light of this perceived ambiguity, the Indiana court overturned a judgment for the insurer and ruled that the status of the pelts with respect to homeowners coverage was a factual question to be determined by a jury. (We will discuss the limit for business property later.)

The common element in both the Indiana and the Alaska courts' divergent readings of the fur limitation is that both interpretations worked to the insured's advantage.

Agent Tip

The lesson is obvious that, if there is any doubt, schedule the articles.

Firearms and Guns

The ISO limit 3.f. of $2,500 for firearms and related equipment is, again, for theft. AAIS special limit c.7)c) is $2,500 for guns and items related to guns. As noted above, ISO HO 00 08 and AAIS HO 0008 do not have this limitation because the overall theft limit is $1,000. When an ISO or AAIS form provides open perils contents coverage, the $2,500 limit includes losing or misplacing. The limitation applies to loss by theft; if the firearms were damaged by fire, the full amount of coverage C would be available.

Firearms is a more limited term than *guns*, usually applying only to small arms capable of being carried easily by an individual, but not to artillery weapons. *Webster's Collegiate Dictionary* defines a firearm as "a weapon from which a shot is discharged by gunpowder, usu. used of small arms." The first definition of a gun, on the other hand, is "a piece of ordnance usu.

with high muzzle velocity and comparatively flat trajectory." The limit in both forms used to apply only to the guns themselves, but now the limit applies to items such as detachable gunsights, carrying cases, slings, cartridges or shells, and extra magazines or clips.

Silverware and Similar Property

The final limitation for theft only (3.g. in the ISO forms; c.7)b) in the AAIS forms) provides $2,500 for silverware, silver-plated ware, goldware, gold-plated ware, platinum and platinum-plated ware, and pewterware. The ISO forms include flatware, hollowware, tea sets, trays and trophies made of or including silver, gold, or pewter. AAIS simply adds that the limitation also applies to items plated with gold, silver, or platinum. Misplacing or losing is included when open perils coverage is added. Note that the limitation applies to flatware and hollowware, tea sets, trays, and trophies made of *or including* any of these metals. Flatware is just that–tableware more or less flat, such as knives, forks, etc. Hollowware, on the other hand, means objects having significant depth, as cups, vases, and bowls. Therefore, objects such as solid sterling silver candelabra or figurines appear to fall outside the limitation. It could be argued that such objects are within special limitation a. (money, etc.) as discussed previously, since they are silver; however, an equally strong argument is that gold and silver are within the list of items readily convertible to cash, as are ingots or bullion. Since the candelabra are not readily convertible, they should not be included. A review of case law for evidence one way or another did not clarify the issue.

Agent Tip

When there is any doubt or question whatsoever, the agent should obtain proper coverage. Few insureds wish to argue semantics following a loss; they simply want the loss to be covered.

Business Property on the Premises

The next two limitations of coverage had been among the most troublesome until the current homeowners forms. The first is for property used in business while on the residence premises. To see how the current editions have solved this problem, we first look at the ISO 1991 edition's limitation:

> $2,500 on property, on the "residence premises," used at any time or in any manner for any "business" purpose.

The AAIS limit was also $2,500 for personal property used in whole or in part for business purposes, while on the residence premises. Included as well in the AAIS limitation was any cost to research, reproduce, replace, or restore business data.

A strict reading of the language of the business property special limit in the ISO 1991 forms would treat any household property—tools, perhaps, used in a grandparent's work as a carpenter—that has ever been used at any time in any way in any business activity as subject to the special limit. It must be remembered, however, that the homeowners contract is between the insured and insurer and not between the insured's ancestor and the insurer. And, under the ISO 1991forms, if the residence premises were rented on an occasional basis, would the limit apply to household furnishings? AAIS does not include this occasional rental within the definition of *business* (see above), thus allowing for coverage. And, as we will discuss, the key to coverage under the current ISO forms is the use of the word *primarily*. If the insured residence is rented on a rare occasion, that hardly qualifies as the furnishings being used primarily for business.

The limitation for property used in business in the current ISO forms now states:

> $2,500 on property, on the "residence premises", used *primarily* [italics added] for "business" purposes.

While the AAIS forms state that the insurer will pay $2,500:

> For loss to personal property used primarily for "business" purposes, other than property rented or held for rental to others.

The use of the adverb *primarily* allows for a much broader interpretation in favor of an insured as opposed to the ISO 1991 "property used at any time or in any manner for any 'business' purpose." Because of this change in wording, the possible coverage gaps noted above no longer exist. So, in the example of grandfather's carpentry tools, the articles are no longer used primarily for business; rather, they are mementos or collectibles. Remember, though, that although there is now coverage for an other structure used to store business property belonging to an insured, the $2,500 limit still applies to the stored property itself.

For example, an insured may own a laptop that is used both personally and for business. If the insured keeps the laptop at work most of the time and uses the bulk of the memory for business files, application of the limitation is likely. However, if the insured takes the laptop to work occasionally, but mostly uses it for personal business, then the limitation should not apply.

AAIS states this limitation does not apply to "property rented or held for rental to others"; this type of property is included in the list of "property not covered" and is discussed later in this chapter. AAIS includes, within this coverage, the cost of research or other expenses necessary to reproduce, replace, or restore business data.

When an acceptable business (studio, office, professional, or private school) is conducted on the insured premises, then endorsements ISO HO 04 12 or AAIS HO 3542 may be used to increase business property limits on furnishings, supplies, and equipment.

Agent Tip

Although both ISO and AAIS have determined that activities generating no more than $2,000 or $2,500 respectively in the year prior to the policy period should not be construed as businesses, the line is still a fine one between non-business and business. For example, an ISO insured decides that his woodworking hobby can bring in some much-needed income. He makes furniture, and sells it, making $2,100. His dwelling burns. Conceivably the insurer could deny coverage for his expensive table saw, router, etc. since they are now used primarily for business purposes. It would be prudent to check with insureds to see if any "hobbies" could potentially fall into the business category.

Business Property Away from the Premises

Coverage for personal property while away from the insured premises or the described location, and primarily used in business, is limited to $500 in the AAIS current forms, and $1,500 in the ISO forms. The 2000 ISO form contained a $500 limit for property used primarily for business *other than* electronic devices. Now, however, the $1,500 limit applies to all property used primarily for business and away from the premises. The limit does not apply to electronic apparatus or accessories; separate limits apply.

These limits can be increased by using endorsement HO 04 12 except with respect to business property (a) in storage or held as a sample or for sale or delivery after sale or (b) pertaining to a business to actually be conducted on the residence premises. Increase in the limit on premises automatically increases the off-premises limit as well, so that the off-premises limit is always 20 percent of the on-premises limit. The AAIS form for coverage of business property away from the described location is HO 6243.

Electronic Apparatus in a Vehicle

AAIS special limit c.3) for $1,500 ($2,500 in HO 0005), and ISO special limit 3.j. for $1,500 apply to portable, adaptable electronic equipment. Adaptable electronic equipment is the kind that is equipped to be operated from the electrical system of a motor vehicle yet can also be operated by other sources of power. The AAIS form limits this coverage to property while in or on a motorized vehicle *or watercraft*. The AAIS category also includes accessories: antennas or tapes, wires, records, discs or other media that can be used with this type of apparatus.

Agent Tip

Laptops are a prime target! While popping in to the local Starbucks for a latte, it is tempting to leave one's laptop in plain view in the passenger seat. And, because many people now store personal information (banking passwords, for example) on laptops, they are high value items for thieves. The $1,500 applies to theft of the laptop itself; if personal data is stolen, then it is to be hoped the insured has identity theft coverage!

Apparatus affected by the ISO limitation is the kind that is designed to be operated by more than one power source. The wording has been changed from the 2000 edition, which referred to the electronic apparatus as being "equipped to be operated by power from the motor vehicle's operating system." Thus, if the item in question had no separate power cord allowing it to be plugged into the cigarette lighter, it could be argued that the unit was not actually equipped but merely capable of being operated, which would be a strong argument for coverage above the limitation. That loophole has been closed.

ISO has also changed the limit in the 2011 form for accessories for electronic equipment. Coverage for antennas, tapes, wires, records, disks or other media used with electronic equipment "that reproduces, receives or transmits audio, visual or data signals" and is in or upon a motor vehicle is now limited to $250.

The AAIS wording states that the limitation applies to devices that *can be* operated from either power source. Included within the limitation are accessories: antennas, films, tapes, wires, discs, records, or other media that can be used with such devices.

Electronic Apparatus Not in a Vehicle

As noted earlier, the ISO 2011 form no longer contains special limit 3.k. for $1,500 for electronic apparatus used primarily for business while away from the residence premises and not in or upon a motor vehicle. Rather, the $1,500 limit 3.i. for property used primarily in business applies.

AAIS special limit c.4) for $1,500 ($2,500 in HO 0005) applies to adaptable electronic apparatus while not in or upon a motor vehicle or other motorized land conveyance, or watercraft. The limit applies to electronic apparatus that is: 1) equipped to be operated from the electrical system of a motor vehicle but is capable of operating from another power source; 2) away from the residence premises; and 3) used primarily for any business purpose. Again, accessories or tapes, records, discs, or other media are included in the limitation.

How the Deductible Applies to the Special Limits

The question has been raised about how the homeowners deductible affects recovery under the special limits. In the earlier ISO forms, application was not clearly spelled out. Therefore, claims adjusters often paid the insured the maximum amount that could be justified.

For example, assume an insured has an ISO HO 00 03, $75,000 coverage C personal property limit, and a standard $500 deductible. She is robbed of jewelry and a watch with a value of $2,500, cash totaling $500, and other personal property amounting to $1,000–for a total loss of $4,000. According to policy provisions regarding the coverage C special limits of liability the insured can recover no more than $1,500 from the special limit for jewelry and watches and $200 from the special money limit, leaving an $1300 excess of loss ($1000 of jewelry; $300 of money).

Since the loss exceeds the special limits that are available (and the coverage C limit is adequate), the $500 deductible can apply against the excess of loss above the special limits ($1300) and does not reduce the available special limit amounts. Therefore, the total recoverable amount is $2,700—$1,500, the total special limit for jewelry and watches; $200, the total special limit for money; and $1,000 towards the other stolen personal property.

Now, though, the ISO forms clearly state that "with respect to any one loss…subject to the applicable limit of liability we will pay only that part of the total of all loss payable that exceeds the deductible amount shown in the Declarations." The wording "all loss payable" would seem to suggest that loss exceeding the special limits is *not* payable and so any excess of loss with regard to the special limits is not taken into account.

The AAIS forms simply state that the deductible applies to all principal property coverages and all incidental coverages except as noted. The insurer will, subject to the "limits" that apply, pay the part of the loss over the deductible.

Property Not Covered

Land

Some independently filed homeowners forms include, within the limit of liability, a certain amount for costs to restore land necessary to support the residence dwelling if the residence sustains a covered loss. However, neither the ISO forms nor the AAIS forms cover land (except as indicated in the AAIS incidental coverage for liquid fuel remediation). The AAIS forms specify this in three places–under coverage A residence, coverage B related private structures, and coverage C personal property; the ISO forms state this under coverages A and B.

Structures Used for Business

As noted previously, other structures used in whole or in part for business purposes are excluded unless rented to a tenant of the insured premises, used strictly for a private garage, or used to store business property belonging to an insured. Coverage for excluded exposures may be arranged; see Chapter 13.

Property Separately Insured

Articles that are separately described and specifically insured in the policy or by means of other insurance are not covered. Both ISO and AAIS add that the property is not covered "regardless of the limit" for which it is insured. Thus, if an insured has scheduled property—jewelry, say—but has insufficient coverage for a fire loss, he or she cannot turn to his or her homeowners to recoup the difference.

The restriction is most often applicable when personal property has also been scheduled under a personal articles floater, scheduled personal property endorsement to the homeowners policy, or an inland marine policy. In any of these situations, a homeowners insured should be certain that the separate scheduled coverage is for the full amount of protection desired on the property because homeowners coverage C will not contribute in the event of a loss. So, for example, a homeowner may schedule specific items of jewelry—perhaps a .75 carat solitaire diamond set in platinum, scheduled at $8,500. If the ring is stolen, the loss is covered, leaving the $1,500 (ISO) or $2,500 (AAIS) under the special limits to apply to other jewelry the insured might possess. But if the ring is only insured for $6,500, and valued at $8,500, the additional amount needed to make up the difference cannot come from the special limits since the ring is specifically insured.

Does the ISO exclusion also apply to property on which there is insurance describing the particular kind of property more specifically than does the homeowners policy, but that covers any property that fits that description? No, the exclusion does not apply in such a case because it refers only to *articles*, meaning specific, identifiable objects, each described separately and insured individually. Therefore, the normal rules for apportioning loss among nonconcurrent policies apply. Note the contrast, however, to the AAIS forms, which do not provide coverage for *property* that is scheduled.

Animals, Birds, Fish, or Insects

The forms do not cover animals, birds, or fish. This is number 4.b. in the ISO forms and number d.2) in the AAIS forms. The AAIS forms include insects in this category. Under the ISO forms, subclasses of insects or lower animal life as separate from the narrow concept of *animals* like fish or birds might conceivably be covered. While the apparent spirit of the exclusion suggests no intent to cover any kind of animal life, the beekeeper or the biology student with a collection of living lower animal specimens might well argue for coverage, and perhaps a court would agree.

Motor Vehicles

ISO has changed the 2011 form so that motor vehicles, and their equipment and parts, are not covered, whether the equipment or parts are on the vehicle or not. Previously, items such as snow tires could fall under homeowners coverage even if removed from the insured's vehicle. This exclusion (4.c.) does not apply to portable electronic equipment that is designed so that it can be operated from a power source other than the motor vehicle's electric system, since limitation j. for $1,500 will apply to such equipment in or on a motor vehicle. The AAIS exclusion is d.3), which excludes motorized vehicles, their parts, equipment, and accessories, and electronic devices. It applies while such items are in or upon a motorized vehicle. But, as we shall see, there are exceptions.

Agent Tip

When a client carries a great number of tapes, discs, or other media designed to be used with a built-in or permanently installed CD changer or tape player, coverage should be arranged by endorsement onto the auto policy.

The exceptions to this exclusion differ. Exempt from the exclusion are vehicles not subject to motor vehicle registration that are used to service an insured's residence or designed to assist the handicapped. The ISO forms have been revised with the 2011 edition. Previously, the forms stated that the exception applied to vehicles "not required to be registered for use on public roads or property which are: (a) used *solely* to service an insured's residence; or (b) designed to assist the handicapped." Under this exception, any vehicle having any other usage other than servicing an insured's premises would not be covered. For example, a thoughtful son might take a riding mower to his elderly parents' home. While there, the mower catches on fire and is destroyed. Since the vehicle was not used *solely* to service an insured's residence, coverage could be denied. Note that the vehicle need not be used to service the *residence premises*; it is enough that it services an insured's residence. Therefore, a riding mower kept, for example, at a summer cottage to cut the grass is covered subject to the limit of personal property at another residence. Now, however, the wording is that the vehicles should not be required to be registered for use on public roads or property, and used solely to service a residence. Obviously, this policy language is much broader than the previous restrictive limitation. The thoughtful son in the above example would find his riding mower covered, should it catch fire at his elderly parents' home.

The AAIS forms take a different approach. They preclude coverage for motorized vehicles, but exempt a vehicle "designed only for use off of public roads; and used only to service an 'insured premises' or a premises of another; if such 'motorized vehicle' is not required by law or governmental regulation to be registered for use on public roads or property and is not used for 'business' purposes."

This exclusion is more encompassing than the motor vehicle exclusion of the section II liability coverage in that golf carts and other unlicensed recreational vehicles, for which there is some liability protection, are excluded for damage under coverage C unless used to service an insured's residence.

A Vehicle Used to Service Premises

An insured resides on an island where no cars or trucks are allowed. He has an all-terrain vehicle that he rides into town to pick up mail and groceries. Is the ATV covered as a vehicle used to service the premises?

The ISO homeowners forms cover motorized vehicles used to service an insured's residence. The verb *service*, according to *Webster's Collegiate Dictionary*, means "to repair or provide maintenance for." Riding the vehicle to pick up mail and run errands for the insured does not seem to constitute providing maintenance for the premises.

Sometimes the argument arises that motor vehicles in dead storage–that is, with the battery removed and gasoline drained–are not considered motor vehicles. That is true only in regard to liability arising from them, as we will discuss in Chapter 8. Whether in dead storage or not, homeowners forms will not provide physical damage coverage for motor vehicles unless they fall within an exception.

Coverage for a Collection of Radiator Caps

An insured has a somewhat unusual hobby. He collects radiator caps and hood ornaments from antique and classic vehicles. The question arises as to whether these items are covered under the homeowners forms or excluded because they are parts of motor vehicles. Under the 2000 ISO forms, the collection would be covered. But now, the forms no longer refer to motor vehicles and *their* equipment or *their* parts, but rather state that "motor vehicles" includes *a* motor vehicle's equipment and parts.

The safest way to cover the collection would be to schedule it.

Aircraft and Hovercraft

Aircraft and parts are excluded from coverage C in homeowners forms. This is exclusion d.4) of the AAIS forms, and 4.d. of the ISO forms. The definition of aircraft—any contrivance used or designed for flight—includes hang gliders and ultra-lites. Similarly to the current ISO motor vehicle exclusion, which also applies to parts, equipment, or accessories away from the vehicle, the aircraft exclusion applies to aircraft parts wherever situated. On the other hand, aircraft accessories or equipment used in the aircraft but not physically attached to it, such as navigational maps, parachutes, etc., are not subject to the exclusion.

An exception to the exclusion clarifies that model and hobby aircraft not used or designed to carry people or cargo are covered property. (A similar exception applies to the section II liability aircraft exclusion, which is discussed in Chapter 8.)

Both ISO (4.e.) and AAIS (c.5)) exclude coverage for hovercraft and parts or equipment. As used in the forms, *hovercraft* means "a self-propelled motorized ground effect vehicle and includes, but is not limited to, flarecraft and air cushion vehicles." While it is common to think of a hovercraft as a type of watercraft, both forms make it clear that any type of vehicle that rides upon a cushion of air is not covered. Flarecraft or wing in ground effect vehicles look like a plane-boat hybrid and rely on a cushion of air to ride some four to five feet above water at up to 130 MPH. The AAIS forms state that model hovercraft not designed or used to carry people or cargo are covered, but the ISO forms do not contain this exception.

Property of Roomers and Boarders

Personal property belonging to roomers, boarders, and other tenants is not covered. This is ISO number 4.f. and AAIS number d.6). But personal property belonging to roomers or boarders who are related to an insured is covered. Note that personal property of a *tenant*, even if related to an insured, is not covered. The distinction is that an apartment for a tenant is generally fitted with housekeeping facilities and so becomes a distinct residence from the insured's. Persons inhabiting such facilities should obtain their own coverage. However, as noted, resident relatives who pay room or board money to an insured do not lose the coverage on personal property that they would otherwise have as insureds if they did not pay.

Property in an Apartment

Personal property of an insured landlord that is located in an apartment regularly rented or held for rental to others is not covered, except as provided in the AAIS and ISO additional coverages for property in rental units or landlord's furnishings (see Chapter 3). As noted previously, property of a relative renting an apartment is not covered even though it would be if the relative rented a room or lived as a boarder. This is ISO number 4.g., and AAIS d.7)

Property Rented or Held for Rental

ISO item 4.h. and AAIS item d.7) in the list of property not covered applies to rented property *away from* the residence premises (furnishings in an off-premises apartment rented to others, for example). This exclusion rules out coverage for *any* property rented by the insured to others while it is off-premises. However, the AAIS form adds that this exclusion of coverage does not apply to property either in that part of the described premises normally occupied by the insured's household while rented to others on an occasional basis, or to property in the portion of the described premises normally occupied by the insured's household that is rented to no more than two roomers of boarders for use as a residence.

Business Data

ISO item 4.i. rules out coverage for business data. This includes data stored in "books of account, drawings or other paper records, or computers and related equipment. The computer *itself* might be covered (subject to any other limitations); it is the business data stored therein that is excluded.

However, the cost of blank recording or storage media and prerecorded computer programs available through retail outlets is covered.

The change in definition of a business has altered this limitation. Under the current edition, activities of an insured resulting in compensation of no more than $2,000 in the twelve months preceding the policy period are not considered a *business*. At this point, it is unclear whether coverage would be limited in some other manner or whether the full coverage C limit would be available to replace the records. Obviously, any ambiguity is resolved in favor of an insured.

The AAIS form covers business data as personal property used in business (limit c.8)), since this coverage limitation states it includes the cost to research or other expenses necessary to reproduce, replace, or restore 'business' data."

Credit Cards

Neither ISO nor AAIS cover credit or fund transfer cards or loss arising from their use except as provided in the additional or incidental coverages. This is item 4.j. in the ISO forms and d.8) in the AAIS forms.

Theft of Calling Card

A thief broke into the insured's residence and stole, among other things, a calling card. The thief ran up a considerable phone bill before the insured realized what had happened.

The card itself is considered personal property that was stolen, so the homeowners policy provides coverage to replace the card. The larger issue is the phone bill. This is not a direct physical loss; it is an economic one. Some coverage is available in the additional coverage of $500 for "the legal obligation of an insured to pay because of the theft...of credit cards." *Credit card* is not defined, so a phone calling card, with which the insured in effect charges calls to the account of his or her phone number, fits the description. If a prepaid phone card had been stolen, coverage would be limited to $200 (as a stored value card) in the current ISO forms.

Trees, Shrubs, Plants

The AAIS forms preclude coverage (d.12)) for "trees, plants, shrubs, or lawns, except as provided under [the] Incidental Property Coverages." The ISO form does not contain a comparable exclusion, referring to this type of property only in the additional coverages.

Water and Steam

The current ISO forms add water and steam to the list of property not covered (4.k.). See the discussion of reasonable repairs in Chapter 3, for possible repercussions if tear-out of a yard to access a pipe is necessary. The AAIS forms exclude coverage for underground water or surface water (d.11)). (Underground water is not usually a term used to describe water coming into an insured dwelling through the water line, so a possibility of yard tear-out coverage because of loss of water as personal property exists.)

Grave Markers

AAIS forms add that no coverage exists for grave markers or mausoleums, except as provided under the incidental coverages for grave markers (except for HO 0008, which does not contain this incidental coverage).

Chapter 5

The Named Perils Coverages

Introduction

Many homeowners policies are written on a named peril basis. In this chapter we will discuss the named perils of the Insurance Services Office (ISO) broad form HO 00 02, contents broad form HO 00 04, condominium unit owners form HO 00 06, and the personal property coverage (coverage C) of special form HO 00 03. The equivalent American Association of Insurance Services (AAIS) forms are broad form HO 0002, contents broad form HO 0004, unit-owners form HO 0006, and special form HO 0003.

Not all homeowners forms contain coverage for all of these named perils. ISO form HO 00 08 covers only ten perils, and coverage for theft is limited. AAIS form HO 0001 has ten, while HO 0008 has eleven. We will discuss these forms in Chapter 12.

The perils are discussed in the order in which they appear in ISO form HO 00 02. Differences in coverage between the ISO and AAIS forms are noted. There are instances in which the coverage limitations of ISO form HO 00 02 and AAIS HO 0002 have been incorporated into the dwellings and other structures coverage of the HO 00 03 and form 3. These instances are noted; however, a more complete discussion is in Chapter 6.

Fire or Lightning

The first of the named perils in both the ISO and AAIS forms is fire or lightning. Of course, direct physical loss caused by fire includes damage by flame, smoke, and soot associated with a fire. But coverage also runs to damage caused by firefighters in extinguishing the blaze. This could be anything from a hole chopped in the roof to extensive water damage. *Fire* is not a defined term in the policy; however, according to *Webster's Collegiate*

Dictionary, fire is "the phenomenon of combustion manifested in light, flame, and heat." Absent one of these ingredients, can there be a fire?

Is Overheating a Fire?

An insured took a two week vacation during the winter, leaving the thermostat of the gas furnace set on sixty-five degrees. While he was gone the furnace malfunctioned, resulting in excessive heat that warped floorboards and damaged some contents. He was insured on an HO 00 03.

The insurer has agreed to pay for the damage to the dwelling but states that, since there was no fire, there is no coverage for contents because contents are covered only for the named perils in the HO 00 03.

Depending upon the jurisdiction, the insured has a strong argument for coverage. Some courts have now broadened the scope of fire to include excessive heat. In the case of *Engel v. Redwood County Farmers Mutual Ins. Co.*, 281 N.W.2d 331 (Minn. 1979), the supreme court held that "fire which causes damage by burning for a greater length of time than intended is no less uncontrolled merely because it continues to burn at its usual rate." However, in the case of *Wasserman v. Caledonia-American Ins. Co.,* 95 N.E.2d 547 (Mass, 1950) excessive heat cracked an empty boiler, and damaged the ceiling above it. But because there was no evidence of charring or smoke stains, the court ruled against recovery. And in *U.S. Fidelity and Guar. Co. v. First State Bank and Trust Co.,* 125 F.3d 680 (C. A. Mo. 8, 1997), an industrial plant's degreaser overheated and caused a chemical reaction. Since there was no actual fire within the meaning of the policy, there was no coverage for the loss.

To see how the approach of *Engel v. Redwood* presents a departure from accepted practice, it is necessary to look at the doctrine of friendly versus hostile fire. A friendly fire is one that is intentionally kindled and remains in the place it was intended to be. A hostile fire, on the other hand, is one that is neither confined to the place intended nor one started intentionally. Courts have traditionally held that the term *fire* as used within the insurance contract means that there must be combustion manifested in a flame or glow, and the result must be hostile. Although many courts have held that coverage is intended only for the hostile fire, that finding is by no means definitive, as seen in *Engel v. Redwood*.

Scorching Caused by a Fire

An HO 00 03 insured watched in dismay as a neighboring house burned to the ground. Although the insured's home did not catch fire, the siding was badly scorched from the heat.

(scenario continues next page)

Traditional interpretation of the fire peril allows coverage for just such an event. To hold otherwise would be to unfairly penalize the insured. One of the advantages of the HO 00 03 is that it is *open perils*; that is, unless excluded, a loss is covered. There is no exclusion for "scorching." The HO 00 02, a named perils form, would also respond in this situation since the proximate cause of the damage was *fire*; that is, the insured's dwelling would not have been damaged but for the fire.

However, had an HO 00 02 insured sustained a loss to personal property caused only by scorching—leaving a hot iron sit on a curtain, perhaps—then there would be no coverage since *scorching* is not a named peril.

Windstorm or Hail

The second named peril in both ISO and AAIS forms is windstorm or hail. It is perhaps fortunate that there is no definition in the policy for windstorm, since a strong gust of unexpected wind can topple a tree onto an insured's residence just as surely as the sustained winds of a hurricane or the short-lived severe winds of a tornado. ISO HO 00 02 and AAIS HO 0002 exclude coverage for damage caused by dust, rain, sand, snow, sleet, or water to the interior of a building or to the property inside unless the direct force of the wind or hail is enough to cause an opening in the structure. (But when the named perils apply to personal property, as in the case of HO 0003 and the HO 00 03, this preclusion of coverage applies only to property contained in a building, not to damage done to the interior of the building.)

It is a common occurrence during a severe rainstorm for water to be driven up under the shingles of a roof and enter a dwelling. In that case, the question of whether or not an opening has been created may be more one of fact rather than of contract. The policy does not state that an obvious hole must be made in a roof, just that the force of the wind creates an opening. Modern weather reporting makes it possible to track wind speeds on any given day, which is important if there is any doubt as to coverage.

Countless court cases arose from the damaging winds and flooding caused by Hurricane Katrina. Many homeowners found themselves facing damage from both covered and excluded causes of loss. In many instances personal property was first damaged by wind-driven rain entering through openings created in the roof, only to be later completely destroyed by the storm surge. One homeowner was forced to act against his insurer, which first denied coverage for the personal property, stating that there was no proof that openings in the roof had been created. The insurer argued that it was the burden of the insureds to segregate covered and excluded damage, and that the insured first needed to prove roof damage. The homeowners had missing turbines as well as evidence of damage to anchoring roof shingles and ridges. It was true that some of the contents were below the four foot water line left by the receding flood; however, the insurer was still liable for the remaining damage. This case is *Johnson v. State Farm Fire & Casualty Co.,* 2008 WL 2178058 (E.D. La. 2008). A similar case is *Gaffney v. State Farm Fire & Casualty Co.,* 2008 WL 941717 (E.D.La. 2008).

Agent Tip

The possibility that there could be no coverage for damage from rain entering a dwelling makes a strong selling point for an open perils policy. It is a long-held principle of insurance that, with named perils coverage, an insured must prove that one of the perils was the cause of a loss. With open perils coverage, it is up to the insurer to prove that an exclusion applies. Of course, the windstorm peril would still come into play with regard to personal property unless the insured chooses an HO 00 05.

What happens, however, when the prudent homeowner decides to have the dwelling reroofed? Two cases illustrate the dilemma. The first is *Homestead Fire Ins. Co. v. De Witt et al.*, 245 P.2d 92 (Okla. 1952). An addition was built onto a school. When the roof of the new addition was being attached to the roof of the school, it was necessary to leave an opening in the school's roof, which was securely covered with canvas. A sudden windstorm blew the canvas off; rain entered and damaged the school's interior. Coverage was denied on the basis that the windstorm did not cause an opening in the roof; rather, the contractor's work caused the opening. In rejecting this argument, the supreme court stated that the fact that the opening was adequately covered by canvas brought it within the provisions of the windstorm clause.

The second case illustrates the opposing view. In the case of *Diep v. California Fair Plan Ass'n.*, 19 Cal. Rptr. 2d 591 (1993), workmen removed a portion of a warehouse roof in order to repair it. They covered the opening with plastic sheeting, but, during a sudden rainstorm, the sheeting was blown open and rain entered. Mattresses inside the warehouse were damaged. The court held that a roof is commonly held to be a permanent part of the structure. The plastic sheeting was nonstructural and of a temporary nature. Further, stated the court, the workmen, not the force of the wind, removed the roof; therefore there was no coverage for the mattresses.

A third case, *Aginsky v. Farmers Insurance Exchange,* 409 F. Supp. 2d 1230 (D. Or. 2005) examined both of the above cases. Here, workers placed a tarp over the insureds' apartment building while doing roof work. A rainstorm blew off the tarp, and damaged the building's interior. The court said it was persuaded by the reasoning of *Diep* that a tarp was not a roof as commonly understood to mean a fixed part of a building, and ruled in favor of the insurer.

A later case, however, looked at the reasoning in *Diep* and was not persuaded that all facts had been examined; notably, the manner in which the plastic sheeting was affixed to the warehouse. In *Dewsnup v. Farmers Insurance Company of Oregon,* 239 P.3d 493 (Or. 2010) the court said that "the opinion provides such a limited recitation of the facts that the breadth of its holding is difficult to gauge." In *Dewsnup*, the insured undertook to repair his roof. He removed the layer of wood shakes, and covered the sublayer with a layer of polyethylene, securing it with staples. The edges were secured with roof tacks, and further secured with wooden bats. Strong winds caused the sheeting to loosen and eventually blow away, allowing rain to enter the dwelling. In finding for the insured, the court opined that a roof sufficiently durable to meet its intended purpose was a roof for coverage purposes, even if it was not necessarily permanent.

In essence, when making a coverage determination under these circumstances, all facts must be considered.

ISO and AAIS also exclude wind or hail damage to watercraft, their trailers, furnishings, equipment, and outboard motors *except* while inside a fully enclosed building. Note that the term *their* makes the exclusion apply only to property specifically used with the particular watercraft and exposed to the same risks as the watercraft, not to boating equipment in general. The earlier AAIS form provided an exception to this exclusion for rowboats and canoes while on an insured premises, but the current form does not.

Wind or Falling Object?

A severe rainstorm dumped enough water on the ground so that a large tree was uprooted. The tree fell across the insured's boat, damaging it. Does the windstorm peril preclude coverage for the boat, or does the peril of "falling objects" provide coverage?

The policy provides coverage for "direct physical damage" caused by any of several perils. In this particular instance, the insured can look to the peril that most directly caused the loss—the falling tree. Although it might well have been particularly windy, and thus assist in the tree's toppling, the efficient proximate cause of the loss was the tree as falling object, not the wind. Had the wind picked up the boat and slammed it against the tree, that would be a different matter.

There is no anti-concurrent causation language here to prevent coverage, and a principle of named peril coverage is that an insured is justified in seeking coverage under the peril that most nearly fits the loss.

Explosion

ISO named peril 3. and AAIS c. is *explosion*. This word is neither defined in the policy, nor is there any modifying language preceding or following the word, so that a broad range of "explosions" may be covered. *Webster's Collegiate Dictionary* says an explosion is "a large-scale, rapid, or spectacular expansion or bursting out or forth."

Attempts have been made to cover frozen or burst pipes under this peril; usually the courts have not accepted this interpretation. See, for example, *Ormsby et ux v. The Travelers Indemnity Co. of Rhode Island*, 601 S.W.2d 779 (Tex. Ct. App. 1980), in which the court said that an explosion was usually thought of as sudden, accidental, and violent bursting usually accompanied by a loud noise.

The peril of *explosion* has been used on at least one occasion to obtain coverage that might otherwise be excluded. In *Fayad v. Clarendon National Insurance Company,* 899 So.2d 1082 (Fla. 2005), nearby blasting caused structural damage to the insureds' home and personal property. The insurer denied the claim based on the exclusion for "settlement, shrinkage, and thermal effects." When a suit was filed, the insurer moved for summary judgment on the earth movement exclusion, which contained this language: "earth movement, meaning earthquake, including land shock waves or tremors before, during or after a volcanic eruption; landslide; mine subsidence; mudflow; earth sinking, rising or shifting…" The court held that this exclusion applied only to earth movement brought about by natural events and did not apply to damage caused by a human event. (But note that the language in both the current ISO and AAIS forms precludes coverage for earth movement whether caused by natural or human forces. See Chapter 6.)

In the case of *Trupo v. Preferred Mutual Insurance Company*, 59 A.D.3d 1044 (N.Y.S. 2009) what appeared to be a clear-cut case of loss caused by explosion was deemed otherwise by the insurer. An explosion at a near-by chemical plant released contaminants into the air, damaging the insureds' home and personal property. The insurer cited the "wear and tear" exclusion, which precludes coverage for loss caused by "wear and tear, marring, deterioration, inherent vice, latent defect….contamination." The court, however, found the exclusion ambiguous, stating that "the title 'Wear and Tear' would lead an average person to believe that the exclusion for 'contamination' therein included only contamination that occurred over time, rather than a sudden occurrence such as the incident here." The editors of FC&S have long held this same position, since these are things that will occur over time and are thus uninsurable. However, when an event certain as to place and time occurs, the resulting loss will often fall outside the exclusion and thus provide coverage. (See Chapter 6 for a discussion of this exclusion.)

Gunfire as Explosion

An insured was cleaning his rifle following a hunting trip. He neglected to check the barrel, and a bullet was discharged into the refrigerator.

The damage is covered under the peril of "explosion." The bullet's exit from the gun meets the definition of *rapid* and *bursting out or forth.*

The case of *Weisman v. The Green Tree Insurance Co.*, 670 A.2d 160 (Pa. Super. Ct. 1995) addressed this point. The insured's tenant committed suicide with a shotgun, damaging the premises. A claim for cleanup and repairs was denied. The trial court found for the appellees, as did the appellate court. The term *explosion* was susceptible to more than one interpretation, and because no further clarification was offered in the policy in question, the claim was covered.

Riot or Civil Commotion

Named peril 4. in the ISO form and d. in the AAIS form is riot or civil commotion. Turning again to *Webster's*, a riot is "a violent public disorder; specifically: a tumultuous disturbance of the public peace by three or more persons assembled together and acting with a common intent." According to *Couch on Insurance Third Edition* (§ 152:6), "The terms 'riot' and 'civil commotion' have a domestic flavor which contrasts sharply with the sense of the terms employed elsewhere [in the war exclusion]… the agents causing the disorder must gather together and cause a disturbance and tumult." *Couch* (§152.16) continues "The common law definition of riot is a tumultuous disturbance of the peace by three persons or more assembling together, of their own authority, with an intent actually to assist each other against any who shall oppose them in the execution of some enterprise of a private nature, and afterwards actually executing the same in a violent and turbulent manner, to the terror of the people." Therefore, acts committed surreptitiously in the dead of night by one person, such as bricks thrown through a plate glass window, would not fall under this peril since it is a single act of vandalism.

However, the distinction between a riot or civil commotion and vandalism is not always clear-cut. An insured owned a piece of rental property insured on a dwelling fire policy. She had not purchased vandalism coverage. When she visited the dwelling to collect overdue rent, she found extensive damage—porch torn off and missing, bottom shingles torn off the roof, water heater missing, and carpeting ruined. She learned the inhabitants had been selling drugs and disrupting the peace of the neighborhood. She turned in a claim to her insurer, seeking coverage under the peril of riot and civil commotion. Although the court found for the insurer, the dissenting judge said the evidence showed the elements of unlawful assembly and violent action were enough to at least justify review by a jury. This case is *Blackledge v. Omega Insurance Co.,* 740 So. 2d 295 (Miss. 1999).

The peril is akin to the excluded peril of "war… meaning civil war, insurrection…" The difference lies in the intent of the action, as well as the number of people involved. In civil war or insurrection, the intent, often organized and widespread, is to overthrow the government, while in a riot or civil commotion the intent appears to be more to make a political statement through force or violence; causing property damage is a side benefit. *Black's Law Dictionary* (Eighth Edition) defines civil commotion as "a public uprising by a large number of people who, acting together, cause harm to people or property. A civil commotion usually involves many more people than a riot."

Aircraft

Aircraft is the fifth named peril in both forms. In the earlier AAIS forms the word stood alone, but in the current forms, as in the ISO forms, it is followed by "This peril includes self-propelled missiles and spacecraft." There is no requirement of direct physical contact between the aircraft and covered property. The policy states that the insurer covers direct physical loss caused by a named peril, but the sonic boom from an aircraft can just as easily cause a direct physical loss by shattering windows as it can by falling from the sky onto an insured dwelling. The peril also covers property damage inflicted by motorized model or hobby aircraft.

Vehicles

Named peril 6. on ISO form HO 00 02 and f. on AAIS form HO 0002 is *vehicles*. While the ISO form excludes damage to fences, driveways, or walks caused by a vehicle owned or operated by a *resident* of the insured premises, the AAIS form states that damage to these same items is excluded if caused by a vehicle owned or operated by an *occupant* of the insured premises. Therefore, under this form, if a relative visiting for a week accidentally hits a fence with her car coverage could be excluded; however, there would be coverage if the relative, over for Sunday dinner, accidentally hits the fence.

This limitation of damage caused by a resident is absent from ISO forms HO 00 03 and HO 00 04 and AAIS forms HO 0003 and HO 0004. In those forms, loss caused by this peril is not subject to any limitations. As we will discuss in Chapter 12, the limited forms, such as AAIS HO 0008, considerably restrict the coverage of this peril.

A vehicle need not come into direct contact with property to cause damage. According to most dictionaries, the word *vehicle* refers to any means of carrying persons or goods and is generally a synonym for *conveyance. Webster's New World College Dictionary* (Third Edition) defines *vehicle* as "any device or contrivance for carrying or conveying persons or objects, esp. over land or in space, as automobiles, bicycles, sleds, spacecraft, etc." Thus, when the proximate cause of a loss is rooted in the functioning or use of a conveyance, recovery should be available under the agreement to insure against "direct physical loss to property . . . caused by . . . vehicles." Some non-standard forms, however, include a statement to the effect that the peril of vehicles means collision with a vehicle. So, before making a coverage determination, check the form.

A Boat as a Conveyance

An insured went sailing and his boat capsized, resulting in the loss of personal property such as binoculars, clothing, and camping equipment.

According to the dictionary, a boat can be a vehicle in that it is a conveyance. There would then be coverage for his personal property. However, some courts have held that a boat is not a vehicle and that the term *vehicle* should be reserved for a conveyance with wheels. Under these jurisdictions, there would be no coverage for the loss. Some forms, such as ISO HO 00 05, exclude loss under coverage C caused by sinking, swamping or stranding of watercraft.

Smoke

Smoke is the next peril. This is number 7. in the ISO form and g. in the AAIS form. The forms state that the *smoke* peril applies to "sudden and accidental damage" and does not encompass damage caused by agricultural smudging or industrial operations (or fireplaces, in ISO HO 00 08 or AAIS HO 0008). These operations are on-going and, as such, are uninsurable. Although much damage from smoke can be directly attributed to fire, there are occasions when no fire need be present, such as when a furnace malfunctions causing smoke to belch into living quarters. The current homeowners forms address this; ISO clarifies that smoke "includ[es] the emission or puffback of smoke, soot, fumes or vapors from a boiler, furnace or related equipment," while AAIS states that the peril "includes sudden and accidental damage from fumes, smoke, soot, or vapors that emit or back up from a boiler, furnace, or related equipment." Previously, it was not unknown for a puffback claim to be mistakenly denied based on the exclusion for mechanical breakdown found in an *open perils* form. The inclusion of *fumes* and *vapors* is interesting in that they are possible pollutants, yet afforded coverage in this peril.

During a holiday season, insureds burned several scented candles, which resulted in significant smoke and soot damage. When they presented a claim, it was denied based on the pollution exclusion. The insureds sued, and the district court's finding for the insurer was upheld by the state supreme court. The exclusion of coverage for pollution specifically included *smoke*; the exception was for pollution caused by a coverage C named peril. Although fire (burning candles) is certainly a coverage C named peril, the smoke must be "sudden and accidental" in nature. Burning candles over a period of weeks was not sudden in the court's view, so whether the damage was *accidental* was not addressed. The case is *Sokoloski v. American West Insurance Company*, 980 P.2d 1043 (Mont. 1999).

Vandalism or Malicious Mischief

Named peril 8. of the ISO form and i. of the AAIS form is *vandalism or malicious mischief*. The current forms restrict coverage if the insured dwelling has been vacant for more than 60 consecutive days immediately before the loss. (This same wording appears in ISO form HO 00 03 and AAIS HO 0003; however, there the limitation applies only to the dwelling and other structures and not to personal property contained within the dwelling.) A building in the course of construction is not considered vacant.

Of course, this begs the question, "What is vacant?" Various courts have attempted to answer this question. Generally, "vacant" means "entirely empty." Sometimes a few items of personal property are left within a dwelling, but generally it is held that the items must be of sufficient value to make it reasonable to believe that the owner has not abandoned the property. The "value" alluded to, though, is the value to the owner thereof; it does not mean that the property must necessarily be expensive or costly. A home containing some furniture, appliances, and personal property, although not fully furnished, was found not to be vacant although the home was not being lived in at the time of the loss (*West American Ins. Co. v. Hernandez*, 669 F. Supp. 2nd 1211 (D. Or. 2009). When making a determination, all facts must be considered.

Both AAIS and ISO have revised this peril, so that any ensuing loss caused by an intentional and wrongful act in the course of the vandalism or malicious mischief will not be covered. This is both broader and more restrictive coverage: broader, because the time a dwelling may stand vacant and still be covered for the peril of vandalism has been extended to sixty days; more restrictive, because any intentional act committed in the course of the vandalism, such as deliberately setting a fire or leaving an outside faucet turned on, is excluded. For example, the named peril policies cover both vandalism and fire. Thus, it has been possible to argue that arson damage done to a vacant building outside the allotted coverage time is attributable to fire rather than vandalism. To clarify coverage intent, then, the policy language has been changed. Prior to this, courts were not particularly helpful to one side or the other of a dispute. To demonstrate: in the case of *American States Ins. Co. v. Rancho San Marcos,* 97 P.3d 775 (Wash. App. 2004), the court held that "arson was not 'vandalism' under vandalism exclusion in property insurance policy, and thus policy covered damage to insured building caused when unknown person drove car into building and set fire to car and another part of building; policy did not exclude arson, and arson was treated differently from vandalism in policy." But in the case of *Battishill v. Farmers Alliance Ins. Co,* 127 P.3d 1111 (N. M. 2006), the court held that arson was a type of vandalism and malicious mischief excluded from coverage. In the case of *Bear River Mutual Ins. Co. v. Williams,* 153 P. 3d 798 (UT App. 2006), the court found vandalism and malicious mischief exclusion clearly precluded coverage for a loss from arson; however, the case was remanded to determine whether the fire was started intentionally or accidentally. If it was started accidentally, then presumably there would be coverage under the fire peril.

Black's Law Dictionary (Eighth Edition) defines *malicious mischief* as "the common-law misdemeanor of intentionally destroying or damaging another's property." Earlier editions of *Black's* indicated that some degree of malice or ill-will toward the owner or possessor of the property being damaged or destroyed had to be present. Now, however, that prerequisite need no longer be present. Dictionary definitions of vandalism are not unanimous in identifying malice as an essential element. *Webster's New Collegiate Dictionary* defines the term as "willful *or* [emphasis added] malicious destruction or defacement of public or private property." The same dictionary also recognizes the use of *willful* simply as a synonym for *intentional.* If this standard dictionary definition is taken as a guide, then coverage for vandalism is understood to be coverage for *intentional* destruction or defacement, malicious or not. The willful act of a child that results in damage to property can be an act of vandalism even if there is no evidence of malicious intent.

However, not all courts would agree with this reasoning. In the case of *Larson v. Fireman's Fund Insurance Co.,* 139 N.W.2d 174 (Iowa 1965), the supreme court held that *malicious mischief* (vandalism was not considered) required proof of malicious intent. A low-flying aircraft, in violation of Civil Aeronautics Board regulations, caused a flock of turkeys to panic, crowd together and smother (domestic turkeys are notoriously prone to this). The farmer attempted to recover for the loss, but the claim was denied on the basis of lack of malice toward the farmer.

But in the case of *Investment Securities Corp. v. Cole*, 194 S.E. 411 (Ga. Ct. App. 1938), the court held that legal malice "need not amount to ill will, hatred, or vindictiveness of purpose; it being sufficient if the [person causing the damage] was guilty of wanton or even a conscious or intentional disregard of the rights of another."

In a by-now classic case, *Stack v. The Hanover Insurance Company*, 329 So. 2d 561, the court determined that the insured's insurance policy's vandalism provision did not apply when a deer crashed through their sliding glass doors, destroying much personal property, since "an animal, such as a deer, to the human mind, and in law, is incapable of forming an intent to commit a wrongful act or to act maliciously…"

Theft

Named peril number 9. on ISO form HO 00 02 and j. on AAIS form HO 0002. is *theft*. Both forms include within this peril losses by attempted theft and loss of property from a known place when it is likely that the property has been stolen or that a theft has occurred. The language eases somewhat the insured's burden of proof in theft claims; circumstantial evidence strong enough to establish that theft is a reasonable explanation of the loss is sufficient to meet coverage requirements. Thus, luggage that fails to materialize after an exhaustive search of an airline facility may be presumed stolen.

Since the ISO and AAIS forms differ somewhat in the coverage limitations, we will deal with the forms separately. General exclusions in the ISO forms applicable to the theft peril rule out coverage for theft: (1) committed by an insured; (2) in or to a dwelling under construction, or of construction materials and supplies used in the construction until the dwelling is finished and occupied; or (3) from that part of a residence premises rented by an insured to someone who is not an insured. To avoid disputes over whether building materials and supplies are building or personal property (as sometimes occurs with cabinetry or other items that have not yet been permanently installed), *open perils* forms HO 00 03 and HO 0003 exclude theft coverage during construction under provisions applicable to coverage on the dwelling and other structures, as well as on personal property.

A separate set of theft coverage restrictions applies to losses away from the residence premises. Property in any other residence owned or occupied by or rented to an insured is covered against theft only while an insured is temporarily living there. The most typical application of this exclusion is to property in a seasonal residence during those periods when the residence is not in use. For coverage to apply, the insured is not required to be physically present in the residence at the time of the loss but must be *living* there. This distinction was explored by a court in *Bryan v. Granite State Insurance Co.*, 185 So. 2d 310 (La. Ct. App. 1966). The court denied recovery for a theft loss to insureds who had not visited their town apartment, the scene of the theft, for four days preceding the loss. In explaining its assessment of the exclusion's scope, the court suggested that there would have been coverage if the insureds had been staying in town on the night of the loss even if they were out attending a social function when the burglary actually took place.

This case is cited in the later case of *Hoff v. Minnesota Mutual Fire and Casualty*, 398 N.W.2d 123 (N.D. 1986). Here, the state supreme court upheld the decision of a district court that a policy insuring a condominium in North Dakota was not required to provide coverage for a theft that occurred at a rented summer cottage in Minnesota. According to the insured's testimony, he was residing at his condominium in North Dakota at the time of the theft. The court felt that the policy language of the HO-6 was unambiguous, and that the condominium policy's coverage extended to the temporary cottage residence only during the periods of time that the insured was residing there.

In *Sanders v. Nationwide Mutual Fire Insurance Co.*, 202 S.E. 2d 477 (N.C. Ct. App. 1974), the court distinguished situations in which the insured had returned home from the temporary residence from circumstances in which the insured had moved on to yet another temporary location. The insured in *Sanders* maintained his household in North Carolina and also kept an apartment in Philadelphia, where he was employed. The insured found it necessary to spend four days in Pittsburgh on business, and, while he was away, the Philadelphia apartment was burglarized. The court of appeals overturned the lower court's decision, ruling in favor of the insured and holding that the interim stay in Pittsburgh did not alter the fact that the insured was "temporarily residing" in Philadelphia at the time of the loss.

The restriction on theft coverage at a secondary residence does not apply to an insured student while away from home, if the student has been at the secondary residence (dormitory, fraternity or sorority house, off-campus apartment, etc.) at any time during the ninety (changed from sixty days in the 2000 forms) immediately preceding the theft. The current form adds a definition of "insured" to include a student "enrolled in school full time, as defined by the school, who was a resident of your household before moving out to attend school, provided the student is under the age of (1) 24 and your relative; or (2) 21 and in your care or the care of a resident of [the named insured's household who is also a relative]." The definition may be broadened by endorsement to include a part-time student or student over age twenty four. But remember, the limitation for property of an insured at another residence still applies unless increased by endorsement. If the 10 percent or $1,000 of coverage C is inadequate, endorsement HO 04 50 can be used to increase the coverage.

There is no off-premises theft coverage in named perils homeowners forms for "watercraft of all types", clarifying that *any* watercraft—from a sailboard to a yacht—is not covered for theft off of the residence premises, and their furnishings, equipment and outboard engines or motors." The forms' use of the word *their* in this exclusion ties the excluded furnishings, equipment, and motors to use with the particular watercraft that are themselves the subject of the exclusion. The exclusionary language is not broad enough to reach all property that might be used to equip or furnish a watercraft. Under the theory of policy interpretation holding that the terms of an exclusion or limitation are to be held to their narrowest reasonable meaning, the terms *furnishings* and *equipment* can be applied to boat cushions, life jackets, oars, etc., but probably not to fishing tackle, ski equipment, and similar items of personal property that might be left in a boat. Such items (that is, items other than furnishings, equipment, and motors) are therefore covered against theft off-premises. And, finally, neither trailers (including semitrailers) nor campers are covered against off-premises theft.

AAIS Theft Peril

For the most, the limitations under the *theft* peril are the same as those on the ISO form. Regarding the exclusion of theft coverage for a dwelling under construction, the AAIS forms state there is no coverage for "theft in or to a dwelling being built, or theft of materials or supplies for use in construction of the dwelling, until the dwelling is occupied for its intended use." Theft coverage for a dwelling under construction can be provided by attaching HO 2722.

The AAIS form makes the same exemption from the theft exclusion for personal property of a student living at a residence away from home as ISO does. The limitation for property at an insured's residence *other than* the residence premises still applies. If additional coverage is needed, endorsement HO 6266 should be attached. The AAIS form, however, unlike the ISO form, stipulates that the student must have been at the residence at some time during the *sixty* days (rather than ninety days) preceding a theft for the loss to be covered.

The AAIS form, unlike the ISO form, declares that loss of a precious or semiprecious stone from a setting is not theft; nonetheless, this loss is not covered. Loss resulting from theft of a credit card, ATM card, and the like is limited to what is provided in the "incidental property coverages." Finally, whereas the ISO form excludes theft coverage for trailers semitrailers, and campers away from the insured premises, the AAIS form adds that *camper bodies* are not covered.

Falling Objects

Falling objects is the tenth of the ISO named perils, and AAIS peril k. In both programs, coverage for the object itself is excluded. Also, there is no coverage for property contained within the dwelling or structure unless the roof or an outside wall has first sustained damage. So, for example, if an insured accidentally drops a bowling ball inside his home, and it damages the flooring, there is no coverage under this peril since the outside of the dwelling did not sustain damage.

Damage from a Falling Object

An HO 00 02 insured lives close by a large water tower. What would happen if the tower were to topple, crashing through the insured's home? What about damage done by the water?

The toppling tower is a falling object. Since an object of this magnitude would certainly damage the roof and/or an outer wall, damage done to the interior of the house and the contents would be covered. Damage done by the water is covered as well. The exclusion for "accidental discharge or overflow" from off the residence premises does not apply, because the discharge takes place *on* the residence premises.

The exclusion for flood is not applicable either, since a *flood* is generally held to be "a rising and overflowing of a body of water" (*Webster's Collegiate Dictionary*). In this case, the container of water fell and released its contents; the proximate cause of the loss is *falling objects*, so the loss would be covered.

Weight of Ice, Snow, or Sleet

ISO named peril number 11. and AAIS named peril i., weight of ice, sleet, and snow, can be contentious. In the forms, the peril means "weight of ice, snow or sleet which causes damage to a building or property contained in a building." Loss to awnings, fences, patios, pavements swimming pools, foundations, retaining walls, piers, wharves, or docks is excluded. Why, exactly, is this peril contentious? If property inside a building is damaged because the roof caves in under the weight of snow, then coverage for *collapse* is triggered. And, if this is the only reason to include the peril, why not simply list it as a covered cause of loss in the additional coverage for collapse?

Granted, the weight of ice or snow may cause a roof to sag (not considered *collapse* under the current forms) or gutters to pull away from the roof, so this might be the reason for inclusion. But why then say that property within a building is covered? Covered for what?

The answer may lie in the meaning of "weight" as "mass." Ice damming—caused by the weight or mass of snow that has compacted and turned to ice—often causes water to back up under shingles or flow under eaves from clogged gutters. If the water stains walls and damages ceilings, there is coverage for the damage to the building under AAIS HO 0003 and ISO HO 00 03 because there is no applicable exclusion for *thawing*. Further, resulting water damage to contents should be covered, since the peril does not say "the weight of the ice, snow or sleet which *damages* property…" but which *causes* damage. Therefore, the scope of the coverage may be broadened to weight of ice as a proximate, not necessarily a direct, cause of loss. And, possibly, the weight of the ice might cause shingles to dislocate just enough to allow water to enter the dwelling. This was the situation in *Nationwide Mut. Fire Ins. Co. v. White*, 167 S.E.2d 125 (Va. 1969), where roof shingles were dislodged by the weight of two heavy snowfalls, and water seeped through the roof, damaging the interior of the dwelling.

Remember, though, that with named perils coverage it is left to the insured to prove that a covered peril was the cause of loss. An advantage to forms HO 00 05 or HO 0005 coverage is that it is left to the insurer to prove the loss is excluded.

Accidental Discharge or Overflow of Water

The following three perils concern themselves with plumbing, heating, or fire sprinkler systems. ISO named peril 12. or n. of the AAIS form is commonly known as *accidental discharge*. The full peril is "accidental discharge or overflow of water or steam" from within [the AAIS form omits "within"] a plumbing, heating, air conditioning or automatic fire protective sprinkler system or from within a household [or domestic] appliance." There are provisions for other coverage as well as limitations within the peril.

Often, people refer to "sudden and accidental discharge." The policy language for this particular peril does not state that the discharge be "sudden"; only that it be accidental. We will discuss "sudden" in policy language in the peril of "sudden and accidental tearing apart" below.

The ISO form excludes loss to the system or appliance from which the water or steam escaped. Water damage from a dishwasher's hose that suddenly springs a leak is covered; the cost to repair the hose is not. Water damage resulting from freezing is not covered under this peril (but see the coverage for *freezing*, discussed later). Water damage that takes place on the residence premises is not covered if the accidental discharge causing the damage occurs off the residence premises. (The HO 00 03 and HO 0003 provide exceptions with regard to coverage for the dwelling and related structures; see Chapter 6.)

Water Damage from Hosepipe Accidentally Left On

An HO 00 02 insured accidentally left his hose running after he finished watering his garden, so that the water ran down into a basement window well, damaging wall-to-wall carpeting, books, and other personal property until the water was shut off.

The accidental discharge peril gives coverage for both the carpeting and personal property. There is no requirement that the plumbing leak or accidental discharge occur from within the dwelling (although, had a neighbor left his hose running, the off-premises limitation would apply). Although it is tempting to apply the exclusion for surface water, it must be remembered that *surface water* is generally held to be run-off of rain or melting snow that meanders over the ground, following no set course. Water from within a man-made contrivance does not have this characteristic. Further, the current ISO form states that "exclusion A.3. water, paragraphs a. and c. that apply to surface water and water below the surface of the ground do not apply to loss by water covered under this peril."

The loss is covered.

Both forms also note that the covered system does not include a sump or sump pump, roof drains, gutters, downspouts, or like equipment. The inclusion of sump pumps is most likely in response to a court case that held that a portable sump pump could be termed an appliance. (See *Stone v. Royal Insurance Co.*, 511 A.2d 717 [N.J. Super. Ct. App. Div. 1986].)

In the ISO form, if the accidental discharge results in mold, fungus, or wet rot that is hidden within the walls or ceilings or beneath the flooring, the cost to clean up or remove the mold is covered. We must emphasize that, to be covered, the mold or wet rot must be hidden. Once damage becomes visible, the insured is obligated by policy conditions to take measures to prevent further damage. (For further discussion of *mold*, see Chapters 6 and Chapter 14.) The AAIS form states it will not cover loss caused by "continuous or repeated seepage or leakage," unless "no 'insured' could reasonably be expected to suspect such discharge, seepage, or leakage of water or the presence or condensation of humidity, moisture, or vapor. (This is a change in the 2006 and 2008 forms; previously such repeated seepage or leakage damage was excluded.)

The accidental discharge peril will not respond to loss on the residence premises if the dwelling has been vacant for more than sixty consecutive days immediately preceding a loss. Forms HO 00 03 and HO 0003 do not contain this limitation. Both the AAIS and ISO forms include the provision that there is coverage for the expense of tearing out the part of the building necessary to get to a covered system. The insurer will also pay to tear out and replace any part of the building *or other structure* on the residence premises to get at the source of the water or steam leak. However, tear-out and replacement of other structures only applies if the water or steam actually damages a building on the residence premises. (Note that the building that sustains the damage need not be the residence dwelling.)

An important provision in the current forms states that the general policy exclusions that apply to surface water and water below the surface of the ground do not apply to loss caused by water as covered under this peril. Heretofore, some losses have been called into question because a water line under a slab broke. It is now clear that loss resulting from an insured's plumbing line, whether inside or outside the insured dwelling, is covered.

The question sometimes arises as to whether a waterbed is an appliance (accidental discharge is covered) or a piece of furniture (accidental discharge is *not* covered). Two cases attempted to answer. The first is *West American Ins. Co. v. Lowrie,* 600 So. 2d 34 (Fla. Dist. Ct. App. 1992), in which the court ruled the waterbed was furniture, so the damage resulting from a leak was not covered. But in the case of *Azze et ux. v. Hanover Ins. Co.*, 765 A.2d 1093 (N.J. Super. Ct. App. Div. 2001) the court found that the presence of a heating element meant the waterbed could be both furniture and an appliance. When the defendant pointed to *West American,* the court stated "We are, of course, not bound by the decisions of Florida courts, and our law suggests that we should treat this particular waterbed otherwise."

Sudden and Accidental Tearing Apart

Named peril 13. on the ISO form, and m. on the AAIS form, is *sudden and accidental tearing apart, cracking, burning or bulging* of a steam or hot water heating system, an air conditioning or automatic fire protective sprinkler system, or an appliance for heating water. This peril cannot be applied in the same way as the peril of accidental discharge, since the use of the word *sudden* can imply that an event almost akin to an explosion takes place. According to *Webster's Collegiate Dictionary*, however, the first definition of *sudden* is "happening or coming unexpectedly; not foreseen or prepared for." It is the second definition—sharp or abrupt—that is often quoted with regard to this peril. Indeed, the use of "cracking, burning, or bulging" implies that an event of some magnitude is being described.

In this peril, there is coverage for the system itself, unlike the peril of accidental discharge. Not included within this peril is coverage for any loss because of freezing (as in, "My pipes froze and burst") which is addressed in a separate peril.

Freezing

The final peril having plumbing or heating as its subject is that of *freezing*; specifically, freezing of a plumbing, heating, air conditioning, automatic fire protective sprinkler system or household appliance. This is ISO peril 14. and AAIS peril o. Earlier editions of the AAIS and ISO forms addressed coverage in instances when the insured dwelling was vacant or unoccupied. But now, in all situations—vacant, occupied, or unoccupied—there is no coverage unless the named insured has taken precautions to maintain heat in the building, or shut off and drain systems and appliances. The exception to this provision is that, if the insured has an automatic fire protection sprinkler system, the named insured must use reasonable care to maintain both the heat and the water supply.

There is no definition of "reasonable care." The best approach, then, in event of a loss, is to use the "prudent man" approach. Generally, keeping a thermostat set at around 55 degrees during the winter months should prevent freezing of pipes. However, if in an unforeseen situation the furnace malfunctions, the insured should be given the benefit of the doubt for attempting to fulfill policy requirements.

Agent Tip

It is important for agents who number snowbirds among their clients to make them aware of this coverage limitation. Too often an insured heads south for a few months to escape the winter weather, and, wishing to save on utility bills, cuts the heat back. Of course, there is no guide in the policy as to what degree of heat is acceptable; presumably keeping the thermostat set on some very low temperature would fulfill the requirement. Obviously, the best solution is for a trustworthy person to check the premises regularly.

Sudden and Accidental Damage– Artificially Generated Current

The next of the ISO named perils is number 15.; p. on the AAIS form. This is the peril of sudden and accidental damage from artificially generated electrical current. The term *artificially generated* needs clarification. It means any electrical current other than naturally generated electrical charges such as lightning or static electricity.

The current forms have added "electronic components or circuitry" to the earlier list of "tubes, transistors, and similar components." If there is any doubt, the forms give examples: electronic apparatus, including but not limited to appliances, fixtures, computers, and home entertainment systems.

The question then sometimes arises as to what is covered by this peril; unfortunately, the answer is, "not much."

Agent Tip

Many insureds do not understand that, while damage caused by lightning through electronic appliances and furnishings is covered, damage done by power surges of artificially generated electricity is not. A tip in the agency newsletter might be advantageous.

Volcanic Eruption

The last of the named perils is number 16. in the ISO form and h. in the AAIS form. This is the peril of *volcanic eruption.* ISO introduced this peril in the 1984 forms edition as a result of the Mount St. Helens eruption. This disaster focused attention on what had been a recurring question, that is, whether the explosion peril covered volcanic eruption. By introducing this covered peril and defining the scope of coverage, insurers hoped to control future potentially severe losses. There is coverage for airborne shock waves, volcanic ash, and lava flow.

Some events arising from volcanic eruption, such as land shock waves, earthquake, or tremors are specifically excluded. This is important to note because many persons automatically think of the ground rumbling and shifting prior to an eruption. Neither form, though, intends to cover damage done by earth movement.

The trigger for debris removal is that the ash or dust from the volcanic eruption must cause direct physical damage to covered property. So, for example, if airborne dust settles on covered property—the roof of the dwelling, perhaps—but not enough to cause structural damage, there is no coverage to clean up the dust.

The section I conditions specify that eruptions that occur within a seventy-two hour period will be considered as one volcanic eruption; this limits the insured's retention to one deductible and also applies one coverage limit to all damage done within the time period.

Sinkhole Collapse

Named peril q. on the AAIS form applies to sinkhole collapse. This peril is not present in the ISO forms. *Sinkhole collapse* is a defined term in the policy, so a loss must result from "the sudden settlement or collapse of earth supporting covered property... resulting from subterranean voids created by the action of water on a limestone or similar rock formation." An insured cannot claim, therefore, as he watches his home slide into a long-abandoned mine shaft, that the loss is caused by a sinkhole. This coverage applies only to damage done to the dwelling or other structures. The cost of filling the sinkhole is not covered, nor is the value of the land.

Chapter 6

Open Perils Coverage; General Policy Exclusions

Introduction

The named perils forms name exactly what is covered. The *open perils* forms, in contrast, state what is *not* covered. It is this distinction that gives the ISO HO 00 03, HO 00 05, or AAIS HO 0003 or HO 0005 insured a coverage advantage. In the named perils forms, the burden of proof to prove there *is* coverage lies with the insured. But in the *open perils* forms, the burden lies with the insurer to prove there is *not* coverage based on the policy exclusions.

Previously, only a few ISO forms provided open perils coverage. Form HO 00 03 provided open perils coverage for the dwelling and other structures and could be endorsed with the HO 00 15 to include this coverage for personal property as well. Now, with the introduction of the HO 00 05, which provides open perils coverage for both dwelling and contents, the HO 00 15 has been withdrawn. Form HO 00 06 (unit owners) by itself provides named perils coverage but can be endorsed with the HO 17 32 to cover building items on an open perils basis and with the HO 17 31 to provide open perils coverage for personal property. Endorsement HO 05 24 provides open perils coverage for the HO 00 04 policyholder.

AAIS form HO 0005 provides open perils coverage for both building and contents on one form, in addition to providing broader coverages and higher limits on certain classes of property. Condominium unit owners form HO 0006 may be endorsed to provide open perils coverage by attaching HO 7032 for coverage A building items, and HO 7029 for coverage C personal property. Endorsement HO 2730 can be used with HO 0004 for the tenant insured.

In this chapter we will discuss exclusions that apply to open perils coverage of the HO 00 03 and HO 0003. The policies contain two sets of exclusions. The first set follows the statement that the forms cover direct physical risk to property insured under coverages A and B. The second set follows the coverage C named perils. These are the section I property exclusions, some of which are prefaced by anti-concurrent causation language. (We will discuss what this means under the heading "General Property Exclusions—Concurrent Causation Language Precludes Coverage.") These exclusions are then followed by a set of exclusions that give back coverage for ensuing losses not otherwise excluded or excepted.

We will describe and discuss the exclusions applicable to open perils personal property coverage in the ISO HO 00 05 and AAIS form HO 0005 in Chapter 12.

Exclusions Applying to Coverages A and B

As noted above, the open perils coverage forms contain two sets of exclusions applying to the property coverages. When reviewing exclusions, therefore, the reader must look in two places. The first set follows the insuring agreement for coverage A dwelling, and coverage B other structures. In many ways, these exclusions are similar to those used in conjunction with the named perils of the other forms. For example, in the named perils forms, *vandalism* is followed by the wording that the coverage does not apply if the dwelling has been vacant for sixty consecutive days preceding the loss. In the HO 00 03 and HO 0003, this provision follows the coverage A and B insuring agreement.

The exclusions noted in this chapter are taken in the order in which they appear in ISO form HO 00 03. The equivalent AAIS exclusions and numbers are included.

Excluded under Section I Exclusions

The ISO form begins by declaring that there is no coverage for any loss excluded under the section I exclusions. The AAIS form states that "'We' do not pay for loss excluded under the Exclusions That Apply To Property Coverages." Possibly this is a way to circumvent a claim whereby an insured sustains an excluded loss, such as earthquake damage, and then attempts to collect for ruptured plumbing under the peril of accidental discharge. For those who read the insurance contract, these statements should make it clear that there is no "all risk" coverage; there will be exclusions.

Collapse

The next exclusion is for collapse (on AAIS form HO 0003 it is exclusion a.7). Both forms exclude coverage except for that provided in the additional or incidental coverages. These coverages were discussed in Chapter 3. The AAIS exclusion not only states that the incidental property coverage is the appropriate place to look, but adds that the insurer will not pay for loss involving "collapse; or impairment of structural integrity, including but not limited to sagging, bowing, bending, leaning, or inadequacy of load bearing capacity." This is not to say that "sagging," for example, is always excluded. If the weight of snow on a roof causes it to sag, there is coverage (unless otherwise excluded); the loss simply will not be treated as a "collapse."

Freezing of Plumbing

Following the exclusion for damage resulting from collapse, ISO form HO 00 03 contains an exclusion discussed in the previous chapter, freezing of a plumbing, heating, air conditioning, or automatic fire protective system, or of a household appliance. The HO 00 03 exclusion also precludes coverage for discharge, leakage, or overflow from within the system or appliance which results from the freezing. In AAIS form HO 0003, this is exclusion 1.a.2).

As we discussed in Chapter 5, the insured is obligated to use reasonable care to maintain heat or turn off the water supply and drain the system even when the dwelling is occupied, *unless* there is an automatic fire protection system; then the water supply and heat must be maintained.

Both the ISO and AAIS forms contain language declaring that with respect to this exclusion, sump pumps and related equipment and roof drains, gutters, and down spouts are not to be considered plumbing systems or domestic appliances. This provision should not be misread; the policy is making the point that coverage for damage from, for example, frozen or ice-dammed gutters should not be precluded by this exclusion.

Freezing of Structures

This exclusion, like that for the named peril of the weight of ice, snow, or sleet, deals with situations common in the winter, whereby the weight of snow or freezing and thawing can cause damage to buildings. The named peril of weight of ice, snow, or sleet precludes coverage for "loss to an awning, fence, patio, pavement, swimming pool, foundation, retaining wall, bulkhead, pier, wharf, or dock," but in the HO 00 03 this exclusion is broader in scope regarding structures. Remember, the open perils forms must clearly exclude what they do *not* intend to cover, unlike a named peril stating what it *does* intend to cover. In the HO 00 03, then, the excluded peril is *freezing, thawing, pressure or weight of water or ice, whether driven by wind or not.* Those structures most susceptible to freezing, thawing, pressure or weight of water or ice, whether wind driven or not, are not covered. These include: (1) fences, pavements, patios, swimming pools; (2) footings, foundations, bulkheads, walls, or any other structure or device that supports all or part of a building or other structure; (3) retaining walls or bulkheads that does not support all or part of a building or other structure; or (4) piers, wharves, or docks. There is no mention of weight of snow, so items such as awnings are covered in the HO 00 03.

The equivalent AAIS exclusion 1.a.3) eliminates coverage for damage caused by freezing, thawing, pressure, or weight of ice or water, whether driven by wind or not. The list of items not covered for this type of loss is similar to ISO's, in that there is no coverage for fences, patios, paved areas, swimming pools, bulkheads, footings, foundations, walls, or any other structures or features that support all or part of a building or other structure; bulkheads or retaining walls that do not support all or part of a building or other structure, or docks, piers, or wharves.

Theft to Dwelling under Construction

This exclusion was discussed in Chapter 5. By placing the exclusion both here and with those applicable to coverage C, any attempt to cover building materials as part of the building or as personal property is forestalled. This is exclusion c.(3) in the ISO HO 00 03 and 1.a.4) in AAIS form HO 0003.

Vandalism

We discussed this coverage and its exception extensively in Chapter 5. Remember that the ISO forms now eliminate coverage for a loss resulting from vandalism or malicious mischief if the dwelling has been vacant for more than sixty consecutive days, and any ensuing loss caused intentionally and wrongfully in the course of the vandalism is excluded. This is exclusion 1.a.5) in AAIS form HO 0003. The earlier AAIS forms limited coverage to thirty consecutive days and did not contain the ensuing loss provision; the current form limits coverage to sixty consecutive days and, like the ISO form, precludes coverage for any wrongful and intentional act committed in the course of the vandalism.

Note that this exclusion applies only to loss to property described in coverages A and B. The named peril coverage for personal property in forms HO 00 03, HO 00 05, and AAIS forms HO 0003 and HO 0005 does not contain the exclusion.

Mold, Fungus, Wet Rot

Exclusion c.(5) of the ISO forms was included in the earlier edition among the kinds of nonfortuitous events that will happen over time and are thus uninsurable. Mold and wet or dry rot were placed with "smog, rust or other corrosion." In the 2000 forms the exclusion was been given its own place within the exclusions, and a clarification—what some may perceive as a broadening of coverage—added. The exclusion continues in the 2011 form. In the AAIS forms it is exclusion 1.j. of the exclusions that apply to property coverages.

The exclusion can be a source of confusion and, at times, much frustration, until one considers its placement in the policy. It is not prefaced by concurrent causation language. Therefore, mold damage caused by an unexcluded cause of loss is covered. For example, a tornado takes off a roof, leaving a dwelling exposed to heavy rains. Perhaps, in the haste to reroof the dwelling, the interior is not sufficiently dried before repairs begin (remember, insureds must take immediate action to mitigate a loss), giving mold a chance to develop. This resulting mold damage is covered. Indeed, the AAIS form states the insurer will not pay for "loss, cost, or expense caused by, consisting of, or relating to the existence of or any activity of bacteria, 'fungi', wet rot, or dry rot that is not the direct result of a Peril Insured Against. 'We' do pay for direct loss to covered property caused by a Peril Insured Against resulting from bacteria, 'fungi', wet rot, or dry rot." (This exclusion is in the AAIS general property exclusions and will be discussed later in this chapter.)

However, mold that develops over time, as in a humid bathroom, is excluded. The insured has been neglectful in maintaining the property, so the ensuing loss is excluded. We will look at the exclusion for neglect later in this chapter.

The ISO exclusion now states the insurer will not cover loss caused by:

> (5) Mold, fungus or wet rot. However, we do insure for loss caused by mold, fungus or wet rot that is hidden within the walls or ceilings or beneath the floors or above the ceilings of a structure if such loss results from the accidental discharge or overflow of water or steam from within:

(a) A plumbing, heating, air conditioning or automatic fire protective sprinkler system, or a household appliance, on the "residence premises"; or

(b) A storm drain, or water, steam or sewer pipes, off the "residence premises".

For purposes of this provision, a plumbing system or household appliancedoes not include a sump, sump pump or related equipment or a roof drain, gutter, downspout or similar fixtures or equipment.

Thus, damage from mold or wet rot that is hidden from view that results from plumbing discharge will be covered unless the insured becomes aware of the damage and does nothing. (Previously, a loss such as wet rot was often denied on the basis of its having occurred over a long period of time.) And, as was stated in the "freezing" peril, a plumbing device does not include a sump pump, downspouts, or guttering, as discussed under this peril in the preceding chapter.

Perhaps a clarification is in order. Water emanating from a storm drain, water, steam, or sewer pipe should not be construed as flood or surface water. Therefore, damage from water from these sources to the property insured under coverages A and B, including any resulting mold damage, is covered. We will look at *mold* in more detail in Chapters 13 and 14.

We will discuss the water damage exclusion in more detail later in this chapter.

Wear and Tear Losses

The next exclusions, applicable only to open perils homeowners coverage, are derived from older all risks policy language and are intended to rule out coverage for two kinds of losses. The first are nonfortuitous events—types of loss that are certain to happen over a period of time and therefore do not represent a *risk* of loss (the possibility that a loss will either occur or *not* occur) because they are certain to occur. These are the perils of wear and tear, marring, deterioration, inherent vice, latent defect (see below for a discussion of *inherent vice* and *latent defect*), mechanical breakdown, and smoke from agricultural smudging or industrial operations, and settling, shrinking, bulging, or expansion, including resultant cracking, of pavements, roofs, walls, floors, or ceilings (perils 2.c.(6)(a),(b), (c), (d) and (f). Over time, aluminum siding will show signs of wear. Furnaces will break down. Constant smoke will mar paint. Buildings are virtually certain to settle over time. Smog caused by human activity cannot be insured against; rust or other corrosion, and dry rot are preventable though adequate maintenance. This peril 2.c.(6)(c) previously included *mold* and *wet rot*, which is now a separate exclusion. See the case of *Trupo v. Preferred Mutual Insurance Company*, 59 A.D.3d 1044 (N.Y.S. 2009), discussed in the previous chapter. In the AAIS form HO 0003, these excluded causes of loss perils are given in three exclusions. The first, exclusion 1.a.8), eliminates coverage for "settling, cracking, shrinking, bulging, or expanding of bulkheads, ceilings, floors, footings, foundations, patios, paved areas, roofs, or walls." Exclusion 1.a.10) states the insurer will not pay for loss caused by smoke from agricultural smudging or industrial operations. Finally, exclusion 1.a.12) excludes "wear and tear" losses: wear and tear, marring or deterioration, mechanical breakdown, latent defect, inherent vice, or any quality, fault, or weakness in property that causes it to damage or destroy itself; rust or other corrosion or smog, or pressure from or the presence of roots of trees, plants, shrubs, or other vegetation." This latter is a welcome edition to the policy. The intent is to eliminate coverage for cracks in a foundation, or blockage of a water pipe, caused by tree roots (but remember, ensuing losses not otherwise excluded are covered). Tree roots will grow; prudent maintenance must be undertaken to prevent damage. The earlier AAIS form contained the "wear and tear" exclusion in the general exclusions applicable to property coverages; the exclusion now appears in the general exclusions following the coverages A and B insuring agreement.

Before continuing with our discussion of inherent vice and latent defect, we will take a look at a recent corrosion situation—the Chinese drywall invasion. Many homeowners were the unknowing victims of the drywall; that is, until they noticed that electrical wiring was damaged, anything made of metal was becoming corroded, appliances and systems such as air conditioners were not working, and the air inside their homes was beginning to smell strongly of sulfur. In a case which affected homeowners brought against manufacturers, distributers, homebuilders and, finally, insurers, *In re Chinese Manufactured Drywall Products Liability Litigation*, 2010 WL 5288032 (E.D.La. 2010), the court agreed that damage from the drywall constituted a direct physical loss. The drywall damage was not excludable as a latent defect, nor as pollution or contamination. However, the "drywall was made of faulty material, and thus fell under faulty material exclusion; and losses were corrosion-related for purposes of corrosion exclusion; insureds' loss of use of home, caused by odors emitting from drywall, was not ensuing loss; damage to electrical wiring, devices, and appliances caused by corrosion from sulfur gasses emitted from drywall were not ensuing losses…"

The two terms "inherent vice" and "latent defect" are sometimes used to deny recovery for losses that should be covered. Quoting *Couch on Insurance, Third Edition,* § 153:77, "An exclusion for inherent vice relates to a loss stemming entirely from some quality within the insured property that renders damage inevitable. An exclusion for inherent vice will not prevent recovery when a loss is caused by a non-inevitable external force, even if the external force combined with some inherent quality of the insured property to cause the loss. A latent defect has been defined as 'an imperfection in the materials used which could not be discovered by any known and customary test. However, in recent years many courts have redefined latent defect even further and held that an exclusion for losses caused by latent or inherent defect was applicable to the insureds' loss if the design and construction defects which caused the loss were not 'readily discoverable'." Thus, a loss may be excluded if it is solely caused by either inherent vice or latent defect. However, if another fortuitous, non-excluded action contributes to the loss, and the exclusion for latent defect or inherent vice is not preceded by anti-concurrent causation language, then there is coverage. As the court said in *State v. Allendale Mutual Ins. Co.,* 154 P.3d 1233 (Mont. 2007), "essentially, the analysis required by 'inherent vice' exclusion of property insurance policy focuses on whether the insured's problem or loss was caused by an internal or external factor or defect; if caused by an internal defect, the problem should be excluded from coverage as an inherent vice." For example, because many diamonds contain flaws, a sharp blow could cause a diamond mounted in a ring to break. It is the external force that has caused the breakage, not the fact that the stone contained a flaw. Without the external force, the diamond would remain intact.

Animal Losses

In the second group of exclusions are those things that happen over time, but are so controllable with reasonable care that only gross disregard by the insured will lead to loss. The first is the exclusion of coverage for damage caused by birds, rodents, or insects. This is exclusions 2.c.(6)(g) and (h) in the ISO HO 00 03. This exclusion has been changed to read that damage caused by "birds, rodents or insects; nesting or infestation, or discharge or release of waste products or secretions by any animals" is not covered. In the earlier forms, an infestation of bats with the concomitant build-up of waste in the space under a roof was covered. But now, since bats are mammals, and hence animals, there is no coverage. Note as well that the word *vermin* has been removed, which also eliminates the discussion as to what "vermin" actually are. (See below for the AAIS solution.)

AAIS exclusion 1.a.9) states that bird, rodent, insect or vermin damage is excluded "except as provided under Incidental Property Coverages"—a reference to the coverage for collapse. The ISO forms cover ensuing losses not otherwise excluded, of which collapse resulting from hidden insect or vermin damage is one.

The absence of definitions for terms used in the open perils exclusions create controversy. While some of the words: wear and tear, deterioration, and inherent vice, for example, have a long history of legal interpretation, others, such as "vermin," are still the subject of disagreement.

Two court decisions have dealt with the meaning of vermin, both determining that particular creatures (carpet beetles and raccoons respectively) are *not* vermin, but leaving open the question of what other kinds of creatures are. In *Sincoff v. Liberty Mutual Fire Insurance Co.*, 183 N.E.2d 899 (N.Y. 1961), the court found that damage to antique fabrics by carpet beetles fell outside the vermin exclusion, while in *Umanoff v. Nationwide Mutual Fire Ins. Co.*, 442 N.Y.S.2d 892 (N.Y. Civ. Ct. 1981), damage in an attic by a family of raccoons was also found not to be vermin damage. In a third case, *North British & Mercantile Ins. Co. v. Mercer*, 84 S.E.2d 570 (Ga. Ct. App. 1954), the court declared that squirrels are not vermin, but squirrel damage, under the current language, is excluded by the term *rodent*. *Webster's Collegiate Dictionary* defines *vermin* as "small common harmful or objectionable animals (as lice or fleas) that are difficult to control; birds and mammals that prey on game; animals that at a particular time and place compete (as for food) with humans or domestic animals." Under this definition, animals such as raccoons are not vermin; they are simply annoying.

The AAIS HO 0003, in order to settle disputes, has now included a definition of *vermin*. "'Vermin' means an animal of a type that is prone to enter or burrow into or under a structure to seek food or shelter, including but not limited to armadillos, bats, opossums, porcupines, raccoons, skunks, and snakes." When *vermin* is so defined, there is little doubt as to intent.

The second exclusion to do with animals owned or kept by an insured. Routine maintenance and care for the dwelling precludes allowing pets to damage carpet, drapes, or furniture. Earlier versions of the homeowners forms referred to *domestic animals*; that is, animals of the house. For clarity, the wording has been changed.

Damage Caused by an Animal

The insured's baby left a container half-filled with grape juice on the wall-to-wall carpet. The family's golden retriever used the bottle as a toy, and the juice spilled onto the carpet. Is there coverage for this loss?

Yes. The exclusion for damage done by animals refers to direct physical damage, such as that caused by a poorly housebroken dog or cat. The exclusion is placed among those kinds of damages that will happen over time. In this case, the juice spillage occurred at an identifiable time; therefore, it is covered.

Pollution Losses

Excluded in both the ISO and AAIS forms is coverage for "discharge, dispersal, seepage, migration, release or escape of pollutants unless the discharge, dispersal, seepage, migration, release or escape is itself caused by a peril insured against under coverage C of this policy." The forms differ as to the definition of a pollutant. Although both essentially define pollutants as solid, liquid, gaseous, or thermal irritants, including smoke, vapor, soot, fumes, acids, alkalis, chemicals, and waste, which includes materials to be recycled, reconditioned, or reclaimed, the AAIS form adds to this definition "radioactive irritant or contaminant" and "electrical, magnetic, or electromagnetic particles or fields, whether visible or invisible, and sound." Since much of the furor that earlier accompanied the damage theoretically done by electro-magnetic fields surrounding high-tension lines has disappeared as a nonevent, the inclusion of this exclusion is interesting. Possibly someone might claim property damage—loss of value—resulting from overhead electric wires.

However, the radioactive pollutant *radon* is often in the news, and the AAIS inclusion of radioactive irritants or contaminants serves to eliminate coverage should an insured claim coverage for, say, additional living expense when forced to vacate the premises while remediation occurs. According to the U.S. Geological Survey (http://energy.cr.usgs.gov/radon/georadon/2.html) ⊠Radon is a gas produced by the radioactive decay of the element radium. Radioactive decay is a natural, spontaneous process in which an atom of one element decays or breaks down to form another element by losing atomic particles (protons, neutrons, or electrons). When solid radium decays to form radon gas, it loses two protons and two neutrons. These two protons and two neutrons are called an alpha particle, which is a type of radiation. The elements that produce radiation are called radioactive. Radon itself is radioactive because it also decays, losing an alpha particle and forming the element polonium." In other words, radon is a naturally occurring element which, when it breaks down into polonium, can be responsible for lung cancer. This pollutant damages persons, not property, and thus should not be seen as a possible cause of loss under a homeowners policy.

Unfortunately, the current pollution exclusion can result in the denial of coverage for losses that have traditionally been covered. For example, paint accidentally spilled on a carpet is now an excluded loss because the paint is a discharged or released pollutant, and *spillage* is not a coverage C named peril. At least the provision of coverage for such losses if they arise from a coverage C peril somewhat reduces the severity of the exclusion.

Coverage for Wind-Driven Oil?

The 2010 Gulf oil spill turned into a non-event when we think of what could have transpired. While we recognize that there was much damage, it could have been so much worse had we sustained a hurricane. But that led us to wonder, what would have happened had hurricane-force winds blown the oil slick, or gobs of oil, onto insured property. Would there have been coverage to clean up insured dwellings under standard homeowners?

The answer is, it depends. While wind is a covered cause of loss, wind-driven water (i.e., storm surge or tidal waves) is not. Damage to property caused by escape, discharge, etc. of pollutants is covered so long as the cause of the escape or migration is caused by a coverage C named peril—wind, in this case. But if it is the water that actually brings the oil on its surface, causing the oil to coat the property, then there is no coverage. And, in any event, there would be no coverage to remove the oil from any land around the dwelling.

Covered Ensuing Water Losses

The ISO HO 00 03 provides coverage for ensuing water damage arising from all eight classes of perils excluded under the "wear and tear, marring," etc., provision unless the ensuing loss is itself excluded. There is coverage for damage caused by the escape of water from heating, air conditioning, automatic fire protective sprinkler systems, and plumbing and household appliances on the residence premises. Therefore, if a worn pipe in the bathroom springs a leak, there is coverage for the cost to get at the leak (but not the cost to repair the pipe itself).

The ISO form contains an explicit provision of coverage for "accidental discharge or overflow of water or steam from within a storm drain, or water, steam or sewer pipe, off the 'residence premises'," unless the loss is otherwise excluded. The section I exclusion for water damage—surface water and water below the surface of the ground—does not apply to a loss covered as an exception to the *mold* exclusion [2.c.(5) above] or a water loss excepted from the wear and tear [2.c.(6)] exclusions. The provision of coverage is intended to apply, for example, as when a nearby municipal drain bursts because the pipe is worn out. It is not intended to give coverage if a flood causes municipal drains or sewers to overflow. The form adds that "for purposes of this provision, a plumbing system or household appliance does not include a sump, sump pump or related equipment of a roof drain, gutter, down spout or similar fixtures or equipment." This reinforces the similar wording found in the named peril of *accidental discharge*. There have been attempts to cover damage to personal property caused by water entering a building by means of worn guttering as accidental discharge of plumbing. This statement circumvents those attempts.

In the AAIS HO 0003, there is also explicit coverage for loss to property insured under coverage A or B that results from water or steam that, due to an excluded cause or event as listed in exclusions a.8) through a.12) results in accidental discharge or overflow from a storm drain, water, steam, or sewer pipe away from the described location. As with the ISO form, the water damage exclusions for surface water or water below the surface do not apply with respect to water damage covered under this provision. And, of course, if one of the excluded perils a.8) through a.12) causes a water or steam loss from an insured's plumbing, heating, air-conditioning, fire protection sprinkler system, hot water heater, or domestic appliance, the insurer will pay to access and replace the part of the building necessary to repair the system or appliance. The insurer will not pay to remove and replace part of a structure that is not a building unless the water or steam has caused direct physical damage to a building on the described location.

The AAIS form differs from the ISO form in its placement of the "mold" exclusion. It is found in the exclusions that apply to the property coverages that follow the coverage C named perils. It is here that the exception to the exclusion is found: the insurer will pay "for direct loss to covered property caused by a Peril Insured Against resulting from bacteria, 'fungi', wet rot, or dry rot." So, there is coverage should a covered off-premises accidental discharge result in mold damage.

Other Covered Ensuing Losses

The application of any of these exclusions—cracking or settling of a foundation, for example—should be governed by the intent behind the entire list, that is, to reinforce the policy's function as a source of protection from *accidental* loss. Homeowners insurance is not intended to cover the wear and tear or gradual marring that wood furniture or kitchen counter tops, for example, are subject to. But when an unexcluded, accidental cause of loss results in sudden damage to such property—a heavy object moved across an oak floor that cracks a board, for instance—it is not appropriate to apply the wear and tear or marring exclusion to such damage. If a foundation cracks so that wires snap and a fire ensues, the fire loss is covered. Or, if birds nest in a chimney resulting in a chimney fire when the fireplace is lit, the damage from the chimney fire is covered.

Unfortunately, a casual reading of the exclusionary language of the policy can result in the impression that there is no coverage for accidental, ensuing damage caused by one of the wear and tear, marring, or other exclusions. The HO 00 03 states that, "under 2.b. and c. above, any ensuing loss to property described in Coverages A and B not precluded by any other provision in this policy is covered." Similar language is in the AAIS form: "'We' pay for an ensuing loss that results from a.2) through a.12) above, unless the ensuing loss itself is excluded."

General Property Exclusions—Concurrent Language Precludes Coverage

The second set of exclusions, the general property exclusions, are found in separate sections of the ISO and AAIS forms (*all* of the property forms, not just the ISO HO 00 03 and AAIS HO 0003). These exclusions apply to *all* the property coverages: A, B, C, and D. Frequently, they apply to events of a more catastrophic nature, such as war, earthquake, or flood. If coverage for an event such as war were available, it would be beyond the means of most homeowners insureds. And, if coverage for earthquake or flood were provided on the standard forms, insureds not needing the coverage would be penalized through higher premiums.

The order of the exclusions in the following discussion is that of the ISO HO 00 03; equivalent AAIS exclusions are incorporated in the discussion. The first set of exclusions is prefaced by what has come to be known as the *concurrent causation doctrine* language. *Black's Law Dictionary (Fifth Edition)* defines concurrent causes as: "causes acting contemporaneously and together causing injury, which would not have resulted in absence of either. Two distinct causes operating at the same time to produce a given result, which might be produced by either, are 'concurrent causes'…" *Black's Law Dictionary (Eighth Edition)* simply states a concurrent cause is "one of two or more causes that simultaneously produce a result." The classic case illustrating this doctrine is *Safeco Insurance Co. v. Guyton*, 692 F.2d 551 (9th Cir. 1982), in which damage caused by flood waters was held to be covered by an all risks homeowners policy, despite its flood exclusion, because the flooding was caused by a third party's negligent maintenance of flood control structures, an unexcluded cause of loss.

As a response to the recoveries not contemplated by the policies, ISO and AAIS drafted policy language to preclude coverage. (The California supreme court, in *Garvey v. State Farm Fire & Casualty Co.*, 770 P.2d 704 [Cal. 1989], refined the doctrine to the "efficient proximate cause" doctrine, so that the unexcluded peril must be the predominant factor in the loss. However, the concurrent language remains a part of the homeowners forms.)

The ISO form states: "'We do not insure for loss caused directly or indirectly by any of the following. Such loss is excluded regardless of any other cause or event contributing concurrently or in any sequence to the loss. These exclusions apply whether or not the loss event results in widespread damage or affects a substantial area." The AAIS form states: "'We' do not pay for loss or damage caused directly or indirectly by one or more of the following excluded causes or events. Such loss or damage is excluded regardless of other causes or events that contribute to or aggravate the loss, whether such causes of events act to produce the loss before, at the same time as, or after the excluded causes or events. These exclusions apply whether or not an extensive area suffers damage from or is affected by the excluded cause or event." Both AAIS and ISO intend that the exclusions will apply, whether or not the excluded event is viewed as catastrophic in nature.

Sometimes the exclusion has been misread to exclude coverage when there should be coverage for a loss (see the case of *Tully*, discussed with regard to the water damage exclusion below). The policy states that the insurer will not pay for loss "caused directly or indirectly by any of the following…Such loss is excluded…" In other words, the policy is referring to a specific loss caused by an excluded peril. It does not mean that a loss occurring at the same time but *not* in any way excluded should not be covered. For example, a thief breaks into an insured dwelling and steals property during a power failure that leaves a neighborhood in darkness. The theft is covered, but not any damage caused directly by the power failure.

Ordinance or Law

The first of the perils so excluded is that of ordinance or law. This is exclusion 1.a. of the AAIS form, and A.1 of the ISO form. Both programs, as noted in Chapter 3, provide some coverage for increased costs because of the enforcement of any ordinance or law. This exclusion clarifies that there is no coverage beyond that already provided.

The exclusion restates restrictions already given in the additional coverage: the policies will not respond to loss in value of the insured property as the result of the enforcement of a building code or ordinance; the policies will not respond to the enforcement of a law, code, or ordinance requiring an insured to test for, monitor, clean up, respond to, or in any way assess the effect of pollutants.

Ordinance or Law—Clean up of Pollutants?

We are concerned about coverage under the following scenario: an insured's dwelling suffers a fire loss. The heating oil tank next to the house ruptures from the heat, and the contents flow into the basement. Is there any coverage for this cleanup? How does the ordinance or law exclusion for cleanup come into play?

Remember that there is coverage for loss or damage caused by release or discharge of pollutants caused by a coverage C peril, which is *fire* in this case. Therefore, the cost to clean up the oil released by the fire into the dwelling is covered. The purpose of the exclusionary language is to preclude coverage where the insured might decide, without an intervening covered event having occurred, to test for or clean up pollutants. In that instance, there is no coverage.

Earth Movement

The second of the *concurrent causation* exclusions is for earth movement; number 1.f. in the AAIS form. Excluded as earth movement are earthquake, including land shock waves before, during, or after a volcanic eruption (there is coverage for airborne volcanic shock waves); landslide, mudslide, or mudflow; subsidence or sinkhole; or any other earth movement including earth sinking, rising, or shifting. The event causing any of these can be caused by an act of nature, or "otherwise" according to ISO. (The 2000 form said "caused by or resulting from human or animal forces or any act of nature.) However, if any of these result in fire, theft, or explosion, that resulting loss is covered.

The AAIS preclusion of coverage is similar, but adds "erosion" to the list. Also, the exclusion does not include sinkhole collapse "as described under the Perils Insured Against that apply to Coverage C." The policy is stating that, if an event meets the description of sinkhole collapse given in the Coverage C peril, it should not be construed as earth movement and thus excluded for purposes of coverage for personal property. Fire or explosion resulting from earth movement is covered; the exclusion does not apply to theft that is otherwise covered by the policy.

Previously, many jurisdictions held that earth movement applied only to naturally-occurring events, usually of a catastrophic nature. Indeed, the words used in the ISO 1991 exclusion describe natural, rather than man-made, events. For this reason, in the case of *Steele v. Statesman Ins. Co.*, 607 A.2d 742 (Pa. 1992), the exclusion was held to apply to natural events only. Thus, there was coverage for damage to a home when the hillside above it collapsed because of a neighbor's construction activity. The court held the exclusion to be ambiguous because, on the one hand, coverage was precluded for naturally occurring events such as earthquake, but, on the other hand, precluded for events such as mudflow that could be man-made, natural, or both. It was therefore reasonable, said the court, to conclude that only natural events were intended to be excluded.

This line of reasoning—that if specific terms precede an ambiguous general term, the general term should be interpreted in light of the specific terms—is called the doctrine of *ejusdem generis*. Courts have often reversed the process so that it does not matter whether earth movement, the ambiguous general term, precedes or follows the specific terms.

But, not all courts held that earth movement in some instances was covered and not in others. In the case of *Miller v. State Farm Fire and Casualty Co.*, 811 P. 2d 1081 (Ariz. 1990), the court held that the exclusion was not ambiguous and so there was no coverage when a leaking lawn sprinkler system caused the earth under the insured's dwelling to compact, resulting in damage. (It is interesting to contemplate whether the outcome of this suit would have been similar had the ISO 2000 (and subsequent) forms been in effect. There is now an explicit exception for water below the surface of the ground that emanates from the insured's plumbing.)

Agent Tip

According to the National Geographic Society, a repeat of the 1811-1812 earthquakes in Missouri could cause widespread damage from St. Louis to Memphis. The ground rock is more rigid than that in the West. Seismic waves do not dissipate and therefore travel further. A useful sales tip, alerting clients to the prevalence of this potential natural disaster, is a map from the National Geographic Society. The Web site is www.nationalgeographic.com. Another useful Web site *vis a vis* both natural and man-made disasters is www.noaa.gov, the National Oceanic and Atmospheric Administration.

Water Damage

The water damage exclusion is the third of the concurrent causation exclusions in the ISO form and number 1.g. in the AAIS form. The water damage exclusion is similar to that for earth movement in that resulting damage from fire or explosion, or theft is covered. *Water* encompasses, in the exclusion, many situations. The water may result from a flood, surface water, or tidal overflow; backup of sewer or drain or overflow from a sump; or occur below the surface of the ground and exert pressure on or seep or leak into buildings or other structures. ISO has added, in the 2011 forms, that damage caused by "tidal wave and tsunami, tides…all whether or not driven by wind, including storm surge…" is not covered. Another addition to the ISO forms is that the exclusion "applies to, but is not limited to, escape, overflow or discharge, for any reason, of water or waterborne material from a dam, levee, seawall or any other boundary or containment system." The AAIS 2008 addition to the water exclusion, no doubt also a response to Hurricane Katrina and its aftermath, states that the exclusion applies, but "is not limited to, water and matter present in or carried or otherwise moved by water, whether driven by wind or not, that: (1) overtops; (2) escapes from; (3) is released from; or (4) is otherwise discharged from; a dam, levee, dike, floodgate, or other device or feature designed or used to retain, contain, or control water." Eliminated as well is coverage for "… waves, including but not limited to tidal wave and tsunami; tides; tidal water…all whether driven by wind or not. This includes, but is not limited to, tidal surge, storm surge, and storm tide."

Agent Tip

Coverage for flood is available through many insurers through the "Write Your Own" program, or directly from the National Flood Insurance Program. If there is any question that a client might need the coverage, it is always best to write it.

A "flood" is held to be "a rising and overflowing of a body of water esp. onto normally dry land" (*Webster's Collegiate Dictionary*). Though most persons can picture a flood—the 1993 Mississippi flood or Fargo, North Dakota, any spring, for example—surface water presents more of a problem. Generally, surface water is held to be water "which is diffused over the surface of the ground, derived from falling rains or melting snows, and continues to be such until it reaches some well defined channel in which it is accustomed to flow and does flow with other waters." This was the ruling in *Georgetown Square v. United States Fidelity and Guaranty Co.*, 523 N.W.2d 380 (Neb. Ct. App. 1994), where the court further found that surface water loses its characteristic as such once it becomes diverted into man-made channels.

Both ISO and AAIS forms exclude loss caused by water that backs up through sewers or drains, or overflows or is otherwise discharged through a sump, sump pump, or related equipment. The AAIS form also states there is no coverage from "any other type of system designed to remove subsurface water which is drained from the foundation area."

The ISO form excludes, as well, "water-borne material" ("matter present in or carried or otherwise moved by water" in the AAIS form) moved by any of the water which is referred to in the exclusion. Two cases highlight the reason for the wording. In *Rodin v. State Farm Fire & Casualty Co.*, 844 S. W.2d 537 (Mo. Ct. App. 1993), the insureds argued that what backed up through their dwelling was sewage and not water; therefore, the resulting damage should be covered. The court held for the insurer, stating that the totality of the exclusion meant that the sewage acted concurrently with its means of transport, the water, and was therefore excluded. A different conclusion, however, was reached by a Florida court. In *Sterling v. City of West Palm Beach*, 595 So. 2d 295 (Fla. Dist. Ct. App. 1992), the court reasoned that, absent mention in the policy of any exclusions for damage caused by raw sewage, the ambiguity must give coverage. In response to this and other cases, the wording of the current exclusions has been amended so that water damage includes damage from, for example, raw sewage carried by the water.

And, similarly to the earth movement exclusion, the excluded water may be caused by "an act of nature or ...otherwise caused."

Coverage for backup of sewer and drain and sump overflow has long been available. Granted the coverage is limited (the ISO endorsement provides $5,000), but the additional premium charge is minimal.

How is the exclusion for backup of sewer and drain to be reconciled with the accidental discharge peril? Perhaps the best position is that expressed by the court in *Hallsted v. Blue Mountain Convalescent Center, Inc.*, 595 P.2d 574 (Wash. Ct. App. 1979). In this case, a sewer under the street in front of the insured's home became clogged, resulting in a sewage backup which flowed out of the toilet in the insured's bathroom. The court found that the loss was not covered, but attempted to reconcile the exclusion with the accidental discharge peril. The court focused on the peril language "from within a plumbing system" and said "if the cause of the discharge is in the [insured's] system, e.g., a clogged sink drain which causes water in the plumbing system to overflow, the [sewer backup exclusion] does not apply. If the cause of the discharge is outside that system, e.g., a clogged sewer pipe which forces water from outside [the insured's] system to overflow, then the [exclusion] is applicable even though the water flowed through [the insured's] plumbing system."

That reasoning takes into account the purpose of the exclusion; that is, to preclude coverage for systems overtaxed by severe rains, flooding, or overbuilding that puts a strain on existing systems. Remember, though, that the HO 00 03 and HO 0003 provide coverage for water damage resulting from off-premises accidental discharge or overflow of water or steam from within a storm drain or water, steam, or sewer lines provided one of the excluded perils, such as wear and tear, was the precipitating cause of the discharge.

The water damage exclusion also precludes coverage for water (or matter within the water) below the surface of the ground that seeps, leaks, or flows through or exerts pressure on foundations, swimming pools, driveways, patios, etc. The covered peril of accidental discharge from within the insured's own plumbing system is exempt from this exclusion. In fact, the AAIS form here specifically states that the exclusions for surface water and water below the surface of the ground do not include water accidentally discharging or overflowing from a plumbing, heating, air-conditioning, or automatic fire protective sprinkling system, water heater, or domestic appliance on the "described location." In the ISO form, this exception is found under the exception to exclusion c.(6), and under the accidental discharge peril.

We cannot leave this topic without a look at Hurricane Katrina and the seemingly innumerable ensuing lawsuits. A quick look at Westlaw® revealed suits filed against insurers based, it seemed, on ingenious theories of coverage, such as against oil companies for causing global warming contributing to major storms. This is not to say that insurers have been entirely without fault. In the case of *Tully v. State Farm Fire and Casualty Co.,* 2007 WL 1459401 (S.D. Miss. 2007), the insurer contended that the insureds had elected to claim coverage under their flood policy, and therefore, under the theory of "election of remedies," could not claim coverage for wind damage under the State Farm policy. (The court said the "election of remedies was not applicable when policies covered different causes of loss.) The insurer also contended that the anti-concurrent causation language precluded coverage for the wind damage, since the insureds sustained water damage as well as wind damage. The court dispensed with this logic, stating "If this argument were accepted, it would follow that in the case of an insured property that took an inch of water and lost its roof to the winds, State Farm would owe the policy holder nothing under its homeowners coverage. I find this logic unpersuasive, and I find the exclusion so poorly drafted and ambiguous that I am uncertain whether it could ever support the interpretation State Farm urges the Court to adopt."

This is not to say, of course, that an insured can recover twice under different insurance policies for the same loss. In *Halmekangas v. State Farm Insurance Company*, 2008 WL 5381603 (E.D. La 2008), the first floor of the insured's home was flooded by Hurricane Katrina; a few days later the home burned completely. The court held that the insured could not recover under the fire policy for the same losses he had recovered under his flood policy. Rather, the damages were to be segregated so that the fire insurer did not pay for the loss that had been paid under the flood policy.

As stated above in the discussion on concurrent causation language, the excluded loss is the "such loss" referred to, not a loss caused by a covered cause of loss. Thus, when, say, wind-driven water (a hurricane) causes "such loss" it is excluded, but when wind causes a loss separately from the water, that loss is covered.

Power Failure

The fourth of the concurrent causation exclusions (number 1.h. on the AAIS form) is loss resulting from the failure of power or other utility service if the failure occurs off of the residence premises. The wording of the ISO 1991 forms added that "if a Peril Insured Against ensues on the 'residence premises,' we will pay only for that ensuing loss." That language resulted in coverage where none was intended. In the case of *Brooklyn Bridge, Inc. v. South Carolina Insurance Company*, 420 S.E.2d 511 (S. C. Ct. App. 1992), the court held for coverage when Hurricane Hugo caused a power outage that resulted in food spoilage. The plaintiff, a deli, argued that windstorm was an insured peril and had ensued on the insured premises, so the exclusion was ambiguous. The court agreed and found for coverage.

The wording of the exclusion has thus been changed in the current forms. Now the wording is clear that no matter what causes the power or other utility failure, a resulting loss must be caused by a covered cause of loss for coverage to apply: "if the failure results in a loss, from a Peril Insured Against on the 'residence premises', we will pay for the loss caused by that peril."

For example, an off-premises power failure occurs, and when the power returns the surge causes a fire in an insured dwelling. This resulting fire damage is covered.

Neglect

An insured who fails to use all reasonable means to protect covered property at and after the time of a loss may find coverage excluded for any ensuing loss. This is the fifth of the concurrent causation perils and number 1.e. on the AAIS form. By way of a somewhat drastic example, if the insured accidentally sets his or her house afire, and then decides to just let it burn rather than calling the fire department, that ensuing fire loss is not covered.

The wording of the exclusion is open to question, however. The AAIS form instructs the insured to "save and preserve covered property," while the ISO form cautions the insured to "save and preserve property." An insured could conceivably expend considerable time and effort at the time of a loss to save property that turned out not to be covered or covered on a limited basis—money or pets, for example—leaving covered property unattended to. It is to be hoped that, should this situation arise, the insurer would take the insured's efforts into account.

War

Concurrent causation peril 6. (1.d. on the AAIS forms) is war. Although *war* is commonly thought of as military action between sovereign countries, or at least recognizable separate entities, the remainder of the exclusion includes civil war, undeclared war, insurrection, rebellion or revolution, warlike acts by military force or personnel, and destruction, seizure, or use for a military purpose. Broad though the terminology is, it must be remembered that, for the exclusion to be applied, the loss must be the *direct* result of a war. In other words, if the loss happens coincidentally with the war, it might be covered. If a dwelling catches fire and burns as the result of a lightning strike, the damage is covered even if a state of war exists. However, one *caveat:* discharge of a nuclear weapon, even if an accident, will be deemed a warlike act, and therefore resulting damage is excluded.

Nuclear Hazard

Excluded peril 7. (AAIS number 1.c) is for nuclear hazard. Damage resulting form any nuclear reaction, radiation, or contamination, no matter how caused, is excluded. This exclusion cites section I property condition N., which states that "loss caused by the nuclear hazard will not be considered loss caused by fire, explosion, or smoke, whether these perils are specifically named in or otherwise included within the Perils Insured Against." An insured cannot, therefore, claim that damage resulting from the detonation of a nuclear device is actually the result of explosion. And, though loss caused directly or indirectly by nuclear hazard is excluded, direct loss by fire resulting from this hazard is covered. The AAIS form, rather than referring to a property condition, contains the definition, exclusion, and exception of coverage for direct loss by fire, explosion, or smoke within the body of the exclusion itself.

Intentional Loss

The eighth of the concurrent causation exclusions in the ISO form (number 1.i. of the AAIS forms) precludes coverage for loss "arising out of any act an 'insured' commits or conspires to commit with the intent to cause a loss. In the event of such loss, no 'insured' is entitled to coverage, even 'insureds' who did not commit or conspire to commit the act causing the loss." The AAIS form words the exclusion slightly differently: "'We' do not pay any 'insured' for loss that results from any act committed: by an 'insured', alone or in collusion with another; or at the direction of an 'insured' with the intent to cause a loss. This exclusion applies even with respect to an 'insured' who was not involved in the commission or direction of the act that caused the loss."

Rightly or wrongly, the exclusion serves to eliminate coverage in cases when, for example, an insured spouse commits arson. The innocent spouse cannot collect. What one spouse knows has traditionally been held to be common knowledge within the marriage. This doctrine has eroded in some jurisdictions. In late 1997, Washington State's Insurance Commissioner Deborah Senn issued a technical assistance advisory notifying insurers that there was "no basis for ignoring losses sustained by innocent co-insureds." The advisory applied to existing policies, so that claims that had been denied were to be reconsidered.

For this reason, the special provisions applicable to any given state must be reviewed if a claim falling under the exclusion occurs. For example, the Washington special provisions (HO 01 46) state that neither the exclusion nor the concealment or fraud condition applies to an insured's claim if the loss was caused by an act of domestic abuse by another insured. Domestic abuse as used in the provision includes "intentionally, knowingly or recklessly causing damage to property so as to intimidate… another household member."

Most jurisdictions, however, hold that the language is clear and unambiguous and serves to deny coverage to the innocent party. See, for example, *Vance v. Pekin Ins. Co.*, 457 N.W.2d 589 (Iowa 1990). Here, the answer to the question "May an innocent coinsured spouse recover under a fire insurance policy when the other coinsured spouse has been convicted of arson?" was an unequivocal "No."

Civil Authority or Governmental Action

The ninth of the ISO exclusions prefaced by anti-concurrent causation language is exclusion 1.b. in the AAIS form. The insurer will not pay for loss caused by "the destruction, confiscation or seizure of property described in Coverage A, B or C by order of any governmental authority." This exclusion is quite restrictive. Although the intent appears to be to circumvent any such outcome as occurred in, for example, *Safeco Insurance v. Guyton* (discussed earlier), or to preclude coverage when a drug dealer's property has been seized, there is little room to maneuver. So, for example, if, as happened some years ago, the Philadelphia mayor ordered an entire square city block of homes blown up, the innocent homeowner whose dwelling was destroyed would have no recourse under either form.

The exclusion, although restrictive, should still be read in context. Say, for example, a police force is attempting to stop an armed murder suspect and, in an ensuing gun battle, bullets damage an insured's dwelling. The governmental authority is responsible for stopping the murder suspect, but the authority has not ordered the police to shoot at or destroy property; they have ordered the police to stop the criminal. Thus, the bullet damage would be covered. In another example, the insured was able to recover for damage caused by tear gas fired into her home when police attempted to force her husband, who was mentally disturbed, out of the house. This case is *Merrimack Mutual Fire Ins. Co. v. Slater*, 2007 WL 2045429 (Mass. Super. 2007). For an extensive treatment of this subject, see the article "Governmental Action—'Destruction, Confiscation, Seizure' of Insured Property" in *FC&S*.

The exception to this exclusion in both forms is for action taken by civil authority to prevent spread of fire, but not if the fire is caused by an excluded peril.

Bacteria, Fungi, Wet Rot, or Dry Rot

The AAIS form has an additional exclusion, 1.j). There is no coverage for bacteria, fungi, wet rot, or dry rot that is not the direct result of a covered cause of loss. In other words, should a tornado take off the roof of an insured dwelling, and mold develop in the days to follow, there would be coverage for the mold. (Of course, the insured is obligated to preserve the property from further loss, but sometimes unforeseen conditions prevent immediate action.) To reinforce the exclusion, and its exception, the policy states "'We' do pay for direct loss to covered property caused by a Peril Insured Against resulting from bacteria, 'fungi', wet rot, or dry rot."

General Property Exclusions—Some Ensuing Losses are Covered

The next set of the general section I property exclusions is not prefaced by anticoncurrent causation language. Both the ISO and AAIS forms state if "any of the following" (ISO) or "one or more of the following" (AAIS) perils result in a loss, that loss is not covered, although any *ensuing* loss not excluded is covered.

Weather Conditions

The first of these exclusions in the ISO forms is for weather conditions. This is exclusion 2.a. in the AAIS form. This exclusion operates so that if the weather conditions contribute to cause any of the excluded causes of loss discussed in the previous "General Property Exclusions—Concurrent

Language Precludes Coverage" section there is no coverage. Say, for example, severe long-term thunder and rainstorms bring lightning and flooding to an area. Any damage done by the flooding is excluded, since that peril is specifically excluded. The insured could not claim damage was actually caused by rain, not by flood. But if there was any lightning damage to insured property, it would be covered since *lightning* is a covered peril.

Acts or Decisions

The second exclusion of the ISO form is for any acts or decisions, including the failure to act or decide, of "any person, group, organization or governmental body." This exclusion is somewhat different in the AAIS form. There, it is part of exclusion 2.b., errors, omissions, and defects. The AAIS form declares that "'We' do not pay for loss caused by one or more of the following…" and exclusion 2.b.1) continues "an act or decision of any person, group, organization, or governmental body or authority, or the failure of any person, group, organization, or governmental body or authority to act or decide…" Quite possibly this exclusion was inserted as a response to the case of *Guyton*, discussed with reference to the development of anti-concurrent causation language. Here, remember, the authority controlling dam overflow opened floodgates and the insureds sustained a flood loss.

As with weather conditions, any ensuing loss not otherwise excepted or excluded is covered.

Faulty, Inadequate, or Defective…

The final ISO exclusion (B.3.) applying to all the property coverages is an extensive one, consisting of four parts. The AAIS exclusion (2.b.2)), which is similar, consists of four parts as well, although the wording is not exactly the same. Again, any ensuing loss not excluded or excepted is covered.

All four parts of this exclusion apply to part or all of any property, whether on or off the residence premises. ISO prefaces the exclusions with "faulty, inadequate or defective" while AAIS uses "a defect, a weakness, the inadequacy, a fault, or unsoundness in" any of the following causes of loss.

Part one excludes coverage for faulty, inadequate or defective planning, zoning, development, surveying, or siting. The exclusion of coverage in the AAIS form is for planning, zoning, development, surveying, or siting. If a new home development is planned and built near a creek that regularly floods so that the homes are damaged, there is no coverage. The development of the site is defective, and the resulting flooding is an excluded peril.

The second exclusion is for faulty, inadequate, or defective design, specifications, workmanship, repair, construction, renovation, remodeling, grading, or compaction. The AAIS exclusion is for design, specification, construction, compaction, remodeling, repair, or workmanship. It is not the purpose of homeowners coverage to respond to damage that should rightly be the responsibility of those performing the work. But remember, however, that ensuing loss resulting from such actions is covered. If, instead of tuck pointing a crumbling chimney the workers negligently mortar it shut—with the result that the first time a fire is lit in the fireplace the house catches fire—the fire loss is covered, but the faulty chimney repair is not. There sometimes appears to be a thin gray line between the faulty workmanship exclusion and an ensuing loss. For example, an insured hires window washers to clean windows. The washers clean the windows, but in doing so manage to scratch them. The work has not been done properly and so the scratching is not covered. However, had the window washers somehow dislodged the window panes with the result that water entered the dwelling at the next rainstorm and damaged the walls, that ensuing loss would be covered.

The third ISO exclusion in this grouping is for faulty or defective materials used in repair, construction, renovation, or remodeling. The similar AAIS exclusion [2.b.2)] precludes coverage for loss caused by a defect, weakness, inadequacy, fault, or unsoundness in materials used in construction or repair. Again, faulty or inadequate materials are the province of those performing the work or of the manufacturer of such materials. Again, however, any ensuing loss not excluded is covered. An exception to keep in mind is that, if defective methods or materials are used in the course of construction, remodeling, or renovation, and the dwelling collapses, the additional coverage of collapse responds. Remember the Chinese drywall case discussed earlier under the "wear and tear" exclusions? The exclusion for faulty or defective materials was found here; however, the ensuing loss—corrosion—was itself excluded.

The fourth ISO exclusion [AAIS exclusion 2.b.2)d)] is for faulty maintenance. And, any ensuing loss not excluded or otherwise excepted is covered. If an insured decides to do some long-needed electrical repairs and inadvertently wires the wrong ends together with the result that every light in the house fails to turn on, the faulty wiring job is not covered. However, if the result is that wiring sets insulation on fire and the house burns down, the fire damage is covered.

Chapter 7

Conditions Applying to Property Coverages

Introduction

There are nineteen conditions that apply only to the section I property coverages of the ISO homeowners 2011 forms. There are eighteen for form HO 00 04 because it does not have a mortgage clause. The AAIS form contains more conditions. The reason is that there are conditions and expansions of conditions that apply to the AAIS forms but do not exist at all in the ISO forms. This discussion follows, as much as possible, the order found in ISO 2011 form HO 00 03. Since the AAIS conditions are not contained in one particular section, as are the ISO conditions, their location is indicated.

One final note. The following appears in the ISO forms after the definition of *insured:*

> Under both Sections I and II, when the word an immediately precedes the word "insured", the words an "insured" together mean one or more "insureds".

Likewise, AAIS has added "The phrase 'an insured', wherever it appears in this policy, means one or more 'insureds'."

In the past, it was possible to argue that a particular provision or exclusion applied only to *the* insured–that is, one particular insured (see "Insurable Interest and Limit of Liability," below, for an example). Now, however, unless disallowed by state law, when *an insured* appears in the form generally all insureds fall under the provision or exclusion.

Insurable Interest and Limit of Liability

Condition A. of the ISO forms, insurable interest and limit of liability, limits the insurer's liability for any section I loss in two ways. The insurer is not liable to an insured for more than the amount of that insured's interest in the property or for more than the applicable limit of liability. Therefore, although it may appear that the insurer will only settle a property loss with an insured, the loss payment condition (discussed later) states that the insurer will adjust all losses with an insured unless another person is legally entitled to receive payment. So, for example, if an insured borrows a neighbor's riding lawnmower, and, while temporarily parked in the insured's garage it catches on fire, the insurer can adjust the loss with the neighbor who is legally entitled to receive payment by virtue of ownership.

The similar condition in the AAIS forms is located in the section entitled "How Much We Pay for Loss or Occurrence." This condition (1.a.) states that the insurer will: "pay the lesser of the 'limit' that applies; or the amount determined under the applicable loss settlement terms; regardless of the number of 'insureds' with an interest in the property. However, no 'insured' will be paid an amount that exceeds his or her interest in the property at the time of loss."

Deductible

Condition B. in the current form is entitled "Deductible." The deductible provision was previously found immediately preceding the section I property coverages.

> Unless otherwise noted in this policy, the following deductible provision applies:
>
> With respect to any one loss:
>
> 1. Subject to the applicable limit of liability, we will pay only that part of the total of all loss payable that exceeds the deductible amount shown in the Declarations.
> 2. If two or more deductibles under this policy apply to the loss, only the highest deductible amount will apply.

The AAIS deductible provision (1.b., located in the section "How Much We Pay for Loss or Occurrence) is more complete; it refers to the deductible as applying to all principal property coverages and all incidental coverages with the exception of the coverages for credit card, etc., fire department service charge, and refrigerated property. It also specifies that the deductible applies per occurrence and, with respect to the association deductible and loss assessment coverages, no matter how many deductibles are charged or assessments levied. Further, the deductible will apply separately at each covered location. So, for example, an insured might schedule property—a garage, perhaps—at another location. Should a tornado damage both the garage and the insured residence, the deductible will apply at each location. The ISO form leaves this situation somewhat ambiguous. Is the tornado responsible for "one loss," or is each piece of property "one loss"?

Duties Following a Loss

Condition C. concerns the duties following a loss:

> In case of a loss to covered property, we have no duty to provide coverage under this policy if the failure to comply with the following duties is prejudicial to us. These duties must be performed either by you, an "insured" seeking coverage, or a representative of either.

The earlier form stated that the duties had to be carried out by the named insured; if the named insured was unable to perform them there could have been a coverage problem. Now, there are options as to who can fulfill the obligations. There are eight duties, with subsections for many. All actions an insured must complete following a loss in order to obtain payment from the insurer for the loss are listed. In the AAIS form, these duties are in the section "What Must Be Done in Case of Loss or Occurrence." The AAIS form contains the duties for both property coverages and liability coverages in this section.

The first requirement is that prompt notice of the loss be given to the insurer or its agent. The AAIS forms add that the insurer may require written notice. The second duty is that, in event of loss by theft, the police must be notified. Third, if the loss falls under the additional coverage for credit card or fund transfer card, the appropriate card company must be notified. These are requirements B.1., 2., and 3. of the ISO forms, and 1.a. of the AAIS section.

The fourth requirement the ISO forms impose following a loss is that the property must be protected from further damage. This might entail making reasonable and necessary repairs to protect the property, in which case the insured must keep accurate records of the repair expenses. Although not stated, the costs of protecting and making necessary repairs to protect the property are covered in addition to the direct property loss, but only to the extent that the entire loss does not exceed the limit of liability. See Chapter 3.

The AAIS forms state (1.b.) that the insured must take all reasonable steps to protect covered property *at and after a covered loss*. Thus, there is a subtle difference between the ISO and AAIS forms. It appears that, in the AAIS forms, the insured must make a determination at the time of loss as to whether or not the loss is covered. This could present a problem. A loss such as a tornado would be obvious. However, not all covered losses are so clear-cut. Many insureds might not realize that scorching damage to their siding, caused by a neighbor's leaf burning, would be covered under the peril of fire. They might ignore the damage or seek coverage under the neighbor's policy.

The safest course of action, therefore, is to advise insureds to take steps to protect the property, even if uncertain as to coverage.

The fifth duty following a loss in the ISO forms is the duty to cooperate with the insurer in the investigation of a claim. This duty has been implicit within the other duties required, but now it is explicit. In the AAIS forms, it is number 1.c. In the ISO forms the duties are to be performed by the named insured, an insured seeking coverage, or the representative of either; in the AAIS forms the cooperation required specifically applies to: "All 'insureds' seeking coverage, and the representative or representatives of all 'insureds' seeking coverage…" The question has arisen as to the scope of persons required to cooperate. Does the duty apply, for example, to a public adjuster? The term "representative" is not limited to any specific type of representative, such as someone holding a power of attorney. Therefore, anyone an insured designates to represent him or her is obligated to cooperate with the insurer.

The courts are in agreement as to the importance of an insured's cooperation. However, "many jurisdictions take the view that an insurer must show not only that the insured breached the contract, but also that it was prejudiced as a result" (*Couch On Insurance Third Edition*, § 199:76) either for denial of a claim or for voiding the policy altogether. See, for example, *Mutual of Enumclaw Ins. Co. v. T & G Construction, Inc.*, 199 P.3d 984 (Wash. App. 2007), where the court held that "an insured's noncompliance with a cooperation clause in a policy releases the insurer from its responsibilities only if the insurer was actually prejudiced by the insured's actions or conduct." And, in *Mefferd v. Sieler and Co., Inc.*, 676 N.W.2d 22 (Neb. 2004) the court held that "an insurer cannot assert a breach of a policy's notice and cooperation provision as a policy defense in the absence of a showing of prejudice or detriment to the insurer."

Many states hold that the clause is met by "substantial compliance," which means, essentially, that the insurer's ability to settle a claim or loss is not prejudiced by the insured's lack of cooperation. See, for example, *Conway v. State Farm Fire & Casualty Co.*, 1999 WL179746 (E.D. Pa. 1999), in which the court said that although the plaintiff had provided some information regarding theft of his boat, there was evidence the information was inaccurate. Therefore, a reasonable jury might conclude the insured had not cooperated.

The sixth ISO duty is to prepare an inventory of the damaged *personal* property. The quantity, description, actual cash value, and amount of loss must be shown. The insured must also include all bills, receipts, and related documents that support the figures. The AAIS form requires similar documentation (1.d.), but in the AAIS form *actual cash value* is a defined term: "the cost to repair or replace property using materials of like kind and quality, to the extent practical, less a deduction for depreciation, however caused."

Agent Tip

Most insureds do not maintain receipts for items, other than for major purchases such as appliances, and then usually only retain them for the warranty period. A recommended practice is to video tape all rooms and personal property in the dwelling. Closet doors and dresser drawers should be open to display their contents. There should be close-ups of all valuables, such as jewelry, silver, antiques, and fine arts. (Presumably proper insurance for these articles has been arranged.) Items stored in a garage, such as a riding lawn mower, should be included. The tape should then be stored in a safe place.

The seventh of the ISO insured's duties following a loss is to show the damaged property to the insurer, provide the insurer with requested records and documents and permit the insurer to make copies, and submit to examination under oath while not in the presence of any other insured and sign the oath. The requirement that an insured submit to questions *without any other insured being present* was inserted into item 7.c. because of the outcome of a Missouri case, *U. S. Fidelity & Guar. Co. v. Hill*, 710 S.W. 2d 171 (Mo. Ct. App. 1986), wherein the court decided that without an express policy provision, an insurer could not require an insured to submit to questioning away from other insureds.

The policy condition to submit to an examination under oath is extremely important, and should not be treated lightly by an insured. A quick review of *Westlaw®* cases indicates just how seriously the courts look at an insured's compliance. Indeed, the instances in which the courts determined that the insured's noncompliance did not allow the insurer to deny coverage are few and far between. One of a few is *First Home Insurance Co. v. Fleurimond*, 36 So.3d 173 (Third Fla. Ct. App. 2010). The insured was allowed to proceed with a suit against the insurer despite a failure to file a sworn proof of loss and fully comply with the examination requirement. This was because the insurer never requested a proof of loss, and the insured testified that when he and his wife appeared for the examination he was required to answer the same questions twice, once in English and once in Creole. They left during a break, and afterwards offered to resume, but the insurer refused to continue.

Of course, in the examination the questions asked by the insurer must be material to the claim. For example, asking about the whereabouts of unrelated personal records is immaterial; asking for records documenting an insured's financial position in a case of suspected arson or theft fraud is within the scope of the request.

The AAIS requirements (1.e., f., and g.) are more stringent. Not only must the insured show the damaged property, but, as in commercial forms, the insured must allow the insurer to take samples of the damaged property for inspection, testing, and analysis. Perhaps this is a precautionary measure to allow the insurer to take samples if arson is suspected. One of the AAIS requirements (similar to the ISO requirement to provide records and documents) is troubling. In event of a covered loss, the insured must show records, "including tax returns and bank records of all cancelled checks that relate to the value, loss, and costs, and permit copies to be made of them…" Although the requirement specifies that the records must pertain to the loss, who makes this determination? Many persons might feel uncomfortable providing tax records for the insurance company to sort through.

However it might be, the courts generally uphold an insurer's reasonable requests. For example, in the case of *DiFrancisco v. Chubb Ins. Co.,* 662 A.2d 1027 (N.J. Super. Ct. App. Div. 1995), the insurer maintained the insured's business was incapable of producing income that would allow the insured to buy items claimed in a theft loss. The court agreed the insurer had the right to income tax records from the insured.

The eighth of the ISO insured's duties following a loss concerns the proof of loss statement, which must be sent to the insurer within sixty days of the insurer's request. This statement must be signed and sworn. Note, the language requires *proof* of loss, not just the insured's stating that he or she suffered a loss. There must be proof that the loss occurred. In the case of a fire loss to a dwelling, the proof is obvious; in the case of the damaged personal property, the importance of accurate record keeping becomes clear. Often, an insurer has specific proof of loss forms that will be sent to the insured with the request to complete and return same.

The importance of submitting the required notice within the allotted time cannot be overstated. *Couch on Insurance Third Edition* §188.25 gives the following explanation: "One obvious purpose in requiring completion of a prepared form of proof is make [*sic*] sure that an insurer has all the information it needs to evaluate the claim. To the extent that alternative claim forms or written narratives fail to do so, they may fail to comply substantially with policy requirements." In the case of *Goodale v. Pioneer,* 614 N.Y.S.

2d 657 (1994) the court not only upheld the requirement, but stated that the insured's failure to comply was an absolute defense when suit was filed after the insurer refused to pay the claim. And, in *Dawkins v. Witt,* 318 F.3d 606 (C.A.4 2003) even though FEMA accepted the insured's proof of loss after sixty days had elapsed, and the flood adjuster told the insured the sixty day requirement would not be enforced, the court enforced the requirement because FEMA had not waived it in writing.

The proof of loss condition also outlines the information that must be included in the proof of loss. The time and cause of the loss must be given. Included as well must be: interests of all insureds and any others (including mortgages and liens) in the property; other insurance that might cover the loss; changes in title or occupancy of the property that occurred during the policy term; and specifications of damaged buildings and detailed repair estimates. (The AAIS forms request "available plans and specifications of buildings"—a much more reasonable way of putting it, since the average homeowner is unlikely to have plans or blueprints). The proof of loss also must include, as noted above, the inventory of any damaged or lost personal property.

It is in completion of the proof of loss that an insurer can cite the insured's failure to cooperate as a reason to deny a claim. Here, as in other areas of the insured's duties following a loss, many courts will accept substantial rather than strict compliance with the requirement. So, for example, an insured substantially complied where the loss was reported the day after the fire, the agent investigated the scene at least twice, and the insured sent five letters to the insurer with additional information as it became available, and the insurer did not object to this form of proof of loss. This case is *Rogers v. Aetna Casualty and Surety Co.*, 601 F.2d 840 (5th Cir. 1979)

Additionally, the insured must provide receipts for any additional living expenses incurred or records documenting the fair rental value lost as the result of a covered loss. Additional living expenses may include, but are not limited to, meals in restaurants, lodging, cost of boarding pets, and additional laundry or dry cleaning costs. If a portion of the insured dwelling is rented or held for rental, careful records of rent receipts and utility bills, if not paid by the tenant, should be kept. Remember, however, that if a loss results in the cessation of utility service, those expenses cannot be claimed.

The coverage for additional living expense should not be viewed as a test of the insurer's deep pockets. For example, receipts for meals at a five-star restaurant from a family that regularly eats at home, with the occasional meal at a burger or pizza restaurant, will probably be viewed unfavorably by the claims adjuster. It is important, however, to remember that the coverage is intended to allow the insureds to maintain their *normal* standard of living and not to force them to accept substandard accommodation simply to save money.

In the case of *Kennett v. Amica Mut. Ins. Co.*, 2010 WL 2977373 (E.D. La. 2010) the court noted that many of the expenses claimed by the insureds (for, among others, gum, cigarettes, and beer) would have been purchased whether or not the insureds continued to live in their home. (This case is also notable for the six hundred and eleven pages of home repair receipts [including receipts for two trips to visit the insured's father] and two hundred and twelve pages of internet shopping receipts.)

For another case involving ALE receipts, see *Grossman*, discussed in Chapter 2, and under Concealment or Fraud later in this chapter.

Finally, records—evidence or affidavit—that support a claim under the coverage for credit card or fund transfer card must be provided to the insurer.

The AAIS forms contain an additional condition (1.i.). The insured is required to assist the insurer in enforcing any right of recovery the insured might have against a party causing the loss.

Loss Settlement Provisions

This is condition C. in the ISO section I property conditions. In the AAIS forms, the provisions governing property loss settlement are found in the section titled "How Much We Pay for Loss or Occurrence." The AAIS forms, in the first provision in this section, state that the insurer will pay the lesser of the limit that applies or the amount determined under the applicable loss settlement terms (such as actual cash value). The insured therefore is advised up front, as it were, as to the insurer's position.

Both the ISO forms and the AAIS forms include a statement that replacement cost and the cost to repair or replace do not include any increased costs incurred to comply with enforcement of any ordinance or law, except to the extent coverage is provided in the additional or the incidental property coverages. Thus, the insured cannot argue that the policy's promise to replace includes these increased costs. Remember that there is an additional amount of insurance—10 percent of the limit of liability that applies to coverage A, which can be increased by endorsement—available for increased costs associated with ordinance or law compliance.

In the ISO forms, personal property, awnings, carpeting, household appliances, outdoor antennas and outdoor equipment whether or not attached to buildings, structures that are not buildings, and grave markers and mausoleums all are valued at actual cash value, but for not more than the amount required to repair or replace them. The AAIS forms contain a somewhat different list of items: replacement cost does not apply to window air-conditioners, awnings and canopies, appliances, carpets, and antennas, all whether or not attached to a building. Although personal property is not listed, the AAIS lead-in language states that the replacement cost terms apply "only to buildings covered under coverages A and B that have a permanent foundation and roof."

Both the ISO and AAIS forms offer replacement cost coverage for buildings under coverages A or B, and, by endorsement, replacement cost coverage for certain other structures that are not buildings. See Chapter 13. At the time of a loss, the amount of insurance carried must be at least 80 percent or more of the full replacement cost of the building immediately before the loss in order for the insurer to pay the cost to repair or replace. The wording of the replacement insuring agreement is important. The insured must carry the replacement cost amount "just before the loss." Following a loss, when perhaps because of scarcity the cost of building materials has been driven up, the insured cannot be penalized for not carrying the amount of replacement the dwelling would require after the loss.

If sufficient insurance is carried the insurer will pay the *lowest* of: 1) the limit of liability applicable to the building; 2) the replacement cost of the damaged part of the building "with material of like kind and quality and for like use"; or 3) the necessary amount actually spent to repair or replace the damaged building. If the insured chooses to replace the dwelling, the replacement dwelling need not be located on the same premises. However, both AAIS and ISO clearly state that if the insured elects to replace a damaged building at another location, replacement cost is limited to the cost that would have been incurred had the building been repaired or replaced on the location where the damage occurred. In other words, an insured cannot decide to build a new dwelling in, say Hawaii, following a loss to a dwelling in Ohio and expect the insurer to pay the increased costs associated with the new location.

If there is less than 80 percent insurance to replacement cost, the insurer pays the *greater* of: 1) the actual cash value of that part of the building damaged, or 2) that proportion of the cost to repair or replace the damage that the amount of insurance on the building bears to 80 percent of the building's replacement cost. The insurer will not, however, pay more than the applicable limit of liability. This provision is similar to a coinsurance clause except that it is applicable only to replacement cost—not actual cash value—recovery.

ISO has changed the wording in the current form with regard to the deductible. Previously, the form stated that the insurer would "pay the cost to repair or replace, after application of any deductible..." or "that proportion of the cost to repair or replace, after application of any deductible..." But because the deductible provision is now condition B., it is clear that the cost to repair or replace should be determined, and the deductible applied to that amount. For example, in a covered loss to a dwelling replacement is $150,000; the deductible of $1,000 is applied to that amount, so $149,000 remains to repair or replace the dwelling.

The AAIS form also spells out actual cash value terms for property not eligible for replacement cost, such as drives, fences, and personal property. The insurer will pay the smaller of: (1) the cost to repair or replace the lost or damaged part of the property with materials of like kind and quality, to the extent practical; or (2) the "actual cash value" of the lost or damaged part of the property just before the loss. Actual cash value is a defined term in the AAIS form; it means "the cost to repair or replace property using materials of like kind and quality, to the extent practical, less a deduction for depreciation, however caused."

There might be a difference of opinion between an insurance company and an insured regarding the appropriate amount of recovery under the replacement cost provision. This is evidenced by the case of *Higginbothan v. New Hampshire Indemnity Co.*, 498 So. 2d 1149 (La. Ct. App. 1987). Here the court reviewed whether the insurer was correct in paying only to *repair* and not to *replace* a roof that was damaged by windstorm. Three expert witnesses testified that, unless the roof was completely replaced, it could not be guaranteed leak-proof. The court ruled that the insurer's original payment for repairs was arbitrary and capricious, and therefore required the insurer to replace the roof and pay all penalties and attorney fees.

When researching cases for this book, it was interesting to note that, rather than using only the term *replacement*, some courts were substituting *replication*. Although the AAIS and ISO forms (and, indeed, insurance custom) refer to *replacement*, *replication* seems to be more in the spirit of the policy intentions—that is, to restore the insured to pre-loss condition. This is not to say that insureds are limited to an exact duplication of the damaged dwelling. See, for example, the case of *Ross v. Metropolitan Property and Casualty Ins. Co.,* 2008 WL 4861698 (S.D. Miss. 2008). Here, the insured's home was virtually destroyed by Hurricane Katrina. There was both a flood policy and standard homeowners policy in place. Coverage under the standard homeowners policy turned on whether the insureds' election to rebuild a substantially different dwelling was allowable under the policy, or whether in fact they had to replicate the home. The court reviewed the policy language, and said "the insurance contract provides only that the insured dwelling may be replaced, and the proper measure of damages under the contract in this situation is replication cost, i.e., the actual cost the plaintiffs would have incurred to duplicate or replicate the insured building using materials of like kind and quality as those in the insured building up to the coverage limit."

In determining the replacement cost of the building, the following items are to be omitted: the value of excavations; foundations (whether brick, stone, or concrete), footings, or any other structures or devices that support all or part of the building; piers, or supports below the lowest basement floor (or below ground inside the foundation walls, if there is no basement); and underground flues, pipes, wiring, and drains. But note that these items are covered if damaged in an insured loss. Note, also, that in a total loss the amount of insurance on the building might be insufficient if there is foundation damage, as could be the case in event of an extremely severe fire.

Agent Tip

The prudent agent will use every means possible to obtain an accurate replacement cost. There are programs on the market that calculate replacement cost for most homes. Remember also that most guaranteed replacement endorsements require the insured to maintain 100 percent of replacement value at the time of a loss and to notify the insurer of any alterations or additions resulting in a 5 percent or greater increase in replacement.

Having said that, many courts are of the opinion that it is the duty of the insured to properly insure his or her property. See, for example, the case of Myers v. Yoder et al., 921 N.E.2d 880 (Ct. App. Ind., 2010) The court held that the agent did not have a duty to advise the homeowners about the policy, and that the agent acted reasonably in issuing the policy without performing a replacement cost estimator. Nonetheless, maintaining insurance to value not only eliminates court visits, but brings in premium dollars.

In no event will the policy pay more than actual cash value unless actual repair or replacement is completed or the cost to repair or replace the damage is both less than $2,500 and less than 5 percent of the amount of insurance on the building. (The AAIS form states that actual cash value will be paid when the repair or replacement cost exceeds the lesser of $2,500 or 5 percent of the amount of insurance.) The insured may claim the actual cash value initially, before repair or replacement is completed, and then make an additional claim based on replacement cost within 180 days *after the date of loss*. This latter provision has been the source of some confusion. In a situation in which an insured cannot immediately rebuild, such as when many homes are damaged in an area because of a tornado, and builders are stretched beyond capacity, the insured should not be penalized for a situation beyond his or her control. The condition is met if the insured notifies the insurer of the intent to claim replacement. Indeed, the current ISO forms clearly state this: "you may then make claim for any additional liability according to the provisions…provided you notify us of your intent to do so within 180 days after the date of loss." The current AAIS form states that "'You' may later make a claim for any additional amount payable under these Replacement Cost Terms, but only if 'you' have informed 'us', within 180 days after the date of loss, that 'you' plan to do so."

Both AAIS and ISO declare that the insurer will pay no more than actual cash value until repair or replacement is completed. Although insureds have tried in the courts to collect replacement prior to fulfilling this condition, the courts have upheld the provision as not placing an undue burden on the insured.

Line-Item Estimates?

Our insured's home burned and it was a total loss. When he and his wife began to rebuild, they were advised that they could only recover actual cash value until the repair or replacement was complete. Further, the insurer is asking for line-item estimates. This seems unreasonable. The insureds also were thinking of making some upgrades to the home as they rebuild—for example, putting in marble countertops and oak instead of laminate cabinetry. Shouldn't they be allowed to do this?

Remember the policy promises to pay replacement cost with the intention of putting the insureds back in their pre-loss condition. If the insureds had Formica® countertops and laminate cabinetry prior to the loss, that is all the insurer is obligated to pay for. If the insureds want to upgrade, perhaps they can work with the insurer to receive the ACV for the pre-upgrades, recognizing that they will be responsible for the difference. As for the line-item estimates, this request is not unreasonable; it's just tedious. And, actual cash value is the only payment available until repair or replacement is complete. Most courts are in agreement on this. For a case that addresses many of these points, see *Burton v. Republic Insurance Co.*, 845 A.2d 889 (Pa. Super. 2004).

Loss to a Pair, Set, or Parts

Both forms state that, in event of a loss to part of a pair or set, the insurer may elect to either repair or replace any part of the pair or set to restore the pair or set to its value before the loss or pay the difference between the actual cash value of the set before and after loss. Note that the choice is the insurer's. This is ISO condition E. and AAIS condition 1.c. in the section "How Much We Pay for Loss or Occurrence."

A novel application of the pair or set clause allows recovery of the actual cash value of a lock set after the theft of a key. Since the value of a lock set is in its ability to prevent unauthorized entry, theft of a key effectively destroys its value. It can be *restored* only by installing a new lock set or having the lock rekeyed. Or, if the insurer elects option b. (paying the difference between actual cash value of the property before and after the loss), the actual cash value of the lock set after theft of a key is zero, so the full actual cash value of the lock set is payable.

The AAIS forms go a step further in condition 1.d. If there is a loss to a part of an item that consists of several parts when complete, the insurer will pay only for the value of the lost or damaged part or the cost to repair or replace it. Although it might appear that such an example as the lock set, above, would not be covered, the limitation applies only when the complete item consists of *several* (more than two) parts. So, for example, if the insured had an expensive stereo system consisting of speakers, turntable, CD hookup, and amplifier, and the amplifier was stolen, he or she could not make a claim for the entire system.

It is sometimes tempting to apply the pair or set clause to situations that do not warrant it. Take, for example, garage doors on a two-car garage, where only one is damaged. If only one door were to be repaired so that there are now two mismatched doors, an insured would not be restored to a preloss condition; i.e., to the value existing before the loss. In such a scenario, application of this condition is not appropriate. The use of the pair and set clause gives the insurer a way to settle a loss when it may be impossible to restore a set. Think, for example, of a one-of-a-kind pair of bookends.

Appraisal

This is condition E. of the ISO forms. The equivalent AAIS condition is located in the section entitled "Conditions Applicable to Property Coverages Only," where it is condition 2. This provision outlines the method for resolving the question of the amount of loss when the insurer and insured cannot agree. This clause is sometimes misunderstood. Its purpose is to determine the *amount* of a loss, not whether or not a loss is covered. Indeed the AAIS form clearly states "Under no circumstance will an appraisal be used to interpret policy 'terms', determine causation, or determine whether or not a loss is covered under this policy." For this reason, a good practice would be to define terms each appraiser is using prior to the process. For example, "scope of loss," depending upon who is using the term, can mean either "amount" or loss or extent of property damaged," which could be two different things entirely.

Each party chooses a competent and impartial appraiser within twenty days of receiving a written request from the other. The two appraisers choose an umpire. If an umpire is not agreed upon within fifteen days, then, either the insured or the insurer requests that the choice be made by a judge of a court of record in the state where the residence premises is located.

The appraisers separately set the amount of the loss. If they agree and submit a written report to the insurer, the amount is binding upon the insurer. If the appraisers fail to agree, the dispute is submitted to the umpire. In that case, the amount set by any two is the amount of loss. The expense of each party's appraiser is borne by that party; the expenses of the umpire and of the appraisal are shared by both parties.

The terms of the appraisal condition can often vary depending upon a state's amendatory provisions. Be sure to check these if there is any question.

The courts have upheld the appraisal clause, including both insured's and insurer's right to demand the same. The condition is part of a legal contract, and the parties thereto are not permitted to pick and choose which parts they will abide by. See, for example, *Farmers Automobile Insurance Association v. Union Pacific Railway Company*, 768 N.W.2d 596 (Wis. 2009), which held that the "appraisal clause in policy compelled homeowner to participate in a binding appraisal process." See also *Woodward v. Liberty Mutual Insurance Company*, 2010 WL 1186323 (N.D. Tex. 2010). Here, the insurer demanded appraisal, and the homeowners decided they did not like the insurer's appraiser's qualifications. Upon that appraiser's withdrawal (because of commitments to work following Hurricane Ike), the insureds appointed their own appraiser, who came up with an estimate. When the estimate was submitted, the insurer declined to pay, and the insureds sued. The court said that the appraiser's withdrawal did not equate with the insurer's withdrawal from the appraisal process, and the appraisal clause was binding on both parties. Therefore, the insurer's request to continue the process was granted. The parties were told to report the outcome to the court in sixty days.

Other Insurance, Service Agreement, and Government Fund

Condition G. of the ISO forms contains two parts. The first applies to other insurance. This provides that, when other insurance also covers a loss that is covered under section I of the homeowners policy, the policies will prorate the loss payment based on the proportional relationship that each policy limit has to the total amount of insurance on the loss. For example, if two policies cover a $10,000 loss, policy A with a limit of $50,000 and policy B with a limit of $70,000, payment under A is $4,200 (50,000/120,000 =.42; $10,000 x .42 = $4,200) and under B is $5,800 (70,000/120,000=.58; $10,000 x .58 = $5,800).

The condition concerning other insurance in the AAIS form is number 6." Insurance under More than One Coverage" in the section "How Much We Pay for Loss or Occurrence." The AAIS form also responds on a proportional basis, except that, when a loss is also covered by the master policy of an association or corporation of property owners, the AAIS form becomes excess. A similar clause is found in the ISO unit owners form HO 00 06, which makes an exception to prorating when the other insurance on the property is in the name of a corporation or association of property owners. In that case, the unit owner's insurance is excess over any such insurance.

The second part of the ISO condition relates to service agreements. It states:

> ...this insurance is excess over any amounts payable under any such agreement. Service agreement means a service plan, property restoration plan, home warranty or other similar service warranty agreement, even if it is characterized as insurance.

For example, insureds may purchase a new home that carries a warranty that the construction and all systems are sound. Three weeks later the roof leaks, and it is learned that the shingles have not been thoroughly nailed in place. The warranty responds first to the loss, and the insurance is then excess. It might be left for a court to determine whether *payable* equates to *collectible*. For example, if the company providing the warranty goes bankrupt, will the homeowners form respond on a primary basis? The AAIS condition is number 7.

Note that both the AAIS and ISO forms state that these warranties or service agreements, even though they might be characterized or have the appearance of insurance, will not force the insurer to participate in a loss on anything other than an excess basis.

The AAIS form contains an additional condition entitled "Government Funds," which states "If loss, cost, or expense covered by this policy is also covered by a government fund, 'we' pay 'our' share of the loss, cost, or expense. 'Our' share is that part of the loss, cost, or expense that the 'limit' of this policy bears to the total amount payable for the loss, cost, or expense permitted by law." Possibly, this condition could be used in the event a tornado destroyed a town, and governmental agencies dispensed funds for living expenses. The insured would then expect his or her additional living expense coverage to take this into account.

Personal Articles Separately Insured

An insured, whose hobby is photography, has an extensive camera collection insured with a specialty lines carrier. Recently, he sustained a theft of all his equipment. He learned that it would cost more to replace all the items than the amount of insurance he had carried. Shouldn't he be able to look to his homeowners policy to make up the rest of the amount? What about the "other insurance" condition?

The clause does not prorate insurance coverage for articles of personal property that are separately described and specifically insured by other insurance. As stated under the coverage C provision for property not covered, the policy does not apply at all to such property and cannot be called on to contribute with other insurance.

Suit Against Us

Condition H. of the ISO forms provides that the insured cannot bring action against the insurer unless all policy provisions have been complied with. The action must be commenced (*filed*, not just thought about) within two years from the date of loss. This is condition 8. of the AAIS section "Conditions Applicable to Property Coverages." The AAIS forms, like the ISO forms, state that a suit must be brought within two years after the loss; however, if a particular state law invalidates this time period the amount of time is governed by that law. Often, a change will be located in the state's amendatory provisions.

Sometimes this condition is misread to deny coverage, as, for example, when an insured learns sometime considerably after a loss that he or she could claim coverage for the loss. That is not at all what the condition refers to; making a claim for coverage is not the same as filing a suit against the insurer.

Our Option

ISO condition I. allows the insurer to elect, within thirty days after receiving the signed proof of loss from the insured, to repair or replace any part of the lost or damaged property with like property. For example, a windstorm blows part of an insured's roof off, resulting in damage to a new suite of bedroom furniture. If the insurer can locate a similar suite and replace the damaged furniture, the insurer has that right. The policy makes it clear that the replacement must be with "material or property of like kind and quality."

The AAIS condition is number 1.b. of the section "Payment of Loss." The wording here is clearer in that it states the insurer has the option to pay the loss in money or, within thirty days after receiving the proof of loss, notify the insured of the intent to rebuild, repair, or replace the property. This same condition also states that the insurer may take all or part of the damaged property at an agreed or appraised value, at which point the property becomes the insurer's. The AAIS condition satisfactorily answers a potential source of dispute in the ISO forms. For example, an insured loses an oil painting in a covered fire. The damage is assessed and the claim settled, but the insured wants to keep the oil painting even though it is damaged. If he or she has been reimbursed for the loss, keeping the painting violates the principle of indemnity (which is not spelled out in the policy). Perhaps the insured knows that, even in a damaged condition, the painting has monetary value. In that case, the insured receives an unwarranted profit. The AAIS forms, by specifically stating the insurer has the right to take the painting after having paid for it, deter a potential dispute.

Use of "May"

We have a question concerning the language of several conditions in the homeowners policies. The appraisal condition, for example, says if the insured and insurer fail to agree on the amount of loss, "either may demand an appraisal..." And, later in the subrogation clause, the form says "an 'insured' may waive in writing before a loss.... If not waived, we may require an assignment of rights..." In common everyday usage, many people use "may" to mean that something might or might not occur. Is that true here? Is the insurer in the last example saying "we might (or might not) require an assignment of rights"?

The use of "may" in any insurance contract is *always* in the sense of "have permission to." Remember the old way of teaching children the difference between "can" and "may"? "Mother, can I go to the movies?" asked the child. "Yes, you can, but no, you may not" was the answer until the child properly asked "May I go?" At which point, the mother said "Yes, you may."

Loss Payment

Condition J. of the ISO form, and condition 1.a. of the AAIS form (in the section "Payment Of Loss"), states that all losses will be adjusted with and paid to the named insured unless some other person is named in the policy or legally entitled to receive payment. For example, property of a guest or resident employee is covered while in any residence occupied by an insured. If this property is destroyed by a covered peril payment is made directly to the guest or residence employee and not to the insured. Loss is payable within sixty days after the proof of loss is received *and* the insurer has reached an agreement with the insured, or there is an entry of a final judgment, or there is an appraisal award filed with the insurer. Under the current AAIS form, the insurer also has sixty days to pay the loss following receipt of an acceptable proof of loss and written agreement as to the amount of the loss. So, for example, if the insured mails the proof of loss and spends some ten days to reach a written agreement with the insurer, the clock does not begin ticking until the agreement has been reached.

This is a condition that may be modified by a state's amendatory endorsement to change the insurer's time to pay a claim.

Abandonment of Property

ISO condition K. and number 1. in the AAIS section "Conditions Applicable to Property Coverages Only" states that an insured cannot just walk away from a property loss and leave the damaged property to the insurer, with the insurer's acceptance of the property (the AAIS form adds "unless 'we' agree."). The insurer has the right, though, to accept any such property.

Mortgage Clause

This is condition L. of the ISO forms number 4. in the AAIS section "Conditions Applicable to Property Coverages Only." The clause protects the mortgagee's interest primarily by providing that the interest of the mortgagee is not invalidated by any act or neglect of the mortgagor. This provision acknowledges the fact that the mortgagee does not usually have direct physical control over the premises. The clause further provides that the mortgagee is to receive payment for any loss, subject, of course, to its interest and the terms and limits of the policy.

According to *Couch on Insurance, Third Edition* §65:46, "The standard mortgage clause, in essence, functions as an independent contract only for the limited purpose of preventing the insurance coverage being defeated by the act of the insured alone; barring specific provisions to the contrary, it does not, in any other way, affect the terms of the policy."

The AAIS form outlines payment in event of a loss payee on personal property. The definition of "insured" is extended to include the loss payee, but only with regard to the personal property. The loss payee is to receive notice if the insurer cancels or nonrenews the policy.

Note that the forms state that the insurer responds to a *valid* claim of the mortgagee. A claim for excluded flood damage will not be covered, even though other conditions have been met.

The question has arisen, particularly with the number of foreclosures, whether the bank's or mortgagee's failing to notify the insurer as to the foreclosure proceedings constitutes a breach of the mortgagee's duty "to notify [the insurer] or any change in ownership, occupancy or substantial change in risk of which the mortgagee is aware." One court answered in the negative. There was a fire which destroyed an insured home while foreclosure proceedings were pending, and the insurer refused to pay the claim, because the bank had not advised the insurer as to the foreclosure. This case is *U.S. Bank., N.A. v. Tennessee Farmers Mutual Insurance Company*, 277 S. W. 3d 381 (Tenn. 2009). It should be noted, however, that the court alluded specifically to Tennessee law as to whether the bank was statutorily required to notify the insurer; other courts might well disagree. If you are an insurer, look to the statutes governing any action required of a mortgagee before making a determination as to coverage.

No Benefit to Bailee

ISO condition M. (because tenant homeowners forms have no mortgage clause, the condition number for those forms will differ from this point on) is a standard property clause. It states that the insurer will not recognize any assignment or grant any coverage that benefits a person or organization holding, storing, or moving property for a fee regardless of any other provision of this policy. For example, if a moving company negligently damages the insured's property, the mover cannot avoid responsibility for payment. Generally a bailee is liable for damage to bailed property if the bailee has failed to exercise due care. In the AAIS forms, this condition is number 5. in the "Conditions Applicable To Property Coverages Only." The wording is much more succinct, stating simply "coverage under this policy will not directly or indirectly benefit those who are paid to assume custody of the covered property."

The condition has sometimes been held to be ambiguous. As one court pointed out, *property* is not defined (nor is *a person or organization*). So, said the court, taken to its logical extreme, an insured depositing an insurer's check (property) in his or her personal banking account could be barred from coverage for the claim because the bank charged a fee for the account but received the benefit of the funds while acting as bailee. Or, if following a covered loss the damaged property was sent to be repaired, the repairer—the bailee—could not be paid with funds received to settle the claim. This case is *Ledyard v. Auto Owners Mutual Ins. Co.*, 739 N.E.2d 1 (Oh. Ct. App. 2000). For the most, though, the intent is to put the responsibility directly on those paid to hold, store, or move property. See *Last v. West American Ins. Co.*, 354 A. 2d 364 (N.J. Super. 1976), where the insured left some guns at a gun shop to be sold. When a fire destroyed them, the insured could not recover under his homeowners policy.

Nuclear Hazard Clause

ISO condition N. is the nuclear hazard clause. Nuclear hazard is defined as "any nuclear reaction, radiation, or radioactive contamination, all whether controlled or uncontrolled or however caused, or any consequence of any of these." Loss caused by the nuclear hazard cannot be considered loss by fire, explosion, or smoke for purposes of obtaining coverage. In other words, if a nuclear explosion levels a dwelling, the insured cannot claim explosion was the cause of loss. However, direct loss by fire resulting from the nuclear hazard is covered.

In the AAIS forms, the nuclear hazard clause is contained within the exclusion of coverage ("Exclusions That Apply to Property Coverages" 1.c.). Also included in the exclusion is the exception of coverage for direct loss resulting from fire.

Recovered Property

ISO condition O. concerns the disposal of any property for which the insurer has made payment. This is number 7. of the AAIS forms in the "Conditions Applicable to All Coverages" section. If any lost or damaged property for which payment has been made is recovered by either insured or insurer, that party is to notify the other. The insured has the option of retaining the recovered property or allowing the insurer to take custody of it. If the insured retains custody, any loss payment may be adjusted to account for the value of the recovered property.

The AAIS forms contain a more detailed agreement in this condition, and refer to property that is recovered "or payment is made by those responsible for the loss." If the claim paid is less than the agreed amount of loss, either because of a deductible or policy limitation, the recovery is prorated between insured and insurer based upon the interest of each in the loss. So, if an insured suffered a theft of personal property in the amount of $10,000 but received only $9,000 because of a $1,000 deductible, the insured's interest in the recovered property will be proportionately greater than the insurer's.

Volcanic Eruption Period

Condition P. of the ISO forms and number 9. of the AAIS "Conditions Applicable to Property Coverages Only" concerns volcanic action. The ISO forms state that all (one or more) eruptions occurring within a seventy-two hour period will be considered as one volcanic eruption. The earlier AAIS forms provided that all action occurring within a *168-hour period* would be considered as one occurrence, but in the 2006 and 2008 forms this period is now seventy-two hours.

Policy Period

Condition Q. of the ISO forms appears separately in the conditions applying to section I and again in the conditions applying to section II. The condition states that the policy applies only to loss that occurs during the policy period.

AAIS condition 6. in the section "Conditions Applicable to Property Coverages Only" states "the policy only covers losses that occur during the policy period." In the earlier AAIS forms, this condition was found in the section "Conditions Applicable to All Coverages," and noted that the policy applied only to bodily injury or property damage that occurred during the policy period. By placing the condition in two locations, as in the ISO forms, there can be no question as to coverage intent.

Concealment or Fraud

Condition R. in the ISO forms is condition 7. in the section "Conditions Applicable to All Coverages" of the AAIS forms.

The condition reads:

> We provide coverage to no "insureds" under this policy if, whether before or after a loss, an "insured" has:
>
> 1. Intentionally concealed or misrepresented any material fact or circumstance;
> 2. Engaged in fraudulent conduct; or
> 3. Made false statements; relating to this insurance.

The earlier AAIS forms stated that the policy would be void "as to 'you' and any other 'insured,'" but now use similar wording as the ISO forms in providing no coverage for any "insured" if, before or after a loss:

> a. an "insured" has willfully concealed or misrepresented a material fact of circumstance that relates to this insurance or the subject thereof; or
>
> b. there has been fraudulent conduct or false swearing by an "insured" with regard to a matter that relates to this insurance or the subject thereof.
>
> This applies even with respect to an "insured" who was not involved in the concealment, misrepresentation, fraudulent conduct, or false swearing.

Fraud means "the intentional perversion of truth in order to induce another to part with something of value," according to *Webster's Collegiate*

Dictionary (Tenth Edition). The act often occurs in connection with a claim, from inflating values of damaged or lost property to outright arson. But what is *material misrepresentation*? Generally, a material misrepresentation is made on an insurance application and is the misstatement of fact if "the knowledge or ignorance of it would naturally influence the judgment of the insurer in making the contract and accepting the risk" (*Bryant v. Nationwide Mutual Ins. Co.*, 313 S.E.2d [N.C. Ct. App. 1984], quoted with approval in *Kinlaw v. North Carolina Farm Bureau Mutual Ins. Co.*, 389 S.E.2d 840 [N.C. Ct. App. 1990].) In other words, if all facts were known, an insurer would not issue the requested policy.

In a case in which material misrepresentations did *not* cause a policy to be voided (or coverage denied under the current forms) the court ruled that the insureds' prior actions did not work a fraud on the insurer since there was no intent to deceive. The insureds forged the signatures of their lien holders in an effort to obtain insurance funds necessary to repair weather-related damages; but they were able to prove to the court's satisfaction that they knew the lien holders would sign them. Further, the lien holders lived in a remote area, only picking up their mail once a week. In *Leasure v. MSI Insurance Company*, 75 Cal. Rptr. 2d 900 (Cal. Ct. App. 1998), the court ruled that, as a matter of law, the insurer was obligated to honor a later claim for vandalism because the prior action had not hindered the insurer from investigating the claim.

Sometimes two (or more) claims are the subject of fraud or misrepresentation, as in *Collins, et al. v. USAA Property and Casualty*, 580 N.W.2d 55 (Minn. Ct. App. 1998). In this instance, the dwelling was broken into and a theft occurred. A few days later, the dwelling, including contents, was completely destroyed by fire. The insureds presented two sworn proofs of loss, one for the break-in and one for the fire. Upon investigation, the insurer learned that both claims for contents were greatly exaggerated and voided the policy. The insureds claimed breach of contract. The district court ruled that their material misrepresentations voided the policy as to the lost property but not for their interest in the dwelling, since that part of the loss was not misrepresented. However, the appellate court reversed the ruling, stating that "voiding the policy for material misrepresentations of substantive amounts is consistent with the reciprocal duties of the insured to its insurer…"

Now, under the current language, if fraudulent acts or misrepresentations are committed, the entire policy is not voided. *All* insureds, however, are barred from coverage under section I property coverages. Taken together with the exclusion of coverage for "any loss arising out of any act an 'insured' commits or conspires to commit with the intent to cause a loss" it is clear that, even in cases of arson ascribed to one insured, innocent insureds will be denied coverage.

Of course, state-specific amendatory endorsements may state otherwise.

Finally, as discussed in Chapter 2, and noted under the heading "Duties Following a Loss," the case of *Grossman v. Homesite Insurance Company*, 2010 WL 1233907 (Conn. Super. 2010) demonstrates that, although the concealment or fraud condition is not to be treated lightly—the courts, for the most part, have resisted any attempts by insureds to circumvent it—there are limits. When no fraud can be demonstrated, the courts uphold the rights of insureds.

Loss Payable Clause

Condition S. in the ISO form is the loss payable clause. This condition amends loss payment clause I., which states that the insurer will adjust all losses with the named insured or certain others, with regard to personal property that may be subject to a lien, such as property bought on time. The definition of "insured" is amended to include the loss payee, but only with respect to the property on which the lien has been placed.

The condition also adds that the loss payee will be notified in writing if the insurer decides to cancel or nonrenew the policy. Note, though, the insurer will not accord the loss payee the same protection as a mortgagee. The insurer does not need to send notice to a loss payee ten days prior to the date of cancellation or nonrenewal; nor will a claim of a loss payee necessarily be honored when an insured's is not.

This is AAIS condition 3. in the section "Conditions Applicable to Property Coverages Only."

Miscellaneous AAIS Property Conditions

Some additional conditions in the AAIS forms are not contained in the ISO forms. The AAIS forms contain a condition (1.c. in the section "Payment of Loss") regarding payment in event of a loss covered under additional living expense coverage. If the insured premises are unfit for use for more than one month, covered costs will be paid on a monthly basis. The insured must furnish proof of such costs, such as receipts from lodging and meals taken in restaurants.

The next condition (3. in the section "Payment of Loss") concerns payment of a claim involving damage to personal property of others. The insurer has the option of adjusting the claim with and making payment to the insured on behalf of the owner, or of adjusting the claim with and making payment directly to the owner of the property. Obviously, if the claim is adjusted with the owner of the property, no payment will be made to the insured.

Chapter 8

Liability Coverages and Exclusions, Part I

Introduction

Personal liability insurance is financial protection against legal obligations of the insured arising out of activities and conditions at the premises where the insured maintains a covered residence. This coverage also extends to the personal (nonbusiness) activities of the named insured and household members anywhere in the world. Section II of the homeowners forms consists of two principal elements. First, coverage E in the ISO forms is personal liability insurance, protecting insureds against liability for both bodily injury and property damage. Coverage F in the ISO forms is medical payments to others. Both coverages are automatically included; neither one is optional. In the AAIS forms, these are coverage L, personal liability, and coverage M, medical payments to others.

Features

There are certain significant features of personal liability coverage. First, coverage for bodily injury (including a limited form of employers liability coverage) and property damage are combined in one insuring clause. Second, the basic package policy premium for this insurance is based on a single limit per occurrence, which applies to any combination of one or more claimants and to claims based on either bodily injury, property damage, or both. Common limits for section II coverage are $100,000 for liability and $1,000 for medical payments to others, although these limits may be increased.

The third feature is the provision of coverage for relatives of the named insured, and of the named insured's spouse, so long as they reside in the named insured's household. The first definition in the ISO form declares that "'you' and 'your' refer to the 'named insured' shown in the Declarations and the spouse if a resident of the same household." The AAIS definition is similar: "The words 'you' and 'your' mean the person or persons named as the insured on the 'declarations'. This includes 'your' spouse if a resident of 'your' household." Both programs have endorsements that give "insured" status to non-related residents of the insured's household; see Chapter 13. And, as we will see, certain others are also covered without additional premium. Residence or domestic employees are insureds under certain circumstances. The definition of a residence employee is discussed later in this section.

Finally, coverage applies not only at the insured's residence (or residences) described in the declarations of the policy, but to any premises that qualify as an insured location as defined in the policy and anywhere with respect to personal activities. Various restrictions in premises liability coverage are considered later in this chapter.

Homeowners section II also contains four additional coverages: claim expenses; first aid expenses; damage to property of others; and loss assessment, which are discussed in Chapter 9. The AAIS forms are constructed differently. They contain eight incidental liability coverages, some of which are the ISO additional coverages, and four of which appear as exceptions to the exclusions in the ISO forms.

Since, except for construction, the forms are much alike in coverage grants and exceptions, the discussion follows the ISO order, with the AAIS location indicated.

Personal Liability Insuring Agreement

There are two parts to the insuring agreements of both the ISO and AAIS forms. First, if a claim is made or suit is brought against an insured for damages arising out of a covered occurrence, the insurer agrees to pay up to the limit of liability for the damages for which the insured is legally liable (including prejudgment interest awarded against the insured; this provision is "Incidental Liability Coverages" 2.e. in the AAIS form). Second, the insurer agrees to provide a defense at its own expense. The insurer promises to defend "even if the suit is groundless, false or fraudulent." Thus, the duty to defend is broader than the duty to pay. This is not to say that *any* suit will be defended; at least one complaint or allegation must potentially fall within coverage. A claim seeking damages for *any* action that conceivably could fall within the coverage provisions of the policy must be investigated and a defense afforded. For example, an insured sells his residence and a year later the purchaser alleges breach of contract in that the insured did not disclose the residence was on a flood plain. Because the homeowners policy responds only to damages because of bodily injury or property damage, not to breach of contract, the insurer will not owe a defense.

The insurer retains the right to make any investigation and settle any claim or suit that it decides is appropriate. The insurer's obligation to defend any claim or suit ends when the amount the insurer pays for damages resulting from the *occurrence* (discussed next) equals its limit of liability. To illustrate, suppose there are multiple claimants injured or suffering property damage from the same occurrence, and the resulting claims exceed the limit of liability for the personal liability coverage. Once the insurer has paid out the limit of liability (and any claim costs in connection with the claimants receiving payment), it is relieved of further responsibility to defend or pay claim costs for additional claimants seeking damages as a result of the same occurrence.

What is an "Occurrence"?

In order for section II coverage to apply, the injury or damage must be caused by an *occurrence*; that is, "an accident, including continuous or repeated exposure to substantially the same general harmful conditions, which results, during the policy period, in: '[b]odily injury'; or b. '[p]roperty damage'." The AAIS form language is similar. It cannot be stressed too greatly that the insurance is intended to apply to activities of an insured that result in *unforeseen, unintentional* bodily injury or property damage.

Although one tends to think of an accident as something immediate in time and place, the definition of *occurrence* includes "continuous or repeated exposure to substantially the same general harmful conditions." So, for example, if an insured child keeps using a neighbor's house as a basketball backboard, with the result that the siding becomes discolored and dented, the resulting property damage falls within the definition.

Sometimes "occurrence" as defined is used with regard to a first person property loss. This is erroneous; "occurrence" in quotation marks—that is, when it is a defined word—only appears in the liability portion of the policy.

Who is an "Insured"?

As noted above, persons other than the named insured and spouse (if resident of the same household) are insureds. Resident relatives of the named insured or resident spouse are insureds. Persons under the age of twenty-one, such as foster children, in the care of the named insured, spouse, or resident relatives, are insureds. ISO has rewritten the definition of *insured* in the 2011 forms; however, this is for clarification rather than a change in the definition. The AAIS definition for *insured* is similar for these persons.

In earlier forms, the status of a student away at school was open to interpretation by insurers as well as the courts. Some held that only students under age twenty-one qualified; others held that status should be determined on a case-by-case basis. But now, *insured* includes "a student enrolled in school full-time, as defined by the school, who was a resident of your household before moving out to attend school, provided the student is under the age of: (1) 24 and your relative; or (2) 21 and in your care or in the care of a resident of your household who is your relative." In the AAIS form, *insured* includes: "'your' relatives under the age of 25 years who: 1) are financially dependent upon 'you'; 2) are students enrolled in school full time, as defined by the school; and 3) were residents of 'your' household just before moving out to attend school." These definitions can be amended; see Chapter 13.

As noted, a person who resides with the named insured but is not a resident relative may be given insured status (for both section I and section II coverage) by endorsement. See Chapter 13.

The above entities are insureds under both section I property and section II liability. We noted earlier, and it bears repeating, that the following language has been added to the ISO and AAIS forms:

> Under both Sections I and II, when the word an immediately precedes the word "insured", the words an "insured" together mean one or more "insureds".

There are, however, additional entities given insured status under section II liability coverage. In the ISO form, any person or organization legally responsible (unless in the course of business—a veterinarian, for example) for animals or watercraft to which the policy applies are also insureds if the animals or watercraft are owned by the named insured, spouse, resident relative, a person in the care of an insured, or a student as described. With respect to a motor vehicle to which the policy applies, persons engaged in the employment of the insured or any person designated an insured are insureds, as are other people using the vehicle on an insured location with consent. The AAIS form adds that persons or organizations legally responsible for a motorized golf cart covered under the policy are insureds, but only with respect to the golf cart. AAIS includes as well persons in the course of acting as the insured's real estate manager for the residence premises, but only with respect to acts falling within the scope of such duties.

What are "Bodily Injury" and "Property Damage"?

Bodily injury is defined as "bodily harm, sickness or disease, including required care, loss of services and death that results." The AAIS definition is that *bodily injury* means "bodily harm to a person and includes sickness, disease, or death. This also includes required care and loss of services." *Bodily injury* thus pertains only to people; the term is not applicable to animals.

Most jurisdictions hold that bodily injury does not include *purely* emotional or mental injury. See, for example, *Allstate Ins. Co. v. Diamant*, 518 N.E.2d 1154 (Mass. 1988). In this case, the Diamants sought defense and coverage from their homeowners policy when suit was brought against them for defamation and intentional infliction of emotional distress. The court held that the policy's definition of bodily injury as "bodily injury, sickness or disease, including resulting death, care and loss of services" was clear and encompassed only physical injuries to the body. And in the case of *Citizens Insurance Co. v. Leiendecker, et al.*, 962 S.W.2d 446 (Mo. Ct. App. 1998), in which the defendants were sued for negligently recommending an insurance agent (who fraudulently obtained money for policies that were never delivered), the court agreed with the majority view that bodily injury refers to conditions of the body and "excludes mental suffering or emotional distress." Thus, there was no coverage under the Leiendeckers' homeowners policy.

However, in the case of *Voorhees v. Preferred Mutual Insurance Co.*, 607 A.2d 1255 (N. J. 1992), the court held that the emotional injuries inflicted by the insured had resulted in physical consequences, which triggered a defense under the homeowners policy. (The dissenting judge asked "What's going on here?" Bodily injury did not encompass "solely subjective nonphysical mental suffering" he added, so reinstatement for the defendant would be in order.) That there is coverage for bodily injury arising out of emotional injury appears to be the minority thinking. In the case of *American Family Mut. Ins. Co. v. Wagner,* 2007 WL 1029004 (Slip Copy W. D. Mo. 2007), the defendant filed a suit against her employer and immediate supervisor, alleging sexual harassment and physical symptoms arising out of emotional injury. The supervisor's insurer, American Family, filed an action seeking a declaration that it had no duty to defend or indemnify the supervisor. The court agreed with the insurer, first saying that the harassment had been no "accident" (the court used a common dictionary), and second, that emotional injuries were not considered bodily injuries unless the emotional distress arose from a definite bodily injury.

Agent Tip

Coverage for some forms of emotional distress, such as libel or slander—usually referred to as personal injury—may be added by endorsement or by purchasing an umbrella policy. See Chapter 13.

Some jurisdictions hold that the term is ambiguous and that coverage should be provided for emotional distress claims. See, for example, *State Farm Mutual Auto Ins. Co. v. Ramsey*, 368 S.E. 2d 477 (S. C. Ct. App. 1988). In this case, a mother witnessed her daughter's death when she was struck by an auto. The court held that the "negligent infliction of emotional distress is a bodily injury," and so the auto policy responded to two bodily injury claims, not one.

Perhaps the most reasonable approach is that taken by a Colorado court. Condo owners sought indemnification from a contractor's insurer, alleging that negligent construction (lack of sufficient soundproofing) caused them mental suffering, including dissatisfaction, embarrassment, frustration, and loss of sleep. The court said that such claims should be analyzed on a case-by-case basis "to determine if alleged emotional injuries are sufficiently akin to physical injury to render the term 'bodily injury' ambiguous." This case is *Admiral Insurance Company v. Hosler et al.*, 626 F. Supp.2d 1105 (D. Col., 2009). We should add that the court also noted that, "under Colorado law, a claim for negligent infliction of emotional distress can be sustained by manifestations of physical or mental illness." As we see, not all jurisdictions agree.

Loss of services is considered to be part of a bodily injury claim. For example, if an insured accidentally trips a woman, causing her to break a leg so that she must hire someone to keep house for her family, that expense is covered.

Property damage is defined as "physical injury to, destruction of, or loss of use of tangible property." Note that the loss of use coverage does not require *physical injury* to property of others; covered damage can arise if the owner is deprived of the property's use. A common example is negligent blocking of access to property of others, with no actual physical damage to the property itself.

Sometimes the question arises as to whether diminution of value is considered property damage, as when, for example, an insured puts up a structure that blocks a neighbor's view of a lake. The neighbor cannot market his property as a view property and claims diminution of value. For the most, courts hold that the damage claimed is solely economic and, as such, is not property damage under the homeowners policy. (This is not to say that a homeowner might not be held liable for the decrease in value of another's property; but the tying of liability coverage to "physical damage to property" should prevent the policy from applying unless the property was actually physically damaged.) Diminution of value may sometimes be recovered, but that has been in cases where the diminution was simply a means of measuring a tangible physical loss when there has been physical damage.

As we noted, the term "bodily injury" applies only to human beings. Although we love our pets, they are, in fact "property." If we negligently injure a neighbor's dog, we are liable for property damage. Courts are much in agreement that economic damages are allowable; emotional damages are not. Thus, when the owner of a dog that wandered onto another's property was fatally shot, the court allowed recovery of economic damage for the destruction of personal property, but not recovery for emotional distress. (See, for example, *Scheele v. Dustin*, 998 A.2d 697 [Vt. 2010]. See also *Kaufman v. Langhofer, D.V.M.*, 222P.3d 272 [Ct. App. Ariz., 2009]. This later case also notes that many courts will apply a "value to owner" theory, which includes such things as purchase of another pet, initial veterinary bills, security, etc., but adds that courts applying this theory "decline to include the pet's sentimental value to its owner.")

What is an "Insured Location"?

Some liability coverage hinges on whether or not an event takes place on an insured location. The current AAIS forms refer to "insured premises" but the categories are the same as in the ISO forms. There are eight categories of insured locations. First, of course, is the residence premises itself; that is, the one- to four-family dwelling, town house, row house, unit, or part of any other building where the named insured resides and which is shown as the residence premises or the described location (AAIS) on the declarations. Included are other structures and grounds at that location.

The second category is the part of other premises used by the named insured as a residence and shown in the declarations (as a seasonal residence), or a residence acquired during the policy period for the named insured's use.

Third is any premises used in connection with the first two categories of premises. There is no geographical limit imposed by the forms, so this category has often led to coverage disputes, with insureds often seeking broader coverage than was intended by the insurer. Commonly, an accident involving use of a motor vehicle covered while being used on an insured location is at the center of the dispute. We will discuss this in more detail when we discuss the exceptions to the motor vehicle exclusion. But to demonstrate that the premises used in connection with a residence premises (or described location) need not be immediately adjacent, the case of *Erie Ins. Exchange v. Szamatowicz,* 597 S. E. 2d 136 (N.C. Ct. App. 2004) is enlightening. Because of the number of invited guests, the insured used a warehouse which he leased for a business and which was some twenty miles from his home to host a birthday party. One of the guests was injured. The insurer denied coverage both because of the distance and because of the warehouse's business use, but the court held that the use of the warehouse was "in connection with" the residence premises. There was no distance limitation in the policy, and the activity was not in any way connected with the business.

The fourth category is any part of a premises not owned by an insured but where an insured is temporarily residing. For example, a hotel room or a rented summer cottage where an insured temporarily resides may be an insured location.

The fifth category involves land: first, vacant land other than farm land owned by or rented to an insured; second, land owned by or rented to an insured on which a one- to four-family dwelling is being built as a residence for an insured. Vacant land is generally held to be land upon which no man-made structure exists. ("When determining if an insured's land qualifies as vacant land under homeowners' insurance policies that include vacant land as insured premises, relevant inquiry centers not on the economic effect of any structures on the property, but rather on the existence of any structures on the property," said the court in *American Family Mut. Ins. Co. v. Page,* 852 N.E.2d 874 [2d Dist. 2006]). Farm land is included in this category. Farm land is often "vacant" in the sense that there are no structures on it; however, it is used for business purposes and a separate set of exclusions applies. For example, in the case of *Metropolitan Property and Casualty Ins. Co. v. Jablonski*, 722 N.W.2d 319 (Minn. Ct. App. 2006), a snowmobiling accident occurred on the insured's land, which he had rented out for farming. The court held that the land was not vacant since the customary use was farming, even though the farming was not taking place when the accident occurred.

Agent Tip

If any doubt exists whether an insured's parcel of land is vacant—perhaps it is enclosed by a fence but no other structures are on it—add the parcel as an additional premises for liability coverage to the homeowners. The cost is minimal.

The sixth category of insured location is individual or family cemetery plots or burial vaults of an insured. Although it is tempting to think of burial vaults or cemetery plots, because they are affixed to the land, as real property, they have the unique distinction of being a hybrid of real and personal property, because their care passes from one generation to the next with no change in title.

The seventh category of insured location is any part of a premises occasionally rented to an insured for other than business use. Thus, a hall rented to an insured for a son's wedding reception is an insured location.

What is a "Residence Employee"?

Before looking at the coverage for medical payments to others we consider the definition of a residence employee, because residence employees are, when in the course of their duties, insureds.

The ISO forms define a residence employee as:

a. An employee of an "insured", or an employee leased to an "insured" by a labor leasing firm under an agreement between an "insured" and the labor leasing firm, whose duties are related to the maintenance or use of the "residence premises", including household or domestic services; or

b. One who performs similar duties elsewhere not related to the "business" of an "insured".

A "residence employee" does not include a temporary employee who is furnished to an "insured" to substitute for a permanent "residence employee" on leave or to meet seasonal or short-term workload conditions.

The AAIS forms use the term "domestic employee," and state these are persons "who perform duties that relate to the use or care of the 'described location'." Persons who are furnished to an insured as temporary substitutes for permanent domestic employees who are on leave, or to meet seasonal or short-term workloads, are not considered domestic employees for coverage purposes.

The intent is to give persons employed on a more or less permanent basis certain coverage. However, for someone hired on a temporary basis, say to help serve at an outdoor party, that person is not an insured. Although this might seem a bit harsh that such persons are not insureds, remember that they also have the right to sue for any injuries they might sustain in the course of their duties.

Medical Payments Insuring Agreement

Coverage F of the ISO forms (coverage M of the AAIS forms) provides medical payments coverage for accidents to persons *other than* insureds who are on an insured location with the permission of any insured or, under certain circumstances only, away from the insured location. The insurer agrees to pay the "necessary medical expenses that are incurred or medically ascertained [found out or learned with certainty] within three years from the date of an accident causing 'bodily injury'." The AAIS provision states that expenses must be incurred or medically determined within three years from the date of the accident that causes bodily injury (as defined) covered by the policy. This clarifies that, for example, should an insured intentionally injure someone, medical payments coverage would not respond. The provision for covering expenses that are ascertained within the three-year period addresses the problems associated with claims that involve treatment beyond one year after the time of an accident. Dental injuries to a child, for example, often cannot be fully treated until the child is older.

ISO defines medical expenses in the insuring agreement as "reasonable charges for medical, surgical, x-ray, dental, ambulance, hospital, professional nursing, prosthetic devices and funeral services." AAIS adds to the list "hearing aids, prescription drugs, and eyeglasses, including contact lenses."

The homeowners medical payments coverage applies to outsiders and residence employees but not to the named insured or other residents of the insured's household. This is emphasized by the name of the coverage—medical payments *to others.* Furthermore, no medical payments coverage applies to anyone (except for residence employees) who regularly resides anywhere on the insured location, such as tenants or boarders. (Residence employees are often given status as insureds, yet they may claim coverage under medical payments to others.)

Medical payments coverage applies, according to ISO, "on the 'insured location'"; according to AAIS, "on the 'insured premises'." See the previously outlined definition of an insured location, and it is apparent how broad the coverage is. The coverage does not apply to persons on the insured premises without permission of an insured; in other words, trespassers. But the permission need not be specific to the occasion for coverage to apply. A neighbor, for instance, making an uninvited but presumably welcome social call, a mail carrier, or other delivery person all have *implied* permission to be on the premises even though not specifically invited.

Additionally, the medical payments coverage applies *away from* the insured location on a more limited basis. There is coverage if the injury occurs in any of the following four circumstances:

1. It arises "out of a condition on the 'insured location' or the ways immediately adjoining." The AAIS form refers to "access ways immediately adjoining an 'insured premises'." Coverage applies, for example, to a neighbor injured by flying debris or overcome by smoke from an explosion or fire originating on the insured premises. There also is coverage for anyone who trips or falls on the public sidewalk adjacent to the premises, even though the insured does not own the sidewalk. Coverage relates to the insured location rather than the residence premises.

2. It is "caused by the activities of an 'insured'." This language has been the subject of many arguments. *Dodge v. Allstate Insurance Co.*, 233 N.E.2d 100 (Ill. App. Ct. 1968), illustrates the intended limitation on coverage. The insured had organized a skating party at a public rink. During the party, three of the guests fell on the ice and required medical attention. Though the insured was not

involved in their fall in any way, the guests subsequently claimed that the party was the activity of the insured, and, since their injuries arose out of this activity, they were entitled to coverage under the medical payments insurance agreement of the insured's homeowners policy. The court, upholding the lower court's reasoning, found that the social party given by the insured did not cause the injuries. In other words, where the activity of an insured is incidental to but not directly the cause of an injury, it is not within the scope of the coverage. In order for coverage to apply, some specific act of the insured must cause the injury; for example, golf ball gone awry that hits a bystander.

3. It is "caused by a 'residence employee' in the course of the 'residence employee's' employment by an 'insured'." As with the second item above, the injury must be caused by the employee. Note, also, that the injury need not "arise out of" the employment but need only be "in the course of" employment by an insured for the medical payments coverage to apply. See also the following discussion of section II coverage for residence employees.

4. It is "caused by an animal owned by or in the care of an 'insured'." There is no definition of *animal* in the policy. Section I of the policy excludes animals, birds, or fish from covered property, but in the medical payments coverage the insured should be allowed the broadest common definition of the term, including all forms of animal life other than humans because there is no limiting definition in the policy.

However, remember that persons legally responsible for animals to which the policy applies are also insureds for liability coverage purposes, although not when in the course of any business or without the owner's consent. For example, a neighbor offers to walk an insured's poodle. The poodle slips his leash, attacks another dog, and bites the other dog's owner when she tries to separate the animals. The neighbor may claim liability coverage as an insured, and the medical payments to others coverage will respond. But, if the poodle bites the kind neighbor, he will not receive any medical payments to others benefits. The neighbor has liability coverage as an insured in charge of the animal; by the same token, an insured is not eligible for medical payments to others coverage.

Note the difference between the wording of provision one—"arising out of a condition on an insured premises"—and the next three—"caused by [an insured, an employee, an animal]." Courts generally hold the wording "arising out of" to be much broader in scope than "caused by." The words "having origin in, growing out of, or flowing from" can be substituted for "arising out of" to clarify the difference. So, for example, in our example of the smoke from a fire on the insured premises injuring the next-door neighbor, the injury arose from a condition on the insured premises; the premises themselves did not cause the injury." "Caused by," on the other hand, implies a direct correlation between the entity causing the injury and the recipient.

Exclusions–Liability and Medical Payments

Both the ISO and the AAIS forms contain three sets of exclusions. The first of these apply to both personal liability and medical payments coverages; the second, to personal liability coverage; and the third, to medical payments coverage. The exclusions for both liability and medical payments are discussed in the order in which they appear in the ISO forms, with the number of the equivalent AAIS exclusion indicated. Note, though, that the AAIS forms are arranged differently from the ISO forms. Whereas ISO excludes certain activities (motor vehicle liability, for example), and then gives coverage by exception to the exclusion, AAIS states what is covered in the section "Incidental Liability Coverages." Then, in the exclusions, the forms will state that motor vehicle liability is excluded except as provided in the Incidental Liability Coverages. Thus, when we discuss the ISO exclusion (and exception) for certain motor vehicles, we will note the AAIS exclusion, and then discuss the coverage for the vehicles.

Exclusions applying only to liability or to medical payments coverage are discussed in Chapter 9.

Motor Vehicle, Watercraft, Aircraft, and Hovercraft Definitions

In the current ISO forms, motor vehicle liability, watercraft liability, aircraft liability, and hovercraft liability are now defined terms:

> "Aircraft Liability", "Hovercraft Liability", "Motor Vehicle Liability" and "Watercraft Liability", subject to the provisions in b. below, mean the following:
>
> a. Liability for "bodily injury" or "property damage" arising out of the:
>
> (1) Ownership of such vehicle or craft by an "insured";
>
> (2) Maintenance, occupancy, operation, use, loading or unloading of such vehicle or craft by any person;
>
> (3) Entrustment of such vehicle or craft by an "insured" to any person;

(4) Failure to supervise or negligent supervision of any person involving such vehicle or craft by an "insured"; or

(5) Vicarious liability, whether or not imposed by law, for the actions of a child or minor involving such vehicle or craft.

b. For the purpose of this definition:

(1) Aircraft means any contrivance used or designed for flight except model or hobby aircraft not used or designed to carry people or cargo;

(2) Hovercraft means a self-propelled motorized ground effect vehicle and includes, but is not limited to, flarecraft and air cushion vehicles;

(3) Watercraft means a craft principally designed to be propelled on or in water by wind, engine power or electric motor; and

(4) Motor vehicle means a "motor vehicle" as defined ... [see below]

The AAIS forms, unlike the ISO, states that a hovercraft does not include a model hovercraft not used to carry people or cargo. A "watercraft" is an apparatus or device primarily designed to be propelled on or in water by engine, motor, or wind."

Before we move on to the definition of a motor vehicle, note that much of what was previously found within the liability exclusions is now in the definitions. Therefore, the exclusions will state, for example, that "coverages E and F do not apply to any 'motor vehicle liability'"... Note as well that hovercraft are now specifically excluded. (Ground effect and flarecraft vehicles do not fly in the sense that aircraft do; they rely on a cushion of air created by their own forward movement. They can operate at heights no greater than about 1-1/2 times wing span.) A somewhat troubling addition is *occupancy*. If a person simply occupies an excluded watercraft, and negligently bumps into another occupant, is there no coverage? This might be a question left for the courts to decide.

As with the medical payments provisions described above, we see the use of "arising out of" with regard to the motor vehicle exclusions. So, a neighbor child can be injured by an insured's changing a tire, which rolls across the street and hits him.

Generally the terms that have given rise to most court cases have been *maintenance*, *use*, and *operation*. To review the many court cases that have had these terms as their subject is not the intent here. Some courts have found that the use or operation of a motor vehicle must constitute the proximate cause of an injury for the exclusion to apply and that there must be an element of control. However, this has not been a universal conclusion, and exactly what constitutes *use* remains ambiguous. For example, if an insured asks his or her neighbor to take his (the insured's own) car and run an errand for him, even though the insured is not driving he could be said to be *using* the car.

Maintenance appears to be clearer to courts than use or operation. In the case of *Indiana Insurance Co. v. Winston et al.*, 377 So. 2d 718 (Fl. Dist. Ct. App. 1979), the insured, his sons, and a friend were adding an air scoop to the insured's car. The hood was removed and the hinges were pushed down. As another friend leaned on the car, a hinge released and struck him in the eye. The court found that, although the injured party was not engaged in maintenance, the injury arose from a condition created during the maintenance of the vehicle. Therefore, the exclusion was upheld.

The next part of the definition refers to *entrustment*. This wording appears redundant in that incidents arising out of ownership, maintenance, use, loading, or unloading are already excluded. However, its inclusion emphasizes that, no matter whose action results in a claim—whether the insured's or another party's—the homeowners form is not the place to find coverage. Both AAIS and ISO forms include *supervision,* including failure to supervise or negligent supervision, to circumvent the argument that bodily injury to another party arose from the insured parents' failure to supervise their teenage daughter's driving. If the mechanism of the loss is an excluded conveyance, the courts have upheld the exclusion. In the case of *Iorio v. Simone*, 773 A.2d 722 (N. J. Super. Ct. App. Div. 2001) the insured allowed his son, age twelve, to drive a go-kart with the insured's nine year-old nephew behind. The son drove the kart into the street and hit a tree. The nephew's parents sued, alleging that the negligent supervision occurred on the premises, and therefore the resulting loss should be covered. But the court upheld the exclusion, saying that the trigger should be the accident itself, which took place in an excluded vehicle, and not the careless conduct of the insured.

Finally, *vicarious liability* for the actions of a child or minor using an excluded conveyance, whether or not imposed by statute, is excluded. *Vicarious liability*, according to *Black's Law Dictionary (Sixth Edition)*, is the "imposition of liability on one person for the actionable conduct of another, based solely on a relationship between the two persons." So, for example, parents are vicariously liable for the actions of their resident minor children, or a person might be liable for the action of a foster child in his care. The AAIS forms state that there is no statutory liability coverage for the use of a motorized vehicle or watercraft, unless provided by incidental motorized vehicle or watercraft coverage (exclusion 1.e.).

A motor vehicle means:

a. A self-propelled land or amphibious vehicle; or

b. Any trailer or semitrailer which is being carried on, towed by or hitched for towing by a vehicle described in a. above.

The current AAIS forms define a *motorized vehicle* similarly to a. and b. above. The trailer or semitrailer meeting the definition of a motor vehicle is one attached to or being carried on or towed by, or that becomes detached while being carried on or towed by, a vehicle as defined in a. This definition clarifies that, even if a trailer being towed by an auto becomes detached during the towing, coverage for any accident arising from this should be found under the auto policy. This is not to say that, once the trailer is detached (as a camper is detached in a camp ground) there is no coverage; "becomes detached" implies that the action has taken place without human intent; for example, the hitch releases while the trailer is being towed. But if a trailer has been detached intentionally, as when a camper detaches the trailer from the towing vehicle, then the trailer no longer meets the definition of a motor vehicle. The earlier AAIS forms also contained definitions for *motor vehicles* and *recreational motor vehicles*, but now a single definition, with appropriate distinctions made in the incidental liability coverages as to which vehicles are covered, have eliminated the need.

Motor Vehicle Exclusions

There are four sets of exclusions applying to motor vehicles, watercraft, aircraft, and hovercraft. Each set of exclusions contains exceptions, except, as noted, the AAIS forms which gives the coverages in the incidental liability coverages. Since the wording of the exclusions and exceptions are similar, they are dealt with together. In the ISO forms these are exclusions A. through D. In the AAIS forms these are exclusions 1.b through 1.e. in the section "Exclusions That Apply to Liability Coverages," and the exceptions to these are in the "Incidental Liability Coverages," numbers 7. and 8.

Exclusion A. eliminates coverage for motor vehicle liability (as defined) if, at the time of the occurrence, the motor vehicle is registered for use on public roads or property, or such registration is required by law or governmental regulation for the vehicle to be used at the place of the occurrence. With the current wording, a vehicle such as a snowmobile might be required to be registered for use on public lands and thus fall within the exclusion (other exclusions might apply as well; these are discussed later).

There is no motor vehicle liability coverage if the motor vehicle is operated in or practicing for any prearranged or organized race, speed contest, or other competition. AAIS adds: "pulling or pushing, demolition, or stunt activity." There is no coverage if the motor vehicle is used to carry persons or cargo for a charge, rented to others, or used for any business purpose other than for a motorized golf cart while on a golf course. (Presumably this is a nod to all those who make business deals while out on a golf course.)

Exceptions to the Motor Vehicle Exclusions

There are exceptions to the motor vehicle liability exclusions. But remember while reading the exceptions below that none of them will apply to give coverage if one of the restrictions discussed above applies.

First, there is liability coverage if the motor vehicle is in dead storage on an insured location. This provision was not in the earlier AAIS forms, but is in the current forms. The term dead storage means "out of action or out of use," according to *Webster's Third New International Dictionary*. A vehicle in dead storage, then, is one that is out of action or out of use because it is incapable of being used in the same sense that a dead electric circuit or a dead telephone line is incapable of being used. An insured's decision simply to discontinue using an auto—an operable sports car kept in the garage for the winter months, for instance—does not qualify as dead storage any more than a phone is dead when not in use, or an electric outlet is dead if nothing is plugged into it. Presumably, dead storage entails removal, at least, of the battery and draining the gas tank.

The issue of what dead storage means, however, has been subject to varying court interpretations, some of which have discounted the issue of operability. For example, in the case of *Sharpe v. State Farm*, 558 F. Supp. 10 (E. D. Tenn. 1982), the vehicles in question were operable. This was evident from the fact that they were sometimes moved around in the insured's yard. The court felt, however, that since they had no license plates and were not driven on the highway, they could be considered to be in dead storage. But a finding to the contrary is *Foremost Signature Insurance Company v. Montgomery*, 266 S.W.3d 868 (Mo. Ct. App. 2008). The insured's pickup struck another, injuring him. The pickup was unregistered and uninsured because the insured intended to sell it; the court said that because it was capable of being started (the insured was demonstrating that it was operational when the injury occurred) it was not in dead storage.

A conflict might arise between situations when a vehicle is in dead storage and when it is undergoing maintenance. In the case of *Westfield Insurance*

Co. v. Herbert et al., 110 F. 3d 24 (Ind. Ct. App. 1997), an insured sixteen year-old was attempting to remove the gasket of a valve cover from a car in dead storage in order to sell the cover. He was using gasoline, and, when that did not work, he tried to burn it off. The resulting explosion severely burned a neighbor child who was playing in the insured's yard. The insurer denied the claim on the basis of the maintenance exclusion, but the court found that the maintenance ended when the insured decided to sell the cover rather than reinstall it on the vehicle. Therefore, maintenance was not the "efficient and predominating" cause of the loss.

Agent Tip

Difficulties of interpretation arise in the case of automobiles being built from kits. Because of court decisions finding that a vehicle cannot simultaneously be in dead storage and be undergoing maintenance, it would be prudent to insure the vehicle under a personal auto policy as it approaches a state of operability. Of course, discussing the situation with the underwriter will help with arranging the proper type of coverage. Under the current personal auto policy (PAP) automatic coverage for a "newly acquired auto" begins on the date the insured becomes the owner, not the date the auto becomes operable.

The next exception to the exclusion is for a motor vehicle used to service an insured's residence. The 2000 ISO forms stated that liability coverage applied to a vehicle "used solely to service an 'insured's' residence." This wording left open the possibility that an insured might take his riding mower to an elderly neighbor's to mow the grass and, while there cause property damage—throwing a rock up and breaking a plate glass window, perhaps—and coverage would be denied. But now this wording has been removed in the 2011 form, so that the exclusion does not apply to a vehicle ⊠used solely to service a residence." The AAIS forms have given coverage by stating the vehicle must be used "only to service an 'insured premises'" with certain exceptions: a premises used in connection with a) the described location, b) one shown on the declarations, or c) a part of any other premises used by the named insured as a residence and acquired during the policy period. The vehicle cannot be used to service burial or cemetery lots. The AAIS form adds that the vehicle is covered if it is used to service the premises of another, but only if the vehicle is designed for use off of public roads.

"Servicing" a Premises

We have some insureds who have summer residences on an island. It is quite common to ride an ATV or a golf cart a mile or so to the local store/ post office to collect mail, pick up a few groceries, and chat with friends.

(scenario continues next page)

Doesn't this constitute "servicing the premises?" Is it necessary to insure these vehicles elsewhere for liability, or will the unendorsed homeowners policy cover them if, say, they accidentally hit and injure someone? Some years ago one of our insureds drove her golf cart into a store's plate glass window, but she had the cart listed on her auto policy. Is this necessary?

One must be careful in drawing conclusions that "servicing" is quite broad and will encompass such things as leaving the premises to collect mail. *Webster's New World College Dictionary* says that the verb means "to make or keep fit; in use, functioning." Taking a golf cart to run errands benefits the occupant of the premises, but not the premises itself. If the ATV was being used to pull a fallen tree off a drive, that would benefit the premises. The unendorsed homeowners will now provide liability coverage if the cart is within the bounds of a residential community. See the exception to the motor vehicle liability exclusion A.2.e.

Both ISO and AAIS forms cover vehicles that are designed to assist the handicapped. But the ISO forms state that at the time of a covered occurrence the vehicle must either be parked on an insured location or being used to assist a handicapped person. This restriction could have unintended consequences—if, perhaps, an insured child were playing on the vehicle and inadvertently ran into someone. The AAIS forms do not add this restriction.

The fourth exception is for motorized vehicles designed for recreational use off of public roads. Bodily injury or property damage caused by an owned vehicle of this type and occurring on an insured location (as defined) is covered. Bodily injury or property damage arising from a nonowned vehicle of this type is covered, wherever occurring. (But remember there is potentially no coverage if the vehicle is registered or required to be registered for use on public roads or property.) Persons using a covered recreational vehicle on an insured location, with the named insured's consent, have "insured" status, as do persons while engaged in an insured's employment. As with golf carts, these persons need not be residence employees; any legitimate employment qualifies so long as the persons are engaged in the employment at the time of the occurrence.

Coverage for recreational motor vehicles has been much debated in the courts. Remember that an insured location includes a premises used by the named insured in connection with the residence premises. In the case of *Nationwide Mutual Ins. Co. v. Prevatte*, 423 S.E.2d 90 (N. C. Ct. App. 1992), the insureds regularly used a neighbor's adjacent property for walks and ATV rides. The court found that property thus constituted an insured location. But in the case of *Safeco Ins. Co. of America v. Clifford et al.*, 896 F. Supp. 1032

(D. Oregon 1995) the insureds' regular use of a relative's adjacent property to store property and burn trash did not make the property an insured location.

There have been many attempts to secure coverage for accidents involving ATVs that occur close to, but not on, the residence premises. (The case of *Prevatte,* above, appears to be a minority position.) See, for example, *Shelter Mut. Ins. Co. v. Davis,* 715 N.W.2d 769 (Iowa App. 2006). The court ruled that "the phrase 'grounds used in connection with the residence premises' contained within policy did not extend to roadway where accident occurred." Even a private road owned by a homeowners association was not enough for a court to decide for the insured in *Royal Indemnity Co. v. King,* 2007 WL 2827844 (F. Supp. 2d 2007). The court said "'insured location' did not encompass every piece of property in which insureds had a property interest, and insured failed to show that they actually used the portion of the road upon which the accident took place."

In the 2011 form, ISO has added an important exception (2.d.(2)(b)) to the motorized vehicle exclusion, and that is for the toy or battery-powered vehicles so commonly seen today. AAIS had an exception for these types of vehicles in the 2006 edition which carries into the 2008 edition. The AAIS exception (7.a.5) is broader, in that it applies to a vehicle "designed for recreational use off of public roads, operated by a battery, and not built or modified after manufacture to exceed a speed of 15 miles per hour on level ground, and not a motorized bicycle, moped, or golf cart." The ISO exception provides coverage so long as the vehicle is "designed as a toy vehicle for use by children under seven years old, powered by one or more batteries, and not built or modified after manufacture to exceed a speed of five miles per hour on level ground."

The fifth exception to the motor vehicle liability exclusion has been broadened in the current forms (quoting ISO):

> A motorized golf cart that is owned by an "insured", designed to carry up to four persons, not built or modified after manufacture to exceed a speed of 25 miles per hour on level ground and, at the time of an "occurrence", is within the legal boundaries of:
>
> (1) A golfing facility and is parked or stored there, or being used by an "insured" to:
>
> (a) Play the game of golf or for other recreational or leisure activity allowed by the facility;
>
> (b) Travel to or from an area where "motor vehicles" or golf carts are parked or stored; or

(c) Cross public roads at designated points to access other parts of the golfing facility; or

(2) A private residential community, including its public roads upon which a motorized golf cart can legally travel, which is subject to the authority of a property owners association and contains an "insured's" residence.

This exception, also found in the AAIS forms, recognizes the prevalence of private communities built around a golf course. As noted under "Who is An Insured," persons in an insured's employment are "insureds" with respect to golf cart liability.

The earlier forms specifically contained coverage for losses arising out of a trailer *not* towed by or carried on a motorized land conveyance. The trailer could be a utility, camp, or boat trailer. (Remember, while a trailer is being towed by, say, an auto, the auto policy provides coverage.) So, if a camp trailer is parked at a campground for an overnight stay, and a visitor trips and falls down its steps, there is coverage for both liability and medical payments. As discussed earlier, in the current forms the exception for coverage is found within the definition of a motor vehicle, so there is no need for an exception within the section II exclusions. However, the ISO definition refers to a "trailer *not hitched for towing*," which means that the trailer must be detached from the auto that tows it in order for the homeowners to respond. The AAIS form states that a motorized vehicle includes a trailer or semitrailer that is attached to or being carried on, or becomes detached from, a self propelled land or amphibious vehicle; therefore, once the trailer is no longer attached to the vehicle pulling it there is coverage.

Watercraft Exclusions

Exclusion B. in the ISO forms applies to watercraft. In the AAIS form, exclusion 8.b. gives the exclusion to the incidental watercraft liability coverage. If, at the time of an occurrence, a watercraft is being operated in or practicing for any prearranged or organized race, speed contest, or other organized competition there is no liability coverage. However, the exclusion does not apply to a sailing vessel or a predicted log cruise. (Predicted log cruises are those in which the operator predicts exactly how much time he or she will take to complete a certain route and touch certain spots; speed is not a factor.) Excluded as well is liability coverage while a watercraft is rented to others, used to carry persons or cargo for a charge, or used for any business purpose. There is no exception to the business exclusion such as that for golf carts.

Exceptions to the Watercraft Exclusions

The ISO exceptions and AAIS incidental coverage 8. provide some liability coverage for bodily injury or property damage arising out of certain types of watercraft. There is coverage in both the ISO and AAIS forms for stored boats. This is similar to the motor vehicle dead storage provision. In the ISO and AAIS forms, there is liability coverage for owned, borrowed, or rented sailboats, with or without auxiliary power, that are under twenty-six feet in overall length. Overall length means length along the longitudinal axis as a person might walk along the top deck—stem to stern, as it were. There is coverage for borrowed sailboats with or without auxiliary power that are greater than twenty-six feet in overall length.

Both the AAIS and ISO forms cover bodily injury or property damage arising out of watercraft powered by inboard or inboard-outdrive (sometimes referred to as inboard-outboard) engine or motor power, including those that power a water jet pump, of fifty horsepower or less *not owned*, i.e., borrowed or rented, by an insured. Both forms also cover watercraft with more than fifty horsepower inboard, inboard-outdrive, or motor power including those powering a water jet pump that are *not owned by or rented to* an insured (borrowed, say).

Watercraft powered by one or more outboard motors totaling twenty-five horsepower or less are covered, whether owned, borrowed, or rented under both ISO and AAIS. There is liability coverage for watercraft having an outboard motor or motors with more than twenty-five total horsepower, if the motor or motors are not owned by an insured. The forms cover watercraft powered by outboard motors totaling more than twenty-five horsepower if they were acquired prior to the policy period and declared at inception, or acquired during the policy period. If that is the case, then the insured must request coverage within forty-five days of acquisition. Coverage applies for the policy period for both circumstances. Obviously, coverage is subject to underwriter approval. Both ISO and AAIS state that "horsepower means the maximum power rating assigned to the engine or motor by the manufacturer."

Remember that insureds are not only, for example, the named insured, spouse, and resident relatives; insureds include any person or organization legally responsible for a watercraft to which the policy applies as long as it is owned by an insured.

Aircraft and Hovercraft Liability

The AAIS and ISO forms state that the policy does not cover aircraft liability or hovercraft liability. These are exclusions C. and D. in the ISO form, and, in the AAIS form, exclusions for aircraft and hovercraft are found throughout the exclusions that apply to liability coverages.

Residence Employee Exception

After having flatly stated that there is no aircraft or hovercraft liability, the forms contain an exception. This exception to the motor vehicle liability, watercraft liability, aircraft, or hovercraft liability is for "bodily injury" to a residence employee arising out of and in the course of the residence employee's employment by an insured. So, for example, if an insured requested that her residence employee unload luggage from an owned private jet (a regular part of the employee's duties), and the employee injured his back in carrying out this order and sued for damages, the insured employer would have liability and defense coverage.

Expected or Intended Injury

This is exclusion E.1. of the ISO forms, and applies to both liability and medical payments coverage. There is no coverage for bodily injury or property damage that is expected or intended by an insured, even if the bodily injury or property damage is different that what was intended, or occurs to a different person or property. The term *an insured* is used, but remember that where *an* prefaces *insured*, the meaning is one or more insureds.

The AAIS exclusion (number 1.i.) is similar. Excluded is bodily injury or property damage that is: "1) expected by, directed by, or intended by an 'insured'; 2) that is the result of a criminal act of an 'insured'; or 3) that is the result of an intentional and malicious act by or at the direction of an 'insured'." The exclusion clarifies that it will apply *even if* the bodily injury or property damage that follows the act is different from what was intended or is inflicted on someone other than the intended recipient. For example, if in a fight an innocent onlooker is hit, the policy will still exclude coverage although the insured did not intend to hit the onlooker.

Both AAIS and ISO forms contain an exception to this exclusion. That is a provision of coverage if the "expected or intended" bodily injury or property damage "arises out of the use of reasonable force to protect persons or property." The ISO forms have been changed with the 2011 edition, so that both intentional bodily injury and property damage resulting from use of reasonable use of force by an insured to protect persons or property is covered. The 2000 edition responded only to bodily injury while protecting persons or property.

The importance of this exception is demonstrated by the case of *Auto Owners Insurance Company v. Harrington*, 565 N.W.2d 839 (Mich. 1997). The language in this policy precluded coverage for "'bodily injury' or 'property damage' which is expected or intended by the 'insured'." The court affirmed that there was no coverage for the insured when he wounded a man who was climbing the insured's garage roof towards the bedroom window where the insured's wife and children were. The man later died. Even though earlier that day the intruder had been heard saying he "felt like killing someone," the court held that the exclusion for intentional injury held. There was no exception to the exclusion in the form.

What is a "Business"?

The next exclusions are those relating to coverage for business activities. The ISO current forms have expanded the definition and as a result given coverage for activities previously excluded or, at best, called into question. The ISO definition of a business is:

a. A trade, profession or occupation engaged in on a full-time, part-time or occasional basis; or

b. Any other activity engaged in for money or other compensation, except the following:

   (1) One or more activities, not described in (2) through (4) below, for which no "insured" receives more than $2,000 in total compensation for the 12 months before the beginning of the policy period;

   (2) Volunteer activities for which no money is received other than payment for expenses incurred to perform the activity;

   (3) Providing home day care services for which no compensation is received, other than the mutual exchange of such services; or

   (4) The rendering of home day care services to a relative of an "insured".

The AAIS forms have much the same definition, but exempt two important areas. (ISO uses exceptions within the exclusion to achieve the same purpose.) The first of these is the occasional rental for residential purposes of the part of the insured premises normally occupied solely by the named insured and his or her household. The second is the rental or holding for rental of a portion of the described location normally occupied by the named insured's household to no more than two roomers or boarders. Additionally, the AAIS forms state that a "business" includes farming, whether full or part time or occasional. The compensation cut-off is $2,500 just before the first day of "this policy period," rather than $2,000.

It should be noted that the wording "compensation" does not equate with "profit." For example, an insured could not argue that, after receiving $3,000 for building and selling furniture, he'd spent an additional $4,000 to purchase exotic wood and therefore was actually in debt. He was compensated for his efforts and so the limitation of $2000 (or $2,500) applies.

The Business Exclusion

The ISO forms exclude bodily injury or property damage arising out of (remember, "arising out of" is broader than, say, "resulting from"), or in connection with, a business conducted from an insured location or engaged in by an insured, whether or not the business is owned or operated by an insured or employs an insured (exclusion E.2.). The exclusion then goes on to include the scope: the exclusion applies "but is not limited to an act or omission, regardless of its nature or circumstance, involving a service or duty rendered, promised, owed, or implied to be provided because of the nature of the 'business'."

In the AAIS forms, as with motorized vehicle and watercraft liability, exclusions that apply to liability and medical payments coverages apply except for coverage provided in incidental liability coverage (1.).

In both the AAIS and ISO forms, the business exclusion applies to the rental or holding for rental of any part of any premises *except for* the rental or holding for rental of an insured location on an occasional basis if used only as a residence. (This was also detailed in the AAIS definition of "business.") For example, often insureds with seasonal homes rent them to others on an occasional basis. (Of course, the exclusion of coverage for theft of personal property applies while the home is rented.) The exclusion does not apply to the rental of other parts of the insured premises for use as a single family residence; the family unit may not include more than two roomers or boarders. This exception applies to renting the other half of a duplex, for example. Next, the exclusion does not apply to renting or holding for rental part of the insured location as an office, school, studio, or private garage. Therefore, bodily injury or property damage arising from these rentals is covered unless otherwise excluded.

The ISO and AAIS forms add that the exclusion does not apply to an insured under age twenty-one involved in a part-time or occasional, self-employed business (as defined) with no employees. Chapter 13 contains information on endorsements that add some coverage for this exposure.

Professional Services Exclusion

Not strictly a business exclusion, but closely allied, is the exclusion for rendering or failing to render professional services. This is ISO exclusion E.3., and AAIS exclusion 1.f. A profession is defined as "a calling requiring specialized knowledge and often long and intensive academic training" (*Webster's Collegiate Dictionary, Tenth Edition*). It would appear that this exclusion is intended to close any gaps in the business exclusion, perhaps to prevent a physician insured from seeking coverage after administering first aid to a traffic accident victim.

Chapter 9

Liability Coverages and Exclusions, Part II

Introduction

Chapter 8 dealt primarily with exclusions (and coverage either through exceptions or incidental liability coverages) that applied to both liability and medical payments coverages. In this chapter, we conclude our discussion of exclusions applicable to both liability and medical payments to others. We then discuss the exclusions applicable only to liability, the exclusions applicable only to medical payments to others, and conclude with the liability additional coverages, or, as some are termed in the AAIS forms, "Incidental Liability Coverages."

Exclusions–Liability and Medical Payments

Premises Not an Insured Location

This is exclusion E.4. of the ISO forms, and AAIS exclusion 1.h. This exclusion eliminates liability and medical payments to others coverage for any incident arising out of a premises that is not an insured location (or, in AAIS, an "insured premises") and is owned by an insured, rented to an insured, or rented to others by an insured. Excepted in the AAIS form is bodily injury to a "residence employee" arising out of and in the course of his or her employment by an insured.

It is usually accepted that, for the exclusion to apply, the bodily injury or property damage must arise out of a condition of the premises (such as a broken sidewalk) and not simply occur there (as an insured negligently swinging a golf club that hits another person). Liability coverage, unless specific events are excluded, applies anywhere in the world. For example, an insured husband and wife rent a hall for their daughter's wedding reception. The hall becomes an insured location by definition, so there is coverage for bodily injury or property damage arising out of that location.

Is Assisted Living Facility an Insured Location?

Our elderly insured moved recently to an assisted living facility, which we were not aware of. She accidentally left a faucet on, and it overflowed into the apartment below hers. We are not sure whether this facility is an insured location because she is not temporarily residing there; she will probably be there the remainder of her life. Is there coverage?

You are correct in that the facility does not qualify as an insured location because she is not a "temporary" resident as she might be in, say, a hotel. However, that is not to say the loss is not covered. The exclusion states that there is no coverage "arising out of" a premises that is not an insured premises, but the damage did not arise out of the premises. It arose out of the insured's negligent act in leaving the faucet on, and so, there is coverage for the resulting damage.

A recent case demonstrating this point involved a dog with a propensity to bite. The dog severely bit a person at an owned property in Massachusetts, and the insured called on both that property's and another homeowners policy on property in New Hampshire to provide coverage. The New Hampshire insurer denied the claim, citing the exclusion for bodily injury arising out of a location that was not an insured location. The court reviewed both the exclusion and the coverage for medical payments to others, and concluded that "arising out of a premises" was intended to apply to a condition of the premises. The court of *Callahan v. Quincy Mutual Fire Ins. Co.*, 736 N.E.2d 857 (Mass. App. Ct. 2000) looked with approval to *Safeco Ins. Co. v. Hale*, 140 Cal. App. 3d 347 (1983), which noted that an animal is "not within the fair connotation of the word 'premises'."

A seemingly different viewpoint is illustrated by the case of *Westfield Insurance Co. v. Hunter*, 2009 WL 3415894 (Oh. App. 12 Dist. 2009). Here, two minor ATV riders, cousins, were injured when their ATVs collided on their grandparents' farm. The grandparents' homeowners insurer stated the farm was not an insured location and so the farm policy should respond. The court reviewed the "arising out of" language of the homeowners form and said the phrase meant there should be a causal connection with the insured property, not that the insured premises should be the proximate cause. Since the ATVs had been brought especially to ride on the farm, that triggered the "arising out of" language and since the farm was not an insured location the homeowners insurer was relieved from the suit.

While this conclusion might appear at odds with the conclusion of *Callahan* (the biting pooch) and our assisted living insured (in the coverage scenario), note that the court in *Westfield* stressed that the ATVs had specifically been bought to be ridden on the farm. The location in *Callahan* was not purchased with the dog in mind, nor was the assisted living facility chosen for the insured for any particular activity that could only be accomplished there.

War Exclusion

The war risks exclusion (ISO exclusion E.5.; AAIS exclusion 1.a.) is similar to the war exclusion of the section I property insurance. It lists all the kinds of activities that are considered to be war (and therefore excluded) in addition to formally declared war. Among these are: undeclared war; civil war; insurrection; rebellion; revolution; warlike acts by a military force or military personnel; action in hindering or defending against actual or expected attack; and destruction, seizure, or use for a military purpose. Any consequence of any of these will be construed as falling within the exclusion. Discharge of a nuclear weapon, even if accidental, will be construed as a warlike act.

Transmission of Disease

This exclusion is E.6. in the ISO forms and 1.j. in the AAIS forms. It was adopted in response to the increased frequency of suits alleging negligent transmission of diseases, particularly those that are sexually transmitted. The exclusion is not limited to diseases that are sexually transmitted, though, applying as it does to any "communicable disease." This term is not defined, leaving some doubt as to the extent of its application. However, the language "*transmission of a communicable disease by an insured*" (emphasis added) suggests only person-to-person transmission by direct physical contact, so the exclusion does not seem to apply to contagious diseases spread by airborne particles—measles, scarlet fever, etc.—nor to diseases that are spread through food or water contamination (such as salmonella, botulism, or typhoid fever), even when their spread may be traced to human carelessness. The exclusion, though, leaves open the possibility that an insured's having a communicable disease and accidentally passing it on ("My Johnny caught chicken pox at day care from your Suzy!") will preclude coverage. A review of Westlaw® could find no cases, however, where courts considered anything other than sexually transmitted disease. The only attempt to enlarge the definition of "communicable disease" was found in the case of *Colony Insurance Co. v. Nicholson*, 2010 WL 3522138 (S.D. Fla. 2010): "Communicable Disease shall include, but not be limited to Acquired Immune Deficiency Syndrome (AIDS) or Human Immunodeficiency Syndrome (HIV), Severe Acute Respiratory Syndrome (SARS), West Nile Disease, chicken pox, any type or strain of influenza (including, but not limited to avian flu), legionella, hepatitis, measles, meningitis, mononucleosis, whooping cough, cholera, bubonic plagues and anthrax." It is perhaps fortunate that this definition was only found in a policy insuring a manicure salon.

Sexual Molestation, Corporal Punishment, or Physical or Mental Abuse

Generally courts have found that as a matter of public policy there is no coverage for bodily injury or property damage arising out of sexual molestation, no matter what attempts are made to find coverage. The remainder of the exclusion is for corporal punishment or physical or mental abuse. Again, as a matter of public policy, coverage for physical abuse is not provided. Some aspects of what might be loosely considered mental abuse—libel, slander, or malicious prosecution, for example—may be covered by endorsements ISO HO 24 82 or AAIS HO 4046, personal injury, or through purchase of an umbrella policy. This is exclusion E.7. of the ISO forms, and exclusions 1.k., 1.l., and 1.m in the AAIS forms.

Agent Tip

Liability for teachers, including administration of corporal punishment, can be added by attaching ISO endorsement HO 24 71 or AAIS endorsement HO 3571. The inclusion of coverage for infliction of corporal punishment depends upon the insurer.

Controlled Substance

This is the final of the ISO exclusions that apply to both liability and medical payments coverage. It is exclusion E.8. and exclusion 1.n. of the AAIS forms. Bodily injury or property damage arising out of the use, sale, manufacture, delivery, transfer, or possession by any person is excluded. Drugs that are included within the scope of the exclusion must meet the definition of a controlled substance as defined by federal law (21 United States Code Annotated Sections 811 and 812). For example, narcotics, hallucinogens, and psychotropic drugs are controlled substances, but alcohol and nicotine are not. The exclusion itself states that controlled substances include, but are not limited to, cocaine, LSD, marijuana, and narcotics, but the exclusion does not preclude coverage for liability arising "from the legitimate use of prescription drugs by a person following the lawful orders of a licensed health care professional." This language has been changed in the 2011 forms; previously the exception read "following the orders of a licensed physician," as does the AAIS form. Thus, the exclusion does not bar coverage if a person correctly using a narcotic or antidepressant that has been prescribed by his doctor causes injury or property damage because of a reaction to the drug. It is uncertain how courts might view the exclusion when applied to liability arising from overuse of a prescription drug due to the insured's negligence, a type of problem that is common with insureds whose short-term memories are impaired.

The intentional acts exclusion will often serve to eliminate coverage, as in the case of *State Farm Fire & Casualty Co. v. Baer*, 745 F. Supp. 595 (U.S. Dist. Cal. 1990), in which the court held that the exclusion for bodily injury that was expected or intended applied when an insured gave a controlled substance to a friend who died as a result. It must be remembered that as a matter of public policy some risks should not and cannot be transferred to the insurance carrier.

To date, the rise in the use of medical marijuana, and the growing acceptance thereof, has not resulted in any change in this policy language. Remember, liability for bodily injury or property damage is excluded, but the exclusion does not apply to the use (*not* the sale, manufacture, or delivery) of marijuana when the person is following the health care professional's lawful orders. Perhaps it will be up to the states to clarify limits of medical marijuana use, as in the case of *County of San Diego v. San Diego NORML*, 81 Cal. Rptr.3d 461 (Cal. App. 4 Dist., 2008), where the legislation legalizing medical marijuana use said "nothing in this section shall be construed to supersede legislation prohibiting person from engaging in conduct that endangers others, nor to condone the diversion of marijuana for nonmedical purposes." In other words, negligent or unlawful conduct that results in harm to others is still negligent or unlawful; the marijuana cannot be used as an excuse.

Exclusion Nine

The standard forms do not contain a ninth exclusion. As we have frequently stressed, state-mandated special provisions must be read when determining coverage. For example, the special provisions form for Ohio adds exclusion 9., which precludes coverage for bodily injury or property damage arising out of the actions of a vicious or dangerous dog, as defined by Ohio Revised Code Sec. 955.11, and the insured's failure to keep the dog restrained.

The exclusion does not apply to bodily injury to a residence employee while the employee is in the course of employment by an insured.

Exclusions Applicable to Liability Only

The following six ISO exclusions only apply to liability coverage. The AAIS forms have ten, but that is because in three instances ISO has one exclusion consisting of two parts; AAIS has split them into separate exclusions and has an additional exclusion.

Loss Assessment

The first of the exclusions that apply to liability coverage only is ISO exclusion F.1.a., and AAIS exclusion 2.i. and 2.c. Remember, the AAIS form contains exclusions, and then gives coverage in the incidental liability coverages. In the ISO forms the coverage is given through exceptions to the exclusions. This exclusion applies to liability of the named insured for any loss assessment charged against him or her as a member of any association, corporation, or community of property owners. Loss assessment coverage is available under the ISO section II additional coverages (discussed later), or the AAIS incidental loss assessment coverage.

The exclusion was added to clarify the intent of the policy rather than to take away coverage. Coverage for loss assessments levied by the association because of inadequate insurance against owners-in-common was never intended to be included in the personal liability coverage.

Contractual Liability

This exclusion, ISO F.1.b., and AAIS 2.c., applies to liability "under any contract or agreement entered into by an 'insured'" but then exempts two major kinds of *written* contracts from the exclusion. Coverage is included for liability assumed under many written contracts unless excluded elsewhere in the policy. Exempt from the exclusion is liability under written contracts: (a) that relate directly to the ownership, maintenance, or use of an insured location, or (b) where the insured has assumed the liability of others prior to an "occurrence" (as defined). AAIS gives coverage for such contractual liability in incidental liability coverage 3. The intent of these exemptions is to provide liability coverage for liability of others *assumed by the insured* before an occurrence under written contracts having to do with an insured location; for example, a lease or a construction or repair contract.

Although it might be tempting to think the policy covers virtually any type of contract that relates to the "ownership, maintenance or use" of an insured premises, such as an insured's contract for the sale of the insured residence, it does not. Perhaps, for example, the insured has not divulged that the property is subject to flooding, and the purchaser sues for negligent misrepresentation. The policy will not respond, because liability coverage is for bodily injury or property damage, and not any possible economic loss, damage, or potential loss or damage.

The AAIS forms tighten the coverage by stating that the loss causing the bodily injury or property damage must have occurred during the policy period.

Coverage for Rented Hall

An insured wishes to rent a large hall for a wedding reception for his daughter. The hall's manager asks him to sign a standard contract, but he is hesitant because he must agree to hold the hall owner harmless if a guest is injured because of, say, a slippery dance floor or a fall in the parking lot.

The insured is also concerned about his liability if someone drinks too much and injures someone while driving. The insured is hiring a caterer and a bartender but is still concerned.

The rented hall is an insured location by definition, since it is a part of a premises occasionally rented to an insured for other than business use. Further, the exclusion for contractual liability excepts liability of others assumed by the insured prior to an occurrence. That is exactly what the insured is doing when signing the hold-harmless agreement.

The caterer should provide its own liquor liability insurance, but that would not protect the insured if someone were to sue him as well as the caterer. At present, there is no host liquor liability exclusion in the homeowners form, so the insured is covered if a guest should drink too much, drive, and injure a third party. Alcohol is not a controlled substance, so exclusion (E.8.) will not apply. The motor vehicle exclusion (A.) should not apply either (unless the insured has entrusted a motor vehicle to the inebriated guest), since the insured does not own, maintain, use, load, or unload the vehicle.

But having said all that, we should add that the insured should not be too much of a "good host" and assist in supplying guests with alcohol. If, for example, the host procures drinks for someone he knows is underage, and that person later injures someone while driving drunk, the insured could well be assumed to have been acting intentionally and so there will be no coverage should he be sued by the injured party.

Damage to Owned Property

The ISO form eliminates coverage for property damage to property owned by *an* ("one or more") insured(s). The equivalent AAIS exclusions are 2.d. and 2.e. The exclusion also precludes coverage for "costs or expenses incurred by an 'insured' or others to repair, replace, enhance, restore or maintain such property to prevent injury to a person or damage to property of others, whether on or away from an 'insured location'."

This wording arose from the case of *Aetna Ins. Co. v. Aaron*, 685 A.2d 858 (Md. Ct. Spec. App. 1996), in which the court held that costs of measures the association took to repair the insured's condominium in order to prevent further damage to a neighboring condominium were potentially a part of property damage liability. The court said the owned property exclusion did not apply, because a third party's property sustained the damage.

Care, Custody or Control Exclusion

This exclusion is a standard liability provision, similar to the "care, custody, or control" exclusion of commercial liability forms. It is exclusion F.3. in the ISO forms, and exclusion 2.f. in the AAIS forms. It eliminates coverage for property damage to property that is rented to, occupied by, used by, or in the care of an insured. By exception there is coverage for property damage caused by fire, explosion, or smoke (sometimes referred to as fire legal liability). So, should an insured inadvertently cause a fire in a hotel room resulting in damage, the damage is covered. In the case of the rented hall discussed previously, the insured would have protection for claims arising out of bodily injury. However, he or she would not have coverage other than the amount given in the additional coverage for property damage to others, discussed later, for property damage should the guests decide to wreck the hall.

Less important is the application of the exclusion to *personal property* in the care of the insured. Coverage C insures personal property owned or *used* by an insured and, at the insured's request, property of guests, so damage by an insured peril to such property can often be paid for under coverage C.

Waterbed Liability

The insured rented an apartment on the second floor of an apartment building. He owns a waterbed. One day, he arrived home to find the waterbed had sprung a leak, drenching the wall-to-wall carpeting of the unit and ruining it. Now the landlord is holding him responsible for the damage. Will his homeowners policy respond?

No. The exclusion of coverage for property damage to property rented to or occupied by an insured precludes coverage, because the damage was not caused by fire, smoke, or explosion. There are endorsements available (AAIS endorsement HO 4009) that will provide coverage. Currently, ISO's waterbed liability endorsement is available in two states only, Hawaii and North Carolina.

Wall-to-wall carpeting is generally held to be part of the realty, so there is no coverage for the loss under coverage C of the insured's policy.

Workers Compensation Exclusion

This exclusion—ISO F.4. and AAIS 2.h.—applies wherever benefits are required by law to be provided or are voluntarily provided by the insured for *any person,* including a domestic or residence employee. Although the most common persons thought of in this regard are domestic or resident employees, note that the forms do not limit the exclusion. The exclusion does not apply to an insured's employers liability protection for injured employees where these benefits are not required by law and have not been provided voluntarily.

As discussed in the previous chapter, there is coverage for bodily injury to a residence employee arising out of and in the course of employment when the bodily injury involves motor vehicles, watercraft, hovercraft, or aircraft. However, if the residence employee is eligible to receive workers compensation benefits that his employer has been providing, there is no liability coverage. So, in the example in the previous chapter, if a residence employee is requested to unload the insured's luggage from his private jet and the employee injures his back, workers compensation benefits will apply; if there are none because they are neither required by law nor voluntarily provided the employee may sue for damages because of bodily injury.

The AAIS forms preclude coverage for sickness, disease, or death of a domestic employee unless a written notice is received by the insurer within thirty-six months after the end of the policy period in which the injury occurred. This is exclusion 2.g., not found in the ISO forms.

Nuclear Energy Exclusion

The exclusion of liability coverage—bodily injury or property damage—for any nuclear occurrence for which the insured is also an insured under a nuclear energy policy, or would be one except that the limits of that policy are exhausted, is standard. In the ISO forms it is F.5., and in the AAIS forms it is exclusion 2.j. In the earlier AAIS forms, it appeared under the exclusions applying to both liability and medical payments. In the current forms, the liability and medical payments exclusions are similar to the ISO format, so there is an exclusion both in the liability exclusions, and in the medical payments to others exclusions.

Bodily Injury to an Insured Exclusion

This exclusion precludes coverage for liability of one family member for bodily injury to another family member. The exclusion eliminates bodily injury coverage for the named insured, spouse, resident relatives, or any one under age twenty-one and in the care of any of these persons. This is exclusion F.6. of the ISO forms, and 2.a. and 2.b. in the AAIS forms.

The ISO form states:

> This exclusion also applies to any claim made or suit brought against you or an "insured" to:
>
> a. Repay; or
>
> b. Share damages with:
>
> another person who may be obligated to pay damages because of "bodily injury" to an "insured".

The AAIS form contains similar language; liability coverage is excluded for: "any claim made or suit brought against an 'insured' seeking 1) reimbursement of; or 2) contribution toward; damages for which another person may be liable because of 'bodily injury' to an 'insured'."

For example, an insured mother takes her children shopping with her. One of the children begins to play on the store escalator and is injured. The mother sues the store for her son's injuries, and the store countersues alleging the mother contributed to the boy's injuries through her negligent supervision. This exclusion would preclude coverage for the insured mother.

This exclusion results in a gap in coverage in states that in whole or part have abrogated the interspousal or intrafamilial immunity doctrine; that is, where children have the right to sue parents, spouses may sue each other, etc. In such states the severability of insurance clause (discussed in Chapter 10) is inapplicable. Sometimes the court is asked to rule on the scope of the exclusion by determining what constitutes a household. This was the situation in the case of *Mutual of Enumclaw Ins. Co. v. Pedersen.*, 983 P.2d 208 (Idaho 1999). A husband, wife, and their two daughters resided with the husband's father. The husband ran over his daughter's foot with a lawn tractor, severely injuring her. The wife sued her husband and father-in-law, claiming that her husband was responsible for the injury and was an insured, and her father-in-law was responsible because he owned the home. The court agreed with the insurer in applying the exclusion, because the evidence proved that the husband, wife, and daughters were all members of the father's household.

Although we might like to think all insureds are trustworthy, one reason for the exclusion is the possibility of collusion between family members. As the court in *Day v. Allstate Indemnity Company*, 784 N.W.2d 694 (Wis. App. 2010) stated, "[The] family exclusion clauses in homeowners' policies are valid regardless of whether the suit involves a direct claim against an insured family member or an indirect action, such as a contribution claim by a third party…Family exclusion clauses in homeowners' policies protect insurers from situations where an insured, because of close family ties, might not completely cooperate and assist an insurance company's administration of the case." In this case, a mother brought a wrongful death action against her son's stepmother; even though the mother was not an insured under the policy, the court said that any amount paid by the insurer would go to the mother and father (her ex husband) who thus would have benefited as the child's legal heir.

An interesting case turned on application of the bodily injury to an insured exclusion and relied on the definition of *insured* as including "any person responsible for...animals owned by you." The insured owned a ranch and employed a father and son to help with driving cattle. The son accidentally shot the rancher's son, and the rancher sued the father and son for his son's injuries. His suit argued that the father and son were insureds by definition so his own policy should provide them a defense and indemnification. He further argued that the "bodily injury to an insured" exclusion was inapplicable because his own son was not a resident of the employee's household; therefore, the severability of insurance clause should prevail. Although the court sympathized with the severe injuries the rancher's son sustained, it added "We cannot stretch our rules of law to grant him the relief he requests." The plain language of the exclusion prevailed. The case is *Page v. Mountain West Farm Bureau Mutual Ins. Co.*, 2 P.3d 506 (Wyo. 2000).

The coverage gap left by this exclusion may have an especially adverse effect with respect to claims brought by persons under age twenty-one in the care of the insured or resident relatives—foster children, for example. In the case of *Jenks v. State of Louisiana*, 507 So. 2d 877 (La. Ct. App. 1987) the court upheld the exclusion in the homeowners policy in a wrongful death action by the natural mother against foster parents who had charge of her fifteen-month-old child.

Agent Tip

In a laudable attempt to give something back to the community, many persons agree to become foster parents. Unfortunately, they frequently do not anticipate that, if a suit seeking damages because of their actions arises, coverage under their homeowners policies might be nonexistent. For example, if a foster child negligently damages a neighbor's property, the foster child is covered as an insured. But, say the foster child is injured during a family outing. Three years later, he sues the foster parents for his injuries because a broken leg has failed to heal properly and left him with a permanent limp. There is no liability coverage for the foster parent insureds. Anyone contemplating becoming a foster parent must make sure that he or she will be covered by the foster care institution's policy.

Other cases involving the exclusion have attempted to obtain coverage using different reasoning. For example, in the case of *National Farmers Union Property and Casualty Co. v. Moore*, 882 P.2d 1168 (Utah Ct. App. 1994), the injured party argued that the insurer's defense based on the exclusion was untenable for several reasons, among them that the exclusion violated both public policy and her reasonable expectations. The insured's stepdaughter was accidentally shot by her brother, the insured's stepson, and the stepdaughter sued. Both children resided with the insured. The Utah court of appeals held that, although the exclusion had been statutorily voided in automobile policies in the state, it had not been voided in the farm owners policy in question. (The reason for the exclusion's invalidation in auto policies is that many courts feel that its use would create a class of innocent victims who are related to and living with the negligent insured. These victims are mandated financial protection by law—financial responsibility, no-fault, uninsured- and underinsured motorist—and the exclusion would circumvent the law's intent.) And, the insured could not pursue this logic because the exclusion was held to be unambiguous and the state of Utah did not have a reasonable expectations doctrine.

Although the exclusion appears to be in conflict with the severability of insurance clause (a section II condition), which provides that the insurance applies separately to each insured, it has been upheld. The purpose of the severability clause is to make the insurance available for any insured for nonexcluded bodily injury or property damage claims against other insureds. (See discussion in Chapter 10.)

Exclusions Applicable to Medical Payments Only

ISO forms contain four exclusions that apply only to medical payments coverage, as do the AAIS forms.

Bodily Injury to a Residence Employee

The first of the exclusions (ISO G.1.; AAIS 3.c.) eliminates coverage for medical payments to a residence or domestic employee if the injury occurs off an insured location or an insured premises (broader terms than residence premises or described location) and does not occur in the course of the employment. Both of these conditions must be present for the exclusion to apply. For example, if the residence employee is on an insured location but not in the course of employment—eating lunch, perhaps—and is injured, the exclusion does not apply.

Workers Compensation Exclusion

The second ISO exclusion applicable to medical payments precludes coverage for any person eligible to receive either voluntary or statutorily imposed workers compensation. This exclusion is similar to that applying to liability coverage, except that it applies to any benefits from any source that the injured person is eligible to receive, not just to benefits required to be or voluntarily provided by an insured. The exclusion applies to any injured person. This is exclusion G.2. of the ISO forms. AAIS exclusion 3.b. states that it applies to "a person, including a 'domestic employee', if a workers' compensation policy covers the injury or if benefits are provided under a workers' compensation, non-occupational disability, occupational disease, or like law."

Nuclear Energy Exclusion

Exclusion G.3. of the ISO forms eliminates medical payments coverage for any nuclear activity, whether controlled or not, or any consequence of these. As noted above, the earlier AAIS forms excluded coverage in the section "Exclusions that Apply to Coverages L and M", but in the current forms it is exclusion 3.d.

Resident Exclusion

The last of the ISO medical payments exclusions, G.4., eliminates coverage for any person regularly residing on any part of an insured location, other than a residence employee. The similar AAIS exclusion (3.a.) states that an insured or other person who resides on an insured premises is not covered. Under both forms, the definitions of *insured location* (ISO) and *insured premises* (AAIS) encompasses more than the premises on which the insured dwelling is located. For example, it can be another premises shown on the declaration, a vacation cottage, for example. Therefore, someone residing on the same premises as the cottage will not be accorded medical payments to others coverage under the insured's homeowners policy should he or she slip and fall. Of course, if the injured person sues for bodily injury caused by a condition of the cottage or premises, the insured has liability coverage.

AAIS Business Exclusion

The earlier AAIS forms contained an exclusion for medical payments to others coverage because of bodily injury to a person who was on the insured premises because a *business* (as defined in the policy) was being conducted or professional services rendered there. However, within the "Incidental

Liability Coverages" the insurer promises to pay for bodily injury or property damage resulting from "the rental of a part of the 'insured premises' for use as a school, studio, office, or private garage." Presumably the exclusion was intended to clarify that only certain activities would be covered.

Section II Additional Coverages

Section II of the AAIS and ISO forms contains additional coverages. In this respect, section II is similar to section I, which provided incidental or additional property coverages. The AAIS forms refer to these as "Incidental Liability Coverages" while, in the ISO forms, they are the "Additional Coverages." However, as indicated several times, the forms are not constructed identically. So, for example, while the ISO forms exclude liability coverage for bodily injury or property damage arising out of motor vehicles and then exempt certain vehicles, the AAIS forms give the exceptions as incidental coverages. We will follow the ISO order and note the similar AAIS provision of coverage.

Claim Expenses

The first of the ISO additional coverages (A.1 though A.4.) and the second (2.a. through 2.e.) of the AAIS incidental coverages provide coverage for claim expenses. There are four parts to the ISO claim expenses provision. First, the insurer promises to pay expenses it incurs and costs taxed against the insured in a suit it defends. Payment under this additional coverage is tied to the second item of the liability coverage—the provision requiring the insurer to provide a defense for liability claims covered by the policy. (Remember the duty to defend is broader than the duty to pay. If it appears that a claim may even remotely be covered, the insurer owes a duty to defend.) However, the liability insuring agreement also exempts the insurer from further responsibility for defense once the limit of liability has been exhausted by payment of claims. When this occurs, the coverage under this additional coverage ceases because all of the expenses payable under this item are related to claims or suits that the insurer must defend.

The second provision included within this coverage is for premium costs on bonds that may be required in a suit, but not for bond amounts that are higher than the limit of liability. The insurer is not required either to apply for or to furnish such a bond. In the ISO forms this is A.2., and in the AAIS forms it is 2.b.

The third provision (ISO A.3.) covers reasonable expenses incurred by an insured at the insurer's request. The AAIS form (2.c.) refers to "necessary costs incurred by an 'insured'." Actual loss of earnings ($250) for time spent away from work to assist the insurer (by attending a trial, perhaps) is covered. Note that *actual* loss of earnings is covered. An insured cannot argue that if only she had been working as a day trader that day she could have made several thousand dollars and expect reimbursement for that amount from the insurer.

The fourth of the claim expenses provisions is that the insurer agrees to pay interest on the entire judgment that accrues after entry and before the insurer pays or deposits in court that part of the judgment that does not exceed the limit of liability. The interest ends when the payment is actually made. This is ISO additional coverage A.4., and AAIS 2.d.

The ISO and AAIS forms differ slightly in their treatment of prejudgment interest. In the ISO forms, this amount is included in the damages awarded against an insured, so the limit of liability is the most that will be paid for both. In the AAIS forms prejudgment interest is a part of the incidental coverage for claims and defense costs (2.e.). The preface to the incidental liability coverages states that "except for Claims And Defense Cost, Damage to Property Of Others, First Aid Expense, and Loss Assessment, they [the incidental liability coverages] do not increase the 'limits' stated for the Principal Liability Coverages." Presumably, therefore, the prejudgment interest amount is not included in the limit of liability. However, the policy does state that if the insurer offers to pay the "'limit' that applies," it will not pay any prejudgment interest based on the period of time after the offer.

The earlier AAIS forms contained as part of the claims and defense costs an additional coverage for a premium up to $500 per bail bond because of an accident or violation arising out of the use of a nonexcluded vehicle. This provision has been removed from the current forms.

First Aid Expenses

In ISO additional coverage B. and AAIS incidental coverage 5., the insurer agrees to pay the expenses incurred by any insured for the first aid rendered to others for any bodily injury covered under the policy. This is entirely apart from the medical payments coverage of the policy. It is payable without limit (other than the practical limits on cost of first aid treatment), and is in addition to any payment that might be made under the medical payments or liability coverages. This provision does not pay for first aid to any insured under the policy. The forms do not define first aid, so the dictionary definition applies. *Webster's Collegiate Dictionary (Tenth Edition)* defines it as "emergency care or treatment given to an ill or injured person before regular medical aid can be obtained."

Damage to Property of Others

ISO additional coverage C. and AAIS incidental coverage 4. are for damage to property of others. The insurer agrees to pay for property damage (as defined) to property of others caused by any insured. Note the difference in wording from the liability insuring agreement, which promises to respond to property damage caused by "an occurrence," meaning an accident. But here we have the wording "caused by." A *cause* may be direct or indirect. For example, an insured child might throw a wild pitch through a neighbor's plate glass window. That is a direct cause. Or, an insured might not saw off a branch hanging near a neighbor's fence. The branch falls and damages the fence. That is an indirect cause. Coverage is per occurrence (as defined). This is, in effect, *good neighbor* coverage, as it allows payment for minor property damage claims without a need to prove the insured's negligence other than that the loss was "caused by" an insured. Indeed, the AAIS forms clarify this by prefacing the coverage with "Regardless of an 'insured's' legal liability, 'we' pay…" Coverage is on a replacement cost basis. The most that will be paid under both AAIS and ISO is $1,000.

Coverage does not apply to the extent that there is recovery under section I of the policy. Section I coverage applies to property owned or *used by* an insured. It also extends, at the request of the insured, to include property of others on the insured's residence premises and property of guests and resident employees in any residence occupied by any insured. Section I coverage, therefore, will more often be involved in paying for loss to personal property in the insured's care, custody, or control (note, in this instance property coverage responds where liability coverage will not) than will the damage to property of others coverage. But losses below the section I deductible or by perils other than those provided for under section I are covered, if "caused by any insured." The policy makes the damage to property of others coverage *excess* over any section I coverage, so the coverage is *in addition to* any section I coverage on property of others.

The coverage is not on a *carte blanche* basis, however. There are limitations. Damage that is caused intentionally by an insured who is thirteen years or older is not covered. So, for example, if the insured's fourteen year-old son takes a dislike to a neighbor family and intentionally throws a brick through their window, the policy will not respond.

There is no coverage for property damage to property owned by an insured, nor to property owned by or rented to (AAIS adds "or leased to") a tenant of an insured or a resident in the insured's household. There is no coverage for property damage arising out of an insured's business. Property damage resulting from an act or omission in connection with a premises owned by, rented to, or controlled by an insured is not covered unless the premises is an insured location.

Finally, there is no coverage for property damage arising out of the ownership, maintenance, occupancy, operation, use, loading, or unloading of watercraft, aircraft, hovercraft, or motor vehicles. The AAIS forms go even further and exclude coverage as well for renting, loaning, entrusting, or supervision of such conveyances. There is an exception, however. The ISO forms declare that if, at the time of the occurrence, the vehicle is designed for recreational use off public roads, is not owned by an insured, and at the time of the occurrence the vehicle is not required by law or governmental regulation to be registered for use on public roads or property, the exclusion will not apply. So, for example, if an insured borrows a snowmobile and damages it, presumably the exception will apply unless another exclusion bars coverage.

AAIS also covers such vehicles, as well as motorized vehicles used only to service an insured premises or the premises of another except in the course of a business, and vehicles designed to assist the handicapped; however, the exception states the motorized vehicle cannot be required to be registered for use on public roads of property.

Loss Assessment

The last of the ISO additional coverages, and AAIS incidental liability coverage 6., is for loss assessment. This coverage is the liability counterpart of the property coverage. The ISO forms limit payment to $1000, while AAIS limits coverage to $1,500. These amounts can be increased by endorsement.

The insured's share of loss assessment must be charged against the insured as an owner or tenant of the *residence premises* by a corporation or association of property owners. Coverage applies to assessments made during the policy term, but the event causing the assessment may occur before the insured's policy takes effect.

Coverage applies when the assessment is made as a result of bodily injury or property damage not excluded under section II of the policy, or liability for an act of an elected, unpaid director, officer, or trustee of the property owners' corporation or association who is acting in his or her official capacity.

The $1,000 or $1,500 of coverage is applied to each loss, not to each assessment. For example, an association makes two separate assessments for one covered bodily injury loss. The policy will respond once. A covered loss is considered to arise from one accident, including continuous or repeated exposure to substantially the same general harmful conditions (that is, an occurrence), or from a covered act of a director, officer, or trustee. The covered act may be perpetuated by any number of directors, officers, or trustees; it is still considered a single act.

Loss assessment coverage does not apply to assessments charged against the insured, corporation, or association by any governmental body. If a condominium association is fined by a local government for violation of a building code, there will no coverage if the assessment is passed on to the association members.

ISO coverage E exclusion F.1.a. states that there is no coverage for the insured's liability for "any loss assessment charged against you as a member of an association, corporation or community of property owners except as provided in D. Loss Assessment under Section II–Additional Coverages." This clarifies that only loss assessment coverage under the terms of the additional coverage is available. Similarly, in the AAIS forms, exclusion 2.i. eliminates coverage for any assessment made by the named insured's homeowners or residential association "except as provided by Incidental Liability Coverage for Loss Assessment."

All section II exclusions apply to loss assessment coverage unless excepted. This means that the scope of the individual homeowner's section II coverage determines whether the assessment is covered. For example, if there is an assessment that arises from a liability claim alleging invasion of privacy that does not arise out of an act of directors or officers, the loss assessment additional coverage will not respond.

Chapter 10

Conditions Applying to Liability Coverages

Introduction

Just as with the property coverages, the liability coverages have conditions applicable only to them. This section of the ISO forms contains the insured's duties following a liability loss, the duties of an injured person seeking coverage under medical payments to others, provisions applying to payment of a claim, and provisions governing the limit of liability and the severability of insurance. As frequently noted in this book, the AAIS forms are constructed differently. The conditions applicable to the liability coverages appear in three sections: "What Must Be Done In Case Of Loss or Occurrence," "How Much We Pay For Loss or Occurrence," and "Policy Conditions," and this latter section is further broken into three sections: "Conditions Applicable To All Coverages," "Conditions Applicable To Property Coverages Only," and "Conditions Applicable To Liability Coverages Only." The order will be that of the ISO forms, with the location of the similar AAIS provision indicated.

Limit of Liability

The first of the ISO conditions (A.) sets forth the limit of liability under coverages E, liability, and F, medical payments to others. These are conditions 2. and 3. in the AAIS section "How Much We Pay For Loss or Occurrence." The AAIS form refers to coverage L, personal liability, and coverage M, medical payments to others. Both forms stress that the limit of liability shown in the policy declarations is the most that will be paid regardless of the number of insureds, claims made, or persons injured in any one occurrence.

An occurrence, remember, is defined as any one accident or continuous or repeated exposure to substantially the same general harmful conditions. Assume the insured regularly mows his lawn using an old mower that releases noxious fumes. Occasionally, the insured's fifteen year-old son, residing in the household, mows the lawn using the same mower. The neighbors' daughter suffers from asthma, and she regularly has an attack when the insured mows his lawn. If the neighbors file a suit against the insured alleging their daughter sustained bodily injury, each asthma attack will be treated as one occurrence. If the neighbors file a separate suit against the son, the claim will still be treated as arising out of the same occurrence. Therefore, the limit of liability shown on the declarations page will be the total amount available to cover the claim or suit(s).

The AAIS forms contain a condition, not present in the ISO forms, in the section "Payment of Loss." Condition 2. states that a person who has secured a judgment against an insured for a covered loss, or who has liability established by written agreement between the claimant, an insured, and the insurer, is entitled to recover under the policy to the extent of coverage provided. Presumably an insured could not therefore demand that his or her insurer refuse to pay a claim on the grounds that the claimant didn't deserve it.

Medical payments to others coverage, unlike the liability coverage, is on a *per person* basis. The limit available to any one person as the result of one accident is the limit shown on the declarations.

Heart Attack Covered under Medical Payments?

An insured is covered under a standard ISO HO 00 03. Recently, his father-in-law was visiting for a few weeks when he suffered what appeared to be a mild heart attack. This entailed his being transported to the local emergency room. Now the insured is being asked to submit a claim to his insurer under the medical payments to others coverage to pay for the ambulance and tests. It turned out that he did not have a heart attack. Is the homeowners policy supposed to cover this sort of thing?

The ISO medical payments coverage promises to pay necessary medical expenses "ascertained within three years from the date of an accident causing 'bodily injury'." According to *Webster's Collegiate Dictionary (Tenth Edition)*, *accident* has many definitions, most relating to an event's being unforeseen or unplanned. However, the definition that would most appear to fit with the overall intent of the liability and medical payments coverage is "an unexpected happening causing loss or injury which is not due to any fault or misconduct on the part of the person injured, but for which legal relief may be sought." Medical payments coverage is often viewed as an immediate means of relief for the person injured, thus averting a potential lawsuit.

In the case of the father-in-law, it would appear that the heart attack was an injury in and of itself and not the result of an outside event. For example, if the father-in-law had tripped, fallen down the insured's stairs, injured himself, and became so stressed he had a heart attack, then the medical payments to others coverage would probably apply. But since there does not appear to have been any event triggering the heart attack—an accident—then the homeowners insurer should not respond.

Severability of Insurance

The "severability of insurance" condition is one that has been given much attention in the courts. This is ISO condition B. The condition states that "This insurance applies separately to each 'insured'. This condition will not increase our limit of liability for any one 'occurrence'." In the AAIS forms, condition 4. in the section "How Much We Pay For Loss or Occurrence" says that "the Liability Coverages provided by this policy apply separately to each 'insured', but this does not increase the 'limit' that applies for any one 'occurrence'."

When this condition is read in isolation, it appears that each person who qualifies as an insured is entitled to coverage—defense and indemnification—even though only one insured might have committed an act resulting in a claim for damages. This condition often comes into question in regards to the exclusion of liability coverage for bodily injury or property damage that is expected or intended by *an*, *one or more*, or *any* insured, depending upon the wording of the exclusion. For example, a teenager gets into a fight and intentionally injures another teen. The injured teen's parents sue for bodily injury and allege negligent supervision on the part of the other parents. At first blush it appears that the parents should be afforded coverage for negligent supervision, even though their son's action was excluded by virtue of being "expected or intended." The majority view of the courts, however, is that the exclusion for expected or intended bodily injury or property damage prevails.

As an example of a case that held that an excluded act did *not* preclude coverage for innocent insureds, see *The Catholic Diocese of Dodge City v. Raymer,* 825 P.2d 1144 (Kan. Ct. App. 1992). The court reviewed other states' interpretations of the severability clause and its relationship to an excluded action, and came to the conclusion that the reasoning used was not persuasive. Here, a minor child engaged in acts of vandalism against a local school. The Diocese filed a cause of action against the son for property damage and against the parents for failure to exercise reasonable parental care and control over their son. A default judgment against the parents was awarded.

The Diocese then filed an order of garnishment against the parents' insurer. The insurer filed an answer stating it was not indebted to the insureds because the property damage had been either expected or intended by an insured. The district court ruled that the son was an insured and that the damage he caused was intentional. But on appeal the court held that a severability clause required that the policy exclusions be applied only against the insured for whom coverage was sought, that is, the insured who committed the excluded action. The policy's severability clause made "*an*" ambiguous in the exclusion for intentional acts of an insured.

And in a more recent case, *Minkler v. Safeco Insurance Company of America*, 232 P.3d 612 (Cal. 2010), the court held that "the exclusion barring coverage for injuries arising out of the intentional acts of 'an insured' does not bar coverage for claims that one insured negligently failed to prevent the intentional acts of another insured." Here, a claimant sued the insured, stating her son had sexually molested him, sometimes in the insured's home. The court agreed that "courts must be wary of liability policy interpretations that encourage artful and sham tort pleading, especially where a sexually molested plaintiff may thereby seek some 'threadbare' means of tapping into the judgment-proof molester's liability insurance, contrary to the public policy against coverage for intentional acts of sexual abuse," but nonetheless held that the insured had not acted in a manner that would trigger the exclusion.

However, as noted, for the most part, courts hold that the severability of insurance condition takes a back seat to the exclusion for expected or intended actions that result in bodily injury or property damage.

In the case of *American Family Mutual Insurance Company v. Moore,* 912 S.W.2d 531 (Mo. Ct. App. 1995), the court found that the severability clause and the exclusion of coverage for business activities did not serve to make the policy's terms ambiguous. The insured provided day care services for two children. One child was bitten by her son's dog. In the ensuing lawsuit, American Family denied coverage, citing the business exclusion. (The policy contained an exception for activities normally incidental to a business.) Summary judgment was entered against the insured and in favor of the insurer. An amended suit was then filed against the insured's husband and son for harboring and owning a dangerous and vicious dog. The plaintiffs argued that the policy's severability clause should give coverage to the husband and son because they were not engaged in a business at the time of the injury and owning a dog was incidental to the business. (Although it might appear unusual that the plaintiff would argue in favor of coverage, remember that a suit seeking thousands of dollars in damages to be paid by an insurer has much greater appeal than a suit seeking thousands of dollars from someone who has few assets.)

The court, however, held that, although owning a dog may be an activity incidental to a nonbusiness pursuit, in this case the dog was in close proximity to small children, who would not have been on the premises had it not been for the business. The activity of owning a dog was therefore not incidental to a business pursuit. The severability of insurance condition did not apply.

A similar case in New Jersey reached the same conclusion, but clarified the application of an exclusion with regard to the severability clause. The insured husband and wife ran a day care center; their son owned a dog that bit one of the children. The court said the "provision in homeowner's insurance policy that excluded liability coverage for damage arising out of 'a business engaged in by an insured,' excluded coverage arising out of a business engaged in by any one of the three insureds under the policy, regardless of whether the person being sued was engaged in those business pursuits." Further, the "severability clause of homeowner's insurance policy, providing that it applied 'separately to each insured,' did not apply to clearly-worded exclusion.... Giving effect to the severability clause in context of the exclusion would rob the exclusion of any meaning... severability clause was not a coverage provision...." This case is *Argent v. Brady*, 901 A.2d 419 (N.J. Super. 2006).

And in the case of *Northwest G. F. Mutual Ins. Co. v. Norgard,* 518 N.W. 2d 179 (N. D. 1994) the husband molested a child attending his wife's day care operation. The day care operation was insured separately from the homeowners, so the exclusion for business pursuits did not apply; the issue was the intentional act resulting in bodily injury. The court found for the insurer. The severability of insurance clause did not serve to provide coverage for the wife in the face of the clearly worded exclusion.

The case of *Mutual of Enumclaw Ins. Co. v. Cross*, 10 P.3d 440 (Wash. Ct. App. 2000), involved the death of a child at the hands of his foster father. The foster father was found guilty of homicide and, following the trial, the biological mother sued the foster mother for negligence in failing to protect the child. In ruling for the insurer, the court said that the exclusionary use of "an" prevailed over the severability of insurance clause.

Indeed, as noted, this appears to be the majority view. When an exclusion is held to apply to each insured the severability of insurance condition will not serve to give coverage back to any insured. Where the clause applies, then, can be illustrated in the scenario we gave earlier, where a father and son are each sued because of their use of the exhaust-spewing lawnmower. The limit that applies to any one occurrence is not increased, but the father and son can each expect the insurer to defend them.

Many agents send a renewal letter to their insureds stating that certain *property* either is not covered or that special limits apply, such as those for theft of guns and jewelry. Rarely does such a letter outline the liability exposures that are not covered. Providing this information to a client is superior service and would go a long way toward closing the door to a potential errors and omissions claim.

Duties After an Occurrence

This is ISO condition C. The similar AAIS condition (number 6.) is located in the section "What Must Be Done In Case Of Loss or Occurrence."

There are six parts to the ISO condition, and six in the AAIS. The duties are to be carried out when there has been an *occurrence,* as defined. This alerts the insured to the fact that an occurrence might turn into a loss, and so the best course is to notify the insurer with all due haste. The language then instructs the insured that the duties listed in this condition may be performed by "another insured" rather than "you." This is important in that the named insured might be incapacitated and unable to carry out the duties.

The ISO forms further state that "We have no duty to provide coverage under this policy if your failure to comply with the following duties is prejudicial to us." But note that the failure to comply allows the insurer to deny coverage *only if* that failure prejudices the insurer in adjusting a claim. For example, an insured may accidentally omit the second named insured shown in the declarations; so long as this does not affect the insurer's ability to adjust a loss, the omission does not allow the insurer to deny coverage. The AAIS forms, however, state that the insurer has no duty to provide the coverages as described in the policy if the duties are not performed; there is nothing to let the insured "off the hook" if any the duties are not fulfilled. In any event, cooperation with the insurer is vital, particularly concerning a liability claim, since the insurer must often provide a defense to the insured.

For this reason, the insured must give written notice to the insurer or its agent, "as soon as is practical," setting forth: 1) the "named insured" and policy number; 2) reasonably available information on the time, place, and circumstances of the occurrence (as defined); and 3) names and addresses of claimants and witnesses. The AAIS forms add "all known *potential* claimants and witnesses." The wording "as soon as practical" is important. Sometimes insureds are not aware there is a pending claim; however, once an insured becomes aware, or even suspects, there might be a claim, a report to the insurer should be made. Where witnesses are involved, memories of an event can often fade over time, thus making a defense difficult.

In the case of *Ostego Mutual Fire Insurance Co. v. Darby et al.*, 358 N.Y.S.2d 314 (1974), the court held that a delay of more than a year in reporting an event to the insurer was not unreasonable, given the circumstances of the case. An insured youth and a friend opened a water valve at a school in September 1969 which resulted in considerable damage. In March 1970 the boy pleaded guilty and was ordered to pay $500 to cover damages not covered by the school's insurance policy. In December 1970, the insured youth's parents received a letter from the school's insurer's attorneys. The parents' insurer declined to defend, citing failure to comply in giving prompt notice. The event was complicated by the fact that the insurance agent for the insured, the friend, and the school was the same person. The court held that knowledge held by the agent was imputable to the insurer and, further, the youth did not know he was an insured under the policy, so the delay was excusable.

Late notice has also been excused where an insured homeowner thought his policy responded only to injuries occurring on his property (*Seemann v. Sterling Ins. Co.*, 699 N.Y.S.2d 542 [App. Div. 1999], four months delay), and where a volunteer scout leader did not know his homeowners policy might provide coverage for an accident involving two scouts being seriously burned while on a camping trip (*State Farm Fire & Cas. Co. v. Hartford Acc. & Indem. Co.*, 347 So. 2d 389 [Ala. 1977], seven months delay).

However, in the case of *Greenway v. Selected Risks Insurance Company*, 307 A.2d 753, a delay of forty-five days was deemed noncompliance with the requirement that notice be given as soon as practicable. Here, the insured owned a bar, and had been aware that one of his employees had been in a dispute with a customer, and was also aware that the customer was likely to sue for assault and battery.

Thus, it cannot be stated strongly enough that if an insured has any reason to suspect an occurrence might result in a claim, the insurer should be put on notice.

A condition in the ISO forms (C.2.) states that one of the named insured's duties following an occurrence is to cooperate with the insurer in the investigation, settlement, or defense of any claim or suit. In the AAIS forms, this is condition 2.c. in "What Must Be Done In Case Of Loss or Occurrence." Then, the insured must forward any notice, demand, summons, or other process relating to the accident or occurrence to the insurer (ISO C.3; AAIS 2.d.).

In the earlier AAIS forms, condition 6. stated that in case of an occurrence that might result in a claim, the insured must promptly forward copies of all notices, demands, and legal papers relating to the occurrence or claim.

Thus, the interpretation could have been that the insured need take no action until the notice of impending lawsuit arrived in the mail, which could be considerably after the event. This wording no longer appears in the current forms. So, if an insured even suspects that an accident or occurrence may result in a claim, the insurer should be notified. For example, if a passer-by trips and falls while negotiating an insured's uneven pavement, and the insured realizes that the passer-by is injured to the extent he needs medical attention, it is best to forward details to the insurer or agent immediately.

At the insurer's request, the insured must provide further assistance (ISO C.4.a. to C.4.d.; AAIS 2.e.1) to 2.e.5) in "What Must Be Done In Case Of Loss Or Occurrence"). The insured must help the insurer make the settlement and enforce any right of contribution or indemnity against anyone (including any organization) who may be liable to an insured. For example, an insured, while in the course of volunteer work, accidentally injures someone and is sued. If the voluntary organization has liability insurance for its volunteers, that insurance might be called upon. The insured cannot prevent its homeowners insurer from seeking contributory indemnity from the voluntary organization.

The insured must help with the conduct of suits and attend hearings and trials. The insured is also required to secure and give evidence and obtain the attendance of witnesses, which could be difficult in some instances. It is to be hoped the insurer would act reasonably with regard to this condition.

With respect to the additional coverage for damage to property of others, the insured must submit to the insurer within sixty days after the loss a sworn statement of loss and must show the damaged property if it is within the insured's control. Note that unlike the requirement for section I claims, the time frame is sixty days *after the loss* rather than after the company's request. The requirement of a statement, rather than a proof of loss, probably reflects the fact that the property's owner, and not the insured, often has control over the damaged property after the loss. This is ISO condition C.5. and AAIS 2.f.

It is important to note that the insured must not, except at his or her own expense, voluntarily make payment, assume obligations, or incur any expense other than for first aid to others at the time of bodily injury. This is because to do so could be misconstrued as an admission of guilt, thus affording the insurer no opportunity for defense. The similar AAIS condition (2.b.) previously applied to *any* loss, property or liability, but now applies to the liability coverages. This condition adds that an insured must not "pay or offer rewards."

Duties of an Injured Person

The next conditions are interesting in that they do not apply to an insured, but rather to a person *other than* an insured; that is, to a person seeking coverage under the medical payments to others. This is ISO condition D., and AAIS condition 2. in the section "Conditions Applicable To Liability Coverages Only." In order to make a claim under the policy, the injured person, or someone acting on behalf of the injured person, must give the insurer written proof of the claim as soon as practical. The proof must be under oath if required. The injured person must authorize the insurer to obtain medical reports and records.

In addition, the injured person must submit to physical examination by a doctor of the insurer's choice when and as often as the insurer may reasonably require. This is not to say the injured person cannot see his or her own personal physician. Rather, the requirement is to prevent any suggestion of collusion between the injured person and his own physician. The proof of claim requirement has long been part of this condition. The difference between requiring a *statement* of a claim or loss, and a *proof* of claim or loss, is that the latter indicates that the insured must submit proof, such as medical records—not merely a sworn statement—to support the claim.

Payment of Claim under Medical Payments

ISO condition F. provides that payment under the coverage of medical payments to others is not an admission of liability by the insured or the insurer. The similar AAIS condition is a part of number 3. of the section "How Much We Pay for Loss or Occurrence", the condition that describes the limit that can be paid for any one accident. (This was discussed above; see ISO condition A. Limit of Liability.)

Although this condition appears aimed at a claimant, it also reminds the insured that the insurer has a duty to defend any suit alleging bodily injury that is potentially covered by the policy.

Suit Against the Insurer

ISO condition F. provides that no action can be brought against the insurer unless there has been compliance with all of the section II policy terms. Failure of the insured to comply with all policy requirements before or after loss will preclude the policy's response, either for defense or for payment of any claim. In the AAIS form, this is condition, number 4., found in the section "Conditions Applicable to Liability Coverages Only."

This condition further provides that no one has the right to join the insurer as a party to any action against any insured. To do so would be to set up an adversarial relationship between the insurer and its own insured.

No action with respect to coverage E (ISO) or coverage L (AAIS) may be brought against the insurer until the amount of an insured's liability has been determined by final judgment or by an agreement signed by the insurer. Under the AAIS forms, liability may be fixed by a final judgment as the result of a trial, or by a written agreement of the insured, the claimant, and the insurer.

Bankruptcy of an Insured

This is condition G. of the ISO forms, and condition 1. in the AAIS section "Conditions Applicable to Liability Coverages Only." Even though an insured declares bankruptcy, the insurer must still fulfill its obligations under the policy. So long as the policy is active at the time of the loss the insurer is obligated to defend and pay covered claims for damages for which the insured is legally liable. In the earlier AAIS forms this condition applied to both property and liability coverages; in the current form it applies only to liability.

Other Insurance

ISO condition H. concerns other insurance and personal liability coverage. It provides that the personal liability coverage is excess over valid and collectible insurance, except for insurance written specifically to cover as excess over the limits of liability of section II of the homeowners policy. This recognizes the possible existence of umbrellas or other excess liability policies purchased to provide coverage in excess of the homeowners personal liability limits.

In the AAIS forms this is condition 6.b, located in the section "How Much We Pay for Loss or Occurrence." The AAIS forms also contain the means of apportioning a loss if the other personal liability insurance is also excess. The insurer will pay the part of the loss that the applicable limit under this policy bears to the total amount of insurance covering a loss.

Policy Period

ISO condition I. states that the policy applies only to bodily injury or property damage that occurs during the policy period. It is condition 3. in the AAIS forms. (It is also condition P. in the conditions that apply to property coverages in the ISO forms, and condition 6. in the AAIS forms; see Chapter 7.) Note that the bodily injury or property damage need not be reported within the policy period. Although the occurrence that results in bodily injury or property damage must take place within the policy period, notification may be at a later time, even after the policy's expiration date. (Remember, though, notice must be given within a reasonable time.)

Therefore, a wise practice is to take note of any event that potentially could result in a loss or future suit. One of the most important duties following an occurrence is to notify the insurer; if the insured fulfills this duty then the insurer cannot deny a potentially covered claim because of late notice.

Agent Tip

A sound agency procedure is to keep track of such notification, including the insurer at the time of the occurrence. If a claim is presented in the future and the insured has since placed insurance elsewhere, obtaining records will be relatively simple.

Concealment or Fraud

ISO condition J. states that the insurer will not provide coverage to an insured "who, whether before or after a loss, has: intentionally concealed or misrepresented any material fact or circumstance; engaged in fraudulent conduct; or made false statements relating to this insurance."

Remember that the forms state, following the definition of "insured," that the use of the word *an* before *insured* means one or more insureds. Therefore, fraud or misrepresentation on the part of one insured will be imputed to all insureds.

In the AAIS forms, this is condition 7. in the section "Conditions Applicable to All Coverages." The AAIS forms add that the "misrepresentation, concealment, or fraud" preclusion of coverage applies "even with respect to an 'insured' who was not involved in the concealment, misrepresentation, fraudulent conduct, or false swearing."

Chapter 11

General Policy Conditions

Introduction

This chapter concludes the discussion of the forms themselves. The final section of the ISO forms contains the conditions that apply to both the property and the liability coverages. Similar AAIS conditions are generally located in the section "Conditions Applicable to All Coverages."

Concealment or Fraud: Voiding a Policy

The ISO forms no longer refer to a policy's being voided; rather, no coverage will apply to a loss. Current AAIS forms have also deleted language giving circumstances that will render a policy void. But, because some forms still contain this condition, we will address it briefly. Earlier policy language stated that if, before or after a loss, an insured had intentionally concealed or misrepresented any material fact or circumstance, engaged in fraudulent conduct, or made false statements concerning the insurance, the entire policy could be voided. In other words, it would be as if the policy never existed.

In the case of *Wagnon v. State Farm Fire and Casualty Company*, 146 F.3d 764 (10th Cir. 1998), the appellate court ruled that the insured's deliberate misrepresentations about tools he claimed had been stolen in a burglary served to void the entire policy. The insured claimed he had no receipts for the tools because his father had given him most of them, and he exaggerated the value of the loss. The insured's intentional and deliberate misrepresentation about the value directly affected the insurer's knowledge of what it was obligated to pay, and therefore these misrepresentations voided the policy.

But consider voiding a policy in the light of the mortgagee clause in the property coverages. In the case of *Norwest Mortgage, Incorporated v. Nationwide Mutual Fire Insurance Co.*, 718 So. 2d 15 (Ala. 1998), the court held that the insured's false statements were not binding on the mortgagee. The insureds represented on their application that they had no prior losses and had not been nonrenewed, when in fact they had had a claim for wind damage and had been nonrenewed by their prior carrier. When fire damaged the premises, the insurer held that the policy was void from the beginning as to *any* insured when the insureds committed the fraudulent act. The court held, however, that the mortgage clause, which contained the wording "denial will not apply to a valid claim of the mortgagee" in effect established a separate contract between the insurer and the mortgagee, so the mortgagee could not be affected by the acts of the insureds.

An insurer must approach voiding a policy with care. In the case of *Florida International Indemnity Co. v. Osgood*, 503 S.E.2d 371 (Ga. Ct. App. 1998), the insured had failed to disclose several significant previous fire losses on his application. The insurer learned of this when investigating a new fire loss which it denied, but the company never notified the insured that it considered the policy void. Instead, several months after learning of the fraud, the insurer sent a notice stating that the policy would soon expire and would not be renewed. This fact, together with the insurer's retention of the premium for nearly five years after the discovery, led to the affirmation of coverage for the fire loss by the appellate court. The court ruled that the insurer had waived its defenses that fraud voided the policy and that it was not justified in its refusal to pay the claim. Had the insured been promptly notified that the policy was considered as void from inception, the outcome might have been different.

A later case before the Georgia court of appeals overturned a lower court's award of summary judgment to an insurer when it attempted to void a policy and deny a claim because of material misrepresentation on the insureds' application. The insureds sustained a total fire loss, and, upon investigation, the insurer learned that they had been nonrenewed following a total fire loss, and had had an earlier total fire loss. The court said there was no question that the application contained misrepresentations, but noted that there was no "bright line" company policy that coverage would have been denied had the underwriter known the truth. The trier of fact would therefore have to resolve the issue (*Lively v. Southern Heritage Ins. Co.*, 568 S.E.2d 98 [Ga. Ct. App. 2002]).

Finally, there is the case of *American Commerce Insurance Company v. Harris*, 2009 WL 3233738 (E.D. Okla. 2009). A fire destroyed the insured's home, and the insurer paid for both the home and contents. The insured hired a public adjuster, and submitted an additional claim for contents, along with requesting a reconsideration of the home's value. The insurer denied the additional claim, and, at trial, the jury found the insured had submitted a fraudulent second claim. The district court was asked to determine if the second (fraudulent) claim meant that the policy could be declared void, and the previous claim payment returned to the insurer. The court found that it would be against public policy if the insured were allowed to keep the first payment "after a vain attempt to defraud American Commerce out of more."

Agent Tip

Agents cannot stress the importance of truth-telling, both on the application and in event of a claim, strongly enough to their clients. Insurers can easily obtain prior loss information, both on automobile and property, and with loss ratios to protect are not hesitant to use the information. Sometimes prior loss history is withheld innocently, as when an insured genuinely believes that an insignificant vandalism claim two years prior doesn't matter or forgets the exact date and so does not disclose a loss. Better to list on the application words to the effect of "prior loss—wind damage to roof—insured unsure of exact date" than not to divulge the claim.

Liberalization Clause

The first of the ISO conditions applicable to both property and liability coverages is the liberalization clause (A.). This is condition 3.b. of the AAIS forms. (The AAIS forms combine the liberalization clause with the "waiver" condition, which is discussed in the next section.)

If the insurer, during the policy period or within sixty days prior to the policy period, adopts a revision that broadens the coverage without additional premium, the broadened coverage applies immediately to the existing policy as of the date it is implemented in the insured's state. In the AAIS forms the insured's policy receives the broadening of coverage as of the date the revision is implemented in the state in which the "described location" is located. For example, an insured's mailing address could be a post office box in one state, with the insured premises actually located in another state. The liberalization therefore applies in the state in which the premises is located, even if a change is implemented sooner in the mailing address state.

The liberalization clause does not apply to changes made through the introduction of subsequent form editions. For example, when the 2000 ISO homeowners program replaced the 1991 program, the liberalization condition did not operate to give broader coverage to policyholders still insured under the 1991 forms. The clause does not apply to any changes brought about by endorsements that amend the policy, such as state amendatory endorsements.

Waiver or Change of Policy Provisions

This clause provides that any waiver or change of policy provisions must be made in writing by the insurer, and that the insurer's request for an appraisal or examination does not waive any of the insurer's rights under the policy. It is the second of the ISO conditions (condition B.) and is a part of condition 3. of the AAIS forms, which includes, as noted previously, the liberalization clause. The statement that the insurer's request for an appraisal or examination will not waive any of its rights appears to be somewhat out of place. The matter is clearer in the AAIS forms, where the condition is entitled "Change, Modification, or Waiver of Policy Terms." Then, there are three conditions: 3.a. relates to waiver or change of terms; 3.b. to liberalization; and 3.c. to the condition that a request for an appraisal or examination under oath does not constitute a waiver of any policy terms.

It is important to note that *any* changes made to the policy *must* be issued by the insurer in writing. An insured cannot decide to alter the terms of the policy except by request to the insurer. The insurer then can either accede to the request or decline it.

Cancellation

ISO cancellation condition C. is number 2. in the AAIS forms. The AAIS condition also contains the nonrenewal provision, which is separate in the ISO form. The AAIS nonrenewal condition is discussed below. State specific special provisions may significantly amend the length of time required to give notice or reasons allowed for a cancellation or nonrenewal. Consult the special provisions in effect in your state for details if in doubt.

The cancellation condition contains four parts. The first part explains that the policy may be cancelled by the insured. The insured may cancel at any time by returning the policy to the insurer or by writing to the insurer, including the date the cancellation is to take place.

Agent Tip

Although the forms do not specify, a request to cancel a policy should always be signed by the named insured or an authorized representative.

The second part of the condition explains the cancellation rights of the insurer. The insurer's rights are more restricted; written notice in advance of cancellation must be given. The notice must be delivered to the insured or mailed to the insured's mailing address shown on the declarations. Proof of mailing (AAIS adds "or delivery") is sufficient proof of notice, so an insured's acknowledgment of receipt is unnecessary. Indeed, an insured might claim he or she never received the notice; if the insurer has kept track of the cancellation (and nonrenewal) notices it has sent, then a court often will accept this as proof.

The question, then, arises as to what constitutes "proof of mailing." Here, we turn to *Couch on Insurance, Third Edition* (§32:20): "In those jurisdictions where a statute which provides that proof of mailing is sufficient to prove valid notice of cancellation the statute may also address the acceptable proof of mailing, as by providing that an affidavit of the individual making or supervising the mailing of an automobile liability policy cancellation shall constitute prima facie evidence of such facts of the mailing as are therein affirmed, or requiring either mailing by certified mail, or a United States postal receipt proof of mailing which shows the name and address of the insured and that the insurer retain a copy of the mailed notice which is certified to be a true copy. Under statutes of this nature, the modern practice by which insurers mail cancellation notices in bulk may be used to establish proof, or at least a presumption, that the notices have been mailed. For example, computer compilations listing the names and addresses of persons to whom notices of cancellation were mailed has been accepted as sufficient evidence of mailing where the compilation was stamped by postal authorities, so long as the insurer establishes that a post office employee confirmed names and addresses on the list prior to entering the post office's date stamp on the list...."

The second part of the cancellation condition also gives the restrictions governing the time an insurer has to cancel a policy. Ten days notice (or more, depending upon the state) is required for cancellation for nonpayment of premium, or for any other reason when a new policy has been in effect for less than sixty days. The AAIS form states "during the first 59 days this policy is in effect, 'we' may cancel for any reason."

But if a policy has been in effect for sixty days or more, or if it is a renewal with the insurer, the insurer may cancel only: 1) if there has been a material misrepresentation that would, if known, have caused the insurer to decline to issue a policy; or 2) if the risk has changed substantially since the policy was issued. In the AAIS form, the reasons are: 1) the policy was obtained through fraud, material misrepresentation, or omission of fact which, if known by the insurer, would have caused the insurer to decline to issue the policy; or 2) there has been a material change or increase in hazard of the risk.

Exactly what constitutes a "substantial change" or "material change" is not spelled out. However, the reason should be significant enough to withstand the scrutiny of the state department of insurance. Generally, a department of insurance will require that the change be hazardous in nature—a dwelling suddenly housing a fireworks plant, for example. However, it might not be so obvious. Unrepaired fire or wind damage so that the dwelling deteriorates is a "substantial change." The important thing is that the risk must have altered *since* the policy was issued. It is assumed that the insurer had ample time during the underwriting period to determine the acceptability; if the policy was issued to a dwelling containing a fireworks operation the insurer cannot use this as a cancellation reason, unless the insured misrepresented that fact to the insurer.

In these instances, at least thirty days notice must be given. (Again, remember that allowable reasons and time vary by state. Check the state amendatory provisions.)

A policy written for more than one year may be cancelled at any anniversary date upon giving thirty days advance notice. This condition does not appear in the AAIS forms.

The third and fourth parts of the cancellation condition describe the procedures the insurer will follow in returning any unearned premium. All premium refunds resulting from an insurer's cancellation are determined from the cancellation date to the expiration date on a pro rata basis. The insurer is required to return the unearned premium "within a reasonable time after the date cancellation takes effect," unless the return premium accompanies the cancellation notice. The AAIS form adds that "payment or tender of the unearned premium is not a condition of cancellation."

Nonrenewal

Condition D. of the ISO forms, and 2. of the AAIS forms, concern nonrenewal. Written notice of the insurer's intent not to renew a policy must be given at least thirty days before the expiration date. Some states have different requirements, which are found in the specific state endorsements. The insurer may nonrenew only at the anniversary date (which is often referred to as the renewal date), while a cancellation may occur either at the anniversary date or another date, depending upon state regulations. States are frequently less restrictive concerning the reasons an insurer may give for nonrenewing a policy than they are for cancelling a policy. For example, an insurer might, depending upon the state, nonrenew for claims frequency, failure to replace a deteriorated roof, or even failure to return a request for underwriting information.

Some states allow a renewal to be issued, but with more restrictive coverage. For example, the New York regulations will not allow nonrenewal of "personal lines insurance," which means homeowners, dwelling fire, or umbrella insurance, except at three year intervals. The insurer may then issue a renewal with no more coverage than is required by law—without a requested schedule, perhaps.

Assignment

ISO condition E. and AAIS condition 1. discuss assignment, which is transferring the policy from one named insured to another person, such as the purchaser of the insured's dwelling. Assignment of the rights under the policy is not valid without the written consent of the insurer. This reflects the concept that the insurance policy is a personal contract between insured and insurer, and so the insurer retains the right to accept or reject assignment of the policy rights to a new insured. Many insurers do not wish to accept an assignment of the policy and prefer instead to use the opportunity to re-underwrite the risk and evaluate the new proposed insureds.

A case illustrating the condition is *Highlands Insurance Company v. Kravecas*, 719 So. 2d 320 (Fla. Dist. Ct. App. 1998). The insured purchased a residence that had been damaged by Hurricane Andrew from another party, who assigned the existing policy and any additional claim for property damage to him. The seller had made claim under the policy for the damages, but he did not make a claim for additional living expense since he was never forced to vacate the premises. Six months later, the new insured advised the insurer that he believed there were additional damages from the storm and made claim for some additional $200,000 in structural repairs, as well as additional living expenses. The claim for additional living expense was denied, and the insured sued. On appeal, the court ruled that the insurer had never given *written* consent to the policy assignment. Further, the purchaser could not assert a claim for *potential* loss of use, only for *actual* loss. Since he had not suffered an actual loss of use, he was only entitled to the additional money to repair the dwelling.

Subrogation

ISO condition F. and AAIS condition 8. describe subrogation, whereby an insured's rights under the policy are subrogated to the insurer. The subrogation clause, a common element of virtually all property insurance policies, was adapted from the standard fire policy and simplified under homeowners '76 and subsequent policies. The clause gives the insured permission to waive rights of recovery against others prior to loss. (For example, an insured suspects that a piece of jewelry has been stolen by a worker at his golf club. He cannot, after the loss, request that the insurer not pursue the worker; however, prior to a loss he could request that any losses occurring at the club not be pursued.) But the waiver must be in writing; oral waiver can jeopardize the insured's right of payment for the loss, as can any waiver of rights of recovery after the loss has occurred.

Also, the condition requires that when assignment of rights is sought by the insurer, the insured will sign and deliver all related papers to, and cooperate with, the insurer in this endeavor. The subrogation clause does not apply to the medical payments to others or the section II additional coverage for damage to property of others.

It has often been accepted that an insurer cannot subrogate against its own insured, but that is not always the case. Subrogation has been allowed in instances where an insurer has paid for a loss it otherwise would not have, as in the case of a payment made to a mortgagee when the insured's claim has been denied (*Parasco v. Pacific Indemnity Co.*, 920 F.Supp 647 [E.D. Pa. 1996]). And, in *Allstate Insurance Company v. LaRandeau,* 622 N.W.2d 646 (Neb. 2001), subrogation was allowed against the named insured, who committed arson, when the insurer made a payment to the innocent coinsured spouse.

Sometimes it might appear that insurers cast about looking for a party to subrogate against. In the case of *Allstate Insurance Company v. Palumbo*, 994 A.2d 174 (Conn. 2010), the insured's fiancé installed a water heater and heat pump which caused a fire. The insurer paid the claim, but then subrogated against the fiancé for negligence. The court said that under the doctrine of equitable subrogation, the subrogee had no rights against a third person beyond what the subrogor had. Because the insured and her fiancé shared the house, jointly paid all bills (including the homeowners insurance bill), and because the fiancé had done considerable work in the home, updating and remodeling it, the court held that "equities dictated that insurer could not prevail against fiancé in equitable subrogation action for fire at homeowner's home caused by fiancé's negligence." The fact that the fiancé was not a resident relative did not sway the court.

Death

ISO condition G. and AAIS condition 5. describe what will happen in the event that a named insured or spouse (if a resident of the same household) dies. The policy extends coverage immediately upon the named insured's death to the deceased's legal representative (executor or administrator of the estate) with respect to the covered premises and property of the deceased. Also, coverage continues for members of the household who were insureds (as defined in the policy) at the time of death, but only while they are residents of the insured premises. Coverage extends with respect to the property to anyone having "proper temporary custody" of the property until appointment and qualification of a legal representative.

In *North Star Mutual Insurance Co. v. Ziebarth*, 386 N.W.2d 238 (Minn. 1986), the court held that the provision for passing coverage to a personal representative or other person having proper temporary custody was not effective when the deceased's spouse, who qualified as an insured, continued to live in the home. After Alois Fisher died, his married daughter, Michelle Ziebarth, returned to her father's home to help sort out the deceased's personal property. Alois's second wife, JoAnn, was living in the home when he died and remained in the residence. The night before Michelle was to return home, she started a fire while making popcorn. Michelle's husband went to help her and was badly burned. In seeking coverage under her father's policy against a claim by her husband, Michelle argued that she was an insured. The court reasoned that she was not an insured since the provision for passing coverage to a legal representative, or, in Michelle's case, to another person until a legal representative could be appointed, was only triggered when no insured had custody of the property. Since JoAnn was an insured who had custody, Michelle was not eligible for insured status. Michelle would have been an insured if both insureds had died and a legal representative had not yet been appointed.

Agent Tip

It is not uncommon for a married couple to list only one name as named insured on the declarations. Even if only one party's name is on the deed, it is best to list both names so that, in the event one person dies, the other may continue to enjoy named insured status.

Additional AAIS Conditions

The AAIS forms contain three additional conditions not found in the ISO forms. The first two are in the section "Conditions Applicable to All Coverages."

Conformity with Statute

The first of these AAIS conditions is 4. It states that, wherever there is a conflict with the laws of the state in which the "described location" is located, the terms of the policy are amended accordingly.

Inspections

AAIS condition 6. provides that the insurer has the right (but not the obligation) to inspect the property and "operations." The inspection may be made by the insurer or by another party acting on the insurer's behalf. However, such an inspection is not to be construed as a warranty that the premises are safe, healthful, or in compliance with any laws or local regulations. For example, after a fire loss an insured cannot claim that the insurer knew a dwelling's wiring was not up to code and failed to warn him or her.

Insurance under More than One Coverage

This condition appears in the section "How Much We Pay for Loss or Occurrence," where it is condition 4. There is no similar ISO condition. It states that, if more than one coverage under the policy applies to a loss, then no more than the actual loss will be paid. So, for example, if an insured suffers a $200 theft of money, and is paid under the special limits, he cannot claim another $200 of money as general personal property and expect to be paid a second time.

Chapter 12

Other Homeowners Forms

Introduction

This chapter contains overviews of the homeowners forms other than the HO 00 03 and HO 0003. Since many of the coverages and exclusions are similar to those already discussed, the forms will be reviewed briefly. Included are the tenant homeowners (HO 00 04 and HO 0004), condominium owners (HO 00 06 and HO 0006), modified or limited homeowners (HO 0001, HO 00 08, and HO 0008), mobile homeowners, and forms HO 00 05 and HO 0005. These latter forms provide open perils coverage for both dwelling and contents. The same exclusions and limitations of coverage apply. Definitions and liability coverages are identical in all the homeowners forms, so they will not be discussed here.

Coverage for Tenant Homeowners

The needs of the renter are different from those of the dwelling or unit owner. ISO's HO 00 04 and AAIS HO 0004 are tailored to address those needs. Both forms begin with coverage C, because the tenant does not insure the dwelling or apartment structure (except for any additions or alterations the tenant installs at his own expense). Likewise, there is no coverage B for other structures; if a tenant insured added a carport, coverage would fall under tenant's improvements. Because the forms do not cover dwelling or other structures, there is no coverage, as in form HO 00 02, for the cost to tear out and replace those parts of the dwelling needed to repair a plumbing system under the peril of accidental discharge, although damage caused by the accidental discharge would be covered.

The perils insured against are similar to those in coverage C of the ISO HO 00 03 and AAIS HO 0003. There is a difference, though, in the coverage for loss arising out of vandalism. The HO 00 03 does not exclude loss caused by vandalism to personal property on the residence premises, nor any ensuing loss caused by an intentional and wrongful act committed in the course of vandalism, even if the dwelling has been vacant for more than sixty consecutive days. The HO 00 04 excludes such loss. Likewise, the AAIS HO 0004 excludes loss to property on the "described location" if the part of the described location where the named insured resides has been vacant for more than sixty consecutive days before the loss. Both forms state that a dwelling being built is not considered vacant.

As was the case with the HO 00 03, the ISO HO 00 04 limits coverage for property contained in a self-storage unit to 10 percent or $1,000 of the coverage C amount.

ISO HO 00 04 Additional Coverages

The ISO additional coverages differ from those in the HO 00 03. Additional coverage 10. for landlord's furnishings has been omitted and replaced with building additions and alterations. This covers items the tenant insured installs in the residential unit, such as built-in book shelves. Coverage applies to *building* items; that is, items considered as a part of the realty and, as such, belonging to the property owner once installed. The tenant, however, has a use interest in the items during the time he resides there. The amount of coverage is 10 percent of the coverage C amount.

Additional coverage 11. allows 10 percent of the limit that applies to the building additions and alterations for ordinance and law coverage. For example, if a tenant has $50,000 in contents, $5,000 may be applied to building additions and alterations. Of that amount, $500 may be used for any increased costs for debris removal, repair, or rebuilding because of enforcement of any ordinance or law.

AAIS HO 0004 Incidental Property Coverages

The incidental property coverages of the AAIS HO 0004 also differ from those in, say, the HO 0003. Incidental coverage 2., debris removal, pays for the cost to remove volcanic ash that causes direct physical damage to property covered under coverage C or tenant's improvements only. A change in the current form is that debris removal coverage also responds to removal of fallen trees that fall and obstruct access to a driveway on the insured premises, as in the other AAIS forms, as well as those that damage property insured under coverage C or tenant's improvements.

Coverage for tenant's improvements applies to *permanent* improvements, fixtures, alterations, decorations, or additions to the insured premises made at the tenant insured's expense. Loss must be caused by a coverage C peril. A tenant's improvement can also include an other structure, but only if it is not rented or held for rental to anyone not a tenant of the insured's residence at the described location (except for a private garage). Coverage is limited to 10 percent of the coverage C limit, but may be increased.

In the earlier AAIS form, ordinance or law coverage was included in the 10 percent of the limit of liability applying to coverage C; now, it is a separate incidental coverage. It is limited to 10 percent of the amount for tenant's improvements, but may be increased.

Coverage D Loss of Use

In the ISO form, a loss to covered property *or the building containing the property* triggers the coverage. Loss of use is limited to 30 percent of the coverage C amount.

In the AAIS form the coverage for additional living expense costs is triggered when a covered loss makes the "part of the 'described location' occupied by 'your' household" unfit for use. Coverage is limited to 40 percent of the coverage C amount.

Amending Coverage for Tenants' Personal Property

AAIS rules allow for open perils coverage, with certain exceptions, to be endorsed to the tenant homeowners form HO 0004. This is endorsement HO 2730.

In the ISO program, endorsement HO 05 24 may be attached to the HO 00 04 to provide open perils coverage. The form was revised with the 2011 edition to reflect the changes that were made in the HO 00 03; for example, loss caused by "nesting or infestation, or discharge or release of waste products or secretions, by any animals" is excluded in the HO 05 24. If it were not, the tenant homeowner would have broader coverage than the HO 00 03 homeowner. Both AAIS and ISO increase the limit of liability applying to certain classes of property when these endorsements are attached. Certain property is also covered for breakage when the breakage is caused by enumerated named perils. For example, collapse is deleted as an additional coverage with respect to coverage C and instead given as a covered cause of loss with regards to fragile property.

Coverage for loss caused by discharge, release, etc., of pollutants applies if the discharge, escape, seepage, etc., "is itself caused by one or more of the Perils Insured Against that would apply under Coverage C of the policy form if this endorsement were not attached to the policy form." So, coverage for loss caused by pollution is limited to what would be a standard coverage C peril.

As will be discussed, the open perils exclusions are similar to those of the ISO HO 00 05 and AAIS HO 0005, which provide open perils coverage for dwelling and contents. For more information see the discussion of those forms later in this chapter.

Coverage for Unit Owners

Although commonly referred to as condominium forms, ISO HO 00 06 and AAIS HO 0006 may be used for the cooperative apartment tenant as well. A cooperative tenant has an ownership interest in the cooperative association or corporation that owns all of the units, and through that ownership has a right to a perpetual lease to occupy a specific unit. However, this difference has not caused any problem in interpreting the intent of the coverage with respect to a resident of a cooperative apartment covered by the forms.

The condominium method of realty ownership involves a number of unique insurance problems. The condominium is a joint enterprise type of ownership in which there is common ownership of certain portions of the premises. The individual also has exclusive ownership of the right to occupy a specific unit and sometimes also individually owns certain items of real property within the unit.

The ownership deed for a condominium, usually called the condominium declaration or, in a few states, the master deed, sets forth the exact provisions of ownership and rights of occupancy of all the unit owners. It usually provides for the establishment of a condominium association, made up of all the unit owners, with membership in the association a mandatory condition of condominium ownership. The association, working through elected officers and a board of directors, provides for the management of the condominium, including purchase of insurance on behalf of the unit owners.

The condominium declaration usually contains a section relating to insurance requirements. Sometimes this is found in the condominium association bylaws. This section describes what insurance the association will carry on behalf of the unit owners. It usually requires that the association purchase insurance on all the common property. In many cases, the association is also assigned the responsibility for insuring all the realty, including portions solely owned by the individual unit owners. Forms such as ISO CP 00 17 are used for this purpose. Any property not insured by the association is the responsibility of the individual unit owners.

Agent Tip

Great care must be taken when arranging coverage for the condominium owner. If the association insures only the condominium building as originally constructed (or for replacement for original equipment only), but not improvements or additions made subsequently by the unit owner or previous owner, additional coverage by the unit owner may be required. Another situation requiring more than the basic amount of coverage is when the association insurance is "bare walls" coverage. This means that the unit owner is responsible for insuring all items in the interior– all fixtures, built-in appliances, interior partitions, plumbing and lighting fixtures; paint, paper, or paneling on the walls and ceilings; tile or carpet on the floors; and, in multi-story units, even the floors, stairs, and ceilings between the lowest floor and highest ceiling.

Coverage A–Dwelling

Both ISO and AAIS amend the definition of a residence or insured premises so that it applies to unit ownership. In ISO form the definition is:

> "Residence premises" means the unit where you reside shown as the "residence premises" in the Declarations.

The AAIS form states:

> Described Location means the unit in which you reside and which is shown on the 'declarations' as the 'described location'.

These definitions are important in analyzing coverage. Note that there is no reference to other structures or grounds as there is in the other homeowners forms, such as the HO 00 03 or HO 0003, because those are generally owned in common and so are not personally insurable.

Unlike the tenant homeowners forms, the condominium owners forms contain coverage A insuring agreements. There are four parts to the coverage. First, there is coverage for alterations, appliances, fixtures, and improvements that are part of the building contained within the residence premises. The AAIS form provides coverage for "fixtures, alterations, decorations, additions, installations, and appliances that are part of the building including within the 'described location'." The second part of coverage A is for items of real property that pertain exclusively to the residence premises, for example, the outdoor condenser that is part of unit's air conditioning system.

The third part of the coverage applies to property that the insured must insure because of an agreement with the association or corporation of property owners. Although this appears to be identical to the first of the coverages, it need not be. The association might require the insured to cover plumbing within the unit, for example.

Finally, the fourth part of coverage A applies to structures at the described location that are owned solely by the insured, such as a garage or carport. The structure does not need to be set apart from the unit by a clear space, as with other structures coverage in the HO 00 03, because the HO 00 06 makes no distinction between attached and detached structures. All structures fall under the full coverage A limit. There is no coverage, however, for structures used in whole or in part for business, other than used solely for a private garage or rented to a tenant of the residence for other than business purposes. (An other structure used to store business property solely owned by an insured or a tenant of the residence falls outside the exclusion, though.)

Although the other homeowners forms include protection under coverage A for building materials and supplies located on or next to the residence premises and used for work on the dwelling or other structures, there is no similar provision in the unit owners coverage A, with the result that such items would fall under personal property coverage. In either case, the theft peril excludes coverage for theft of construction materials and supplies until the unit is finished and occupied. Note, the *unit* must be finished and occupied, not the entire complex in which the unit may be situated.

The ISO coverage A limit is $5,000, on a named perils basis. The AAIS form provides 10 percent of the coverage C amount, also on a named perils basis. Both may be changed to open perils coverage (see below). The amounts of coverage may be increased in both forms as well. Whether the basic coverage limit is sufficient or not depends largely on how the association insurance is written. If the association insurance covers the entire unit, including all interior fixtures, pipes, wiring, partitions, and other building items within the unit, and if the association carries enough coverage to provide full replacement of the entire building, the unit owner might not require additional individual coverage.

Loss Settlement and Other Insurance

This is a good place to pause for a moment in our discussion of the coverages, and take a look at the 2011 other insurance condition.

The 2000 HO 00 06 forms contained a provision (F.2.) stating that:

> If, at the time of loss, there is other insurance or a service agreement in the name of a corporation or association of property owners covering the same property covered by this policy, this insurance will be excess over the amount recoverable under such other insurance or service agreement.

This left open the possibility that an insured could be in the hole for a large amount of money in event of a covered loss, since the HO 00 06 stated it was excess over any amount recoverable under the master policy. Of course, given that many master policies maintain high deductibles, nothing would be recoverable. So, ISO developed an endorsement to address this situation. The endorsement (HO 17 34 10 00) read:

> 2. If, at the time of loss, there is other insurance or a service agreement, in the name of a corporation or association of property owners covering the same property covered by this policy, we will pay only for the amount of the loss in excess of the amount due from that other insurance or service agreement, whether they can collect on it or not.

It is immediately apparent that the hoped-for results would be subject to question. The insurer still pays for the amount of the loss that is in excess of the amount due, whether "they" (who is *they*?) can collect on it or not.

In the current (2011) form, the revised wording is:

> 2. Subject to Paragraph G.1., if, at the time of loss, there is other insurance or a service agreement in the name of a corporation or association of property owners covering the same property covered by this policy, this insurance is:
>
>   a. Excess over the amount due under such other insurance or service agreement, whether the corporation or association of property owners has collected that amount or not; and
>
>   b. Primary with respect to any amount of the loss covered by this policy and not due under such other insurance or service agreement because of the application of a deductible.

So, the condo owner who has paid for coverage should be able to collect for a covered loss, even if the master policy would normally respond to the loss, but, because of a high deductible, will not.

Additional or Incidental Coverages

There are eleven additional coverages in the ISO HO 00 06. The coverages are: debris removal; reasonable repairs; trees, shrubs, and plants (limited to $500 for any one tree, plant, or shrub); fire department service charge; property removed; credit and fund transfer card; loss assessment; collapse; glass; ordinance and law; and grave markers.

The AAIS incidental coverages are: association deductible, emergency removal; debris removal; ordinance or law; fire department service charge; credit card; grave markers; collapse; glass breakage; liquid fuel remediation; reasonable repairs; refrigerated food spoilage; trees, lawns, and shrubs; and loss assessment.

The additional coverages are identical to those of the other ISO and AAIS homeowners HO 00 03 and HO 0003, with these exceptions. First, glass breakage coverage applies to glass covered under coverage A. Second, the coverage for trees, shrubs, and other plants is 10 percent of the limit of liability applying to coverage C, rather than the 5 percent of the dwelling limit as in the HO 00 03 and HO 0003. Coverage for debris removal will not respond to the cost to remove a tree that blocks access to the premises. There is no coverage for landlord's furnishings in the ISO form, or for property in rental units in the AAIS form.

Coverage C—Personal Property

Most of the provisions included in coverage C of form HO 00 06 and HO 0006 are identical to form HO 00 03 and HO 0003, with an exception worth noting. Both the condo forms cover personal property owned by others while the property is on the part of the residence premises occupied by an insured, but the extent of coverage may differ from the HO 00 03 and HO 0003 because of the definitions of "residence premises" or "described location" (see definitions given previously). The HO 00 06 limits the meaning to the *unit* (an undefined term in the policy, but understood to be the individually-owned area in the condo building) in which the insured resides, and HO 0006 refers to "parts of the described location …occupied solely by an insured household." Therefore, in the case of coverage for personal property of others, a narrow interpretation might leave a unit owner without the option of extending coverage to a guest's property taken from the garage or the lawn appurtenant to his unit.

As was discussed earlier in this book, ISO has now, in the 2011 edition, limited the coverage for personal property owned or used by an insured and located in a self-storage facility to 10 percent of the coverage C limit, or $1,000, whichever is greater. The limit does not apply if the property is in the self-storage unit because the residence premises is being repaired, renovated, or rebuilt, or if the premises is not fit to live in or store property in.

The named perils coverages in the unit owners forms apply to coverages A and C. Some of these perils differ from those found in the forms HO 00 03 and HO 0003 coverage C. Often, these reflect the difference in property ownership. The peril of *vehicles* does not include loss to fences, driveways, or walks caused by a vehicle owned or operated by a resident of the insured premises or an occupant of the described location. The peril of *vandalism* is amended so that there is no coverage for loss or an ensuing loss to property pertaining to the residence premises if the building containing the residence premises or described location has been vacant for more than sixty consecutive days before the loss. A building in the course of construction is not vacant. Because so many condo owners often rent their condos to others for brief periods, it is important to note that the peril of *theft,* as was the case in the HO 00 03, does not apply to theft "from that part of a 'residence premises' rented by an 'insured' to someone other than another 'insured'."

Both programs amend the named peril of *weight of ice, snow, and sleet* that causes damage to property inside a structure so that it is similar to the named peril found in the HO 0002 and HO 00 02. The HO 0006 and HO 00 06 peril applies to "weight of ice, snow or sleet which damages a building or the property inside a building." However, coverage does not apply to awnings or canopies and their supports, or to swimming pools, retaining walls, fences, piers, wharves, foundations, patios, or paved areas.

Some differences exist between the language of forms HO 00 03 and HO 00 06 (and forms HO 0003 and HO 0006) regarding the peril of *accidental discharge or overflow*. The cost to get to and repair a leak applies only to property covered under coverage A, or, in the AAIS form, "those parts of a building or other structure, owned solely by 'you', covered by Coverage A, and on the site of the 'described location'." For example, if the pipe in an upstairs unit leaked and damaged the insured unit, this repair part of the coverage would not apply, although, of course, the damage caused by the water to the insured's unit would be covered. Both the condo forms eliminate coverage for accidental discharge or overflow occurring away from the building where the 'residence premises' is located" in the ISO form, and "from off the 'described location'" in the AAIS form. Both the ISO HO 00 06 and AAIS HO 0006 exclude coverage under the accidental discharge peril if the building containing the unit has been vacant for more than sixty consecutive days.

Coverage D—Loss of Use

The coverage D insuring agreement of the ISO HO 00 06 has been adapted to take into account the multiple occupancy of the building. Rather than providing coverage if the insured's part of the premises is not fit to live in, the unit owners form provides coverage if a loss by a covered peril "to covered property or the building containing the property" renders the unit unfit for habitation. Thus, unit owners coverage D can apply even when there has been no direct physical loss to the insured's particular unit. Coverage D in AAIS form HO 0006 is identical in wording to the other AAIS forms. The ISO program provides 50 percent of the coverage C amount for coverage D. The AAIS program provides 40 percent of coverage C.

Amending Coverage for Unit Owners

Named perils coverage for a unit owner's additions and alterations (coverage A) and personal property (coverage C) may be changed to open perils. When ISO HO 17 32 or AAIS HO 7032 is attached, coverage for additions and alterations will be similar to the coverage of forms HO 00 03 and HO 0003.

Coverage for personal property may also be changed from named perils to an open perils basis. ISO utilizes HO 17 31, and AAIS HO 7029. Open perils coverage for dwellings and other structures was discussed in Chapter 6; we will discuss open perils coverage for personal property later in this chapter in conjunction with forms HO 0005 and HO 00 05. Adding the HO 17 31 or HO 7029 will not, however, give theft coverage while the unit is rented; exclusion 2. eliminates coverage for loss "to property in a unit regularly rented or held for rental to others by you." Endorsement HO 17 33 should be attached if the unit is regularly rented or held for rental to others. The endorsement states that property in an apartment *other than the residence premises* regularly rented is not covered, and eliminates coverage for theft from the residence premises of money, jewelry, silver, etc. The exclusion for business is amended so that it does not apply to the rental or holding for rental of the residence premises. The AAIS endorsement HO 7033 accomplishes the same result by amending the exclusion for property rented or held for rental by an insured, so it does not apply to property in the described location while rented to others for residential purposes. Theft from the insured premises of money, silver, securities, jewelry, etc., is excluded. Liability coverage is amended to include the rental of the insured premises for residential purposes.

As we noted in the discussion of amending the coverage for personal property for the tenant homeowner to open perils, the 2011 forms for the condo owner have likewise been amended so there is no coverage for loss caused by nesting, infestation, discharge or release of waste products or secretions by any animals.

Form HO 0001

ISO has discontinued this form, but the AAIS program retains it. The form does not contain all of the incidental property coverages; there is no coverage for collapse or liquid fuel remediation. Coverage for glass breakage is limited to $100.

In this form, the covered perils are: fire or lightning; windstorm or hail; explosion; riot or civil commotion; aircraft; vehicles (but no coverage for fences, drives, or walks damaged by a vehicle driven by an occupant of the described location); smoke, sinkhole collapse; volcanic eruption; vandalism or malicious mischief; or theft. There is thus no coverage for: falling objects; weight of ice, snow or sleet; sudden and accidental discharge of water; sudden and accidental bursting, burning, or bulging; freezing; or sudden and accidental damage from artificial electrical current.

The replacement cost settlement terms are the same as in form HO 0003.

Form HO 0008 and HO 00 08—Limited Coverage

For many insureds the ISO HO 00 08 and AAIS HO 0008 provide the best alternative to purchasing a replacement cost policy. Those insureds with ornate homes built earlier in the century, or those whose homes are in declining neighborhoods, may be provided less costly insurance with these forms. The coverages are not as broad as in the other forms, except for the section II liability coverages.

Named Perils Coverage for Dwelling and Contents

The named perils coverages apply to both dwelling and personal property. Both the ISO and AAIS forms only cover personal property *while on the residence premises*, except that 10 percent of the coverage C amount or $1,000, whichever is greater, may be applied to personal property away from the premises. (Personal property contained in a bank vault or other similar site, or a self-storage unit, is considered to be on the residence premises.) This is in sharp contrast to, for example, the HO 00 03 coverage C insuring agreement, which states "we cover personal property owned or used by an 'insured' while it is anywhere in the world."

The ten perils insured against on the ISO form are: fire or lightning; windstorm or hail; explosion; riot or civil commotion; aircraft; vehicles (excluding loss caused by a vehicle owned or operated by a resident); smoke (excluding agricultural, industrial, or fireplace smoke); vandalism or malicious mischief (unless dwelling has been vacant for the sixty days preceding the loss); theft (limited to $1,000 and excluding theft away from the insured premises); and volcanic eruption.

The AAIS form insures against eleven perils: fire or lightning; windstorm or hail; explosion; riot or civil commotion; aircraft; vehicles (excluding loss to fences, driveways, or walks caused by a vehicle owned or operated by an occupant of the described location); smoke (except for agricultural, industrial, or fireplace smoke); sinkhole collapse; vandalism (unless dwelling has been vacant for the sixty days preceding the loss); theft (limited to $1000 and only if theft is from described location); and volcanic action.

Additional or Incidental Property Coverages

ISO HO 00 08 contains eight additional coverages. These are: debris removal; reasonable repairs; trees, shrubs and other plants; fire department service charge; property removed; credit and fund transfer card; loss assessment, and glass or safety glazing material. They are identical to those in the HO 00 03, except that loss to glass is limited to $100 per occurrence. Notable is the fact that there is no coverage for landlord's furnishings, collapse, or ordinance and law. Ordinance and law coverage may be added by attaching endorsement HO 23 73 if the insurer agrees. Note, though, that this form might not be available. It is not listed in the 2011 manual, and the edition date of the form is June 1994.

AAIS form HO 0008 contains ten incidental coverages. These are: association deductible; emergency removal; debris removal; reasonable repairs; fire department service charge; credit card; trees, plants, shrubs, or lawns; glass breakage (limited to $100); refrigerated food spoilage; and loss assessment. Like the ISO form, there is no coverage for collapse, ordinance or law, or for property in rental units. Coverage for ordinance or law is not available with this form.

Limits on Certain Classes of Property

Both the ISO and AAIS forms limit certain classes of property, such as money, jewelry, guns, silver, etc. in the other homeowners forms. These limitations, however, are even more stringent in forms HO 0008 and HO 00 08. In the ISO forms the limits are: $200 for money, $1,500 for securities, $1,500 for watercraft, $1,500 for trailers, $2,500 for business property on the residence premises, $500 for business property away from the residence premises, and $1,500 each for the two categories of electronic apparatus.

Immediately obvious is the fact that there are no limits for theft of firearms, silver, or jewelry. This is because the overall limit of coverage for theft is $1,000, and then only for theft occurring on the residence premises or from a bank vault, safe deposit company, or public warehouse. This is true as well for the AAIS form.

The limits on the AAIS form are: $250 on money, $1,500 on securities, $1,500 each for the two classes of electronic devices, $1,500 on watercraft, $1,500 on trailers, $2,500 for business property on the residence premises, and $500 for business property away from the residence premises.

Loss of Use

Coverage for loss of use in both AAIS and ISO is identical to that in forms HO 00 03 and HO 0003.

Loss Settlement Provisions

The ISO loss settlement provisions contain a repair cost loss condition, but many states require actual cash value loss adjustment because it might result in a greater amount. In those states that do not permit losses to be handled on a repair cost basis loss settlement endorsement HO 04 81 is attached to form HO 00 08. When this endorsement is attached, losses are settled on an actual cash value basis, but for no more than the amount required to repair or replace.

The insured may repair or replace the damaged building for the same occupancy and use at the same site within 180 days. In this case the insurer pays the lesser of the limit that applies to the building or the "necessary amount actually spent to repair or replace" the damaged property "using common construction materials and methods where functionally equivalent to and less costly than obsolete, antique or custom construction materials and methods." If the conditions under the repair cost provision are not met, settlement becomes the *smallest* of: 1) the applicable limit of liability; 2) the market value of the building at the time of loss excluding land; or 3) repair or replacement at actual cash value.

Likewise, the AAIS form omits the replacement cost terms found in form HO 0003. Loss settlement terms are on an actual cash value basis, which includes a deduction for depreciation no matter how caused. Payment will be the smallest of: 1) the cost to repair or replace the damaged property with materials of like kind and quality to the extent practical, or 2) the actual cash value of the property just before the time of loss. Actual cash value is defined as "the cost to repair or replace property using materials of like kind and quality, to the extent practical, less a deduction for depreciation, however, caused."

Mobile Homeowners

Many companies do not wish to insure mobile homes. Other insurers specialize in these risks. Eligibility is subject to the particular insurer's underwriting criteria. For this reason, this book contains only a cursory look at the forms.

ISO forms HO 00 02 and HO 00 03 may be used for mobile homes; endorsement MH 04 01 is attached. This endorsement provides that the residence premises means the mobile home and other structures located on land that is owned by or leased to the insured, where the insured resides, and which is shown as the "residence premises" in the declarations. Coverage A includes structures and utility tanks attached to the mobile home, as well as floor coverings, appliances, and dressers and cabinets and similar items that are permanently installed. The coverage for other structures is not more than 10 percent of the limit applying to coverage A; however, if the 10 percent is less than $2,000, the insurer will provide a minimum limit of $2,000. This amount does not reduce the amount of the coverage A limit.

Additional coverage 5, property removed, is amended so that up to $500 is available to move the mobile home (and return it to its site) in case a covered peril endangers it. There is no coverage for ordinance or law unless added by endorsement. Finally, the pair or set condition is amended so that the insurer pays the reasonable cost to repair or replace a series of pieces or panels, or if not feasible, pays to provide a decoratively pleasing effect. In the event of a loss to a part, the insurer will not be liable for the value, repair, or replacement of the entire series of pieces or panels.

The ISO form provides for replacement cost or actual cash value (the HO 00 02 or HO 00 03 provisions), or, by endorsement, these provisions may be changed so that the insurer may elect to: 1) pay the cost of repair; 2) replace the damaged property with similar property, not necessarily the same manufacturer; or 3) pay the least of : a) the difference between actual cash value before and after the loss; b) the cost of repair; or c) the cost of replacing the damaged property with similar property.

AAIS forms are similar; form 3 Ed. 2.0, for example, may be used to write mobile homes. The definition of "residence" is "a one-to four-family house, a townhouse, a row house, or a one-or two-family mobile home used mainly for family residential purposes.

If the mobile homeowner decides to relocate, then endorsement MH 04 03 transportation/permission to move should be attached. The endorsement provides collision coverage while the home is in transit. The comparable

AAIS forms are ML 25 consent to move, and ML 26 collision or upset. The latter may not be attached unless ML 25 is attached.

Open Perils Coverage–ISO HO 00 05 and AAIS HO 0005

AAIS HO 0005 is a special building and contents form. It provides open perils coverage for both building and contents and also provides coverage enhancements not found in the other forms. The ISO form, HO 00 05, provides open perils coverage for both dwelling and contents, but not the coverage enhancements found in the AAIS form. And, as discussed below, the AAIS form's replacement cost coverage applies to personal property as well as to the dwelling.

Special Limitations to Certain Classes of Property

Some of the special limits applying to certain classes of property are increased in AAIS HO 0005. The amounts for securities, electronic devices, watercraft (including their trailers), and trailers not otherwise provided for are increased from $1,500 to $2,500. Further, the limit of $2,500 for theft of jewelry, silver, and guns is broadened so that losing or misplacing items is included.

ISO form HO 00 05 does not change the amounts of the special limits. However, it does add "misplacing or losing" to the special limits for theft of jewelry, firearms, and silverware.

Incidental Coverages—AAIS HO 0005

AAIS increases the limits applying to certain of the incidental property coverages and adds a new coverage. The amount available for debris removal is equal to the limit applying to the damaged property, with an additional 5 percent of the applicable limit available should that amount be insufficient.

Ordinance or law coverage is limited to 10 percent of the coverage A limit. The limit for a fire department service charge is $1,000 per occurrence. The limit applying to loss resulting from credit card, forgery, or acceptance of counterfeit money is $5,000 per occurrence, as is the limit applying to grave markers.

Finally, the AAIS form adds an incidental coverage for lock and garage door transmitter replacement. If the keys to the insured residence are lost or stolen, or the transmitter to the automatic garage door is lost or stolen, $500 is available to replace the exterior locks and transmitter. The insured must notify the insurer in writing within seventy-two hours of discovering the loss.

The ISO HO 00 05 does not alter or amend the additional coverages; they are identical to those of the HO 00 03.

Open Perils Exclusions

Both AAIS HO 0005 and ISO HO 00 05 provide open perils coverage for dwelling, related private structures, and contents and promise to insure property described under coverages A, B, and C for risks of direct physical loss, unless the cause of loss is excluded. The HO 0003 and HO 00 03 general exclusions applying to coverages A and B apply as well in forms HO 0005 and HO 00 05 to coverages A, B, and C; they were discussed in Chapter 6. (These are the exclusions such as the one for freezing if the insured has not used reasonable care to maintain heat or shut off the water supply.)

A separate set of exclusions, therefore, applies only to property insured under coverage C. The first exclusion is for loss caused by breakage of fragile articles such as eyeglasses, glassware, marble, and porcelains. Jewelry, watches, bronzes, cameras, and photographic lenses are excepted. However, any breakage caused by the following is covered (quoting the ISO form):

a. Fire, lightning, windstorm, hail;

b. Smoke, other than smoke from agricultural smudging or industrial operations;

c. Explosion, riot, civil commotion;

d. Aircraft, vehicles, vandalism and malicious mischief;

e. Collapse of a building or any part of a building;

f. Water not otherwise excluded;

g. Theft or attempted theft; or

h. Sudden and accidental tearing apart, cracking, burning or bulging of:

   (1) A steam or hot water heating system;

   (2) An air conditioning or automatic fire protective sprinkler system; or

   (3) An appliance for heating water.

The AAIS form adds that breakage caused by "collapse of a building or a part of a building or the impairment of the structural integrity of a building or a part of a building" is covered, as well as breakage caused by one of the "specified perils," which are essentially the AAIS broad form (HO 0002) named perils.

Certain other exclusions apply to coverage C. Loss caused by dampness or extremes of temperature is not covered unless the direct cause of loss is rain, snow, sleet, or hail. Loss caused by refinishing, renovating, or repairing property other than jewelry, watches, or furs is not covered. If property is being restored by a professional, that person is presumed to know what he is doing. This exclusion can be mistakenly applied. It is intended to apply to work in progress, and not to an unrelated event, or even a related event but one distant in time. For example, an antiques restorer might be refinishing a table. If he applies too much solvent and mars the table, there is no coverage. But say he accidentally knocks over a can of solvent, and a lighted cigarette falls and ignites the solvent. In the resulting fire the table is destroyed. There is coverage since the loss did not result from the act of refinishing.

AAIS form HO 0005 excludes loss to watercraft caused by collision, sinking, swamping, or stranding, except for collision of the watercraft with a motorized vehicle. ISO form HO 00 05 excludes loss under coverage C caused by "collision, other than collision with a land vehicle, sinking, swamping or stranding of watercraft, including their trailers, furnishings, equipment and outboard engines or motors." Thus, the ISO insured is left with the possibility of a claim's being denied if a cruise ship sinks and he loses personal property, since the exclusion appears to apply to any property insured under coverage C and not just to an insured's own watercraft.

The coverage C exclusion for loss resulting from destruction, confiscation or seizure by order of any government or public authority (C.5. in the 2000 form) has been deleted. Since the exclusion appears in the Section I exclusions (those prefaced by the anti-concurrent language), where it refers to coverages A, B, and C, there is no need to include it here. There is no coverage for loss caused by any act or failure to act of a person, group, organization, or government body. The ISO form excepts any ensuing loss not otherwise excluded. The AAIS form's exclusion for seizure of property is found in the section "Exclusions That Apply to Property Coverages." Like the ISO form, the exclusion for acts or failure to act contains an exception for an ensuing loss not otherwise covered.

Both forms provide coverage for personal property in an exception to the water damage exclusion. Water damage to coverage C property is covered *if* the property is away from a premises or location owned, rented, occupied, or controlled by an insured. Property could be left in a packing crate in a warehouse and damaged by a sewer backup, for example. The loss would be covered.

Loss Settlement Provisions

The loss settlement provisions of the HO 00 05 are identical to those found in the HO 00 03.

AAIS form HO 0005, however, includes replacement cost coverage for personal property in the policy itself, rather than adding the coverage by endorsement. Replacement cost coverage applies to property covered under coverage C, and these classes of personal property if scheduled on the policy and not subject to agreed value loss settlement: jewelry, furs, cameras, musical instruments, silverware, golfer's equipment, and bicycles. Obviously, replacement cost will not apply to articles such as antiques or artwork that cannot be duplicated, memorabilia, poorly maintained items, or outdated and stored items. Settlement for these items is subject to actual cash value terms. Replacement settlement is the smallest of: 1) the cost to replace without deduction for depreciation; or 2) the full cost, at the time of loss, to repair the damaged part of the property. The insurer pays no more than actual cash value, if the loss is more than $500, until actual repair or replacement is completed.

Chapter 13

Common Endorsements

Introduction

Although many people are adequately insured by unendorsed homeowners forms, a careful review soon indicates many clients need modified, enhanced, or broadened coverage. Simply put, it is rare today for a policy to exist in a completely unendorsed form. The endorsements included in this chapter are those most commonly used to tailor coverage. Both AAIS and ISO have a broad range of useful endorsements that might be considered for any particular client's needs.

Because of the new edition, ISO has developed transition forms to be used with the HO 00 02 (HO 00 22 05 11), HO 00 03 (HO 00 23 05 11), HO 00 04 (HO 00 23 05 11), HO 00 05 (HO 00 25 05 11), HO 00 06 (HO 00 26 05 11), and HO 00 08 (HO 00 28 05 11). These forms contain the new or revised language, and effectively transition a 2000 form into a 2011 form.

Three final notes: 1) the following are brief descriptions. Please refer to the endorsement itself to verify the coverage and any restrictive language. 2) Not all endorsements may be used with all homeowners forms. For example, AAIS endorsement HO 2708 water backup and sump discharge or overflow, may not be used with HO 0008. 3) Many endorsements for the HO 00 06 were discussed in Chapter 12, so they are not included here.

Following are descriptions of commonly used endorsements, grouped by category.

Modifying the Insured

Insuring a Personal Trust

The ISO program includes an endorsement that provides coverage for a residence held in trust. Previously, coverage for this type of arrangement depended upon an insurer's agreeing to show a trust as a named insured. An obvious hindrance to insuring this type of property is policy language itself. For example, "you" and "your" refer to the named insured shown in the declarations and the spouse. A trust cannot have a spouse. And, if the trustee shown as named insured does not reside in the insured residence, who is responsible for maintaining the dwelling and the premises? Although some insurers permitted use of the additional insured endorsement (HO 04 41) this arrangement was never entirely satisfactory.

Endorsement HO 05 43, residence held in trust, has been replaced in the 2011 forms edition. The current endorsement is HO 06 15 05 11, entitled "trust endorsement." The policy can be issued in the name of the trust holding legal title (the trust must be recognized under applicable state law as a legal entity with the capacity to sue or be sued, according to the endorsement) to the insured residence. ISO notes that not all states recognize a trust as a legal entity; in those states an alternative endorsement will be filed. It is assumed that the trustee regularly resides in the residence. The definition of "business" is amended to include activities performed by the trustee in connection with administering the trust. Liability for the trustee is limited to bodily injury or property damage arising out of the ownership, maintenance, or use of the residence premises.

AAIS has two endorsements that may be used for a personal trust. Both are additional insured endorsements and provide coverage for the trust as an additional insured rather than as a named insured as in the ISO endorsement. Endorsement HO 6072 (ML 0672) provides coverages A, B, C, L, and M, while HO 6041 (ML-41) provides coverages A, B, L, and M. As in the ISO endorsement, liability coverage is limited to incidents arising out of the insured premises.

Nonrelated Residents

Both programs have endorsements that give insured status to residents of the named insured's household who are not relatives of the named insured's. ISO endorsement HO 04 58, other members of your household, insures the person scheduled for coverages C, E, and F. The insurer must be notified within thirty days of a change in residency or status of the person scheduled.

AAIS endorsement HO 6033 (ML-433), other residents of your household, extends certain property and liability coverages to the person identified in the endorsement's schedule. The earlier endorsement amended the definition of "insured" to include the person; the current one does not. The endorsement specifically states that this person has no coverage under A, B, or fair rental value under D. The person has insured status only while resident of the named insured's household; if the person stops living with the named insured the named insured has thirty days to notify the insurer.

Relative in Assisted Living Facility

Endorsement HO 04 59, assisted living care coverage, attaches to an insured's homeowners policy and provides coverage for a relative who resides in an assisted living facility. The name of the relative and the name and location of the facility are scheduled. Coverage C and coverage E limits are scheduled. The special limits of liability are amended so that coverage is limited for certain items, such as medical alert devices. The endorsement also provides additional living expense (limited to $500 per month for no more than twelve consecutive months) if a coverage C named peril makes the facility unfit to live in.

The 2011 form has been revised in that the deductible provision has been removed. The deductible in the underlying policy applies (as it did in the earlier edition); the earlier wording stated that if a single loss event resulted in damage to both personal property in the underlying policy and the personal property of the assisted living resident, then the deductible applied only once. The changed language in the forms (e.g., the HO 00 03 05 11) states that only the total of all loss payable exceeding the deductible will be paid. Therefore, there is no need to repeat the deductible provision in the HO 04 59.

The equivalent AAIS endorsement is HO 6235, coverage for resident of assisted living facility. There was no previous endorsement. Amounts of coverage (up to $10,000 coverage C, $6,000 coverage D, and $100,000 coverage L) are scheduled. As with the ISO form, coverage for certain items, such as walking aids, wheelchairs, and medical alert devices, is limited. Additional living expense is limited to $500 per month for no more than twelve consecutive months. Increased costs due to action of civil authority are limited to $50 per day not to exceed two weeks.

Student Away at School

As discussed in Chapter 5, the ISO forms have amended the definition of *insured* to include full-time student relatives under age twenty-four or full-time unrelated students under age twenty-one in the care of an insured. Many times related or unrelated students attend school part-time or beyond age twenty-four. ISO endorsement HO 05 27, additional insured—student living away from the residence premises, allows relative students or others under age twenty-one in the care of an insured to be given insured status. The name, address, and school must be scheduled. These insureds must have been residents of the named insured's household prior to leaving to attend school.

The equivalent AAIS endorsement is HO 6036 (there was no previous endorsement), additional insured—student living away from the described location. Because the current AAIS forms define "insured" as including the named insured's relatives under age 25 who were residents of the named insured's household prior to moving out to attend school, the endorsement is for students over age twenty-five or those under age twenty-one in the care of an insured; in other words, those who do not qualify as insureds as defined in the policy. As with the ISO form, the name, address, and school must be indicated on the endorsement.

Additional Interest or Insured

It is often necessary to provide coverage for someone other than a mortgagee who possesses an insurable interest in the dwelling. This may be accomplished by attaching ISO endorsement HO 04 10, additional interests. This endorsement states that if the policy is cancelled the named parties will be notified in writing, although no time frame for doing this is given. The equivalent AAIS endorsement is HO 6034, additional interests. There was no previous endorsement.

An *additional interest* is different from an *additional insured*. An additional interest has an insurable interest in the property; an additional insured may have the same insurable interest but additionally needs coverage for liability exposures arising from the insured premises. AAIS form HO 6041, additional insured, may be used for both purposes: to cover the insurable interest in the described property and the necessary premises liability. The equivalent ISO form is HO 04 41, additional insured, which provides for insurable interest coverage in the dwelling as well as coverage for bodily injury or property damage arising out of the insured premises.

These endorsements do not provide comprehensive liability coverage to the additional insured. They provide premises liability coverage only. Medical payments to others coverage applies only with respect to the insured residence premises.

Modifying Coverage A

Although many of the endorsements that follow modify dwelling coverage, remember that coverage A means additions and alterations for the condominium or unit owner.

Dwelling Under Construction–Theft

Both ISO and AAIS exclude coverage for theft in or to a dwelling being built or of building materials. AAIS also excludes theft in or to a newly constructed dwelling until it is occupied. Currently, only AAIS allows an insured to purchase coverage for this exposure by attaching endorsement HO 2722, residence under construction (theft). A dollar amount is chosen, which applies on a per occurrence basis. This amount does not increase the limit of liability applying to the dwelling. Because of the wording of the endorsement—theft in or to a dwelling under construction—the coverage can apply to items of real or personal property in the dwelling.

ISO has developed an endorsement, HO 06 07 05 11 limited coverage for theft of personal property located in a dwelling under construction. It is discussed under the **Modifying Coverage C** heading.

Earthquake Coverage

Homeowners forms exclude coverage for loss resulting from *earth movement*. An ISO insured may add earthquake as an insured peril for coverages A (dwelling), B (other structures), and C (contents) by adding endorsement HO 04 54, earthquake. The AAIS insured may add the coverage by attaching endorsement HO 2754, earthquake coverage.

Both forms define the peril of earthquake as including land shock waves or tremors accompanying a volcanic eruption. (The unendorsed policies cover damage resulting from the *airborne* shock waves of a volcanic eruption but not damage caused by land shock waves.) In both ISO and AAIS forms, a single earthquake includes all earthquake shocks that occur within a seventy-two hour period.

Like other forms of earthquake insurance, these endorsements exclude flood, tidal wave, or tsunami (a new addition in ISO's 05 11 form), even when caused or contributed to by earthquake. By adding earthquake coverage the insured is adding two named perils; earthquake and land shock waves in conjunction with volcanic eruption.

Masonry veneer coverage is optional in both forms; if excluded, the deductible applies to the applicable limit minus the value of this veneer. Stucco is not included within the meaning of masonry veneer.

Coverage under the endorsement is provided *within the applicable limits of liability* and does not include the cost of filling land. In effect, the endorsement provides an *extension* of coverages A, B, and C. Both forms contain a percentage deductible provision. The dollar amount of the deductible is determined by multiplying either coverage A, dwelling, or coverage C, personal property, whichever is greater, by the percentage. This deductible then applies to all loss under section I property, except for coverage D and the additional or, in the AAIS form, certain incidental coverages. ISO does not permit a deductible of less than $500; The AAIS minimum is $250.

Inflation Guard

These endorsements (ISO HO 04 46 and AAIS HO 2584) provide for automatic increases in the limits of liability for all section I property coverages in order to avoid underinsurance due to inflation. The specified percentage increase is effective on a pro rata basis during the policy period.

Thus, if a loss occurs during the policy period, the percentage is multiplied by the coverage A limit, and prorated from the prior renewal date until the date of loss. The insured then has an additional amount of insurance, even though it might be small.

Ordinance or Law

Loss resulting from the operation of laws regulating the construction, repair, or demolition of a structure is an additional coverage in both the standard AAIS and ISO programs, except for HO 0008 and HO 00 08. ISO endorsement HO 04 77, ordinance or law increased amount of coverage, therefore may be used to provide an increased amount of coverage. The AAIS equivalent is AAIS endorsement HO 2557, increased cost—ordinance or law.

Unit Owners Special Coverage

Coverage for a unit owners' additions and alterations on the HO 00 06 and HO 0006 is on a named peril basis. ISO's unit-owners coverage A special coverage, HO 17 32, and AAIS's unit-owners additions special coverage, HO 7032, provide open perils coverage, similar to that of the HO 00 03 and HO 0003. The endorsements were discussed in Chapter 12.

Water Back Up and Sump Discharge or Overflow

Loss caused by water, whether flood, surface water, or water that backs up through a sewer or drain, is excluded (see Chapter 6). Insureds may, however, purchase limited coverage for this exposure. AAIS HO 2708, water back up and sump discharge or overflow, and ISO HO 04 95, water back up and sump discharge or overflow, provide up to $5,000 (more in the case of the 2011 ISO form) to cover water (or water-borne material or matter present in water) that backs up through sewers or drains or water that overflows from within a sump or sump pump.

As noted, ISO insureds are now able to purchase additional amounts of insurance—$10,000, $15,000, $20,000, or $25,000 amounts are available.

ISO has revised the 2011 form somewhat. It now states that the insurer pays for direct physical loss not caused by the negligence of an insured, caused by water or waterborne material which "originates from within the dwelling where you reside" and backs up through sewers or drains. Although it was always the intent to cover water coming up through a drain, say, because of a heavy downpour and the municipal's system's inability to handle the water, this language now clarifies that the water must actually come up into—originate from within—the dwelling, rather than entering the dwelling in some other manner.

The AAIS form includes that loss caused by water that "enters into and overflows from within a sump ... or other type of system designed to remove subsurface water which is drained from the foundation area" is covered, leaving open the possibility that water overflowing a system of drain tiles is covered.

Both forms add that backup of sewer, drain, or sump pump overflow that is a result of flood is not covered. The AAIS form applies a $250 deductible; in the 2011 ISO form, the deductible is that in the policy itself. Although loss resulting from mechanical breakdown of a sump pump is covered, loss to the pump itself is not.

Modifying Coverage B

The normal homeowners forms allow 10 percent of the coverage A amount to be applied to other unattached structures not used for business purposes on the residence premises. There are times when this amount is insufficient or when the structures are not located on the residence premises. These endorsements fill that void. (Endorsements relating to business use appear later in this chapter.)

Increased Limit—Other Structures

The coverage for other or related private structures on the insured premises may be increased. Individual structures may be scheduled on these endorsements with a designated amount of insurance applying to each. Use of these endorsements does not increase the coverage B amount of the policy; instead, the endorsements make available an *additional* amount of coverage for the described structure. For example, if the coverage B amount is $5,000, and $10,000 is needed for adequate coverage on a particular structure, ISO HO 04 48, other structures on the residence premises—increased limits, or AAIS HO 3048 (ML-48), related private structures, are used to write the *additional* $5,000 insurance on that building. If two or more eligible structures are on the premises, thought should be given to the risk of their *simultaneous* destruction when considering the adequacy of coverage B.

Other Structures Away From Premises

Many times insureds have other structures that are at another location, a barn or shed on a garden plot, for example. So long as the structure is not capable of being used as a dwelling and is not used for business purposes (other than rented to a tenant of the insured premises and not used for business), the structure may be insured in either of two ways. The first method is to attach AAIS HO 6217, related private structures—away from premises, or ISO HO 04 91, coverage B—other structures away from the residence premises. Coverage B then applies to other structures off the residence premises. These endorsements do not provide an additional amount of insurance, so if the insured has structures both on the residence premises and away, this must be taken into account.

The second method is to schedule individual structures (with a limit of insurance for each) by attaching AAIS HO 6218, scheduled related private structures, or ISO HO 04 92, specific structures away from the residence premises. Since the structures are away from the insured premises, the regular homeowners coverage B amount *does not* apply. This must be considered when arranging coverage.

Modifying Coverage C

Basic homeowners forms (obviously not the unit owners or tenants forms) allot 50 percent of the coverage A dwelling amount for personal property coverage. Although some insurers automatically provide up to 70 percent of the coverage A amount, this is by no means standard. Coverage C may be increased by showing the new limit on the declarations page. An additional premium applies. Below are other ways of enhancing coverage.

Coverage for Property in a Self-Storage Unit

As discussed in Chapter 2, ISO limits coverage to 10 percent or $1,000, whichever is greater, for personal property contained in a self-storage unit. By attaching endorsement HO 06 14 05 11, the insured can schedule an amount of coverage. The scheduled amount then replaces the 10 percent or $1,000. The policy deductible applies to any loss.

Computer Coverage

ISO endorsement HO 04 14, special computer coverage, may be used by homeowners or unit owners who do not have *open perils* coverage on personal property to provide coverage for computers and computer equipment against additional covered causes of loss. The ISO form defines computer equipment as: "1. computer hardware, software, operating systems or networks; and 2.

other electronic parts, equipment or systems solely designed for use with or connected to equipment in 1. above." Subject to certain exclusions, coverage is modified to cover such property on an *open perils* basis.

This endorsement does not give an additional amount of insurance, nor does it delete the limitation for property used in business. It merely provides broader coverage for computer equipment.

AAIS endorsement HO 2770, computer coverage, provides open perils coverage and, like the ISO endorsement, does not provide an additional amount of insurance or delete the limitations on certain property or delete the exclusions for certain property. Coverage is an open perils basis, subject to certain exclusions. The policy deductible applies. Computer equipment means computer hardware, including pcs, laptops, and peripherals, and computer software, including media, programs, and data.

Open Perils Coverage for Personal Property

AAIS endorsement HO 7029, unit-owners coverage C, and ISO endorsement HO 17 31, unit-owners coverage C special coverage, provide open perils coverage for unit owners. These were discussed in Chapter 12. A tenant may attach either AAIS HO 2730, coverage C—personal property, or ISO HO 05 24, special personal property coverage, for open perils coverage.

The 1991 ISO program did not include an HO 00 05. Open perils coverage could be added to the HO 00 03 by attaching HO 00 15. But with the advent of the ISO 2000 homeowners program, which includes the HO 00 05, endorsement HO 00 15 has been withdrawn. (Many insurers still use the 1991 form. Please check with your insurer.) ISO HO 00 05 and AAIS HO 0005 were discussed in Chapter 12.

Scheduling Personal Property

Agent Tip

Many insureds do not realize the need for scheduled coverage until after a loss. Unfortunately, for many agents, questioning about rare, unique, or valuable items is limited to "Got any expensive jewelry?" The client might not have any one piece valued at more than $2,000 (an engagement ring, perhaps), but those gold necklaces and a diamond tennis bracelet add up quickly. That camcorder and the Nikon camera could use special treatment. How about artwork? The average homeowner has property that should be afforded scheduled coverage.

Agents must educate their clients when property is scheduled. Although some insurers' schedules are on an agreed value basis for

> *all* items scheduled, until recently standard forms provided agreed value coverage only for fine arts. (See the following discussion.) In that case, the amount the fine art is scheduled for is agreed to be the value of the piece. Other items are adjusted as discussed later in this section. Many insureds think that, since they pay premium on a diamond ring valued at $10,000, they should receive that amount in event of a loss. But the settlement provisions without the agreed value provisions allow the insurer to replace the ring for $7,000 if able to do so.

Personal articles insurance may be written in conjunction with a homeowners policy by using ISO endorsement HO 04 61, scheduled personal property endorsement, or AAIS endorsement HO 3061, scheduled personal property coverage. This makes it convenient for a homeowners insured who wishes to broaden the scope of coverage on personal property to an *open perils* basis or who has value in excess of the limits specified in the homeowners form for certain categories of property, such as jewelry, furs, cameras, musical instruments, silverware, golfer's equipment, fine arts, postage stamps, and coins. Damage resulting from flood or earthquake is covered; only causes of loss that are virtually impossible to insure against are excluded, such as war, nuclear hazard, and wear and tear. (This is not a complete list. Consult the endorsement.)

Both programs now allow property such as jewelry and cameras, as well as fine arts, to be scheduled on an agreed value basis. Loss settlement thus results in fewer acrimonious feelings on an insured's part. Under the ISO form, in the event of loss to a pair or set consisting of several parts, the agreed amount is paid. The insurer has the right to take any property not lost or stolen after payment has been made. This is endorsement HO 04 60. The AAIS form is HO 3063 for agreed value loss settlement. The AAIS loss settlement for pairs or sets differs from the ISO. The insurer agrees to pay to restore the pair or set, or to pay the difference in actual cash value immediately before the loss and immediately afterward. If there is a loss to a part of an item consisting of several parts, the value of the lost or damaged part, or the cost to repair or replace it, is paid.

It is important to remember the coverage C exclusion of "articles separately described and specifically insured in this or any other insurance" or "property covered by scheduled insurance" when deciding on amounts of insurance to be inserted in the endorsement. The coverage C amount will not contribute in case of loss to any property insured in the endorsement, so it is important that each item be scheduled for an adequate amount of coverage.

The full effect of the "other insurance" provision can be avoided if an insured chooses not to schedule blanket items (such as *silverware*) in the endorsement, but instead lists only the more valuable items specifically, i.e., "a four-piece service for eight of ABC brand silverware, ~'Huntress' pattern." Other silverware items in the household thus escape the "other insurance" provision and continue to have the protection of coverage C. (The special limits may be increased by using HO 04 65, HO 04 66, or HO 2565).

Losses on the HO 04 61 and HO 3061 are settled at the lesser of: the actual cash value at the time of loss, the amount for which the property could reasonably be repaired or replaced. Losses to fine arts are settled on an agreed value basis on both forms.

Coverage for fine arts is limited to the United States and Canada in the ISO form. Other classes of property are covered anywhere in the world. AAIS covers scheduled property anywhere in the world, but with regard to fine arts, the premium is based on the insured's statement that the property is on the described location, or at another address shown on the schedule. Each form provides coverage (limited as to time and amount) for certain newly acquired classes of property.

Theft Coverage–Rented Unit

It is not uncommon for a homeowner to hold for rent, say, a seasonal dwelling on an occasional basis, particularly if it is located in a desirable area. Remember, a dwelling regularly rented to others should be covered on a dwelling fire policy.

AAIS has two endorsements that may be used when the insured premises is rented on an occasional basis. The first is HO 2736, residence rented to others, which may be used when an insured residence is rented on an occasional basis. The endorsement cannot be used with the form HO 0005. Theft caused by: a tenant, roomer, or boarder; or a member of a household of one of these; or an employee of one of these, is covered while the insured premises usually occupied by the insured is rented. There is no coverage, though, for theft of valuable property such as money, silver, securities, jewelry, etc.

ISO also has two endorsements that may be used when the insured premises is rented. Endorsement HO 05 41, extended theft coverage for residence premises occasionally rented to others, provides coverage for theft of personal property *even if* the theft is caused by a tenant, roomer, or boarder, members of the tenant's household, or their employees. Excluded is coverage for theft of money, silver, securities, jewelry, etc. The endorsement may not be used with the HO 00 05.

The second endorsements of each program, to be used with forms HO 0006 and HO 00 06, are the HO 7033 (AAIS) and HO 17 33 (ISO) These endorsements were discussed in Chapter 12.

Theft Coverage—Personal Property in a Dwelling under Construction

ISO has developed an endorsement (HO 06 07 05 11) which may be used to provide theft coverage for personal property located in a dwelling under construction. The coverage begins on the inception date shown in the schedule, and ends on the earliest of the termination date shown in the schedule, or the date the dwelling is completed and occupied. Because the endorsement deletes paragraph B.9.b.(2) of the HO 00 03, the elimination of coverage for theft of personal property in or to a dwelling under construction, or of materials and supplies for use in the construction, it is clear that the endorsement would not apply to give coverage if, for example, a thief stole copper piping already installed in the dwelling.

Physical Damage Coverage for a Golf Cart

AAIS endorsement HO 3831, scheduled motorized golf cart coverage, and ISO endorsement HO 05 28, owned motorized golf cart physical loss coverage, provide physical damage coverage for golf carts. Collision is an optional peril. ISO rules specify a $500 deductible applied separately to each scheduled golf cart; the AAIS rules allow choice of deductible, although the rating information is based on a $500 deductible.

Refrigerated Property Coverage

ISO endorsement HO 04 98, refrigerated property coverage, provides coverage for loss of up to $500 worth of refrigerated property if loss results from interruption of electrical service to the refrigeration unit or mechanical failure of the unit storing the property. A $100 deductible applies.

The AAIS endorsement HO 2530 allows an increase in coverage above the $500 for refrigerated property found in the incidental coverages. This endorsement can also be used to increase the incidental coverages for: association deductible; credit card; fire department service charge; liquid fuel remediation; and tenant's improvements.

Modifying Loss Settlement

The following endorsements may be used to modify various loss settlement provisions.

Actual Cash Value

Some states have determined that actual cash value must be used as a loss settlement provision rather than cost to repair or replace. Therefore, before attaching either ISO HO 04 81, which is required with the HO 00 08, or AAIS HO 4815, check carefully to see if this form is applicable.

"Guaranteed" Rebuilding

Although neither ISO nor AAIS has a "guaranteed" rebuilding endorsement, both programs have endorsements that will fill the needs of many insureds. ISO has two endorsements, which may be used only with an HO 02, HO 03, or HO 00 05. The first, HO 04 20, specified additional amount of insurance for coverage A—dwelling, makes an additional amount equal to either 25 percent or 50 percent of the coverage A limit to apply to a covered loss. This amount cannot be used to apply to coverages B, C, or D. The second is HO 04 11, additional limits of liability for coverages A, B, C, and D. In the event of a covered loss, the limits of liability on the policy will be amended to equal the current replacement cost of the dwelling. Coverages B, C, and D will be increased, by the same percentage applied to coverage A, retroactive to the date of the loss. Both endorsements require that the insured maintain insurance at full replacement value and report any alterations that increase the dwelling's value by 5 percent or more.

AAIS likewise has two endorsements. HO 4844, specified additional amount of insurance, is used to increase coverage A by the percentage selected by the insured. HO 4843, additional limits, is used to increase coverage A, and therefore coverages B, C, and D, in event of a loss.

Functional Replacement

Standard homeowners forms promise to repair or replace with like kind and quality in event of a covered loss. However, the cost to insure many older, ornate dwellings for full replacement value may be prohibitive. It is possible to insure a dwelling for *functional* replacement so that a covered loss will be settled with the amount to repair or replace using common construction methods and materials. Functional replacement cost means "the amount which it would cost to repair or replace the damaged building with less costly common construction materials and methods which are functionally equivalent to obsolete, antique or custom construction materials and methods used in the original construction of the building." For example, a coved plaster ceiling may be replaced with drywall. Endorsement HO 05 30, functional replacement cost loss settlement, may be attached to an HO 00 02, HO 00 03, or HO 00 05. AAIS rules permit HO 4857 functional replacement cost loss settlement terms, to be attached to forms HO 0001, HO 0002, or HO 0003.

Coverage B Replacement Cost

Full replacement is available for buildings insured under coverage B of the standard homeowners forms. ISO has introduced endorsement HO 04 43, replacement cost loss settlement for certain nonbuilding structures on the residence premises. Replacement loss settlement is provided for driveways; reinforced masonry walls; metal, PVC, or fiberglass fences; and patios or walks not made of wood. The 2011 form now includes inground or semi-inground swimming pools, therapeutic baths, or hot tubs that have walls and floors made of reinforced masonry, cement, metal, or fiberglass. Note that hot tubs simply sitting on a patio or deck are not reached by this endorsement, since they are neither inground nor semi-inground.

The AAIS endorsement for this coverage is HO 4832. Replacement loss settlement terms apply to reinforced masonry walls, fences made of metal, fiberglass, or plastic and/or resin, patios and walks not made of wood or wood products, and driveways.

Personal Property Replacement Cost

Loss settlement provisions for personal property, carpeting, awnings, and other items are on an actual cash value basis in the unendorsed policy forms (except for AAIS form HO 0005). ISO endorsement HO 04 90, personal property cost loss settlement, and AAIS endorsement HO 4855, replacement cost loss settlement terms, are used to provide homeowners replacement cost coverage (otherwise available only for buildings) on personal property, awnings, carpeting, household appliances, and outdoor equipment (including antennas). Certain items of property that are separately described and specifically insured in the policy also receive replacement cost treatment under these endorsements. The forms specify that items in this second category are limited to: jewelry; furs and fur-trimmed or fur garments; cameras, projection machines, films, and related equipment; musical equipment and related items; silverware, silverplated ware, goldware, goldplated ware, platinum, platinum-plated ware, and pewterware (but not pens, pencils, flasks, smoking implements, or jewelry in the ISO form); golf clubs, golf clothing, or golf equipment. The AAIS form includes bicycles.

Recovery for all property insured under the ISO endorsement is limited to the smallest of five amounts: 1) replacement cost at the time of loss; 2) the full repair cost; 3) the coverage C limit, if applicable; 4) any applicable special limits; or 5) the limit that applies to any item separately described and specifically insured in the policy. However, this last loss settlement provision does not apply to items that are subject to agreed value loss settlement. The AAIS form's loss settlement terms for replacement cost are the smaller of the cost to replace the lost or damaged property without a deduction for depreciation, or the full cost, at the time of loss, to repair the damaged part of the property.

Four categories of property are not eligible for replacement cost coverage: 1) antiques, fine arts, and similar property; 2) memorabilia, souvenirs, collector's items, and the like; 3) property not kept in good or workable condition; and 4) obsolete articles that are stored or not being used. The first two categories represent types of property for which an accurate replacement value cannot be determined. (Fine arts and antiques are often scheduled for *agreed value* coverage. If allowed to remain under the homeowners policy's actual cash value provisions such property is covered for its market value.) The last two categories comprise property for which replacement cost recovery would violate the indemnity principle and perhaps invite a moral hazard.

For losses with a replacement value of more than $500, actual repair or replacement must be made before the replacement cost provisions are applicable. An actual cash value claim can be made at the time of loss and amended to replacement cost within 180 days.

Modifying "Business" Coverage

There are various methods that may be used to amend coverage for property, both real and personal, used in business, as well as the liability exposures. Remember, however, that for the most part these endorsements provide only *incidental* coverage and are subordinate to the homeowners forms' primary purpose—to insure the dwelling *as a residence*. Both AAIS and ISO have developed coverage forms that address the current explosion of home-based businesses. These forms will be touched upon briefly, since they are, in many respects, akin to the commercial businessowners forms.

Home-based Business

The number of home-based businesses in the country is growing rapidly, thanks in large part to the computer and the Internet. Both ISO and AAIS have developed extensive endorsements to fill this need. The ISO endorsement is IIO 07 01 (but chcck; othcr cndorscmcnts arc spccific to statcs; for cxamplc, Missouri's form is HO 07 02); the AAIS endorsement is ML-450 (there is no newer edition). Target markets and acceptability vary, so consult the underwriting guidelines of any given insurer.

The endorsements provide coverage for both business property and liability for a variety of home businesses. The business must be owned by the named insured, or by a partnership, joint venture, or organization comprised solely of the named insured and resident relatives. Coverage is included for business property, property of others in the insured's care because of the business, and business property leased by the insured so long as there is a contractual responsibility to insure it. There is coverage for valuable papers and records and accounts receivable (optional on the AAIS form). The AAIS form, since it may be used to insure a bed and breakfast, includes as optional coverages guests' personal property, related private structures, and spoilage of perishable stock.

Time element coverages include business income, extended business income, extra expense, and loss of business income because of the action of civil authority (subject to a seventy-two hour time deductible in the ISO form).

There is liability coverage for premises operations, products, advertising injury, and personal injury (the latter two are optional in the AAIS form). The exclusion of liability arising out of or in connection with a *business* is changed so that the exclusion does not apply to *your product* (ISO) or *products* (AAIS), or *your work,* all defined terms. There is, however, no coverage for professional services, many of which are listed in the ISO endorsement.

Home Day Care

Property and liability coverage for a home day care business is available to a homeowner under ISO endorsement HO 04 97, home day care coverage. The ISO manual rules do not specify a limit as to number of persons; however, premium is based on one to three persons, other than insureds, receiving care. The AAIS rules specify no more than three persons. The AAIS endorsement is HO 3557 care provided for others. If the business is conducted in another structure on the residence premises, a limit of liability for that structure must be scheduled on the endorsement. The endorsement protects personal property of the described business under the total coverage C limit.

In addition to the standard policy liability exclusions, liability coverage is excluded for: maintenance, use, loading, unloading, or entrustment by the insured to others of draft or saddle animals, or vehicles used with them; aircraft; and all motorized land conveyances or watercraft, whether owned, operated, or hired by or for the insured or employee, or used by the insured for instruction in their use. Excluded also is injury to any employee of an insured (other than a residence employee) arising out of the day care operation.

Since the current homeowners forms exclude coverage for bodily injury or property damage arising out of sexual molestation, there is no exclusion in the endorsements.

These endorsements also impose a policy year aggregate limit for liability and medical payments combined. The limit corresponds to the ISO coverage E or AAIS coverage L limit shown in the declarations, with a further per person accident sublimit for day care related medical payments equal to the coverage F or M limit. The sublimit applies within the aggregate limit of liability. Limits described on the endorsement apply even if contrary to those contained in the policy or declarations. The severability of insurance clause specifies that coverage applies separately to insureds *except with respect to the aggregate limit*, so the aggregate limit remains unaffected by the number of insureds.

Before adding either endorsement, consult your insurer to verify their acceptance.

Business Not Owned by Insured—Liability Coverage

When the insured does not own, financially control, or have a partnership interest in a business, these endorsements may provide needed liability coverage. Of particular interest is the provision for liability coverage for teachers, including (at an extra charge) administering corporal punishment. Salespersons, messengers, collectors, or clerical workers may be covered for liability. The ISO endorsement is HO 24 71, business pursuits; the AAIS endorsement is HO 3571, business activities.

Incidental Business on Premises—Liability Coverage

Many homeowners exclusions apply to business activities of an insured. These endorsements, AAIS HO 3542, office, professional, private school, or studio occupancy, and ISO HO 04 42, permitted incidental occupancies—residence premises, delete the exclusions as they pertain to a business conducted *on the residence premises.* The premises must be occupied principally as the insured's residence; the business must be conducted by an insured; and there can be no other business conducted on the premises. Office, studio, or private school (such as music or dance instruction) purposes are the contemplated exposures.

Because coverage B of the homeowners form does not apply to any structures used for business purposes, the endorsement provides for scheduling a specified amount of coverage for an other structure on the residence premises that is used in a business. The homeowners forms limit the amount of coverage for on-premises business property to $2,500. This endorsement increases coverage for on-premises business furnishings, supplies, and equipment to the coverage C limit.

The section II exclusions of liability and medical payments coverages in connection with business pursuits of the insured is likewise modified so that section II coverage applies to the "necessary and incidental use of the premises" for the business described on the endorsement. The liability coverage provided under the endorsement does not include coverage for two types of bodily injury claims: 1) bodily injury to any employee of the insured, except residence employees in the course of their employment; or 2) bodily injury to a pupil arising out of corporal punishment administered by or at the direction of the insured.

Neither of these endorsements provides the broad coverage of the home-based business endorsements.

Increased Limits on Business Property

The insured can increase the amount of coverage for business property on the premises. The ISO endorsement is HO 04 12, and the AAIS is HO 3565. The increased limit is scheduled. In the current ISO form, the special limit of liability applying to business property off premises is increased to 60 percent of the total limit shown in the schedule; the AAIS form provides 20% of the limit.

Modifying Liability Coverage

Agent Tip

Unfortunately, in their zeal to insure property exposures, insured clients often overlook the necessity of reviewing liability exposures. "Those jet skis? What do you mean it's not covered if I run one into someone's dock at the lake?" "So I wrote a letter to the editor of the local paper calling my neighbor an idiot. That's not covered either? But he *is* an idiot." Although, of course, not all activities are insurable, many of them are. The prudent agent will check all possible sources for potential claims for damages arising out of covered bodily injury or property damage.

Additional Residence–Rented to Others

It is very common for insureds to own rental property. For example, the "starter home" may be kept for investment purposes. Although the dwelling itself must be insured on a dwelling fire policy, liability coverage arising from the rental premises can be extended from the homeowners policy. AAIS endorsement HO 6270, additional residence rented to others, allows additional residence premises to be scheduled; the definition of "residence premises" therefore encompasses the rental property. Similarly, ISO endorsement HO 24 70, additional residence rented to others—1, 2, 3, or 4 families, provides personal liability and medical payments coverage with respect to the insured's liability arising out of the ownership of a residence regularly rented to others. The mechanism for providing these coverages is the definition on the endorsement listing the rented premises as an "insured location." Neither of the endorsements insures the rental property for other than the liability exposure. Dwelling fire policies should be written to cover dwellings and other structures.

Liability coverage for other locations owned by and resided in by an insured are usually indicated on the declarations. No separate endorsement is required.

Farmers Liability

Homeowners policies are not designed to provide coverage for full-scale farming operations. Both ISO and AAIS have farm programs in place. What *can* be endorsed onto the homeowners policy, however, is coverage for the gentleman farmer whose activities do not comprise his or her major source of income.

For liability arising out of incidental farming activities on the insured premises, such as a market garden or grazing of a small number of animals, attach AAIS HO 7540, incidental farming, which amends coverages L and M to apply to the designated farming operations, or ISO HO 24 72, incidental farming personal liability, which amends coverages E and F to apply. Both endorsements may also be used for incidental farming activities at another location away from the insured premises.

Coverage for liability arising out of a farm premises *away from* the insured premises may be endorsed using HO 7500, farm liability coverage, for the AAIS homeowners, and HO 24 73, farmers personal liability, for the ISO homeowners. Both forms amend the definition of "business" so that it does not include farming. Since use of these forms varies significantly by insurer, any farming exposure should be checked carefully with the homeowners underwriter to determine acceptability.

Personal Injury

Personal injury is a frequently overlooked coverage. Endorsements extend coverage for injury arising out of false arrest or imprisonment, wrongful eviction or entry, detention, invasion of privacy, malicious prosecution, libel, slander, or defamation of character. The ISO endorsement is HO 24 82, personal injury, and the AAIS endorsement is HO 4046, personal injury. ISO has introduced endorsement HO 24 10 personal injury coverage—aggregate limit of liability. This endorsement states that the insurer pays damages for which an insured is legally liable "subject to the aggregate limit of liability as shown in the schedule." The aggregate is on an annual basis.

Several exclusions apply. There is no coverage for: 1) oral or written publication of material if done by or at the direction of an insured with knowledge of its falsity; 2) any personal injury to a person if the injury is in any way related to the employment of that person by an insured; 3) injury arising out of a criminal act committed by or at the direction of an insured; 4) personal injury caused by or at the direction of an insured with the knowledge that the act would violate the rights of another. Other exclusions apply; consult the forms.

Recreational Motor Vehicles

Liability coverage for off-premises use of golf carts, snowmobiles, and certain other recreational motor vehicles not subject to motor vehicle registration and capable of achieving no more than 15 mph may be endorsed onto an AAIS homeowners policy. AAIS endorsement HO 3832, golf cart liability coverage, may be used for a golf cart used on a golf course or on public roads within a private residential community.

Liability coverage for snowmobiles used away from the insured premises is provided by endorsement HO 3864, snowmobile liability coverage only. Liability coverage for low power motor vehicles used away from the insured premises is provided by endorsement HO 3828, incidental coverage for motorized vehicles. The endorsement provides liability coverage for vehicles not built to exceed a speed of fifteen miles per hour, and that are not mopeds, golf carts, or motorized bicycles. Remember that both ISO and AAIS now include liability coverage for battery-powered toy vehicles; the miles per hour limit is no more than 15 for the AAIS homeowners, and 5 for the ISO.

The ISO rules allow off-premises liability coverage to be endorsed onto the homeowners for snowmobiles, and recreational motor vehicles not subject to motor vehicle registration and capable of speeds no greater than 15 mph. ISO rules require golf cart liability (for exposures other than those contemplated by the homeowners forms) to be endorsed onto an auto policy. Endorsement HO 24 13, incidental low power recreational motor vehicles, provides liability coverage for vehicles not built to exceed a speed of fifteen miles per hour, and that are not mopeds, golf carts, or motorized bicycles, no matter what speed these vehicles might attain. Endorsement HO 24 64, owned snowmobile, is used for off-premises use of these vehicles. Again, these endorsements provide liability coverage only.

Underwriting requirements of individual insurers may not permit insuring these vehicles. Consult the insurer's underwriting guidelines.

Snowbird alert! It is not uncommon for snowbirds to spend their winters in a community centered around a golf course. Remember that, while the ISO 1991 homeowners policy extends liability coverage for golf carts used for golfing purposes, many persons tend to use the carts to make a trip to the local store. The current ISO and AAIS homeowners cover liability for use of a golf cart within a private residential community. (See Chapter 8.) Make sure your clients are covered.

Waterbed Liability

The AAIS program has an endorsement that a tenant homeowner may well need—coverage for liability arising out of a waterbed. For example, if an insured's waterbed springs a leak, drenching the apartment, there is no coverage under the unendorsed homeowners policy, because only liability coverage for fire, smoke, or explosion damage to property rented to the insured is covered. Endorsement HO 4009, waterbed liability, amends the exclusion so that damage arising out of the insured's ownership of the waterbed is covered. (Coverage for damage to an insured's covered property may be added by endorsement HO 2721.) ISO has two endorsements, HO 24 99 and HO 32 40, for use in Hawaii and North Carolina respectively.

Watercraft Liability

The homeowners policy provides limited coverage for liability arising out of the use of watercraft. When coverage for both the boat and liability is desired, then the best course of action is to write coverage on a boatowners policy. There are times, though, when all that is necessary is liability coverage. In those instances, either AAIS endorsement HO 3875, watercraft, or ISO HO 24 75, watercraft, may be used. The endorsements amend the liability exclusions of the homeowners forms so that "bodily injury" or "property damage" arising out of the ownership, maintenance, use, loading, or unloading of the described watercraft is covered.

Caution! Many types of watercraft are unacceptable, and an agent should not attempt to place these on the homeowners policy. Few companies jump at the chance, for example, to insure a jet boat. Most watercraft of the type termed "personal watercraft" such as jet skis and wet bikes are also unacceptable. Any questionable watercraft should be discussed with the underwriter.

Amending the Mobile Homeowners

The common endorsements used to amend mobile homeowners coverage were discussed in Chapter 12.

Miscellaneous Endorsements

The following endorsements are not easily categorized.

Amending Loss Assessment

The homeowners forms provide a certain amount of loss assessment (ISO $1,000; AAIS $1,500) for assessments made against the insured by his or her property owners association resulting from a loss to commonly owned property or because of a claim for bodily injury or property damage arising out of the property. Additional coverage may be purchased. AAIS endorsement HO 2550 (ML-50), loss assessment coverage, allows limits to be increased both at the described location and at additional locations. ISO endorsement HO 04 35, loss assessment coverage, also allows increased limits both at the insured residence and at additional locations. (If an insured owns a rental condo as well as his or her own, the endorsements may be used to insure all locations.) Neither program will respond to a loss assessed because of a deductible in the association's insurance greater than the basic limit in the unendorsed policy. Remember, though, the current AAIS program includes coverage for association deductible of $1,500, which can be increased.

Loss assessment arising out of an earthquake may be purchased. ISO endorsement HO 04 36, loss assessment coverage for earthquake, and AAIS endorsement HO 2753, earthquake loss assessment, provide coverage. A percentage deductible applies.

Pollution

There is an ISO endorsement that gives limited property and liability coverage for escaped fuel or lead. Endorsement HO 05 80, property remediation for escaped liquid fuel and limited lead and escaped liquid fuel liability coverages, is actually a decrease in coverage and thus subject to a premium credit. Some insurers have been attaching the endorsement to all homeowners policies, when in fact it would not appear to have relevance for the homeowner insured who does not heat with propane or heating oil.

The endorsement allows a scheduled amount of coverage for property remediation and an aggregate limit of liability for lead or escaped fuel.

AAIS allows up to $10,000 for liquid fuel remediation for covered property as an incidental property coverage.

Identity Theft

Both AAIS and ISO offer endorsements to cover the expenses resulting from identity theft or fraud. The AAIS endorsement is HO 2786, identity fraud expense; the ISO endorsement is HO 04 55, identity fraud expense coverage. AAIS allows the limit of coverage to be selected; consult the manual. Identity fraud expense is treated as an additional coverage. A $100 deductible applies. The ISO endorsement limits coverage to up to $15,000 with a $500 deductible (the deductible has been increased from $250 to $500 in the 2011 edition).

Both forms respond to costs often incurred with identity fraud, such as for certified mail to law enforcement agencies and credit bureaus, charges for long distance calls to merchants, etc., to report or discuss an actual identity fraud, notarizing documents attesting to fraud, application fees for re-applying for a loan when the original was denied because of incorrect credit information. Both pay reasonable and necessary attorney fees: to defend suits against an insured by financial institutions, merchants, or collection agencies; to challenge the accuracy of consumer credit reports; and to remove any criminal or civil judgments. Both pay actual loss of earnings from time taken from work to deal with the fraud. The ISO endorsement allows up to a maximum of $200 per day with a total of $5,000 available; the AAIS a maximum of $250 per day, with a total of $5,000 available.

Chapter 14

"Hot Topics"

Certain subjects are regularly brought before the courts for interpretation of coverage. While the courts may unanimously agree on certain things—for example, sexual molestation of a minor by an adult, no matter what the motive, reason, or expressed intent, is not covered as a matter of public policy—there are still many areas of dispute.

Following are three "hot topics": 1) "where you reside" 2) alcohol, drugs, and the homeowners exclusion; and 3) malicious prosecution. Each discussion is of a general nature and contains references to various court interpretations. No discussion should be construed as advocating any one position or offering legal advice. Interpretations of coverage vary according to state statute and jurisdiction; in questionable matters consult an attorney.

Where You Reside....

The recent uptick in the number of foreclosures has brought this particular issue to the forefront of discussion in the insurance community. Because of the number of vacant properties for sale, people who might not have thought about buying a new home are jumping into the "joys" of home ownership.

So, wherein lies the problem? In many instances the insureds bring a new homeowners policy to closing with the effective date being the same date as the closing, as the mortgagee demands. Then, they decide that a fresh coat of paint, new countertops, and ceiling fans should be in place before they actually move in. (It should be noted that the author pleads guilty as charged—closing on July 14th and actually moving in on August 1.) They estimate that this work should take no more than fifteen days at the outset. So, again, what is the problem? A week into the fifteen days, a severe thunderstorm occurs. Lightning hits the home's chimney, causing a fire which burns a substantial portion of the dwelling before being contained. Now **here** is the problem. What action is the insurer to take? Unquestioningly pay the claim, or deny the loss? After all, the insureds do not actually reside in the dwelling, nor do painting, installing countertops and ceiling fans constitute the dwelling's being under construction. The situation can be compounded by the fact that in some instances the sellers are allowed to remain in the dwelling after the closing for a period of time, perhaps because their own new home's not being yet ready for occupancy. Does this then make the home a rental property, and not an owner-occupied residence?

The insurer covers "the dwelling on the 'residence premises' shown in the Declarations..." The homeowners policy explicitly defines the "residence premises" as "the one-family dwelling where you reside; the two-, three-, or four-family dwelling where you reside in at least one of the family units ... and which is shown as the 'residence premises' in the Declarations." According to *Webster's New World College Dictionary,* "residence" means "the place in which a person or thing resides; dwelling place; abode, esp. a house." And "reside" means "to dwell in for a long time; have one's residence; live (*in* or *at*)."

Clearly, our new homeowners do not reside in the home. They intend to reside there, but intentions are not covered under the policy.

At present, there are three solutions, none of which appears entirely satisfactory. The first is to write a dwelling fire policy for the closing, which should satisfy the mortgagee's demands. The policy would then need to be cancelled and rewritten as a homeowners policy when the new owners moved in. This solution would give coverage whether the sellers were allowed to stay in the dwelling for a period of time or not. The new homeowners could also take a bit longer in moving into the residence, if the painting did not go as planned. Of course, writing a dwelling fire under these circumstances can mean that the insurer is issuing a policy on a (temporarily) vacant dwelling, which is certainly not an underwriting delight.

The next option is to look to the homeowners policy conditions (ISO Sections I and II condition B., AAIS Policy Conditions 3.). This is the waiver or change of policy provisions (AAIS uses policy terms), which states that only the insurer can waive or change policy provisions, and that such waiver must be in writing to be valid. The insurer, upon being advised that the insureds will not actually be in their new home until a date after the closing, can then write an addendum to the effect that "It is agreed that we cover the premises shown in the declarations as the named insured's residence premises even though the named insured will not take up residence therein until (X) days following the policy's inception date." Of course, the named insured would then be responsible for making sure he or she actually resided in the residence premises on the scheduled date.

The third option would be for ISO and AAIS to develop an endorsement with wording that would also convey the same meaning as the change of policy provisions above. It would be the agent's (or the insurer's) responsibility to discuss the endorsement with the prospective insured who phones to request a homeowners policy "because I'm going to close on a new home." At that point the closing and the prospective moving date could be ascertained. The endorsement could then add language to the effect that "It is agreed that if you do not reside in the residence premises by such-and-such a date, then in event of loss following that date we may have the right to deny coverage for that loss." Having the insured sign and date the endorsement might drive home the point.

(For a look at this and other scenarios where the insured does not reside in the dwelling insured on the homeowners policy, look at "'Where You Reside'—The 'Where's Waldo?®' Catastrophic Homeowners Policy 'Exclusion' That Could Bankrupt Your Insureds" by William C. Wilson, Jr., CPCU, ARM, AAM, in the CPCU eJournal, March 2011.)

Alcohol, Controlled Substances, and the Homeowners Exclusion

We discussed earlier in this book the coverage an insured can find for renting, say, a hall for a wedding reception (see Chapter 9). We left unaddressed the possibility of the host's acting as bartender and providing alcohol to minors. It is becoming common these days for parents to host prom-night parties; the theory being that if the kids are drinking at someone's home, they are not on the road driving while drunk. Along with this, we must consider the increased use of drugs—both illegal and prescription. What are the consequences of alcohol or drug use by others for the homeowner? Is there any coverage? And, with states jumping on the "medical marijuana" bandwagon, what are the implications for a homeowner who grows his or her own? (See the excellent article by Christine Barlow, CPCU, Medical Marijuana, in *FC&S Online* for more information on this topic.)

First, the alcohol question. Unfortunately, the alcohol question usually arises in connection with use of a motor vehicle, as when an intoxicated person (often a minor) consumes alcohol given to him or her by a family member or a friend, gets into a car, and crashes. In these instances the insurer is often on safe ground denying the claim on the basis of the motor vehicle liability exclusion (a vehicle registered for use on public roads or property, for example). Now, giving alcohol to a minor might seem to be unconnected with the actual use of a motor vehicle—at least so far as the insured is concerned—but many courts have ruled the exclusion applies. And, if the link appears tenuous, we might look at a Hawai'i case to see where the courts find the connection. The case is *Allstate Insurance Company v. Miller*, F. Supp. 2d 1128 (2010). Here, two minors consumed alcohol at the insured's home. Following this, the minor driver had an accident and his passenger died. The court agreed that the insurer had no duty to defend the wrongful death suit, citing the exclusion for bodily injury arising out of the use of a motor vehicle. The court saw no "independent act breaking the causal link" between the accident and the death. Further, said the court, the exclusion for bodily injury intended by, or which could reasonably be expected to result from the intentional or criminal acts or omissions of any insured person also applied. Hawai'i statute made it illegal to serve alcohol to a minor. Even though the insured was not charged criminally, nonetheless the alcohol was consumed on the insured's premises, which were in his control.

A slightly different approach was taken in the case of *American Modern Home Insurance Company v. Corra*, 671 S.E.2d 802 (WVA, 2008). The insured's daughter invited several friends to a party at her father's home. He was present at the time, although not actually in the house. One of the guests helped herself to a beer from the refrigerator, and then went with a fake ID to purchase more. After consuming several cans of beer, she drove off in a car with three friends. She was involved in an auto accident resulting in one friend seriously injured, and two dead. The claim against the insured was denied by his insurer on the grounds that giving alcohol (or at least, turning a blind eye to its consumption) to minors was not an occurrence as defined by the policy. That is, the occurrence was not "an accident." The homeowner knowingly permitted underage adults to consume alcohol on his premises; the court, therefore, did not need to go further to evaluate the motor vehicle or intentional act exclusions.

Sounds simple and straight-forward enough, but is it? We turn to the case of *Salem Group v. Oliver*, 607 A.2d 138 (NJ 1992). (We should note at the outset that this case represents the New Jersey jurisdiction; the outcome is markedly different from the similar case in Hawai'i [*Allstate Insurance Company v. Miller*] we discussed above.) The insured supplied alcohol to his minor nephew, who then (with the insured's permission) operated the insured's ATV. He took the vehicle off the insured's property, fell off several times, and then crashed the vehicle. He sued his uncle for his injuries. In this case, the court held that the reasonable expectations of the insured were that "insurers are generally obligated to defend their insureds on social host claims. The critical question is whether the insurer can avoid that obligation because a separate excluded risk, the operation of an all-terrain vehicle (ATV), constitutes an additional cause of the injury. We find that the insurer remains obligated to defend the covered risk. It may not avoid that obligation simply because the operation of an ATV constitutes an additional cause of the injury." The court also pointed out that had the nephew remained on the insured's property, the injury would have been covered regardless of the alcohol. In differentiating other cases where the motor vehicle exclusion had applied to eliminate coverage, the court said that serving alcohol did not depend on the ownership of a motor vehicle. Further, one count of the complaint alleged serving alcohol, which was not excluded. (Again, note the difference between the *Allstate* case; Hawai'i making it illegal to serve alcohol to minors. The *Salem Group* case does not reference any such statute.) In reaching its decision the court said it did not go to the extreme of the California supreme court in *State Farm Mutual Automobile Insurance Co. v. Partridge*, 514 P. 2d 123 (Cal. 1973), which essentially applied concurrent causation to liability coverage; that is, where two risks constituted concurrent proximate causes of an accident, the insurer is liable so long as one of the causes is covered by the policy. The policy was, however, silent about concurrent causation and that made the motor vehicle exclusion ambiguous. However, lest one is left with the impression that the *Salem Group* court was essentially finding coverage for the insured, that is not the case. The court said "We hold not that the insurer may ultimately be liable under the policy, but only that it must honor its duty to defend." We should add that, in this case, the exclusion for intentional acts reasonably seen to result in bodily injury or property damage was not brought into this case.

Next, we move on to drugs and the homeowners exclusion for controlled substances. Bodily injury and property damage "arising out of the use, sale, manufacture, delivery, transfer or possession by any person of a Controlled Substance as defined by the Federal Food and Drug Law at 21 U.S.C.A. Section 811 and 812 are excluded. Controlled Substances include but are not limited to cocaine, LSD, marijuana and all narcotic drugs." The exclusion excepts "the legitimate use of prescription drugs by a person following the lawful orders of a licensed health care professional" (ISO HO 00 03 05 11, exclusion 8.). It appears that the exclusion's exception must be read to apply only to an insured's use of prescription drugs. For example, if an insured's use of a prescription drug causes him or her to have a reaction, step completely out of character, and throw rocks through the neighbor's windows that action would be covered. With the number of states legalizing medical marijuana for personal use, this exclusion's exception is one that bears watching.

A recent case involving a prescription drug is enlightening as to how broadly the exclusion might be applied. In *Massachusetts Property Insurance Underwriting Association v. Gallagher,* 911 N.E.2d 808 (Mass. App. 2009), a suit was filed against the insured alleging that he negligently left a prescription drug in a place accessible to a guest, and the guest died from an overdose.

The eighteen year old and his mother were spending the night at the insured's (apparently a fairly regular occurrence, since the mother argued that they were members of the insured's household, and therefore her son's suicide should be covered). The argument presented by the mother was that her son's death "arose out of" the insured's legitimate prescription use of the drug (propoxyphene; included on the list of controlled substances) that caused her son's death, in the sense that the drug would not have been available to the boy without the insured's use. The court admitted "the argument is not without persuasive force," but said the argument was flawed in that "it overlooks the separate and independent application of the exclusion to McMaster's own use of the [drug]... the fact remains that McMaster's *own* (italics added) use of the [drug] clearly does not fall within the exception." The immediate cause of the boy's death was his excluded use of the drug, and "whatever causal contribution [the insured's] use may have furnished was decidedly more remote."

We next turn to the case of *Flomerfelt v. Cardiello*, 997 A.2d 991 (NJ 2010). Here, the plaintiff brought action against the insured, alleging that she was injured when she overdosed on alcohol and drugs provided by the insured at a party at his parents' home (they were out of town), and that he failed to get prompt help for her. This case illustrates the necessity of considering all the facts in a case before reaching a verdict. At first blush, a denial of coverage would appear to be appropriate, since it became clear that illegal drugs were involved. The insured, age twenty, hosted a party at his parents' house while they were out of town. One of the party guests overdosed on alcohol and drugs. The next afternoon, when the host awoke, he found her passed out on the porch. He admitted he called her sister to pick her up and take her to the hospital, since he did not want his parents to find out about the party. When the sister did not come, he called a rescue service. The insurer denied coverage for her injuries, citing the exclusion for bodily injury arising out of the use, transfer (the host provided beer and Ultracet, a prescription medication, to his guests).

The trial court agreed that the exclusion did not apply, since the plaintiff had no recollection of what she might have drunk or ingested either before or during the party. And, because her injuries might have resulted from her own actions prior to the party, the exclusion did not apply. Further, failing to summon help is not an excluded action. The insurer appealed, holding that the injuries were tied at least in part to the illegal drugs at the party (as confirmed by a toxicology report), and the trial verdict was overturned. The insured appealed, and the case was then heard by the New Jersey supreme court. The court carefully reviewed all evidence and arguments. The court reiterated the oft-stated principle that exclusions are to be narrowly construed, and the burden is on the insurer to bring the case within the exclusion. The court also noted that "courts are often required to evaluate whether the insurer owes its insured a duty to defend in advance of a conclusive decision about coverage." The court must then compare the allegations set forth with the language of the insurance policy. (Remember, the duty to defend is broader than the duty to indemnify.)

The court noted that it had rejected, with regard to property coverage cases, that a loss would be covered if one cause was covered even though another cause was excluded; particularly if it was impossible to separate the covered from the non-covered cause. The court also noted that it had addressed a concurrent causation third-party claim in the case of *Salem Group*, discussed above. The court stated, though, that in the *Salem Group* decision it did not necessarily represent concurrent causation, but rather a sequence of causes. And, when one cause was covered and the other not, a duty to defend was owed. The duty to defend continued so long as there was a potentially covered claim. The court said, "In evaluating the duty to defend, we can lay the complaint and the policy side by side and see that in this dispute some theories of liability would be covered and others would not. If, for example, the finder of fact were to conclude that alcohol ingestion, either in the context of the social host serving plaintiff when she was visibly intoxicated… or in combination with a delay in summoning aid, was the cause for the injuries, or set the chain of events in motion, and that there was not a substantial nexus between drugs at the party and the injuries, the claim would fall within the coverage of the policy and would not be barred by the exclusion. If the finder of fact were to conclude that plaintiff's injuries were caused by use of drugs before she arrived at the party, by genetic predisposition, or by long term drug use such that the injuries did not 'originate in,' grow out of' or have a 'substantial nexus [all terms used to describe 'arising out of'] to her use of drugs at the party, the claim would also be covered. Whether any of those possibilities is the likeliest outcome is of no consequence, because our traditional analysis of the duty to defend requires that Pennsylvania General provide a defense."

The court was not saying that the allegations should be covered, but rather that the insurer owed a defense. The court was not unsympathetic to the insurer in this case, since it noted that the insurer had several options: it could defend under a reservation or rights; decline to defend but reimburse the insured if the finder of fact found the injury did not arise out of drug use at the party; or litigate the coverage issue in advance of a trial on the plaintiff's claim.

Malicious Prosecution: What is That?

The endorsement for personal injury coverage (ISO 24 82 05 11) defines "personal injury" as injury arising out of, among other things, "malicious prosecution." The form states the insurer will pay damages up to the limit of liability, and provide a defense "even if the suit is groundless, false or fraudulent." The form excludes, however, personal injury caused "by or at the direction of an 'insured' with the knowledge that the act would violate the rights of another and would inflict 'personal injury'" is excluded. This appears to be a coverage paradox. *Black's Law Dictionary (Eighth Edition)* defines *malicious prosecution* as "the institution of a criminal or civil proceeding for an improper purpose and without probable cause. The tort requires an adversary to prove four elements: (1) the initiation or continuation of a lawsuit; (2) lack of probable cause; (3) malice; and (4) favorable termination of the lawsuit." In other words, party A sues party B for slander, and the case is resolved in party A's favor. Party B cannot therefore sue for malicious prosecution, since the outcome of the underlying suit had a termination favorable to party A. So, again, given that malicious prosecution would appear to entail acting with intent to inflict injury, how can the policy cover something that it appears to deny coverage for?

We should note at the outset that there are very few cases addressing malicious prosecution and, of those reviewed, none involved either this endorsement or an umbrella policy (the coverage for personal injury is similar). So, we content ourselves with the review of a few cases having malicious prosecution as the focus. Perhaps it will be to the courts to decide this paradox.

In the case of *Cohen v. Corwin*, 980 So.2d 1153 (4th Fla. App., 2008), Corwin sued the Cohens for leaving garbage cans in plain view and parking on the cul-de-sac. Corwin also alleged that the Cohens had told others that he was an unsavory character. Corwin voluntarily dismissed the counts, but subsequently the Cohens sued Corwin for defamation claims amounting to malicious prosecution. The action turned on whether Corwin's dismissal of the claims was a "favorable termination of the lawsuit" (see *Black*, above), such that the first suit's lack of merit was demonstrated. The court held that Corwin's dismissal of the complaint demonstrated that there was no factual basis to support the claim and, therefore, the Cohen's suit for malicious prosecution could continue.

In *Giannamore v. Shevchuk*, 947 A.2d 1012 (Conn. App. 2008), a malicious prosecution action was brought against Shevchuk (the homeowner) by Giannamore (a painter), hired by the homeowner to paint both the interior and exterior of his home. The underlying action was brought by the homeowner, alleging larceny when the painter failed to finish the paint job in a timely manner and had stolen the down payment. There was no suggestion of wrongdoing by the painter; rather, he had explained the delay to the homeowner and had thought the homeowner understood. The trial court found for the painter. The court found that the homeowner lacked probable cause to initiate criminal proceedings against the painter and acted with malice in pursuing criminal charges. In finding for the painter, the court said "The use of criminal proceedings to recover a debt, even money lawfully owed to an accuser, is improper and subjects a person to liability for malicious prosecution." Since the outcome of the suit was favorable to the painter, the malicious prosecution action could proceed.

Finally, for another look at neighbor v. neighbor, as in *Cohen*, above, we turn to *Turnage v. Kasper*, 704 S.E.2d 842 (Ga. App. 2010). At one time the Kaspers and Turnages were friends, but the "friendship" fell apart to the extent that the Turnages and other neighbors blocked Kasper and her son in the middle of a public street while they were riding their motorbikes; took Kasper's son's football and destroyed it, etc. That is not to say Kasper was without fault, since there was some evidence that she shoved Turnage at one point and, as the saying goes, "got in his face." Needless to say, the police were involved on several occasions. Turnage even went so far as to demand that a police officer arrest Kasper on battery charges, and issue a warrant to stay away from him. This was done, and Kasper released. But Kasper daily walked to the school bus stop to meet her children. One day Turnage and another man blocked her way, took her picture, and then called the police, claiming Kasper had violated her release and she should be charged with aggravated stalking. She was in jail for about two weeks. Upon her release, she sued for malicious prosecution (and intentional infliction of emotional distress).

The defendants (Turnage and other neighbors) claimed the police officer's action meant they were not liable for malicious prosecution, but the court found the initial arrest was not supported by probable cause, and so the police actions did not hinder their liability. The court said several factors supported the malicious prosecution action: Turnage urged a law enforcement officer to begin criminal proceedings, and he provided information to the officer that he knew to be false. So, Turnage was guilty of malicious prosecution.

As pointed out when introducing this topic, the underlying action must have a favorable outcome to the person then initiating a malicious prosecution suit, and, not only a favorable outcome, but a clear indication that the underlying suit had no merit. Otherwise, there can be no malicious prosecution.

So where does that leave the holder of a personal injury coverage endorsement or an umbrella? There must first be an underlying lawsuit with an outcome favorable to the person not holding personal injury coverage or an umbrella, and then said holder must be sued for malicious prosecution for bringing the underlying suit in the first place. At this point, remember the insurer promises to defend even if the suit is groundless, false, or fraudulent. But given the circumstances necessary to trigger the coverage, the outcome should be interesting, to say the least.

Appendix A

An Agent's Miscellany

Tailoring a policy to meet a client's needs is a necessary part of providing good service, and building a lasting relationship, since shopping the internet for insurance is a reality. In all probability complex commercial accounts will continue to be sold in a traditional manner; however, for many consumers the ease of internet shopping will win out over dealing with an agent.

The key to retaining loyal clients and building a strong customer base lies in the quality of the service provided. Granted commission dollars rarely offset the cost of getting business on the books and doing account follow-up, and, unfortunately, agents have the job of educating their clients as well. For example, most people know that they need to contact their insurance agent when there is a new driver in the household, but few remember to call when they decide to build an addition.

Therefore, this portion of the book is designed primarily to assist the agent. There are check lists to use in tailoring a homeowners policy. (Please feel free to copy them and modify them for your own use.) Although for many clients a stand-alone homeowners policy will fill the bill, there are times when a more affluent client will not be best served by the standard policy. The agent must be prepared to dig— diplomatically, of course—to access the information necessary to do the best job possible. And, of course, as well as asking questions, the agent must be prepared to answer questions and educate the client.

Following the checklists, there are sample letters for use in renewal or requesting a change of agent (agent of record), and, following those, agency E&O checklists.

Rating a Policy

Agents are frequently asked how an insurer arrives at a final premium. Each state is broken up into rating territories, reflecting differences in such things as crime, vandalism, susceptibility to windstorm, etc. Within each territory, dwellings are classified according to two factors: construction type and protection class. Construction type is generally frame or brick. Frame dwellings carry a slightly higher rate than brick because of flammability. "Protection class" is a system of rating local fire department capabilities and the availability of water supply. (The ISO system rates departments on a scale of 1 to 10, with 1 being the best and 10 having essentially no fire protection.)

Fairly recent is ISO's Building Code Effectiveness Grading System. Grades of one to ten are issued to a community based on the adequacy of its building code, and the effectiveness of the enforcement of that code. For example, following the rebuilding in Florida after Hurricane Andrew, many partially destroyed dwellings were not rebuilt to the standard then in effect; rather, their rebuilding was grandfathered to the earlier standard. The new code effectiveness system, along with the premium credits available, promotes adherence to effective building standards.

The final premium for a standard unendorsed homeowners policy is then based upon the type of policy chosen, i.e., HO 00 02, HO 00 03, or HO 00 05, and the limits of coverage. Additional coverages beyond the standard policy – backup of sewer or drain, replacement cost for contents, personal injury, etc. – add premium dollars. By the same token, there are discounts for a higher deductible, smoke detectors or alarm systems, or, with an older home, updated systems.

Many clients do not understand that rates for personal lines insurance are subject to state review and approval. A few years ago a politically active group was collecting signatures in Ohio because "it wasn't fair that insurance companies could just charge anything they wanted and the customer had to accept it." Ohio is a "file and use" state, so yes, the insurer could begin to charge new rates, but the state had the power to approve or deny the rate increase. This is something an agent can help the ordinary customer understand.

Personal Liability Checklist

Date:
Named Insured:
Spouse, if applicable:
Residents other than foster children or those related by marriage, blood, or adoption:
Address:
City/State/Zip:
Business phone:

Home phone:
Cell:
E-mail:
X-date:

	Yes	No
<u>Exposures:</u>		
Other dwellings	❒	❒
Are there other residences?	❒	❒
If so, where insured?	❒	❒
Are there any domestic or residence employees?	❒	❒
If yes, is workers compensation required?	❒	❒
Business activities on residence premises?	❒	❒
Describe:____________________	❒	❒
Special coverage necessary?	❒	❒
Is there an in-home business?	❒	❒
Is there on-premises day care?	❒	❒
Is professional liability coverage required?	❒	❒
Is any portion of any residence premises rented to others?	❒	❒
if so, usage:____________________________________	❒	❒
Are there any unusual pets?	❒	❒
If yes, describe:__________________	❒	❒
Describe any dogs, giving breeds:____________________	❒	❒
Any pleasure horses?	❒	❒
Any horses boarded on premises?	❒	❒
<u>Farming:</u>		
Does insured engage in farming operations?	❒	❒
If yes, specify type:__________________	❒	❒
incidental	❒	❒
custom farming	❒	❒
farm employees	❒	❒
livestock	❒	❒
<u>Motorized Vehicles:</u>		
Does insured own a snowmobile?	❒	❒
Does insured own an ATV?	❒	❒
Does insured own a go-kart?	❒	❒
Does insured own a dune buggy?	❒	❒
Does insured own a golf cart?	❒	❒
Does insured own a motor bike?	❒	❒
Any battery powered vehicles?	❒	❒
Describe, including speed________________________		

Watercraft:

Does insured own a boat/yacht? ❐ ❐
Sail boat: ❐ ❐
length:________ ❐ ❐
Power boat: ❐ ❐
length:________ ❐ ❐
outboard: give horsepower____________ ❐ ❐
inboard/outdrive: give horsepower:_______ ❐ ❐
jet ski or wet bike? ❐ ❐
Is boat used for water skiing? ❐ ❐
Is it rented to others? ❐ ❐
Principal operator(s)/ages:__________________
Coast Guard or Power Squadron training? ❐ ❐

Aircraft:

Does the insured own aircraft? ❐ ❐
How titled:____________________ ❐ ❐
How used:____________________ ❐ ❐
Is it rented to others? ❐ ❐

Rental Residential Property:

Does the insured have rental (residential) property? ❐ ❐
number of families:__________________ ❐ ❐
Is there any business conducted on premises? ❐ ❐
If yes, describe:_________________ ❐ ❐

Miscellaneous:

Are there any foster children cared for? ❐ ❐
If yes, number and ages:___________________ ❐ ❐
Does insured volunteer for non-profit org.? ❐ ❐
Does the insured have paid civic/public duties? ❐ ❐
Is insured a corporate director? ❐ ❐
Does insured's children do any babysitting on premises? ❐ ❐
Is there a swimming pool on premises? ❐ ❐
If yes, is it fenced? ❐ ❐
Any other "attractive nuisances"? ❐ ❐
If yes, describe____________ ❐ ❐
Does insured own guns?
If yes, how stored?________________________ ❐ ❐
Is kidnap/ransom coverage needed? ❐ ❐
Is umbrella coverage needed? ❐ ❐
Identity theft coverage? ❐ ❐

General comments: ________________________

Personal Property Checklist

Date:
Named Insured:
Spouse:
Residents other than those related by marriage, blood or adoption, or foster children:
Address:
City/State/Zip:
Business phone:
Home phone:
Cell phone:
e-mail:
X-date:
Amount:
Coverage: Named peril or open peril________________

	Yes	**No**
Increased amount personal property	❒	❒
Replacement cost contents	❒	❒
Increased limits special classes property	❒	❒
Personal property at another residence	❒	❒
Personal property at rental location	❒	❒
Property of others	❒	❒
Property stored in a rental unit	❒	❒
Scheduled property:		
Coin or stamp collection	❒	❒
Appraisal and date__________________		
exhibited?	❒	❒
Jewelry, watches	❒	❒
Appraisal and date__________________		
in vault?	❒	❒
Furs	❒	❒
Appraisal and date:_____________________	❒	❒
Guns	❒	❒
If antique, appraisal and date:________________		
Silver-, gold-, or pewter ware	❒	❒
If yes, describe:______________		
Antiques	❒	❒
If yes, appraisal(s) and date:________________		

Artwork	❒	❒
If yes, describe:____________________		
If yes, breakage needed?	❒	❒
any on loan or exhibited?	❒	❒
agreed or replacement value?	❒	❒
special collections; rare or unique items	❒	❒
Appraisals or bills of sale:____________________		
Tools	❒	❒
business use?	❒	❒
Oriental rugs:	❒	❒
If yes, give value(s):______________________		
Computers or other electronics:	❒	❒
If yes, describe:__________________		
Used in business?	❒	❒
Special computer endorsement?	❒	❒
Sports equipment:	❒	❒
If yes, describe:______________________		
Cameras (incl. camcorders)	❒	❒
Breakage	❒	❒
professional usage?	❒	❒
Musical Instruments:	❒	❒
Describe:__________________		
If yes, professional usage?	❒	❒
Valuable papers?	❒	❒
Accounts Receivable?	❒	❒
Describe:_________________________		
Other (indicate): ______		
Any scheduled property not at the insured's residence?	❒	❒
Business property **on premises**	❒	❒
If yes, describe:___________________________		
Property with student away at school	❒	❒
If yes, increased coverage? Tenant H/O?	❒	❒
Watercraft	❒	❒
If yes, where insured?		
Motorized vehicles not required to be licensed:		
Snowmobile	❒	❒
ATV	❒	❒
go-kart	❒	❒
dune buggy	❒	❒
golf cart	❒	❒
other: (describe)___________________________		

Aircraft ❒ ❒
If yes, where insured? ___________________________
Livestock ❒ ❒

Real Property Checklist

Date:
Named Insured:
Spouse, if applicable:
Additional/other interests:
Address:
City/State/Zip:
Home phone: ( )__________________ Business phone: ( )______________
e-mail______________________________
Occupation:
Social Security number (if applicable):______-______-_______
Renewal date:
Comments:
Primary Residence:
Address: (if different from above)
If property is in a trust, describe:_____________________________________
Titled to:
Mortgagor:
Occupancy: ❒ single family ❒ duplex ❒ 3-family ❒ 4-family
Construction: ❒ frame ❒ masonry ❒ masonry veneer ❒ other
No. of stories:______
Roofing material: _______________________________________

	Yes	No
Sprinkler system?	❒	❒
Smoke detectors?	❒	❒
Alarm?	❒	❒

If so, local? ❒ central station? ❒ other ❒
(describe:___________________________
Replacement cost (refer to costimator): $________________
Actual cash value if applicable: $________________
Detached structures (describe):
Used for business? ❒ ❒
Comments:
Optional Coverages:
earthquake ❒ ❒
include masonry veneer? ❒ ❒
flood ❒ ❒

sinkhole/mine ❒ ❒
ordinance/law ❒ ❒
backup sewer/drain ❒ ❒
rebuilding end. ❒ ❒
windstorm ded ❒ ❒
replacement cost for patios, drives, etc? ❒ ❒
If a condo:
increased cov. A ❒ ❒
open perils cov. A ❒ ❒
add'l loss asses. ❒ ❒
Rented to others? ❒ ❒
If yes, HO 17 33 ❒ ❒
Comments:
Secondary Residence: ❒ ❒
Address:
City/State/Zip:
Titled to:
Mortgagor:
If in a trust, describe:_________________
Occupancy: ❒ single family ❒ duplex ❒ 3-family ❒ 4-family
Construction: ❒ frame ❒ masonry ❒ masonry veneer ❒ other
No. of stories:_______
Roofing material:
Sprinkler system? ❒ ❒
Smoke detectors? ❒ ❒
Alarm? ❒ ❒
If so, local? ❒centralstation?❒other❒describe:______________________
Replacement cost (refer to costimator): $_________________
Actual cash value if applicable: $_________________
Detached structures (describe):
Used for business? ❒ ❒
Comments:
Optional Coverages::
earthquake ❒ ❒
include masonry veneer? ❒ ❒
flood ❒ ❒
sinkhole/mine ❒ ❒
ordinance/law ❒ ❒
backup sewer/drain ❒ ❒
rebuilding end. ❒ ❒
windstorm ded ❒ ❒

replacement cost for walls, drives, etc? ❐ ❐
If a condo:
increased cov. A ❐ ❐
open perils cov. A ❐ ❐
add'l loss asses. ❐ ❐
Rented to others? ❐ ❐
If yes, HO 17 33? ❐ ❐
Comments:
Rental Property:
Address:
City/State/Zip:
Titled to:
Mortgagor:
If in a trust, describe:________________________
Occupancy: ❐ single family ❐ duplex ❐ 3-family ❐ 4-family
Construction: ❐ frame ❐ masonry ❐ masonry veneer ❐ other
No. of stories:______
Roofing material:
Sprinkler system? ❐ ❐
Smoke detectors? ❐ ❐
Alarm? ❐ ❐
If so, local? ❐centralstation?❐other❐describe:________________________
Replacement cost (refer to costimator): $__________________
Actual cash value if applicable: $__________________
Detached structures (describe):
Used for business? ❐ ❐
Comments:

Farm or Vacant Property:

Describe:

Sample Renewal Letter

Date:
Dear (Customer Name):
Your homeowners renewal has been issued and we'd like to review the coverages briefly with you. Your policy provides ($.......) for the dwelling itself, and ($.......) in unscheduled personal property. You have ($.......) for other structures—your swimming pool, concrete patio, and detached garage—on your property. If you do not think this amount is adequate, please contact us. We show scheduled jewelry for you with a total value of ($.......), and fine arts valued at ($.........), with breakage included. Please review the schedule you received from (Company name), and advise us immediately of any changes.

Theft coverage for unscheduled jewelry is limited to $1,000; guns, $2,000; and silverware, $2,500. Coverage for money is limited to $200. Coverage for property primarily used in business, while at your residence, is limited to $2,500; while away from your residence, $250.

Your policy includes personal liability coverage for $100,000. The homeowners policy does not cover any business or professional activities. There are other restrictions as well, such as for use of motorized vehicles.

If you have any questions, or wish to review your coverages in more detail, please contact us.

Sincerely,

(Name)

(XYZ Agency)

Sample Agent of Record Letter

A word of advice: DO NOT attempt to switch a policy in the middle of a term. Do it only at the renewal date. The reason for this is that the prior agent will get the commission until the end of the policy term, and the new agent will be charged with any losses that occur after the switch.

Date:

Insurer Name:

Address:

City/State/Zip:

Re: (Client Name and Policy Number)

Gentlemen:

Please be advised that effective this date I have appointed (Agency Name) as my agent of record with regard to the above captioned p olic(y)(ies). This letter also constitutes your authority to furnish the representatives of (Agency Name) with all information they may request regarding my policy, including schedules, loss information, or other data.

Sincerely,

(Insured's signature)

Insured's name

Insured's address

Errors & Omissions Prevention Suggestions

Careful risk management and attention to detail can prevent the majority of acts that result in errors and omissions allegations against an insurance agency. Making agency personnel aware of proper procedures in a number of areas is essential to the successful operation of an agency. The following is a compendium of suggestions on avoiding errors and omissions, broken down into various facets of agency operations.

Communications with Insureds:

In General

- Use care when explaining or delivering "all risks," comprehensive, and specific coverages. All policies have exclusions. Explain them to the insured.
- Confirm in writing the insured's declination to purchase important coverages or limits.
- Explore every market, standard, excess and surplus, before advising an insured coverage is not available.
- Advise insureds in writing if needed coverage previously unavailable can now be written.
- Do not indicate to an insured you can place a policy until you know for certain it can be placed.
- Do not place property coverages until you have physically visited the premises to be insured.
- Stay within your own field. Don't try to be an attorney, accountant, engineer, etc.
- If you don't know, say so. Find out and report back in writing.
- Never reveal you are insured for errors and omissions.

Binders and Orders:

- Prepare all binders immediately.
- Indicate the time and date that binder is effective.
- Indicate the company, the type of coverage, property to be insured, limits, address to be insured, and the correct name and mailing address of the insured.
- Pick up the binder when you deliver the policy.
- An oral request for a binder should be followed up immediately with a written binder and the insured sent a copy.
- All agency personnel should be informed of agency binder procedures.
- When possible, use standardized binder forms.
- Use agency binders to effect new coverages on existing policies.
- Do not exceed your binding authority for either limits or coverages.
- Inform agency personnel of binding authority and the prohibited and restricted lists of each company.
- Binders should be executed in triplicate. The original to the insured, a copy to the company, and an office copy.
- Never use a binder to provide free insurance. Advise the insured that coverage is in force and will have to be paid for.

Endorsements:

- Prepare endorsements at once. If not possible, acknowledge request in writing and issue binder.
- Indicate on the face of the office copy of the policy that the policy has been endorsed, the date, and whether coverage was added, deleted, or modified, e.g., increase in limits in mid-term.
- Determine whether endorsement or cancellation and rewrite of policy is the best method to accomplish a change in the policy, e.g., assignment, change of address, agent, etc.

Expirations and Renewals:

- A renewal policy should be issued and delivered prior to expiration of existing policy.
- Advise insured in writing if the renewal differs from the expiring policy. If necessary, request insurer issue corrected policy.
- Cross-check renewal lists with office expiration records and company expiration lists.
- The renewal list should be reviewed 60 to 90 days prior to expiration, and the insured contacted so any changes can be made.
- Advise insureds in writing of non-renewal of policies in sufficient time. Obtain replacement coverage when possible. If unable, advise the insured in time for the insured to obtain coverage elsewhere. Many state insurance regulations on cancellations and non-renewals require at least 30 days prior notice of non-renewal for policies covering family automobiles, dwellings, or governmental properties.
- Unless proper notice of non-renewal has been given, a renewal must be issued.

Cancellations:

- Valid cancellation is only obtained by strict adherence to cancellation provisions of the policy and insurance regulations on cancellations and non-renewals.
- Policies cancelled by the insured should be picked up at once.
- If it is not possible to obtain physical possession of the policy, obtain a lost policy receipt signed by the insured.
- Be certain that additional insureds, mortgagees, loss payees, governmental agencies, etc., are all included in the notice of cancellation.
- Check office copy of policy changes in address, assignment, etc., when a notice of cancellation is received.
- Do not divulge reasons for cancellation unless requested to by law and with immunity from suit.

- If a policy is reinstated, make sure that the insured is aware if there is a gap in coverage.
- Never send an invoice on a policy that has been cancelled and the earned premium paid thereon. Be certain accounts receivable records indicate clearly that policy has been cancelled. Indicate on invoice that balances due on cancelled policies are for the earned premium.

Claims:

- All reported claims must be in writing and on claim report forms. Often, insurers prefer ACORD forms. Use or devise a telephone report form and/or log.
- Never indicate there is or is not coverage unless you are absolutely certain.
- Get the company's answer in writing when requesting coverage information before relaying it to the insured or claimant.
- Take the report and advise that you or the adjuster will be in touch with the insured or claimant.
- Obtain the telephone number where the insured or claimant can be reached.
- Advise the company in writing of the reported claim as soon as possible.
- Advise company at once of all reported claims. Use the phone in an emergency and follow up in writing.
- Advise the insured of his responsibilities to protect property and to do nothing that will increase the loss. Lack of cooperation on the part of the insured could result in the claim being denied.

Communications with Insurers:

Binders

- Company must be sent copies of all binders.
- Binders must be cancelled in the same manner as policies are cancelled.
- If company requests cancellation of the binder, comply with that request immediately and replace binder with another company.
- Never bind a company for coverage or limits beyond your binding authority or for which there is no authority.

Renewals:

- Check renewals issued by company with the renewal list sent to the company.

- If you don't receive policy renewal by expiration date, issue a binder, or advise company policy has been renewed with another company.
- Check renewal policy for correctness. Do not assume it has been prepared correctly.
- Do not endorse an incorrectly prepared renewal. Request the insurer to issue a corrected renewal before delivery to the insured.
- Check renewals as to form. Form changes should be brought to the attention of the insured.

Requests for New Policies:

- Do not misrepresent the risk or withhold any underwriting information on new risk submissions.
- Applications should be completed thoroughly. Applications may become part of the policy or statements made therein may modify or void the coverage.
- Check the policy against the application for correctness.
- Notify the insured immediately if company declines coverage or modifies coverage it is willing to write.
- Company requests to alter or modify the coverage requested in the application should be in writing.

Endorsements:

- Check endorsements for accuracy.
- Send company copies of endorsements prepared in agency as soon as possible. If endorsements can't be prepared at once, prepare binders.
- Use standard endorsement request forms whenever possible.

Office Procedures:

- Instruct office personnel they must use your standard procedures to handle claims, cancellations, endorsements, renewals, and orders for new policies.
- All personnel must record all in-person or telephone conversations. Use a telephone memo or a call sheet.
- Hand written records of communications are invaluable when agency is questioned on performance or the lack of it.
- Check and re-check office personnel on compliance with standard procedures.
- Order, prepare, and deliver policies, renewals, binders, and endorsements as soon as possible. Insureds and agents often forget what was ordered.

- Review files on a scheduled basis with other members of the agency and, when requested, company representatives.
- Establish a system to advise insureds of new policies and coverages and changes in company underwriting attitudes.
- Upgrade your personnel by their attendance at conferences, seminars, and schools relating to their functions and responsibilities in the agency.
- Know your companies. Placing coverage in an unsound company may result in a claim against you as well as damage to your agency's reputation.

Appendix B

ISO and AAIS Forms

Forms to illustrate the discussions in this book follow. We have included representative forms from the 2011 ISO Homeowners program, and the 2008 AAIS Homeowners program.

ISO Homeowners Broad Form, Entire Policy HO 00 02 (05 11)

ISO Homeowners Special Form, Entire Policy HO 00 03 (05 11)

ISO Homeowners 5–Comprehensive Form, Entire Policy
HO 00 05 (05 11)

AAIS Homeowners Special Form, Entire Policy HO 0003 (09 08)

AAIS Special Building and Contents Form, Entire Policy
HO 0005 (09 08)

HOMEOWNERS
HO 00 02 05 11

HOMEOWNERS 2 – BROAD FORM

AGREEMENT

We will provide the insurance described in this policy in return for the premium and compliance with all applicable provisions of this policy.

DEFINITIONS

A. In this policy, "you" and "your" refer to the "named insured" shown in the Declarations and the spouse if a resident of the same household. "We", "us" and "our" refer to the Company providing this insurance.

B. In addition, certain words and phrases are defined as follows:

1. "Aircraft Liability", "Hovercraft Liability", "Motor Vehicle Liability" and "Watercraft Liability", subject to the provisions in **b.** below, mean the following:

a. Liability for "bodily injury" or "property damage" arising out of the:

(1) Ownership of such vehicle or craft by an "insured";

(2) Maintenance, occupancy, operation, use, loading or unloading of such vehicle or craft by any person;

(3) Entrustment of such vehicle or craft by an "insured" to any person;

(4) Failure to supervise or negligent supervision of any person involving such vehicle or craft by an "insured"; or

(5) Vicarious liability, whether or not imposed by law, for the actions of a child or minor involving such vehicle or craft.

b. For the purpose of this definition:

(1) Aircraft means any contrivance used or designed for flight, except model or hobby aircraft not used or designed to carry people or cargo;

(2) Hovercraft means a self-propelled motorized ground effect vehicle and includes, but is not limited to, flarecraft and air cushion vehicles;

(3) Watercraft means a craft principally designed to be propelled on or in water by wind, engine power or electric motor; and

(4) Motor vehicle means a "motor vehicle" as defined in **7.** below.

2. "Bodily injury" means bodily harm, sickness or disease, including required care, loss of services and death that results.

3. "Business" means:

a. A trade, profession or occupation engaged in on a full-time, part-time or occasional basis; or

b. Any other activity engaged in for money or other compensation, except the following:

(1) One or more activities, not described in **(2)** through **(4)** below, for which no "insured" receives more than $2,000 in total compensation for the 12 months before the beginning of the policy period;

(2) Volunteer activities for which no money is received other than payment for expenses incurred to perform the activity;

(3) Providing home day care services for which no compensation is received, other than the mutual exchange of such services; or

(4) The rendering of home day care services to a relative of an "insured".

4. "Employee" means an employee of an "insured", or an employee leased to an "insured" by a labor leasing firm under an agreement between an "insured" and the labor leasing firm, whose duties are other than those performed by a "residence employee".

5. "Insured" means:

a. You and residents of your household who are:

(1) Your relatives; or

(2) Other persons under the age of 21 and in your care or the care of a resident of your household who is your relative;

b. A student enrolled in school full-time, as defined by the school, who was a resident of your household before moving out to attend school, provided the student is under the age of:

(1) 24 and your relative; or

(2) 21 and in your care or the care of a resident of your household who is your relative; or

c. Under Section **II:**

(1) With respect to animals or watercraft to which this policy applies, any person or organization legally responsible for these animals or watercraft which are owned by you or any person described in **5.a.** or **b.** "Insured" does not mean a person or organization using or having custody of these animals or watercraft in the course of any "business" or without consent of the owner; or

(2) With respect to a "motor vehicle" to which this policy applies:

(a) Persons while engaged in your employ or that of any person described in **5.a.** or **b.**; or

(b) Other persons using the vehicle on an "insured location" with your consent.

Under both Sections **I** and **II,** when the word an immediately precedes the word "insured", the words an "insured" together mean one or more "insureds".

6. "Insured location" means:

a. The "residence premises";

b. The part of other premises, other structures and grounds used by you as a residence; and

(1) Which is shown in the Declarations; or

(2) Which is acquired by you during the policy period for your use as a residence;

c. Any premises used by you in connection with a premises described in **a.** and **b.** above;

d. Any part of a premises:

(1) Not owned by an "insured"; and

(2) Where an "insured" is temporarily residing;

e. Vacant land, other than farm land, owned by or rented to an "insured";

f. Land owned by or rented to an "insured" on which a one-, two-, three- or four-family dwelling is being built as a residence for an "insured";

g. Individual or family cemetery plots or burial vaults of an "insured"; or

h. Any part of a premises occasionally rented to an "insured" for other than "business" use.

7. "Motor vehicle" means:

a. A self-propelled land or amphibious vehicle; or

b. Any trailer or semitrailer which is being carried on, towed by or hitched for towing by a vehicle described in **a.** above.

8. "Occurrence" means an accident, including continuous or repeated exposure to substantially the same general harmful conditions, which results, during the policy period, in:

a. "Bodily injury"; or

b. "Property damage".

9. "Property damage" means physical injury to, destruction of, or loss of use of tangible property.

10. "Residence employee" means:

a. An employee of an "insured", or an employee leased to an "insured" by a labor leasing firm, under an agreement between an "insured" and the labor leasing firm, whose duties are related to the maintenance or use of the "residence premises", including household or domestic services; or

b. One who performs similar duties elsewhere not related to the "business" of an "insured".

A "residence employee" does not include a temporary employee who is furnished to an "insured" to substitute for a permanent "residence employee" on leave or to meet seasonal or short-term workload conditions.

11. "Residence premises" means:

a. The one-family dwelling where you reside;

b. The two-, three- or four-family dwelling where you reside in at least one of the family units; or

c. That part of any other building where you reside;

and which is shown as the "residence premises" in the Declarations.

"Residence premises" also includes other structures and grounds at that location.

SECTION I – PROPERTY COVERAGES

A. Coverage A – Dwelling

1. We cover:

a. The dwelling on the "residence premises" shown in the Declarations, including structures attached to the dwelling; and

b. Materials and supplies located on or next to the "residence premises" used to construct, alter or repair the dwelling or other structures on the "residence premises".

2. We do not cover land, including land on which the dwelling is located.

B. Coverage B – Other Structures

1. We cover other structures on the "residence premises" set apart from the dwelling by clear space. This includes structures connected to the dwelling by only a fence, utility line, or similar connection.

2. We do not cover:

a. Land, including land on which the other structures are located;

b. Other structures rented or held for rental to any person not a tenant of the dwelling, unless used solely as a private garage;

c. Other structures from which any "business" is conducted; or

d. Other structures used to store "business" property. However, we do cover a structure that contains "business" property solely owned by an "insured" or a tenant of the dwelling, provided that "business" property does not include gaseous or liquid fuel, other than fuel in a permanently installed fuel tank of a vehicle or craft parked or stored in the structure.

3. The limit of liability for this coverage will not be more than 10% of the limit of liability that applies to Coverage **A.** Use of this coverage does not reduce the Coverage **A** limit of liability.

C. Coverage C – Personal Property

1. Covered Property

We cover personal property owned or used by an "insured" while it is anywhere in the world. After a loss and at your request, we will cover personal property owned by:

a. Others while the property is on the part of the "residence premises" occupied by an "insured"; or

b. A guest or a "residence employee", while the property is in any residence occupied by an "insured".

2. Limit For Property At Other Locations

a. Other Residences

Our limit of liability for personal property usually located at an "insured's" residence, other than the "residence premises", is 10% of the limit of liability for Coverage **C,** or $1,000, whichever is greater. However, this limitation does not apply to personal property:

(1) Moved from the "residence premises" because it is:

(a) Being repaired, renovated or rebuilt; and

(b) Not fit to live in or store property in; or

(2) In a newly acquired principal residence for 30 days from the time you begin to move the property there.

b. Self-storage Facilities

Our limit of liability for personal property owned or used by an "insured" and located in a self-storage facility is 10% of the limit of liability for Coverage **C,** or $1,000, whichever is greater. However, this limitation does not apply to personal property:

(1) Moved from the "residence premises" because it is:

(a) Being repaired, renovated or rebuilt; and

(b) Not fit to live in or store property in; or

(2) Usually located in an "insured's" residence, other than the "residence premises".

3. Special Limits Of Liability

The special limit for each category shown below is the total limit for each loss for all property in that category. These special limits do not increase the Coverage **C** limit of liability.

a. $200 on money, bank notes, bullion, gold other than goldware, silver other than silverware, platinum other than platinumware, coins, medals, scrip, stored value cards and smart cards.

b. $1,500 on securities, accounts, deeds, evidences of debt, letters of credit, notes other than bank notes, manuscripts, personal records, passports, tickets and stamps. This dollar limit applies to these categories regardless of the medium (such as paper or computer software) on which the material exists.

This limit includes the cost to research, replace or restore the information from the lost or damaged material.

c. $1,500 on watercraft of all types, including their trailers, furnishings, equipment and outboard engines or motors.

d. $1,500 on trailers or semitrailers not used with watercraft of all types.

e. $1,500 for loss by theft of jewelry, watches, furs, precious and semiprecious stones.

f. $2,500 for loss by theft of firearms and related equipment.

g. $2,500 for loss by theft of silverware, silver-plated ware, goldware, gold-plated ware, platinumware, platinum-plated ware and pewterware. This includes flatware, hollowware, tea sets, trays and trophies made of or including silver, gold or pewter.

h. $2,500 on property, on the "residence premises", used primarily for "business" purposes.

i. $1,500 on property, away from the "residence premises", used primarily for "business" purposes. However, this limit does not apply to antennas, tapes, wires, records, disks or other media that are:

(1) Used with electronic equipment that reproduces, receives or transmits audio, visual or data signals; and

(2) In or upon a "motor vehicle".

j. $1,500 on portable electronic equipment that:

(1) Reproduces, receives or transmits audio, visual or data signals;

(2) Is designed to be operated by more than one power source, one of which is a "motor vehicle's" electrical system; and

(3) Is in or upon a "motor vehicle".

k. $250 on antennas, tapes, wires, records, disks or other media that are:

(1) Used with electronic equipment that reproduces, receives or transmits audio, visual or data signals; and

(2) In or upon a "motor vehicle".

4. Property Not Covered

We do not cover:

a. Articles separately described and specifically insured, regardless of the limit for which they are insured, in this or other insurance;

b. Animals, birds or fish;

c. "Motor vehicles".

This includes a "motor vehicle's" equipment and parts.

However, this Paragraph **4.c.** does not apply to:

(1) Portable electronic equipment that:

(a) Reproduces, receives or transmits audio, visual or data signals; and

(b) Is designed so that it may be operated from a power source other than a "motor vehicle's" electrical system.

(2) "Motor vehicles" not required to be registered for use on public roads or property which are:

(a) Used solely to service a residence; or

(b) Designed to assist the handicapped;

d. Aircraft, meaning any contrivance used or designed for flight, including any parts whether or not attached to the aircraft.

We do cover model or hobby aircraft not used or designed to carry people or cargo;

e. Hovercraft and parts. Hovercraft means a self-propelled motorized ground effect vehicle and includes, but is not limited to, flarecraft and air cushion vehicles;

f. Property of roomers, boarders and other tenants, except property of roomers and boarders related to an "insured";

g. Property in an apartment regularly rented or held for rental to others by an "insured", except as provided under **E.10.** Landlord's Furnishings under Section **I** – Property Coverages;

h. Property rented or held for rental to others off the "residence premises";

i. "Business" data, including such data stored in:

(1) Books of account, drawings or other paper records; or

(2) Computers and related equipment.

We do cover the cost of blank recording or storage media and of prerecorded computer programs available on the retail market;

j. Credit cards, electronic fund transfer cards or access devices used solely for deposit, withdrawal or transfer of funds except as provided in **E.6.** Credit Card, Electronic Fund Transfer Card Or Access Device, Forgery And Counterfeit Money under Section **I** – Property Coverages; or

k. Water or steam.

D. Coverage D – Loss Of Use

The limit of liability for Coverage **D** is the total limit for the coverages in **1.** Additional Living Expense, **2.** Fair Rental Value and **3.** Civil Authority Prohibits Use below.

1. Additional Living Expense

If a loss covered under Section **I** makes that part of the "residence premises" where you reside not fit to live in, we cover any necessary increase in living expenses incurred by you so that your household can maintain its normal standard of living.

Payment will be for the shortest time required to repair or replace the damage or, if you permanently relocate, the shortest time required for your household to settle elsewhere.

2. Fair Rental Value

If a loss covered under Section **I** makes that part of the "residence premises" rented to others or held for rental by you not fit to live in, we cover the fair rental value of such premises less any expenses that do not continue while it is not fit to live in.

Payment will be for the shortest time required to repair or replace such premises.

3. Civil Authority Prohibits Use

If a civil authority prohibits you from use of the "residence premises" as a result of direct damage to neighboring premises by a Peril Insured Against, we cover the loss as provided in **1.** Additional Living Expense and **2.** Fair Rental Value above for no more than two weeks.

4. Loss Or Expense Not Covered

We do not cover loss or expense due to cancellation of a lease or agreement.

The periods of time under **1.** Additional Living Expense, **2.** Fair Rental Value and **3.** Civil Authority Prohibits Use above are not limited by expiration of this policy.

E. Additional Coverages

1. Debris Removal

a. We will pay your reasonable expense for the removal of:

(1) Debris of covered property if a Peril Insured Against that applies to the damaged property causes the loss; or

(2) Ash, dust or particles from a volcanic eruption that has caused direct loss to a building or property contained in a building.

This expense is included in the limit of liability that applies to the damaged property. If the amount to be paid for the actual damage to the property plus the debris removal expense is more than the limit of liability for the damaged property, an additional 5% of that limit is available for such expense.

b. We will also pay your reasonable expense, up to $1,000, for the removal from the "residence premises" of:

(1) Your trees felled by the peril of Windstorm or Hail or Weight of Ice, Snow or Sleet; or

(2) A neighbor's trees felled by a Peril Insured Against under Coverage **C;**

provided the trees:

(3) Damage a covered structure; or

(4) Do not damage a covered structure, but:

(a) Block a driveway on the "residence premises" which prevents a "motor vehicle", that is registered for use on public roads or property, from entering or leaving the "residence premises"; or

(b) Block a ramp or other fixture designed to assist a handicapped person to enter or leave the dwelling building.

The $1,000 limit is the most we will pay in any one loss, regardless of the number of fallen trees. No more than $500 of this limit will be paid for the removal of any one tree.

This coverage is additional insurance.

2. Reasonable Repairs

a. We will pay the reasonable cost incurred by you for the necessary measures taken solely to protect covered property that is damaged by a Peril Insured Against from further damage.

b. If the measures taken involve repair to other damaged property, we will only pay if that property is covered under this policy and the damage is caused by a Peril Insured Against. This coverage does not:

(1) Increase the limit of liability that applies to the covered property; or

(2) Relieve you of your duties, in case of a loss to covered property, described in **C.4.** under Section **I** – Conditions.

3. Trees, Shrubs And Other Plants

We cover trees, shrubs, plants or lawns, on the "residence premises", for loss caused by the following Perils Insured Against:

a. Fire or Lightning;

b. Explosion;

c. Riot or Civil Commotion;

d. Aircraft;

e. Vehicles not owned or operated by a resident of the "residence premises";

f. Vandalism or Malicious Mischief; or

g. Theft.

We will pay up to 5% of the limit of liability that applies to the dwelling for all trees, shrubs, plants or lawns. No more than $500 of this limit will be paid for any one tree, shrub or plant. We do not cover property grown for "business" purposes.

This coverage is additional insurance.

4. Fire Department Service Charge

We will pay up to $500 for your liability assumed by contract or agreement for fire department charges incurred when the fire department is called to save or protect covered property from a Peril Insured Against. We do not cover fire department service charges if the property is located within the limits of the city, municipality or protection district furnishing the fire department response.

This coverage is additional insurance. No deductible applies to this coverage.

5. Property Removed

We insure covered property against direct loss from any cause while being removed from a premises endangered by a Peril Insured Against and for no more than 30 days while removed.

This coverage does not change the limit of liability that applies to the property being removed.

6. Credit Card, Electronic Fund Transfer Card Or Access Device, Forgery And Counterfeit Money

a. We will pay up to $500 for:

(1) The legal obligation of an "insured" to pay because of the theft or unauthorized use of credit cards issued to or registered in an "insured's" name;

(2) Loss resulting from theft or unauthorized use of an electronic fund transfer card or access device used for deposit, withdrawal or transfer of funds, issued to or registered in an "insured's" name;

(3) Loss to an "insured" caused by forgery or alteration of any check or negotiable instrument; and

(4) Loss to an "insured" through acceptance in good faith of counterfeit United States or Canadian paper currency.

All loss resulting from a series of acts committed by any one person or in which any one person is concerned or implicated is considered to be one loss.

This coverage is additional insurance. No deductible applies to this coverage.

b. We do not cover:

(1) Use of a credit card, electronic fund transfer card or access device:

(a) By a resident of your household;

(b) By a person who has been entrusted with either type of card or access device; or

(c) If an "insured" has not complied with all terms and conditions under which the cards are issued or the devices accessed; or

(2) Loss arising out of "business" use or dishonesty of an "insured".

c. If the coverage in **a.** applies, the following defense provisions also apply:

(1) We may investigate and settle any claim or suit that we decide is appropriate. Our duty to defend a claim or suit ends when the amount we pay for the loss equals our limit of liability.

(2) If a suit is brought against an "insured" for liability under **a.(1)** or **(2)** above, we will provide a defense at our expense by counsel of our choice.

(3) We have the option to defend at our expense an "insured" or an "insured's" bank against any suit for the enforcement of payment under **a.(3)** above.

7. Loss Assessment

a. We will pay up to $1,000 for your share of loss assessment charged during the policy period against you, as owner or tenant of the "residence premises", by a corporation or association of property owners. The assessment must be made as a result of direct loss to property, owned by all members collectively, of the type that would be covered by this policy if owned by you, caused by a Peril Insured Against under Coverage **A,** other than:

(1) Earthquake; or

(2) Land shock waves or tremors before, during or after a volcanic eruption.

The limit of $1,000 is the most we will pay with respect to any one loss, regardless of the number of assessments. We will only apply one deductible, per unit, to the total amount of any one loss to the property described above, regardless of the number of assessments.

b. We do not cover assessments charged against you or a corporation or association of property owners by any governmental body.

c. Paragraph **Q.** Policy Period under Section **I** – Conditions does not apply to this coverage.

This coverage is additional insurance.

8. Collapse

a. The coverage provided under this Additional Coverage – Collapse applies only to an abrupt collapse.

b. For the purpose of this Additional Coverage – Collapse, abrupt collapse means an abrupt falling down or caving in of a building or any part of a building with the result that the building or part of the building cannot be occupied for its intended purpose.

c. This Additional Coverage – Collapse does not apply to:

(1) A building or any part of a building that is in danger of falling down or caving in;

(2) A part of a building that is standing, even if it has separated from another part of the building; or

(3) A building or any part of a building that is standing, even if it shows evidence of cracking, bulging, sagging, bending, leaning, settling, shrinkage or expansion.

d. We insure for direct physical loss to covered property involving abrupt collapse of a building or any part of a building if such collapse was caused by one or more of the following:

(1) The Perils Insured Against;

(2) Decay, of a building or any part of a building, that is hidden from view, unless the presence of such decay is known to an "insured" prior to collapse;

(3) Insect or vermin damage, to a building or any part of a building, that is hidden from view, unless the presence of such damage is known to an "insured" prior to collapse;

(4) Weight of contents, equipment, animals or people;

(5) Weight of rain which collects on a roof; or

(6) Use of defective material or methods in construction, remodeling or renovation if the collapse occurs during the course of the construction, remodeling or renovation.

e. Loss to an awning, fence, patio, deck, pavement, swimming pool, underground pipe, flue, drain, cesspool, septic tank, foundation, retaining wall, bulkhead, pier, wharf or dock is not included under **d.(2)** through **(6)** above, unless the loss is a direct result of the collapse of a building or any part of a building.

f. This coverage does not increase the limit of liability that applies to the damaged covered property.

9. Glass Or Safety Glazing Material

a. We cover:

(1) The breakage of glass or safety glazing material which is part of a covered building, storm door or storm window;

(2) The breakage of glass or safety glazing material which is part of a covered building, storm door or storm window when caused directly by earth movement; and

(3) The direct physical loss to covered property caused solely by the pieces, fragments or splinters of broken glass or safety glazing material which is part of a building, storm door or storm window.

b. This coverage does not include loss:

(1) To covered property which results because the glass or safety glazing material has been broken, except as provided in **a.(3)** above; or

(2) On the "residence premises" if the dwelling has been vacant for more than 60 consecutive days immediately before the loss, except when the breakage results directly from earth movement as provided in **a.(2)** above. A dwelling being constructed is not considered vacant.

c. This coverage does not increase the limit of liability that applies to the damaged property.

10. Landlord's Furnishings

We will pay up to $2,500 for your appliances, carpeting and other household furnishings, in each apartment on the "residence premises" regularly rented or held for rental to others by an "insured", for loss caused by a Peril Insured Against other than Theft.

This limit is the most we will pay in any one loss regardless of the number of appliances, carpeting or other household furnishings involved in the loss.

This coverage does not increase the limit of liability applying to the damaged property.

11. Ordinance Or Law

a. You may use up to 10% of the limit of liability that applies to Coverage **A** for the increased costs you incur due to the enforcement of any ordinance or law which requires or regulates:

(1) The construction, demolition, remodeling, renovation or repair of that part of a covered building or other structure damaged by a Peril Insured Against;

(2) The demolition and reconstruction of the undamaged part of a covered building or other structure, when that building or other structure must be totally demolished because of damage by a Peril Insured Against to another part of that covered building or other structure; or

(3) The remodeling, removal or replacement of the portion of the undamaged part of a covered building or other structure necessary to complete the remodeling, repair or replacement of that part of the covered building or other structure damaged by a Peril Insured Against.

b. You may use all or part of this ordinance or law coverage to pay for the increased costs you incur to remove debris resulting from the construction, demolition, remodeling, renovation, repair or replacement of property as stated in **a.** above.

c. We do not cover:

(1) The loss in value to any covered building or other structure due to the requirements of any ordinance or law; or

(2) The costs to comply with any ordinance or law which requires any "insured" or others to test for, monitor, clean up, remove, contain, treat, detoxify or neutralize, or in any way respond to, or assess the effects of, pollutants in or on any covered building or other structure.

Pollutants means any solid, liquid, gaseous or thermal irritant or contaminant, including smoke, vapor, soot, fumes, acids, alkalis, chemicals and waste. Waste includes materials to be recycled, reconditioned or reclaimed.

This coverage is additional insurance.

12. Grave Markers

We will pay up to $5,000 for grave markers, including mausoleums, on or away from the "residence premises" for loss caused by a Peril Insured Against.

This coverage does not increase the limits of liability that apply to the damaged covered property.

SECTION I – PERILS INSURED AGAINST

We insure for direct physical loss to the property described in Coverages **A, B** and **C** caused by any of the following perils unless the loss is excluded under Section **I** – Exclusions.

1. Fire Or Lightning

2. Windstorm Or Hail

This peril includes loss to watercraft of all types and their trailers, furnishings, equipment, and outboard engines or motors, only while inside a fully enclosed building.

This peril does not include loss to the inside of a building or the property contained in a building caused by rain, snow, sleet, sand or dust unless the direct force of wind or hail damages the building causing an opening in a roof or wall and the rain, snow, sleet, sand or dust enters through this opening.

3. **Explosion**
4. **Riot Or Civil Commotion**
5. **Aircraft**

   This peril includes self-propelled missiles and spacecraft.

6. **Vehicles**

   This peril does not include loss to a fence, driveway or walk caused by a vehicle owned or operated by a resident of the "residence premises".

7. **Smoke**

   This peril means sudden and accidental damage from smoke, including the emission or puffback of smoke, soot, fumes or vapors from a boiler, furnace or related equipment.

   This peril does not include loss caused by smoke from agricultural smudging or industrial operations.

8. **Vandalism Or Malicious Mischief**

   This peril does not include loss to property on the "residence premises", and any ensuing loss caused by any intentional and wrongful act committed in the course of the vandalism or malicious mischief, if the dwelling has been vacant for more than 60 consecutive days immediately before the loss. A dwelling being constructed is not considered vacant.

9. **Theft**

   a. This peril includes attempted theft and loss of property from a known place when it is likely that the property has been stolen.

   b. This peril does not include loss caused by theft:

   (1) Committed by an "insured";

   (2) In or to a dwelling under construction, or of materials and supplies for use in the construction until the dwelling is finished and occupied;

   (3) From that part of a "residence premises" rented by an "insured" to someone other than another "insured"; or

   (4) That occurs off the "residence premises" of:

   (a) Trailers, semitrailers and campers;

   (b) Watercraft of all types, and their furnishings, equipment and outboard engines or motors; or

   (c) Property while at any other residence owned by, rented to, or occupied by an "insured", except while an "insured" is temporarily living there. Property of an "insured" who is a student is covered while at the residence the student occupies to attend school as long as the student has been there at any time during the 90 days immediately before the loss.

10. **Falling Objects**

    This peril does not include loss to the inside of a building or property contained in the building unless the roof or an outside wall of the building is first damaged by a falling object. Damage to the falling object itself is not included.

11. **Weight Of Ice, Snow Or Sleet**

    This peril means weight of ice, snow or sleet which causes damage to a building or property contained in a building.

    This peril does not include loss to an awning, fence, patio, pavement, swimming pool, foundation, retaining wall, bulkhead, pier, wharf, or dock.

12. **Accidental Discharge Or Overflow Of Water Or Steam**

    a. This peril means accidental discharge or overflow of water or steam from within a plumbing, heating, air conditioning or automatic fire protective sprinkler system or from within a household appliance. We also pay to tear out and replace any part of the building, or other structure, on the "residence premises", but only when necessary to repair the system or appliance from which the water or steam escaped. However, such tear out and replacement coverage only applies to other structures if the water or steam causes actual damage to a building on the "residence premises".

    b. This peril does not include loss:

    (1) On the "residence premises", if the dwelling has been vacant for more than 60 consecutive days immediately before the loss. A dwelling being constructed is not considered vacant;

    (2) To the system or appliance from which the water or steam escaped;

    (3) Caused by or resulting from freezing except as provided in Peril Insured Against **14.** Freezing;

(4) On the "residence premises" caused by accidental discharge or overflow which occurs off the "residence premises"; or

(5) Caused by mold, fungus or wet rot unless hidden within the walls or ceilings or beneath the floors or above the ceilings of a structure.

c. In this peril, a plumbing system or household appliance does not include a sump, sump pump or related equipment or a roof drain, gutter, downspout or similar fixtures or equipment.

d. Section **I** – Exclusion **3.** Water, Paragraphs **a.** and **c.** that apply to surface water and water below the surface of the ground do not apply to loss by water covered under this peril.

13. Sudden And Accidental Tearing Apart, Cracking, Burning Or Bulging

This peril means sudden and accidental tearing apart, cracking, burning or bulging of a steam or hot water heating system, an air conditioning or automatic fire protective sprinkler system, or an appliance for heating water.

This peril does not include loss caused by or resulting from freezing except as provided in Peril Insured Against **14.** Freezing below.

14. Freezing

a. This peril means freezing of a plumbing, heating, air conditioning or automatic fire protective sprinkler system or of a household appliance, but only if you have used reasonable care to:

(1) Maintain heat in the building; or

(2) Shut off the water supply and drain all systems and appliances of water.

However, if the building is protected by an automatic fire protective sprinkler system, you must use reasonable care to continue the water supply and maintain heat in the building for coverage to apply.

b. In this peril, a plumbing system or household appliance does not include a sump, sump pump or related equipment or a roof drain, gutter, downspout or similar fixtures or equipment.

15. Sudden And Accidental Damage From Artificially Generated Electrical Current

This peril does not include loss to tubes, transistors, electronic components or circuitry that is a part of appliances, fixtures, computers, home entertainment units or other types of electronic apparatus.

16. Volcanic Eruption

This peril does not include loss caused by earthquake, land shock waves or tremors.

SECTION I – EXCLUSIONS

We do not insure for loss caused directly or indirectly by any of the following. Such loss is excluded regardless of any other cause or event contributing concurrently or in any sequence to the loss. These exclusions apply whether or not the loss event results in widespread damage or affects a substantial area.

1. Ordinance Or Law

Ordinance or Law means any ordinance or law:

a. Requiring or regulating the construction, demolition, remodeling, renovation or repair of property, including removal of any resulting debris. This Exclusion **1.a.** does not apply to the amount of coverage that may be provided for in **E.11.** Ordinance Or Law under Section **I** – Property Coverages;

b. The requirements of which result in a loss in value to property; or

c. Requiring any "insured" or others to test for, monitor, clean up, remove, contain, treat, detoxify or neutralize, or in any way respond to, or assess the effects of, pollutants.

Pollutants means any solid, liquid, gaseous or thermal irritant or contaminant, including smoke, vapor, soot, fumes, acids, alkalis, chemicals and waste. Waste includes materials to be recycled, reconditioned or reclaimed.

This Exclusion **1.** applies whether or not the property has been physically damaged.

2. Earth Movement

Earth Movement means:

a. Earthquake, including land shock waves or tremors before, during or after a volcanic eruption;

b. Landslide, mudslide or mudflow;

c. Subsidence or sinkhole; or

d. Any other earth movement including earth sinking, rising or shifting.

This Exclusion **2.** applies regardless of whether any of the above, in **2.a.** through **2.d.,** is caused by an act of nature or is otherwise caused.

However, direct loss by fire, explosion or theft resulting from any of the above, in **2.a.** through **2.d.,** is covered.

3. **Water**

This means:

a. Flood, surface water, waves, including tidal wave and tsunami, tides, tidal water, overflow of any body of water, or spray from any of these, all whether or not driven by wind, including storm surge;

b. Water which:

(1) Backs up through sewers or drains; or

(2) Overflows or is otherwise discharged from a sump, sump pump or related equipment;

c. Water below the surface of the ground, including water which exerts pressure on, or seeps, leaks or flows through a building, sidewalk, driveway, patio, foundation, swimming pool or other structure; or

d. Waterborne material carried or otherwise moved by any of the water referred to in **3.a.** through **3.c.** of this exclusion.

This Exclusion **3.** applies regardless of whether any of the above, in **3.a.** through **3.d.,** is caused by an act of nature or is otherwise caused.

This Exclusion **3.** applies to, but is not limited to, escape, overflow or discharge, for any reason, of water or waterborne material from a dam, levee, seawall or any other boundary or containment system.

However, direct loss by fire, explosion or theft resulting from any of the above, in **3.a.** through **3.d.,** is covered.

4. **Power Failure**

Power Failure means the failure of power or other utility service if the failure takes place off the "residence premises". But if the failure results in a loss, from a Peril Insured Against on the "residence premises", we will pay for the loss caused by that peril.

5. **Neglect**

Neglect means neglect of an "insured" to use all reasonable means to save and preserve property at and after the time of a loss.

6. **War**

War includes the following and any consequence of any of the following:

a. Undeclared war, civil war, insurrection, rebellion or revolution;

b. Warlike act by a military force or military personnel; or

c. Destruction, seizure or use for a military purpose.

Discharge of a nuclear weapon will be deemed a warlike act even if accidental.

7. **Nuclear Hazard**

This Exclusion **7.** pertains to Nuclear Hazard to the extent set forth in **N.** Nuclear Hazard Clause under Section **I** – Conditions.

8. **Intentional Loss**

Intentional Loss means any loss arising out of any act an "insured" commits or conspires to commit with the intent to cause a loss.

In the event of such loss, no "insured" is entitled to coverage, even "insureds" who did not commit or conspire to commit the act causing the loss.

9. **Governmental Action**

Governmental Action means the destruction, confiscation or seizure of property described in Coverage **A, B** or **C** by order of any governmental or public authority.

This exclusion does not apply to such acts ordered by any governmental or public authority that are taken at the time of a fire to prevent its spread, if the loss caused by fire would be covered under this policy.

SECTION I – CONDITIONS

A. Insurable Interest And Limit Of Liability

Even if more than one person has an insurable interest in the property covered, we will not be liable in any one loss:

1. To an "insured" for more than the amount of such "insured's" interest at the time of loss; or
2. For more than the applicable limit of liability.

B. Deductible

Unless otherwise noted in this policy, the following deductible provision applies:

With respect to any one loss:

1. Subject to the applicable limit of liability, we will pay only that part of the total of all loss payable that exceeds the deductible amount shown in the Declarations.
2. If two or more deductibles under this policy apply to the loss, only the highest deductible amount will apply.

C. Duties After Loss

In case of a loss to covered property, we have no duty to provide coverage under this policy if the failure to comply with the following duties is prejudicial to us. These duties must be performed either by you, an "insured" seeking coverage, or a representative of either:

1. Give prompt notice to us or our agent;
2. Notify the police in case of loss by theft;

3. Notify the credit card or electronic fund transfer card or access device company in case of loss as provided for in **E.6.** Credit Card, Electronic Fund Transfer Card Or Access Device, Forgery And Counterfeit Money under Section **I** – Property Coverages;
4. Protect the property from further damage. If repairs to the property are required, you must:
   a. Make reasonable and necessary repairs to protect the property; and
   b. Keep an accurate record of repair expenses;
5. Cooperate with us in the investigation of a claim;
6. Prepare an inventory of damaged personal property showing the quantity, description, actual cash value and amount of loss. Attach all bills, receipts and related documents that justify the figures in the inventory;
7. As often as we reasonably require:
   a. Show the damaged property;
   b. Provide us with records and documents we request and permit us to make copies; and
   c. Submit to examination under oath, while not in the presence of another "insured", and sign the same;
8. Send to us, within 60 days after our request, your signed, sworn proof of loss which sets forth, to the best of your knowledge and belief:
   a. The time and cause of loss;
   b. The interests of all "insureds" and all others in the property involved and all liens on the property;
   c. Other insurance which may cover the loss;
   d. Changes in title or occupancy of the property during the term of the policy;
   e. Specifications of damaged buildings and detailed repair estimates;
   f. The inventory of damaged personal property described in **6.** above;
   g. Receipts for additional living expenses incurred and records that support the fair rental value loss; and
   h. Evidence or affidavit that supports a claim under **E.6.** Credit Card, Electronic Fund Transfer Card Or Access Device, Forgery And Counterfeit Money under Section **I** – Property Coverages, stating the amount and cause of loss.

D. Loss Settlement

In this Condition **D.**, the terms "cost to repair or replace" and "replacement cost" do not include the increased costs incurred to comply with the enforcement of any ordinance or law, except to the extent that coverage for these increased costs is provided in **E.11.** Ordinance Or Law under Section **I** – Property Coverages. Covered property losses are settled as follows:

1. Property of the following types:
   a. Personal property;
   b. Awnings, carpeting, household appliances, outdoor antennas and outdoor equipment, whether or not attached to buildings;
   c. Structures that are not buildings; and
   d. Grave markers, including mausoleums;

   at actual cash value at the time of loss but not more than the amount required to repair or replace.
2. Buildings covered under Coverage **A** or **B** at replacement cost without deduction for depreciation, subject to the following:
   a. If, at the time of loss, the amount of insurance in this policy on the damaged building is 80% or more of the full replacement cost of the building immediately before the loss, we will pay the cost to repair or replace, without deduction for depreciation, but not more than the least of the following amounts:
      (1) The limit of liability under this policy that applies to the building;
      (2) The replacement cost of that part of the building damaged with material of like kind and quality and for like use; or
      (3) The necessary amount actually spent to repair or replace the damaged building.

      If the building is rebuilt at a new premises, the cost described in **(2)** above is limited to the cost which would have been incurred if the building had been built at the original premises.
   b. If, at the time of loss, the amount of insurance in this policy on the damaged building is less than 80% of the full replacement cost of the building immediately before the loss, we will pay the greater of the following amounts, but not more than the limit of liability under this policy that applies to the building:
      (1) The actual cash value of that part of the building damaged; or

(2) That proportion of the cost to repair or replace, without deduction for depreciation, that part of the building damaged, which the total amount of insurance in this policy on the damaged building bears to 80% of the replacement cost of the building.

c. To determine the amount of insurance required to equal 80% of the full replacement cost of the building immediately before the loss, do not include the value of:

(1) Excavations, footings, foundations, piers, or any other structures or devices that support all or part of the building, which are below the undersurface of the lowest basement floor;

(2) Those supports described in **(1)** above which are below the surface of the ground inside the foundation walls, if there is no basement; and

(3) Underground flues, pipes, wiring and drains.

d. We will pay no more than the actual cash value of the damage until actual repair or replacement is complete. Once actual repair or replacement is complete, we will settle the loss as noted in **2.a.** and **b.** above.

However, if the cost to repair or replace the damage is both:

(1) Less than 5% of the amount of insurance in this policy on the building; and

(2) Less than $2,500;

we will settle the loss as noted in **2.a.** and **b.** above whether or not actual repair or replacement is complete.

e. You may disregard the replacement cost loss settlement provisions and make claim under this policy for loss to buildings on an actual cash value basis. You may then make claim for any additional liability according to the provisions of this Condition **D.** Loss Settlement, provided you notify us, within 180 days after the date of loss, of your intent to repair or replace the damaged building.

E. Loss To A Pair Or Set

In case of loss to a pair or set we may elect to:

1. Repair or replace any part to restore the pair or set to its value before the loss; or

2. Pay the difference between actual cash value of the property before and after the loss.

F. Appraisal

If you and we fail to agree on the amount of loss, either may demand an appraisal of the loss. In this event, each party will choose a competent and impartial appraiser within 20 days after receiving a written request from the other. The two appraisers will choose an umpire. If they cannot agree upon an umpire within 15 days, you or we may request that the choice be made by a judge of a court of record in the state where the "residence premises" is located. The appraisers will separately set the amount of loss. If the appraisers submit a written report of an agreement to us, the amount agreed upon will be the amount of loss. If they fail to agree, they will submit their differences to the umpire. A decision agreed to by any two will set the amount of loss.

Each party will:

1. Pay its own appraiser; and

2. Bear the other expenses of the appraisal and umpire equally.

G. Other Insurance And Service Agreement

If a loss covered by this policy is also covered by:

1. Other insurance, we will pay only the proportion of the loss that the limit of liability that applies under this policy bears to the total amount of insurance covering the loss; or

2. A service agreement, this insurance is excess over any amounts payable under any such agreement. Service agreement means a service plan, property restoration plan, home warranty or other similar service warranty agreement, even if it is characterized as insurance.

H. Suit Against Us

No action can be brought against us unless there has been full compliance with all of the terms under Section **I** of this policy and the action is started within two years after the date of loss.

I. Our Option

If we give you written notice within 30 days after we receive your signed, sworn proof of loss, we may repair or replace any part of the damaged property with material or property of like kind and quality.

J. Loss Payment

We will adjust all losses with you. We will pay you unless some other person is named in the policy or is legally entitled to receive payment. Loss will be payable 60 days after we receive your proof of loss and:

1. Reach an agreement with you;

2. There is an entry of a final judgment; or

3. There is a filing of an appraisal award with us.

K. Abandonment Of Property

We need not accept any property abandoned by an "insured".

L. Mortgage Clause

1. If a mortgagee is named in this policy, any loss payable under Coverage **A** or **B** will be paid to the mortgagee and you, as interests appear. If more than one mortgagee is named, the order of payment will be the same as the order of precedence of the mortgages.

2. If we deny your claim, that denial will not apply to a valid claim of the mortgagee, if the mortgagee:

a. Notifies us of any change in ownership, occupancy or substantial change in risk of which the mortgagee is aware;

b. Pays any premium due under this policy on demand if you have neglected to pay the premium; and

c. Submits a signed, sworn statement of loss within 60 days after receiving notice from us of your failure to do so. Paragraphs **F.** Appraisal, **H.** Suit Against Us and **J.** Loss Payment under Section **I** – Conditions also apply to the mortgagee.

3. If we decide to cancel or not to renew this policy, the mortgagee will be notified at least 10 days before the date cancellation or nonrenewal takes effect.

4. If we pay the mortgagee for any loss and deny payment to you:

a. We are subrogated to all the rights of the mortgagee granted under the mortgage on the property; or

b. At our option, we may pay to the mortgagee the whole principal on the mortgage plus any accrued interest. In this event, we will receive a full assignment and transfer of the mortgage and all securities held as collateral to the mortgage debt.

5. Subrogation will not impair the right of the mortgagee to recover the full amount of the mortgagee's claim.

M. No Benefit To Bailee

We will not recognize any assignment or grant any coverage that benefits a person or organization holding, storing or moving property for a fee regardless of any other provision of this policy.

N. Nuclear Hazard Clause

1. "Nuclear Hazard" means any nuclear reaction, radiation, or radioactive contamination, all whether controlled or uncontrolled or however caused, or any consequence of any of these.

2. Loss caused by the nuclear hazard will not be considered loss caused by fire, explosion, or smoke, whether these perils are specifically named in or otherwise included within the Perils Insured Against.

3. This policy does not apply under Section **I** to loss caused directly or indirectly by nuclear hazard, except that direct loss by fire resulting from the nuclear hazard is covered.

O. Recovered Property

If you or we recover any property for which we have made payment under this policy, you or we will notify the other of the recovery. At your option, the property will be returned to or retained by you or it will become our property. If the recovered property is returned to or retained by you, the loss payment will be adjusted based on the amount you received for the recovered property.

P. Volcanic Eruption Period

One or more volcanic eruptions that occur within a 72-hour period will be considered as one volcanic eruption.

Q. Policy Period

This policy applies only to loss which occurs during the policy period.

R. Concealment Or Fraud

We provide coverage to no "insureds" under this policy if, whether before or after a loss, an "insured" has:

1. Intentionally concealed or misrepresented any material fact or circumstance;

2. Engaged in fraudulent conduct; or

3. Made false statements;

relating to this insurance.

S. Loss Payable Clause

If the Declarations shows a loss payee for certain listed insured personal property, the definition of "insured" is changed to include that loss payee with respect to that property.

If we decide to cancel or not renew this policy, that loss payee will be notified in writing.

SECTION II – LIABILITY COVERAGES

A. Coverage E – Personal Liability

If a claim is made or a suit is brought against an "insured" for damages because of "bodily injury" or "property damage" caused by an "occurrence" to which this coverage applies, we will:

1. Pay up to our limit of liability for the damages for which an "insured" is legally liable. Damages include prejudgment interest awarded against an "insured"; and
2. Provide a defense at our expense by counsel of our choice, even if the suit is groundless, false or fraudulent. We may investigate and settle any claim or suit that we decide is appropriate. Our duty to settle or defend ends when our limit of liability for the "occurrence" has been exhausted by payment of a judgment or settlement.

B. Coverage F – Medical Payments To Others

We will pay the necessary medical expenses that are incurred or medically ascertained within three years from the date of an accident causing "bodily injury". Medical expenses means reasonable charges for medical, surgical, x-ray, dental, ambulance, hospital, professional nursing, prosthetic devices and funeral services. This coverage does not apply to you or regular residents of your household except "residence employees". As to others, this coverage applies only:

1. To a person on the "insured location" with the permission of an "insured"; or
2. To a person off the "insured location", if the "bodily injury":
   a. Arises out of a condition on the "insured location" or the ways immediately adjoining;
   b. Is caused by the activities of an "insured";
   c. Is caused by a "residence employee" in the course of the "residence employee's" employment by an "insured"; or
   d. Is caused by an animal owned by or in the care of an "insured".

SECTION II – EXCLUSIONS

A. "Motor Vehicle Liability"

1. Coverages **E** and **F** do not apply to any "motor vehicle liability" if, at the time and place of an "occurrence", the involved "motor vehicle":
   a. Is registered for use on public roads or property;
   b. Is not registered for use on public roads or property, but such registration is required by a law, or regulation issued by a government agency, for it to be used at the place of the "occurrence"; or
   c. Is being:
      (1) Operated in, or practicing for, any prearranged or organized race, speed contest or other competition;
      (2) Rented to others;
      (3) Used to carry persons or cargo for a charge; or
      (4) Used for any "business" purpose except for a motorized golf cart while on a golfing facility.
2. If Exclusion **A.1.** does not apply, there is still no coverage for "motor vehicle liability", unless the "motor vehicle" is:
   a. In dead storage on an "insured location";
   b. Used solely to service a residence;
   c. Designed to assist the handicapped and, at the time of an "occurrence", it is:
      (1) Being used to assist a handicapped person; or
      (2) Parked on an "insured location";
   d. Designed for recreational use off public roads and:
      (1) Not owned by an "insured"; or
      (2) Owned by an "insured" provided the "occurrence" takes place:
         (a) On an "insured location" as defined in Definition **B.6.a., b., d., e.** or **h.**; or
         (b) Off an "insured location" and the "motor vehicle" is:
            (i) Designed as a toy vehicle for use by children under seven years of age;
            (ii) Powered by one or more batteries; and
            (iii) Not built or modified after manufacture to exceed a speed of five miles per hour on level ground;

e. A motorized golf cart that is owned by an "insured", designed to carry up to four persons, not built or modified after manufacture to exceed a speed of 25 miles per hour on level ground and, at the time of an "occurrence", is within the legal boundaries of:

(1) A golfing facility and is parked or stored there, or being used by an "insured" to:

(a) Play the game of golf or for other recreational or leisure activity allowed by the facility;

(b) Travel to or from an area where "motor vehicles" or golf carts are parked or stored; or

(c) Cross public roads at designated points to access other parts of the golfing facility; or

(2) A private residential community, including its public roads upon which a motorized golf cart can legally travel, which is subject to the authority of a property owners association and contains an "insured's" residence.

B. "Watercraft Liability"

1. Coverages **E** and **F** do not apply to any "watercraft liability" if, at the time of an "occurrence", the involved watercraft is being:

a. Operated in, or practicing for, any prearranged or organized race, speed contest or other competition. This exclusion does not apply to a sailing vessel or a predicted log cruise;

b. Rented to others;

c. Used to carry persons or cargo for a charge; or

d. Used for any "business" purpose.

2. If Exclusion **B.1.** does not apply, there is still no coverage for "watercraft liability" unless, at the time of the "occurrence", the watercraft:

a. Is stored;

b. Is a sailing vessel, with or without auxiliary power, that is:

(1) Less than 26 feet in overall length; or

(2) 26 feet or more in overall length and not owned by or rented to an "insured"; or

c. Is not a sailing vessel and is powered by:

(1) An inboard or inboard-outdrive engine or motor, including those that power a water jet pump, of:

(a) 50 horsepower or less and not owned by an "insured"; or

(b) More than 50 horsepower and not owned by or rented to an "insured"; or

(2) One or more outboard engines or motors with:

(a) 25 total horsepower or less;

(b) More than 25 horsepower if the outboard engine or motor is not owned by an "insured";

(c) More than 25 horsepower if the outboard engine or motor is owned by an "insured" who acquired it during the policy period; or

(d) More than 25 horsepower if the outboard engine or motor is owned by an "insured" who acquired it before the policy period, but only if:

(i) You declare them at policy inception; or

(ii) Your intent to insure them is reported to us in writing within 45 days after you acquire them.

The coverages in **(c)** and **(d)** above apply for the policy period.

Horsepower means the maximum power rating assigned to the engine or motor by the manufacturer.

C. "Aircraft Liability"

This policy does not cover "aircraft liability".

D. "Hovercraft Liability"

This policy does not cover "hovercraft liability".

E. Coverage E – Personal Liability And Coverage F – Medical Payments To Others

Coverages **E** and **F** do not apply to the following:

1. Expected Or Intended Injury

"Bodily injury" or "property damage" which is expected or intended by an "insured", even if the resulting "bodily injury" or "property damage":

a. Is of a different kind, quality or degree than initially expected or intended; or

b. Is sustained by a different person, entity or property than initially expected or intended.

However, this Exclusion **E.1.** does not apply to "bodily injury" or "property damage" resulting from the use of reasonable force by an "insured" to protect persons or property;

2. **"Business"**

   a. "Bodily injury" or "property damage" arising out of or in connection with a "business" conducted from an "insured location" or engaged in by an "insured", whether or not the "business" is owned or operated by an "insured" or employs an "insured".

   This Exclusion **E.2.** applies but is not limited to an act or omission, regardless of its nature or circumstance, involving a service or duty rendered, promised, owed, or implied to be provided because of the nature of the "business".

   b. This Exclusion **E.2.** does not apply to:

   (1) The rental or holding for rental of an "insured location";

   (a) On an occasional basis if used only as a residence;

   (b) In part for use only as a residence, unless a single-family unit is intended for use by the occupying family to lodge more than two roomers or boarders; or

   (c) In part, as an office, school, studio or private garage; and

   (2) An "insured" under the age of 21 years involved in a part-time or occasional, self-employed "business" with no employees;

3. **Professional Services**

   "Bodily injury" or "property damage" arising out of the rendering of or failure to render professional services;

4. **"Insured's" Premises Not An "Insured Location"**

   "Bodily injury" or "property damage" arising out of a premises:

   a. Owned by an "insured";

   b. Rented to an "insured"; or

   c. Rented to others by an "insured";

   that is not an "insured location";

5. **War**

   "Bodily injury" or "property damage" caused directly or indirectly by war, including the following and any consequence of any of the following:

   a. Undeclared war, civil war, insurrection, rebellion or revolution;

   b. Warlike act by a military force or military personnel; or

   c. Destruction, seizure or use for a military purpose.

   Discharge of a nuclear weapon will be deemed a warlike act even if accidental;

6. **Communicable Disease**

   "Bodily injury" or "property damage" which arises out of the transmission of a communicable disease by an "insured";

7. **Sexual Molestation, Corporal Punishment Or Physical Or Mental Abuse**

   "Bodily injury" or "property damage" arising out of sexual molestation, corporal punishment or physical or mental abuse; or

8. **Controlled Substance**

   "Bodily injury" or "property damage" arising out of the use, sale, manufacture, delivery, transfer or possession by any person of a Controlled Substance as defined by the Federal Food and Drug Law at 21 U.S.C.A. Sections 811 and 812. Controlled Substances include but are not limited to cocaine, LSD, marijuana and all narcotic drugs. However, this exclusion does not apply to the legitimate use of prescription drugs by a person following the lawful orders of a licensed health care professional.

Exclusions **A.** "Motor Vehicle Liability", **B.** "Watercraft Liability", **C.** "Aircraft Liability", **D.** "Hovercraft Liability" and **E.4.** "Insured's" Premises Not An "Insured Location" do not apply to "bodily injury" to a "residence employee" arising out of and in the course of the "residence employee's" employment by an "insured".

F. Coverage E – Personal Liability

Coverage **E** does not apply to:

1. Liability:

   a. For any loss assessment charged against you as a member of an association, corporation or community of property owners, except as provided in **D.** Loss Assessment under Section **II** – Additional Coverages;

   b. Under any contract or agreement entered into by an "insured". However, this exclusion does not apply to written contracts:

   (1) That directly relate to the ownership, maintenance or use of an "insured location"; or

   (2) Where the liability of others is assumed by you prior to an "occurrence";

   unless excluded in **a.** above or elsewhere in this policy;

2. "Property damage" to property owned by an "insured". This includes costs or expenses incurred by an "insured" or others to repair, replace, enhance, restore or maintain such property to prevent injury to a person or damage to property of others, whether on or away from an "insured location";

3. "Property damage" to property rented to, occupied or used by or in the care of an "insured". This exclusion does not apply to "property damage" caused by fire, smoke or explosion;

4. "Bodily injury" to any person eligible to receive any benefits voluntarily provided or required to be provided by an "insured" under any:

a. Workers' compensation law;

b. Non-occupational disability law; or

c. Occupational disease law;

5. "Bodily injury" or "property damage" for which an "insured" under this policy:

a. Is also an insured under a nuclear energy liability policy issued by the:

(1) Nuclear Energy Liability Insurance Association;

(2) Mutual Atomic Energy Liability Underwriters;

(3) Nuclear Insurance Association of Canada;

or any of their successors; or

b. Would be an insured under such a policy but for the exhaustion of its limit of liability; or

6. "Bodily injury" to you or an "insured" as defined under Definition **5.a.** or **b.**

This exclusion also applies to any claim made or suit brought against you or an "insured" to:

a. Repay; or

b. Share damages with;

another person who may be obligated to pay damages because of "bodily injury" to an "insured".

G. Coverage F – Medical Payments To Others

Coverage **F** does not apply to "bodily injury":

1. To a "residence employee" if the "bodily injury":

a. Occurs off the "insured location"; and

b. Does not arise out of or in the course of the "residence employee's" employment by an "insured";

2. To any person eligible to receive benefits voluntarily provided or required to be provided under any:

a. Workers' compensation law;

b. Non-occupational disability law; or

c. Occupational disease law;

3. From any:

a. Nuclear reaction;

b. Nuclear radiation; or

c. Radioactive contamination;

all whether controlled or uncontrolled or however caused; or

d. Any consequence of any of these; or

4. To any person, other than a "residence employee" of an "insured", regularly residing on any part of the "insured location".

SECTION II – ADDITIONAL COVERAGES

We cover the following in addition to the limits of liability:

A. Claim Expenses

We pay:

1. Expenses we incur and costs taxed against an "insured" in any suit we defend;

2. Premiums on bonds required in a suit we defend, but not for bond amounts more than the Coverage **E** limit of liability. We need not apply for or furnish any bond;

3. Reasonable expenses incurred by an "insured" at our request, including actual loss of earnings (but not loss of other income) up to $250 per day, for assisting us in the investigation or defense of a claim or suit; and

4. Interest on the entire judgment which accrues after entry of the judgment and before we pay or tender, or deposit in court that part of the judgment which does not exceed the limit of liability that applies.

B. First Aid Expenses

We will pay expenses for first aid to others incurred by an "insured" for "bodily injury" covered under this policy. We will not pay for first aid to an "insured".

C. Damage To Property Of Others

1. We will pay, at replacement cost, up to $1,000 per "occurrence" for "property damage" to property of others caused by an "insured".

2. We will not pay for "property damage":

a. To the extent of any amount recoverable under Section **I;**

b. Caused intentionally by an "insured" who is 13 years of age or older;

c. To property owned by an "insured";

d. To property owned by or rented to a tenant of an "insured" or a resident in your household; or

e. Arising out of:

(1) A "business" engaged in by an "insured";

(2) Any act or omission in connection with a premises owned, rented or controlled by an "insured", other than the "insured location"; or

(3) The ownership, maintenance, occupancy, operation, use, loading or unloading of aircraft, hovercraft, watercraft or "motor vehicles".

This Exclusion **e.(3)** does not apply to a "motor vehicle" that:

(a) Is designed for recreational use off public roads;

(b) Is not owned by an "insured"; and

(c) At the time of the "occurrence", is not required by law, or regulation issued by a government agency, to have been registered for it to be used on public roads or property.

D. Loss Assessment

1. We will pay up to $1,000 for your share of loss assessment charged against you, as owner or tenant of the "residence premises", during the policy period by a corporation or association of property owners, when the assessment is made as a result of:

a. "Bodily injury" or "property damage" not excluded from coverage under Section **II** – Exclusions; or

b. Liability for an act of a director, officer or trustee in the capacity as a director, officer or trustee, provided such person:

(1) Is elected by the members of a corporation or association of property owners; and

(2) Serves without deriving any income from the exercise of duties which are solely on behalf of a corporation or association of property owners.

2. Paragraph **I.** Policy Period under Section **II** – Conditions does not apply to this Loss Assessment Coverage.

3. Regardless of the number of assessments, the limit of $1,000 is the most we will pay for loss arising out of:

a. One accident, including continuous or repeated exposure to substantially the same general harmful condition; or

b. A covered act of a director, officer or trustee. An act involving more than one director, officer or trustee is considered to be a single act.

4. We do not cover assessments charged against you or a corporation or association of property owners by any governmental body.

SECTION II – CONDITIONS

A. Limit Of Liability

Our total liability under Coverage **E** for all damages resulting from any one "occurrence" will not be more than the Coverage **E** Limit Of Liability shown in the Declarations. This limit is the same regardless of the number of "insureds", claims made or persons injured. All "bodily injury" and "property damage" resulting from any one accident or from continuous or repeated exposure to substantially the same general harmful conditions shall be considered to be the result of one "occurrence".

Our total liability under Coverage **F** for all medical expense payable for "bodily injury" to one person as the result of one accident will not be more than the Coverage **F** Limit Of Liability shown in the Declarations.

B. Severability Of Insurance

This insurance applies separately to each "insured". This condition will not increase our limit of liability for any one "occurrence".

C. Duties After "Occurrence"

In case of an "occurrence", you or another "insured" will perform the following duties that apply. We have no duty to provide coverage under this policy if your failure to comply with the following duties is prejudicial to us. You will help us by seeing that these duties are performed:

1. Give written notice to us or our agent as soon as is practical, which sets forth:

a. The identity of the policy and the "named insured" shown in the Declarations;

b. Reasonably available information on the time, place and circumstances of the "occurrence"; and

c. Names and addresses of any claimants and witnesses;

2. Cooperate with us in the investigation, settlement or defense of any claim or suit;
3. Promptly forward to us every notice, demand, summons or other process relating to the "occurrence";
4. At our request, help us:
   a. To make settlement;
   b. To enforce any right of contribution or indemnity against any person or organization who may be liable to an "insured";
   c. With the conduct of suits and attend hearings and trials; and
   d. To secure and give evidence and obtain the attendance of witnesses;
5. With respect to **C.** Damage To Property Of Others under Section **II** – Additional Coverages, submit to us within 60 days after the loss a sworn statement of loss and show the damaged property, if in an "insured's" control;
6. No "insured" shall, except at such "insured's" own cost, voluntarily make payment, assume obligation or incur expense other than for first aid to others at the time of the "bodily injury".

D. Duties Of An Injured Person – Coverage F – Medical Payments To Others

1. The injured person or someone acting for the injured person will:
   a. Give us written proof of claim, under oath if required, as soon as is practical; and
   b. Authorize us to obtain copies of medical reports and records.
2. The injured person will submit to a physical exam by a doctor of our choice when and as often as we reasonably require.

E. Payment Of Claim – Coverage F – Medical Payments To Others

Payment under this coverage is not an admission of liability by an "insured" or us.

F. Suit Against Us

1. No action can be brought against us unless there has been full compliance with all of the terms under this Section **II.**
2. No one will have the right to join us as a party to any action against an "insured".
3. Also, no action with respect to Coverage **E** can be brought against us until the obligation of such "insured" has been determined by final judgment or agreement signed by us.

G. Bankruptcy Of An "Insured"

Bankruptcy or insolvency of an "insured" will not relieve us of our obligations under this policy.

H. Other Insurance

This insurance is excess over other valid and collectible insurance except insurance written specifically to cover as excess over the limits of liability that apply in this policy.

I. Policy Period

This policy applies only to "bodily injury" or "property damage" which occurs during the policy period.

J. Concealment Or Fraud

We do not provide coverage to an "insured" who, whether before or after a loss, has:

1. Intentionally concealed or misrepresented any material fact or circumstance;
2. Engaged in fraudulent conduct; or
3. Made false statements;

relating to this insurance.

SECTIONS I AND II – CONDITIONS

A. Liberalization Clause

If we make a change which broadens coverage under this edition of our policy without additional premium charge, that change will automatically apply to your insurance as of the date we implement the change in your state, provided that this implementation date falls within 60 days prior to or during the policy period stated in the Declarations.

This Liberalization Clause does not apply to changes implemented with a general program revision that includes both broadenings and restrictions in coverage, whether that general program revision is implemented through introduction of:

1. A subsequent edition of this policy; or
2. An amendatory endorsement.

B. Waiver Or Change Of Policy Provisions

A waiver or change of a provision of this policy must be in writing by us to be valid. Our request for an appraisal or examination will not waive any of our rights.

C. Cancellation

1. You may cancel this policy at any time by returning it to us or by letting us know in writing of the date cancellation is to take effect.

2. We may cancel this policy only for the reasons stated below by letting you know in writing of the date cancellation takes effect. This cancellation notice may be delivered to you, or mailed to you at your mailing address shown in the Declarations. Proof of mailing will be sufficient proof of notice.

a. When you have not paid the premium, we may cancel at any time by letting you know at least 10 days before the date cancellation takes effect.

b. When this policy has been in effect for less than 60 days and is not a renewal with us, we may cancel for any reason by letting you know at least 10 days before the date cancellation takes effect.

c. When this policy has been in effect for 60 days or more, or at any time if it is a renewal with us, we may cancel:

(1) If there has been a material misrepresentation of fact which if known to us would have caused us not to issue the policy; or

(2) If the risk has changed substantially since the policy was issued.

This can be done by letting you know at least 30 days before the date cancellation takes effect.

d. When this policy is written for a period of more than one year, we may cancel for any reason at anniversary by letting you know at least 30 days before the date cancellation takes effect.

3. When this policy is canceled, the premium for the period from the date of cancellation to the expiration date will be refunded pro rata.

4. If the return premium is not refunded with the notice of cancellation or when this policy is returned to us, we will refund it within a reasonable time after the date cancellation takes effect.

D. Nonrenewal

We may elect not to renew this policy. We may do so by delivering to you, or mailing to you at your mailing address shown in the Declarations, written notice at least 30 days before the expiration date of this policy. Proof of mailing will be sufficient proof of notice.

E. Assignment

Assignment of this policy will not be valid unless we give our written consent.

F. Subrogation

An "insured" may waive in writing before a loss all rights of recovery against any person. If not waived, we may require an assignment of rights of recovery for a loss to the extent that payment is made by us.

If an assignment is sought, an "insured" must sign and deliver all related papers and cooperate with us.

Subrogation does not apply to Coverage **F** or Paragraph **C.** Damage To Property Of Others under Section **II** – Additional Coverages.

G. Death

If any person named in the Declarations or the spouse, if a resident of the same household, dies, the following apply:

1. We insure the legal representative of the deceased but only with respect to the premises and property of the deceased covered under the policy at the time of death; and

2. "Insured" includes:

a. An "insured" who is a member of your household at the time of your death, but only while a resident of the "residence premises"; and

b. With respect to your property, the person having proper temporary custody of the property until appointment and qualification of a legal representative.

HOMEOWNERS 3 – SPECIAL FORM

AGREEMENT

We will provide the insurance described in this policy in return for the premium and compliance with all applicable provisions of this policy.

DEFINITIONS

A. In this policy, "you" and "your" refer to the "named insured" shown in the Declarations and the spouse if a resident of the same household. "We", "us" and "our" refer to the Company providing this insurance.

B. In addition, certain words and phrases are defined as follows:

1. "Aircraft Liability", "Hovercraft Liability", "Motor Vehicle Liability" and "Watercraft Liability", subject to the provisions in **b.** below, mean the following:

a. Liability for "bodily injury" or "property damage" arising out of the:

(1) Ownership of such vehicle or craft by an "insured";

(2) Maintenance, occupancy, operation, use, loading or unloading of such vehicle or craft by any person;

(3) Entrustment of such vehicle or craft by an "insured" to any person;

(4) Failure to supervise or negligent supervision of any person involving such vehicle or craft by an "insured"; or

(5) Vicarious liability, whether or not imposed by law, for the actions of a child or minor involving such vehicle or craft.

b. For the purpose of this definition:

(1) Aircraft means any contrivance used or designed for flight except model or hobby aircraft not used or designed to carry people or cargo;

(2) Hovercraft means a self-propelled motorized ground effect vehicle and includes, but is not limited to, flarecraft and air cushion vehicles;

(3) Watercraft means a craft principally designed to be propelled on or in water by wind, engine power or electric motor; and

(4) Motor vehicle means a "motor vehicle" as defined in **7.** below.

2. "Bodily injury" means bodily harm, sickness or disease, including required care, loss of services and death that results.

3. "Business" means:

a. A trade, profession or occupation engaged in on a full-time, part-time or occasional basis; or

b. Any other activity engaged in for money or other compensation, except the following:

(1) One or more activities, not described in **(2)** through **(4)** below, for which no "insured" receives more than $2,000 in total compensation for the 12 months before the beginning of the policy period;

(2) Volunteer activities for which no money is received other than payment for expenses incurred to perform the activity;

(3) Providing home day care services for which no compensation is received, other than the mutual exchange of such services; or

(4) The rendering of home day care services to a relative of an "insured".

4. "Employee" means an employee of an "insured", or an employee leased to an "insured" by a labor leasing firm under an agreement between an "insured" and the labor leasing firm, whose duties are other than those performed by a "residence employee".

5. "Insured" means:

a. You and residents of your household who are:

(1) Your relatives; or

(2) Other persons under the age of 21 and in your care or the care of a resident of your household who is your relative;

b. A student enrolled in school full-time, as defined by the school, who was a resident of your household before moving out to attend school, provided the student is under the age of:

(1) 24 and your relative; or

(2) 21 and in your care or the care of a resident of your household who is your relative; or

c. Under Section **II:**

(1) With respect to animals or watercraft to which this policy applies, any person or organization legally responsible for these animals or watercraft which are owned by you or any person described in **5.a.** or **b.** "Insured" does not mean a person or organization using or having custody of these animals or watercraft in the course of any "business" or without consent of the owner; or

(2) With respect to a "motor vehicle" to which this policy applies:

(a) Persons while engaged in your employ or that of any person described in **5.a.** or **b.;** or

(b) Other persons using the vehicle on an "insured location" with your consent.

Under both Sections **I** and **II,** when the word an immediately precedes the word "insured", the words an "insured" together mean one or more "insureds".

6. "Insured location" means:

a. The "residence premises";

b. The part of other premises, other structures and grounds used by you as a residence; and

(1) Which is shown in the Declarations; or

(2) Which is acquired by you during the policy period for your use as a residence;

c. Any premises used by you in connection with a premises described in **a.** and **b.** above;

d. Any part of a premises:

(1) Not owned by an "insured"; and

(2) Where an "insured" is temporarily residing;

e. Vacant land, other than farm land, owned by or rented to an "insured";

f. Land owned by or rented to an "insured" on which a one-, two-, three- or four-family dwelling is being built as a residence for an "insured";

g. Individual or family cemetery plots or burial vaults of an "insured"; or

h. Any part of a premises occasionally rented to an "insured" for other than "business" use.

7. "Motor vehicle" means:

a. A self-propelled land or amphibious vehicle; or

b. Any trailer or semitrailer which is being carried on, towed by or hitched for towing by a vehicle described in **a.** above.

8. "Occurrence" means an accident, including continuous or repeated exposure to substantially the same general harmful conditions, which results, during the policy period, in:

a. "Bodily injury"; or

b. "Property damage".

9. "Property damage" means physical injury to, destruction of, or loss of use of tangible property.

10. "Residence employee" means:

a. An employee of an "insured", or an employee leased to an "insured" by a labor leasing firm, under an agreement between an "insured" and the labor leasing firm, whose duties are related to the maintenance or use of the "residence premises", including household or domestic services; or

b. One who performs similar duties elsewhere not related to the "business" of an "insured".

A "residence employee" does not include a temporary employee who is furnished to an "insured" to substitute for a permanent "residence employee" on leave or to meet seasonal or short-term workload conditions.

11. "Residence premises" means:

a. The one-family dwelling where you reside;

b. The two-, three- or four-family dwelling where you reside in at least one of the family units; or

c. That part of any other building where you reside;

and which is shown as the "residence premises" in the Declarations.

"Residence premises" also includes other structures and grounds at that location.

SECTION I – PROPERTY COVERAGES

A. Coverage A – Dwelling

1. We cover:
   a. The dwelling on the "residence premises" shown in the Declarations, including structures attached to the dwelling; and
   b. Materials and supplies located on or next to the "residence premises" used to construct, alter or repair the dwelling or other structures on the "residence premises".
2. We do not cover land, including land on which the dwelling is located.

B. Coverage B – Other Structures

1. We cover other structures on the "residence premises" set apart from the dwelling by clear space. This includes structures connected to the dwelling by only a fence, utility line, or similar connection.
2. We do not cover:
   a. Land, including land on which the other structures are located;
   b. Other structures rented or held for rental to any person not a tenant of the dwelling, unless used solely as a private garage;
   c. Other structures from which any "business" is conducted; or
   d. Other structures used to store "business" property. However, we do cover a structure that contains "business" property solely owned by an "insured" or a tenant of the dwelling, provided that "business" property does not include gaseous or liquid fuel, other than fuel in a permanently installed fuel tank of a vehicle or craft parked or stored in the structure.
3. The limit of liability for this coverage will not be more than 10% of the limit of liability that applies to Coverage **A.** Use of this coverage does not reduce the Coverage **A** limit of liability.

C. Coverage C – Personal Property

1. **Covered Property**

   We cover personal property owned or used by an "insured" while it is anywhere in the world. After a loss and at your request, we will cover personal property owned by:
   a. Others while the property is on the part of the "residence premises" occupied by an "insured"; or
   b. A guest or a "residence employee", while the property is in any residence occupied by an "insured".
2. **Limit For Property At Other Locations**
   a. **Other Residences**

      Our limit of liability for personal property usually located at an "insured's" residence, other than the "residence premises", is 10% of the limit of liability for Coverage **C,** or $1,000, whichever is greater. However, this limitation does not apply to personal property:

      (1) Moved from the "residence premises" because it is:

         (a) Being repaired, renovated or rebuilt; and

         (b) Not fit to live in or store property in; or

      (2) In a newly acquired principal residence for 30 days from the time you begin to move the property there.
   b. **Self-storage Facilities**

      Our limit of liability for personal property owned or used by an "insured" and located in a self-storage facility is 10% of the limit of liability for Coverage **C,** or $1,000, whichever is greater. However, this limitation does not apply to personal property:

      (1) Moved from the "residence premises" because it is:

         (a) Being repaired, renovated or rebuilt; and

         (b) Not fit to live in or store property in; or

      (2) Usually located in an "insured's" residence, other than the "residence premises".

3. Special Limits Of Liability

The special limit for each category shown below is the total limit for each loss for all property in that category. These special limits do not increase the Coverage **C** limit of liability.

a. $200 on money, bank notes, bullion, gold other than goldware, silver other than silverware, platinum other than platinumware, coins, medals, scrip, stored value cards and smart cards.

b. $1,500 on securities, accounts, deeds, evidences of debt, letters of credit, notes other than bank notes, manuscripts, personal records, passports, tickets and stamps. This dollar limit applies to these categories regardless of the medium (such as paper or computer software) on which the material exists.

This limit includes the cost to research, replace or restore the information from the lost or damaged material.

c. $1,500 on watercraft of all types, including their trailers, furnishings, equipment and outboard engines or motors.

d. $1,500 on trailers or semitrailers not used with watercraft of all types.

e. $1,500 for loss by theft of jewelry, watches, furs, precious and semiprecious stones.

f. $2,500 for loss by theft of firearms and related equipment.

g. $2,500 for loss by theft of silverware, silver-plated ware, goldware, gold-plated ware, platinumware, platinum-plated ware and pewterware. This includes flatware, hollowware, tea sets, trays and trophies made of or including silver, gold or pewter.

h. $2,500 on property, on the "residence premises", used primarily for "business" purposes.

i. $1,500 on property, away from the "residence premises", used primarily for "business" purposes. However, this limit does not apply to antennas, tapes, wires, records, disks or other media that are:

(1) Used with electronic equipment that reproduces, receives or transmits audio, visual or data signals; and

(2) In or upon a "motor vehicle".

j. $1,500 on portable electronic equipment that:

(1) Reproduces, receives or transmits audio, visual or data signals;

(2) Is designed to be operated by more than one power source, one of which is a "motor vehicle's" electrical system; and

(3) Is in or upon a "motor vehicle".

k. $250 for antennas, tapes, wires, records, disks or other media that are:

(1) Used with electronic equipment that reproduces, receives or transmits audio, visual or data signals; and

(2) In or upon a "motor vehicle".

4. Property Not Covered

We do not cover:

a. Articles separately described and specifically insured, regardless of the limit for which they are insured, in this or other insurance;

b. Animals, birds or fish;

c. "Motor vehicles".

This includes a "motor vehicle's" equipment and parts. However, this Paragraph **4.c.** does not apply to:

(1) Portable electronic equipment that:

(a) Reproduces, receives or transmits audio, visual or data signals; and

(b) Is designed so that it may be operated from a power source other than a "motor vehicle's" electrical system.

(2) "Motor vehicles" not required to be registered for use on public roads or property which are:

(a) Used solely to service a residence; or

(b) Designed to assist the handicapped;

d. Aircraft, meaning any contrivance used or designed for flight, including any parts whether or not attached to the aircraft.

We do cover model or hobby aircraft not used or designed to carry people or cargo;

e. Hovercraft and parts. Hovercraft means a self-propelled motorized ground effect vehicle and includes, but is not limited to, flarecraft and air cushion vehicles;

f. Property of roomers, boarders and other tenants, except property of roomers and boarders related to an "insured";

g. Property in an apartment regularly rented or held for rental to others by an "insured", except as provided in **E.10.** Landlord's Furnishings under Section **I** – Property Coverages;

h. Property rented or held for rental to others off the "residence premises";

i. "Business" data, including such data stored in:

(1) Books of account, drawings or other paper records; or

(2) Computers and related equipment.

We do cover the cost of blank recording or storage media and of prerecorded computer programs available on the retail market;

j. Credit cards, electronic fund transfer cards or access devices used solely for deposit, withdrawal or transfer of funds except as provided in **E.6.** Credit Card, Electronic Fund Transfer Card Or Access Device, Forgery And Counterfeit Money under Section **I** – Property Coverages; or

k. Water or steam.

D. Coverage D – Loss Of Use

The limit of liability for Coverage **D** is the total limit for the coverages in **1.** Additional Living Expense, **2.** Fair Rental Value and **3.** Civil Authority Prohibits Use below.

1. Additional Living Expense

If a loss covered under Section **I** makes that part of the "residence premises" where you reside not fit to live in, we cover any necessary increase in living expenses incurred by you so that your household can maintain its normal standard of living.

Payment will be for the shortest time required to repair or replace the damage or, if you permanently relocate, the shortest time required for your household to settle elsewhere.

2. Fair Rental Value

If a loss covered under Section **I** makes that part of the "residence premises" rented to others or held for rental by you not fit to live in, we cover the fair rental value of such premises less any expenses that do not continue while it is not fit to live in.

Payment will be for the shortest time required to repair or replace such premises.

3. Civil Authority Prohibits Use

If a civil authority prohibits you from use of the "residence premises" as a result of direct damage to neighboring premises by a Peril Insured Against, we cover the loss as provided in **1.** Additional Living Expense and **2.** Fair Rental Value above for no more than two weeks.

4. Loss Or Expense Not Covered

We do not cover loss or expense due to cancellation of a lease or agreement.

The periods of time under **1.** Additional Living Expense, **2.** Fair Rental Value and **3.** Civil Authority Prohibits Use above are not limited by expiration of this policy.

E. Additional Coverages

1. Debris Removal

a. We will pay your reasonable expense for the removal of:

(1) Debris of covered property if a Peril Insured Against that applies to the damaged property causes the loss; or

(2) Ash, dust or particles from a volcanic eruption that has caused direct loss to a building or property contained in a building.

This expense is included in the limit of liability that applies to the damaged property. If the amount to be paid for the actual damage to the property plus the debris removal expense is more than the limit of liability for the damaged property, an additional 5% of that limit is available for such expense.

b. We will also pay your reasonable expense, up to $1,000, for the removal from the "residence premises" of:

(1) Your trees felled by the peril of Windstorm or Hail or Weight of Ice, Snow or Sleet; or

(2) A neighbor's trees felled by a Peril Insured Against under Coverage **C;**

provided the trees:

(3) Damage a covered structure; or

(4) Do not damage a covered structure, but:

(a) Block a driveway on the "residence premises" which prevents a "motor vehicle", that is registered for use on public roads or property, from entering or leaving the "residence premises"; or

(b) Block a ramp or other fixture designed to assist a handicapped person to enter or leave the dwelling building.

The $1,000 limit is the most we will pay in any one loss, regardless of the number of fallen trees. No more than $500 of this limit will be paid for the removal of any one tree.

This coverage is additional insurance.

2. Reasonable Repairs

a. We will pay the reasonable cost incurred by you for the necessary measures taken solely to protect covered property that is damaged by a Peril Insured Against from further damage.

b. If the measures taken involve repair to other damaged property, we will only pay if that property is covered under this policy and the damage is caused by a Peril Insured Against. This coverage does not:

(1) Increase the limit of liability that applies to the covered property; or

(2) Relieve you of your duties, in case of a loss to covered property, described in **C.4.** under Section **I** – Conditions.

3. Trees, Shrubs And Other Plants

We cover trees, shrubs, plants or lawns, on the "residence premises", for loss caused by the following Perils Insured Against:

a. Fire or Lightning;

b. Explosion;

c. Riot or Civil Commotion;

d. Aircraft;

e. Vehicles not owned or operated by a resident of the "residence premises";

f. Vandalism or Malicious Mischief; or

g. Theft.

We will pay up to 5% of the limit of liability that applies to the dwelling for all trees, shrubs, plants or lawns. No more than $500 of this limit will be paid for any one tree, shrub or plant. We do not cover property grown for "business" purposes.

This coverage is additional insurance.

4. Fire Department Service Charge

We will pay up to $500 for your liability assumed by contract or agreement for fire department charges incurred when the fire department is called to save or protect covered property from a Peril Insured Against. We do not cover fire department service charges if the property is located within the limits of the city, municipality or protection district furnishing the fire department response.

This coverage is additional insurance. No deductible applies to this coverage.

5. Property Removed

We insure covered property against direct loss from any cause while being removed from a premises endangered by a Peril Insured Against and for no more than 30 days while removed.

This coverage does not change the limit of liability that applies to the property being removed.

6. Credit Card, Electronic Fund Transfer Card Or Access Device, Forgery And Counterfeit Money

a. We will pay up to $500 for:

(1) The legal obligation of an "insured" to pay because of the theft or unauthorized use of credit cards issued to or registered in an "insured's" name;

(2) Loss resulting from theft or unauthorized use of an electronic fund transfer card or access device used for deposit, withdrawal or transfer of funds, issued to or registered in an "insured's" name;

(3) Loss to an "insured" caused by forgery or alteration of any check or negotiable instrument; and

(4) Loss to an "insured" through acceptance in good faith of counterfeit United States or Canadian paper currency.

All loss resulting from a series of acts committed by any one person or in which any one person is concerned or implicated is considered to be one loss.

This coverage is additional insurance. No deductible applies to this coverage.

b. We do not cover:

(1) Use of a credit card, electronic fund transfer card or access device:

(a) By a resident of your household;

(b) By a person who has been entrusted with either type of card or access device; or

(c) If an "insured" has not complied with all terms and conditions under which the cards are issued or the devices accessed; or

(2) Loss arising out of "business" use or dishonesty of an "insured".

c. If the coverage in **a.** above applies, the following defense provisions also apply:

(1) We may investigate and settle any claim or suit that we decide is appropriate. Our duty to defend a claim or suit ends when the amount we pay for the loss equals our limit of liability.

(2) If a suit is brought against an "insured" for liability under **a.(1)** or **(2)** above, we will provide a defense at our expense by counsel of our choice.

(3) We have the option to defend at our expense an "insured" or an "insured's" bank against any suit for the enforcement of payment under **a.(3)** above.

7. Loss Assessment

a. We will pay up to $1,000 for your share of loss assessment charged during the policy period against you, as owner or tenant of the "residence premises", by a corporation or association of property owners. The assessment must be made as a result of direct loss to property, owned by all members collectively, of the type that would be covered by this policy if owned by you, caused by a Peril Insured Against under Coverage **A,** other than:

(1) Earthquake; or

(2) Land shock waves or tremors before, during or after a volcanic eruption.

The limit of $1,000 is the most we will pay with respect to any one loss, regardless of the number of assessments. We will only apply one deductible, per unit, to the total amount of any one loss to the property described above, regardless of the number of assessments.

b. We do not cover assessments charged against you or a corporation or association of property owners by any governmental body.

c. Paragraph **Q.** Policy Period under Section **I** – Conditions does not apply to this coverage.

This coverage is additional insurance.

8. Collapse

a. The coverage provided under this Additional Coverage – Collapse applies only to an abrupt collapse.

b. For the purpose of this Additional Coverage – Collapse, abrupt collapse means an abrupt falling down or caving in of a building or any part of a building with the result that the building or part of the building cannot be occupied for its intended purpose.

c. This Additional Coverage – Collapse does not apply to:

(1) A building or any part of a building that is in danger of falling down or caving in;

(2) A part of a building that is standing, even if it has separated from another part of the building; or

(3) A building or any part of a building that is standing, even if it shows evidence of cracking, bulging, sagging, bending, leaning, settling, shrinkage or expansion.

d. We insure for direct physical loss to covered property involving abrupt collapse of a building or any part of a building if such collapse was caused by one or more of the following:

(1) The Perils Insured Against named under Coverage **C;**

(2) Decay, of a building or any part of a building, that is hidden from view, unless the presence of such decay is known to an "insured" prior to collapse;

(3) Insect or vermin damage, to a building or any part of a building, that is hidden from view, unless the presence of such damage is known to an "insured" prior to collapse;

(4) Weight of contents, equipment, animals or people;

(5) Weight of rain which collects on a roof; or

(6) Use of defective material or methods in construction, remodeling or renovation if the collapse occurs during the course of the construction, remodeling or renovation.

e. Loss to an awning, fence, patio, deck, pavement, swimming pool, underground pipe, flue, drain, cesspool, septic tank, foundation, retaining wall, bulkhead, pier, wharf or dock is not included under **d.(2)** through **(6)** above, unless the loss is a direct result of the collapse of a building or any part of a building.

f. This coverage does not increase the limit of liability that applies to the damaged covered property.

9. Glass Or Safety Glazing Material

a. We cover:

(1) The breakage of glass or safety glazing material which is part of a covered building, storm door or storm window;

(2) The breakage of glass or safety glazing material which is part of a covered building, storm door or storm window when caused directly by earth movement; and

(3) The direct physical loss to covered property caused solely by the pieces, fragments or splinters of broken glass or safety glazing material which is part of a building, storm door or storm window.

b. This coverage does not include loss:

(1) To covered property which results because the glass or safety glazing material has been broken, except as provided in **a.(3)** above; or

(2) On the "residence premises" if the dwelling has been vacant for more than 60 consecutive days immediately before the loss, except when the breakage results directly from earth movement as provided in **a.(2)** above. A dwelling being constructed is not considered vacant.

c. This coverage does not increase the limit of liability that applies to the damaged property.

10. Landlord's Furnishings

We will pay up to $2,500 for your appliances, carpeting and other household furnishings, in each apartment on the "residence premises" regularly rented or held for rental to others by an "insured", for loss caused by a Peril Insured Against in Coverage **C,** other than Theft.

This limit is the most we will pay in any one loss regardless of the number of appliances, carpeting or other household furnishings involved in the loss.

This coverage does not increase the limit of liability applying to the damaged property.

11. Ordinance Or Law

a. You may use up to 10% of the limit of liability that applies to Coverage **A** for the increased costs you incur due to the enforcement of any ordinance or law which requires or regulates:

(1) The construction, demolition, remodeling, renovation or repair of that part of a covered building or other structure damaged by a Peril Insured Against;

(2) The demolition and reconstruction of the undamaged part of a covered building or other structure, when that building or other structure must be totally demolished because of damage by a Peril Insured Against to another part of that covered building or other structure; or

(3) The remodeling, removal or replacement of the portion of the undamaged part of a covered building or other structure necessary to complete the remodeling, repair or replacement of that part of the covered building or other structure damaged by a Peril Insured Against.

b. You may use all or part of this ordinance or law coverage to pay for the increased costs you incur to remove debris resulting from the construction, demolition, remodeling, renovation, repair or replacement of property as stated in **a.** above.

c. We do not cover:

(1) The loss in value to any covered building or other structure due to the requirements of any ordinance or law; or

(2) The costs to comply with any ordinance or law which requires any "insured" or others to test for, monitor, clean up, remove, contain, treat, detoxify or neutralize, or in any way respond to, or assess the effects of, pollutants in or on any covered building or other structure.

Pollutants means any solid, liquid, gaseous or thermal irritant or contaminant, including smoke, vapor, soot, fumes, acids, alkalis, chemicals and waste. Waste includes materials to be recycled, reconditioned or reclaimed.

This coverage is additional insurance.

12. Grave Markers

We will pay up to $5,000 for grave markers, including mausoleums, on or away from the "residence premises" for loss caused by a Peril Insured Against under Coverage **C.**

This coverage does not increase the limits of liability that apply to the damaged covered property.

SECTION I – PERILS INSURED AGAINST

A. Coverage A – Dwelling And Coverage B – Other Structures

1. We insure against direct physical loss to property described in Coverages **A** and **B.**

2. We do not insure, however, for loss:

a. Excluded under Section **I** – Exclusions;

b. Involving collapse, including any of the following conditions of property or any part of the property:

(1) An abrupt falling down or caving in;

(2) Loss of structural integrity, including separation of parts of the property or property in danger of falling down or caving in; or

(3) Any cracking, bulging, sagging, bending, leaning, settling, shrinkage or expansion as such condition relates to **(1)** or **(2)** above;

except as provided in **E.8.** Collapse under Section **I** – Property Coverages; or

c. Caused by:

(1) Freezing of a plumbing, heating, air conditioning or automatic fire protective sprinkler system or of a household appliance, or by discharge, leakage or overflow from within the system or appliance caused by freezing. This provision does not apply if you have used reasonable care to:

(a) Maintain heat in the building; or

(b) Shut off the water supply and drain all systems and appliances of water.

However, if the building is protected by an automatic fire protective sprinkler system, you must use reasonable care to continue the water supply and maintain heat in the building for coverage to apply.

For purposes of this provision, a plumbing system or household appliance does not include a sump, sump pump or related equipment or a roof drain, gutter, downspout or similar fixtures or equipment;

(2) Freezing, thawing, pressure or weight of water or ice, whether driven by wind or not, to a:

(a) Fence, pavement, patio or swimming pool;

(b) Footing, foundation, bulkhead, wall, or any other structure or device that supports all or part of a building, or other structure;

(c) Retaining wall or bulkhead that does not support all or part of a building or other structure; or

(d) Pier, wharf or dock;

(3) Theft in or to a dwelling under construction, or of materials and supplies for use in the construction until the dwelling is finished and occupied;

(4) Vandalism and malicious mischief, and any ensuing loss caused by any intentional and wrongful act committed in the course of the vandalism or malicious mischief, if the dwelling has been vacant for more than 60 consecutive days immediately before the loss. A dwelling being constructed is not considered vacant;

(5) Mold, fungus or wet rot. However, we do insure for loss caused by mold, fungus or wet rot that is hidden within the walls or ceilings or beneath the floors or above the ceilings of a structure if such loss results from the accidental discharge or overflow of water or steam from within:

(a) A plumbing, heating, air conditioning or automatic fire protective sprinkler system, or a household appliance, on the "residence premises"; or

(b) A storm drain, or water, steam or sewer pipes, off the "residence premises".

For purposes of this provision, a plumbing system or household appliance does not include a sump, sump pump or related equipment or a roof drain, gutter, downspout or similar fixtures or equipment; or

(6) Any of the following:

(a) Wear and tear, marring, deterioration;

(b) Mechanical breakdown, latent defect, inherent vice or any quality in property that causes it to damage or destroy itself;

(c) Smog, rust or other corrosion, or dry rot;

(d) Smoke from agricultural smudging or industrial operations;

(e) Discharge, dispersal, seepage, migration, release or escape of pollutants unless the discharge, dispersal, seepage, migration, release or escape is itself caused by a Peril Insured Against named under Coverage **C.**

Pollutants means any solid, liquid, gaseous or thermal irritant or contaminant, including smoke, vapor, soot, fumes, acids, alkalis, chemicals and waste. Waste includes materials to be recycled, reconditioned or reclaimed;

(f) Settling, shrinking, bulging or expansion, including resultant cracking, of bulkheads, pavements, patios, footings, foundations, walls, floors, roofs or ceilings;

(g) Birds, rodents or insects;

(h) Nesting or infestation, or discharge or release of waste products or secretions, by any animals; or

(i) Animals owned or kept by an "insured".

Exception To c.(6)

Unless the loss is otherwise excluded, we cover loss to property covered under Coverage **A** or **B** resulting from an accidental discharge or overflow of water or steam from within a:

(i) Storm drain, or water, steam or sewer pipe, off the "residence premises"; or

(ii) Plumbing, heating, air conditioning or automatic fire protective sprinkler system or household appliance on the "residence premises". This includes the cost to tear out and replace any part of a building, or other structure, on the "residence premises", but only when necessary to repair the system or appliance. However, such tear out and replacement coverage only applies to other structures if the water or steam causes actual damage to a building on the "residence premises".

We do not cover loss to the system or appliance from which this water or steam escaped.

For purposes of this provision, a plumbing system or household appliance does not include a sump, sump pump or related equipment or a roof drain, gutter, downspout or similar fixtures or equipment.

Section **I** – Exclusion **A.3.** Water, Paragraphs **a.** and **c.** that apply to surface water and water below the surface of the ground do not apply to loss by water covered under **c.(5)** and **(6)** above.

Under **2.b.** and **c.** above, any ensuing loss to property described in Coverages **A** and **B** not precluded by any other provision in this policy is covered.

B. Coverage C – Personal Property

We insure for direct physical loss to the property described in Coverage **C** caused by any of the following perils unless the loss is excluded in Section **I** – Exclusions.

1. Fire Or Lightning

2. Windstorm Or Hail

This peril includes loss to watercraft of all types and their trailers, furnishings, equipment, and outboard engines or motors, only while inside a fully enclosed building.

This peril does not include loss to the property contained in a building caused by rain, snow, sleet, sand or dust unless the direct force of wind or hail damages the building causing an opening in a roof or wall and the rain, snow, sleet, sand or dust enters through this opening.

3. Explosion

4. Riot Or Civil Commotion

5. Aircraft

This peril includes self-propelled missiles and spacecraft.

6. Vehicles

7. Smoke

This peril means sudden and accidental damage from smoke, including the emission or puffback of smoke, soot, fumes or vapors from a boiler, furnace or related equipment.

This peril does not include loss caused by smoke from agricultural smudging or industrial operations.

8. Vandalism Or Malicious Mischief

9. Theft

a. This peril includes attempted theft and loss of property from a known place when it is likely that the property has been stolen.

b. This peril does not include loss caused by theft:

(1) Committed by an "insured";

(2) In or to a dwelling under construction, or of materials and supplies for use in the construction until the dwelling is finished and occupied;

(3) From that part of a "residence premises" rented by an "insured" to someone other than another "insured"; or

(4) That occurs off the "residence premises" of:

(a) Trailers, semitrailers and campers;

(b) Watercraft of all types, and their furnishings, equipment and outboard engines or motors; or

(c) Property while at any other residence owned by, rented to, or occupied by an "insured", except while an "insured" is temporarily living there. Property of an "insured" who is a student is covered while at the residence the student occupies to attend school as long as the student has been there at any time during the 90 days immediately before the loss.

10. Falling Objects

This peril does not include loss to property contained in a building unless the roof or an outside wall of the building is first damaged by a falling object. Damage to the falling object itself is not included.

11. Weight Of Ice, Snow Or Sleet

This peril means weight of ice, snow or sleet which causes damage to property contained in a building.

12. Accidental Discharge Or Overflow Of Water Or Steam

a. This peril means accidental discharge or overflow of water or steam from within a plumbing, heating, air conditioning or automatic fire protective sprinkler system or from within a household appliance.

b. This peril does not include loss:

(1) To the system or appliance from which the water or steam escaped;

(2) Caused by or resulting from freezing except as provided in Peril Insured Against **14.** Freezing;

(3) On the "residence premises" caused by accidental discharge or overflow which occurs off the "residence premises"; or

(4) Caused by mold, fungus or wet rot unless hidden within the walls or ceilings or beneath the floors or above the ceilings of a structure.

c. In this peril, a plumbing system or household appliance does not include a sump, sump pump or related equipment or a roof drain, gutter, downspout or similar fixtures or equipment.

d. Section **I** – Exclusion **A.3.** Water, Paragraphs **a.** and **c.** that apply to surface water and water below the surface of the ground do not apply to loss by water covered under this peril.

13. Sudden And Accidental Tearing Apart, Cracking, Burning Or Bulging

This peril means sudden and accidental tearing apart, cracking, burning or bulging of a steam or hot water heating system, an air conditioning or automatic fire protective sprinkler system, or an appliance for heating water.

We do not cover loss caused by or resulting from freezing under this peril.

14. Freezing

a. This peril means freezing of a plumbing, heating, air conditioning or automatic fire protective sprinkler system or of a household appliance, but only if you have used reasonable care to:

(1) Maintain heat in the building; or

(2) Shut off the water supply and drain all systems and appliances of water.

However, if the building is protected by an automatic fire protective sprinkler system, you must use reasonable care to continue the water supply and maintain heat in the building for coverage to apply.

b. In this peril, a plumbing system or household appliance does not include a sump, sump pump or related equipment or a roof drain, gutter, downspout or similar fixtures or equipment.

15. Sudden And Accidental Damage From Artificially Generated Electrical Current

This peril does not include loss to tubes, transistors, electronic components or circuitry that is a part of appliances, fixtures, computers, home entertainment units or other types of electronic apparatus.

16. Volcanic Eruption

This peril does not include loss caused by earthquake, land shock waves or tremors.

SECTION I – EXCLUSIONS

A. We do not insure for loss caused directly or indirectly by any of the following. Such loss is excluded regardless of any other cause or event contributing concurrently or in any sequence to the loss. These exclusions apply whether or not the loss event results in widespread damage or affects a substantial area.

1. Ordinance Or Law

Ordinance Or Law means any ordinance or law:

a. Requiring or regulating the construction, demolition, remodeling, renovation or repair of property, including removal of any resulting debris. This Exclusion **A.1.a.** does not apply to the amount of coverage that may be provided for in **E.11.** Ordinance Or Law under Section **I** – Property Coverages;

b. The requirements of which result in a loss in value to property; or

c. Requiring any "insured" or others to test for, monitor, clean up, remove, contain, treat, detoxify or neutralize, or in any way respond to, or assess the effects of, pollutants.

Pollutants means any solid, liquid, gaseous or thermal irritant or contaminant, including smoke, vapor, soot, fumes, acids, alkalis, chemicals and waste. Waste includes materials to be recycled, reconditioned or reclaimed.

This Exclusion **A.1.** applies whether or not the property has been physically damaged.

2. Earth Movement

Earth Movement means:

a. Earthquake, including land shock waves or tremors before, during or after a volcanic eruption;

b. Landslide, mudslide or mudflow;

c. Subsidence or sinkhole; or

d. Any other earth movement including earth sinking, rising or shifting.

This Exclusion **A.2.** applies regardless of whether any of the above, in **A.2.a.** through **A.2.d.**, is caused by an act of nature or is otherwise caused.

However, direct loss by fire, explosion or theft resulting from any of the above, in **A.2.a.** through **A.2.d.**, is covered.

3. Water

This means:

a. Flood, surface water, waves, including tidal wave and tsunami, tides, tidal water, overflow of any body of water, or spray from any of these, all whether or not driven by wind, including storm surge;

b. Water which:

(1) Backs up through sewers or drains; or

(2) Overflows or is otherwise discharged from a sump, sump pump or related equipment;

c. Water below the surface of the ground, including water which exerts pressure on, or seeps, leaks or flows through a building, sidewalk, driveway, patio, foundation, swimming pool or other structure; or

d. Waterborne material carried or otherwise moved by any of the water referred to in **A.3.a.** through **A.3.c.** of this exclusion.

This Exclusion **A.3.** applies regardless of whether any of the above, in **A.3.a.** through **A.3.d.,** is caused by an act of nature or is otherwise caused.

This Exclusion **A.3.** applies to, but is not limited to, escape, overflow or discharge, for any reason, of water or waterborne material from a dam, levee, seawall or any other boundary or containment system.

However, direct loss by fire, explosion or theft resulting from any of the above, in **A.3.a.** through **A.3.d.,** is covered.

4. Power Failure

Power Failure means the failure of power or other utility service if the failure takes place off the "residence premises". But if the failure results in a loss, from a Peril Insured Against on the "residence premises", we will pay for the loss caused by that peril.

5. Neglect

Neglect means neglect of an "insured" to use all reasonable means to save and preserve property at and after the time of a loss.

6. War

War includes the following and any consequence of any of the following:

a. Undeclared war, civil war, insurrection, rebellion or revolution;

b. Warlike act by a military force or military personnel; or

c. Destruction, seizure or use for a military purpose.

Discharge of a nuclear weapon will be deemed a warlike act even if accidental.

7. Nuclear Hazard

This Exclusion **A.7.** pertains to Nuclear Hazard to the extent set forth in **N.** Nuclear Hazard Clause under Section **I** – Conditions.

8. Intentional Loss

Intentional Loss means any loss arising out of any act an "insured" commits or conspires to commit with the intent to cause a loss.

In the event of such loss, no "insured" is entitled to coverage, even "insureds" who did not commit or conspire to commit the act causing the loss.

9. Governmental Action

Governmental Action means the destruction, confiscation or seizure of property described in Coverage **A, B** or **C** by order of any governmental or public authority.

This exclusion does not apply to such acts ordered by any governmental or public authority that are taken at the time of a fire to prevent its spread, if the loss caused by fire would be covered under this policy.

B. We do not insure for loss to property described in Coverages **A** and **B** caused by any of the following. However, any ensuing loss to property described in Coverages **A** and **B** not precluded by any other provision in this policy is covered.

1. Weather conditions. However, this exclusion only applies if weather conditions contribute in any way with a cause or event excluded in **A.** above to produce the loss.

2. Acts or decisions, including the failure to act or decide, of any person, group, organization or governmental body.

3. Faulty, inadequate or defective:

a. Planning, zoning, development, surveying, siting;

b. Design, specifications, workmanship, repair, construction, renovation, remodeling, grading, compaction;

c. Materials used in repair, construction, renovation or remodeling; or

d. Maintenance;

of part or all of any property whether on or off the "residence premises".

SECTION I – CONDITIONS

A. Insurable Interest And Limit Of Liability

Even if more than one person has an insurable interest in the property covered, we will not be liable in any one loss:

1. To an "insured" for more than the amount of such "insured's" interest at the time of loss; or

2. For more than the applicable limit of liability.

B. Deductible

Unless otherwise noted in this policy, the following deductible provision applies:

With respect to any one loss:

1. Subject to the applicable limit of liability, we will pay only that part of the total of all loss payable that exceeds the deductible amount shown in the Declarations.

2. If two or more deductibles under this policy apply to the loss, only the highest deductible amount will apply.

C. Duties After Loss

In case of a loss to covered property, we have no duty to provide coverage under this policy if the failure to comply with the following duties is prejudicial to us. These duties must be performed either by you, an "insured" seeking coverage, or a representative of either:

1. Give prompt notice to us or our agent;
2. Notify the police in case of loss by theft;
3. Notify the credit card or electronic fund transfer card or access device company in case of loss as provided for in **E.6.** Credit Card, Electronic Fund Transfer Card Or Access Device, Forgery And Counterfeit Money under Section **I** – Property Coverages;
4. Protect the property from further damage. If repairs to the property are required, you must:
   - **a.** Make reasonable and necessary repairs to protect the property; and
   - **b.** Keep an accurate record of repair expenses;
5. Cooperate with us in the investigation of a claim;
6. Prepare an inventory of damaged personal property showing the quantity, description, actual cash value and amount of loss. Attach all bills, receipts and related documents that justify the figures in the inventory;
7. As often as we reasonably require:
   - **a.** Show the damaged property;
   - **b.** Provide us with records and documents we request and permit us to make copies; and
   - **c.** Submit to examination under oath, while not in the presence of another "insured", and sign the same;
8. Send to us, within 60 days after our request, your signed, sworn proof of loss which sets forth, to the best of your knowledge and belief:
   - **a.** The time and cause of loss;
   - **b.** The interests of all "insureds" and all others in the property involved and all liens on the property;
   - **c.** Other insurance which may cover the loss;
   - **d.** Changes in title or occupancy of the property during the term of the policy;
   - **e.** Specifications of damaged buildings and detailed repair estimates;
   - **f.** The inventory of damaged personal property described in **6.** above;
   - **g.** Receipts for additional living expenses incurred and records that support the fair rental value loss; and
   - **h.** Evidence or affidavit that supports a claim under **E.6.** Credit Card, Electronic Fund Transfer Card Or Access Device, Forgery And Counterfeit Money under Section **I** – Property Coverages, stating the amount and cause of loss.

D. Loss Settlement

In this Condition **D.**, the terms "cost to repair or replace" and "replacement cost" do not include the increased costs incurred to comply with the enforcement of any ordinance or law, except to the extent that coverage for these increased costs is provided in **E.11.** Ordinance Or Law under Section **I** – Property Coverages. Covered property losses are settled as follows:

1. Property of the following types:
   - **a.** Personal property;
   - **b.** Awnings, carpeting, household appliances, outdoor antennas and outdoor equipment, whether or not attached to buildings;
   - **c.** Structures that are not buildings; and
   - **d.** Grave markers, including mausoleums;

   at actual cash value at the time of loss but not more than the amount required to repair or replace.
2. Buildings covered under Coverage **A** or **B** at replacement cost without deduction for depreciation, subject to the following:
   - **a.** If, at the time of loss, the amount of insurance in this policy on the damaged building is 80% or more of the full replacement cost of the building immediately before the loss, we will pay the cost to repair or replace, without deduction for depreciation, but not more than the least of the following amounts:
     - **(1)** The limit of liability under this policy that applies to the building;
     - **(2)** The replacement cost of that part of the building damaged with material of like kind and quality and for like use; or
     - **(3)** The necessary amount actually spent to repair or replace the damaged building.

     If the building is rebuilt at a new premises, the cost described in **(2)** above is limited to the cost which would have been incurred if the building had been built at the original premises.

b. If, at the time of loss, the amount of insurance in this policy on the damaged building is less than 80% of the full replacement cost of the building immediately before the loss, we will pay the greater of the following amounts, but not more than the limit of liability under this policy that applies to the building:

(1) The actual cash value of that part of the building damaged; or

(2) That proportion of the cost to repair or replace, without deduction for depreciation, that part of the building damaged, which the total amount of insurance in this policy on the damaged building bears to 80% of the replacement cost of the building.

c. To determine the amount of insurance required to equal 80% of the full replacement cost of the building immediately before the loss, do not include the value of:

(1) Excavations, footings, foundations, piers, or any other structures or devices that support all or part of the building, which are below the undersurface of the lowest basement floor;

(2) Those supports described in **(1)** above which are below the surface of the ground inside the foundation walls, if there is no basement; and

(3) Underground flues, pipes, wiring and drains.

d. We will pay no more than the actual cash value of the damage until actual repair or replacement is complete. Once actual repair or replacement is complete, we will settle the loss as noted in **2.a.** and **b.** above.

However, if the cost to repair or replace the damage is both:

(1) Less than 5% of the amount of insurance in this policy on the building; and

(2) Less than $2,500;

we will settle the loss as noted in **2.a.** and **b.** above whether or not actual repair or replacement is complete.

e. You may disregard the replacement cost loss settlement provisions and make claim under this policy for loss to buildings on an actual cash value basis. You may then make claim for any additional liability according to the provisions of this Condition **D.** Loss Settlement, provided you notify us, within 180 days after the date of loss, of your intent to repair or replace the damaged building.

E. Loss To A Pair Or Set

In case of loss to a pair or set we may elect to:

1. Repair or replace any part to restore the pair or set to its value before the loss; or

2. Pay the difference between actual cash value of the property before and after the loss.

F. Appraisal

If you and we fail to agree on the amount of loss, either may demand an appraisal of the loss. In this event, each party will choose a competent and impartial appraiser within 20 days after receiving a written request from the other. The two appraisers will choose an umpire. If they cannot agree upon an umpire within 15 days, you or we may request that the choice be made by a judge of a court of record in the state where the "residence premises" is located. The appraisers will separately set the amount of loss. If the appraisers submit a written report of an agreement to us, the amount agreed upon will be the amount of loss. If they fail to agree, they will submit their differences to the umpire. A decision agreed to by any two will set the amount of loss.

Each party will:

1. Pay its own appraiser; and

2. Bear the other expenses of the appraisal and umpire equally.

G. Other Insurance And Service Agreement

If a loss covered by this policy is also covered by:

1. Other insurance, we will pay only the proportion of the loss that the limit of liability that applies under this policy bears to the total amount of insurance covering the loss; or

2. A service agreement, this insurance is excess over any amounts payable under any such agreement. Service agreement means a service plan, property restoration plan, home warranty or other similar service warranty agreement, even if it is characterized as insurance.

H. Suit Against Us

No action can be brought against us unless there has been full compliance with all of the terms under Section **I** of this policy and the action is started within two years after the date of loss.

I. Our Option

If we give you written notice within 30 days after we receive your signed, sworn proof of loss, we may repair or replace any part of the damaged property with material or property of like kind and quality.

J. Loss Payment

We will adjust all losses with you. We will pay you unless some other person is named in the policy or is legally entitled to receive payment. Loss will be payable 60 days after we receive your proof of loss and:

1. Reach an agreement with you;

2. There is an entry of a final judgment; or

3. There is a filing of an appraisal award with us.

K. Abandonment Of Property

We need not accept any property abandoned by an "insured".

L. Mortgage Clause

1. If a mortgagee is named in this policy, any loss payable under Coverage **A** or **B** will be paid to the mortgagee and you, as interests appear. If more than one mortgagee is named, the order of payment will be the same as the order of precedence of the mortgages.

2. If we deny your claim, that denial will not apply to a valid claim of the mortgagee, if the mortgagee:

a. Notifies us of any change in ownership, occupancy or substantial change in risk of which the mortgagee is aware;

b. Pays any premium due under this policy on demand if you have neglected to pay the premium; and

c. Submits a signed, sworn statement of loss within 60 days after receiving notice from us of your failure to do so. Paragraphs **F.** Appraisal, **H.** Suit Against Us and **J.** Loss Payment under Section **I** – Conditions also apply to the mortgagee.

3. If we decide to cancel or not to renew this policy, the mortgagee will be notified at least 10 days before the date cancellation or nonrenewal takes effect.

4. If we pay the mortgagee for any loss and deny payment to you:

a. We are subrogated to all the rights of the mortgagee granted under the mortgage on the property; or

b. At our option, we may pay to the mortgagee the whole principal on the mortgage plus any accrued interest. In this event, we will receive a full assignment and transfer of the mortgage and all securities held as collateral to the mortgage debt.

5. Subrogation will not impair the right of the mortgagee to recover the full amount of the mortgagee's claim.

M. No Benefit To Bailee

We will not recognize any assignment or grant any coverage that benefits a person or organization holding, storing or moving property for a fee regardless of any other provision of this policy.

N. Nuclear Hazard Clause

1. "Nuclear Hazard" means any nuclear reaction, radiation, or radioactive contamination, all whether controlled or uncontrolled or however caused, or any consequence of any of these.

2. Loss caused by the nuclear hazard will not be considered loss caused by fire, explosion, or smoke, whether these perils are specifically named in or otherwise included within the Perils Insured Against.

3. This policy does not apply under Section **I** to loss caused directly or indirectly by nuclear hazard, except that direct loss by fire resulting from the nuclear hazard is covered.

O. Recovered Property

If you or we recover any property for which we have made payment under this policy, you or we will notify the other of the recovery. At your option, the property will be returned to or retained by you or it will become our property. If the recovered property is returned to or retained by you, the loss payment will be adjusted based on the amount you received for the recovered property.

P. Volcanic Eruption Period

One or more volcanic eruptions that occur within a 72-hour period will be considered as one volcanic eruption.

Q. Policy Period

This policy applies only to loss which occurs during the policy period.

R. Concealment Or Fraud

We provide coverage to no "insureds" under this policy if, whether before or after a loss, an "insured" has:

1. Intentionally concealed or misrepresented any material fact or circumstance;
2. Engaged in fraudulent conduct; or
3. Made false statements;

relating to this insurance.

S. Loss Payable Clause

If the Declarations shows a loss payee for certain listed insured personal property, the definition of "insured" is changed to include that loss payee with respect to that property.

If we decide to cancel or not renew this policy, that loss payee will be notified in writing.

SECTION II – LIABILITY COVERAGES

A. Coverage E – Personal Liability

If a claim is made or a suit is brought against an "insured" for damages because of "bodily injury" or "property damage" caused by an "occurrence" to which this coverage applies, we will:

1. Pay up to our limit of liability for the damages for which an "insured" is legally liable. Damages include prejudgment interest awarded against an "insured"; and
2. Provide a defense at our expense by counsel of our choice, even if the suit is groundless, false or fraudulent. We may investigate and settle any claim or suit that we decide is appropriate. Our duty to settle or defend ends when our limit of liability for the "occurrence" has been exhausted by payment of a judgment or settlement.

B. Coverage F – Medical Payments To Others

We will pay the necessary medical expenses that are incurred or medically ascertained within three years from the date of an accident causing "bodily injury". Medical expenses means reasonable charges for medical, surgical, x-ray, dental, ambulance, hospital, professional nursing, prosthetic devices and funeral services. This coverage does not apply to you or regular residents of your household except "residence employees". As to others, this coverage applies only:

1. To a person on the "insured location" with the permission of an "insured"; or
2. To a person off the "insured location", if the "bodily injury":
   - **a.** Arises out of a condition on the "insured location" or the ways immediately adjoining;
   - **b.** Is caused by the activities of an "insured";
   - **c.** Is caused by a "residence employee" in the course of the "residence employee's" employment by an "insured"; or
   - **d.** Is caused by an animal owned by or in the care of an "insured".

SECTION II – EXCLUSIONS

A. "Motor Vehicle Liability"

1. Coverages **E** and **F** do not apply to any "motor vehicle liability" if, at the time and place of an "occurrence", the involved "motor vehicle":
   - **a.** Is registered for use on public roads or property;
   - **b.** Is not registered for use on public roads or property, but such registration is required by a law, or regulation issued by a government agency, for it to be used at the place of the "occurrence"; or
   - **c.** Is being:
     - **(1)** Operated in, or practicing for, any prearranged or organized race, speed contest or other competition;
     - **(2)** Rented to others;
     - **(3)** Used to carry persons or cargo for a charge; or
     - **(4)** Used for any "business" purpose except for a motorized golf cart while on a golfing facility.
2. If Exclusion **A.1.** does not apply, there is still no coverage for "motor vehicle liability", unless the "motor vehicle" is:
   - **a.** In dead storage on an "insured location";
   - **b.** Used solely to service a residence;
   - **c.** Designed to assist the handicapped and, at the time of an "occurrence", it is:
     - **(1)** Being used to assist a handicapped person; or
     - **(2)** Parked on an "insured location";
   - **d.** Designed for recreational use off public roads and:
     - **(1)** Not owned by an "insured"; or

(2) Owned by an "insured" provided the "occurrence" takes place:

(a) On an "insured location" as defined in Definition **B.6.a., b., d., e.** or **h.**; or

(b) Off an "insured location" and the "motor vehicle" is:

(i) Designed as a toy vehicle for use by children under seven years of age;

(ii) Powered by one or more batteries; and

(iii) Not built or modified after manufacture to exceed a speed of five miles per hour on level ground;

e. A motorized golf cart that is owned by an "insured", designed to carry up to four persons, not built or modified after manufacture to exceed a speed of 25 miles per hour on level ground and, at the time of an "occurrence", is within the legal boundaries of:

(1) A golfing facility and is parked or stored there, or being used by an "insured" to:

(a) Play the game of golf or for other recreational or leisure activity allowed by the facility;

(b) Travel to or from an area where "motor vehicles" or golf carts are parked or stored; or

(c) Cross public roads at designated points to access other parts of the golfing facility; or

(2) A private residential community, including its public roads upon which a motorized golf cart can legally travel, which is subject to the authority of a property owners association and contains an "insured's" residence.

B. "Watercraft Liability"

1. Coverages **E** and **F** do not apply to any "watercraft liability" if, at the time of an "occurrence", the involved watercraft is being:

a. Operated in, or practicing for, any prearranged or organized race, speed contest or other competition. This exclusion does not apply to a sailing vessel or a predicted log cruise;

b. Rented to others;

c. Used to carry persons or cargo for a charge; or

d. Used for any "business" purpose.

2. If Exclusion **B.1.** does not apply, there is still no coverage for "watercraft liability" unless, at the time of the "occurrence", the watercraft:

a. Is stored;

b. Is a sailing vessel, with or without auxiliary power, that is:

(1) Less than 26 feet in overall length; or

(2) 26 feet or more in overall length and not owned by or rented to an "insured"; or

c. Is not a sailing vessel and is powered by:

(1) An inboard or inboard-outdrive engine or motor, including those that power a water jet pump, of:

(a) 50 horsepower or less and not owned by an "insured"; or

(b) More than 50 horsepower and not owned by or rented to an "insured"; or

(2) One or more outboard engines or motors with:

(a) 25 total horsepower or less;

(b) More than 25 horsepower if the outboard engine or motor is not owned by an "insured";

(c) More than 25 horsepower if the outboard engine or motor is owned by an "insured" who acquired it during the policy period; or

(d) More than 25 horsepower if the outboard engine or motor is owned by an "insured" who acquired it before the policy period, but only if:

(i) You declare them at policy inception; or

(ii) Your intent to insure them is reported to us in writing within 45 days after you acquire them.

The coverages in **(c)** and **(d)** above apply for the policy period.

Horsepower means the maximum power rating assigned to the engine or motor by the manufacturer.

C. "Aircraft Liability"

This policy does not cover "aircraft liability".

D. "Hovercraft Liability"

This policy does not cover "hovercraft liability".

E. Coverage E – Personal Liability And Coverage F – Medical Payments To Others

Coverages **E** and **F** do not apply to the following:

1. Expected Or Intended Injury

"Bodily injury" or "property damage" which is expected or intended by an "insured", even if the resulting "bodily injury" or "property damage":

a. Is of a different kind, quality or degree than initially expected or intended; or

b. Is sustained by a different person, entity or property than initially expected or intended.

However, this Exclusion **E.1.** does not apply to "bodily injury" or "property damage" resulting from the use of reasonable force by an "insured" to protect persons or property;

2. "Business"

a. "Bodily injury" or "property damage" arising out of or in connection with a "business" conducted from an "insured location" or engaged in by an "insured", whether or not the "business" is owned or operated by an "insured" or employs an "insured".

This Exclusion **E.2.** applies but is not limited to an act or omission, regardless of its nature or circumstance, involving a service or duty rendered, promised, owed, or implied to be provided because of the nature of the "business".

b. This Exclusion **E.2.** does not apply to:

(1) The rental or holding for rental of an "insured location";

(a) On an occasional basis if used only as a residence;

(b) In part for use only as a residence, unless a single-family unit is intended for use by the occupying family to lodge more than two roomers or boarders; or

(c) In part, as an office, school, studio or private garage; and

(2) An "insured" under the age of 21 years involved in a part-time or occasional, self-employed "business" with no employees;

3. Professional Services

"Bodily injury" or "property damage" arising out of the rendering of or failure to render professional services;

4. "Insured's" Premises Not An "Insured Location"

"Bodily injury" or "property damage" arising out of a premises:

a. Owned by an "insured";

b. Rented to an "insured"; or

c. Rented to others by an "insured";

that is not an "insured location";

5. War

"Bodily injury" or "property damage" caused directly or indirectly by war, including the following and any consequence of any of the following:

a. Undeclared war, civil war, insurrection, rebellion or revolution;

b. Warlike act by a military force or military personnel; or

c. Destruction, seizure or use for a military purpose.

Discharge of a nuclear weapon will be deemed a warlike act even if accidental;

6. Communicable Disease

"Bodily injury" or "property damage" which arises out of the transmission of a communicable disease by an "insured";

7. Sexual Molestation, Corporal Punishment Or Physical Or Mental Abuse

"Bodily injury" or "property damage" arising out of sexual molestation, corporal punishment or physical or mental abuse; or

8. Controlled Substance

"Bodily injury" or "property damage" arising out of the use, sale, manufacture, delivery, transfer or possession by any person of a Controlled Substance as defined by the Federal Food and Drug Law at 21 U.S.C.A. Sections 811 and 812. Controlled Substances include but are not limited to cocaine, LSD, marijuana and all narcotic drugs. However, this exclusion does not apply to the legitimate use of prescription drugs by a person following the lawful orders of a licensed health care professional.

Exclusions **A.** "Motor Vehicle Liability", **B.** "Watercraft Liability", **C.** "Aircraft Liability", **D.** "Hovercraft Liability" and **E.4.** "Insured's" Premises Not An "Insured Location" do not apply to "bodily injury" to a "residence employee" arising out of and in the course of the "residence employee's" employment by an "insured".

F. Coverage E – Personal Liability

Coverage **E** does not apply to:

1. Liability:
   - **a.** For any loss assessment charged against you as a member of an association, corporation or community of property owners, except as provided in **D.** Loss Assessment under Section **II** – Additional Coverages;
   - **b.** Under any contract or agreement entered into by an "insured". However, this exclusion does not apply to written contracts:
     - **(1)** That directly relate to the ownership, maintenance or use of an "insured location"; or
     - **(2)** Where the liability of others is assumed by you prior to an "occurrence";

     unless excluded in **a.** above or elsewhere in this policy;
2. "Property damage" to property owned by an "insured". This includes costs or expenses incurred by an "insured" or others to repair, replace, enhance, restore or maintain such property to prevent injury to a person or damage to property of others, whether on or away from an "insured location";
3. "Property damage" to property rented to, occupied or used by or in the care of an "insured". This exclusion does not apply to "property damage" caused by fire, smoke or explosion;
4. "Bodily injury" to any person eligible to receive any benefits voluntarily provided or required to be provided by an "insured" under any:
   - **a.** Workers' compensation law;
   - **b.** Non-occupational disability law; or
   - **c.** Occupational disease law;
5. "Bodily injury" or "property damage" for which an "insured" under this policy:
   - **a.** Is also an insured under a nuclear energy liability policy issued by the:
     - **(1)** Nuclear Energy Liability Insurance Association;
     - **(2)** Mutual Atomic Energy Liability Underwriters;
     - **(3)** Nuclear Insurance Association of Canada;

     or any of their successors; or
   - **b.** Would be an insured under such a policy but for the exhaustion of its limit of liability; or
6. "Bodily injury" to you or an "insured" as defined under Definition **5.a.** or **b.**

   This exclusion also applies to any claim made or suit brought against you or an "insured" to:
   - **a.** Repay; or
   - **b.** Share damages with;

   another person who may be obligated to pay damages because of "bodily injury" to an "insured".

G. Coverage F – Medical Payments To Others

Coverage **F** does not apply to "bodily injury":

1. To a "residence employee" if the "bodily injury":
   - **a.** Occurs off the "insured location"; and
   - **b.** Does not arise out of or in the course of the "residence employee's" employment by an "insured";
2. To any person eligible to receive benefits voluntarily provided or required to be provided under any:
   - **a.** Workers' compensation law;
   - **b.** Non-occupational disability law; or
   - **c.** Occupational disease law;
3. From any:
   - **a.** Nuclear reaction;
   - **b.** Nuclear radiation; or
   - **c.** Radioactive contamination;

   all whether controlled or uncontrolled or however caused; or
   - **d.** Any consequence of any of these; or
4. To any person, other than a "residence employee" of an "insured", regularly residing on any part of the "insured location".

SECTION II – ADDITIONAL COVERAGES

We cover the following in addition to the limits of liability:

A. Claim Expenses

We pay:

1. Expenses we incur and costs taxed against an "insured" in any suit we defend;
2. Premiums on bonds required in a suit we defend, but not for bond amounts more than the Coverage **E** limit of liability. We need not apply for or furnish any bond;

3. Reasonable expenses incurred by an "insured" at our request, including actual loss of earnings (but not loss of other income) up to $250 per day, for assisting us in the investigation or defense of a claim or suit; and
4. Interest on the entire judgment which accrues after entry of the judgment and before we pay or tender, or deposit in court that part of the judgment which does not exceed the limit of liability that applies.

B. First Aid Expenses

We will pay expenses for first aid to others incurred by an "insured" for "bodily injury" covered under this policy. We will not pay for first aid to an "insured".

C. Damage To Property Of Others

1. We will pay, at replacement cost, up to $1,000 per "occurrence" for "property damage" to property of others caused by an "insured".
2. We will not pay for "property damage":
   a. To the extent of any amount recoverable under Section **I;**
   b. Caused intentionally by an "insured" who is 13 years of age or older;
   c. To property owned by an "insured";
   d. To property owned by or rented to a tenant of an "insured" or a resident in your household; or
   e. Arising out of:
      (1) A "business" engaged in by an "insured";
      (2) Any act or omission in connection with a premises owned, rented or controlled by an "insured", other than the "insured location"; or
      (3) The ownership, maintenance, occupancy, operation, use, loading or unloading of aircraft, hovercraft, watercraft or "motor vehicles".
      This Exclusion **e.(3)** does not apply to a "motor vehicle" that:
         (a) Is designed for recreational use off public roads;
         (b) Is not owned by an "insured"; and
         (c) At the time of the "occurrence", is not required by law, or regulation issued by a government agency, to have been registered for it to be used on public roads or property.

D. Loss Assessment

1. We will pay up to $1,000 for your share of loss assessment charged against you, as owner or tenant of the "residence premises", during the policy period by a corporation or association of property owners, when the assessment is made as a result of:
   a. "Bodily injury" or "property damage" not excluded from coverage under Section **II** – Exclusions; or
   b. Liability for an act of a director, officer or trustee in the capacity as a director, officer or trustee, provided such person:
      (1) Is elected by the members of a corporation or association of property owners; and
      (2) Serves without deriving any income from the exercise of duties which are solely on behalf of a corporation or association of property owners.
2. Paragraph **I.** Policy Period under Section **II** – Conditions does not apply to this Loss Assessment Coverage.
3. Regardless of the number of assessments, the limit of $1,000 is the most we will pay for loss arising out of:
   a. One accident, including continuous or repeated exposure to substantially the same general harmful condition; or
   b. A covered act of a director, officer or trustee. An act involving more than one director, officer or trustee is considered to be a single act.
4. We do not cover assessments charged against you or a corporation or association of property owners by any governmental body.

SECTION II – CONDITIONS

A. Limit Of Liability

Our total liability under Coverage **E** for all damages resulting from any one "occurrence" will not be more than the Coverage **E** Limit Of Liability shown in the Declarations. This limit is the same regardless of the number of "insureds", claims made or persons injured. All "bodily injury" and "property damage" resulting from any one accident or from continuous or repeated exposure to substantially the same general harmful conditions shall be considered to be the result of one "occurrence".

Our total liability under Coverage **F** for all medical expense payable for "bodily injury" to one person as the result of one accident will not be more than the Coverage **F** Limit Of Liability shown in the Declarations.

B. Severability Of Insurance

This insurance applies separately to each "insured". This condition will not increase our limit of liability for any one "occurrence".

C. Duties After "Occurrence"

In case of an "occurrence", you or another "insured" will perform the following duties that apply. We have no duty to provide coverage under this policy if your failure to comply with the following duties is prejudicial to us. You will help us by seeing that these duties are performed:

1. Give written notice to us or our agent as soon as is practical, which sets forth:

a. The identity of the policy and the "named insured" shown in the Declarations;

b. Reasonably available information on the time, place and circumstances of the "occurrence"; and

c. Names and addresses of any claimants and witnesses;

2. Cooperate with us in the investigation, settlement or defense of any claim or suit;

3. Promptly forward to us every notice, demand, summons or other process relating to the "occurrence";

4. At our request, help us:

a. To make settlement;

b. To enforce any right of contribution or indemnity against any person or organization who may be liable to an "insured";

c. With the conduct of suits and attend hearings and trials; and

d. To secure and give evidence and obtain the attendance of witnesses;

5. With respect to **C.** Damage To Property Of Others under Section **II** – Additional Coverages, submit to us within 60 days after the loss a sworn statement of loss and show the damaged property, if in an "insured's" control;

6. No "insured" shall, except at such "insured's" own cost, voluntarily make payment, assume obligation or incur expense other than for first aid to others at the time of the "bodily injury".

D. Duties Of An Injured Person – Coverage F – Medical Payments To Others

1. The injured person or someone acting for the injured person will:

a. Give us written proof of claim, under oath if required, as soon as is practical; and

b. Authorize us to obtain copies of medical reports and records.

2. The injured person will submit to a physical exam by a doctor of our choice when and as often as we reasonably require.

E. Payment Of Claim – Coverage F – Medical Payments To Others

Payment under this coverage is not an admission of liability by an "insured" or us.

F. Suit Against Us

1. No action can be brought against us unless there has been full compliance with all of the terms under this Section **II.**

2. No one will have the right to join us as a party to any action against an "insured".

3. Also, no action with respect to Coverage **E** can be brought against us until the obligation of such "insured" has been determined by final judgment or agreement signed by us.

G. Bankruptcy Of An "Insured"

Bankruptcy or insolvency of an "insured" will not relieve us of our obligations under this policy.

H. Other Insurance

This insurance is excess over other valid and collectible insurance except insurance written specifically to cover as excess over the limits of liability that apply in this policy.

I. Policy Period

This policy applies only to "bodily injury" or "property damage" which occurs during the policy period.

J. Concealment Or Fraud

We do not provide coverage to an "insured" who, whether before or after a loss, has:

1. Intentionally concealed or misrepresented any material fact or circumstance;

2. Engaged in fraudulent conduct; or

3. Made false statements;

relating to this insurance.

SECTIONS I AND II – CONDITIONS

A. Liberalization Clause

If we make a change which broadens coverage under this edition of our policy without additional premium charge, that change will automatically apply to your insurance as of the date we implement the change in your state, provided that this implementation date falls within 60 days prior to or during the policy period stated in the Declarations.

This Liberalization Clause does not apply to changes implemented with a general program revision that includes both broadenings and restrictions in coverage, whether that general program revision is implemented through introduction of:

1. A subsequent edition of this policy; or

2. An amendatory endorsement.

B. Waiver Or Change Of Policy Provisions

A waiver or change of a provision of this policy must be in writing by us to be valid. Our request for an appraisal or examination will not waive any of our rights.

C. Cancellation

1. You may cancel this policy at any time by returning it to us or by letting us know in writing of the date cancellation is to take effect.

2. We may cancel this policy only for the reasons stated below by letting you know in writing of the date cancellation takes effect. This cancellation notice may be delivered to you, or mailed to you at your mailing address shown in the Declarations. Proof of mailing will be sufficient proof of notice.

a. When you have not paid the premium, we may cancel at any time by letting you know at least 10 days before the date cancellation takes effect.

b. When this policy has been in effect for less than 60 days and is not a renewal with us, we may cancel for any reason by letting you know at least 10 days before the date cancellation takes effect.

c. When this policy has been in effect for 60 days or more, or at any time if it is a renewal with us, we may cancel:

(1) If there has been a material misrepresentation of fact which if known to us would have caused us not to issue the policy; or

(2) If the risk has changed substantially since the policy was issued.

This can be done by letting you know at least 30 days before the date cancellation takes effect.

d. When this policy is written for a period of more than one year, we may cancel for any reason at anniversary by letting you know at least 30 days before the date cancellation takes effect.

3. When this policy is canceled, the premium for the period from the date of cancellation to the expiration date will be refunded pro rata.

4. If the return premium is not refunded with the notice of cancellation or when this policy is returned to us, we will refund it within a reasonable time after the date cancellation takes effect.

D. Nonrenewal

We may elect not to renew this policy. We may do so by delivering to you, or mailing to you at your mailing address shown in the Declarations, written notice at least 30 days before the expiration date of this policy. Proof of mailing will be sufficient proof of notice.

E. Assignment

Assignment of this policy will not be valid unless we give our written consent.

F. Subrogation

An "insured" may waive in writing before a loss all rights of recovery against any person. If not waived, we may require an assignment of rights of recovery for a loss to the extent that payment is made by us.

If an assignment is sought, an "insured" must sign and deliver all related papers and cooperate with us.

Subrogation does not apply to Coverage **F** or Paragraph **C.** Damage To Property Of Others under Section **II** – Additional Coverages.

G. Death

If any person named in the Declarations or the spouse, if a resident of the same household, dies, the following apply:

1. We insure the legal representative of the deceased but only with respect to the premises and property of the deceased covered under the policy at the time of death; and

2. "Insured" includes:

a. An "insured" who is a member of your household at the time of your death, but only while a resident of the "residence premises"; and

b. With respect to your property, the person having proper temporary custody of the property until appointment and qualification of a legal representative.

HOMEOWNERS 5 – COMPREHENSIVE FORM

AGREEMENT

We will provide the insurance described in this policy in return for the premium and compliance with all applicable provisions of this policy.

DEFINITIONS

A. In this policy, "you" and "your" refer to the "named insured" shown in the Declarations and the spouse if a resident of the same household. "We", "us" and "our" refer to the Company providing this insurance.

B. In addition, certain words and phrases are defined as follows:

1. "Aircraft Liability", "Hovercraft Liability", "Motor Vehicle Liability" and "Watercraft Liability", subject to the provisions in **b.** below, mean the following:

a. Liability for "bodily injury" or "property damage" arising out of the:

(1) Ownership of such vehicle or craft by an "insured";

(2) Maintenance, occupancy, operation, use, loading or unloading of such vehicle or craft by any person;

(3) Entrustment of such vehicle or craft by an "insured" to any person;

(4) Failure to supervise or negligent supervision of any person involving such vehicle or craft by an "insured"; or

(5) Vicarious liability, whether or not imposed by law, for the actions of a child or minor involving such vehicle or craft.

b. For the purpose of this definition:

(1) Aircraft means any contrivance used or designed for flight except model or hobby aircraft not used or designed to carry people or cargo;

(2) Hovercraft means a self-propelled motorized ground effect vehicle and includes, but is not limited to, flarecraft and air cushion vehicles;

(3) Watercraft means a craft principally designed to be propelled on or in water by wind, engine power or electric motor; and

(4) Motor vehicle means a "motor vehicle" as defined in **7.** below.

2. "Bodily injury" means bodily harm, sickness or disease, including required care, loss of services and death that results.

3. "Business" means:

a. A trade, profession or occupation engaged in on a full-time, part-time or occasional basis; or

b. Any other activity engaged in for money or other compensation, except the following:

(1) One or more activities, not described in **(2)** through **(4)** below, for which no "insured" receives more than $2,000 in total compensation for the 12 months before the beginning of the policy period;

(2) Volunteer activities for which no money is received other than payment for expenses incurred to perform the activity;

(3) Providing home day care services for which no compensation is received, other than the mutual exchange of such services; or

(4) The rendering of home day care services to a relative of an "insured".

4. "Employee" means an employee of an "insured", or an employee leased to an "insured" by a labor leasing firm under an agreement between an "insured" and the labor leasing firm, whose duties are other than those performed by a "residence employee".

5. "Insured" means:

a. You and residents of your household who are:

(1) Your relatives; or

(2) Other persons under the age of 21 and in your care or the care of a resident of your household who is your relative;

b. A student enrolled in school full-time, as defined by the school, who was a resident of your household before moving out to attend school, provided the student is under the age of:

(1) 24 and your relative; or

(2) 21 and in your care or the care of a resident of your household who is your relative; or

c. Under Section **II:**

(1) With respect to animals or watercraft to which this policy applies, any person or organization legally responsible for these animals or watercraft which are owned by you or any person described in **5.a.** or **b.** "Insured" does not mean a person or organization using or having custody of these animals or watercraft in the course of any "business" or without consent of the owner; or

(2) With respect to a "motor vehicle" to which this policy applies:

(a) Persons while engaged in your employ or that of any person described in **5.a.** or **b.**; or

(b) Other persons using the vehicle on an "insured location" with your consent.

Under both Sections **I** and **II,** when the word an immediately precedes the word "insured", the words an "insured" together mean one or more "insureds".

6. "Insured location" means:

a. The "residence premises";

b. The part of other premises, other structures and grounds used by you as a residence; and

(1) Which is shown in the Declarations; or

(2) Which is acquired by you during the policy period for your use as a residence;

c. Any premises used by you in connection with a premises described in **a.** and **b.** above;

d. Any part of a premises:

(1) Not owned by an "insured"; and

(2) Where an "insured" is temporarily residing;

e. Vacant land, other than farm land, owned by or rented to an "insured";

f. Land owned by or rented to an "insured" on which a one-, two-, three- or four-family dwelling is being built as a residence for an "insured";

g. Individual or family cemetery plots or burial vaults of an "insured"; or

h. Any part of a premises occasionally rented to an "insured" for other than "business" use.

7. "Motor vehicle" means:

a. A self-propelled land or amphibious vehicle; or

b. Any trailer or semitrailer which is being carried on, towed by or hitched for towing by a vehicle described in **a.** above.

8. "Occurrence" means an accident, including continuous or repeated exposure to substantially the same general harmful conditions, which results, during the policy period, in:

a. "Bodily injury"; or

b. "Property damage".

9. "Property damage" means physical injury to, destruction of, or loss of use of tangible property.

10. "Residence employee" means:

a. An employee of an "insured", or an employee leased to an "insured" by a labor leasing firm, under an agreement between an "insured" and the labor leasing firm, whose duties are related to the maintenance or use of the "residence premises", including household or domestic services; or

b. One who performs similar duties elsewhere not related to the "business" of an "insured".

A "residence employee" does not include a temporary employee who is furnished to an "insured" to substitute for a permanent "residence employee" on leave or to meet seasonal or short-term workload conditions.

11. "Residence premises" means:

a. The one-family dwelling where you reside;

b. The two-, three- or four-family dwelling where you reside in at least one of the family units; or

c. That part of any other building where you reside;

and which is shown as the "residence premises" in the Declarations.

"Residence premises" also includes other structures and grounds at that location.

SECTION I – PROPERTY COVERAGES

A. Coverage A – Dwelling

1. We cover:

a. The dwelling on the "residence premises" shown in the Declarations, including structures attached to the dwelling; and

b. Materials and supplies located on or next to the "residence premises" used to construct, alter or repair the dwelling or other structures on the "residence premises".

2. We do not cover land, including land on which the dwelling is located.

B. Coverage B – Other Structures

1. We cover other structures on the "residence premises" set apart from the dwelling by clear space. This includes structures connected to the dwelling by only a fence, utility line, or similar connection.

2. We do not cover:

a. Land, including land on which the other structures are located;

b. Other structures rented or held for rental to any person not a tenant of the dwelling, unless used solely as a private garage;

c. Other structures from which any "business" is conducted; or

d. Other structures used to store "business" property. However, we do cover a structure that contains "business" property solely owned by an "insured" or a tenant of the dwelling, provided that "business" property does not include gaseous or liquid fuel, other than fuel in a permanently installed fuel tank of a vehicle or craft parked or stored in the structure.

3. The limit of liability for this coverage will not be more than 10% of the limit of liability that applies to Coverage **A.** Use of this coverage does not reduce the Coverage **A** limit of liability.

C. Coverage C – Personal Property

1. Covered Property

We cover personal property owned or used by an "insured" while it is anywhere in the world. After a loss and at your request, we will cover personal property owned by:

a. Others while the property is on the part of the "residence premises" occupied by an "insured"; or

b. A guest or a "residence employee", while the property is in any residence occupied by an "insured".

2. Limit For Property At Other Locations

a. Other Residences

Our limit of liability for personal property usually located at an "insured's" residence, other than the "residence premises", is 10% of the limit of liability for Coverage **C,** or $1,000, whichever is greater. However, this limitation does not apply to personal property:

(1) Moved from the "residence premises" because it is:

(a) Being repaired, renovated or rebuilt; and

(b) Not fit to live in or store property in; or

(2) In a newly acquired principal residence for 30 days from the time you begin to move the property there.

b. Self-storage Facilities

Our limit of liability for personal property owned or used by an "insured" and located in a self-storage facility is 10% of the limit of liability for Coverage **C,** or $1,000, whichever is greater. However, this limitation does not apply to personal property:

(1) Moved from the "residence premises" because it is:

(a) Being repaired, renovated or rebuilt; and

(b) Not fit to live in or store property in; or

(2) Usually located in an "insured's" residence, other than the "residence premises".

3. Special Limits Of Liability

The special limit for each category shown below is the total limit for each loss for all property in that category. These special limits do not increase the Coverage **C** limit of liability.

a. $200 on money, bank notes, bullion, gold other than goldware, silver other than silverware, platinum other than platinumware, coins, medals, scrip, stored value cards and smart cards.

b. $1,500 on securities, accounts, deeds, evidences of debt, letters of credit, notes other than bank notes, manuscripts, personal records, passports, tickets and stamps. This dollar limit applies to these categories regardless of the medium (such as paper or computer software) on which the material exists.

This limit includes the cost to research, replace or restore the information from the lost or damaged material.

c. $1,500 on watercraft of all types, including their trailers, furnishings, equipment and outboard engines or motors.

d. $1,500 on trailers or semitrailers not used with watercraft of all types.

e. $1,500 for loss by theft, misplacing or losing of jewelry, watches, furs, precious and semiprecious stones.

f. $2,500 for loss by theft, misplacing or losing of firearms and related equipment.

g. $2,500 for loss by theft, misplacing or losing of silverware, silver-plated ware, goldware, gold-plated ware, platinumware, platinum-plated ware and pewterware. This includes flatware, hollowware, tea sets, trays and trophies made of or including silver, gold or pewter.

h. $2,500 on property, on the "residence premises", used primarily for "business" purposes.

i. $1,500 on property, away from the "residence premises", used primarily for "business" purposes. However, this limit does not apply to antennas, tapes, wires, records, disks or other media that are:

(1) Used with electronic equipment that reproduces, receives or transmits audio, visual or data signals; and

(2) In or upon a "motor vehicle".

j. $1,500 on portable electronic equipment that:

(1) Reproduces, receives or transmits audio, visual or data signals;

(2) Is designed to be operated by more than one power source, one of which is a "motor vehicle's" electrical system; and

(3) Is in or upon a "motor vehicle".

k. $250 on antennas, tapes, wires, records, disks or other media that are:

(1) Used with electronic equipment that reproduces, receives or transmits audio, visual or data signals; and

(2) In or upon a "motor vehicle".

4. Property Not Covered

We do not cover:

a. Articles separately described and specifically insured, regardless of the limit for which they are insured, in this or other insurance;

b. Animals, birds or fish;

c. "Motor vehicles".

This includes a "motor vehicle's" equipment and parts.

However, this Paragraph **4.c.** does not apply to:

(1) Portable electronic equipment that:

(a) Reproduces, receives or transmits audio, visual or data signals; and

(b) Is designed so that it may be operated from a power source other than a "motor vehicle's" electrical system.

(2) "Motor vehicles" not required to be registered for use on public roads or property which are:

(a) Used solely to service a residence; or

(b) Designed to assist the handicapped;

d. Aircraft, meaning any contrivance used or designed for flight, including any parts whether or not attached to the aircraft.

We do cover model or hobby aircraft not used or designed to carry people or cargo;

e. Hovercraft and parts. Hovercraft means a self-propelled motorized ground effect vehicle and includes, but is not limited to, flarecraft and air cushion vehicles;

f. Property of roomers, boarders and other tenants, except property of roomers and boarders related to an "insured";

g. Property in an apartment regularly rented or held for rental to others by an "insured", except as provided under **E.10.** Landlord's Furnishings under Section **I** – Property Coverages;

h. Property rented or held for rental to others off the "residence premises";

i. "Business" data, including such data stored in:

(1) Books of account, drawings or other paper records; or

(2) Computers and related equipment.

We do cover the cost of blank recording or storage media and of prerecorded computer programs available on the retail market;

j. Credit cards, electronic fund transfer cards or access devices used solely for deposit, withdrawal or transfer of funds except as provided in **E.6.** Credit Card, Electronic Fund Transfer Card Or Access Device, Forgery And Counterfeit Money under Section **I** – Property Coverages; or

k. Water or steam.

D. Coverage D – Loss Of Use

The limit of liability for Coverage **D** is the total limit for the coverages in **1.** Additional Living Expense, **2.** Fair Rental Value and **3.** Civil Authority Prohibits Use below.

1. Additional Living Expense

If a loss covered under Section **I** makes that part of the "residence premises" where you reside not fit to live in, we cover any necessary increase in living expenses incurred by you so that your household can maintain its normal standard of living.

Payment will be for the shortest time required to repair or replace the damage or, if you permanently relocate, the shortest time required for your household to settle elsewhere.

2. Fair Rental Value

If a loss covered under Section **I** makes that part of the "residence premises" rented to others or held for rental by you not fit to live in, we cover the fair rental value of such premises less any expenses that do not continue while it is not fit to live in.

Payment will be for the shortest time required to repair or replace such premises.

3. Civil Authority Prohibits Use

If a civil authority prohibits you from use of the "residence premises" as a result of direct damage to neighboring premises by a Peril Insured Against, we cover the loss as provided in **1.** Additional Living Expense and **2.** Fair Rental Value above for no more than two weeks.

4. Loss Or Expense Not Covered

We do not cover loss or expense due to cancellation of a lease or agreement.

The periods of time under **1.** Additional Living Expense, **2.** Fair Rental Value and **3.** Civil Authority Prohibits Use above are not limited by expiration of this policy.

E. Additional Coverages

1. Debris Removal

a. We will pay your reasonable expense for the removal of:

(1) Debris of covered property if a Peril Insured Against that applies to the damaged property causes the loss; or

(2) Ash, dust or particles from a volcanic eruption that has caused direct loss to a building or property contained in a building.

This expense is included in the limit of liability that applies to the damaged property. If the amount to be paid for the actual damage to the property plus the debris removal expense is more than the limit of liability for the damaged property, an additional 5% of that limit is available for such expense.

b. We will also pay your reasonable expense, up to $1,000, for the removal from the "residence premises" of:

(1) Your trees felled by the peril of Windstorm or Hail or Weight of Ice, Snow or Sleet; or

(2) A neighbor's trees felled by a Peril Insured Against;

provided the trees:

(3) Damage a covered structure; or

(4) Do not damage a covered structure, but:

(a) Block a driveway on the "residence premises" which prevents a "motor vehicle", that is registered for use on public roads or property, from entering or leaving the "residence premises"; or

(b) Block a ramp or other fixture designed to assist a handicapped person to enter or leave the dwelling building.

The $1,000 limit is the most we will pay in any one loss, regardless of the number of fallen trees. No more than $500 of this limit will be paid for the removal of any one tree.

This coverage is additional insurance.

2. Reasonable Repairs

a. We will pay the reasonable cost incurred by you for the necessary measures taken solely to protect covered property that is damaged by a Peril Insured Against from further damage.

b. If the measures taken involve repair to other damaged property, we will only pay if that property is covered under this policy and the damage is caused by a Peril Insured Against. This coverage does not:

(1) Increase the limit of liability that applies to the covered property; or

(2) Relieve you of your duties, in case of a loss to covered property, described in **C.4.** under Section **I** – Conditions.

3. **Trees, Shrubs And Other Plants**

We cover trees, shrubs, plants or lawns, on the "residence premises", for loss caused by the following Perils Insured Against:

a. Fire or Lightning;

b. Explosion;

c. Riot or Civil Commotion;

d. Aircraft;

e. Vehicles not owned or operated by a resident of the "residence premises";

f. Vandalism or Malicious Mischief; or

g. Theft.

We will pay up to 5% of the limit of liability that applies to the dwelling for all trees, shrubs, plants or lawns. No more than $500 of this limit will be paid for any one tree, shrub or plant. We do not cover property grown for "business" purposes.

This coverage is additional insurance.

4. **Fire Department Service Charge**

We will pay up to $500 for your liability assumed by contract or agreement for fire department charges incurred when the fire department is called to save or protect covered property from a Peril Insured Against. We do not cover fire department service charges if the property is located within the limits of the city, municipality or protection district furnishing the fire department response.

This coverage is additional insurance. No deductible applies to this coverage.

5. **Property Removed**

We insure covered property against direct loss from any cause while being removed from a premises endangered by a Peril Insured Against and for no more than 30 days while removed.

This coverage does not change the limit of liability that applies to the property being removed.

6. **Credit Card, Electronic Fund Transfer Card Or Access Device, Forgery And Counterfeit Money**

a. We will pay up to $500 for:

(1) The legal obligation of an "insured" to pay because of the theft or unauthorized use of credit cards issued to or registered in an "insured's" name;

(2) Loss resulting from theft or unauthorized use of an electronic fund transfer card or access device used for deposit, withdrawal or transfer of funds, issued to or registered in an "insured's" name;

(3) Loss to an "insured" caused by forgery or alteration of any check or negotiable instrument; and

(4) Loss to an "insured" through acceptance in good faith of counterfeit United States or Canadian paper currency.

All loss resulting from a series of acts committed by any one person or in which any one person is concerned or implicated is considered to be one loss.

This coverage is additional insurance. No deductible applies to this coverage.

b. We do not cover:

(1) Use of a credit card, electronic fund transfer card or access device:

(a) By a resident of your household;

(b) By a person who has been entrusted with either type of card or access device; or

(c) If an "insured" has not complied with all terms and conditions under which the cards are issued or the devices accessed; or

(2) Loss arising out of "business" use or dishonesty of an "insured".

c. If the coverage in **a.** above applies, the following defense provisions also apply:

(1) We may investigate and settle any claim or suit that we decide is appropriate. Our duty to defend a claim or suit ends when the amount we pay for the loss equals our limit of liability.

(2) If a suit is brought against an "insured" for liability under **a.(1)** or **(2)** above, we will provide a defense at our expense by counsel of our choice.

(3) We have the option to defend at our expense an "insured" or an "insured's" bank against any suit for the enforcement of payment under **a.(3)** above.

7. Loss Assessment

a. We will pay up to $1,000 for your share of loss assessment charged during the policy period against you, as owner or tenant of the "residence premises", by a corporation or association of property owners. The assessment must be made as a result of direct loss to property, owned by all members collectively, of the type that would be covered by this policy if owned by you, caused by a Peril Insured Against, other than:

(1) Earthquake; or

(2) Land shock waves or tremors before, during or after a volcanic eruption.

The limit of $1,000 is the most we will pay with respect to any one loss, regardless of the number of assessments. We will only apply one deductible, per unit, to the total amount of any one loss to the property described above, regardless of the number of assessments.

b. We do not cover assessments charged against you or a corporation or association of property owners by any governmental body.

c. Paragraph **Q.** Policy Period under Section **I** – Conditions does not apply to this coverage.

This coverage is additional insurance.

8. Collapse

This Additional Coverage applies to property covered under Coverages **A** and **B.**

a. The coverage provided under this Additional Coverage – Collapse applies only to an abrupt collapse.

b. For the purpose of this Additional Coverage – Collapse, abrupt collapse means an abrupt falling down or caving in of a building or any part of a building with the result that the building or part of the building cannot be occupied for its intended purpose.

c. This Additional Coverage – Collapse does not apply to:

(1) A building or any part of a building that is in danger of falling down or caving in;

(2) A part of a building that is standing, even if it has separated from another part of the building; or

(3) A building or any part of a building that is standing, even if it shows evidence of cracking, bulging, sagging, bending, leaning, settling, shrinkage or expansion.

d. We insure for direct physical loss to covered property involving abrupt collapse of a building or any part of a building if such collapse was caused by one or more of the following:

(1) The Perils Insured Against under Coverages **A** and **B;**

(2) Decay, of a building or any part of a building, that is hidden from view, unless the presence of such decay is known to an "insured" prior to collapse;

(3) Insect or vermin damage, to a building or any part of a building, that is hidden from view, unless the presence of such damage is known to an "insured" prior to collapse;

(4) Weight of contents, equipment, animals or people;

(5) Weight of rain which collects on a roof; or

(6) Use of defective material or methods in construction, remodeling or renovation if the collapse occurs during the course of the construction, remodeling or renovation.

e. Loss to an awning, fence, patio, deck, pavement, swimming pool, underground pipe, flue, drain, cesspool, septic tank, foundation, retaining wall, bulkhead, pier, wharf or dock is not included under **d.(2)** through **(6)** above, unless the loss is a direct result of the collapse of a building or any part of a building.

f. This coverage does not increase the limit of liability that applies to the damaged covered property.

9. Glass Or Safety Glazing Material

a. We cover:

(1) The breakage of glass or safety glazing material which is part of a covered building, storm door or storm window;

(2) The breakage of glass or safety glazing material which is part of a covered building, storm door or storm window when caused directly by earth movement; and

(3) The direct physical loss to covered property caused solely by the pieces, fragments or splinters of broken glass or safety glazing material which is part of a building, storm door or storm window.

b. This coverage does not include loss:

(1) To covered property which results because the glass or safety glazing material has been broken, except as provided in **a.(3)** above; or

(2) On the "residence premises" if the dwelling has been vacant for more than 60 consecutive days immediately before the loss, except when the breakage results directly from earth movement as provided in **a.(2)** above. A dwelling being constructed is not considered vacant.

c. This coverage does not increase the limit of liability that applies to the damaged property.

10. Landlord's Furnishings

We will pay up to $2,500 for your appliances, carpeting and other household furnishings, in each apartment on the "residence premises" regularly rented or held for rental to others by an "insured", for loss caused only by the following Perils Insured Against:

a. Fire Or Lightning

b. Windstorm Or Hail

This peril includes loss to watercraft of all types and their trailers, furnishings, equipment, and outboard engines or motors, only while inside a fully enclosed building.

This peril does not include loss to the property contained in a building caused by rain, snow, sleet, sand or dust unless the direct force of wind or hail damages the building causing an opening in a roof or wall and the rain, snow, sleet, sand or dust enters through this opening.

c. Explosion

d. Riot Or Civil Commotion

e. Aircraft

This peril includes self-propelled missiles and spacecraft.

f. Vehicles

g. Smoke

This peril means sudden and accidental damage from smoke, including the emission or puffback of smoke, soot, fumes or vapors from a boiler, furnace or related equipment.

This peril does not include loss caused by smoke from agricultural smudging or industrial operations.

h. Vandalism Or Malicious Mischief

i. Falling Objects

This peril does not include loss to property contained in a building unless the roof or an outside wall of the building is first damaged by a falling object. Damage to the falling object itself is not included.

j. Weight Of Ice, Snow Or Sleet

This peril means weight of ice, snow or sleet which causes damage to property contained in a building.

k. Accidental Discharge Or Overflow Of Water Or Steam

(1) This peril means accidental discharge or overflow of water or steam from within a plumbing, heating, air conditioning or automatic fire protective sprinkler system or from within a household appliance.

(2) This peril does not include loss:

(a) To the system or appliance from which the water or steam escaped;

(b) Caused by or resulting from freezing except as provided in **m.** Freezing below;

(c) On the "residence premises" caused by accidental discharge or overflow which occurs off the "residence premises"; or

(d) Caused by mold, fungus or wet rot unless hidden within the walls or ceilings or beneath the floors or above the ceilings of a structure.

(3) In this peril, a plumbing system or household appliance does not include a sump, sump pump or related equipment or a roof drain, gutter, downspout or similar fixtures or equipment.

l. Sudden And Accidental Tearing Apart, Cracking, Burning Or Bulging

This peril means sudden and accidental tearing apart, cracking, burning or bulging of a steam or hot water heating system, an air conditioning or automatic fire protective sprinkler system, or an appliance for heating water.

We do not cover loss caused by or resulting from freezing under this peril.

m. Freezing

(1) This peril means freezing of a plumbing, heating, air conditioning or automatic fire protective sprinkler system or of a household appliance but only if you have used reasonable care to:

(a) Maintain heat in the building; or

(b) Shut off the water supply and drain all systems and appliances of water.

However, if the building is protected by an automatic fire protective sprinkler system, you must use reasonable care to continue the water supply and maintain heat in the building for coverage to apply.

(2) In this peril, a plumbing system or household appliance does not include a sump, sump pump or related equipment or a roof drain, gutter, downspout or similar fixtures or equipment.

n. Sudden And Accidental Damage From Artificially Generated Electrical Current

This peril does not include loss to tubes, transistors, electronic components or circuitry that is a part of appliances, fixtures, computers, home entertainment units or other types of electronic apparatus.

o. Volcanic Eruption

This peril does not include loss caused by earthquake, land shock waves or tremors.

This limit is the most we will pay in any one loss regardless of the number of appliances, carpeting or other household furnishings involved in the loss.

This coverage does not increase the limit of liability applying to the damaged property.

11. Ordinance Or Law

a. You may use up to 10% of the limit of liability that applies to Coverage **A** for the increased costs you incur due to the enforcement of any ordinance or law which requires or regulates:

(1) The construction, demolition, remodeling, renovation or repair of that part of a covered building or other structure damaged by a Peril Insured Against;

(2) The demolition and reconstruction of the undamaged part of a covered building or other structure, when that building or other structure must be totally demolished because of damage by a Peril Insured Against to another part of that covered building or other structure; or

(3) The remodeling, removal or replacement of the portion of the undamaged part of a covered building or other structure necessary to complete the remodeling, repair or replacement of that part of the covered building or other structure damaged by a Peril Insured Against.

b. You may use all or part of this ordinance or law coverage to pay for the increased costs you incur to remove debris resulting from the construction, demolition, remodeling, renovation, repair or replacement of property as stated in **a.** above.

c. We do not cover:

(1) The loss in value to any covered building or other structure due to the requirements of any ordinance or law; or

(2) The costs to comply with any ordinance or law which requires any "insured" or others to test for, monitor, clean up, remove, contain, treat, detoxify or neutralize, or in any way respond to, or assess the effects of, pollutants in or on any covered building or other structure.

Pollutants means any solid, liquid, gaseous or thermal irritant or contaminant, including smoke, vapor, soot, fumes, acids, alkalis, chemicals and waste. Waste includes materials to be recycled, reconditioned or reclaimed.

This coverage is additional insurance.

12. Grave Markers

We will pay up to $5,000 for grave markers, including mausoleums, on or away from the "residence premises" for loss caused by a Peril Insured Against.

This coverage does not increase the limits of liability that apply to the damaged covered property.

SECTION I – PERILS INSURED AGAINST

We insure against direct physical loss to property described in Coverages **A, B** and **C.**

We do not insure, however, for loss:

A. Under Coverages **A, B** and **C:**

1. Excluded under Section **I** – Exclusions;

2. Caused by:

a. Freezing of a plumbing, heating, air conditioning or automatic fire protective sprinkler system or of a household appliance, or by discharge, leakage or overflow from within the system or appliance caused by freezing. This provision does not apply if you have used reasonable care to:

(1) Maintain heat in the building; or

(2) Shut off the water supply and drain all systems and appliances of water.

However, if the building is protected by an automatic fire protective sprinkler system, you must use reasonable care to continue the water supply and maintain heat in the building for coverage to apply.

For purposes of this provision, a plumbing system or household appliance does not include a sump, sump pump or related equipment or a roof drain, gutter, downspout or similar fixtures or equipment;

b. Freezing, thawing, pressure or weight of water or ice, whether driven by wind or not, to a:

(1) Fence, pavement, patio or swimming pool;

(2) Footing, foundation, bulkhead, wall, or any other structure or device, that supports all or part of a building or other structure;

(3) Retaining wall or bulkhead that does not support all or part of a building or other structure; or

(4) Pier, wharf or dock;

c. Theft in or to a dwelling under construction, or of materials and supplies for use in the construction until the dwelling is finished and occupied;

d. Mold, fungus or wet rot. However, we do insure for loss caused by mold, fungus or wet rot that is hidden within the walls or ceilings or beneath the floors or above the ceilings of a structure if such loss results from the accidental discharge or overflow of water or steam from within:

(1) A plumbing, heating, air conditioning or automatic fire protective sprinkler system, or a household appliance, on the "residence premises"; or

(2) A storm drain, or water, steam or sewer pipes, off the "residence premises".

For purposes of this provision, a plumbing system or household appliance does not include a sump, sump pump or related equipment or a roof drain, gutter, downspout or similar fixtures or equipment; or

e. Any of the following:

(1) Wear and tear, marring, deterioration;

(2) Mechanical breakdown, latent defect, inherent vice or any quality in property that causes it to damage or destroy itself;

(3) Smog, rust or other corrosion, or dry rot;

(4) Smoke from agricultural smudging or industrial operations;

(5) Discharge, dispersal, seepage, migration, release or escape of pollutants unless the discharge, dispersal, seepage, migration, release or escape is itself caused by a Peril Insured Against in **a.** through **o.** as listed in **E.10.** Landlord's Furnishings under Section **I** – Property Coverages.

Pollutants means any solid, liquid, gaseous or thermal irritant or contaminant, including smoke, vapor, soot, fumes, acids, alkalis, chemicals and waste. Waste includes materials to be recycled, reconditioned or reclaimed;

(6) Settling, shrinking, bulging or expansion, including resultant cracking, of bulkheads, pavements, patios, footings, foundations, walls, floors, roofs or ceilings;

(7) Birds, rodents or insects;

(8) Nesting or infestation, or discharge or release of waste products or secretions, by any animals; or

(9) Animals owned or kept by an "insured".

Exception To 2.e.

Unless the loss is otherwise excluded, we cover loss to property covered under Coverage **A, B** or **C** resulting from an accidental discharge or overflow of water or steam from within a:

(i) Storm drain, or water, steam or sewer pipe, off the "residence premises"; or

(ii) Plumbing, heating, air conditioning or automatic fire protective sprinkler system or household appliance on the "residence premises". This includes the cost to tear out and replace any part of a building, or other structure, on the "residence premises", but only when necessary to repair the system or appliance. However, such tear out and replacement coverage only applies to other structures if the water or steam causes actual damage to a building on the "residence premises".

We do not cover loss to the system or appliance from which this water or steam escaped.

For purposes of this provision, a plumbing system or household appliance does not include a sump, sump pump or related equipment or a roof drain, gutter, downspout or similar fixtures or equipment.

Section **I** – Exclusion **A.3.** Water, Paragraphs **a.** and **c.** that apply to surface water and water below the surface of the ground do not apply to loss by water covered under **d.** and **e.** above.

Under **2.a.** through **e.** above, any ensuing loss to property described in Coverages **A, B** and **C** not precluded by any other provision in this policy is covered.

B. Under Coverages **A** and **B:**

1. Caused by vandalism and malicious mischief, and any ensuing loss caused by any intentional and wrongful act committed in the course of the vandalism or malicious mischief, if the dwelling has been vacant for more than 60 consecutive days immediately before the loss. A dwelling being constructed is not considered vacant;

2. Involving collapse, including any of the following conditions of property or any part of the property:

a. An abrupt falling down or caving in;

b. Loss of structural integrity, including separation of parts of the property or property in danger of falling down or caving in; or

c. Any cracking, bulging, sagging, bending, leaning, settling, shrinkage or expansion as such condition relates to **a.** or **b.** above;

other than as provided in **E.8.** Collapse under Section **I** – Property Coverages. However, any ensuing loss to property described in Coverages **A** and **B** not precluded by any other provision in this policy is covered.

C. Under Coverage **C** caused by:

1. Breakage of eyeglasses, glassware, statuary, marble, bric-a-brac, porcelains and similar fragile articles other than jewelry, watches bronzes, cameras and photographic lenses.

However, there is coverage for breakage of the property by or resulting from:

a. Fire, lightning, windstorm, hail;

b. Smoke, other than smoke from agricultural smudging or industrial operations;

c. Explosion, riot, civil commotion;

d. Aircraft, vehicles, vandalism and malicious mischief;

e. Collapse of a building or any part of a building;

f. Water not otherwise excluded;

g. Theft or attempted theft; or

h. Sudden and accidental tearing apart, cracking, burning or bulging of:

(1) A steam or hot water heating system;

(2) An air conditioning or automatic fire protective sprinkler system; or

(3) An appliance for heating water;

2. Dampness of atmosphere or extremes of temperature unless the direct cause of loss is rain, snow, sleet or hail;

3. Refinishing, renovating or repairing property other than watches, jewelry and furs;

4. Collision, other than collision with a land vehicle, sinking, swamping or stranding of watercraft, including their trailers, furnishings, equipment and outboard engines or motors; or

5. Acts or decisions, including the failure to act or decide, of any person, group, organization or governmental body. However, any ensuing loss to property described in Coverage **C** not precluded by any other provision in this policy is covered.

SECTION I – EXCLUSIONS

A. We do not insure for loss caused directly or indirectly by any of the following. Such loss is excluded regardless of any other cause or event contributing concurrently or in any sequence to the loss. These exclusions apply whether or not the loss event results in widespread damage or affects a substantial area.

1. Ordinance Or Law

Ordinance Or Law means any ordinance or law:

a. Requiring or regulating the construction, demolition, remodeling, renovation or repair of property, including removal of any resulting debris. This Exclusion **A.1.a.** does not apply to the amount of coverage that may be provided for in **E.11.** Ordinance Or Law under Section **I** – Property Coverages;

b. The requirements of which result in a loss in value to property; or

c. Requiring any "insured" or others to test for, monitor, clean up, remove, contain, treat, detoxify or neutralize, or in any way respond to, or assess the effects of, pollutants.

Pollutants means any solid, liquid, gaseous or thermal irritant or contaminant, including smoke, vapor, soot, fumes, acids, alkalis, chemicals and waste. Waste includes materials to be recycled, reconditioned or reclaimed.

This Exclusion **A.1.** applies whether or not the property has been physically damaged.

2. Earth Movement

Earth Movement means:

a. Earthquake, including land shock waves or tremors before, during or after a volcanic eruption;

b. Landslide, mudslide or mudflow;

c. Subsidence or sinkhole; or

d. Any other earth movement including earth sinking, rising or shifting.

This Exclusion **A.2.** applies regardless of whether any of the above, in **A.2.a.** through **A.2.d.,** is caused by an act of nature or is otherwise caused.

However, direct loss by fire, explosion or theft resulting from any of the above, in **A.2.a.** through **A.2.d.,** is covered.

3. Water

This means:

a. Flood, surface water, waves, including tidal wave and tsunami, tides, tidal water, overflow of any body of water, or spray from any of these, all whether or not driven by wind, including storm surge;

b. Water which:

(1) Backs up through sewers or drains; or

(2) Overflows or is otherwise discharged from a sump, sump pump or related equipment;

c. Water below the surface of the ground, including water which exerts pressure on, or seeps, leaks or flows through a building, sidewalk, driveway, patio, foundation, swimming pool or other structure; or

d. Waterborne material carried or otherwise moved by any of the water referred to in **A.3.a.** through **A.3.c.** of this exclusion.

This Exclusion **A.3.** applies regardless of whether any of the above, in **A.3.a.** through **A.3.d.,** is caused by an act of nature or is otherwise caused.

This Exclusion **A.3.** applies to, but is not limited to, escape, overflow or discharge, for any reason, of water or waterborne material from a dam, levee, seawall or any other boundary or containment system.

However, direct loss by fire, explosion or theft resulting from any of the above, in **A.3.a.** through **A.3.d.,** is covered.

This exclusion does not apply to property described in Coverage **C** that is away from a premises or location owned, rented, occupied or controlled by an "insured".

This exclusion applies to property described in Coverage **C** that is on a premises or location owned, rented, occupied or controlled by an "insured" even if weather conditions contribute in any way to produce the loss.

4. Power Failure

Power Failure means the failure of power or other utility service if the failure takes place off the "residence premises". But if the failure results in a loss, from a Peril Insured Against on the "residence premises", we will pay for the loss caused by that peril.

5. **Neglect**

   Neglect means neglect of an "insured" to use all reasonable means to save and preserve property at and after the time of a loss.

6. **War**

   War includes the following and any consequence of any of the following:

   a. Undeclared war, civil war, insurrection, rebellion or revolution;

   b. Warlike act by a military force or military personnel; or

   c. Destruction, seizure or use for a military purpose.

   Discharge of a nuclear weapon will be deemed a warlike act even if accidental.

7. **Nuclear Hazard**

   This Exclusion **A.7.** pertains to Nuclear Hazard to the extent set forth in **N.** Nuclear Hazard Clause under Section **I** – Conditions.

8. **Intentional Loss**

   Intentional Loss means any loss arising out of any act an "insured" commits or conspires to commit with the intent to cause a loss.

   In the event of such loss, no "insured" is entitled to coverage, even "insureds" who did not commit or conspire to commit the act causing the loss.

9. **Governmental Action**

   Governmental Action means the destruction, confiscation or seizure of property described in Coverage **A, B** or **C** by order of any governmental or public authority.

   This exclusion does not apply to such acts ordered by any governmental or public authority that are taken at the time of a fire to prevent its spread, if the loss caused by fire would be covered under this policy.

B. We do not insure for loss to property described in Coverages **A** and **B** caused by any of the following. However, any ensuing loss to property described in Coverages **A** and **B** not precluded by any other provision in this policy is covered.

1. Weather conditions. However, this exclusion only applies if weather conditions contribute in any way with a cause or event excluded in **A.** above to produce the loss.

2. Acts or decisions, including the failure to act or decide, of any person, group, organization or governmental body.

3. Faulty, inadequate or defective:

   a. Planning, zoning, development, surveying, siting;

   b. Design, specifications, workmanship, repair, construction, renovation, remodeling, grading, compaction;

   c. Materials used in repair, construction, renovation or remodeling; or

   d. Maintenance;

   of part or all of any property whether on or off the "residence premises".

SECTION I – CONDITIONS

A. Insurable Interest And Limit Of Liability

Even if more than one person has an insurable interest in the property covered, we will not be liable in any one loss:

1. To an "insured" for more than the amount of such "insured's" interest at the time of loss; or

2. For more than the applicable limit of liability.

B. Deductible

Unless otherwise noted in this policy, the following deductible provision applies:

With respect to any one loss:

1. Subject to the applicable limit of liability, we will pay only that part of the total of all loss payable that exceeds the deductible amount shown in the Declarations.

2. If two or more deductibles under this policy apply to the loss, only the highest deductible amount will apply.

C. Duties After Loss

In case of a loss to covered property, we have no duty to provide coverage under this policy if the failure to comply with the following duties is prejudicial to us. These duties must be performed either by you, or an "insured" seeking coverage, or a representative of either:

1. Give prompt notice to us or our agent;

2. Notify the police in case of loss by theft;

3. Notify the credit card or electronic fund transfer card or access device company in case of loss as provided for in **E.6.** Credit Card, Electronic Fund Transfer Card Or Access Device, Forgery And Counterfeit Money under Section **I** – Property Coverages;

4. Protect the property from further damage. If repairs to the property are required, you must:

   a. Make reasonable and necessary repairs to protect the property; and

   b. Keep an accurate record of repair expenses;

5. Cooperate with us in the investigation of a claim;

6. Prepare an inventory of damaged personal property showing the quantity, description, actual cash value and amount of loss. Attach all bills, receipts and related documents that justify the figures in the inventory;
7. As often as we reasonably require:
   a. Show the damaged property;
   b. Provide us with records and documents we request and permit us to make copies; and
   c. Submit to examination under oath, while not in the presence of another "insured", and sign the same;
8. Send to us, within 60 days after our request, your signed, sworn proof of loss which sets forth, to the best of your knowledge and belief:
   a. The time and cause of loss;
   b. The interests of all "insureds" and all others in the property involved and all liens on the property;
   c. Other insurance which may cover the loss;
   d. Changes in title or occupancy of the property during the term of the policy;
   e. Specifications of damaged buildings and detailed repair estimates;
   f. The inventory of damaged personal property described in **6.** above;
   g. Receipts for additional living expenses incurred and records that support the fair rental value loss; and
   h. Evidence or affidavit that supports a claim under **E.6.** Credit Card, Electronic Fund Transfer Card Or Access Device, Forgery And Counterfeit Money under Section **I** – Property Coverages, stating the amount and cause of loss.

D. Loss Settlement

In this Condition **D.**, the terms "cost to repair or replace" and "replacement cost" do not include the increased costs incurred to comply with the enforcement of any ordinance or law, except to the extent that coverage for these increased costs is provided in **E.11.** Ordinance Or Law under Section **I** – Property Coverages. Covered property losses are settled as follows:

1. Property of the following types:
   a. Personal property;
   b. Awnings, carpeting, household appliances, outdoor antennas and outdoor equipment, whether or not attached to buildings;
   c. Structures that are not buildings; and
   d. Grave markers, including mausoleums;

   at actual cash value at the time of loss but not more than the amount required to repair or replace.
2. Buildings covered under Coverage **A** or **B** at replacement cost without deduction for depreciation, subject to the following:
   a. If, at the time of loss, the amount of insurance in this policy on the damaged building is 80% or more of the full replacement cost of the building immediately before the loss, we will pay the cost to repair or replace, without deduction for depreciation, but not more than the least of the following amounts:
      (1) The limit of liability under this policy that applies to the building;
      (2) The replacement cost of that part of the building damaged with material of like kind and quality and for like use; or
      (3) The necessary amount actually spent to repair or replace the damaged building.

      If the building is rebuilt at a new premises, the cost described in **(2)** above is limited to the cost which would have been incurred if the building had been built at the original premises.
   b. If, at the time of loss, the amount of insurance in this policy on the damaged building is less than 80% of the full replacement cost of the building immediately before the loss, we will pay the greater of the following amounts, but not more than the limit of liability under this policy that applies to the building:
      (1) The actual cash value of that part of the building damaged; or
      (2) That proportion of the cost to repair or replace, without deduction for depreciation, that part of the building damaged, which the total amount of insurance in this policy on the damaged building bears to 80% of the replacement cost of the building.
   c. To determine the amount of insurance required to equal 80% of the full replacement cost of the building immediately before the loss, do not include the value of:
      (1) Excavations, footings, foundations, piers, or any other structures or devices that support all or part of the building, which are below the undersurface of the lowest basement floor;

(2) Those supports described in **(1)** above which are below the surface of the ground inside the foundation walls, if there is no basement; and

(3) Underground flues, pipes, wiring and drains.

d. We will pay no more than the actual cash value of the damage until actual repair or replacement is complete. Once actual repair or replacement is complete, we will settle the loss as noted in **2.a.** and **b.** above.

However, if the cost to repair or replace the damage is both:

(1) Less than 5% of the amount of insurance in this policy on the building; and

(2) Less than $2,500;

we will settle the loss as noted in **2.a.** and **b.** above whether or not actual repair or replacement is complete.

e. You may disregard the replacement cost loss settlement provisions and make claim under this policy for loss to buildings on an actual cash value basis. You may then make claim for any additional liability according to the provisions of this Condition **D.** Loss Settlement, provided you notify us, within 180 days after the date of loss, of your intent to repair or replace the damaged building.

E. Loss To A Pair Or Set

In case of loss to a pair or set we may elect to:

1. Repair or replace any part to restore the pair or set to its value before the loss; or

2. Pay the difference between actual cash value of the property before and after the loss.

F. Appraisal

If you and we fail to agree on the amount of loss, either may demand an appraisal of the loss. In this event, each party will choose a competent and impartial appraiser within 20 days after receiving a written request from the other. The two appraisers will choose an umpire. If they cannot agree upon an umpire within 15 days, you or we may request that the choice be made by a judge of a court of record in the state where the "residence premises" is located. The appraisers will separately set the amount of loss. If the appraisers submit a written report of an agreement to us, the amount agreed upon will be the amount of loss. If they fail to agree, they will submit their differences to the umpire. A decision agreed to by any two will set the amount of loss.

Each party will:

1. Pay its own appraiser; and

2. Bear the other expenses of the appraisal and umpire equally.

G. Other Insurance And Service Agreement

If a loss covered by this policy is also covered by:

1. Other insurance, we will pay only the proportion of the loss that the limit of liability that applies under this policy bears to the total amount of insurance covering the loss; or

2. A service agreement, this insurance is excess over any amounts payable under any such agreement. Service agreement means a service plan, property restoration plan, home warranty or other similar service warranty agreement, even if it is characterized as insurance.

H. Suit Against Us

No action can be brought against us unless there has been full compliance with all of the terms under Section **I** of this policy and the action is started within two years after the date of loss.

I. Our Option

If we give you written notice within 30 days after we receive your signed, sworn proof of loss, we may repair or replace any part of the damaged property with material or property of like kind and quality.

J. Loss Payment

We will adjust all losses with you. We will pay you unless some other person is named in the policy or is legally entitled to receive payment. Loss will be payable 60 days after we receive your proof of loss and:

1. Reach an agreement with you;

2. There is an entry of a final judgment; or

3. There is a filing of an appraisal award with us.

K. Abandonment Of Property

We need not accept any property abandoned by an "insured".

L. Mortgage Clause

1. If a mortgagee is named in this policy, any loss payable under Coverage **A** or **B** will be paid to the mortgagee and you, as interests appear. If more than one mortgagee is named, the order of payment will be the same as the order of precedence of the mortgages.

2. If we deny your claim, that denial will not apply to a valid claim of the mortgagee, if the mortgagee:
   a. Notifies us of any change in ownership, occupancy or substantial change in risk of which the mortgagee is aware;
   b. Pays any premium due under this policy on demand if you have neglected to pay the premium; and
   c. Submits a signed, sworn statement of loss within 60 days after receiving notice from us of your failure to do so. Paragraphs **F.** Appraisal, **H.** Suit Against Us and **J.** Loss Payment under Section **I** – Conditions also apply to the mortgagee.
3. If we decide to cancel or not to renew this policy, the mortgagee will be notified at least 10 days before the date cancellation or nonrenewal takes effect.
4. If we pay the mortgagee for any loss and deny payment to you:
   a. We are subrogated to all the rights of the mortgagee granted under the mortgage on the property; or
   b. At our option, we may pay to the mortgagee the whole principal on the mortgage plus any accrued interest. In this event, we will receive a full assignment and transfer of the mortgage and all securities held as collateral to the mortgage debt.
5. Subrogation will not impair the right of the mortgagee to recover the full amount of the mortgagee's claim.

M. No Benefit To Bailee

We will not recognize any assignment or grant any coverage that benefits a person or organization holding, storing or moving property for a fee regardless of any other provision of this policy.

N. Nuclear Hazard Clause

1. "Nuclear Hazard" means any nuclear reaction, radiation, or radioactive contamination, all whether controlled or uncontrolled or however caused, or any consequence of any of these.
2. Loss caused by the nuclear hazard will not be considered loss caused by fire, explosion, or smoke, whether these perils are specifically named in or otherwise included within the Perils Insured Against.
3. This policy does not apply under Section **I** to loss caused directly or indirectly by nuclear hazard, except that direct loss by fire resulting from the nuclear hazard is covered.

O. Recovered Property

If you or we recover any property for which we have made payment under this policy, you or we will notify the other of the recovery. At your option, the property will be returned to or retained by you or it will become our property. If the recovered property is returned to or retained by you, the loss payment will be adjusted based on the amount you received for the recovered property.

P. Volcanic Eruption Period

One or more volcanic eruptions that occur within a 72-hour period will be considered as one volcanic eruption.

Q. Policy Period

This policy applies only to loss which occurs during the policy period.

R. Concealment Or Fraud

We provide coverage to no "insureds" under this policy if, whether before or after a loss, an "insured" has:

1. Intentionally concealed or misrepresented any material fact or circumstance;
2. Engaged in fraudulent conduct; or
3. Made false statements;

relating to this insurance.

S. Loss Payable Clause

If the Declarations shows a loss payee for certain listed insured personal property, the definition of "insured" is changed to include that loss payee with respect to that property.

If we decide to cancel or not renew this policy, that loss payee will be notified in writing.

SECTION II – LIABILITY COVERAGES

A. Coverage E – Personal Liability

If a claim is made or a suit is brought against an "insured" for damages because of "bodily injury" or "property damage" caused by an "occurrence" to which this coverage applies, we will:

1. Pay up to our limit of liability for the damages for which an "insured" is legally liable. Damages include prejudgment interest awarded against an "insured"; and
2. Provide a defense at our expense by counsel of our choice, even if the suit is groundless, false or fraudulent. We may investigate and settle any claim or suit that we decide is appropriate. Our duty to settle or defend ends when our limit of liability for the "occurrence" has been exhausted by payment of a judgment or settlement.

B. Coverage F – Medical Payments To Others

We will pay the necessary medical expenses that are incurred or medically ascertained within three years from the date of an accident causing "bodily injury". Medical expenses means reasonable charges for medical, surgical, x-ray, dental, ambulance, hospital, professional nursing, prosthetic devices and funeral services. This coverage does not apply to you or regular residents of your household except "residence employees". As to others, this coverage applies only:

1. To a person on the "insured location" with the permission of an "insured"; or
2. To a person off the "insured location", if the "bodily injury":
   a. Arises out of a condition on the "insured location" or the ways immediately adjoining;
   b. Is caused by the activities of an "insured";
   c. Is caused by a "residence employee" in the course of the "residence employee's" employment by an "insured"; or
   d. Is caused by an animal owned by or in the care of an "insured".

SECTION II – EXCLUSIONS

A. "Motor Vehicle Liability"

1. Coverages **E** and **F** do not apply to any "motor vehicle liability" if, at the time and place of an "occurrence", the involved "motor vehicle":
   a. Is registered for use on public roads or property;
   b. Is not registered for use on public roads or property, but such registration is required by a law, or regulation issued by a government agency, for it to be used at the place of the "occurrence"; or
   c. Is being:
      (1) Operated in, or practicing for, any prearranged or organized race, speed contest or other competition;
      (2) Rented to others;
      (3) Used to carry persons or cargo for a charge; or
      (4) Used for any "business" purpose except for a motorized golf cart while on a golfing facility.
2. If Exclusion **A.1.** does not apply, there is still no coverage for "motor vehicle liability", unless the "motor vehicle" is:
   a. In dead storage on an "insured location";
   b. Used solely to service a residence;
   c. Designed to assist the handicapped and, at the time of an "occurrence", it is:
      (1) Being used to assist a handicapped person; or
      (2) Parked on an "insured location";
   d. Designed for recreational use off public roads and:
      (1) Not owned by an "insured"; or
      (2) Owned by an "insured" provided the "occurrence" takes place:
         (a) On an "insured location" as defined in Definition **B.6.a., b., d., e.** or **h.;** or
         (b) Off an "insured location" and the "motor vehicle" is:
            (i) Designed as a toy vehicle for use by children under seven years of age;
            (ii) Powered by one or more batteries; and
            (iii) Not built or modified after manufacture to exceed a speed of five miles per hour on level ground;
   e. A motorized golf cart that is owned by an "insured", designed to carry up to four persons, not built or modified after manufacture to exceed a speed of 25 miles per hour on level ground and, at the time of an "occurrence", is within the legal boundaries of:
      (1) A golfing facility and is parked or stored there, or being used by an "insured" to:
         (a) Play the game of golf or for other recreational or leisure activity allowed by the facility;
         (b) Travel to or from an area where "motor vehicles" or golf carts are parked or stored; or
         (c) Cross public roads at designated points to access other parts of the golfing facility; or
      (2) A private residential community, including its public roads upon which a motorized golf cart can legally travel, which is subject to the authority of a property owners association and contains an "insured's" residence.

B. "Watercraft Liability"

1. Coverages **E** and **F** do not apply to any "watercraft liability" if, at the time of an "occurrence", the involved watercraft is being:
   a. Operated in, or practicing for, any prearranged or organized race, speed contest or other competition. This exclusion does not apply to a sailing vessel or a predicted log cruise;
   b. Rented to others;
   c. Used to carry persons or cargo for a charge; or
   d. Used for any "business" purpose.
2. If Exclusion **B.1.** does not apply, there is still no coverage for "watercraft liability" unless, at the time of the "occurrence", the watercraft:
   a. Is stored;
   b. Is a sailing vessel, with or without auxiliary power, that is:
   (1) Less than 26 feet in overall length; or
   (2) 26 feet or more in overall length and not owned by or rented to an "insured"; or
   c. Is not a sailing vessel and is powered by:
   (1) An inboard or inboard-outdrive engine or motor, including those that power a water jet pump, of:
   (a) 50 horsepower or less and not owned by an "insured"; or
   (b) More than 50 horsepower and not owned by or rented to an "insured"; or
   (2) One or more outboard engines or motors with:
   (a) 25 total horsepower or less;
   (b) More than 25 horsepower if the outboard engine or motor is not owned by an "insured";
   (c) More than 25 horsepower if the outboard engine or motor is owned by an "insured" who acquired it during the policy period; or
   (d) More than 25 horsepower if the outboard engine or motor is owned by an "insured" who acquired it before the policy period, but only if:
   (i) You declare them at policy inception; or
   (ii) Your intent to insure them is reported to us in writing within 45 days after you acquire them.

   The coverages in **(c)** and **(d)** above apply for the policy period.

   Horsepower means the maximum power rating assigned to the engine or motor by the manufacturer.

C. "Aircraft Liability"

This policy does not cover "aircraft liability".

D. "Hovercraft Liability"

This policy does not cover "hovercraft liability".

E. Coverage E – Personal Liability And Coverage F – Medical Payments To Others

Coverages **E** and **F** do not apply to the following:

1. **Expected Or Intended Injury**

   "Bodily injury" or "property damage" which is expected or intended by an "insured", even if the resulting "bodily injury" or "property damage":
   a. Is of a different kind, quality or degree than initially expected or intended; or
   b. Is sustained by a different person, entity or property than initially expected or intended.

   However, this Exclusion **E.1.** does not apply to "bodily injury" or "property damage" resulting from the use of reasonable force by an "insured" to protect persons or property;
2. **"Business"**
   a. "Bodily injury" or "property damage" arising out of or in connection with a "business" conducted from an "insured location" or engaged in by an "insured", whether or not the "business" is owned or operated by an "insured" or employs an "insured".

   This Exclusion **E.2.** applies but is not limited to an act or omission, regardless of its nature or circumstance, involving a service or duty rendered, promised, owed, or implied to be provided because of the nature of the "business".
   b. This Exclusion **E.2.** does not apply to:
   (1) The rental or holding for rental of an "insured location";
   (a) On an occasional basis if used only as a residence;
   (b) In part for use only as a residence, unless a single-family unit is intended for use by the occupying family to lodge more than two roomers or boarders; or
   (c) In part, as an office, school, studio or private garage; and

(2) An "insured" under the age of 21 years involved in a part-time or occasional, self-employed "business" with no employees;

3. **Professional Services**

"Bodily injury" or "property damage" arising out of the rendering of or failure to render professional services;

4. **"Insured's" Premises Not An "Insured Location"**

"Bodily injury" or "property damage" arising out of a premises:

a. Owned by an "insured";

b. Rented to an "insured"; or

c. Rented to others by an "insured";

that is not an "insured location";

5. **War**

"Bodily injury" or "property damage" caused directly or indirectly by war, including the following and any consequence of any of the following:

a. Undeclared war, civil war, insurrection, rebellion or revolution;

b. Warlike act by a military force or military personnel; or

c. Destruction, seizure or use for a military purpose.

Discharge of a nuclear weapon will be deemed a warlike act even if accidental;

6. **Communicable Disease**

"Bodily injury" or "property damage" which arises out of the transmission of a communicable disease by an "insured";

7. **Sexual Molestation, Corporal Punishment Or Physical Or Mental Abuse**

"Bodily injury" or "property damage" arising out of sexual molestation, corporal punishment or physical or mental abuse; or

8. **Controlled Substance**

"Bodily injury" or "property damage" arising out of the use, sale, manufacture, delivery, transfer or possession by any person of a Controlled Substance as defined by the Federal Food and Drug Law at 21 U.S.C.A. Sections 811 and 812. Controlled Substances include but are not limited to cocaine, LSD, marijuana and all narcotic drugs. However, this exclusion does not apply to the legitimate use of prescription drugs by a person following the lawful orders of a licensed health care professional.

Exclusions **A.** "Motor Vehicle Liability", **B.** "Watercraft Liability", **C.** "Aircraft Liability", **D.** "Hovercraft Liability" and **E.4.** "Insured's" Premises Not An "Insured Location" do not apply to "bodily injury" to a "residence employee" arising out of and in the course of the "residence employee's" employment by an "insured".

F. **Coverage E – Personal Liability**

Coverage **E** does not apply to:

1. Liability:

a. For any loss assessment charged against you as a member of an association, corporation or community of property owners, except as provided in **D.** Loss Assessment under Section **II** – Additional Coverages;

b. Under any contract or agreement entered into by an "insured". However, this exclusion does not apply to written contracts:

(1) That directly relate to the ownership, maintenance or use of an "insured location"; or

(2) Where the liability of others is assumed by you prior to an "occurrence";

unless excluded in **a.** above or elsewhere in this policy;

2. "Property damage" to property owned by an "insured". This includes costs or expenses incurred by an "insured" or others to repair, replace, enhance, restore or maintain such property to prevent injury to a person or damage to property of others, whether on or away from an "insured location";

3. "Property damage" to property rented to, occupied or used by or in the care of an "insured". This exclusion does not apply to "property damage" caused by fire, smoke or explosion;

4. "Bodily injury" to any person eligible to receive any benefits voluntarily provided or required to be provided by an "insured" under any:

a. Workers' compensation law;

b. Non-occupational disability law; or

c. Occupational disease law;

5. "Bodily injury" or "property damage" for which an "insured" under this policy:

a. Is also an insured under a nuclear energy liability policy issued by the:

(1) Nuclear Energy Liability Insurance Association;

(2) Mutual Atomic Energy Liability Underwriters;

(3) Nuclear Insurance Association of Canada;

or any of their successors; or

b. Would be an insured under such a policy but for the exhaustion of its limit of liability; or

6. "Bodily injury" to you or an "insured" as defined under Definition **5.a.** or **b.**

This exclusion also applies to any claim made or suit brought against you or an "insured" to:

a. Repay; or

b. Share damages with;

another person who may be obligated to pay damages because of "bodily injury" to an "insured".

G. Coverage F – Medical Payments To Others

Coverage **F** does not apply to "bodily injury":

1. To a "residence employee" if the "bodily injury":

a. Occurs off the "insured location"; and

b. Does not arise out of or in the course of the "residence employee's" employment by an "insured";

2. To any person eligible to receive benefits voluntarily provided or required to be provided under any:

a. Workers' compensation law;

b. Non-occupational disability law; or

c. Occupational disease law;

3. From any:

a. Nuclear reaction;

b. Nuclear radiation; or

c. Radioactive contamination;

all whether controlled or uncontrolled or however caused; or

d. Any consequence of any of these; or

4. To any person, other than a "residence employee" of an "insured", regularly residing on any part of the "insured location".

SECTION II – ADDITIONAL COVERAGES

We cover the following in addition to the limits of liability:

A. Claim Expenses

We pay:

1. Expenses we incur and costs taxed against an "insured" in any suit we defend;

2. Premiums on bonds required in a suit we defend, but not for bond amounts more than the Coverage **E** limit of liability. We need not apply for or furnish any bond;

3. Reasonable expenses incurred by an "insured" at our request, including actual loss of earnings (but not loss of other income) up to $250 per day, for assisting us in the investigation or defense of a claim or suit; and

4. Interest on the entire judgment which accrues after entry of the judgment and before we pay or tender, or deposit in court that part of the judgment which does not exceed the limit of liability that applies.

B. First Aid Expenses

We will pay expenses for first aid to others incurred by an "insured" for "bodily injury" covered under this policy. We will not pay for first aid to an "insured".

C. Damage To Property Of Others

1. We will pay, at replacement cost, up to $1,000 per "occurrence" for "property damage" to property of others caused by an "insured".

2. We will not pay for "property damage":

a. To the extent of any amount recoverable under Section **I;**

b. Caused intentionally by an "insured" who is 13 years of age or older;

c. To property owned by an "insured";

d. To property owned by or rented to a tenant of an "insured" or a resident in your household; or

e. Arising out of:

(1) A "business" engaged in by an "insured";

(2) Any act or omission in connection with a premises owned, rented or controlled by an "insured", other than the "insured location"; or

(3) The ownership, maintenance, occupancy, operation, use, loading or unloading of aircraft, hovercraft, watercraft or "motor vehicles".

This Exclusion **e.(3)** does not apply to a "motor vehicle" that:

(a) Is designed for recreational use off public roads;

(b) Is not owned by an "insured"; and

(c) At the time of the "occurrence", is not required by law, or regulation issued by a government agency, to have been registered for it to be used on public roads or property.

D. Loss Assessment

1. We will pay up to $1,000 for your share of loss assessment charged against you, as owner or tenant of the "residence premises", during the policy period by a corporation or association of property owners, when the assessment is made as a result of:

a. "Bodily injury" or "property damage" not excluded from coverage under Section **II** – Exclusions; or

b. Liability for an act of a director, officer or trustee in the capacity as a director, officer or trustee, provided such person:

(1) Is elected by the members of a corporation or association of property owners; and

(2) Serves without deriving any income from the exercise of duties which are solely on behalf of a corporation or association of property owners.

2. Paragraph **I.** Policy Period under Section **II** – Conditions does not apply to this Loss Assessment Coverage.

3. Regardless of the number of assessments, the limit of $1,000 is the most we will pay for loss arising out of:

a. One accident, including continuous or repeated exposure to substantially the same general harmful condition; or

b. A covered act of a director, officer or trustee. An act involving more than one director, officer or trustee is considered to be a single act.

4. We do not cover assessments charged against you or a corporation or association of property owners by any governmental body.

SECTION II – CONDITIONS

A. Limit Of Liability

Our total liability under Coverage **E** for all damages resulting from any one "occurrence" will not be more than the Coverage **E** Limit Of Liability shown in the Declarations. This limit is the same regardless of the number of "insureds", claims made or persons injured. All "bodily injury" and "property damage" resulting from any one accident or from continuous or repeated exposure to substantially the same general harmful conditions shall be considered to be the result of one "occurrence".

Our total liability under Coverage **F** for all medical expense payable for "bodily injury" to one person as the result of one accident will not be more than the Coverage **F** Limit Of Liability shown in the Declarations.

B. Severability Of Insurance

This insurance applies separately to each "insured". This condition will not increase our limit of liability for any one "occurrence".

C. Duties After "Occurrence"

In case of an "occurrence", you or another "insured" will perform the following duties that apply. We have no duty to provide coverage under this policy if your failure to comply with the following duties is prejudicial to us. You will help us by seeing that these duties are performed:

1. Give written notice to us or our agent as soon as is practical, which sets forth:

a. The identity of the policy and the "named insured" shown in the Declarations;

b. Reasonably available information on the time, place and circumstances of the "occurrence"; and

c. Names and addresses of any claimants and witnesses;

2. Cooperate with us in the investigation, settlement or defense of any claim or suit;

3. Promptly forward to us every notice, demand, summons or other process relating to the "occurrence";

4. At our request, help us:

a. To make settlement;

b. To enforce any right of contribution or indemnity against any person or organization who may be liable to an "insured";

c. With the conduct of suits and attend hearings and trials; and

d. To secure and give evidence and obtain the attendance of witnesses;

5. With respect to **C.** Damage To Property Of Others under Section **II** – Additional Coverages, submit to us within 60 days after the loss a sworn statement of loss and show the damaged property, if in an "insured's" control;

6. No "insured" shall, except at such "insured's" own cost, voluntarily make payment, assume obligation or incur expense other than for first aid to others at the time of the "bodily injury".

D. Duties Of An Injured Person – Coverage F – Medical Payments To Others

1. The injured person or someone acting for the injured person will:
   a. Give us written proof of claim, under oath if required, as soon as is practical; and
   b. Authorize us to obtain copies of medical reports and records.
2. The injured person will submit to a physical exam by a doctor of our choice when and as often as we reasonably require.

E. Payment Of Claim – Coverage F – Medical Payments To Others

Payment under this coverage is not an admission of liability by an "insured" or us.

F. Suit Against Us

1. No action can be brought against us unless there has been full compliance with all of the terms under this Section **II**.
2. No one will have the right to join us as a party to any action against an "insured".
3. Also, no action with respect to Coverage **E** can be brought against us until the obligation of such "insured" has been determined by final judgment or agreement signed by us.

G. Bankruptcy Of An "Insured"

Bankruptcy or insolvency of an "insured" will not relieve us of our obligations under this policy.

H. Other Insurance

This insurance is excess over other valid and collectible insurance except insurance written specifically to cover as excess over the limits of liability that apply in this policy.

I. Policy Period

This policy applies only to "bodily injury" or "property damage" which occurs during the policy period.

J. Concealment Or Fraud

We do not provide coverage to an "insured" who, whether before or after a loss, has:

1. Intentionally concealed or misrepresented any material fact or circumstance;
2. Engaged in fraudulent conduct; or
3. Made false statements;

relating to this insurance.

SECTIONS I AND II – CONDITIONS

A. Liberalization Clause

If we make a change which broadens coverage under this edition of our policy without additional premium charge, that change will automatically apply to your insurance as of the date we implement the change in your state, provided that this implementation date falls within 60 days prior to or during the policy period stated in the Declarations.

This Liberalization Clause does not apply to changes implemented with a general program revision that includes both broadenings and restrictions in coverage, whether that general program revision is implemented through introduction of:

1. A subsequent edition of this policy; or
2. An amendatory endorsement.

B. Waiver Or Change Of Policy Provisions

A waiver or change of a provision of this policy must be in writing by us to be valid. Our request for an appraisal or examination will not waive any of our rights.

C. Cancellation

1. You may cancel this policy at any time by returning it to us or by letting us know in writing of the date cancellation is to take effect.
2. We may cancel this policy only for the reasons stated below by letting you know in writing of the date cancellation takes effect. This cancellation notice may be delivered to you, or mailed to you at your mailing address shown in the Declarations. Proof of mailing will be sufficient proof of notice.
   a. When you have not paid the premium, we may cancel at any time by letting you know at least 10 days before the date cancellation takes effect.
   b. When this policy has been in effect for less than 60 days and is not a renewal with us, we may cancel for any reason by letting you know at least 10 days before the date cancellation takes effect.
   c. When this policy has been in effect for 60 days or more, or at any time if it is a renewal with us, we may cancel:
      (1) If there has been a material misrepresentation of fact which if known to us would have caused us not to issue the policy; or

(2) If the risk has changed substantially since the policy was issued.

This can be done by letting you know at least 30 days before the date cancellation takes effect.

d. When this policy is written for a period of more than one year, we may cancel for any reason at anniversary by letting you know at least 30 days before the date cancellation takes effect.

3. When this policy is canceled, the premium for the period from the date of cancellation to the expiration date will be refunded pro rata.

4. If the return premium is not refunded with the notice of cancellation or when this policy is returned to us, we will refund it within a reasonable time after the date cancellation takes effect.

D. Nonrenewal

We may elect not to renew this policy. We may do so by delivering to you, or mailing to you at your mailing address shown in the Declarations, written notice at least 30 days before the expiration date of this policy. Proof of mailing will be sufficient proof of notice.

E. Assignment

Assignment of this policy will not be valid unless we give our written consent.

F. Subrogation

An "insured" may waive in writing before a loss all rights of recovery against any person. If not waived, we may require an assignment of rights of recovery for a loss to the extent that payment is made by us.

If an assignment is sought, an "insured" must sign and deliver all related papers and cooperate with us.

Subrogation does not apply to Coverage **F** or Paragraph **C.** Damage To Property Of Others under Section **II** – Additional Coverages.

G. Death

If any person named in the Declarations or the spouse, if a resident of the same household, dies, the following apply:

1. We insure the legal representative of the deceased but only with respect to the premises and property of the deceased covered under the policy at the time of death; and

2. "Insured" includes:

a. An "insured" who is a member of your household at the time of your death, but only while a resident of the "residence premises"; and

b. With respect to your property, the person having proper temporary custody of the property until appointment and qualification of a legal representative.

THIS IS A LEGAL CONTRACT
-- PLEASE READ IT CAREFULLY --

SPECIAL FORM

The following Table of Contents shows how the policy is organized. It will help "you" locate particular sections of the policy.

TABLE OF CONTENTS

Page

Endorsements and schedules may also be part of this policy. They are identified on the "declarations".

Words and phrases that have special meaning are shown in quotation marks. The special meanings for these words and phrases are set forth in Definitions.

AGREEMENT

This policy, subject to all of its "terms", provides the described insurance coverages during the policy period. In return "you" must pay the required premium. Each of the Principal Coverages described in this policy applies only if a "limit" is shown on the "declarations" for that coverage.

DEFINITIONS

1. The words "you" and "your" mean the person or persons named as the insured on the "declarations". This includes "your" spouse if a resident of "your" household.

2. The words "we", "us", and "our" mean the company providing this insurance.

3. "Actual cash value" means the cost to repair or replace property using materials of like kind and quality, to the extent practical, less a deduction for depreciation, however caused.

4. Under the Liability Coverages provided by this policy, "aircraft" means an apparatus or a device designed or used for flight, but this does not include:

   a. a model aircraft that is not designed or used to carry people or cargo;

   b. a "hovercraft"; or

   c. a model hovercraft that is not designed or used to carry people or cargo.

5. "Bodily injury" means bodily harm to a person and includes sickness, disease, or death. This also includes required care and loss of services.

   However, "bodily injury" does not mean bodily harm, sickness, disease, or death that arises out of mental or emotional injury, suffering, or distress that does not result from actual physical injury to a person.

6. "Business" means:

   a. a trade, a profession, or an occupation, including farming, all whether full time, part time, or occasional. This includes the rental of property to others, but does not include:

      1) the occasional rental for residential purposes of that part of the "described location" normally occupied solely by "your" household; or
      2) the rental or holding for rental of a portion of that part of the "described location" normally occupied by "your" household to no more than two roomers or boarders for use as a residence; or

   b. any other activity undertaken for money or other compensation, but this does not include:

      1) providing care services to a relative of an "insured";
      2) providing services for the care of persons who are not relatives of an "insured" and for which the only compensation is the mutual exchange of like services;
      3) a volunteer activity for which:

         a) an "insured" receives no compensation; or
         b) an "insured's" only compensation is the reimbursement of expenses incurred to carry out the activity; or

      4) an activity not described in 1) through 3) above for which no "insured's" total compensation for the 12 month period just before the first day of this policy period was more than $2,500.

7. "Declarations" means all pages labeled declarations, supplemental declarations, or schedule that pertain to this policy.

8. "Described location" means the one- to four-family house, the townhouse, or the row house where "you" reside and which is shown on the "declarations" as the "described location". It includes related private structures and grounds at that location.

However, if the "described location" is a townhouse or a row house, it includes only related private structures and grounds at that location that are used or occupied solely by "your" household for residential purposes.

9. "Domestic employee" means a person employed by an "insured", or a person leased to an "insured" under a contract or an agreement with a labor leasing firm, to perform duties that relate to the use or care of the "described location". This includes a person who performs duties of a similar nature elsewhere for an "insured", provided such duties are not in connection with an "insured's" "business".

   However, "domestic employee" does not include a person who is furnished to an "insured":

   a. as a temporary substitute for a permanent "domestic employee" who is on leave; or

   b. to meet seasonal or short-term workloads.

10. "Employee" means a person employed by an "insured", or a person leased to an "insured" under a contract or an agreement with a labor leasing firm, to perform duties other than those performed by a "domestic employee".

11. "Fungi" means any kind or form of fungus, including but not limited to mildew and mold, and any chemical, matter, or compound produced or released by a fungus, including but not limited to toxins, spores, fragments, and metabolites such as microbial volatile organic compounds.

12. Under the Liability Coverages provided by this policy, "hovercraft" means a self-propelled motorized ground effect machine or air cushion vehicle designed or used to travel over land or water. This includes, but is not limited to, a flarecraft.

    However, "hovercraft" does not include:

    a. a model hovercraft that is not designed or used to carry people or cargo;

    b. an "aircraft";

    c. a model aircraft that is not designed or used to carry people or cargo;

    d. a "motorized vehicle";

    e. a "watercraft"; or

    f. a model watercraft that is not designed or used to carry people or cargo.

13. "Insured" means:

    a. "you";

    b. "your" relatives if residents of "your" household;

    c. "your" relatives under the age of 25 years who:

       1) are financially dependent upon "you";
       2) are students enrolled in school full time, as defined by the school; and
       3) were residents of "your" household just before moving out to attend school;

    d. persons, other than "your" relatives, under the age of 21 years who:

       1) reside in "your" household; and
       2) are in "your" care or in the care of "your" resident relatives;

    e. persons, other than "your" relatives, under the age of 21 years who:

       1) are in "your" care or in the care of "your" resident relatives;
       2) are students enrolled in school full time, as defined by the school; and
       3) were residents of "your" household just before moving out to attend school; or

f. solely with respect to the Liability Coverages provided by this policy:

   1) persons in the course of acting as "your" real estate manager for the "described location", but only with respect to acts falling within the scope of such duties;
   2) persons while engaged in the employ of an "insured" as defined in a., b., c., d., or e. above, but only with respect to a "motorized vehicle" to which this insurance applies;
   3) persons using a "motorized vehicle" to which this insurance applies on an "insured premises" with "your" consent, but only with respect to such use;
   4) persons or organizations accountable by law for "watercraft" or animals:

      a) owned by an "insured" as defined in a., b., c., d., or e. above; and
      b) to which this insurance applies;

      but only with respect to such "watercraft" or animals.

      However, this does not include persons or organizations using or having charge or control of such "watercraft" or animals in the course of "business" or without the owner's consent; or

   5) persons or organizations accountable by law for a motorized golf cart:

      a) owned by an "insured" as defined in a., b., c., d., or e. above; and
      b) to which this insurance applies;

      but only with respect to such golf cart.

      However, this does not include persons or organizations using or having charge or control of such golf cart without the owner's consent.

The phrase an "insured", wherever it appears in this policy, means one or more "insureds".

14. "Insured premises" means:

   a. the "described location";

   b. that part of any other premises used by "you" as a residence and shown on the "declarations" as an "insured premises";

   c. that part of any other premises used by "you" as a residence and that is acquired by "you" during the policy period for such use;

   d. premises used by "you" in connection with a premises described in a., b., or c. above;

   e. cemetery lots and burial vaults of an "insured";

   f. that part of a premises not owned by an "insured" and that is temporarily used by an "insured" as a residence;

   g. that part of a premises occasionally rented to an "insured" for other than "business" purposes; and

   h. vacant land owned by or rented to an "insured". This includes land where a one- to four-family house, a townhouse, or a row house is being built for use as an "insured's" residence. This does not include farm land.

15. "Limit" means amount of insurance.

16. "Motorized vehicle" means:

   a. a self-propelled land or amphibious vehicle, regardless of method of surface contact, but this does not include a:

      1) "hovercraft";
      2) model hovercraft that is not designed or used to carry people or cargo;
      3) "watercraft"; or

4) model watercraft that is not designed or used to carry people or cargo; or

b. a trailer or semitrailer that:

1) is attached to or being carried on or towed by; or
2) becomes detached while being carried on or towed by;

a vehicle described in a. above.

17. "Occurrence" means an accident, including repeated exposures to similar conditions, that results in "bodily injury" or "property damage" during the policy period.

18. "Pollutant" means:

a. any solid, liquid, gaseous, thermal, or radioactive irritant or contaminant, including acids, alkalis, chemicals, fumes, smoke, soot, vapor, and waste. Waste includes materials to be disposed of as well as recycled, reclaimed, or reconditioned; and

b. electrical, magnetic, or electromagnetic particles or fields, whether visible or invisible, and sound.

19. "Property damage" means:

a. physical injury to or destruction of tangible property; or

b. the loss of use of tangible property whether or not it is physically damaged.

20. "Terms" means all provisions, limitations, exclusions, conditions, "declarations", and definitions used in this policy.

21. "Vermin" means an animal of a type that is prone to enter or burrow into or under a structure to seek food or shelter, including but not limited to:

a. armadillos;

b. bats;

c. opossums;

d. porcupines;

e. raccoons;

f. skunks; and

g. snakes.

22. Under the Liability Coverages provided by this policy, "watercraft" means an apparatus or a device primarily designed to be propelled on or in water by engine, motor, or wind, but this does not include:

a. a model watercraft that is not designed or used to carry people or cargo;

b. a "hovercraft";

c. a model hovercraft that is not designed or used to carry people or cargo;

d. a "motorized vehicle";

e. an "aircraft"; or

f. a model aircraft that is not designed or used to carry people or cargo.

PROPERTY COVERAGES

PRINCIPAL PROPERTY COVERAGES

1. **Coverage A -- Residence**

a. "We" cover the residence on the "described location". This includes additions attached to the residence and built-in components and fixtures, as well as building materials and supplies located on or adjacent to the "described location" for use in the construction, alteration, or repair of the residence or related private structures on the "described location".

b. "We" do not cover:

1) land, including the land on which covered property is located, except as provided under the Incidental Property Coverage for Liquid Fuel Remediation;
2) underground water or surface water;
3) trees, plants, shrubs, or lawns, except as provided under the Incidental Property Coverage for Debris Removal and the Incidental Property Coverage for Trees, Plants, Shrubs, Or Lawns; or
4) grave markers or mausoleums, except as provided under the Incidental Property Coverage for Grave Markers.

c. The "limit" that applies to Coverage A is the most "we" pay per occurrence for all property covered under Coverage A.

2. **Coverage B -- Related Private Structures**

a. "We" cover related private structures on the "described location" that are not attached to the residence covered under Coverage A. Structures that are connected to the residence covered under Coverage A by only a fence, a utility line, or a similar connection are not considered attached.

b. "We" also cover fences, driveways, sidewalks, and other permanently installed outdoor fixtures.

c. "We" do not cover:

1) land, including the land on which covered property is located, except as provided under the Incidental Property Coverage for Liquid Fuel Remediation;
2) underground water or surface water;
3) trees, plants, shrubs, or lawns, except as provided under the Incidental Property Coverage for Debris Removal and the Incidental Property Coverage for Trees, Plants, Shrubs, Or Lawns;
4) grave markers or mausoleums, except as provided under the Incidental Property Coverage for Grave Markers; or
5) any structure:

a) rented or held for rental to any person who is not a tenant of the residence covered under Coverage A, other than a structure used solely for private garage purposes;
b) used, in whole or in part, for the direction or operation of a "business"; or
c) used, in whole or in part, for the storage of "business" property.

However, this exclusion does not apply to a structure used by an "insured" or a tenant of the residence covered under Coverage A to store "business" property that:

(1) is a private passenger auto, a pickup truck, a van, or a "motorized vehicle" designed for grounds maintenance activities such as lawn mowing or snow plowing; or
(2) is owned solely by such "insured" or tenant and is not a "motorized vehicle"; and

does not consist of or contain gaseous or liquid fuel, other than fuel contained in a permanently installed fuel tank of a vehicle, craft, or grounds maintenance machine or in a portable container that is designed to hold fuel and has a capacity of no more than five U.S. gallons.

d. The "limit" that applies to Coverage B is the most "we" pay per occurrence for all property covered under Coverage B.

3. **Coverage C -- Personal Property**

a. "We" cover personal property owned or used by an "insured". At "your" option:

1) personal property owned by a guest or "domestic employee" is covered while it is in that part of any residential premises occupied by an "insured"; and
2) personal property owned by a person other than a guest or "domestic employee" is covered while it is in that part of the "described location" occupied by an "insured".

b. **Limitation On Property At Residential Premises Other Than The Described Location** -- Coverage for personal property usually on residential premises of an "insured" other than the "described location" is limited to 10% of the Coverage C "limit" or $1,000, whichever is greater.

However, this limitation does not apply to personal property:

1) that is removed from the "described location" because the "described location" is undergoing alteration, reconstruction, or repair and is unfit for use as a residence or a place in which to store property; or
2) in "your" newly acquired principal place of residence for 30 days from the date that "you" first move property there.

c. **Limitations On Certain Property** -- The special "limits" shown below do not increase the Coverage C "limit". The "limit" for each class is the total "limit" per occurrence for all items in that class.

1) $250 on money; bank notes; bullion; gold other than goldware and gold-plated ware; silver other than silverware and silver-plated ware; platinum other than platinumware and platinum-plated ware; coins; medals; scrip; smart cards; and cards or other devices on which a cash value is stored electronically.
2) $1,500 on securities, stamps, letters of credit, notes other than bank notes, personal records, tickets, accounts, deeds, evidence of debt, passports, and manuscripts. This special "limit" applies regardless of the medium on which these items exist, and includes the cost of research or other expenses necessary to reproduce, replace, or restore the item.
3) $1,500 on electronic devices and accessories while in or on a "motorized vehicle" or watercraft, if the device can be operated from the electrical system of the "motorized vehicle" or watercraft and by another source of power. Accessories include antennas, films, tapes, wires, discs, records, or other media that can be used with such devices.
4) $1,500 on electronic devices and accessories used primarily for "business" purposes while away from the "described location" and not in or on a "motorized vehicle" or watercraft, if the device can be operated from the electrical system of a "motorized vehicle" or watercraft and by another source of power. Accessories include antennas, films, tapes, wires, discs, records, or other media that can be used with such devices.
5) $1,500 on watercraft, including their furnishings, equipment, engines, motors, trailers, and semitrailers.

However, this does not apply to:

a) model watercraft that is not designed or used to carry people or cargo; or
b) hovercraft.

6) $1,500 on trailers and semitrailers, other than trailers and semitrailers designed for or used with watercraft.
7) For loss by theft:

a) $2,500 on jewelry, watches, precious and semiprecious stones, gems, and furs;
b) $2,500 on silverware, goldware, platinumware, pewterware, and items plated with gold, silver, or platinum; and
c) $2,500 on guns and items related to guns.

8) For loss to personal property used primarily for "business" purposes, other than property rented or held for rental to others:

a) $2,500 on property while on the "described location"; and
b) $500 on property while away from the "described location".

However, this special "limit" does not apply to electronic devices and accessories described in 3) and 4) above.

These special "limits" include the cost of research or other expenses necessary to reproduce, replace, or restore "business" data.

d. **Personal Property Not Covered** -- "We" do not cover:

1) property separately described and specifically insured by this or any other policy, regardless of the "limit" that applies to such property under such insurance;
2) animals, birds, fish, or insects;
3) "motorized vehicles".

a) This includes:

(1) their parts, equipment, and accessories, other than property described in c.3) above; and
(2) electronic devices and accessories that can be operated only from the electrical system of a "motorized vehicle", including antennas, films, tapes, wires, discs, records, or other media that can be used with such devices;

while in or on a "motorized vehicle".

b) However, this does not include a "motorized vehicle":

(1) that is designed to assist the handicapped; or
(2) that is:

(a) owned by an "insured";
(b) designed only for use off of public roads; and
(c) used only to service an "insured premises" or a premises of another;

if such "motorized vehicle" is not required by law or governmental regulation to be registered for use on public roads or property and is not used for "business" purposes;

4) aircraft, meaning apparatus or devices designed or used for flight. This includes parts or equipment of aircraft, whether or not attached.

However, this does not include model aircraft that are not designed or used to carry people or cargo;

5) hovercraft, meaning self-propelled motorized ground effect machines or air cushion vehicles, including but not limited to flarecraft, designed or used to travel over land or water. This includes parts or equipment of hovercraft, whether or not attached.

However, this does not include model hovercraft that are not designed or used to carry people or cargo;

6) property of roomers, boarders, or other tenants, but this does not include property of roomers or boarders who are related to an "insured";
7) property rented or held for rental to others by an "insured", but this does not include property in:

   a) that part of the "described location" normally occupied solely by "your" household while rented to others on an occasional basis for residential purposes;
   b) the portion of that part of the "described location" normally occupied by "your" household that is rented or held for rental to no more than two roomers or boarders for use as a residence; or
   c) an apartment on the "described location" regularly rented or held for rental to others by an "insured", but only to the extent that coverage for such property is provided under the Incidental Property Coverage for Property In Rental Units;

8) loss that results from credit cards, electronic fund transfer cards, or electronic access devices that make possible the deposit, withdrawal, or transfer of funds, except as provided under the Incidental Property Coverage for Credit Card; Electronic Fund Transfer Card Or Access Device; Forgery; And Counterfeit Money;
9) grave markers or mausoleums, except as provided under the Incidental Property Coverage for Grave Markers;
10) land, including the land on which covered property is located, except as provided under the Incidental Property Coverage for Liquid Fuel Remediation;
11) underground water or surface water; or
12) trees, plants, shrubs, or lawns, except as provided under the Incidental Property Coverage for Debris Removal or the Incidental Property Coverage for Trees, Plants, Shrubs, Or Lawns.

e. Subject to the limitations described in b. and c. above, the "limit" that applies to Coverage C is the most "we" pay per occurrence for all property covered under Coverage C.

4. **Coverage D -- Additional Living Costs And Loss Of Rent**

a. "We" pay for the necessary and reasonable increase in living costs "you" incur to maintain the normal standard of living of "your" household if that part of the "described location" occupied by "your" household is made unfit for use as a residence by a loss covered under the Property Coverages.

"We" pay only for the period of time reasonably required to make the "described location" fit for use or, if "your" household is permanently relocated, only for the period of time reasonably required for relocation. This period of time is not limited by the policy period.

b. "We" pay for the fair rental value of that part of the "described location" rented or held for rental to others by "you" if it is made unfit for use as a residence by a loss covered under the Property Coverages.

However, "we" will deduct from the fair rental value any charges or expenses that do not continue while the part of the "described location" rented or held for rental to others is unfit for use.

"We" pay only for the period of time reasonably required to repair or replace the part of the "described location" rented or held for rental to others. This period of time is not limited by the policy period.

c. "We" pay for "your" additional living costs and fair rental value as described in a. and b. above for up to two weeks if a premises neighboring the "described location" is directly damaged by a Peril Insured Against covered by this policy and "you" may not, by order of civil authority, use the "described location". This period of time is not limited by the policy period.

d. "We" do not pay for loss, cost, or expense due to the cancellation of a lease or an agreement.

e. The "limit" that applies to Coverage D is the most "we" pay for all of the coverages described in a., b., and c. above.

INCIDENTAL PROPERTY COVERAGES

This policy provides the following Incidental Property Coverages. They are subject to all of the "terms" of the applicable Coverage A, Coverage B, or Coverage C. These coverages provide additional insurance unless otherwise stated.

1. **Association Deductible**

   a. "We" pay for "your" share of a deductible applicable to the insurance held by a homeowners, condominium, or similar residential association. Coverage applies only when the deductible:

      1) is charged against "you", during the policy period, as owner or tenant of the "described location"; and
      2) results from direct loss to property that:

         a) would be eligible for coverage by this policy if it were owned by "you";
         b) is covered under the insurance held by "your" association; and
         c) is caused by a Peril Insured Against described under Coverage A in this policy, but this does not include:

            (1) earthquake; or
            (2) land shock waves or tremors before, during, or after a volcanic eruption.

   b. The most "we" pay is $1,500 per occurrence unless a higher "limit" for Association Deductible is shown on the "declarations". The "limit" that applies is the most "we" pay for any one loss, regardless of the number of deductibles charged against "you".

   c. The Policy Period condition under Conditions Applicable To Property Coverages Only does not apply to this Incidental Property Coverage.

2. **Collapse**

   a. "We" pay for direct physical loss to covered property involving the collapse of a building or a part of a building if the collapse was caused only by one or more of the following:

      1) a Peril Insured Against described under Coverage C;
      2) insect, rodent, or "vermin" damage, but only if no "insured" knew of or could reasonably be expected to suspect the presence of such damage prior to the collapse;
      3) decay, but only if no "insured" knew of or could reasonably be expected to suspect the presence of such decay prior to the collapse;

4) weight of animals, equipment, people, or personal property;
5) weight of rain that collects on a roof; or
6) the use of defective materials or methods in construction or repair if the collapse occurs during the course of construction or repair.

However, "we" do not pay for loss to awnings, bulkheads, cesspools, decks, docks, drains, fences, flues, foundations, patios, paved areas, piers, retaining walls, septic tanks, swimming pools, underground pipes, or wharves caused by a peril described in 2) through 6) above unless the loss is the direct result of the collapse of a building or a part of a building. With respect to loss caused by a peril described in 2) through 6) above, awnings, bulkheads, cesspools, decks, docks, drains, fences, flues, foundations, patios, paved areas, piers, retaining walls, septic tanks, swimming pools, underground pipes, and wharves are not considered to be buildings or parts of buildings, whether or not such property is attached to or connected to one or more buildings.

b. In this Incidental Property Coverage:

1) collapse of a building or a part of a building means an abrupt caving in, falling in, falling down, or giving way of the building or the part of the building that prevents the building or the part of the building from being occupied for the purpose for which it was intended just before caving in, falling in, falling down, or giving way; and
2) the following are not considered to be in a state of collapse:

a) a building or a part of a building that has not caved in, fallen in, fallen down, or given way even if it displays evidence of bending, bowing, bulging, cracking, expansion, inadequate load bearing capacity, leaning, sagging, settling, or shrinkage;
b) a building or a part of a building in danger of caving in, falling in, falling down, or giving way; or
c) a part of a building that has not caved in, fallen in, fallen down, or given way even if it has separated from another part of the building.

However, the "terms" stated in 1) and 2) above do not limit coverage for direct loss to covered property caused by a Peril Insured Against described under Coverage C.

c. With respect to this Incidental Property Coverage, the peril of Weight Of Ice, Snow, Or Sleet means the weight of ice, snow, or sleet that causes damage to a building.

d. This coverage does not increase the "limits" that apply to the property covered.

e. The Bacteria, Fungi, Wet Rot, Or Dry Rot and Errors, Omissions, And Defects exclusions under Exclusions That Apply To Property Coverages do not apply to this Incidental Property Coverage.

3. **Credit Card; Electronic Fund Transfer Card Or Access Device; Forgery; And Counterfeit Money**

a. "We" pay for loss if an "insured":

1) by law must pay for the theft or unauthorized use of credit cards issued or registered in the name of an "insured";
2) has a loss resulting from the theft or unauthorized use of:

a) an electronic fund transfer card; or
b) an electronic access device that makes possible the deposit, withdrawal, or transfer of funds;

issued or registered in the name of an "insured";

3) has a loss when checks, drafts, or negotiable instruments are forged or altered; or
4) accepts in good faith counterfeit United States or Canadian paper money.

The most "we" pay is $1,500 per occurrence unless a higher "limit" for Credit Card; Electronic Fund Transfer Card Or Access Device; Forgery; And Counterfeit Money is shown on the "declarations". All loss resulting from a series of acts committed by any one person or in which any one person is involved or implicated is considered one occurrence.

b. "We" will defend a suit seeking damages against an "insured" if the suit results from the theft or unauthorized use of:

1) a credit card;
2) an electronic fund transfer card; or
3) an electronic access device that makes possible the deposit, withdrawal, or transfer of funds;

issued or registered in an "insured's" name.

Subject to the limitation set forth in d. below, "we" will pay for the expense of such defense. Defense will be provided by counsel that "we" choose.

c. At "our" option, "we" may defend an "insured" or an "insured's" bank against a suit for the enforcement of payment when checks, drafts, or negotiable instruments are forged or altered. If "we" choose to provide such defense, "we" will pay for the expense. Defense will be provided by counsel that "we" choose.

d. "We" may make investigations and settle all claims or suits under this coverage that "we" decide are appropriate. "We" do not have to provide a defense after "we" have paid an amount equal to the "limit" that applies to Credit Card; Electronic Fund Transfer Card Or Access Device; Forgery; And Counterfeit Money as a result of a judgment or a written settlement agreed to by "us".

e. "We" do not pay for loss:

1) that results from the use of a credit card, an electronic fund transfer card, or an electronic access device that makes possible the deposit, withdrawal, or transfer of funds:

   a) if an "insured" has not complied with all rules under which the credit card, fund transfer card, or access device was issued or granted;
   b) by a resident of "your" household; or
   c) by a person who has the credit card, fund transfer card, or access device with the consent of an "insured";

2) caused by the dishonesty of an "insured"; or
3) that results from the "business" of an "insured";

nor do "we" provide a defense for suits resulting from such loss.

4. **Debris Removal**

a. "We" pay for the reasonable cost to remove the debris of covered property after a loss. The loss must be caused by a Peril Insured Against that applies to the damaged property. "We" also pay for the reasonable cost to remove volcanic ash, dust, or particulate matter that causes direct physical loss to a covered building or covered property contained in a building.

"We" will not pay more for direct physical loss to property and debris removal combined than the "limit" that applies to the damaged property. However, if the covered loss plus the cost of debris removal is more than the applicable "limit", "we" will pay up to an extra 5% of the applicable "limit" to cover the cost of debris removal.

This coverage does not include any cost or expense to test for, monitor, clean up, remove, contain, treat, detoxify, neutralize, or in any way respond to or assess the effects of "pollutants".

b. Subject to the limitations set forth in c. below, "we" also pay for the reasonable cost to remove from the "described location":

1) "your" fallen tree or trees if the falling of the tree or trees is caused by the peril of:

a) Windstorm Or Hail; or
b) Weight Of Ice, Snow, Or Sleet; or

2) a neighbor's fallen tree or trees if the falling of the tree or trees is caused by any of the Perils Insured Against described under Coverage C in this policy.

Regardless of the number of fallen trees, the most "we" pay is $1,000 per occurrence.

However, "we" pay no more than $500 of this "limit" to remove any one tree.

With respect to this Incidental Property Coverage, the peril of Weight Of Ice, Snow, Or Sleet means the weight of ice, snow, or sleet that causes a tree to fall.

c. The coverage described in b. above applies only to a fallen tree that:

1) causes damage to a covered structure;
2) prevents a "motorized vehicle" that is registered for use on public roads or property from using a driveway on the "described location"; or
3) obstructs a ramp or other fixture designed to make the residence on the "described location" accessible to a handicapped person.

5. **Emergency Removal** -- "We" pay for direct physical loss to covered property that is moved from a premises to prevent a loss from a Peril Insured Against. The property is covered for up to 30 days, however this coverage does not extend past the date on which this policy expires.

This coverage does not increase the "limits" that apply to the property being removed.

The Exclusions That Apply To Coverage A And Coverage B and the Exclusions That Apply To Property Coverages do not apply to such property while removed.

However, "we" do not pay any "insured" for loss that results from any act committed by or at the direction of an "insured" with the intent to cause a loss. This applies even with respect to an "insured" who was not involved in the commission or direction of the act that caused the loss.

6. **Fire Department Service Charge** -- "We" pay for charges assumed by "you" under a contract or an agreement when a fire department is called to save or protect covered property from a Peril Insured Against.

However, "we" do not pay for such charges when the property is located within the limits of the city, municipality, or protection district that provides the fire department response.

The most "we" pay is $500 per occurrence unless a higher "limit" for Fire Department Service Charge is shown on the "declarations".

7. **Glass Or Safety Glazing Material**

   a. "We" pay for:

      1) the breakage of glass or safety glazing material that is part of a covered building or storm door or window; and
      2) direct physical loss to covered property caused only by broken pieces of glass or safety glazing material that, before breaking, was part of a building or storm door or window.

   b. The Earth Movement exclusion under Exclusions That Apply To Property Coverages does not apply with respect to the coverage described in a. above.

   c. Under this Incidental Property Coverage, "we" do not pay for loss:

      1) to covered property that occurs because of the breakage of glass or safety glazing material, except as provided in a.2) above; or
      2) on the "described location" if the residence covered under Coverage A was vacant for more than 60 days in a row just before the loss.

         However, this does not apply to loss caused by breakage of glass or safety glazing material that is the direct result of earth movement.

         A residence being built is not vacant.

   d. This coverage does not increase the "limits" that apply to the property covered.

8. **Grave Markers** -- "We" pay up to $2,500 for direct physical loss to grave markers and mausoleums on or away from the "described location" caused by a Peril Insured Against described under Coverage C.

   With respect to this Incidental Property Coverage, the peril of Weight Of Ice, Snow, Or Sleet includes the weight of ice, snow, or sleet that causes damage to a mausoleum.

9. **Increased Cost -- Ordinance Or Law**

   a. When loss to the residence covered under Coverage A or a related private structure covered under Coverage B is caused by a Peril Insured Against and "you" elect to repair or replace the damage, "you" may apply up to 10% of the Coverage A "limit" to cover the increased cost that "you" incur due to the enforcement of a code, ordinance, or law that regulates the construction, repair, replacement, or demolition of the damaged residence or structure.

   b. "You" may use all or part of this Increased Cost -- Ordinance Or Law coverage to cover the increased cost "you" incur to remove debris resulting from the construction, repair, replacement, or demolition of the residence covered under Coverage A or a related private structure covered under Coverage B when:

      1) loss to the residence or structure is caused by a Peril Insured Against; and
      2) a code, ordinance, or law regulates its construction, repair, replacement, or demolition.

      This does not increase the "limit" that applies to this Incidental Property Coverage.

   c. However, "we" do not pay for:

      1) any loss in value of property that results from the enforcement of a code, ordinance, or law; or

2) any loss, cost, or expense that results from the enforcement of a code, ordinance, or law requiring that an "insured" or others test for, monitor, clean up, remove, contain, treat, detoxify, neutralize, or in any way respond to or assess the effects of "pollutants".

10. **Liquid Fuel Remediation**

a. "We" pay for loss to:

1) property covered under Coverage A, Coverage B, or Coverage C;
2) land:

a) within the "described location";
b) owned by an "insured"; and
c) on which the residence covered under Coverage A or a structure covered under Coverage B is located;

but this does not include farm land; or

3) property covered under the Incidental Property Coverage for Trees, Plants, Shrubs, Or Lawns;

caused directly or indirectly by the discharge, dispersal, emission, escape, leaching, leakage, migration, release, seepage, or spillage of liquid fuel from the fuel system of a heating or air-conditioning system, water heater, or domestic appliance located on the "described location".

b. When there is discharge, dispersal, emission, escape, leaching, leakage, migration, release, seepage, or spillage of liquid fuel from a fuel system described in a. above, "we" also pay for:

1) cost or expense "you" incur to take temporary measures to stop any further discharge, dispersal, emission, escape, leaching, leakage, migration, release, seepage, or spillage of such fuel from such system;
2) cost or expense "you" incur to prevent or hinder the spread of the discharged, dispersed, emitted, escaped, leached, leaked, migrated, released, seeped, or spilled fuel over a larger area;
3) cost or expense "you" incur to clean up or treat such fuel on or remove such fuel from:

a) property covered under Coverage A, Coverage B, or Coverage C;
b) land:

(1) within the "described location";
(2) owned by an "insured"; and
(3) on which the residence covered under Coverage A or a structure covered under Coverage B is located;

but this does not include farm land; or

c) property covered under the Incidental Property Coverage for Trees, Plants, Shrubs, Or Lawns.

This includes cost or expense to remove the debris of such property or land;

4) cost or expense "you" incur to remove and replace those parts of covered property necessary to gain access to the system from which such fuel discharged, dispersed, emitted, escaped, leached, leaked, migrated, released, seeped, or spilled;
5) the necessary and reasonable increase in living costs "you" incur to maintain the normal standard of living of "your" household if that part of the "described location" occupied by "your" household is made unfit for use as a residence; and

6) cost or expense "you" incur to assess, monitor, or test the effects of discharged, dispersed, emitted, escaped, leached, leaked, migrated, released, seeped, or spilled liquid fuel.

   However, "we" will pay for such cost or expense only if the assessment, monitoring, or testing:

   a) is necessitated by a statutory or regulatory requirement or is in response to a request, demand, or order by a governmental body or authority or court of law; and
   b) arises out of loss for which payment is made under a., b.1), b.2), or b.3) above.

c. The Policy Period condition under Conditions Applicable To Property Coverages Only does not apply to this Incidental Property Coverage.

d. Under Exclusions That Apply To Coverage A And Coverage B, the exclusion for loss caused by the discharge, dispersal, disposal, emission, escape, leaching, leakage, migration, release, seepage, or spillage of "pollutants" does not apply to the coverage provided under this Incidental Property Coverage for the discharge, dispersal, emission, escape, leaching, leakage, migration, release, seepage, or spillage of liquid fuel.

e. "We" do not pay for:

   1) loss, cost, or expense involving underground water or surface water;
   2) loss, cost, or expense involving trees, plants, shrubs, or lawns grown for "business";
   3) loss, cost, or expense due to the cancellation of a lease or an agreement;
   4) the replacement of discharged, dispersed, emitted, escaped, leached, leaked, migrated, released, seeped, or spilled fuel;
   5) any loss in the market value of property or land, whether or not damaged by discharged, dispersed, emitted, escaped, leached, leaked, migrated, released, seeped, or spilled fuel;
   6) any damages resulting from:

      a) a loss of; or
      b) a reduction in value of;

      an agreement to sell property or land; or

   7) any cost or expense to repair, replace, remove, or demolish any part of the fuel system from which the fuel discharged, dispersed, emitted, escaped, leached, leaked, migrated, released, seeped, or spilled, except as provided under b. above.

f. The "terms" and "limits" applicable to:

   1) Coverage D -- Additional Living Costs And Loss Of Rent; and
   2) the Incidental Property Coverage for Debris Removal;

   do not apply to any loss, cost, or expense arising out of the discharge, dispersal, emission, escape, leaching, leakage, migration, release, seepage, or spillage of fuel from a fuel system described in a. above.

g. The most "we" pay for this Incidental Property Coverage for Liquid Fuel Remediation is $10,000 unless a higher "limit" for Liquid Fuel Remediation is shown on the "declarations". The "limit" for this Incidental Property Coverage for Liquid Fuel Remediation:

   1) is the most "we" pay for the total of:

a) all discharges, dispersals, emissions, escapes, leachings, leakages, migrations, releases, seepages, or spillages of liquid fuel that an "insured" first discovers or is made aware of during the policy period; and
b) all coverages described in a. and b. above; and

2) applies regardless of the number of:

a) claims made;
b) discharges, dispersals, emissions, escapes, leachings, leakages, migrations, releases, seepages, or spillages of liquid fuel that an "insured" first discovers or is made aware of during the policy period; or
c) locations insured under this policy.

With respect to loss to property covered under the Incidental Property Coverage for Trees, Plants, Shrubs, Or Lawns, the most "we" pay is an amount equal to 5% of the Coverage A "limit", but not more than $500 for any lawn or any one tree, plant, or shrub. This does not increase the "limit" that applies to this Incidental Property Coverage for Liquid Fuel Remediation.

With respect to coverage for the necessary and reasonable increase in living costs incurred to maintain the normal standard of living of "your" household, "we" pay only for the period of time reasonably required to make the "described location" fit for use or, if "your" household is permanently relocated, only for the period of time reasonably required for relocation. This period of time is not limited by the policy period. This does not increase the "limit" that applies to this Incidental Property Coverage for Liquid Fuel Remediation.

h. The "terms" stated in a. through g. above do not limit coverage for direct loss to covered property caused by the discharge, dispersal, emission, escape, leaching, leakage, migration, release, seepage, or spillage of liquid fuel when the discharge, dispersal, disposal, emission, escape, leaching, leakage, migration, release, seepage, or spillage is caused by a Peril Insured Against described under Coverage C.

11. **Loss Assessment**

a. "We" pay for "your" share of an assessment levied by a homeowners, condominium, or similar residential association. Coverage applies only when the assessment:

1) is levied during the policy period;
2) results from direct loss to property that is:

a) owned collectively by all association members;
b) of the type that would be eligible for coverage by this policy if it were owned by "you"; and
c) caused by a Peril Insured Against described under Coverage A in this policy, but this does not include:

(1) earthquake; or
(2) land shock waves or tremors before, during, or after a volcanic eruption; and

3) is levied against "you" as owner or tenant of the "described location".

b. However, "we" do not pay for an assessment that:

1) results from a deductible in the insurance held by the association; or
2) is levied against "you" or the association by any governmental body or authority.

c. The most "we" pay is $1,500 per occurrence unless a higher "limit" for Loss Assessment is shown on the "declarations". The "limit" that applies is the most "we" pay for any one loss, regardless of the number of assessments.

d. The Policy Period condition under Conditions Applicable To Property Coverages Only does not apply to this Incidental Property Coverage.

12. **Property In Rental Units** -- "We" pay for direct physical loss to "your" appliances, carpeting, and other household furnishings in an apartment on the "described location" regularly rented or held for rental to others by an "insured" when the loss is caused by a Peril Insured Against described under Coverage C, other than the peril of Theft.

    The most "we" pay for loss to such property in each apartment rented or held for rental to others is $2,500 per occurrence. The "limit" applies regardless of the quantity of appliances, carpeting, or other household furnishings damaged.

    This coverage does not increase the "limits" that apply to the property covered.

13. **Reasonable Repairs**

    a. "We" pay for the reasonable costs incurred by "you" for necessary measures performed solely to protect covered property from further damage by a Peril Insured Against if a Peril Insured Against has already caused a loss.

    b. If the measures described in a. above involve repair to other damaged property, "we" pay only if the property that is repaired is covered by this policy and only if the damage that necessitates the repair is caused by a Peril Insured Against.

    This coverage does not:

    1) increase the "limit" that applies to the property covered; or
    2) relieve "you" of the duties described in 1.b., Protecting Property, under What Must Be Done In Case Of Loss Or Occurrence.

14. **Refrigerated Property** -- "We" pay for direct loss to covered property stored in a freezer or refrigerated unit on the "described location" caused by:

    a. complete or partial disruption of electrical power due to conditions beyond an "insured's" control, if such disruption is caused by damage to the generating or transmission equipment; or

    b. mechanical breakdown of the freezer or refrigerated unit.

    Coverage applies only if the freezer or refrigerated unit had been maintained in proper working order prior to the loss.

    The most "we" pay is $500 per occurrence unless a higher "limit" for Refrigerated Property is shown on the "declarations".

    The Power Failure and Bacteria, Fungi, Wet Rot, Or Dry Rot exclusions under Exclusions That Apply To Property Coverages do not apply to this Incidental Property Coverage.

15. **Trees, Plants, Shrubs, Or Lawns** -- "We" pay for direct physical loss to trees, plants, shrubs, or lawns on the "described location" caused by:

    a. Fire Or Lightning, Explosion, Riot Or Civil Commotion, Aircraft;

    b. Vehicles if not owned or operated by an occupant of the "described location"; or

    c. Vandalism Or Malicious Mischief or Theft.

"You" may apply up to 5% of the Coverage A "limit" to cover trees, plants, shrubs, or lawns. "We" do not pay more than $500 for each tree, plant, or shrub. This includes the cost to remove the debris of the covered item.

"We" do not cover trees, plants, shrubs, or lawns grown for "business".

PERILS INSURED AGAINST -- COVERAGES A, B, C, AND D

1. **Coverage A -- Residence And Coverage B -- Related Private Structures** -- "We" insure property covered under Coverage A or Coverage B for risks of direct physical loss, unless the loss is excluded under the Exclusions That Apply To Coverage A And Coverage B.

   a. **Exclusions That Apply To Coverage A And Coverage B**

      1) "We" do not pay for loss excluded under the Exclusions That Apply To Property Coverages.
      2) **Freezing, Discharge, Leakage, Or Overflow** -- Subject to the exceptions stated in a) and b) below, "we" do not pay for loss caused by freezing of, or the resulting discharge, leakage, or overflow from, a plumbing, heating, air-conditioning, or automatic fire protective sprinkling system, water heater, or domestic appliance.

         a) When the building is protected by an automatic fire protective sprinkling system, this exclusion does not apply if "you" have taken reasonable care to:

            (1) maintain heat in the building; and
            (2) continue the water supply.

         b) When the building is not protected by an automatic fire protective sprinkling system, this exclusion does not apply if "you" have taken reasonable care to:

            (1) maintain heat in the building; or
            (2) shut off the water supply and completely empty water from all systems, heaters, and appliances.

         With respect to this exclusion and the exceptions stated in a) and b) above, plumbing systems and domestic appliances do not include sumps, sump pumps, or related equipment; any other type of system designed to remove subsurface water which is drained from the foundation area; or roof drains, gutters, downspouts, or like equipment.

      3) **Freezing, Thawing, Pressure, Or Weight Of Ice Or Water** -- "We" do not pay for loss caused by freezing, thawing, pressure, or weight of ice or water, whether driven by wind or not, to:

         a) fences, patios, paved areas, or swimming pools;
         b) bulkheads, footings, foundations, walls, or any other structures or features that support all or part of a building or other structure;
         c) bulkheads or retaining walls that do not support all or part of a building or other structure; or
         d) docks, piers, or wharves.

      4) **Theft** -- "We" do not pay for loss caused by theft in or to a residence being built, or theft of materials or supplies for use in construction of the residence, until the residence is occupied for its intended use.

5) **Vandalism Or Malicious Mischief** -- "We" do not pay for loss:

   a) caused by vandalism or malicious mischief; or
   b) that ensues from a wrongful act committed intentionally in the course of vandalism or malicious mischief;

   if the residence covered under Coverage A was vacant for more than 60 days in a row just before the loss. A residence being built is not vacant.

6) **Water, Humidity, Moisture, Or Vapor** -- "We" do not pay for loss caused by:

   a) continuous or repeated discharge, seepage, or leakage of water; or
   b) the presence or condensation of humidity, moisture, or vapor;

   over a period of weeks, months, or years, unless no "insured" knew of or could reasonably be expected to suspect such discharge, seepage, or leakage of water or the presence or condensation of humidity, moisture, or vapor.

   Under Exclusions That Apply To Property Coverages, 1)b) and 3) of the Water exclusion that apply to surface water and water below the surface of the ground do not apply with respect to loss caused by continuous or repeated discharge, seepage, or leakage of water from a plumbing, heating, air-conditioning, or automatic fire protective sprinkling system, water heater, or domestic appliance on the "described location" if no "insured" knew of or could reasonably be expected to suspect such discharge, seepage, or leakage of water. Plumbing systems and domestic appliances do not include sumps, sump pumps, or related equipment; any other type of system designed to remove subsurface water which is drained from the foundation area; or roof drains, gutters, downspouts, or like equipment.

7) **Collapse Or Impairment** -- "We" do not pay for loss involving:

   a) collapse; or
   b) impairment of structural integrity, including but not limited to sagging, bowing, bending, leaning, or inadequacy of load bearing capacity;

   except as provided under the Incidental Property Coverage for Collapse.

8) **Settling, Cracking, Shrinking, Bulging, Or Expanding** -- "We" do not pay for loss caused by the settling, cracking, shrinking, bulging, or expanding of:

   a) bulkheads;
   b) ceilings;
   c) floors;
   d) footings;
   e) foundations;
   f) patios;
   g) paved areas;
   h) roofs; or
   i) walls.

9) **Birds, Vermin, Rodents, Insects, Or Animals** -- "We" do not pay for loss caused by:

   a) birds;
   b) "vermin";
   c) rodents;
   d) insects; or
   e) any animal owned or kept by an "insured";

   except as provided under the Incidental Property Coverages.

10) **Smoke** -- "We" do not pay for loss caused by smoke from agricultural smudging or industrial operations.
11) **Pollutants** -- "We" do not pay for loss caused by the discharge, dispersal, disposal, emission, escape, leaching, leakage, migration, release, seepage, or spillage of "pollutants", unless the discharge, dispersal, disposal, emission, escape, leaching, leakage, migration, release, seepage, or spillage is caused by a Peril Insured Against described under Coverage C.
12) **Wear And Tear** -- "We" do not pay for loss caused by:

    a) wear and tear, marring, or deterioration;
    b) mechanical breakdown, latent defect, inherent vice, or any quality, fault, or weakness in property that causes it to damage or destroy itself;
    c) rust or other corrosion or smog; or
    d) pressure from or the presence of roots of trees, plants, shrubs, or other vegetation.

b. **Exceptions To Exclusions That Apply To Coverage A And Coverage B**

1) "We" pay for an ensuing loss that results from a.2) through a.12) above, unless the ensuing loss itself is excluded.
2) Unless the loss is otherwise excluded by this policy, "we" pay for loss to property covered under Coverage A or Coverage B that results from water or steam that, due to a cause or event excluded under a.8) through a.12) above, accidentally discharges or overflows from:

    a) a storm drain, or a water, steam, or sewer pipe, away from the "described location"; or
    b) a plumbing, heating, air-conditioning, or automatic fire protective sprinkling system, water heater, or domestic appliance on the "described location". This includes the reasonable cost of removing and replacing those parts of a building or other structure on the "described location" needed to repair the system, heater, or appliance.

    However, "we" will pay the cost of removing and replacing part of a structure that is not a building only if the water or steam causes direct physical loss to a building on the "described location".

    "We" do not pay for loss to the system, heater, or appliance from which the water or steam escaped.

    In this exception, plumbing systems and domestic appliances do not include sumps, sump pumps, or related equipment; any other type of system designed to remove subsurface water which is drained from the foundation area; or roof drains, gutters, downspouts, or like equipment.

Under Exclusions That Apply To Property Coverages, 1)b) and 3) of the Water exclusion that apply to surface water and water below the surface of the ground do not apply with respect to loss by water covered under this exception.

2. **Coverage C -- Personal Property** -- "We" insure against direct physical loss to property covered under Coverage C caused by the following perils, unless the loss is excluded under the Exclusions That Apply To Property Coverages:

    a. **Fire Or Lightning**

b. **Windstorm Or Hail**

However, "we" do not pay for loss:

1) to property inside a building caused by dust, rain, sand, sleet, or snow, all whether driven by wind or not, that enters through an opening in the building not made by the direct force of wind or hail; or
2) to watercraft or their furnishings, equipment, engines, motors, trailers, or semitrailers unless inside a fully enclosed building.

c. **Explosion**

d. **Riot Or Civil Commotion**

e. **Aircraft** -- This includes self-propelled missiles and spacecraft.

f. **Vehicles**

g. **Sudden And Accidental Damage From Smoke** -- This includes sudden and accidental damage from fumes, smoke, soot, or vapors that emit or back up from a boiler, furnace, or related equipment.

However, "we" do not pay for loss caused by smoke from agricultural smudging or industrial operations.

h. **Volcanic Eruption**

However, this does not include loss caused by earthquake, land shock waves, or tremors.

i. **Vandalism Or Malicious Mischief**

j. **Theft** -- This includes attempted theft and loss of property from a known place when it is likely that theft occurred.

However, "we" do not pay for loss:

1) caused by theft by an "insured";
2) caused by theft in or to a residence being built, or theft of materials or supplies for use in construction of the residence, until the residence is occupied for its intended use;
3) of a precious or semiprecious stone from its setting;
4) that results from the theft of:

   a) a credit card;
   b) an electronic fund transfer card; or
   c) an electronic access device that makes possible the deposit, withdrawal, or transfer of funds;

   except as provided under the Incidental Property Coverage for Credit Card; Electronic Fund Transfer Card Or Access Device; Forgery; And Counterfeit Money;

5) caused by theft from a part of the "described location" rented by an "insured" to a person other than another "insured"; or
6) caused by theft that occurs away from the "described location" of:

   a) trailers or semitrailers;
   b) campers or camper bodies;
   c) watercraft or their furnishings, equipment, engines, or motors; or
   d) property while on the part of residential premises that an "insured" owns, rents, or occupies, except for the time while an "insured" temporarily resides there. "We" do cover the property of an "insured" who is a student while it is in the living quarters occupied by the student at school if the student has been at such living quarters at any time during the 60 days just before the loss.

k. **Falling Objects**

However, "we" do not pay for loss to:

1) property inside a building, unless the falling object has first damaged an outside wall or the roof of the building by impact; or
2) the object that falls.

l. **Weight Of Ice, Snow, Or Sleet** that causes damage to property inside a building.

m. **Sudden And Accidental Tearing Apart, Cracking, Burning, Or Bulging** of a steam or hot water heating system, an air-conditioning or automatic fire protective sprinkling system, or a water heater.

However, "we" do not pay for loss caused by or resulting from freezing, except as provided under the peril of Freezing.

n. **Accidental Discharge Or Overflow Of Water Or Steam** from a plumbing, heating, air-conditioning, or automatic fire protective sprinkling system, water heater, or domestic appliance.

However, "we" do not pay for loss:

1) caused by continuous or repeated discharge, seepage, or leakage of water, or the presence or condensation of humidity, moisture, or vapor, over a period of weeks, months, or years, unless no "insured" knew of or could reasonably be expected to suspect such discharge, seepage, or leakage of water or the presence or condensation of humidity, moisture, or vapor;
2) caused by or resulting from freezing, except as provided under the peril of Freezing;
3) on the "described location" caused by accidental discharge or overflow that comes from off the "described location"; or
4) to the system or appliance from which the water or steam escaped.

In this peril, plumbing systems and domestic appliances do not include sumps, sump pumps, or related equipment; any other type of system designed to remove subsurface water which is drained from the foundation area; or roof drains, gutters, downspouts, or like equipment.

Under Exclusions That Apply To Property Coverages, 1)b) and 3) of the Water exclusion that apply to surface water and water below the surface of the ground do not apply with respect to loss by water covered under this peril.

o. **Freezing** -- This means freezing of a plumbing, heating, air-conditioning, or automatic fire protective sprinkling system, water heater, or domestic appliance, subject to the requirements stated in 1) and 2) below. In this peril, plumbing systems and domestic appliances do not include sumps, sump pumps, or related equipment; any other type of system designed to remove subsurface water which is drained from the foundation area; or roof drains, gutters, downspouts, or like equipment.

1) When the building is protected by an automatic fire protective sprinkling system, coverage for loss caused by the peril of Freezing applies only if "you" have taken reasonable care to:

    a) maintain heat in the building; and
    b) continue the water supply.

2) When the building is not protected by an automatic fire protective sprinkling system, coverage for loss caused by the peril of Freezing applies only if "you" have taken reasonable care to:

    a) maintain heat in the building; or

b) shut off the water supply and completely empty water from all systems, heaters, and appliances.

p. **Sudden And Accidental Damage From Artificially Generated Electrical Currents**

However, "we" do not pay for loss to tubes, transistors, electronic components, or circuitry that are a part of any type of an electronic apparatus, including but not limited to appliances, fixtures, computers, and home entertainment units.

q. **Sinkhole Collapse** -- This means the sudden settlement or collapse of earth supporting covered property. The earth settlement or collapse must result from subterranean voids created by the action of water on a limestone or similar rock formation.

However, "we" do not cover the cost of filling sinkholes.

EXCLUSIONS THAT APPLY TO PROPERTY COVERAGES

1. "We" do not pay for loss or damage caused directly or indirectly by one or more of the following excluded causes or events. Such loss or damage is excluded regardless of other causes or events that contribute to or aggravate the loss, whether such causes or events act to produce the loss before, at the same time as, or after the excluded causes or events.

These exclusions apply whether or not an extensive area suffers damage from or is affected by the excluded cause or event.

a. **Ordinance Or Law** -- "We" do not pay for:

1) any loss or increased cost that results from the enforcement of a code, ordinance, or law that regulates the construction, repair, or demolition of property or the removal of its debris, except as provided under the Incidental Property Coverage for Increased Cost -- Ordinance Or Law;
2) any loss in value of property that results from the enforcement of a code, ordinance, or law; or
3) any loss, cost, or expense that results from the enforcement of a code, ordinance, or law requiring that an "insured" or others test for, monitor, clean up, remove, contain, treat, detoxify, neutralize, or in any way respond to or assess the effects of "pollutants".

This exclusion applies whether or not there has been physical damage to covered property.

b. **Civil Authority** -- "We" do not pay for loss caused by the confiscation, destruction, or seizure of property covered under Coverage A, Coverage B, or Coverage C by order of civil authority.

"We" do pay for loss caused by acts ordered by a civil authority at the time of a fire to prevent its spread, but only if loss caused by the fire would be covered by this policy.

c. **Nuclear Hazard**

1) "We" do not pay for loss caused by nuclear reaction, radiation, or radioactive contamination:

a) whether controlled or uncontrolled; or
b) however caused;

or any consequence of such reaction, radiation, or contamination.

2) Loss caused by nuclear reaction, radiation, or radioactive contamination is not considered loss caused by:

   a) fire;
   b) explosion; or
   c) smoke;

   even if this policy provides coverage for loss caused by one or more of these perils.

3) Direct loss by fire resulting from nuclear reaction, radiation, or radioactive contamination is covered.

d. **War And Military Action** -- "We" do not pay for loss caused by:

   1) war, including undeclared or civil war;
   2) warlike action by a military force, including action in hindering or defending against an actual or expected attack, by any government, sovereign, or other authority using military personnel or other agents; or
   3) insurrection, rebellion, revolution, usurped power, or action taken by governmental authority in hindering or defending against any of these.

   With respect to any action that comes within the "terms" of this exclusion and involves nuclear reaction, radiation, or radioactive contamination, this War And Military Action exclusion supersedes the Nuclear Hazard exclusion.

   Discharge of a nuclear weapon is deemed a warlike action even if it is accidental.

e. **Neglect** -- "We" do not pay for loss caused by the neglect of an "insured" to use all reasonable means to save and preserve covered property at and after the time of a loss.

f. **Earth Movement** -- "We" do not pay for loss caused by earth movement whether the earth movement results from or is caused by human or animal forces or an act of nature.

   Earth movement means:

   1) earthquake;
   2) land shock waves or tremors before, during, or after a volcanic eruption;
   3) landslide, mudflow, mudslide;
   4) subsidence, erosion; or
   5) any other earth movement, including but not limited to earth sinking, rising, shifting, expanding, or contracting.

      However, this does not include Sinkhole Collapse as described under the Perils Insured Against that apply to Coverage C.

   "We" do pay for direct loss to covered property caused by fire or explosion resulting from earth movement.

   This exclusion does not apply to loss caused by theft that is otherwise covered by this policy.

g. **Water**

   1) "We" do not pay for loss caused by:

      a) flood;
      b) surface water;
      c) waves, including but not limited to tidal wave and tsunami;
      d) tides;
      e) tidal water;
      f) overflow of any body of water; or
      g) spray from a) through f) above;

      whether driven by wind or not.

      This includes, but is not limited to, tidal surge, storm surge, and storm tide.

2) "We" do not pay for loss caused by water that:

   a) backs up through sewers or drains; or
   b) overflows or otherwise discharges from:

      (1) a sump, sump pump, or related equipment; or
      (2) any other type of system designed to remove subsurface water which is drained from the foundation area.

3) "We" do not pay for loss caused by water below the surface of the ground. This includes, but is not limited to, water that exerts pressure on, or seeps, leaks, or flows through or into, a building, sidewalk, driveway, patio, foundation, swimming pool, or other structure.
4) "We" do not pay for loss caused by matter present in or carried or otherwise moved by water described in 1) through 3) above.
5) The exclusions set forth in 1) through 4) above:

   a) apply regardless of the cause of the excluded event, whether or not such cause is an act of nature; and
   b) apply to, but are not limited to, water and matter present in or carried or otherwise moved by water, whether driven by wind or not, that:

      (1) overtops;
      (2) escapes from;
      (3) is released from; or
      (4) is otherwise discharged from;

   a dam, levee, dike, floodgate, or other device or feature designed or used to retain, contain, or control water.

6) "We" do pay for direct loss to covered property caused by fire or explosion resulting from an event excluded in 1) through 4) above.
7) These exclusions do not apply to loss caused by theft that is otherwise covered by this policy.
8) With respect to these exclusions, surface water and water below the surface of the ground do not include water that accidentally discharges or overflows from a plumbing, heating, air-conditioning, or automatic fire protective sprinkling system, water heater, or domestic appliance on the "described location" when loss caused by such water is not otherwise excluded by this policy. Plumbing systems and domestic appliances do not include sumps, sump pumps, or related equipment; any other type of system designed to remove subsurface water which is drained from the foundation area; or roof drains, gutters, downspouts, or like equipment.

h. **Power Failure** -- "We" do not pay for loss caused by the failure of power or other utility service, whether or not it is caused by a Peril Insured Against, if the cause of the failure is not on the "described location".

   "We" do pay for direct loss that is otherwise covered by this policy that occurs on the "described location" as a result of the failure of power or other utility service.

i. **Intentional Acts** -- "We" do not pay any "insured" for loss that results from any act committed:

   1) by an "insured", alone or in collusion with another; or
   2) at the direction of an "insured";

   with the intent to cause a loss.

This exclusion applies even with respect to an "insured" who was not involved in the commission or direction of the act that caused the loss.

j. **Bacteria, Fungi, Wet Rot, Or Dry Rot** -- "We" do not pay for loss, cost, or expense caused by, consisting of, or relating to the existence of or any activity of bacteria, "fungi", wet rot, or dry rot that is not the direct result of a Peril Insured Against.

"We" do pay for direct loss to covered property caused by a Peril Insured Against resulting from bacteria, "fungi", wet rot, or dry rot.

2. "We" do not pay for loss or damage to property covered under Coverage A or Coverage B that is caused by or results from one or more of the following excluded causes or events. However, "we" do pay for an ensuing loss to property covered under Coverage A or Coverage B that is otherwise covered by this policy.

   a. **Weather Conditions** -- "We" do not pay for loss caused by weather conditions that initiate, set in motion, or in any way contribute to a cause or event excluded under the preceding Exclusions That Apply To Property Coverages (Numbers 1.a. through 1.j).

   b. **Errors, Omissions, And Defects** -- "We" do not pay for loss caused by one or more of the following:

      1) an act or decision of any person, group, organization, or governmental body or authority, or the failure of any person, group, organization, or governmental body or authority to act or decide; or
      2) a defect, a weakness, the inadequacy, a fault, or unsoundness in the:

         a) development, planning, siting, surveying, zoning;
         b) construction, compaction, design, grading, remodeling, renovation, repair, specification, workmanship;
         c) materials used in construction, remodeling, renovation, or repair; or
         d) maintenance;

      of any property, whether in whole or in part, and whether on or away from the "described location", except as provided under the Incidental Property Coverage for Collapse.

LIABILITY COVERAGES

PRINCIPAL LIABILITY COVERAGES

1. **Coverage L -- Personal Liability** -- "We" pay, up to the "limit" that applies, all sums for which an "insured" is legally liable because of "bodily injury" or "property damage" caused by an "occurrence" to which this coverage applies.

   "We" will defend a suit seeking damages if the suit resulted from "bodily injury" or "property damage" caused by an "occurrence" to which this coverage applies. Such defense will be provided at "our" expense by counsel that "we" choose.

   "We" may make investigations and settle claims or suits that "we" decide are appropriate. "We" do not have to settle or provide a defense after "we" have paid an amount equal to the "limit" that applies as a result of a judgment or written settlement.

2. **Coverage M -- Medical Payments To Others** -- "We" pay the necessary medical expenses if they are incurred or medically determined within three years from the date of an accident causing "bodily injury" covered by this policy. Medical expenses means the reasonable charges for medical, surgical, X-ray, dental, ambulance, hospital, professional nursing, and funeral services; prosthetic devices; hearing aids; prescription drugs; and eyeglasses, including contact lenses.

   This coverage does not apply to "you" or to any person who is a regular resident of "your" household, other than a "domestic employee". With respect to others, this coverage applies only to:

   a. a person on an "insured premises" with the permission of an "insured"; or

   b. a person away from an "insured premises" if the "bodily injury":

      1) arises out of a condition on an "insured premises" or the access ways immediately adjoining an "insured premises";
      2) is caused by an activity of an "insured";
      3) is caused by a "domestic employee" in the course of his or her employment by an "insured"; or
      4) is caused by an animal owned by or in the care of an "insured".

INCIDENTAL LIABILITY COVERAGES

This policy provides the following Incidental Liability Coverages. They are subject to all of the "terms" of Coverage L and Coverage M. Except for Claims And Defense Cost, Damage To Property Of Others, First Aid Expense, and Loss Assessment, they do not increase the "limits" stated for the Principal Liability Coverages.

1. **Business**

   a. "We" pay for "bodily injury" or "property damage" that arises out of:

      1) the rental or holding for rental of an "insured premises":

         a) on an occasional basis for use only as a residence;
         b) in part for use only as a residence (No family unit may include more than two roomers or boarders.); or
         c) in part for use as a school, studio, office, or private garage; or

      2) the "business" activities of an "insured" under the age of 21 years, but only if such "insured" is involved in a part-time or occasional, self-employed "business" that does not employ others and the "bodily injury" or "property damage" arises out of activities related to that "business".

   b. This Incidental Liability Coverage for Business is subject to all of the:

      1) Exclusions That Apply To Coverage L And Coverage M, other than exclusion g.;
      2) Additional Exclusions That Apply Only To Coverage L; and
      3) Additional Exclusions That Apply Only To Coverage M.

2. **Claims And Defense Cost** -- "We" pay for:

   a. the costs incurred by "us" and the costs taxed to an "insured" in a suit "we" defend;

   b. the premiums on required bonds in a suit "we" defend, but only for bond amounts up to the "limit" that applies. "We" are not required to apply for or furnish bonds;

   c. the necessary costs incurred by an "insured" at "our" request for assisting "us" in the investigation or defense of a claim or suit. This includes up to $250 per day, per "insured", for the actual loss of earnings, but not loss of other income, for time spent away from work at "our" request;

d. the interest on the entire judgment that accrues after the entry of the judgment, but ending when "we" tender, pay, or deposit in court that part of the judgment that does not exceed the "limit" that applies; and

e. prejudgment interest awarded against an "insured" on that part of the judgment "we" pay. If "we" offer to pay the "limit" that applies, "we" will not pay any prejudgment interest based on that period of time after the offer.

3. **Contracts**

   a. "We" pay for "bodily injury" or "property damage":

      1) for which an "insured" is liable under a written contract that directly relates to the ownership, maintenance, or use of an "insured premises"; or
      2) for which "you" are liable under a written contract, made before the loss, in which "you" have assumed the liability of others.

      The loss causing the "bodily injury" or "property damage" must have occurred during the policy period.

   b. This Incidental Liability Coverage for Contracts is subject to all of the:

      1) Exclusions That Apply To Coverage L And Coverage M;
      2) Additional Exclusions That Apply Only To Coverage L, other than exclusion c.; and
      3) Additional Exclusions That Apply Only To Coverage M.

4. **Damage To Property Of Others** -- Regardless of an "insured's" legal liability, "we" pay, at replacement cost, for "property damage" to property of others caused by an "insured". The "limit" that applies to this coverage is $1,000 per "occurrence".

   The exclusions that apply to Coverage L and Coverage M do not apply to this coverage.

   However, "we" do not pay for "property damage":

   a. covered under the Property Coverages section of this policy.

      However, "we" will pay for "property damage" in excess of the amount recoverable under the Property Coverages, to the extent that such "property damage" is covered under the "terms" of this Incidental Liability Coverage;

   b. to property owned by an "insured", or owned by, rented to, or leased to another resident of "your" household or a tenant of an "insured";

   c. caused intentionally by an "insured" who has attained the age of 13 years;

   d. arising out of an act or omission in any way related to a:

      1) "business" undertaken by an "insured"; or
      2) premises owned, rented, or controlled by an "insured", other than an "insured premises"; or

   e. arising out of the ownership, operation, maintenance, use, occupancy, loaning, entrusting, supervision, leasing, loading, or unloading of "aircraft", "hovercraft", "motorized vehicles", or "watercraft".

      However, this exclusion does not apply to "property damage" arising out of a "motorized vehicle":

      1) that is not owned by an "insured" and is designed:

         a) for recreational use off of public roads; or
         b) to assist the handicapped; or

2) that is not owned by an "insured" and is used only to service:

a) an "insured premises"; or
b) a premises of another, not in the course of "business";

if, at the time of the "occurrence", such "motorized vehicle" is not required by law or governmental regulation to be registered for use on public roads or property.

5. **First Aid Expense** -- "We" pay the expenses incurred by an "insured" for first aid to persons, other than "insureds", for "bodily injury" covered by this policy.

6. **Loss Assessment**

a. "We" pay for "your" share of an assessment levied by a homeowners, condominium, or similar residential association if the assessment is levied as a result of:

1) "bodily injury" or "property damage" to which Coverage L and Coverage M apply; or
2) damages or legal fees the association legally must pay for the acts of a director, officer, or trustee that result from the exercise of his or her duties solely on behalf of the association. This applies only to the acts of a director, officer, or trustee who is elected by the members of the association and who serves without receiving a fee, salary, or other compensation, other than reimbursement of expenses incurred.

b. However, "we" do not pay for assessments levied against "you" or a homeowners, condominium, or similar residential association by any governmental body or authority.

c. Coverage applies only when the assessment is levied during the policy period and is levied against "you" as owner or tenant of the "described location".

d. The most "we" pay is $1,500 per occurrence. Regardless of the number of assessments, this "limit" is the most "we" pay for loss arising out of:

1) any one accident, including repeated exposures to similar conditions; or
2) an act of a director or trustee. An act involving more than one director or trustee is considered a single act.

e. The Policy Period condition under Conditions Applicable To Liability Coverages Only does not apply to this Incidental Liability Coverage.

7. **Motorized Vehicles**

a. Subject to the limitations set forth in b. and c. below, "we" pay for "bodily injury" or "property damage" that arises out of a "motorized vehicle" that:

1) is in dead storage on an "insured premises";
2) is used only to service:

a) an "insured premises", but only if the "occurrence" takes place on an "insured premises" as defined in 14.a., 14.b., 14.c., 14.f., 14.g., or 14.h. under Definitions; or
b) an "insured premises" or a premises of another, but only if such "motorized vehicle" is designed only for use off of public roads;

3) is designed to assist the handicapped;
4) is designed for recreational use off of public roads and is:

a) not owned by an "insured"; or

b) owned by an "insured", but only if the "occurrence" takes place on an "insured premises" as defined in 14.a., 14.b., 14.c., 14.f., 14.g., or 14.h. under Definitions;

5) is operated only from electrical current supplied by a battery and is:

a) not built or modified after manufacture to exceed a speed of 15 miles per hour on level ground; and
b) not a motorized bicycle, moped, or golf cart; or

6) is a motorized golf cart that:

a) is owned by an "insured";
b) is designed to carry no more than four persons;
c) is not built or modified after manufacture to exceed a speed of 25 miles per hour on level ground; and
d) at the time of the "occurrence", is within the legal boundaries of:

(1) a golfing establishment and is:

(a) parked or stored there; or
(b) being used by an "insured" to:

(i) play the game of golf or for other recreational or leisure activity allowed by the establishment;
(ii) travel to or from an area where "motorized vehicles" or golf carts are parked or stored; or
(iii) cross public roads at designated points to access other parts of the golfing establishment; or

(2) a private residential community, including its public roads upon which a motorized golf cart can legally travel:

(a) that is subject to the authority of an association of property owners; and
(b) in which an "insured premises" is located.

b. The coverage described in a. above applies only to a "motorized vehicle" that, at the time of the "occurrence", is not:

1) registered for use on public roads or property;
2) required by law or governmental regulation to be registered for use at the location of the "occurrence";
3) being used in, or in the practice or the preparation for, a prearranged or organized racing, speed, pulling or pushing, demolition, or stunt activity or contest;
4) being rented to others;
5) being used to carry people or cargo for a fee; or
6) being used for any "business" purpose, except a motorized golf cart while on a golfing establishment.

c. This Incidental Liability Coverage for Motorized Vehicles is subject to all of the:

1) Exclusions That Apply To Coverage L And Coverage M, other than:

a) exclusions c. and e.; and
b) solely with respect to the use of a motorized golf cart while on a golfing establishment, exclusion g.;

2) Additional Exclusions That Apply Only To Coverage L; and
3) Additional Exclusions That Apply Only To Coverage M.

8. **Watercraft**

a. Subject to the limitations set forth in b. and c. below, "we" pay for "bodily injury" or "property damage" that arises out of a "watercraft" that:

1) is in storage;
2) is a sailing vessel, with or without auxiliary power, that is:

a) less than 26 feet in overall length; or
b) 26 feet or more in overall length and not owned by or rented to an "insured"; or

3) is not a sailing vessel and is powered by:

a) an inboard or inboard-outdrive engine or motor, including an engine or motor that powers a water jet pump, of:

(1) 50 horsepower or less if not owned by an "insured"; or
(2) more than 50 horsepower if not owned by or rented to an "insured"; or

b) one or more outboard engines or motors with:

(1) 25 total horsepower or less;
(2) more than 25 horsepower if the outboard engine or motor is not owned by an "insured";
(3) more than 25 horsepower if the outboard engine or motor is owned by an "insured" who acquired it during the policy period; or
(4) more than 25 horsepower if the outboard engine or motor is owned by an "insured" who acquired it before the policy period, but only if:

(a) it is listed on the "declarations" as insured for personal liability; or
(b) a written request for liability coverage is received by "us" within 45 days after it is acquired.

In this Incidental Liability Coverage for Watercraft, horsepower means the maximum power rating assigned to the engine or motor by the manufacturer.

b. The coverage described in a. above applies only to a "watercraft" that, at the time of the "occurrence", is not being:

1) rented to others;
2) used to carry people or cargo for a fee;
3) used for any "business" purpose; or
4) used in, or in the practice or the preparation for, a prearranged or organized racing, speed, pulling or pushing, demolition, or stunt activity or contest.

However, this does not apply to a sailing vessel or to a "watercraft" being used in a predicted log contest or cruise.

c. This Incidental Liability Coverage for Watercraft is subject to all of the:

1) Exclusions That Apply To Coverage L And Coverage M, other than exclusions c. and e.;
2) Additional Exclusions That Apply Only To Coverage L; and
3) Additional Exclusions That Apply Only To Coverage M.

EXCLUSIONS THAT APPLY TO LIABILITY COVERAGES

1. **Exclusions That Apply To Coverage L And Coverage M** -- Coverage L and Coverage M do not apply to:

   a. "bodily injury" or "property damage" caused directly or indirectly by:

      1) war, including undeclared or civil war;
      2) warlike action by a military force, including action in hindering or defending against an actual or expected attack, by any government, sovereign, or other authority using military personnel or other agents; or
      3) insurrection, rebellion, revolution, usurped power, or action taken by governmental authority in hindering or defending against any of these.

      Discharge of a nuclear weapon is deemed a warlike action even if it is accidental.

   b. "bodily injury" or "property damage" arising out of:

      1) the ownership or leasing of "aircraft" or "hovercraft" by an "insured";
      2) the operation, maintenance, use, occupancy, loading, or unloading of "aircraft" or "hovercraft" by any person;
      3) the entrustment or loaning of "aircraft" or "hovercraft" by an "insured" to any person; or
      4) an "insured's" negligent supervision of or failure to supervise any person with respect to "aircraft" or "hovercraft".

      However, this exclusion does not apply to "bodily injury" to a "domestic employee" arising out of and in the course of his or her employment by an "insured".

   c. "bodily injury" or "property damage" arising out of:

      1) the ownership or leasing of a "motorized vehicle" or "watercraft" by an "insured";
      2) the operation, maintenance, use, occupancy, loading, or unloading of a "motorized vehicle" or "watercraft" by any person;
      3) the entrustment or loaning of a "motorized vehicle" or "watercraft" by an "insured" to any person; or
      4) an "insured's" negligent supervision of or failure to supervise any person with respect to a "motorized vehicle" or "watercraft".

      However, this exclusion does not apply to "bodily injury" to a "domestic employee" arising out of and in the course of his or her employment by an "insured" or if coverage is provided under the Incidental Liability Coverage for Motorized Vehicles or the Incidental Liability Coverage for Watercraft.

   d. "bodily injury" or "property damage" for which an "insured" is vicariously liable if the "bodily injury" or "property damage" arises out of the actions of a child or minor with respect to:

      1) "aircraft"; or
      2) "hovercraft".

      This applies whether or not such liability is imposed by law.

   e. "bodily injury" or "property damage" for which an "insured" is vicariously liable if the "bodily injury" or "property damage" arises out of the actions of a child or minor with respect to a:

      1) "motorized vehicle"; or
      2) "watercraft".

      This applies whether or not such liability is imposed by law.

However, this exclusion does not apply to the extent that coverage for the "motorized vehicle" or "watercraft" is provided under the Incidental Liability Coverage for Motorized Vehicles or the Incidental Liability Coverage for Watercraft.

f. "bodily injury" or "property damage" arising out of the rendering of or the failing to render a professional service.

g. "bodily injury" or "property damage" arising out of or in any way related to a "business" conducted from an "insured premises" or undertaken by an "insured", regardless of location, whether or not the "business" is owned or operated by an "insured" or employs an "insured".

This includes but is not limited to "bodily injury" or "property damage" arising out of an act or a failure to act, regardless of its circumstance, involving a service or duty owed, promised, provided, or implied to be provided because of the nature of the "business".

However, this exclusion does not apply to the extent that coverage is provided:

1) for the use of a motorized golf cart while on a golfing establishment under the Incidental Liability Coverage for Motorized Vehicles; or
2) under the Incidental Liability Coverage for Business.

h. "bodily injury" or "property damage" that arises out of premises that are:

1) owned by an "insured";
2) rented to an "insured"; or
3) rented to others by an "insured";

and that are not "insured premises".

However, this exclusion does not apply to "bodily injury" to a "domestic employee" arising out of and in the course of his or her employment by an "insured".

i. "bodily injury" or "property damage" that is:

1) expected by, directed by, or intended by an "insured";
2) the result of a criminal act of an "insured"; or
3) the result of an intentional and malicious act by or at the direction of an "insured".

This exclusion applies even if the "bodily injury" or "property damage":

1) that occurs is different than what was expected, directed, or intended; or
2) is suffered by persons, entities, or property not expected, directed, or intended.

However, this exclusion does not apply to "bodily injury" or "property damage" that arises out of the use of reasonable force by an "insured" to protect people or property.

j. "bodily injury" or "property damage" that arises out of the transmission of a communicable disease by an "insured".

k. "bodily injury" or "property damage" that arises out of sexual molestation.

l. "bodily injury" or "property damage" that arises out of physical or mental abuse.

m. "bodily injury" or "property damage" that arises out of corporal punishment.

n. "bodily injury" or "property damage" that arises out of the use, sale, manufacture, delivery, transfer, or possession by any person of a Controlled Substance as defined by the Federal Food and Drug Law at 21 U.S.C.A. Sections 811 and 812, including any amendments. Controlled Substances include but are not limited to cocaine, LSD, marijuana, and all narcotic or hallucinogenic drugs.

However, this exclusion does not apply to the legitimate use of prescription drugs by a person following the orders of a licensed physician.

2. **Additional Exclusions That Apply Only To Coverage L** -- Coverage L does not apply to:

   a. "bodily injury" to an "insured" as defined in 13.a., 13.b., 13.c., 13.d., or 13.e. under Definitions.

   b. any claim made or suit brought against an "insured" seeking:

      1) reimbursement of; or
      2) contribution toward;

      damages for which another person may be liable because of "bodily injury" to an "insured".

   c. liability under a contract or an agreement entered into by an "insured", except as provided under the Incidental Liability Coverage for Contracts.

   d. "property damage" to property owned by an "insured".

   e. cost or expense for measures performed on property owned by an "insured" to prevent:

      1) injury to a person; or
      2) damage to property of others;

      on or away from an "insured premises", whether such cost or expense is incurred by an "insured" or others.

   f. "property damage" to property that is rented to, occupied by, used by, or in the care of an "insured".

      However, this exclusion does not apply to "property damage" to such property caused by fire, smoke, or explosion.

   g. sickness, disease, or death of a "domestic employee" unless a written notice is received by "us" within 36 months after the end of the policy period in which the injury occurred.

   h. "bodily injury" to a person, including a "domestic employee", if:

      1) an "insured" has a workers' compensation policy covering the injury; or
      2) benefits are payable or are required to be provided by an "insured" under a workers' compensation, non-occupational disability, occupational disease, or like law.

   i. liability for any assessment levied by a homeowners, condominium, or similar residential association, except as provided under the Incidental Liability Coverage for Loss Assessment.

   j. "bodily injury" or "property damage" for which an "insured" under this policy is also an insured under a nuclear energy liability policy or would be an insured under a nuclear energy liability policy but for the exhaustion of its "limits". (A nuclear energy liability policy is a policy issued by Mutual Atomic Energy Liability Underwriters, Nuclear Energy Liability Insurance Association, or Nuclear Insurance Association of Canada or their successors.)

3. **Additional Exclusions That Apply Only To Coverage M** -- Coverage M does not apply to "bodily injury":

   a. to an "insured" or any other person, other than a "domestic employee", who regularly resides on any part of the "insured premises".

   b. to a person, including a "domestic employee", if a workers' compensation policy covers the injury or if benefits are provided or required to be provided under a workers' compensation, non-occupational disability, occupational disease, or like law.

c. to a "domestic employee" if the "bodily injury":

   1) occurs away from an "insured premises"; and
   2) does not arise out of or in the course of his or her employment by an "insured".

d. from any:

   1) nuclear reaction;
   2) nuclear radiation; or
   3) radioactive contamination;

   whether controlled or uncontrolled or however caused; or

   4) any consequence of 1), 2), or 3) above.

WHAT MUST BE DONE IN CASE OF LOSS OR OCCURRENCE

1. **Property Coverages**

   The following duties apply when there is loss to covered property. These duties must be performed by "you", "your" representative, an "insured" seeking coverage, or the representative of an "insured" seeking coverage.

   "We" are not obligated to provide the coverages described in this policy if these duties are not performed.

   a. **Notice** -- Prompt notice must be given to "us" or "our" agent. "We" may request written notice.

      Notice must be given to the police when the loss involves theft.

      Notice must be given to the credit card, electronic fund transfer card, or electronic access device company when the loss involves a credit card, an electronic fund transfer card, or an electronic access device.

   b. **Protecting Property** -- All reasonable measures must be taken to protect covered property at and after a covered loss to avoid further loss.

      If the property must be repaired, "you" must:

      1) make reasonable and necessary repairs to protect the property; and
      2) keep an accurate record of the costs of such repairs.

   c. **Cooperation** -- All "insureds" seeking coverage, and the representative or representatives of all "insureds" seeking coverage, must cooperate with "us" in the investigation of a claim.

   d. **Inventory Of Damaged Personal Property** -- "We" must be given an inventory of personal property involved in a loss that shows, in detail, the:

      1) quantity;
      2) description;
      3) "actual cash value"; and
      4) amount of loss.

      Copies of all bills, receipts, and related documents that confirm the figures stated in the inventory must be attached.

   e. **Showing Damaged Property** -- As often as "we" reasonably request, "we" must be:

      1) shown the damaged property; and
      2) allowed to take samples of damaged property for inspection, testing, and analysis.

   f. **Records And Documents** -- As often as "we" reasonably request, "we" must be:

      1) given requested records and documents, including but not limited to tax returns and bank records of all canceled checks that relate to the value, loss, and costs; and

2) permitted to make copies of such records and documents.

g. **Examination Under Oath** -- As often as "we" reasonably request, all "insureds" must:

1) submit to examination under oath in matters that relate to the loss or claim; and
2) sign such statement made under oath.

If more than one person is examined, "we" have the right to examine and receive statements separately from each person and not in the presence of other "insureds".

h. **Proof Of Loss** -- "We" must be given a signed, sworn proof of loss, within 60 days after "our" request, that:

1) states, to the best of "your" knowledge and belief, the:

a) time and cause of the loss; and
b) interests of all "insureds" and the interests of all others, including all mortgages and liens, in the property involved in the loss;

2) identifies:

a) other policies that may cover the loss; and
b) any changes in title or use of the property during the policy period; and

3) provides:

a) available plans and specifications of damaged buildings;
b) detailed estimates for repair;
c) the inventory of damaged personal property described in d. above;
d) receipts for additional living costs incurred and records that prove the fair rental value; and
e) evidence or affidavit supporting a claim under the Incidental Property Coverage for Credit Card; Electronic Fund Transfer Card Or Access Device; Forgery; And Counterfeit Money and stating the amount and cause of loss.

i. **Assistance With Enforcing Right Of Recovery** -- At "our" request, "we" must be given assistance with enforcing any right of recovery that an "insured" may have against a party causing the loss.

2. **Liability Coverages**

The following duties apply when there has been an "occurrence". These duties must be performed by "you" or another "insured". "You" must assist "us" by seeing that they are performed.

"We" are not obligated to provide the coverages described in this policy if these duties are not performed.

a. **Notice** -- Written notice must be given to "us" or "our" agent as soon as is practical. The notice must state:

1) "your" name and the policy number;
2) reasonably available information regarding the time, location, and other details of the "occurrence"; and
3) the names and addresses of all known potential claimants and witnesses.

b. **Volunteer Payments** -- Any:

1) payments made;
2) rewards paid or offered; or
3) obligations or other costs assumed;

by an "insured" will be at the "insured's" own cost.

However, this does not apply to costs that are covered under the Incidental Liability Coverage for First Aid Expense.

c. **Cooperation** -- The "insured" must cooperate with "us" in the investigation, defense, or settlement of a claim or suit.

d. **Notices, Demands, And Legal Papers** -- The "insured" must promptly give "us" copies of all notices, demands, and legal papers that relate to the "occurrence".

e. **Assistance With Claims And Suits** -- At "our" request, the "insured" must help "us":

1) to settle a claim;
2) to enforce the right of recovery or indemnification against all parties who may be liable to an "insured";
3) to conduct suits. This includes being at trials and hearings;
4) in the securing of and giving of evidence; and
5) in obtaining the attendance of all witnesses.

f. **Other Duties -- Damage To Property Of Others** -- "We" must be given a sworn statement of loss within 60 days after the loss. The damaged property must be shown to "us" if it is within an "insured's" control.

HOW MUCH WE PAY FOR LOSS OR OCCURRENCE

1. **Property Coverages**

a. **Our Limit** -- "We" pay the lesser of:

1) the "limit" that applies; or
2) the amount determined under the applicable Loss Settlement Terms;

regardless of the number of "insureds" with an interest in the property.

However, no "insured" will be paid an amount that exceeds his or her interest in the property at the time of loss.

b. **Deductible**

1) This applies to all Principal Property Coverages and all Incidental Property Coverages except:

a) Credit Card; Electronic Fund Transfer Card Or Access Device; Forgery; And Counterfeit Money;
b) Fire Department Service Charge; and
c) Refrigerated Property.

It applies to all Perils Insured Against unless otherwise stated.

2) Subject to the "limits" that apply, "we" pay that part of the loss over the deductible. The deductible applies:

a) per occurrence and, with respect to the Incidental Property Coverages for Association Deductible and Loss Assessment, regardless of the number of deductibles charged or assessments levied; and
b) separately at each covered location. Only one deductible applies at each location.

c. **Loss To A Pair Or Set** -- If there is a loss to an item that is part of a pair or set, "we" pay only to replace or repair the item, or "we" pay the difference in the "actual cash value" of the pair or set just before the loss and the "actual cash value" just after the loss.

d. **Loss To Parts** -- If there is a loss to a part of an item that consists of several parts when it is complete, "we" pay only for the value of the lost or damaged part or the cost to repair or replace it.

e. **Loss Settlement Terms** -- Subject to the "terms" shown above, "we" settle losses according to the Replacement Cost Terms. If the Replacement Cost Terms do not apply, "we" settle losses according to the Actual Cash Value Terms.

In the Replacement Cost Terms and the Actual Cash Value Terms, replacement cost and cost to repair or replace do not include any increased cost that results from the enforcement of a code, ordinance, or law, except to the extent that coverage for such increased cost is provided under the Incidental Property Coverage for Increased Cost -- Ordinance Or Law.

1) **Replacement Cost Terms**

a) The Replacement Cost Terms apply only to buildings covered under Coverage A or Coverage B that have a permanent foundation and roof.

However, Replacement Cost Terms do not apply to:

(1) window air-conditioners;
(2) awnings and canopies;
(3) appliances;
(4) carpets; and
(5) antennas;

whether or not attached to a building.

b) If the "limit" that applies to the damaged building at the time of loss is less than 80% of its full replacement cost just before the loss, the larger of the following amounts is used in applying the "terms" under Our Limit:

(1) the "actual cash value" of the damaged part of the building just before the loss; or
(2) that part of the cost to repair or replace the damaged part, after application of any deductible, which the "limit" on the damaged building bears to 80% of its full replacement cost just before the loss.

c) If the "limit" that applies to the damaged building at the time of loss is at least 80% of its full replacement cost just before the loss, the smaller of the following amounts is used in applying the "terms" under Our Limit:

(1) the amount actually and necessarily spent to repair or replace the damaged building; or
(2) the cost to repair or replace the damage:

(a) using materials of like kind and quality; and
(b) for like use.

However, when a damaged building is rebuilt at another location, such cost is limited to the cost that would have been incurred if the building had been repaired or replaced at the location where the damage occurred.

d) In determining the replacement cost, do not include the cost of:

(1) excavations; brick, stone, or concrete foundations; piers; footings; or other structures or features that support all or part of the building that are:

(a) below the undersurface of the lowest basement floor; or

(b) below the surface of the ground inside the foundation walls, if there is no basement; or

(2) underground flues, pipes, wiring, or drains.

e) When the cost to repair or replace exceeds the lesser of $2,500 or 5% of the "limit" that applies to the damaged building, "we" will pay no more than the "actual cash value" of the loss until repair or replacement is completed. Once repair or replacement is completed, "we" will settle the loss as described in b) and c) above.

f) At "your" option, "you" may make a claim under the Actual Cash Value Terms instead of these Replacement Cost Terms. "You" may later make a claim for any additional amount payable under these Replacement Cost Terms, but only if "you" have informed "us", within 180 days after the date of loss, that "you" plan to do so.

2) **Actual Cash Value Terms**

a) The Actual Cash Value Terms apply to all property not subject to the Replacement Cost Terms.

b) The smaller of the following amounts is used in applying the "terms" under Our Limit:

(1) the cost to repair or replace the lost or damaged part of the property with materials of like kind and quality, to the extent practical; or

(2) the "actual cash value" of the lost or damaged part of the property just before the loss.

2. **Coverage L -- Personal Liability** -- The "limit" shown on the "declarations" for Coverage L is the most "we" pay for loss for each "occurrence". This applies regardless of the number of:

a. persons insured under this policy;

b. parties who sustain injury or damage;

c. claims made or suits brought; or

d. policy periods involved.

All "bodily injury" and "property damage" arising out of any one accident or out of repeated exposures to similar conditions will be considered one "occurrence".

3. **Coverage M -- Medical Payments To Others** -- The "limit" shown on the "declarations" per person for Coverage M is the most "we" pay for all medical expenses payable for "bodily injury" to one person as the result of one accident.

When a "limit" is shown on the "declarations" per accident for Coverage M, that "limit" is the most "we" pay for any one accident.

The payment of a claim under Coverage M does not mean an admission of liability on "our" part or on the part of any "insured".

4. **Severability** -- The Liability Coverages provided by this policy apply separately to each "insured", but this does not increase the "limit" that applies for any one "occurrence".

5. **Insurance Under More Than One Coverage** -- If more than one coverage of this policy applies to a loss, "we" pay no more than the actual loss.

6. **Insurance Under More Than One Policy**

a. **Property Coverages**

1) If there is other insurance that applies to a loss, cost, or expense, other than insurance in the name of an association or a corporation of property owners, "we" pay "our" share of the loss, cost, or expense. "Our" share is that part of the loss, cost, or expense that the "limit" of this policy bears to the total amount of insurance that applies to the loss, cost, or expense.

   However, this does not apply to loss, cost, or expense that is also covered by:

   a) a home warranty, a service or maintenance plan or agreement, or any other warranty, plan, or agreement that provides for the repair or replacement of property, even if such warranty, plan, or agreement has the characteristics or qualities of insurance; or
   b) a government fund.

2) When a loss, cost, or expense is also covered by insurance in the name of an association or a corporation of property owners, this insurance is excess over the "limit" that applies under such other insurance.

   However, this excess provision does not apply with respect to the coverage provided under the Incidental Property Coverage for Association Deductible.

b. **Coverage L -- Personal Liability** -- This insurance is excess over other valid and collectible insurance that applies to the loss or claim, other than insurance written specifically to provide coverage in excess of the "limits" that apply in this policy.

If the other insurance is also excess, "we" pay only "our" share of the loss. "We" pay only that part of the loss that the applicable "limit" under this policy bears to the total amount of insurance covering the loss.

7. **Warranties And Service Or Maintenance Plans Or Agreements** -- If loss, cost, or expense covered by this policy is also covered by a home warranty, a service or maintenance plan or agreement, or any other warranty, plan, or agreement that provides for the repair or replacement of property, this insurance is excess over any amount payable by such warranty, plan, or agreement. This applies even if such warranty, plan, or agreement has the characteristics or qualities of insurance.

8. **Government Funds** -- If loss, cost, or expense covered by this policy is also covered by a government fund, "we" pay "our" share of the loss, cost, or expense. "Our" share is that part of the loss, cost, or expense that the "limit" of this policy bears to the total amount payable for the loss, cost, or expense to the extent permitted by law.

PAYMENT OF LOSS

1. **Property Coverages**

   a. Except as provided in 3. below, "we" adjust each loss with "you". "We" pay a covered loss within 60 days after an acceptable proof of loss is received and:

      1) "we" reach an agreement with "you";
      2) there is an entry of a final judgment; or
      3) there is a filing of an appraisal award with "us".

      Payment is made to "you" unless a loss payee or some other person or entity is named in the policy or is legally entitled to receive payment.

b. "We" may:

1) pay the loss in money; or
2) rebuild, repair, or replace the property. "We" must give "you" written notice of "our" intent to do so within 30 days after "we" receive an acceptable proof of loss.

If "we" pay the loss in money, "we" may take all or part of the damaged property at the agreed or appraised value. Property paid for or replaced by "us" becomes "ours".

c. If the "described location" is made unfit for use for more than one month, loss, cost, or expense covered under Coverage D is paid on a monthly basis. "You" must give "us" proof of such loss, cost, or expense.

2. **Liability Coverages** -- A person who has secured a judgment against an "insured" for a covered loss or has liability established by a written agreement between the claimant, an "insured", and "us" is entitled to recover under this policy to the extent of coverage provided.

3. **Damage To Personal Property Of Others** -- At "our" option, a covered loss may be adjusted with and paid:

a. to "you" on behalf of the owner; or

b. to the owner. If "we" pay the owner, "we" do not have to pay an "insured".

POLICY CONDITIONS

CONDITIONS APPLICABLE TO ALL COVERAGES

1. **Assignment** -- This policy may not be assigned without "our" written consent.

2. **Cancellation And Nonrenewal** -- "You" may cancel this policy by returning the policy to "us" or by giving "us" written notice and stating at what future date coverage is to stop.

"We" may cancel or not renew this policy by written notice to "you" at the address shown on the "declarations". Proof of delivery or mailing is sufficient proof of notice.

During the first 59 days this policy is in effect, "we" may cancel for any reason. "We" will give "you" notice at least ten days before cancellation is effective.

When this policy has been in effect 60 days or more, or if it is a renewal of a policy issued by "us", "we" may cancel or not renew only at the anniversary date unless:

a. the premium has not been paid when due;

b. the policy was obtained through fraud, material misrepresentation, or omission of fact, which, if known by "us", would have caused "us" not to issue the policy; or

c. there has been a material change or increase in hazard of the risk.

If "we" cancel this policy for nonpayment of premium, "we" will give "you" notice at least ten days before cancellation is effective. If "we" cancel this policy for any other reason when it has been in effect for 60 days or more, "we" will give "you" notice at least 30 days before cancellation is effective.

If "we" do not renew this policy, "we" will give "you" notice at least 30 days before nonrenewal is effective.

"Your" return premium, if any, will be calculated on a pro rata basis and will be refunded at the time of cancellation or as soon as practical. Payment or tender of the unearned premium is not a condition of cancellation.

3. **Change, Modification, Or Waiver Of Policy Terms**

   a. A waiver or change of the "terms" of this policy must be issued by "us" in writing to be valid.

   b. If "we" adopt a revision that broadens coverage under this edition of "our" policy without an additional premium, the broadened coverage will apply to "your" policy as of the date "we" adopt the revision in the state in which the "described location" is located. This applies only to revisions adopted within 60 days prior to or during the policy period shown on the "declarations".

      However, this does not apply to revisions adopted as part of an overall program revision that both broadens and restricts coverage, whether "we" bring about the program revision by introducing:

      1) a subsequent edition of "our" policy; or
      2) an endorsement that amends "our" policy.

   c. "Our" request for an appraisal or examination under oath does not waive policy "terms".

4. **Conformity With Statute** -- "Terms" in conflict with the laws of the state in which the "described location" is located are changed to conform to such laws.

5. **Death** -- The "terms" in a. and b. below apply if any person named as the insured on the "declarations" or that person's spouse, if a resident of the same household, dies.

   a. "We" provide coverage for the legal representative of the deceased person:

      1) but only with respect to the deceased person's premises and property covered by this policy at the time of death; and
      2) only to the extent that coverage is provided by this policy.

   b. "Insured" includes:

      1) an "insured" who is a member of the deceased person's household at the time of the deceased person's death, but only while a resident of the "described location"; and
      2) persons having proper, temporary custody of the deceased person's covered property, but only with respect to such property and only until such time as a legal representative is appointed and qualified.

6. **Inspections** -- "We" have the right, but are not obligated, to inspect "your" property and operations. This inspection may be made by "us" or may be made on "our" behalf. An inspection or its resulting advice or report does not warrant that "your" property or operations are safe, healthful, or in compliance with laws, rules, or regulations. Inspections or reports are for "our" benefit only.

7. **Misrepresentation, Concealment, Or Fraud** -- "We" do not provide coverage for any "insured" if, before or after a loss:

   a. an "insured" has willfully concealed or misrepresented a material fact or circumstance that relates to this insurance or the subject thereof; or

   b. there has been fraudulent conduct or false swearing by an "insured" with regard to a matter that relates to this insurance or the subject thereof.

   This applies even with respect to an "insured" who was not involved in the concealment, misrepresentation, fraudulent conduct, or false swearing.

8. **Subrogation** -- If "we" pay for a loss, "we" may require that the "insured" assign to "us" the right of recovery up to the amount "we" pay. "We" are not liable for a loss if, after the loss, an "insured" impairs "our" right to recover against others. An "insured" may waive his or her right to recover, in writing and before a loss occurs, without affecting coverage.

   In the event that "we" require such an assignment, the "insured" must:

   a. sign and give to "us" all related documents; and

   b. cooperate with "us".

   Subrogation does not apply to Coverage M -- Medical Payments To Others or to the Incidental Liability Coverage for Damage To Property Of Others.

CONDITIONS APPLICABLE TO PROPERTY COVERAGES ONLY

1. **Abandonment Of Property** -- An "insured" may not abandon property to "us" unless "we" agree.

2. **Appraisal** -- If "you" and "we" do not agree as to the value or amount of loss, either may demand an appraisal of such loss. In this event, "you" and "we" will each select a competent and impartial appraiser within 20 days after receiving a written request from the other. The two appraisers will select a competent and impartial umpire. If they do not agree on an umpire within 15 days, "you" or "we" may ask a judge of a court of record of the state where the "described location" is located to make the selection.

   A written agreement of the two appraisers will set the amount of loss. If the appraisers fail to agree, they will submit their differences to the umpire. The written agreement of any two of these three will set the amount of the loss.

   "You" will pay the expense of "your" appraiser and "we" will pay the expense of "our" appraiser. "You" and "we" will share equally the expense of the umpire and the other expenses of the appraisal.

   Under no circumstance will an appraisal be used to interpret policy "terms", determine causation, or determine whether or not a loss is covered under this policy.

3. **Loss Payable Clause** -- With respect to those items of personal property for which a loss payee is shown on the "declarations", the definition of "insured" is extended to include that loss payee, but only with respect to those items of personal property.

   If "we" cancel or do not renew this policy, "we" will so notify, in writing, any loss payees shown on the "declarations".

4. **Mortgage Clause**

   a. If a mortgagee is named on the "declarations", a loss payable under Coverage A or Coverage B will be paid to the mortgagee and "you", as interests appear. If more than one mortgagee is named, the order of payment will be the same as the order of precedence of the mortgages. The word mortgagee includes trustee.

   b. If "we" deny "your" claim, that denial does not apply to a valid claim of the mortgagee if the mortgagee has:

      1) notified "us" of change in ownership, occupancy, or substantial change in risk of which the mortgagee became aware;
      2) paid the premium due under this policy on demand if "you" neglected to pay the premium; and
      3) submitted a signed, sworn statement of loss within 60 days after receiving notice from "us" if "you" failed to do so.

All "terms" of this policy apply to the mortgagee unless changed by this clause.

c. If "we" cancel or do not renew this policy, "we" will notify any mortgagees named on the "declarations" at least ten days before the date cancellation or nonrenewal takes effect.

d. If "we" pay the mortgagee for a loss and deny payment to "you", "we" are subrogated, up to the amount "we" paid for the loss, to all the rights of the mortgagee granted under the mortgage on the property. Subrogation will not impair the right of the mortgagee to recover the full amount of the mortgagee's claim.

At "our" option, "we" may pay to the mortgagee the whole principal on the mortgage plus the accrued interest. In this event, "we" will receive a full assignment and transfer of the mortgage and all securities held as collateral to the mortgage debt.

5. **No Benefit To Bailee** -- Coverage under this policy will not directly or indirectly benefit those who are paid to assume custody of covered property.

6. **Policy Period** -- This policy covers only losses that occur during the policy period.

7. **Recoveries** -- This applies if "we" pay for a loss and lost or damaged property is recovered or payment is made by those responsible for the loss.

"You" must inform "us" or "we" must inform "you" if either recovers property or receives payment. Proper costs incurred by either party are paid first.

At "your" option, "you" may keep the recovered property. If "you" keep the recovered property, the amount of the claim paid, or a lesser amount to which "we" agree, must be returned to "us".

If the claim paid is less than the agreed loss due to a deductible or other limiting "terms", the recovery is prorated between "you" and "us" based on the interest of each in the loss.

8. **Suit Against Us** -- No suit may be brought against "us" unless all of the "terms" that apply to the Property Coverages have been complied with and the suit is brought within two years after the loss.

If a law of the state where the "described location" is located makes this time period invalid, the suit must be brought within the time period allowed by the law.

9. **Volcanic Eruption** -- All volcanic eruption that occurs within a 72-hour period constitutes a single occurrence.

CONDITIONS APPLICABLE TO LIABILITY COVERAGES ONLY

1. **Bankruptcy Of An Insured** -- Bankruptcy or insolvency of an "insured" does not relieve "us" of "our" obligations under this policy.

2. **Duties Of An Injured Person -- Medical Payments To Others Coverage** -- In case of a loss, the injured person or someone acting on behalf of that person must:

   a. give "us" written proof of claim (under oath if "we" request) as soon as practical; and

   b. authorize "us" to get copies of medical records.

   The injured person must submit to medical exams by doctors chosen by "us" when and as often as "we" may reasonably require.

3. **Policy Period** -- This policy covers only "bodily injury" and "property damage" that occur during the policy period.

4. **Suit Against Us** -- No suit may be brought against "us" unless all of the "terms" that apply to the Liability Coverages have been complied with and the amount of the "insured's" liability has been fixed by:

   a. a final judgment against the "insured" as a result of a trial; or

   b. a written agreement of the "insured", the claimant, and "us".

   No person has a right under this policy to join "us" or implead "us" in actions that are brought to fix the liability of an "insured".

HO 0003 09 08

AAIS
HO 0005 09 08
Page 1 of 47

THIS IS A LEGAL CONTRACT
-- PLEASE READ IT CAREFULLY --

SPECIAL BUILDING AND CONTENTS FORM

The following Table of Contents shows how the policy is organized. It will help "you" locate particular sections of the policy.

TABLE OF CONTENTS

Endorsements and schedules may also be part of this policy. They are identified on the "declarations".

Words and phrases that have special meaning are shown in quotation marks. The special meanings for these words and phrases are set forth in Definitions.

AGREEMENT

This policy, subject to all of its "terms", provides the described insurance coverages during the policy period. In return "you" must pay the required premium. Each of the Principal Coverages described in this policy applies only if a "limit" is shown on the "declarations" for that coverage.

DEFINITIONS

1. The words "you" and "your" mean the person or persons named as the insured on the "declarations". This includes "your" spouse if a resident of "your" household.

2. The words "we", "us", and "our" mean the company providing this insurance.

3. "Actual cash value" means the cost to repair or replace property using materials of like kind and quality, to the extent practical, less a deduction for depreciation, however caused.

4. Under the Liability Coverages provided by this policy, "aircraft" means an apparatus or a device designed or used for flight, but this does not include:

   a. a model aircraft that is not designed or used to carry people or cargo;

   b. a "hovercraft"; or

   c. a model hovercraft that is not designed or used to carry people or cargo.

5. "Bodily injury" means bodily harm to a person and includes sickness, disease, or death. This also includes required care and loss of services.

   However, "bodily injury" does not mean bodily harm, sickness, disease, or death that arises out of mental or emotional injury, suffering, or distress that does not result from actual physical injury to a person.

6. "Business" means:

   a. a trade, a profession, or an occupation, including farming, all whether full time, part time, or occasional. This includes the rental of property to others, but does not include:

      1) the occasional rental for residential purposes of that part of the "described location" normally occupied solely by "your" household; or
      2) the rental or holding for rental of a portion of that part of the "described location" normally occupied by "your" household to no more than two roomers or boarders for use as a residence; or

   b. any other activity undertaken for money or other compensation, but this does not include:

      1) providing care services to a relative of an "insured";
      2) providing services for the care of persons who are not relatives of an "insured" and for which the only compensation is the mutual exchange of like services;
      3) a volunteer activity for which:

         a) an "insured" receives no compensation; or
         b) an "insured's" only compensation is the reimbursement of expenses incurred to carry out the activity; or

      4) an activity not described in 1) through 3) above for which no "insured's" total compensation for the 12 month period just before the first day of this policy period was more than $2,500.

7. "Declarations" means all pages labeled declarations, supplemental declarations, or schedule that pertain to this policy.

8. "Described location" means the one- to four-family house, the townhouse, or the row house where "you" reside and which is shown on the "declarations" as the "described location". It includes related private structures and grounds at that location.

However, if the "described location" is a townhouse or a row house, it includes only related private structures and grounds at that location that are used or occupied solely by "your" household for residential purposes.

9. "Domestic employee" means a person employed by an "insured", or a person leased to an "insured" under a contract or an agreement with a labor leasing firm, to perform duties that relate to the use or care of the "described location". This includes a person who performs duties of a similar nature elsewhere for an "insured", provided such duties are not in connection with an "insured's" "business".

   However, "domestic employee" does not include a person who is furnished to an "insured":

   a. as a temporary substitute for a permanent "domestic employee" who is on leave; or

   b. to meet seasonal or short-term workloads.

10. "Employee" means a person employed by an "insured", or a person leased to an "insured" under a contract or an agreement with a labor leasing firm, to perform duties other than those performed by a "domestic employee".

11. "Fungi" means any kind or form of fungus, including but not limited to mildew and mold, and any chemical, matter, or compound produced or released by a fungus, including but not limited to toxins, spores, fragments, and metabolites such as microbial volatile organic compounds.

12. Under the Liability Coverages provided by this policy, "hovercraft" means a self-propelled motorized ground effect machine or air cushion vehicle designed or used to travel over land or water. This includes, but is not limited to, a flarecraft.

    However, "hovercraft" does not include:

    a. a model hovercraft that is not designed or used to carry people or cargo;

    b. an "aircraft";

    c. a model aircraft that is not designed or used to carry people or cargo;

    d. a "motorized vehicle";

    e. a "watercraft"; or

    f. a model watercraft that is not designed or used to carry people or cargo.

13. "Insured" means:

    a. "you";

    b. "your" relatives if residents of "your" household;

    c. "your" relatives under the age of 25 years who:

       1) are financially dependent upon "you";
       2) are students enrolled in school full time, as defined by the school; and
       3) were residents of "your" household just before moving out to attend school;

    d. persons, other than "your" relatives, under the age of 21 years who:

       1) reside in "your" household; and
       2) are in "your" care or in the care of "your" resident relatives;

    e. persons, other than "your" relatives, under the age of 21 years who:

       1) are in "your" care or in the care of "your" resident relatives;
       2) are students enrolled in school full time, as defined by the school; and
       3) were residents of "your" household just before moving out to attend school; or

f. solely with respect to the Liability Coverages provided by this policy:

1) persons in the course of acting as "your" real estate manager for the "described location", but only with respect to acts falling within the scope of such duties;
2) persons while engaged in the employ of an "insured" as defined in a., b., c., d., or e. above, but only with respect to a "motorized vehicle" to which this insurance applies;
3) persons using a "motorized vehicle" to which this insurance applies on an "insured premises" with "your" consent, but only with respect to such use;
4) persons or organizations accountable by law for "watercraft" or animals:

   a) owned by an "insured" as defined in a., b., c., d., or e. above; and
   b) to which this insurance applies;

   but only with respect to such "watercraft" or animals.

   However, this does not include persons or organizations using or having charge or control of such "watercraft" or animals in the course of "business" or without the owner's consent; or

5) persons or organizations accountable by law for a motorized golf cart:

   a) owned by an "insured" as defined in a., b., c., d., or e. above; and
   b) to which this insurance applies;

   but only with respect to such golf cart.

   However, this does not include persons or organizations using or having charge or control of such golf cart without the owner's consent.

The phrase an "insured", wherever it appears in this policy, means one or more "insureds".

14. "Insured premises" means:

a. the "described location";

b. that part of any other premises used by "you" as a residence and shown on the "declarations" as an "insured premises";

c. that part of any other premises used by "you" as a residence and that is acquired by "you" during the policy period for such use;

d. premises used by "you" in connection with a premises described in a., b., or c. above;

e. cemetery lots and burial vaults of an "insured";

f. that part of a premises not owned by an "insured" and that is temporarily used by an "insured" as a residence;

g. that part of a premises occasionally rented to an "insured" for other than "business" purposes; and

h. vacant land owned by or rented to an "insured". This includes land where a one- to four-family house, a townhouse, or a row house is being built for use as an "insured's" residence. This does not include farm land.

15. "Limit" means amount of insurance.

16. "Motorized vehicle" means:

a. a self-propelled land or amphibious vehicle, regardless of method of surface contact, but this does not include a:

1) "hovercraft";
2) model hovercraft that is not designed or used to carry people or cargo;
3) "watercraft"; or
4) model watercraft that is not designed or used to carry people or cargo; or

b. a trailer or semitrailer that:

1) is attached to or being carried on or towed by; or
2) becomes detached while being carried on or towed by;

a vehicle described in a. above.

17. "Occurrence" means an accident, including repeated exposures to similar conditions, that results in "bodily injury" or "property damage" during the policy period.

18. "Pollutant" means:

a. any solid, liquid, gaseous, thermal, or radioactive irritant or contaminant, including acids, alkalis, chemicals, fumes, smoke, soot, vapor, and waste. Waste includes materials to be disposed of as well as recycled, reclaimed, or reconditioned; and

b. electrical, magnetic, or electromagnetic particles or fields, whether visible or invisible, and sound.

19. "Property damage" means:

a. physical injury to or destruction of tangible property; or

b. the loss of use of tangible property whether or not it is physically damaged.

20. "Sinkhole collapse" means the sudden settlement or collapse of earth supporting covered property. The earth settlement or collapse must result from subterranean voids created by the action of water on a limestone or similar rock formation.

"Sinkhole collapse" does not include the cost of filling sinkholes.

21. "Specified perils" means the following perils:

a. Accidental Discharge Or Overflow Of Water Or Steam from a plumbing, heating, air-conditioning, or automatic fire protective sprinkling system, water heater, or domestic appliance.

However, "we" do not pay for loss:

1) caused by continuous or repeated discharge, seepage, or leakage of water, or the presence or condensation of humidity, moisture, or vapor, over a period of weeks, months, or years, unless no "insured" knew of or could reasonably be expected to suspect such discharge, seepage, or leakage of water or the presence or condensation of humidity, moisture, or vapor;
2) on the "described location" if the residence covered under Coverage A has been vacant for more than 60 days in a row just before the loss. A residence being built is not vacant;
3) caused by or resulting from freezing, except as provided in f. below; or
4) to the system or appliance from which the water or steam escaped.

In this peril, plumbing systems and domestic appliances do not include sumps, sump pumps, or related equipment; any other type of system designed to remove subsurface water which is drained from the foundation area; or roof drains, gutters, downspouts, or like equipment.

Under Exclusions That Apply To Property Coverages, 1)b) and 3) of the Water exclusion that apply to surface water and water below the surface of the ground do not apply with respect to loss by water covered under this peril.

b. Aircraft -- This includes self-propelled missiles and spacecraft.

c. Explosion

d. Falling Objects

However, "we" do not pay for loss to:

1) the interior of a building, or to property inside a building, unless the falling object has first damaged an outside wall or the roof of the building by impact; or
2) the object that falls.

e. Fire Or Lightning

f. Freezing -- This means freezing of a plumbing, heating, air-conditioning, or automatic fire protective sprinkling system, water heater, or domestic appliance, subject to the requirements stated in 1) and 2) below. In this peril, plumbing systems and domestic appliances do not include sumps, sump pumps, or related equipment; any other type of system designed to remove subsurface water which is drained from the foundation area; or roof drains, gutters, downspouts, or like equipment.

1) When the building is protected by an automatic fire protective sprinkling system, coverage for loss caused by the peril of Freezing applies only if "you" have taken reasonable care to:

a) maintain heat in the building; and
b) continue the water supply.

2) When the building is not protected by an automatic fire protective sprinkling system, coverage for loss caused by the peril of Freezing applies only if "you" have taken reasonable care to:

a) maintain heat in the building; or
b) shut off the water supply and completely empty water from all systems, heaters, and appliances.

g. Riot Or Civil Commotion

h. "Sinkhole collapse"

i. Sudden And Accidental Damage From Smoke -- This includes sudden and accidental damage from fumes, smoke, soot, or vapors that emit or back up from a boiler, furnace, or related equipment.

However, "we" do not pay for loss caused by smoke from agricultural smudging or industrial operations.

j. Sudden And Accidental Damage From Artificially Generated Electrical Currents

However, "we" do not pay for loss to tubes, transistors, electronic components, or circuitry that are a part of any type of an electronic apparatus, including but not limited to appliances, fixtures, computers, and home entertainment units.

k. Sudden And Accidental Tearing Apart, Cracking, Burning, Or Bulging of a steam or hot water heating system, an air-conditioning or automatic fire protective sprinkling system, or a water heater.

However, "we" do not pay for loss caused by or resulting from freezing under this peril.

l. Theft -- This includes attempted theft and loss of property from a known place when it is likely that theft occurred.

However, "we" do not pay for loss caused by:

1) theft by an "insured";

2) theft in or to a residence being built, or theft of materials or supplies for use in construction of the residence, until the residence is occupied for its intended use;
3) theft from a part of the "described location" rented by an "insured" to a person other than another "insured"; or
4) theft that occurs away from the "described location" of property while on the part of residential premises that an "insured" owns, rents, or occupies, except for the time while an "insured" temporarily resides there.

m. Vandalism Or Malicious Mischief

However, "we" do not pay for loss to property on the "described location":

1) caused by vandalism or malicious mischief; or
2) that ensues from a wrongful act committed intentionally in the course of vandalism or malicious mischief;

if the residence covered under Coverage A was vacant for more than 60 days in a row just before the loss. A residence being built is not vacant.

n. Vehicles

o. Volcanic Eruption

However, this does not include loss caused by earthquake, land shock waves, or tremors.

p. Weight Of Ice, Snow, Or Sleet that causes damage to a building or property inside a building.

q. Windstorm Or Hail

However, "we" do not pay for loss:

1) to the interior of a building, or to property inside, caused by dust, rain, sand, sleet, or snow, all whether driven by wind or not, that enters through an opening in the building not made by the direct force of wind or hail; or
2) to watercraft or their furnishings, equipment, engines, motors, trailers, or semitrailers unless inside a fully enclosed building.

22. "Terms" means all provisions, limitations, exclusions, conditions, "declarations", and definitions used in this policy.

23. "Vermin" means an animal of a type that is prone to enter or burrow into or under a structure to seek food or shelter, including but not limited to:

a. armadillos;

b. bats;

c. opossums;

d. porcupines;

e. raccoons;

f. skunks; and

g. snakes.

24. Under the Liability Coverages provided by this policy, "watercraft" means an apparatus or a device primarily designed to be propelled on or in water by engine, motor, or wind, but this does not include:

a. a model watercraft that is not designed or used to carry people or cargo;

b. a "hovercraft";

c. a model hovercraft that is not designed or used to carry people or cargo;

d. a "motorized vehicle";

e. an "aircraft"; or

f. a model aircraft that is not designed or used to carry people or cargo.

PROPERTY COVERAGES

PRINCIPAL PROPERTY COVERAGES

1. **Coverage A -- Residence**

   a. "We" cover the residence on the "described location". This includes additions attached to the residence and built-in components and fixtures, as well as building materials and supplies located on or adjacent to the "described location" for use in the construction, alteration, or repair of the residence or related private structures on the "described location".

   b. "We" do not cover:

      1) land, including the land on which covered property is located, except as provided under the Incidental Property Coverage for Liquid Fuel Remediation;
      2) underground water or surface water;
      3) trees, plants, shrubs, or lawns, except as provided under the Incidental Property Coverage for Debris Removal and the Incidental Property Coverage for Trees, Plants, Shrubs, Or Lawns; or
      4) grave markers or mausoleums, except as provided under the Incidental Property Coverage for Grave Markers.

   c. The "limit" that applies to Coverage A is the most "we" pay per occurrence for all property covered under Coverage A.

2. **Coverage B -- Related Private Structures**

   a. "We" cover related private structures on the "described location" that are not attached to the residence covered under Coverage A. Structures that are connected to the residence covered under Coverage A by only a fence, a utility line, or a similar connection are not considered attached.

   b. "We" also cover fences, driveways, sidewalks, and other permanently installed outdoor fixtures.

   c. "We" do not cover:

      1) land, including the land on which covered property is located, except as provided under the Incidental Property Coverage for Liquid Fuel Remediation;
      2) underground water or surface water;
      3) trees, plants, shrubs, or lawns, except as provided under the Incidental Property Coverage for Debris Removal and the Incidental Property Coverage for Trees, Plants, Shrubs, Or Lawns;
      4) grave markers or mausoleums, except as provided under the Incidental Property Coverage for Grave Markers; or
      5) any structure:

         a) rented or held for rental to any person who is not a tenant of the residence covered under Coverage A, other than a structure used solely for private garage purposes;
         b) used, in whole or in part, for the direction or operation of a "business"; or
         c) used, in whole or in part, for the storage of "business" property.

However, this exclusion does not apply to a structure used by an "insured" or a tenant of the residence covered under Coverage A to store "business" property that:

(1) is a private passenger auto, a pickup truck, a van, or a "motorized vehicle" designed for grounds maintenance activities such as lawn mowing or snow plowing; or
(2) is owned solely by such "insured" or tenant and is not a "motorized vehicle"; and

does not consist of or contain gaseous or liquid fuel, other than fuel contained in a permanently installed fuel tank of a vehicle, craft, or grounds maintenance machine or in a portable container that is designed to hold fuel and has a capacity of no more than five U.S. gallons.

d. The "limit" that applies to Coverage B is the most "we" pay per occurrence for all property covered under Coverage B.

3. **Coverage C -- Personal Property**

a. "We" cover personal property owned or used by an "insured". At "your" option:

1) personal property owned by a guest or "domestic employee" is covered while it is in that part of any residential premises occupied by an "insured"; and
2) personal property owned by a person other than a guest or "domestic employee" is covered while it is in that part of the "described location" occupied by an "insured".

b. **Limitation On Property At Residential Premises Other Than The Described Location** -- Coverage for personal property usually on residential premises of an "insured" other than the "described location" is limited to 10% of the Coverage C "limit" or $1,000, whichever is greater.

However, this limitation does not apply to personal property:

1) that is removed from the "described location" because the "described location" is undergoing alteration, reconstruction, or repair and is unfit for use as a residence or a place in which to store property; or
2) in "your" newly acquired principal place of residence for 30 days from the date that "you" first move property there.

c. **Limitations On Certain Property** -- The special "limits" shown below do not increase the Coverage C "limit". The "limit" for each class is the total "limit" per occurrence for all items in that class.

1) $250 on money; bank notes; bullion; gold other than goldware and gold-plated ware; silver other than silverware and silver-plated ware; platinum other than platinumware and platinum-plated ware; coins; medals; scrip; smart cards; and cards or other devices on which a cash value is stored electronically.
2) $2,500 on securities, stamps, letters of credit, notes other than bank notes, personal records, tickets, accounts, deeds, evidence of debt, passports, and manuscripts. This special "limit" applies regardless of the medium on which these items exist, and includes the cost of research or other expenses necessary to reproduce, replace, or restore the item.

3) $2,500 on electronic devices and accessories while in or on a "motorized vehicle" or watercraft, if the device can be operated from the electrical system of the "motorized vehicle" or watercraft and by another source of power. Accessories include antennas, films, tapes, wires, discs, records, or other media that can be used with such devices.
4) $2,500 on electronic devices and accessories used primarily for "business" purposes while away from the "described location" and not in or on a "motorized vehicle" or watercraft, if the device can be operated from the electrical system of a "motorized vehicle" or watercraft and by another source of power. Accessories include antennas, films, tapes, wires, discs, records, or other media that can be used with such devices.
5) $2,500 on watercraft, including their furnishings, equipment, engines, motors, trailers, and semitrailers.

   However, this does not apply to:

   a) model watercraft that is not designed or used to carry people or cargo; or
   b) hovercraft.

6) $2,500 on trailers and semitrailers, other than trailers and semitrailers designed for or used with watercraft.
7) For loss by theft, misplacing, or losing:

   a) $2,500 on jewelry, watches, precious and semiprecious stones, gems, and furs;
   b) $2,500 on silverware, goldware, platinumware, pewterware, and items plated with gold, silver, or platinum; and
   c) $2,500 on guns and items related to guns.

8) For loss to personal property used primarily for "business" purposes, other than property rented or held for rental to others:

   a) $2,500 on property while on the "described location"; and
   b) $500 on property while away from the "described location".

      However, this special "limit" does not apply to electronic devices and accessories described in 3) and 4) above.

   These special "limits" include the cost of research or other expenses necessary to reproduce, replace, or restore "business" data.

d. **Personal Property Not Covered** -- "We" do not cover:

   1) property separately described and specifically insured by this or any other policy, regardless of the "limit" that applies to such property under such insurance;
   2) animals, birds, fish, or insects;
   3) "motorized vehicles".

      a) This includes:

         (1) their parts, equipment, and accessories, other than property described in c.3) above; and
         (2) electronic devices and accessories that can be operated only from the electrical system of a "motorized vehicle", including antennas, films, tapes, wires, discs, records, or other media that can be used with such devices;

         while in or on a "motorized vehicle".

b) However, this does not include a "motorized vehicle":

(1) that is designed to assist the handicapped; or
(2) that is:

(a) owned by an "insured";
(b) designed only for use off of public roads; and
(c) used only to service an "insured premises" or a premises of another;

if such "motorized vehicle" is not required by law or governmental regulation to be registered for use on public roads or property and is not used for "business" purposes;

4) aircraft, meaning apparatus or devices designed or used for flight. This includes parts or equipment of aircraft, whether or not attached.

However, this does not include model aircraft that are not designed or used to carry people or cargo;

5) hovercraft, meaning self-propelled motorized ground effect machines or air cushion vehicles, including but not limited to flarecraft, designed or used to travel over land or water. This includes parts or equipment of hovercraft, whether or not attached.

However, this does not include model hovercraft that are not designed or used to carry people or cargo;

6) property of roomers, boarders, or other tenants, but this does not include property of roomers or boarders who are related to an "insured";
7) property rented or held for rental to others by an "insured", but this does not include property in:

a) that part of the "described location" normally occupied solely by "your" household while rented to others on an occasional basis for residential purposes;
b) the portion of that part of the "described location" normally occupied by "your" household that is rented or held for rental to no more than two roomers or boarders for use as a residence; or
c) an apartment on the "described location" regularly rented or held for rental to others by an "insured", but only to the extent that coverage for such property is provided under the Incidental Property Coverage for Property In Rental Units;

8) loss that results from credit cards, electronic fund transfer cards, or electronic access devices that make possible the deposit, withdrawal, or transfer of funds, except as provided under the Incidental Property Coverage for Credit Card; Electronic Fund Transfer Card Or Access Device; Forgery; And Counterfeit Money;
9) grave markers or mausoleums, except as provided under the Incidental Property Coverage for Grave Markers;
10) land, including the land on which covered property is located, except as provided under the Incidental Property Coverage for Liquid Fuel Remediation;
11) underground water or surface water; or
12) trees, plants, shrubs, or lawns, except as provided under the Incidental Property Coverage for Debris Removal or the Incidental Property Coverage for Trees, Plants, Shrubs, Or Lawns.

e. Subject to the limitations described in b. and c. above, the "limit" that applies to Coverage C is the most "we" pay per occurrence for all property covered under Coverage C.

4. **Coverage D -- Additional Living Costs And Loss Of Rent**

   a. "We" pay for the necessary and reasonable increase in living costs "you" incur to maintain the normal standard of living of "your" household if that part of the "described location" occupied by "your" household is made unfit for use as a residence by a loss covered under the Property Coverages.

      "We" pay only for the period of time reasonably required to make the "described location" fit for use or, if "your" household is permanently relocated, only for the period of time reasonably required for relocation. This period of time is not limited by the policy period.

   b. "We" pay for the fair rental value of that part of the "described location" rented or held for rental to others by "you" if it is made unfit for use as a residence by a loss covered under the Property Coverages.

      However, "we" will deduct from the fair rental value any charges or expenses that do not continue while the part of the "described location" rented or held for rental to others is unfit for use.

      "We" pay only for the period of time reasonably required to repair or replace the part of the "described location" rented or held for rental to others. This period of time is not limited by the policy period.

   c. "We" pay for "your" additional living costs and fair rental value as described in a. and b. above for up to two weeks if a premises neighboring the "described location" is directly damaged by a Peril Insured Against covered by this policy and "you" may not, by order of civil authority, use the "described location". This period of time is not limited by the policy period.

   d. "We" do not pay for loss, cost, or expense due to the cancellation of a lease or an agreement.

   e. The "limit" that applies to Coverage D is the most "we" pay for all of the coverages described in a., b., and c. above.

INCIDENTAL PROPERTY COVERAGES

This policy provides the following Incidental Property Coverages. They are subject to all of the "terms" of the applicable Coverage A, Coverage B, or Coverage C. These coverages provide additional insurance unless otherwise stated.

1. **Association Deductible**

   a. "We" pay for "your" share of a deductible applicable to the insurance held by a homeowners, condominium, or similar residential association. Coverage applies only when the deductible:

      1) is charged against "you", during the policy period, as owner or tenant of the "described location"; and
      2) results from direct loss to property that:

         a) would be eligible for coverage by this policy if it were owned by "you";
         b) is covered under the insurance held by "your" association; and

c) is caused by a Peril Insured Against covered by this policy, but this does not include:

(1) earthquake; or
(2) land shock waves or tremors before, during, or after a volcanic eruption.

b. The most "we" pay is $1,500 per occurrence unless a higher "limit" for Association Deductible is shown on the "declarations". The "limit" that applies is the most "we" pay for any one loss, regardless of the number of deductibles charged against "you".

c. The Policy Period condition under Conditions Applicable To Property Coverages Only does not apply to this Incidental Property Coverage.

2. **Collapse**

a. "We" pay for direct physical loss to covered property involving the collapse of a building or a part of a building if the collapse was caused only by one or more of the following:

1) a Peril Insured Against described under Coverage A and Coverage B;
2) insect, rodent, or "vermin" damage, but only if no "insured" knew of or could reasonably be expected to suspect the presence of such damage prior to the collapse;
3) decay, but only if no "insured" knew of or could reasonably be expected to suspect the presence of such decay prior to the collapse;
4) weight of animals, equipment, people, or personal property;
5) weight of rain that collects on a roof; or
6) the use of defective materials or methods in construction or repair if the collapse occurs during the course of construction or repair.

However, "we" do not pay for loss to awnings, bulkheads, cesspools, decks, docks, drains, fences, flues, foundations, patios, paved areas, piers, retaining walls, septic tanks, swimming pools, underground pipes, or wharves caused by a peril described in 2) through 6) above unless the loss is the direct result of the collapse of a building or a part of a building. With respect to loss caused by a peril described in 2) through 6) above, awnings, bulkheads, cesspools, decks, docks, drains, fences, flues, foundations, patios, paved areas, piers, retaining walls, septic tanks, swimming pools, underground pipes, and wharves are not considered to be buildings or parts of buildings, whether or not such property is attached to or connected to one or more buildings.

b. In this Incidental Property Coverage:

1) collapse of a building or a part of a building means an abrupt caving in, falling in, falling down, or giving way of the building or the part of the building that prevents the building or the part of the building from being occupied for the purpose for which it was intended just before caving in, falling in, falling down, or giving way; and
2) the following are not considered to be in a state of collapse:

a) a building or a part of a building that has not caved in, fallen in, fallen down, or given way even if it displays evidence of bending, bowing, bulging, cracking, expansion, inadequate load bearing capacity, leaning, sagging, settling, or shrinkage;
b) a building or a part of a building in danger of caving in, falling in, falling down, or giving way; or
c) a part of a building that has not caved in, fallen in, fallen down, or given way even if it has separated from another part of the building.

However, the "terms" stated in 1) and 2) above do not limit coverage for direct loss to covered property caused by one or more of the "specified perils" and not otherwise excluded under this policy.

c. This coverage does not increase the "limits" that apply to the property covered.

d. The Bacteria, Fungi, Wet Rot, Or Dry Rot and Errors, Omissions, And Defects exclusions under Exclusions That Apply To Property Coverages do not apply to this Incidental Property Coverage.

3. **Credit Card; Electronic Fund Transfer Card Or Access Device; Forgery; And Counterfeit Money**

   a. "We" pay for loss if an "insured":

      1) by law must pay for the theft or unauthorized use of credit cards issued or registered in the name of an "insured";
      2) has a loss resulting from the theft or unauthorized use of:

         a) an electronic fund transfer card; or
         b) an electronic access device that makes possible the deposit, withdrawal, or transfer of funds;

         issued or registered in the name of an "insured";

      3) has a loss when checks, drafts, or negotiable instruments are forged or altered; or
      4) accepts in good faith counterfeit United States or Canadian paper money.

   The most "we" pay is $5,000 per occurrence unless a higher "limit" for Credit Card; Electronic Fund Transfer Card Or Access Device; Forgery; And Counterfeit Money is shown on the "declarations". All loss resulting from a series of acts committed by any one person or in which any one person is involved or implicated is considered one occurrence.

   b. "We" will defend a suit seeking damages against an "insured" if the suit results from the theft or unauthorized use of:

      1) a credit card;
      2) an electronic fund transfer card; or
      3) an electronic access device that makes possible the deposit, withdrawal, or transfer of funds;

      issued or registered in an "insured's" name.

   Subject to the limitation set forth in d. below, "we" will pay for the expense of such defense. Defense will be provided by counsel that "we" choose.

   c. At "our" option, "we" may defend an "insured" or an "insured's" bank against a suit for the enforcement of payment when checks, drafts, or negotiable instruments are forged or altered. If "we" choose to provide such defense, "we" will pay for the expense. Defense will be provided by counsel that "we" choose.

   d. "We" may make investigations and settle all claims or suits under this coverage that "we" decide are appropriate. "We" do not have to provide a defense after "we" have paid an amount equal to the "limit" that applies to Credit Card; Electronic Fund Transfer Card Or Access Device; Forgery; And Counterfeit Money as a result of a judgment or a written settlement agreed to by "us".

e. "We" do not pay for loss:

1) that results from the use of a credit card, an electronic fund transfer card, or an electronic access device that makes possible the deposit, withdrawal, or transfer of funds:

a) if an "insured" has not complied with all rules under which the credit card, fund transfer card, or access device was issued or granted;
b) by a resident of "your" household; or
c) by a person who has the credit card, fund transfer card, or access device with the consent of an "insured";

2) caused by the dishonesty of an "insured"; or
3) that results from the "business" of an "insured";

nor do "we" provide a defense for suits resulting from such loss.

4. **Debris Removal**

a. "We" pay for the reasonable cost to remove the debris of covered property after a loss. The loss must be caused by a Peril Insured Against that applies to the damaged property. "We" also pay for the reasonable cost to remove volcanic ash, dust, or particulate matter that causes direct physical loss to a covered building or covered property contained in a building.

"We" will not pay more for direct physical loss to property and debris removal combined than the "limit" that applies to the damaged property. However, if the covered loss plus the cost of debris removal is more than the applicable "limit", "we" will pay up to an extra 5% of the applicable "limit" to cover the cost of debris removal.

This coverage does not include any cost or expense to test for, monitor, clean up, remove, contain, treat, detoxify, neutralize, or in any way respond to or assess the effects of "pollutants".

b. Subject to the limitations set forth in c. below, "we" also pay for the reasonable cost to remove from the "described location":

1) "your" fallen tree or trees if the falling of the tree or trees is caused by the peril of:

a) Windstorm Or Hail; or
b) Weight Of Ice, Snow, Or Sleet; or

2) a neighbor's fallen tree or trees if the falling of the tree or trees is caused by any of the Perils Insured Against covered by this policy.

Regardless of the number of fallen trees, the most "we" pay is $1,000 per occurrence.

However, "we" pay no more than $500 of this "limit" to remove any one tree.

With respect to this Incidental Property Coverage, the peril of Weight Of Ice, Snow, Or Sleet means the weight of ice, snow, or sleet that causes a tree to fall.

c. The coverage described in b. above applies only to a fallen tree that:

1) causes damage to a covered structure;
2) prevents a "motorized vehicle" that is registered for use on public roads or property from using a driveway on the "described location"; or
3) obstructs a ramp or other fixture designed to make the residence on the "described location" accessible to a handicapped person.

5. **Emergency Removal** -- "We" pay for direct physical loss to covered property that is moved from a premises to prevent a loss from a Peril Insured Against. The property is covered for up to 30 days, however this coverage does not extend past the date on which this policy expires.

   This coverage does not increase the "limits" that apply to the property being removed.

   The Exclusions That Apply To Coverage A, Coverage B, And Coverage C; the Exclusions That Apply Only To Coverage A And Coverage B; the Exclusions That Apply Only To Coverage C; and the Exclusions That Apply To Property Coverages do not apply to such property while removed.

   However, "we" do not pay any "insured" for loss that results from any act committed by or at the direction of an "insured" with the intent to cause a loss. This applies even with respect to an "insured" who was not involved in the commission or direction of the act that caused the loss.

6. **Fire Department Service Charge** -- "We" pay for charges assumed by "you" under a contract or an agreement when a fire department is called to save or protect covered property from a Peril Insured Against.

   However, "we" do not pay for such charges when the property is located within the limits of the city, municipality, or protection district that provides the fire department response.

   The most "we" pay is $1,000 per occurrence unless a higher "limit" for Fire Department Service Charge is shown on the "declarations".

7. **Glass Or Safety Glazing Material**

   a. "We" pay for:

      1) the breakage of glass or safety glazing material that is part of a covered building or storm door or window; and
      2) direct physical loss to covered property caused only by broken pieces of glass or safety glazing material that, before breaking, was part of a building or storm door or window.

   b. The Earth Movement exclusion under Exclusions That Apply To Property Coverages does not apply with respect to the coverage described in a. above.

   c. Under this Incidental Property Coverage, "we" do not pay for loss:

      1) to covered property that occurs because of the breakage of glass or safety glazing material, except as provided in a.2) above; or
      2) on the "described location" if the residence covered under Coverage A was vacant for more than 60 days in a row just before the loss.

         However, this does not apply to loss caused by breakage of glass or safety glazing material that is the direct result of earth movement.

         A residence being built is not vacant.

   d. This coverage does not increase the "limits" that apply to the property covered.

8. **Grave Markers** -- "We" pay up to $5,000 for direct physical loss to grave markers and mausoleums on or away from the "described location" caused by a Peril Insured Against.

9. **Increased Cost -- Ordinance Or Law**

   a. When loss to the residence covered under Coverage A or a related private structure covered under Coverage B is caused by a Peril Insured Against and "you" elect to repair or replace the damage, "you" may apply up to 10% of the Coverage A "limit" to cover the increased cost that "you" incur due to the enforcement of a code, ordinance, or law that regulates the construction, repair, replacement, or demolition of the damaged residence or structure.

   b. "You" may use all or part of this Increased Cost -- Ordinance Or Law coverage to cover the increased cost "you" incur to remove debris resulting from the construction, repair, replacement, or demolition of the residence covered under Coverage A or a related private structure covered under Coverage B when:

      1) loss to the residence or structure is caused by a Peril Insured Against; and
      2) a code, ordinance, or law regulates its construction, repair, replacement, or demolition.

      This does not increase the "limit" that applies to this Incidental Property Coverage.

   c. However, "we" do not pay for:

      1) any loss in value of property that results from the enforcement of a code, ordinance, or law; or
      2) any loss, cost, or expense that results from the enforcement of a code, ordinance, or law requiring that an "insured" or others test for, monitor, clean up, remove, contain, treat, detoxify, neutralize, or in any way respond to or assess the effects of "pollutants".

10. **Liquid Fuel Remediation**

   a. "We" pay for loss to:

      1) property covered under Coverage A, Coverage B, or Coverage C;
      2) land:

         a) within the "described location";
         b) owned by an "insured"; and
         c) on which the residence covered under Coverage A or a structure covered under Coverage B is located;

         but this does not include farm land; or

      3) property covered under the Incidental Property Coverage for Trees, Plants, Shrubs, Or Lawns;

      caused directly or indirectly by the discharge, dispersal, emission, escape, leaching, leakage, migration, release, seepage, or spillage of liquid fuel from the fuel system of a heating or air-conditioning system, water heater, or domestic appliance located on the "described location".

   b. When there is discharge, dispersal, emission, escape, leaching, leakage, migration, release, seepage, or spillage of liquid fuel from a fuel system described in a. above, "we" also pay for:

      1) cost or expense "you" incur to take temporary measures to stop any further discharge, dispersal, emission, escape, leaching, leakage, migration, release, seepage, or spillage of such fuel from such system;
      2) cost or expense "you" incur to prevent or hinder the spread of the discharged, dispersed, emitted, escaped, leached, leaked, migrated, released, seeped, or spilled fuel over a larger area;

3) cost or expense "you" incur to clean up or treat such fuel on or remove such fuel from:

   a) property covered under Coverage A, Coverage B, or Coverage C;
   b) land:

      (1) within the "described location";
      (2) owned by an "insured"; and
      (3) on which the residence covered under Coverage A or a structure covered under Coverage B is located;

   but this does not include farm land; or

   c) property covered under the Incidental Property Coverage for Trees, Plants, Shrubs, Or Lawns.

   This includes cost or expense to remove the debris of such property or land;

4) cost or expense "you" incur to remove and replace those parts of covered property necessary to gain access to the system from which such fuel discharged, dispersed, emitted, escaped, leached, leaked, migrated, released, seeped, or spilled;
5) the necessary and reasonable increase in living costs "you" incur to maintain the normal standard of living of "your" household if that part of the "described location" occupied by "your" household is made unfit for use as a residence; and
6) cost or expense "you" incur to assess, monitor, or test the effects of discharged, dispersed, emitted, escaped, leached, leaked, migrated, released, seeped, or spilled liquid fuel.

   However, "we" will pay for such cost or expense only if the assessment, monitoring, or testing:

   a) is necessitated by a statutory or regulatory requirement or is in response to a request, demand, or order by a governmental body or authority or court of law; and
   b) arises out of loss for which payment is made under a., b.1), b.2), or b.3) above.

c. The Policy Period condition under Conditions Applicable To Property Coverages Only does not apply to this Incidental Property Coverage.

d. Under Exclusions That Apply To Coverage A, Coverage B, And Coverage C, the exclusion for loss caused by the discharge, dispersal, disposal, emission, escape, leaching, leakage, migration, release, seepage, or spillage of "pollutants" does not apply to the coverage provided under this Incidental Property Coverage for the discharge, dispersal, emission, escape, leaching, leakage, migration, release, seepage, or spillage of liquid fuel.

e. "We" do not pay for:

   1) loss, cost, or expense involving underground water or surface water;
   2) loss, cost, or expense involving trees, plants, shrubs, or lawns grown for "business";
   3) loss, cost, or expense due to the cancellation of a lease or an agreement;
   4) the replacement of discharged, dispersed, emitted, escaped, leached, leaked, migrated, released, seeped, or spilled fuel;
   5) any loss in the market value of property or land, whether or not damaged by discharged, dispersed, emitted, escaped, leached, leaked, migrated, released, seeped, or spilled fuel;

6) any damages resulting from:

a) a loss of; or
b) a reduction in value of;

an agreement to sell property or land; or

7) any cost or expense to repair, replace, remove, or demolish any part of the fuel system from which the fuel discharged, dispersed, emitted, escaped, leached, leaked, migrated, released, seeped, or spilled, except as provided under b. above.

f. The "terms" and "limits" applicable to:

1) Coverage D -- Additional Living Costs And Loss Of Rent; and
2) the Incidental Property Coverage for Debris Removal;

do not apply to any loss, cost, or expense arising out of the discharge, dispersal, emission, escape, leaching, leakage, migration, release, seepage, or spillage of fuel from a fuel system described in a. above.

g. The most "we" pay for this Incidental Property Coverage for Liquid Fuel Remediation is $10,000 unless a higher "limit" for Liquid Fuel Remediation is shown on the "declarations". The "limit" for this Incidental Property Coverage for Liquid Fuel Remediation:

1) is the most "we" pay for the total of:

a) all discharges, dispersals, emissions, escapes, leachings, leakages, migrations, releases, seepages, or spillages of liquid fuel that an "insured" first discovers or is made aware of during the policy period; and
b) all coverages described in a. and b. above; and

2) applies regardless of the number of:

a) claims made;
b) discharges, dispersals, emissions, escapes, leachings, leakages, migrations, releases, seepages, or spillages of liquid fuel that an "insured" first discovers or is made aware of during the policy period; or
c) locations insured under this policy.

With respect to loss to property covered under the Incidental Property Coverage for Trees, Plants, Shrubs, Or Lawns, the most "we" pay is an amount equal to 5% of the Coverage A "limit", but not more than $500 for any lawn or any one tree, plant, or shrub. This does not increase the "limit" that applies to this Incidental Property Coverage for Liquid Fuel Remediation.

With respect to coverage for the necessary and reasonable increase in living costs incurred to maintain the normal standard of living of "your" household, "we" pay only for the period of time reasonably required to make the "described location" fit for use or, if "your" household is permanently relocated, only for the period of time reasonably required for relocation. This period of time is not limited by the policy period. This does not increase the "limit" that applies to this Incidental Property Coverage for Liquid Fuel Remediation.

h. The "terms" stated in a. through g. above do not limit coverage for direct loss to covered property caused by the discharge, dispersal, emission, escape, leaching, leakage, migration, release, seepage, or spillage of liquid fuel when the discharge, dispersal, disposal, emission, escape, leaching, leakage, migration, release, seepage, or spillage is caused by one or more of the "specified perils" and is not otherwise excluded under this policy.

11. **Lock And Garage Door Transmitter Replacement** -- "We" pay to replace the locks on exterior doors of the residence covered under Coverage A if the keys to such locks are lost or stolen. "We" also pay to replace a portable transmitter that is part of an automatic garage door opening system on the "described location" if such transmitter is lost or stolen.

    "You" must notify "us" in writing within 72 hours of discovering the loss. The most "we" pay is $500 per occurrence.

12. **Loss Assessment**

    a. "We" pay for "your" share of an assessment levied by a homeowners, condominium, or similar residential association. Coverage applies only when the assessment:

        1) is levied during the policy period;
        2) results from direct loss to property that is:

            a) owned collectively by all association members;
            b) of the type that would be eligible for coverage by this policy if it were owned by "you"; and
            c) caused by a Peril Insured Against covered by this policy, but this does not include:

                (1) earthquake; or
                (2) land shock waves or tremors before, during, or after a volcanic eruption; and

        3) is levied against "you" as owner or tenant of the "described location".

    b. However, "we" do not pay for an assessment that:

        1) results from a deductible in the insurance held by the association; or
        2) is levied against "you" or the association by any governmental body or authority.

    c. The most "we" pay is $1,500 per occurrence unless a higher "limit" for Loss Assessment is shown on the "declarations". The "limit" that applies is the most "we" pay for any one loss, regardless of the number of assessments.

    d. The Policy Period condition under Conditions Applicable To Property Coverages Only does not apply to this Incidental Property Coverage.

13. **Property In Rental Units** -- "We" pay for direct physical loss to "your" appliances, carpeting, and other household furnishings in an apartment on the "described location" regularly rented or held for rental to others by an "insured", but only when the loss is caused by one or more of the "specified perils", other than Theft, and is not otherwise excluded under this policy.

    The most "we" pay for loss to such property in each apartment rented or held for rental to others is $2,500 per occurrence. The "limit" applies regardless of the quantity of appliances, carpeting, or other household furnishings damaged.

    This coverage does not increase the "limits" that apply to the property covered.

14. **Reasonable Repairs**

    a. "We" pay for the reasonable costs incurred by "you" for necessary measures performed solely to protect covered property from further damage by a Peril Insured Against if a Peril Insured Against has already caused a loss.

b. If the measures described in a. above involve repair to other damaged property, "we" pay only if the property that is repaired is covered by this policy and only if the damage that necessitates the repair is caused by a Peril Insured Against.

This coverage does not:

1) increase the "limit" that applies to the property covered; or
2) relieve "you" of the duties described in 1.b., Protecting Property, under What Must Be Done In Case Of Loss Or Occurrence.

15. **Refrigerated Property** -- "We" pay for direct loss to covered property stored in a freezer or refrigerated unit on the "described location" caused by:

a. complete or partial disruption of electrical power due to conditions beyond an "insured's" control, if such disruption is caused by damage to the generating or transmission equipment; or

b. mechanical breakdown of the freezer or refrigerated unit.

Coverage applies only if the freezer or refrigerated unit had been maintained in proper working order prior to the loss.

The most "we" pay is $500 per occurrence unless a higher "limit" for Refrigerated Property is shown on the "declarations".

The reference to mechanical breakdown in the Wear And Tear exclusion under Exclusions That Apply To Coverage A, Coverage B, And Coverage C and the Power Failure and Bacteria, Fungi, Wet Rot, Or Dry Rot exclusions under Exclusions That Apply To Property Coverages do not apply to this Incidental Property Coverage.

16. **Trees, Plants, Shrubs, Or Lawns** -- "We" pay for direct physical loss to trees, plants, shrubs, or lawns on the "described location" caused by:

a. Fire Or Lightning, Explosion, Riot Or Civil Commotion, Aircraft;

b. Vehicles if not owned or operated by an occupant of the "described location"; or

c. Vandalism Or Malicious Mischief or Theft.

"You" may apply up to 5% of the Coverage A "limit" to cover trees, plants, shrubs, or lawns. "We" do not pay more than $500 for each tree, plant, or shrub. This includes the cost to remove the debris of the covered item.

"We" do not cover trees, plants, shrubs, or lawns grown for "business".

PERILS INSURED AGAINST -- COVERAGES A, B, C, AND D

Coverage A -- Residence, Coverage B -- Related Private Structures, And Coverage C -- Personal Property -- "We" insure property covered under Coverage A, Coverage B, or Coverage C for risks of direct physical loss, unless the loss is excluded under the Exclusions That Apply To Coverage A, Coverage B, And Coverage C, the Exclusions That Apply Only To Coverage A And Coverage B, or the Exclusions That Apply Only To Coverage C.

1. **Exclusions That Apply To Coverage A, Coverage B, And Coverage C**

   a. "We" do not pay for loss excluded under the Exclusions That Apply To Property Coverages.

b. **Freezing, Discharge, Leakage, Or Overflow** -- Subject to the exceptions stated in 1) and 2) below, "we" do not pay for loss caused by freezing of, or the resulting discharge, leakage, or overflow from, a plumbing, heating, air-conditioning, or automatic fire protective sprinkling system, water heater, or domestic appliance.

   1) When the building is protected by an automatic fire protective sprinkling system, this exclusion does not apply if "you" have taken reasonable care to:

      a) maintain heat in the building; and
      b) continue the water supply.

   2) When the building is not protected by an automatic fire protective sprinkling system, this exclusion does not apply if "you" have taken reasonable care to:

      a) maintain heat in the building; or
      b) shut off the water supply and completely empty water from all systems, heaters, and appliances.

   With respect to this exclusion and the exceptions stated in 1) and 2) above, plumbing systems and domestic appliances do not include sumps, sump pumps, or related equipment; any other type of system designed to remove subsurface water which is drained from the foundation area; or roof drains, gutters, downspouts, or like equipment.

c. **Freezing, Thawing, Pressure, Or Weight Of Ice Or Water** -- "We" do not pay for loss caused by freezing, thawing, pressure, or weight of ice or water, whether driven by wind or not, to:

   1) fences, patios, paved areas, or swimming pools;
   2) bulkheads, footings, foundations, walls, or any other structures or features that support all or part of a building or other structure;
   3) bulkheads or retaining walls that do not support all or part of a building or other structure; or
   4) docks, piers, or wharves.

d. **Theft** -- "We" do not pay for loss caused by theft in or to a residence being built, or theft of materials or supplies for use in construction of the residence, until the residence is occupied for its intended use.

e. **Water, Humidity, Moisture, Or Vapor** -- "We" do not pay for loss caused by:

   1) continuous or repeated discharge, seepage, or leakage of water; or
   2) the presence or condensation of humidity, moisture, or vapor;

   over a period of weeks, months, or years, unless no "insured" knew of or could reasonably be expected to suspect such discharge, seepage, or leakage of water or the presence or condensation of humidity, moisture, or vapor.

   Under Exclusions That Apply To Property Coverages, 1)b) and 3) of the Water exclusion that apply to surface water and water below the surface of the ground do not apply with respect to loss caused by continuous or repeated discharge, seepage, or leakage of water from a plumbing, heating, air-conditioning, or automatic fire protective sprinkling system, water heater, or domestic appliance on the "described location" if no "insured" knew of or could reasonably be expected to suspect such discharge, seepage, or leakage of water. Plumbing systems and domestic appliances do not include sumps, sump pumps, or related equipment; any other type of system designed to remove subsurface water which is drained from the foundation area; or roof drains, gutters, downspouts, or like equipment.

f. **Settling, Cracking, Shrinking, Bulging, Or Expanding** -- "We" do not pay for loss caused by the settling, cracking, shrinking, bulging, or expanding of:

1) bulkheads;
2) ceilings;
3) floors;
4) footings;
5) foundations;
6) patios;
7) paved areas;
8) roofs; or
9) walls.

g. **Birds, Vermin, Rodents, Insects, Or Animals** -- "We" do not pay for loss caused by:

1) birds;
2) "vermin";
3) rodents;
4) insects; or
5) any animal owned or kept by an "insured";

except as provided under the Incidental Property Coverages.

h. **Smoke** -- "We" do not pay for loss caused by smoke from agricultural smudging or industrial operations.

i. **Pollutants** -- "We" do not pay for loss caused by the discharge, dispersal, disposal, emission, escape, leaching, leakage, migration, release, seepage, or spillage of "pollutants", unless the discharge, dispersal, disposal, emission, escape, leaching, leakage, migration, release, seepage, or spillage is caused by one or more of the "specified perils" and is not otherwise excluded under this policy.

j. **Wear And Tear** -- "We" do not pay for loss caused by:

1) wear and tear, marring, or deterioration;
2) mechanical breakdown, latent defect, inherent vice, or any quality, fault, or weakness in property that causes it to damage or destroy itself;
3) rust or other corrosion or smog; or
4) pressure from or the presence of roots of trees, plants, shrubs, or other vegetation.

2. **Exceptions To Exclusions That Apply To Coverage A, Coverage B, And Coverage C**

a. "We" pay for an ensuing loss that results from 1.b. through 1.j. above, unless the ensuing loss itself is excluded.

b. Unless the loss is otherwise excluded by this policy, "we" pay for loss to property covered under Coverage A, Coverage B, or Coverage C that results from water or steam that, due to a cause or event excluded under 1.f. through 1.j. above, accidentally discharges or overflows from:

1) a storm drain, or a water, steam, or sewer pipe, away from the "described location"; or
2) a plumbing, heating, air-conditioning, or automatic fire protective sprinkling system, water heater, or domestic appliance on the "described location". This includes the reasonable cost of removing and replacing those parts of a building or other structure on the "described location" needed to repair the system, heater, or appliance.

   However, "we" will pay the cost of removing and replacing part of a structure that is not a building only if the water or steam causes direct physical loss to a building on the "described location".

"We" do not pay for loss to the system, heater, or appliance from which the water or steam escaped.

In this exception, plumbing systems and domestic appliances do not include sumps, sump pumps, or related equipment; any other type of system designed to remove subsurface water which is drained from the foundation area; or roof drains, gutters, downspouts, or like equipment.

Under Exclusions That Apply To Property Coverages, 1)b) and 3) of the Water exclusion that apply to surface water and water below the surface of the ground do not apply with respect to loss by water covered under this exception.

3. **Exclusions That Apply Only To Coverage A And Coverage B**

   a. **Vandalism Or Malicious Mischief** -- "We" do not pay for loss:

      1) caused by vandalism or malicious mischief; or
      2) that ensues from a wrongful act committed intentionally in the course of vandalism or malicious mischief;

      if the residence covered under Coverage A was vacant for more than 60 days in a row just before the loss. A residence being built is not vacant.

   b. **Collapse Or Impairment** -- "We" do not pay for loss involving:

      1) collapse; or
      2) impairment of structural integrity, including but not limited to sagging, bowing, bending, leaning, or inadequacy of load bearing capacity;

      except as provided under the Incidental Property Coverage for Collapse.

      However, "we" do pay for an ensuing loss to property covered under Coverage A or Coverage B unless the ensuing loss itself is excluded.

4. **Exclusions That Apply Only To Coverage C**

   a. **Breakage** -- "We" do not pay for loss caused by breakage of eyeglasses, glassware, statuary, marble, bric-a-brac, porcelains, and similar fragile articles.

      However, this exclusion does not apply to:

      1) jewelry; watches; bronzes; cameras and photographic lenses; or
      2) loss caused by or resulting from:

         a) the collapse of a building or a part of a building or the impairment of the structural integrity of a building or a part of a building; or
         b) one or more of the "specified perils", other than Falling Objects, that is not otherwise excluded under this policy.

   b. **Watercraft** -- "We" do not pay for loss to watercraft, including their trailers, semitrailers, furnishings, equipment, engines, and motors, caused by collision, sinking, swamping, or stranding. This exclusion does not apply to collision of watercraft with a land vehicle.

   c. **Dampness And Temperature** -- "We" do not pay for loss caused by dampness of atmosphere or extremes of temperature. This does not apply to loss caused directly by rain, snow, sleet, or hail.

   d. **Refinishing, Renovating, Or Repairing** -- "We" do not pay for loss to property, other than jewelry, watches, and furs, caused by a refinishing, renovating, or repairing process.

However, if such process results in a fire or explosion, "we" do cover the loss or damage caused by that fire or explosion.

EXCLUSIONS THAT APPLY TO PROPERTY COVERAGES

1. "We" do not pay for loss or damage caused directly or indirectly by one or more of the following excluded causes or events. Such loss or damage is excluded regardless of other causes or events that contribute to or aggravate the loss, whether such causes or events act to produce the loss before, at the same time as, or after the excluded causes or events.

   These exclusions apply whether or not an extensive area suffers damage from or is affected by the excluded cause or event.

   a. **Ordinance Or Law** -- "We" do not pay for:

      1) any loss or increased cost that results from the enforcement of a code, ordinance, or law that regulates the construction, repair, or demolition of property or the removal of its debris, except as provided under the Incidental Property Coverage for Increased Cost -- Ordinance Or Law;
      2) any loss in value of property that results from the enforcement of a code, ordinance, or law; or
      3) any loss, cost, or expense that results from the enforcement of a code, ordinance, or law requiring that an "insured" or others test for, monitor, clean up, remove, contain, treat, detoxify, neutralize, or in any way respond to or assess the effects of "pollutants".

      This exclusion applies whether or not there has been physical damage to covered property.

   b. **Civil Authority** -- "We" do not pay for loss caused by the confiscation, destruction, or seizure of property covered under Coverage A, Coverage B, or Coverage C by order of civil authority.

      "We" do pay for loss caused by acts ordered by a civil authority at the time of a fire to prevent its spread, but only if loss caused by the fire would be covered by this policy.

   c. **Nuclear Hazard**

      1) "We" do not pay for loss caused by nuclear reaction, radiation, or radioactive contamination:

         a) whether controlled or uncontrolled; or
         b) however caused;

         or any consequence of such reaction, radiation, or contamination.

      2) Loss caused by nuclear reaction, radiation, or radioactive contamination is not considered loss caused by:

         a) fire;
         b) explosion; or
         c) smoke;

         even if this policy provides coverage for loss caused by one or more of these perils.

      3) Direct loss by fire resulting from nuclear reaction, radiation, or radioactive contamination is covered.

   d. **War And Military Action** -- "We" do not pay for loss caused by:

      1) war, including undeclared or civil war;

2) warlike action by a military force, including action in hindering or defending against an actual or expected attack, by any government, sovereign, or other authority using military personnel or other agents; or
3) insurrection, rebellion, revolution, usurped power, or action taken by governmental authority in hindering or defending against any of these.

With respect to any action that comes within the "terms" of this exclusion and involves nuclear reaction, radiation, or radioactive contamination, this War And Military Action exclusion supersedes the Nuclear Hazard exclusion.

Discharge of a nuclear weapon is deemed a warlike action even if it is accidental.

e. **Neglect** -- "We" do not pay for loss caused by the neglect of an "insured" to use all reasonable means to save and preserve covered property at and after the time of a loss.

f. **Earth Movement** -- "We" do not pay for loss caused by earth movement whether the earth movement results from or is caused by human or animal forces or an act of nature.

Earth movement means:

1) earthquake;
2) land shock waves or tremors before, during, or after a volcanic eruption;
3) landslide, mudflow, mudslide;
4) subsidence, erosion; or
5) any other earth movement, including but not limited to earth sinking, rising, shifting, expanding, or contracting.

However, this does not include "sinkhole collapse".

"We" do pay for direct loss to covered property caused by fire or explosion resulting from earth movement.

This exclusion does not apply to loss caused by theft that is otherwise covered by this policy.

g. **Water**

1) "We" do not pay for loss caused by:

a) flood;
b) surface water;
c) waves, including but not limited to tidal wave and tsunami;
d) tides;
e) tidal water;
f) overflow of any body of water; or
g) spray from a) through f) above;

whether driven by wind or not.

This includes, but is not limited to, tidal surge, storm surge, and storm tide.

2) "We" do not pay for loss caused by water that:

a) backs up through sewers or drains; or
b) overflows or otherwise discharges from:

(1) a sump, sump pump, or related equipment; or
(2) any other type of system designed to remove subsurface water which is drained from the foundation area.

3) "We" do not pay for loss caused by water below the surface of the ground. This includes, but is not limited to, water that exerts pressure on, or seeps, leaks, or flows through or into, a building, sidewalk, driveway, patio, foundation, swimming pool, or other structure.

4) "We" do not pay for loss caused by matter present in or carried or otherwise moved by water described in 1) through 3) above.
5) The exclusions set forth in 1) through 4) above:

   a) apply regardless of the cause of the excluded event, whether or not such cause is an act of nature; and
   b) apply to, but are not limited to, water and matter present in or carried or otherwise moved by water, whether driven by wind or not, that:

      (1) overtops;
      (2) escapes from;
      (3) is released from; or
      (4) is otherwise discharged from;

   a dam, levee, dike, floodgate, or other device or feature designed or used to retain, contain, or control water.

6) "We" do pay for direct loss to covered property caused by fire or explosion resulting from an event excluded in 1) through 4) above.
7) These exclusions do not apply to loss caused by theft that is otherwise covered by this policy.
8) With respect to these exclusions, surface water and water below the surface of the ground do not include water that accidentally discharges or overflows from a plumbing, heating, air-conditioning, or automatic fire protective sprinkling system, water heater, or domestic appliance on the "described location" when loss caused by such water is not otherwise excluded by this policy. Plumbing systems and domestic appliances do not include sumps, sump pumps, or related equipment; any other type of system designed to remove subsurface water which is drained from the foundation area; or roof drains, gutters, downspouts, or like equipment.
9) These exclusions do not apply with respect to direct physical loss to property covered under Coverage C while such property is away from a premises or location owned by, rented to, occupied by, or controlled by an "insured". With respect to such loss, the Weather Conditions exclusion under Exclusions That Apply To Property Coverages does not apply.

h. **Power Failure** -- "We" do not pay for loss caused by the failure of power or other utility service, whether or not it is caused by a Peril Insured Against, if the cause of the failure is not on the "described location".

   "We" do pay for direct loss that is otherwise covered by this policy that occurs on the "described location" as a result of the failure of power or other utility service.

i. **Intentional Acts** -- "We" do not pay any "insured" for loss that results from any act committed:

   1) by an "insured", alone or in collusion with another; or
   2) at the direction of an "insured";

   with the intent to cause a loss.

   This exclusion applies even with respect to an "insured" who was not involved in the commission or direction of the act that caused the loss.

j. **Bacteria, Fungi, Wet Rot, Or Dry Rot** -- "We" do not pay for loss, cost, or expense caused by, consisting of, or relating to the existence of or any activity of bacteria, "fungi", wet rot, or dry rot that is not the direct result of a Peril Insured Against.

"We" do pay for direct loss to covered property caused by a Peril Insured Against resulting from bacteria, "fungi", wet rot, or dry rot.

2. "We" do not pay for loss or damage caused by or resulting from one or more of the following excluded causes or events. However, "we" do pay for an ensuing loss that is otherwise covered by this policy.

   a. **Weather Conditions** -- "We" do not pay for loss caused by weather conditions that initiate, set in motion, or in any way contribute to a cause or event excluded under the preceding Exclusions That Apply To Property Coverages (Numbers 1.a. through 1.j).

   b. **Errors, Omissions, And Defects** -- "We" do not pay for loss caused by one or more of the following:

      1) an act or decision of any person, group, organization, or governmental body or authority, or the failure of any person, group, organization, or governmental body or authority to act or decide; or
      2) a defect, a weakness, the inadequacy, a fault, or unsoundness in the:

         a) development, planning, siting, surveying, zoning;
         b) construction, compaction, design, grading, remodeling, renovation, repair, specification, workmanship;
         c) materials used in construction, remodeling, renovation, or repair; or
         d) maintenance;

      of any property, whether in whole or in part, and whether on or away from the "described location", except as provided under the Incidental Property Coverage for Collapse.

LIABILITY COVERAGES

PRINCIPAL LIABILITY COVERAGES

1. **Coverage L -- Personal Liability** -- "We" pay, up to the "limit" that applies, all sums for which an "insured" is legally liable because of "bodily injury" or "property damage" caused by an "occurrence" to which this coverage applies.

   "We" will defend a suit seeking damages if the suit resulted from "bodily injury" or "property damage" caused by an "occurrence" to which this coverage applies. Such defense will be provided at "our" expense by counsel that "we" choose.

   "We" may make investigations and settle claims or suits that "we" decide are appropriate. "We" do not have to settle or provide a defense after "we" have paid an amount equal to the "limit" that applies as a result of a judgment or written settlement.

2. **Coverage M -- Medical Payments To Others** -- "We" pay the necessary medical expenses if they are incurred or medically determined within three years from the date of an accident causing "bodily injury" covered by this policy. Medical expenses means the reasonable charges for medical, surgical, X-ray, dental, ambulance, hospital, professional nursing, and funeral services; prosthetic devices; hearing aids; prescription drugs; and eyeglasses, including contact lenses.

   This coverage does not apply to "you" or to any person who is a regular resident of "your" household, other than a "domestic employee". With respect to others, this coverage applies only to:

   a. a person on an "insured premises" with the permission of an "insured"; or

   b. a person away from an "insured premises" if the "bodily injury":

1) arises out of a condition on an "insured premises" or the access ways immediately adjoining an "insured premises";
2) is caused by an activity of an "insured";
3) is caused by a "domestic employee" in the course of his or her employment by an "insured"; or
4) is caused by an animal owned by or in the care of an "insured".

INCIDENTAL LIABILITY COVERAGES

This policy provides the following Incidental Liability Coverages. They are subject to all of the "terms" of Coverage L and Coverage M. Except for Claims And Defense Cost, Damage To Property Of Others, First Aid Expense, and Loss Assessment, they do not increase the "limits" stated for the Principal Liability Coverages.

1. **Business**

   a. "We" pay for "bodily injury" or "property damage" that arises out of:

      1) the rental or holding for rental of an "insured premises":

         a) on an occasional basis for use only as a residence;
         b) in part for use only as a residence (No family unit may include more than two roomers or boarders.); or
         c) in part for use as a school, studio, office, or private garage; or

      2) the "business" activities of an "insured" under the age of 21 years, but only if such "insured" is involved in a part-time or occasional, self-employed "business" that does not employ others and the "bodily injury" or "property damage" arises out of activities related to that "business".

   b. This Incidental Liability Coverage for Business is subject to all of the:

      1) Exclusions That Apply To Coverage L And Coverage M, other than exclusion g.;
      2) Additional Exclusions That Apply Only To Coverage L; and
      3) Additional Exclusions That Apply Only To Coverage M.

2. **Claims And Defense Cost** -- "We" pay for:

   a. the costs incurred by "us" and the costs taxed to an "insured" in a suit "we" defend;

   b. the premiums on required bonds in a suit "we" defend, but only for bond amounts up to the "limit" that applies. "We" are not required to apply for or furnish bonds;

   c. the necessary costs incurred by an "insured" at "our" request for assisting "us" in the investigation or defense of a claim or suit. This includes up to $250 per day, per "insured", for the actual loss of earnings, but not loss of other income, for time spent away from work at "our" request;

   d. the interest on the entire judgment that accrues after the entry of the judgment, but ending when "we" tender, pay, or deposit in court that part of the judgment that does not exceed the "limit" that applies; and

   e. prejudgment interest awarded against an "insured" on that part of the judgment "we" pay. If "we" offer to pay the "limit" that applies, "we" will not pay any prejudgment interest based on that period of time after the offer.

3. **Contracts**

   a. "We" pay for "bodily injury" or "property damage":

1) for which an "insured" is liable under a written contract that directly relates to the ownership, maintenance, or use of an "insured premises"; or
2) for which "you" are liable under a written contract, made before the loss, in which "you" have assumed the liability of others.

The loss causing the "bodily injury" or "property damage" must have occurred during the policy period.

b. This Incidental Liability Coverage for Contracts is subject to all of the:

1) Exclusions That Apply To Coverage L And Coverage M;
2) Additional Exclusions That Apply Only To Coverage L, other than exclusion c.; and
3) Additional Exclusions That Apply Only To Coverage M.

4. **Damage To Property Of Others** -- Regardless of an "insured's" legal liability, "we" pay, at replacement cost, for "property damage" to property of others caused by an "insured". The "limit" that applies to this coverage is $1,000 per "occurrence".

The exclusions that apply to Coverage L and Coverage M do not apply to this coverage.

However, "we" do not pay for "property damage":

a. covered under the Property Coverages section of this policy.

However, "we" will pay for "property damage" in excess of the amount recoverable under the Property Coverages, to the extent that such "property damage" is covered under the "terms" of this Incidental Liability Coverage;

b. to property owned by an "insured", or owned by, rented to, or leased to another resident of "your" household or a tenant of an "insured";

c. caused intentionally by an "insured" who has attained the age of 13 years;

d. arising out of an act or omission in any way related to a:

1) "business" undertaken by an "insured"; or
2) premises owned, rented, or controlled by an "insured", other than an "insured premises"; or

e. arising out of the ownership, operation, maintenance, use, occupancy, loaning, entrusting, supervision, leasing, loading, or unloading of "aircraft", "hovercraft", "motorized vehicles", or "watercraft".

However, this exclusion does not apply to "property damage" arising out of a "motorized vehicle":

1) that is not owned by an "insured" and is designed:

a) for recreational use off of public roads; or
b) to assist the handicapped; or

2) that is not owned by an "insured" and is used only to service:

a) an "insured premises"; or
b) a premises of another, not in the course of "business";

if, at the time of the "occurrence", such "motorized vehicle" is not required by law or governmental regulation to be registered for use on public roads or property.

5. **First Aid Expense** -- "We" pay the expenses incurred by an "insured" for first aid to persons, other than "insureds", for "bodily injury" covered by this policy.

6. **Loss Assessment**

   a. "We" pay for "your" share of an assessment levied by a homeowners, condominium, or similar residential association if the assessment is levied as a result of:

      1) "bodily injury" or "property damage" to which Coverage L and Coverage M apply; or
      2) damages or legal fees the association legally must pay for the acts of a director, officer, or trustee that result from the exercise of his or her duties solely on behalf of the association. This applies only to the acts of a director, officer, or trustee who is elected by the members of the association and who serves without receiving a fee, salary, or other compensation, other than reimbursement of expenses incurred.

   b. However, "we" do not pay for assessments levied against "you" or a homeowners, condominium, or similar residential association by any governmental body or authority.

   c. Coverage applies only when the assessment is levied during the policy period and is levied against "you" as owner or tenant of the "described location".

   d. The most "we" pay is $1,500 per occurrence. Regardless of the number of assessments, this "limit" is the most "we" pay for loss arising out of:

      1) any one accident, including repeated exposures to similar conditions; or
      2) an act of a director or trustee. An act involving more than one director or trustee is considered a single act.

   e. The Policy Period condition under Conditions Applicable To Liability Coverages Only does not apply to this Incidental Liability Coverage

7. **Motorized Vehicles**

   a. Subject to the limitations set forth in b. and c. below, "we" pay for "bodily injury" or "property damage" that arises out of a "motorized vehicle" that:

      1) is in dead storage on an "insured premises";
      2) is used only to service:

         a) an "insured premises", but only if the "occurrence" takes place on an "insured premises" as defined in 14.a., 14.b., 14.c., 14.f., 14.g., or 14.h. under Definitions; or
         b) an "insured premises" or a premises of another, but only if such "motorized vehicle" is designed only for use off of public roads;

      3) is designed to assist the handicapped;
      4) is designed for recreational use off of public roads and is:

         a) not owned by an "insured"; or
         b) owned by an "insured", but only if the "occurrence" takes place on an "insured premises" as defined in 14.a., 14.b., 14.c., 14.f., 14.g., or 14.h. under Definitions;

      5) is operated only from electrical current supplied by a battery and is:

         a) not built or modified after manufacture to exceed a speed of 15 miles per hour on level ground; and
         b) not a motorized bicycle, moped, or golf cart; or

      6) is a motorized golf cart that:

         a) is owned by an "insured";
         b) is designed to carry no more than four persons;

c) is not built or modified after manufacture to exceed a speed of 25 miles per hour on level ground; and
d) at the time of the "occurrence", is within the legal boundaries of:

(1) a golfing establishment and is:

(a) parked or stored there; or
(b) being used by an "insured" to:

(i) play the game of golf or for other recreational or leisure activity allowed by the establishment;
(ii) travel to or from an area where "motorized vehicles" or golf carts are parked or stored; or
(iii) cross public roads at designated points to access other parts of the golfing establishment; or

(2) a private residential community, including its public roads upon which a motorized golf cart can legally travel:

(a) that is subject to the authority of an association of property owners; and
(b) in which an "insured premises" is located.

b. The coverage described in a. above applies only to a "motorized vehicle" that, at the time of the "occurrence", is not:

1) registered for use on public roads or property;
2) required by law or governmental regulation to be registered for use at the location of the "occurrence";
3) being used in, or in the practice or the preparation for, a prearranged or organized racing, speed, pulling or pushing, demolition, or stunt activity or contest;
4) being rented to others;
5) being used to carry people or cargo for a fee; or
6) being used for any "business" purpose, except a motorized golf cart while on a golfing establishment.

c. This Incidental Liability Coverage for Motorized Vehicles is subject to all of the:

1) Exclusions That Apply To Coverage L And Coverage M, other than:

a) exclusions c. and e.; and
b) solely with respect to the use of a motorized golf cart while on a golfing establishment, exclusion g.;

2) Additional Exclusions That Apply Only To Coverage L; and
3) Additional Exclusions That Apply Only To Coverage M.

8. **Watercraft**

a. Subject to the limitations set forth in b. and c. below, "we" pay for "bodily injury" or "property damage" that arises out of a "watercraft" that:

1) is in storage;
2) is a sailing vessel, with or without auxiliary power, that is:

a) less than 26 feet in overall length; or
b) 26 feet or more in overall length and not owned by or rented to an "insured"; or

3) is not a sailing vessel and is powered by:

   a) an inboard or inboard-outdrive engine or motor, including an engine or motor that powers a water jet pump, of:

      (1) 50 horsepower or less if not owned by an "insured"; or
      (2) more than 50 horsepower if not owned by or rented to an "insured"; or

   b) one or more outboard engines or motors with:

      (1) 25 total horsepower or less;
      (2) more than 25 horsepower if the outboard engine or motor is not owned by an "insured";
      (3) more than 25 horsepower if the outboard engine or motor is owned by an "insured" who acquired it during the policy period; or
      (4) more than 25 horsepower if the outboard engine or motor is owned by an "insured" who acquired it before the policy period, but only if:

         (a) it is listed on the "declarations" as insured for personal liability; or
         (b) a written request for liability coverage is received by "us" within 45 days after it is acquired.

In this Incidental Liability Coverage for Watercraft, horsepower means the maximum power rating assigned to the engine or motor by the manufacturer.

b. The coverage described in a. above applies only to a "watercraft" that, at the time of the "occurrence", is not being:

   1) rented to others;
   2) used to carry people or cargo for a fee;
   3) used for any "business" purpose; or
   4) used in, or in the practice or the preparation for, a prearranged or organized racing, speed, pulling or pushing, demolition, or stunt activity or contest.

   However, this does not apply to a sailing vessel or to a "watercraft" being used in a predicted log contest or cruise.

c. This Incidental Liability Coverage for Watercraft is subject to all of the:

   1) Exclusions That Apply To Coverage L And Coverage M, other than exclusions c. and e.;
   2) Additional Exclusions That Apply Only To Coverage L; and
   3) Additional Exclusions That Apply Only To Coverage M.

EXCLUSIONS THAT APPLY TO LIABILITY COVERAGES

1. **Exclusions That Apply To Coverage L And Coverage M** -- Coverage L and Coverage M do not apply to:

   a. "bodily injury" or "property damage" caused directly or indirectly by:

      1) war, including undeclared or civil war;
      2) warlike action by a military force, including action in hindering or defending against an actual or expected attack, by any government, sovereign, or other authority using military personnel or other agents; or

3) insurrection, rebellion, revolution, usurped power, or action taken by governmental authority in hindering or defending against any of these.

Discharge of a nuclear weapon is deemed a warlike action even if it is accidental.

b. "bodily injury" or "property damage" arising out of:

1) the ownership or leasing of "aircraft" or "hovercraft" by an "insured";
2) the operation, maintenance, use, occupancy, loading, or unloading of "aircraft" or "hovercraft" by any person;
3) the entrustment or loaning of "aircraft" or "hovercraft" by an "insured" to any person; or
4) an "insured's" negligent supervision of or failure to supervise any person with respect to "aircraft" or "hovercraft".

However, this exclusion does not apply to "bodily injury" to a "domestic employee" arising out of and in the course of his or her employment by an "insured".

c. "bodily injury" or "property damage" arising out of:

1) the ownership or leasing of a "motorized vehicle" or "watercraft" by an "insured";
2) the operation, maintenance, use, occupancy, loading, or unloading of a "motorized vehicle" or "watercraft" by any person;
3) the entrustment or loaning of a "motorized vehicle" or "watercraft" by an "insured" to any person; or
4) an "insured's" negligent supervision of or failure to supervise any person with respect to a "motorized vehicle" or "watercraft".

However, this exclusion does not apply to "bodily injury" to a "domestic employee" arising out of and in the course of his or her employment by an "insured" or if coverage is provided under the Incidental Liability Coverage for Motorized Vehicles or the Incidental Liability Coverage for Watercraft.

d. "bodily injury" or "property damage" for which an "insured" is vicariously liable if the "bodily injury" or "property damage" arises out of the actions of a child or minor with respect to:

1) "aircraft"; or
2) "hovercraft".

This applies whether or not such liability is imposed by law.

e. "bodily injury" or "property damage" for which an "insured" is vicariously liable if the "bodily injury" or "property damage" arises out of the actions of a child or minor with respect to a:

1) "motorized vehicle"; or
2) "watercraft".

This applies whether or not such liability is imposed by law.

However, this exclusion does not apply to the extent that coverage for the "motorized vehicle" or "watercraft" is provided under the Incidental Liability Coverage for Motorized Vehicles or the Incidental Liability Coverage for Watercraft.

f. "bodily injury" or "property damage" arising out of the rendering of or the failing to render a professional service.

g. "bodily injury" or "property damage" arising out of or in any way related to a "business" conducted from an "insured premises" or undertaken by an "insured", regardless of location, whether or not the "business" is owned or operated by an "insured" or employs an "insured".

This includes but is not limited to "bodily injury" or "property damage" arising out of an act or a failure to act, regardless of its circumstance, involving a service or duty owed, promised, provided, or implied to be provided because of the nature of the "business".

However, this exclusion does not apply to the extent that coverage is provided:

1) for the use of a motorized golf cart while on a golfing establishment under the Incidental Liability Coverage for Motorized Vehicles; or
2) under the Incidental Liability Coverage for Business.

h. "bodily injury" or "property damage" that arises out of premises that are:

1) owned by an "insured";
2) rented to an "insured"; or
3) rented to others by an "insured";

and that are not "insured premises".

However, this exclusion does not apply to "bodily injury" to a "domestic employee" arising out of and in the course of his or her employment by an "insured".

i. "bodily injury" or "property damage" that is:

1) expected by, directed by, or intended by an "insured";
2) the result of a criminal act of an "insured"; or
3) the result of an intentional and malicious act by or at the direction of an "insured".

This exclusion applies even if the "bodily injury" or "property damage":

1) that occurs is different than what was expected, directed, or intended; or
2) is suffered by persons, entities, or property not expected, directed, or intended.

However, this exclusion does not apply to "bodily injury" or "property damage" that arises out of the use of reasonable force by an "insured" to protect people or property.

j. "bodily injury" or "property damage" that arises out of the transmission of a communicable disease by an "insured".

k. "bodily injury" or "property damage" that arises out of sexual molestation.

l. "bodily injury" or "property damage" that arises out of physical or mental abuse.

m. "bodily injury" or "property damage" that arises out of corporal punishment.

n. "bodily injury" or "property damage" that arises out of the use, sale, manufacture, delivery, transfer, or possession by any person of a Controlled Substance as defined by the Federal Food and Drug Law at 21 U.S.C.A. Sections 811 and 812, including any amendments. Controlled Substances include but are not limited to cocaine, LSD, marijuana, and all narcotic or hallucinogenic drugs.

However, this exclusion does not apply to the legitimate use of prescription drugs by a person following the orders of a licensed physician.

2. **Additional Exclusions That Apply Only To Coverage L** -- Coverage L does not apply to:

a. "bodily injury" to an "insured" as defined in 13.a., 13.b., 13.c., 13.d., or 13.e. under Definitions.

b. any claim made or suit brought against an "insured" seeking:

1) reimbursement of; or
2) contribution toward;

damages for which another person may be liable because of "bodily injury" to an "insured".

c. liability under a contract or an agreement entered into by an "insured", except as provided under the Incidental Liability Coverage for Contracts.

d. "property damage" to property owned by an "insured".

e. cost or expense for measures performed on property owned by an "insured" to prevent:

   1) injury to a person; or
   2) damage to property of others;

   on or away from an "insured premises", whether such cost or expense is incurred by an "insured" or others.

f. "property damage" to property that is rented to, occupied by, used by, or in the care of an "insured".

   However, this exclusion does not apply to "property damage" to such property caused by fire, smoke, or explosion.

g. sickness, disease, or death of a "domestic employee" unless a written notice is received by "us" within 36 months after the end of the policy period in which the injury occurred.

h. "bodily injury" to a person, including a "domestic employee", if:

   1) an "insured" has a workers' compensation policy covering the injury; or
   2) benefits are payable or are required to be provided by an "insured" under a workers' compensation, non-occupational disability, occupational disease, or like law.

i. liability for any assessment levied by a homeowners, condominium, or similar residential association, except as provided under the Incidental Liability Coverage for Loss Assessment.

j. "bodily injury" or "property damage" for which an "insured" under this policy is also an insured under a nuclear energy liability policy or would be an insured under a nuclear energy liability policy but for the exhaustion of its "limits". (A nuclear energy liability policy is a policy issued by Mutual Atomic Energy Liability Underwriters, Nuclear Energy Liability Insurance Association, or Nuclear Insurance Association of Canada or their successors.)

3. **Additional Exclusions That Apply Only To Coverage M** -- Coverage M does not apply to "bodily injury":

   a. to an "insured" or any other person, other than a "domestic employee", who regularly resides on any part of the "insured premises".

   b. to a person, including a "domestic employee", if a workers' compensation policy covers the injury or if benefits are provided or required to be provided under a workers' compensation, non-occupational disability, occupational disease, or like law.

   c. to a "domestic employee" if the "bodily injury":

      1) occurs away from an "insured premises"; and
      2) does not arise out of or in the course of his or her employment by an "insured".

   d. from any:

      1) nuclear reaction;
      2) nuclear radiation; or
      3) radioactive contamination;

whether controlled or uncontrolled or however caused; or

4) any consequence of 1), 2), or 3) above.

WHAT MUST BE DONE IN CASE OF LOSS OR OCCURRENCE

1. **Property Coverages**

The following duties apply when there is loss to covered property. These duties must be performed by "you", "your" representative, an "insured" seeking coverage, or the representative of an "insured" seeking coverage.

"We" are not obligated to provide the coverages described in this policy if these duties are not performed.

a. **Notice** -- Prompt notice must be given to "us" or "our" agent. "We" may request written notice.

Notice must be given to the police when the loss involves theft.

Notice must be given to the credit card, electronic fund transfer card, or electronic access device company when the loss involves a credit card, an electronic fund transfer card, or an electronic access device.

b. **Protecting Property** -- All reasonable measures must be taken to protect covered property at and after a covered loss to avoid further loss.

If the property must be repaired, "you" must:

1) make reasonable and necessary repairs to protect the property; and
2) keep an accurate record of the costs of such repairs.

c. **Cooperation** -- All "insureds" seeking coverage, and the representative or representatives of all "insureds" seeking coverage, must cooperate with "us" in the investigation of a claim.

d. **Inventory Of Damaged Personal Property** -- "We" must be given an inventory of personal property involved in a loss that shows, in detail, the:

1) quantity;
2) description;
3) "actual cash value"; and
4) amount of loss.

Copies of all bills, receipts, and related documents that confirm the figures stated in the inventory must be attached.

e. **Showing Damaged Property** -- As often as "we" reasonably request, "we" must be:

1) shown the damaged property; and
2) allowed to take samples of damaged property for inspection, testing, and analysis.

f. **Records And Documents** -- As often as "we" reasonably request, "we" must be:

1) given requested records and documents, including but not limited to tax returns and bank records of all canceled checks that relate to the value, loss, and costs; and
2) permitted to make copies of such records and documents.

g. **Examination Under Oath** -- As often as "we" reasonably request, all "insureds" must:

1) submit to examination under oath in matters that relate to the loss or claim; and
2) sign such statement made under oath.

If more than one person is examined, "we" have the right to examine and receive statements separately from each person and not in the presence of other "insureds".

h. **Proof Of Loss** -- "We" must be given a signed, sworn proof of loss, within 60 days after "our" request, that:

1) states, to the best of "your" knowledge and belief, the:

a) time and cause of the loss; and
b) interests of all "insureds" and the interests of all others, including all mortgages and liens, in the property involved in the loss;

2) identifies:

a) other policies that may cover the loss; and
b) any changes in title or use of the property during the policy period; and

3) provides:

a) available plans and specifications of damaged buildings;
b) detailed estimates for repair;
c) the inventory of damaged personal property described in d. above;
d) receipts for additional living costs incurred and records that prove the fair rental value; and
e) evidence or affidavit supporting a claim under the Incidental Property Coverage for Credit Card; Electronic Fund Transfer Card Or Access Device; Forgery; And Counterfeit Money and stating the amount and cause of loss.

i. **Assistance With Enforcing Right Of Recovery** -- At "our" request, "we" must be given assistance with enforcing any right of recovery that an "insured" may have against a party causing the loss.

2. **Liability Coverages**

The following duties apply when there has been an "occurrence". These duties must be performed by "you" or another "insured". "You" must assist "us" by seeing that they are performed.

"We" are not obligated to provide the coverages described in this policy if these duties are not performed.

a. **Notice** -- Written notice must be given to "us" or "our" agent as soon as is practical. The notice must state:

1) "your" name and the policy number;
2) reasonably available information regarding the time, location, and other details of the "occurrence"; and
3) the names and addresses of all known potential claimants and witnesses.

b. **Volunteer Payments** -- Any:

1) payments made;
2) rewards paid or offered; or
3) obligations or other costs assumed;

by an "insured" will be at the "insured's" own cost.

However, this does not apply to costs that are covered under the Incidental Liability Coverage for First Aid Expense.

c. **Cooperation** -- The "insured" must cooperate with "us" in the investigation, defense, or settlement of a claim or suit.

d. **Notices, Demands, And Legal Papers** -- The "insured" must promptly give "us" copies of all notices, demands, and legal papers that relate to the "occurrence".

e. **Assistance With Claims And Suits** -- At "our" request, the "insured" must help "us":

1) to settle a claim;
2) to enforce the right of recovery or indemnification against all parties who may be liable to an "insured";
3) to conduct suits. This includes being at trials and hearings;
4) in the securing of and giving of evidence; and
5) in obtaining the attendance of all witnesses.

f. **Other Duties -- Damage To Property Of Others** -- "We" must be given a sworn statement of loss within 60 days after the loss. The damaged property must be shown to "us" if it is within an "insured's" control.

HOW MUCH WE PAY FOR LOSS OR OCCURRENCE

1. **Property Coverages**

a. **Our Limit** -- "We" pay the lesser of:

1) the "limit" that applies; or
2) the amount determined under the applicable Loss Settlement Terms;

regardless of the number of "insureds" with an interest in the property.

However, no "insured" will be paid an amount that exceeds his or her interest in the property at the time of loss.

b. **Deductible**

1) This applies to all Principal Property Coverages and all Incidental Property Coverages except:

a) Credit Card; Electronic Fund Transfer Card Or Access Device; Forgery; And Counterfeit Money;
b) Fire Department Service Charge;
c) Lock And Garage Door Transmitter Replacement; and
d) Refrigerated Property.

It applies to all Perils Insured Against unless otherwise stated.

2) Subject to the "limits" that apply, "we" pay that part of the loss over the deductible. The deductible applies:

a) per occurrence and, with respect to the Incidental Property Coverages for Association Deductible and Loss Assessment, regardless of the number of deductibles charged or assessments levied; and
b) separately at each covered location. Only one deductible applies at each location.

c. **Loss To A Pair Or Set** -- If there is a loss to an item that is part of a pair or set, "we" pay only to replace or repair the item, or "we" pay the difference in the "actual cash value" of the pair or set just before the loss and the "actual cash value" just after the loss.

d. **Loss To Parts** -- If there is a loss to a part of an item that consists of several parts when it is complete, "we" pay only for the value of the lost or damaged part or the cost to repair or replace it.

e. **Loss Settlement Terms** -- Subject to the "terms" shown above, "we" settle losses according to the Replacement Cost Terms. If the Replacement Cost Terms do not apply, "we" settle losses according to the Actual Cash Value Terms.

In the Replacement Cost Terms and the Actual Cash Value Terms, replacement cost and cost to repair or replace do not include any increased cost that results from the enforcement of a code, ordinance, or law, except to the extent that coverage for such increased cost is provided under the Incidental Property Coverage for Increased Cost -- Ordinance Or Law.

1) **Replacement Cost Terms That Apply To Coverage A And Coverage B Only**

a) These Replacement Cost Terms apply only to buildings covered under Coverage A or Coverage B that have a permanent foundation and roof.

b) If the "limit" that applies to the damaged building at the time of loss is less than 80% of its full replacement cost just before the loss, the larger of the following amounts is used in applying the "terms" under Our Limit:

(1) the "actual cash value" of the damaged part of the building just before the loss; or

(2) that part of the cost to repair or replace the damaged part, after application of any deductible, which the "limit" on the damaged building bears to 80% of its full replacement cost just before the loss.

c) If the "limit" that applies to the damaged building at the time of loss is at least 80% of its full replacement cost just before the loss, the smaller of the following amounts is used in applying the "terms" under Our Limit:

(1) the amount actually and necessarily spent to repair or replace the damaged building; or

(2) the cost to repair or replace the damage:

(a) using materials of like kind and quality; and
(b) for like use.

However, when a damaged building is rebuilt at another location, such cost is limited to the cost that would have been incurred if the building had been repaired or replaced at the location where the damage occurred.

d) In determining the replacement cost, do not include the cost of:

(1) excavations; brick, stone, or concrete foundations; piers; footings; or other structures or features that support all or part of the building that are:

(a) below the undersurface of the lowest basement floor; or
(b) below the surface of the ground inside the foundation walls, if there is no basement; or

(2) underground flues, pipes, wiring, or drains.

e) When the cost to repair or replace exceeds the lesser of $2,500 or 5% of the "limit" that applies to the damaged building, "we" will pay no more than the "actual cash value" of the loss until repair or replacement is completed. Once repair or replacement is completed, "we" will settle the loss as described in b) and c) above.

f) At "your" option, "you" may make a claim under the Actual Cash Value Terms instead of these Replacement Cost Terms. "You" may later make a claim for any additional amount payable under these Replacement Cost Terms, but only if "you" have informed "us", within 180 days after the date of loss, that "you" plan to do so.

2) **Replacement Cost Terms That Apply To Personal Property Only**

a) These "terms" apply to:

(1) property covered under Coverage C; and
(2) the following classes of personal property, if covered under this policy by scheduled insurance and such coverage is not subject to Agreed Value Loss Settlement Terms:

(a) jewelry;
(b) furs and garments trimmed with fur or consisting principally of fur;
(c) cameras, projection machines, films, and related items of equipment;
(d) musical instruments and related items of equipment;
(e) silverware, goldware, platinumware, pewterware, and items plated with silver, gold, or platinum;
(f) golf clubs, golf clothing, and golf equipment; and
(g) bicycles.

b) However, these "terms" do not apply to:

(1) items of antiquity, art, or rarity that cannot be duplicated;
(2) memorabilia, souvenirs, collector's items, and similar items whose age or history contribute to their value;
(3) items not maintained in good or workable condition; or
(4) items that are outdated or obsolete and are stored or not being used.

Property described in (1) through (4) above is subject to Actual Cash Value Terms.

c) The smaller of the following amounts is used in applying the "terms" under Our Limit:

(1) the cost, at the time of loss, to replace the lost or damaged part of the property, without deduction for depreciation; or
(2) the full cost, at the time of loss, to repair the damaged part of the property.

d) When the total cost to repair or replace all property involved in any one occurrence is more than $500, "we" do not pay for more than the "actual cash value" of the loss until actual repair or replacement is completed.

e) At "your" option, "you" may make a claim under the Actual Cash Value Terms instead of these Replacement Cost Terms. "You" may later make a claim for any additional amount payable under these Replacement Cost Terms, but only if "you" have informed "us", within 180 days after the date of loss, that "you" plan to do so.

3) **Actual Cash Value Terms**

a) The Actual Cash Value Terms apply to all property not subject to the Replacement Cost Terms.
b) The smaller of the following amounts is used in applying the "terms" under Our Limit:

(1) the cost to repair or replace the lost or damaged part of the property with materials of like kind and quality, to the extent practical; or
(2) the "actual cash value" of the lost or damaged part of the property just before the loss.

2. **Coverage L -- Personal Liability** -- The "limit" shown on the "declarations" for Coverage L is the most "we" pay for loss for each "occurrence". This applies regardless of the number of:

a. persons insured under this policy;

b. parties who sustain injury or damage;

c. claims made or suits brought; or

d. policy periods involved.

All "bodily injury" and "property damage" arising out of any one accident or out of repeated exposures to similar conditions will be considered one "occurrence".

3. **Coverage M -- Medical Payments To Others** -- The "limit" shown on the "declarations" per person for Coverage M is the most "we" pay for all medical expenses payable for "bodily injury" to one person as the result of one accident.

When a "limit" is shown on the "declarations" per accident for Coverage M, that "limit" is the most "we" pay for any one accident.

The payment of a claim under Coverage M does not mean an admission of liability on "our" part or on the part of any "insured".

4. **Severability** -- The Liability Coverages provided by this policy apply separately to each "insured", but this does not increase the "limit" that applies for any one "occurrence".

5. **Insurance Under More Than One Coverage** -- If more than one coverage of this policy applies to a loss, "we" pay no more than the actual loss.

6. **Insurance Under More Than One Policy**

a. **Property Coverages**

1) If there is other insurance that applies to a loss, cost, or expense, other than insurance in the name of an association or a corporation of property owners, "we" pay "our" share of the loss, cost, or expense. "Our" share is that part of the loss, cost, or expense that the "limit" of this policy bears to the total amount of insurance that applies to the loss, cost, or expense.

However, this does not apply to loss, cost, or expense that is also covered by:

a) a home warranty, a service or maintenance plan or agreement, or any other warranty, plan, or agreement that provides for the repair or replacement of property, even if such warranty, plan, or agreement has the characteristics or qualities of insurance; or
b) a government fund.

2) When a loss, cost, or expense is also covered by insurance in the name of an association or a corporation of property owners, this insurance is excess over the "limit" that applies under such other insurance.

However, this excess provision does not apply with respect to the coverage provided under the Incidental Property Coverage for Association Deductible.

b. **Coverage L -- Personal Liability** -- This insurance is excess over other valid and collectible insurance that applies to the loss or claim, other than insurance written specifically to provide coverage in excess of the "limits" that apply in this policy.

If the other insurance is also excess, "we" pay only "our" share of the loss. "We" pay only that part of the loss that the applicable "limit" under this policy bears to the total amount of insurance covering the loss.

7. **Warranties And Service Or Maintenance Plans Or Agreements** -- If loss, cost, or expense covered by this policy is also covered by a home warranty, a service or maintenance plan or agreement, or any other warranty, plan, or agreement that provides for the repair or replacement of property, this insurance is excess over any amount payable by such warranty, plan, or agreement. This applies even if such warranty, plan, or agreement has the characteristics or qualities of insurance.

8. **Government Funds** -- If loss, cost, or expense covered by this policy is also covered by a government fund, "we" pay "our" share of the loss, cost, or expense. "Our" share is that part of the loss, cost, or expense that the "limit" of this policy bears to the total amount payable for the loss, cost, or expense to the extent permitted by law.

PAYMENT OF LOSS

1. **Property Coverages**

a. Except as provided in 3. below, "we" adjust each loss with "you". "We" pay a covered loss within 60 days after an acceptable proof of loss is received and:

1) "we" reach an agreement with "you";
2) there is an entry of a final judgment; or
3) there is a filing of an appraisal award with "us".

Payment is made to "you" unless a loss payee or some other person or entity is named in the policy or is legally entitled to receive payment.

b. "We" may:

1) pay the loss in money; or
2) rebuild, repair, or replace the property. "We" must give "you" written notice of "our" intent to do so within 30 days after "we" receive an acceptable proof of loss.

If "we" pay the loss in money, "we" may take all or part of the damaged property at the agreed or appraised value. Property paid for or replaced by "us" becomes "ours".

c. If the "described location" is made unfit for use for more than one month, loss, cost, or expense covered under Coverage D is paid on a monthly basis. "You" must give "us" proof of such loss, cost, or expense.

2. **Liability Coverages** -- A person who has secured a judgment against an "insured" for a covered loss or has liability established by a written agreement between the claimant, an "insured", and "us" is entitled to recover under this policy to the extent of coverage provided.

3. **Damage To Personal Property Of Others** -- At "our" option, a covered loss may be adjusted with and paid:

   a. to "you" on behalf of the owner; or

   b. to the owner. If "we" pay the owner, "we" do not have to pay an "insured".

POLICY CONDITIONS

CONDITIONS APPLICABLE TO ALL COVERAGES

1. **Assignment** -- This policy may not be assigned without "our" written consent.

2. **Cancellation And Nonrenewal** -- "You" may cancel this policy by returning the policy to "us" or by giving "us" written notice and stating at what future date coverage is to stop.

   "We" may cancel or not renew this policy by written notice to "you" at the address shown on the "declarations". Proof of delivery or mailing is sufficient proof of notice.

   During the first 59 days this policy is in effect, "we" may cancel for any reason. "We" will give "you" notice at least ten days before cancellation is effective.

   When this policy has been in effect 60 days or more, or if it is a renewal of a policy issued by "us", "we" may cancel or not renew only at the anniversary date unless:

   a. the premium has not been paid when due;

   b. the policy was obtained through fraud, material misrepresentation, or omission of fact, which, if known by "us", would have caused "us" not to issue the policy; or

   c. there has been a material change or increase in hazard of the risk.

   If "we" cancel this policy for nonpayment of premium, "we" will give "you" notice at least ten days before cancellation is effective. If "we" cancel this policy for any other reason when it has been in effect for 60 days or more, "we" will give "you" notice at least 30 days before cancellation is effective.

   If "we" do not renew this policy, "we" will give "you" notice at least 30 days before nonrenewal is effective.

   "Your" return premium, if any, will be calculated on a pro rata basis and will be refunded at the time of cancellation or as soon as practical. Payment or tender of the unearned premium is not a condition of cancellation.

3. **Change, Modification, Or Waiver Of Policy Terms**

   a. A waiver or change of the "terms" of this policy must be issued by "us" in writing to be valid.

   b. If "we" adopt a revision that broadens coverage under this edition of "our" policy without an additional premium, the broadened coverage will apply to "your" policy as of the date "we" adopt the revision in the state in which the "described location" is located. This applies only to revisions adopted within 60 days prior to or during the policy period shown on the "declarations".

      However, this does not apply to revisions adopted as part of an overall program revision that both broadens and restricts coverage, whether "we" bring about the program revision by introducing:

      1) a subsequent edition of "our" policy; or
      2) an endorsement that amends "our" policy.

   c. "Our" request for an appraisal or examination under oath does not waive policy "terms".

4. **Conformity With Statute** -- "Terms" in conflict with the laws of the state in which the "described location" is located are changed to conform to such laws.

5. **Death** -- The "terms" in a. and b. below apply if any person named as the insured on the "declarations" or that person's spouse, if a resident of the same household, dies.

   a. "We" provide coverage for the legal representative of the deceased person:

      1) but only with respect to the deceased person's premises and property covered by this policy at the time of death; and
      2) only to the extent that coverage is provided by this policy.

   b. "Insured" includes:

      1) an "insured" who is a member of the deceased person's household at the time of the deceased person's death, but only while a resident of the "described location"; and
      2) persons having proper, temporary custody of the deceased person's covered property, but only with respect to such property and only until such time as a legal representative is appointed and qualified.

6. **Inspections** -- "We" have the right, but are not obligated, to inspect "your" property and operations. This inspection may be made by "us" or may be made on "our" behalf. An inspection or its resulting advice or report does not warrant that "your" property or operations are safe, healthful, or in compliance with laws, rules, or regulations. Inspections or reports are for "our" benefit only.

7. **Misrepresentation, Concealment, Or Fraud** -- "We" do not provide coverage for any "insured" if, before or after a loss:

   a. an "insured" has willfully concealed or misrepresented a material fact or circumstance that relates to this insurance or the subject thereof; or

   b. there has been fraudulent conduct or false swearing by an "insured" with regard to a matter that relates to this insurance or the subject thereof.

   This applies even with respect to an "insured" who was not involved in the concealment, misrepresentation, fraudulent conduct, or false swearing.

8. **Subrogation** -- If "we" pay for a loss, "we" may require that the "insured" assign to "us" the right of recovery up to the amount "we" pay. "We" are not liable for a loss if, after the loss, an "insured" impairs "our" right to recover against others. An "insured" may waive his or her right to recover, in writing and before a loss occurs, without affecting coverage.

   In the event that "we" require such an assignment, the "insured" must:

   a. sign and give to "us" all related documents; and

   b. cooperate with "us".

   Subrogation does not apply to Coverage M -- Medical Payments To Others or to the Incidental Liability Coverage for Damage To Property Of Others.

CONDITIONS APPLICABLE TO PROPERTY COVERAGES ONLY

1. **Abandonment Of Property** -- An "insured" may not abandon property to "us" unless "we" agree.

2. **Appraisal** -- If "you" and "we" do not agree as to the value or amount of loss, either may demand an appraisal of such loss. In this event, "you" and "we" will each select a competent and impartial appraiser within 20 days after receiving a written request from the other. The two appraisers will select a competent and impartial umpire. If they do not agree on an umpire within 15 days, "you" or "we" may ask a judge of a court of record of the state where the "described location" is located to make the selection.

   A written agreement of the two appraisers will set the amount of loss. If the appraisers fail to agree, they will submit their differences to the umpire. The written agreement of any two of these three will set the amount of the loss.

   "You" will pay the expense of "your" appraiser and "we" will pay the expense of "our" appraiser. "You" and "we" will share equally the expense of the umpire and the other expenses of the appraisal.

   Under no circumstance will an appraisal be used to interpret policy "terms", determine causation, or determine whether or not a loss is covered under this policy.

3. **Loss Payable Clause** -- With respect to those items of personal property for which a loss payee is shown on the "declarations", the definition of "insured" is extended to include that loss payee, but only with respect to those items of personal property.

   If "we" cancel or do not renew this policy, "we" will so notify, in writing, any loss payees shown on the "declarations".

4. **Mortgage Clause**

   a. If a mortgagee is named on the "declarations", a loss payable under Coverage A or Coverage B will be paid to the mortgagee and "you", as interests appear. If more than one mortgagee is named, the order of payment will be the same as the order of precedence of the mortgages. The word mortgagee includes trustee.

   b. If "we" deny "your" claim, that denial does not apply to a valid claim of the mortgagee if the mortgagee has:

      1) notified "us" of change in ownership, occupancy, or substantial change in risk of which the mortgagee became aware;
      2) paid the premium due under this policy on demand if "you" neglected to pay the premium; and
      3) submitted a signed, sworn statement of loss within 60 days after receiving notice from "us" if "you" failed to do so.

      All "terms" of this policy apply to the mortgagee unless changed by this clause.

   c. If "we" cancel or do not renew this policy, "we" will notify any mortgagees named on the "declarations" at least ten days before the date cancellation or nonrenewal takes effect.

   d. If "we" pay the mortgagee for a loss and deny payment to "you", "we" are subrogated, up to the amount "we" paid for the loss, to all the rights of the mortgagee granted under the mortgage on the property. Subrogation will not impair the right of the mortgagee to recover the full amount of the mortgagee's claim.

      At "our" option, "we" may pay to the mortgagee the whole principal on the mortgage plus the accrued interest. In this event, "we" will receive a full assignment and transfer of the mortgage and all securities held as collateral to the mortgage debt.

5. **No Benefit To Bailee** -- Coverage under this policy will not directly or indirectly benefit those who are paid to assume custody of covered property.

6. **Policy Period** -- This policy covers only losses that occur during the policy period.

7. **Recoveries** -- This applies if "we" pay for a loss and lost or damaged property is recovered or payment is made by those responsible for the loss.

   "You" must inform "us" or "we" must inform "you" if either recovers property or receives payment. Proper costs incurred by either party are paid first.

   At "your" option, "you" may keep the recovered property. If "you" keep the recovered property, the amount of the claim paid, or a lesser amount to which "we" agree, must be returned to "us".

   If the claim paid is less than the agreed loss due to a deductible or other limiting "terms", the recovery is prorated between "you" and "us" based on the interest of each in the loss.

8. **Suit Against Us** -- No suit may be brought against "us" unless all of the "terms" that apply to the Property Coverages have been complied with and the suit is brought within two years after the loss.

   If a law of the state where the "described location" is located makes this time period invalid, the suit must be brought within the time period allowed by the law.

9. **Volcanic Eruption** -- All volcanic eruption that occurs within a 72-hour period constitutes a single occurrence.

CONDITIONS APPLICABLE TO LIABILITY COVERAGES ONLY

1. **Bankruptcy Of An Insured** -- Bankruptcy or insolvency of an "insured" does not relieve "us" of "our" obligations under this policy.

2. **Duties Of An Injured Person -- Medical Payments To Others Coverage** -- In case of a loss, the injured person or someone acting on behalf of that person must:

   a. give "us" written proof of claim (under oath if "we" request) as soon as practical; and

   b. authorize "us" to get copies of medical records.

   The injured person must submit to medical exams by doctors chosen by "us" when and as often as "we" may reasonably require.

3. **Policy Period** -- This policy covers only "bodily injury" and "property damage" that occur during the policy period.

4. **Suit Against Us** -- No suit may be brought against "us" unless all of the "terms" that apply to the Liability Coverages have been complied with and the amount of the "insured's" liability has been fixed by:

   a. a final judgment against the "insured" as a result of a trial; or

   b. a written agreement of the "insured", the claimant, and "us".

   No person has a right under this policy to join "us" or implead "us" in actions that are brought to fix the liability of an "insured".

Index